READINGS
—*for*—
WRITERS

READINGS
—— *for* ——
WRITERS

ELEVENTH EDITION

JO RAY MCCUEN
Glendale College

ANTHONY C. WINKLER

THOMSON
———✦———™
HEINLE

Australia Canada Mexico Singapore Spain United Kingdom United States

THOMSON
™

HEINLE

Readings for Writers,
Eleventh Edition
Jo Ray McCuen and Anthony Winkler

Publisher: *Michael Rosenberg*
Acquisitions Editor: *Dickson Musslewhite*
Development Editor: *Julie McBurney*
Production Editor: *Eunice Yeates-Fogle*
Director of Marketing: *Lisa Kimball*
Senior Print Buyer: *Mary Beth Hennebury*

Compositor, Text Designer:
Carlisle Communications, Ltd.
Project Manager: *Mary Jo Graham*
Photo Manager: *Sheri Blaney*
Cover Designer: *Circa 86, Inc.*
Printer: *Maple Vail Printers*

For more information contact Heinle,
25 Thomson Place, Boston, Massachusetts 02210 USA. or you can visit out Internet site at
http://www.heinle.com.

For permission to use material from this text or product, contact us by

Tel   1-800- 730-2214
Fax   1-800-730-2215
www.thomsonrights.com

ISBN: 0-8584-0546-0 (InfoTrac® College Edition)

**Library of Congress
Cataloging-in-Publication Data**

Readings for writers / [compiled by] Jo Ray McCuen, Anthony C. Winkler.—11th ed.
p.   cm.
Includes bibliographical references and index.
ISBN 0-8384-0546-0 (alk. paper)
1. College readers. 2. English language—Rhetoric—Problems, exercises, etc. 3. Report writing—Problems, exercises, etc. I. McCuen, Jo Ray, 1929- II. Winkler, Anthony C.
PE1417.R423 2003
808'.0427—dc21

2003047387

For Allwyn and Cathy—spouses,
silent backers, patient listeners—
with gratitude and love

Preface

Readings for Writers, like all textbooks, has evolved over time in response to changes in the field and the emergence of new trends in freshman composition. Because the first principle of sensible change is to avoid needless change, this eleventh edition of *Readings for Writers*, though the most substantially revised, remains unchanged in those core features instructors tell us they especially appreciate.

- Unchanged in this eleventh edition is the unique labeling system that identifies the intended function of every anthologized piece as either giving advice about some fundamental principle of writing or a being a model of it.

- Unchanged is the broad sweep of topics, styles, and interests of the included works. Here, gathered under one roof, are works from writers as varied and different as Oscar Wilde and Paul Roberts; as venerable as Shakespeare and as homespun as Louis L'Amour; as beloved as James Herriot and as stormy as Kate Chopin. Their topics range from the practical discussion of sharing housework to the philosophical musings of an insomniac anthropologist. *Readings for Writers*, because of the enormous range of its contents, has become known as the one book that has something for everyone and every taste.

- Unchanged is the popular "Student Corner," which showcases the essays of real students along with their commentary on their own work and their writing tips.

- Each chapter still ends with chapter Writing Assignments, a Writing Assignment for a Specific Audience, and a Collaborative Writing Project.

- Each selection is still prefaced by a headnote and followed by questions under the headings of the facts, the strategies, and the issues.

New editions, however, are justified not by what they don't change, but by what they do. And all the changes in this eleventh edition—and they are substantial—have one aim in common: to make *Readings for Writers* even more practical and easier to use than ever before. Specifically, we have done the following:

- We have added an entirely new feature called *Editors' Counsel* that contains editor-written instructional text rarely found in a reader as well as exercises on the topic of every chapter.

- We have expanded the section on critical reading and included an exercise demonstrating exactly how one would go about applying a particular skill to an actual essay.

- We have added a feature to the first six chapters called *Real-Life Student Writing* in which we reproduce examples of actual student writing. Examples range from a breezy e-mail to a somber eulogy, the intent being to tie together the principles of writing as taught in the classroom and as practiced in real life.

- Each rhetorical mode is now covered in a separate chapter complete with editor-written instructional material organized under recurring headings—what the mode does and when and how to use it—followed by warming-up exercises.

- We have added a new chapter, "Combining the Modes," in which we discuss the realistic use of the rhetorical modes by professional writers.

- We have added a unique feature we call "the Editing Booth," which pulls together a systematic list of editing tips students can use to edit and revise their first drafts.

- We have changed three of the issues for critical thinking, adding the topics of terrorism, spanking children, and the separation of church and state.

- We have added to chapter 2 a module on writing about visual images in which we cover basic techniques and provide examples.

- We have added the occasional text box to introduce a touch of humor to the instructional material.

Because of these changes, *Readings for Writers*, can be used unaccompanied by any other book. The advice of its anthologized experts, combined with the editors' additions, provides all the help a freshman student would need to become a better writer. This new edition anthologizes 113 pieces consisting of 69 essays, 5 short stories, 12 poems, 3 speeches, 9 student essays, 1 sermon, 4 letters, 2 text boxes, 6 sample paragraphs, 2 annotated research papers—one in the MLA style, the other in the APA—and 1 literary paper, making it the most comprehensive of all the readers available for freshman English.

In this revision, we have been ably guided by the advice of our development editor, Julie McBurney, and by the wise counsel of Dickson Musslewhite, Eunice Yeates-Fogle, and Lisa Kimball. To all of them we offer our heartfelt thanks.

We would like to gratefully acknowledge the reviewers whose insightful suggestions helped shape this edition:

Joseph Alvarez, *Central Piedmont Community College*
Lee Barnes, *Community College of Southern Nevada*
Karen Davis, *Pasco-Hernando Community College*
Pat Ecker, *Kentucky Community and Technical College*
Julie Fleenor, *William Rainey Harper College*
Joe Glaser, *Western Kentucky University*
Thomas Alan Holmes, *Eastern Tennessee State University*
Howard Kerner, *Polk Community College*
Lindsay Lewan, *Arapahoe Community College*
Teri Maddox, *Jackson State Community College*
Troy Nordham, *Butler County Community College*
Lois Reynolds, *Pellissippi State Technical Community College*
Jude Ryan, *Polk Community College*
Richard Sheehan, *North Hennepin Community College*

JO RAY MCCUEN
ANTHONY C. WINKLER

Contents

PART 2
PATTERNS OF DEVELOPMENT   191

---

11   DEFINITION   359

---

12   COMPARISON/CONTRAST   411

PART 3
REWRITING YOUR WRITING   651

The Editing Booth   653

APPENDIX   677

SAMPLE STUDENT PAPERS   685

Thematic Table of Contents

(Listed alphabetically within sections)

SCIENCE

SOCIAL PROBLEMS

THINKING

PART I

Introduction:
From Reading to Writing

A veteran English teacher once remarked to us that she had known readers who were not writers, but she had never known writers who were not readers. Neither have we. All writers begin as eager readers and continue to read throughout their lives. Their lifelong pleasure in reading wanes only in the presence of the greater pleasure they take in writing.

You may not be a writer, in the sense of making a living from what you write, and you may not even write every day. But like it or not, you read every day, even if it is nothing more than the sign on a passing bus or the words on a billboard. But unless you live in a cave or on a desert island, modern life compels you to read.

All of us begin life as nonreaders. Reading is a skill that begins in childhood and has effects on our intellect that are still not completely understood. And though we might have learned to read under peculiarly similar or different conditions, we all more or less share a similar reading history.

It began with the delight we felt when we first were taught to read. And once we were able to read on our own, many of us found ourselves swept away into magical worlds. Books took us on exotic journeys to places that existed only on the page and in our heads. We were visited by cats wearing hats, by talking rabbits, and by children who never grow old. We walked down yellow brick roads, sailed a balloon to the moon, and went with a crusty pirate in search of buried treasure on a remote island. Reading had planted in our heads a delightful high-definition TV, called imagination, and never were colors brighter or images sharper.

But as we grew older a curious thing happened: Reading became associated with schoolwork as we were forced to read textbooks we disliked on subjects we hated. The very act of opening a book became a labor. Soon we were watching television to relax and reading only when we had to because of schoolwork. For many, reading changed from fun to drudgery. A lucky few retained a deep love of reading and will continue throughout their lives to read for fun. Speaking for them, the famous 18th-century British historian Edward Gibbon wrote in his *Memoirs*: "My early and invincible love of reading, I would not exchange for the treasures of India."

If you wish to write, you should develop the habit of reading. The skill of writing well is essentially a kind of mimicry, and the more writers we read, the more examples we have to imitate. And although reading constantly is no guarantee that you will write well, the likelihood is that your writing will get better if you continue to be a reader.

The first part of this book—*Reading and Writing*—covers the preliminary topics of a writing course. Chapter 1 covers critical reading and introduces us to one of America's most prolific writers, himself an avid reader who devoured hundreds of books each year. Chapter 2 examines the role of rhetoric, an ancient discipline that is much misunderstood today. Chapter 3 covers the writer's voice, while Chapters 4, 5, and 6 deal with the nuts-and-bolts of choosing a thesis topic and organizing a paper, and the indispensable craft of paragraph writing.

Among the lessons Part 1 teaches is this: Writing is not an isolated skill that exists apart from the intellect of the individual. It is, instead, ingrained in the whole person. Read widely and your writing is likely to get better as your judgment of good writing matures. You are also likely to rediscover pleasures you once derived from memorable storybooks—pleasures that have no box office charge, no crowds, and require no hardware more elaborate than a library card.

1

Guidelines for Critical Reading

KINDS OF READING

There are at least four different kinds of reading. *Casual reading* is the most common. Everyone does it. The casual reader glances at magazines, newspaper headlines, letters, and roadside signs. Casual readers read not because they want to, but because they must. Many people, if not most, fall into this category.

Reading for pleasure—whether mystery novels, romances, or tales of adventure—is the second common kind of reading. Reading of this kind is relaxed and uncritical. Many readers do it at bedtime to help them fall asleep. Pleasure readers don't worry about grasping the writer's full meaning as long as they get the gist of it and are transported by the writing to an imaginary world.

Reading for information, the third kind of reading, is practiced by information seekers who use reading as a tool. This type of reading is usually related to work or school. The pleasure derived from reading for information is the result not of reading, but of doing a job well or completing an assignment on schedule. This kind of reading requires attention, understanding, and memorization.

Finally, there is *critical reading*—the kind of reading you must do for your college classes. Critical reading is active reading. You engage in a kind of mental dialogue with the writer. The writer says so-and-so is the case and you reply, "Maybe so, but what about this?" You annotate the margins of the book you're reading with your reactions and comments. You not only try to understand the author's main point, you also try to deduce any consequences of it. To be a critical reader, you must take the following steps:

1. Read actively. Determine the author's main point as well as any secondary effects that stem from it. Ask yourself whether you agree or disagree with the author's opinions. If you disagree, make a note in the margin saying why. If the author makes a mistake of logic or fact, make a note on the page where it occurred.

2. Demystify the writer. Many of us have the tendency to regard writers as Godlike and to take everything they say as the gospel. But writers are only human and are just as likely to make mistakes as anyone

else. Reading critically begins with kicking the writer off the throne of public esteem and regarding the writer's work as you would any other human production—which is to say, prone to error.

3. Understand what you read. Reread difficult passages, looking up in a dictionary all the unfamiliar words. You cannot form an opinion of what you have read unless you understand what the author is saying. Some students find it helpful to summarize aloud any difficult ideas they encounter. Reread any difficult chapter or essay whose meaning you didn't completely comprehend. A difficult-to-understand point usually seems clearer the second time around. For example, Tolstoy's massive novel *War and Peace,* on first reading, seems like a tangled plot cluttered by an overwhelming mass of scenes and characters. On second reading, however, the plot will seem clearer and the scenes and characters more understandable.

4. Imagine an opposing point of view for all opinions. If the writer says that the Arab punishment of cutting off the hands of a thief is more humane than the American equivalent of imprisonment, reverse the argument and see what happens. In other words, look for reasons that support the other side. For example, if an essay is passionately against the use of dogs in medical research, try to see the opposing point of view—namely, the benefits of such research to the lives of millions who suffer terrible diseases. A little digging will reveal that insulin, whose introduction has prolonged the lives of millions of diabetics, was discovered through research on dogs. The argument boils down to this question: Does a puppy have the same worth as a human baby?

5. Look for biases and hidden assumptions. For example, an atheist arguing for abortion will not attribute a soul to the unborn fetus; a devout Catholic will. To ferret out possible biases and hidden assumptions, check the author's age, sex, education, and ethnic background. These and other personal biographical facts might have influenced the opinions expressed in the work, but you cannot know to what extent unless you know something about the author. (That is the rationale behind the use of biographical headnotes, which accompany the readings in this book.)

6. Separate emotion from fact. Talented writers frequently color an issue with emotionally charged language, thus casting their opinions in the best possible light. For example, a condemned murderer may be described in sympathetic language that draws attention away from his or her horrifying crime. Be alert to sloganeering, to bumper-sticker philosophizing about complex issues. To the neutral observer, few issues are as simple as black and white. Abortion is a more complex issue than either side presents. Capital punishment is not simply a matter of vengeance versus mercy. The tendency in public debate is to demonize the opposition and reduce issues to emotional

slogans. As a critical reader, you must evaluate an argument by logic and reason and not be swayed by the emotionality of either side.

7. If the issue is new to you, look up the facts. If you are reading about an unfamiliar issue, be willing to fill in the gaps in your knowledge with research. For example, if you are reading an editorial that proposes raising home insurance rates for families taking care of foster children, you will want to know why. Is it because foster children do more property damage than other children? Is it because natural parents are apt to file lawsuits against foster parents? You can find answers to these questions by asking representatives of the affected parties: the State Department of Social Services, typical insurance agencies, foster parents associations, the county welfare directors association, any children's lobby, and others. To make a critical judgment you must know, and carefully weigh, the facts.

8. Use insights from one subject to illuminate or correct another. Be prepared to apply what you already know to whatever you read. History can inform psychology; literature can give you insights into geography. For example, if a writer in psychology argues that most oppressed people develop a defeatist air that gives them a subconscious desire to be subjugated and makes them prey to tyrants, your knowledge of American history should tell you otherwise. As proof that oppressed people often fight oppression unto death, you can point to the *Battle of Fallen Timbers* in 1794, to the *Battle of Tippecanoe* in 1811, and to the *Black Hawk War* of 1832— conflicts in which the Indians fought desperately to retain their territories rather than go meekly to the reservations. In other words, you can use what you have learned from history to refute a falsehood from psychology.

9. Evaluate the evidence. Critical readers do not accept evidence at face value. They question its source, its verifiability, its appropriateness. Here are some practical tips for evaluating evidence:

    ■ Verify a questionable opinion by cross-checking with other sources. For example, if a medical writer argues that heavy smoking tends to cause serious bladder diseases in males, check the medical journals for confirmation of this view. Diligent research often turns up a consensus of opinion among the experts in any field.

    ■ Check the date of the evidence. In science especially, evidence varies from year to year. Before 1987, no one really knew exactly how the immune system worked. Then Susumu Tonegawa, a geneticist at the Massachusetts Institute of Technology, discovered how the immune system protects the body from foreign substances by manufacturing antibodies. In 1980, the evidence would say that the working of the immune system was a mystery; that evidence would be inaccurate in 1987.

- Use common sense in evaluating evidence. For example, if a writer argues that a child's handwriting can accurately predict his or her life as an adult, your own experience with human nature should lead you to reject this conclusion as speculative. No convincing evidence exists to corroborate it.

10. Ponder the values behind an argument. In writing the Declaration of Independence, Thomas Jefferson based his arguments on the value that "all men are created equal." On the other hand, Karl Marx based the arguments of his *Communist Manifesto* on the value that the laborer is society's greatest good. Critical reading means thinking about the values implicit in an argument. For instance, to argue that murderers should be hanged in public to satisfy society's need for revenge is to value revenge over human dignity. On the other hand, to argue that democracy can exist only with free speech is to value freedom of speech.

11. Look for logical fallacies. These typical, logical flaws occur in a wide range of arguments: the *ad hominem* attack (attacking the person instead of the issue or the argument); the *ad populum* appeal (the use of simplistic popular slogans to convince); the *false analogy* (comparing situations that have no bearing on each other); *begging the question* (arguing in circles); and *ignoring the question* (focusing on matters that are beside the point). For a better understanding of logical fallacies, review chapter 15, "Argumentation."

12. Don't be seduced by bogus claims. Arguments are often based on unsubstantiated statements. For example, a writer may warn that "recent studies show women becoming increasingly hostile to men." Or, another writer might announce, "Statistics have shown beyond doubt that most well-educated males oppose gun control." You should always remain skeptical of these and similar claims when they are unaccompanied by hard-headed evidence. A proper claim will always be documented with verifiable evidence.

13. Annotate your reading. Many of us have the tendency to become lazy readers. We sit back with a book and almost immediately lapse into a daze. One way to avoid being a lazy reader is to annotate your reading—making notes in the margins as you read. Many students are reluctant to scribble in the margins of a book because they hope to resell it at the end of the term. But this is a penny-wise-and-pound-foolish outlook. Instead of aiming to resell the book, your focus should be on getting the most out of it; annotating is one way to do that. Indeed, to make notes in the margins of books is, in a way, to interact with the reading—almost like chatting with the author. If you can't bring yourself to write directly on the printed page of this book, we suggest you make notes on a separate sheet as you read. Here are some suggestions for annotating your reading:

■ Write down your immediate impression of the essay.

   a. Did the subject interest you?

   b. Did the reading leave you inspired, worried, angry, tickled, or better informed?

   c. Did the reading remind you of something in your own experience? (Cite the experience.)

   d. Did you agree or disagree with the author? (Note specific passages.)

   e. Did the reading give you any new ideas?

■ Note the author's style, especially the words or expressions used.

   a. What specific passages really made you think?

   b. Where did the writer use an especially apt expression or image? What was it? What made it so good?

   c. Where, if any place, did the author write "over your head"?

   d. What kind of audience did the author seem to address? Did it include you or did you feel left out?

■ Make marginal notes that express your response to the author's ideas.

   a. Supplement the author's idea or example with one of your own.

   b. Underline passages that seem essential to the author's point.

   c. Write any questions you might want to ask the author if he or she were sitting next to you.

   d. Write any sudden insight you experienced.

   e. Write why you disagree with the author.

   f. Write a marginal explanation of any allusion made by the writer. For example, in the fourth paragraph of this chapter, we wrote "We were visited by cats wearing hats, by talking rabbits, and by children who never grow old." Did you understand these three allusions? The first is a reference to *The Cat in the Hat* by Dr. Seuss; the second, to *Alice in Wonderland*; the third, to *Peter Pan*.

14. Finally, be sure you understand the writer's opening context. The writing may be part of an ongoing debate that began before you arrived and will continue after you've left. Some essays begin by plunging right into an ongoing discussion, taking for granted that the reader is familiar with the opening context. The effect can be mystifying, like hearing an answer but not knowing the question.

Here are the principles of critical reading applied to a brief essay by CBS News commentator Andy Rooney. The annotations in the margins raise questions that we think any reasonable critical reader would ask. At the end of the essay, we provide the answers.

1. What is the opening context of this article?	1 I would choose to have written Fowler's *Modern English Usage.*
	2 My book, known far and wide and for all time as Rooney's *Modern English Usage* and comparable in sales to the Bible, would have assured my fame and fortune. Even more than that, if I'd had the kind of command of the language it would take to have written it, I would never again be uncertain about whether to use *further* or *farther, hung* or *hanged, dived* or *dove.* When I felt lousy and wanted to write about it, I'd know whether to say felt *nauseous* or *nauseated.*
2. Who is Fowler? *3. What is his book about?*	
	3 If I was the intellectual guru of grammar, as author of that tome, I would issue updated decrees on usage such as an end to the pretentious subjunctive. Not if I *were.*
4. What do we learn about Fowler's book in this paragraph?	
	4 I would split infinitives at will when I damn well felt like it, secure in my knowledge that I was setting the standard for when to and when not to. Challenged by some petty grammarian quoting a high school English textbook I would quote myself and say, as Fowler does "Those upon whom the fear of infinity-splitting sits heavy should remember that to give conclusive evidence, by distortions, of misconceiving the nature of the split infinitive is far more damaging to their literary pretensions than an actual lapse could be for it exhibits them as deaf to the normal rhythm of English sentences."
5. What is Rooney doing here?	
6. What does this quotation tell us about Fowler?	5 Never again would I suffer indecision over matters like whether it was necessary for me to use an "of " after "a propos." I would not be looking up "arcane" eight or ten times a year. I would not use "like" when I meant "such as."
	6 The fine difference between sophisticated bits of usage such as syllepsis and zeugma would be clear in my mind. ("She ate an omelet and her heart out" is either syllepsis or zeugma. I am unclear which.)
7. What do these terms mean?	
	7 Having produced the best book on English usage ever written, I would berate the editors of the newly issued *New York Times Manual of Style and Usage* for their insistence that the President of The United States be referred to as merely president except when used as a title immediately preceding his name. In my book he's The President. Corporate chief executives are plain president.
8. What is the best book ever written on English usage?	
	8 I would conduct a nationwide poll to choose a satisfactory gender neutral replacement for both "he" "she", "him" and "her". This would relieve writers of the cumbersome but socially correct necessity of "he and she", "him or her" or the grammatically incorrect "they" or "their" with a singular precedent. ("Someone left their keys.")
9. What does this paragraph mean?	
	9 Eventually, I'd expect Oliver Stone to buy the movie rights to Rooney's *Modern English Usage.* His film would prove it was neither I nor me who murdered the English language.
10. What is the significance of either "I nor me"?	

Answers to Critical Reading Questions on Andy Rooney

   1. If you do not know the opening context of this essay, you're likely to miss the writer's intent—although you could probably reconstruct it from his essay. Rooney's essay initially appeared in the 2000 annual awards *Journal of the Screenwriters' Guild* under the feature, *A Writer's Fantasy—What I Wish I Had Written.* Various writers, Rooney among them, were asked to select the one work they wish they had written and say why.

2. Henry Watson Fowler (1858–1933) was an English lexicographer and philologist—someone who studies linguistics—who, in collaboration with his younger brother Frank, published in 1906 *The King's English*, a witty book on English usage and misusage. After the death of his brother, Fowler completed the classic Rooney wished he had written, *A Dictionary of Modern English Usage* (1926). Fowler was known for being definitive and blunt in his grammatical and literary opinions. He wrote, "Anyone who wishes to become a good writer should endeavor, before he allows himself to be tempted by the more showy qualities, to be direct, simple, brief, vigorous, and lucid," certainly good advice for anyone who writes.

3. Many people consider *A Dictionary of Modern English Usage* to be the definitive book on English usage and grammar. Grammarians often consult it to settle arguments over the fine points of acceptable usage.

4. We learn in this paragraph that Fowler's book sold as well as the Bible and that its popularity ensured fame and fortune to its writer.

5. He's mocking the rule of the subjunctive, which many people think is an ugly Latin holdover.

6. It gives us a glimpse of the sometimes starchy writing style of Fowler, who is capable of going from clarity and plainness to a scholastic denseness in a single page.

7. These are examples of the kind of arcane topics that Fowler deals with in his book. *Syllepsis* refers to the use of a word in the same grammatical relationship with two other words while disagreeing in case, gender, number, or sense with one of them. An example is "Neither she nor they are coming," where *are* agrees with *they* but not with *she*. Syllepsis is also a figure of speech in which a single word is linked to two others but in different senses, as in this use of *write*, "I write with enthusiasm and a pen." *Zeugma* refers to the linking of one word to two, one of which it does not grammatically fit, as in this use of *were*: "The seeds were devoured but the banana uneaten."

8. Obviously Fowler's, in Rooney's opinion.

9. Rooney is referring here to the quest for a nonsexist, third-person pronoun so that a sentence like "A doctor should take care of his patients" can be written without the sexiest bias implicit in the use of "his." In 1858, Charles Crozat Converse, of Erie, Pennsylvania, proposed the use of *thon*, a shortened form of *that one*, as a neutral, third-person pronoun—"A doctor should take care of thon patients"—but the word never caught on.

10. Again, Rooney is spoofing another fusty rule from English grammar—namely, that the verb "to be" takes no object. Rigorous practice of this rule is responsible for the snooty construction one hears over the telephone occasionally, "It is I" or "This is he."

EDUCATION OF A WANDERING MAN

Louis L'Amour

Louis L'Amour (1908–1988) was a prolific writer of western stories. Born March 22, 1908, Louis Dearborn LaMoore, in Jamestown, North Dakota, the family's seventh and youngest child, L'Amour dropped out of high school when he was 15 and wandered around the country, working in odd jobs as a lumberjack, elephant handler, and longshoreman. After serving in World War II, L'Amour turned his attention to becoming a writer, publishing pulp short stories in popular magazines. He eventually turned his focus to western stories, producing over three books a year until his death in 1988. A voracious reader his entire life, L'Amour kept a running tally of every book he read, recording, for example, the titles of 115 books and plays he read in 1930.

In this chapter from his autobiography, Education of a Wandering Man, *L'Amour shares his thoughts about books, civilizations, writing, and people. The chapter is included here to give you an opportunity to exercise your newly learned skill of critical reading. As you read the material, ask yourself what portrait of L'Amour, the man, emerges.*

~

1 Only one who has learned much can fully appreciate his ignorance. He knows so well the limits of his knowledge and how much lies waiting to be learned.

2   What had men thought? What had men believed? How did they come by those thoughts and beliefs? How had men learned to govern themselves? Were the processes the same everywhere?

3   Did man build cities because of an inner drive, like that of the beaver to build dams? How much of what we do is free will, and how much programmed in our genes? Why is each people so narrow that it believes that it, and it alone, has all the answers? In religion, is there but one road to salvation? Or are there many, all equally good, all going in the same general direction?

4   I have read my books by many lights, hoarding their beauty, their wit or wisdom against the dark days when I would have no book, nor a place to read.

5   I have known hunger of the belly kind many times over, but I have known a worse hunger: the need to know and to learn.

6   Once, when hitchhiking, I was picked up by a professor from some small college. He noticed I carried a book in my coat pocket, and was curious. It was a Modern Library edition, in the limp bindings they used to have, which sold at the time for 95 cents. This one contained Nietzsche's *Ecce Homo*, and *The Birth of Tragedy*.

7   The professor was a pedantic man of limited imagination and seemed almost offended that I was reading such a book. (I suspected after a few minutes'

conversation that he had not read it himself.) He plied me with questions. Obviously I did not fit some category in which he decided I belonged, and when he dropped me off in town, I suspect he was relieved to be rid of me.

8   He kept asking me why I wanted to read such a book. At first, he doubted I was reading it. Where had I heard of Nietzsche?

9   When I told him I thought it was in the preface to a book on Schopenhauer, he was even more disturbed and probably believed I was lying. Fortunately, there seem to be few of his kind, and my subsequent friendships with university professors have proved exciting, stimulating, and fun. Perhaps I was fortunate in that the first group I met was at the University of Oklahoma in the 1930's. At that time I met Kenneth C. Kaufman, Ben Botkin, Walter Stanley Campbell (who also wrote as Stanley Vestal), Carl Coke Rister, Paul Sears, and others. Sears had just written *Deserts on the March*, one of the very first books on ecology, when that word was scarcely known. I believe also that the book was the first best seller to come from a university press. Stuart Chase followed it a bit later with *Rich Land, Poor Land*, also on the subject, in 1936.

10   Having been over a lot of country I had seen what was happening to the land, and was pleased to get a chance to review Sears's book for a farm magazine. Ecology had been getting into some of my stories, principally one titled "Merrano of the Dry Country." It appeared in a pulp magazine and dealt not only with proper usage of the land but with the race question. That story first appeared about forty years ago, or a bit more.

11   The lists of books I read in my earlier years have largely been lost, but my memory for some is clear. It was a knock-about time for me: of going to sea, working in mines, lumber camps, and sawmills, doing whatever was available to make an honest dollar. Many of the activities of young men of the time I missed entirely, or in part. Either I was working, traveling from one place to another, or else I did not have the money to afford it.

12   At the time I thought that I might make a career of fighting. My early training had been good, and in knocking about the country I had picked up a few dollars here and there in small-town boxing rings. For that reason, among others, I never smoked and rarely had a drink. The idea that it might be fun to get drunk never appealed to me, for I had come to believe I could cope with any situation that might arise if I had my wits about me. There was one night in Shanghai when I was in more trouble than one man could handle. Three drunken British sailors pitched in to help, and help they did, but at bitter cost to themselves. Had they been sober, with the right coordination and reflexes, I think they would have made it.

13   Several times while traveling in Asia I hired students to read sight translations of books unavailable, so far as I knew, in English. On occasion this took place on a riverbank. Several times it was in coffee- or teahouses, where we never failed to pick up an interested audience. In one case a rather violent argument developed between the reader and a listener over a line from an Indian poet, Bhartrihari. I thought the Indus River was about to flow with fresh blood, but after a good deal of shouting and waving of arms and flashing eyes, the listener strode away. When he was well out of hearing, my reader said, "He may be right, at that."

14   (It was Bhartrihari, incidentally, who said of a woman: "She talks to one man, looks at a second, and thinks of a third.")

15   One book always led to another and occasionally my discoveries led to a whole succession of books, but there was no intent in my reading except to learn and to know. Later, when I actually began doing research on various eras of history, from curiosity or because of something I wished to write, all that changed.

16   I read *Crime and Punishment* while in Klamath Falls, Oregon. I had heard much of Dostoevsky but was surprised by this book—surprised and very impressed. Several times I turned back to reread sections of the book. At the time I was working in a sawmill, off bearing on the green chain. And that, my friends, is purely hard work.

17   When a log is cut into planks, those planks (in this case three inches thick and twelve inches wide) are green, fresh-cut lumber, and heavy. One takes a plank from the chain and puts it aboard a truck standing nearby. Meanwhile, the chain from the saw is bringing more planks, and more and more. If one is strong, reasonably agile, and gets his timing right, he can put in an eight-hour shift without too much trouble, but for hours at a stretch those planks keep coming. That is one description of off-bearing on the green chain.

18   (It has been years since I have been in a sawmill, and it is probably all done by machinery now, as are most of the jobs I used to do. I feel very sorry indeed for any young man without an education in these days, for there is literally nowhere to go.)

19   Also while on that job I read *The Moonstone* by Wilkie Collins, as well as *Plain Tales from the Hills* and *Kim* (for the second time), both by Kipling.

20   We hear a lot of talk these days about violence; but we forget the many generations that have grown up on stories of violence. The bloodiest of all, perhaps, were the so-called fairy tales, but I would have missed none of them and doubt if I did, yet I see little difference between Jack killing a fabled giant and Wyatt Earp shooting it out with an outlaw.

21   It often appears that violence is bad unless it is cloaked with enough tradition. There is much violence in the Bible, and the story could have been told in no other way. Many of Shakespeare's plays end with nearly everybody killed or dead by suicide. If we were to eliminate violence from our reading, we would have to eliminate all history, much of the world's great drama, as well as the daily newspaper.

22   What many people do not understand is that a child in growing up repeats within his early years much of the life history of man upon the earth, and it is necessary that he or she do this to become a human being.

23   At first a baby is simply a small animal that eats and sleeps, but there will come a time when he will want to build a shelter, to find some place he can crawl into, even if it is only a blanket over a chair or a table. Then there will be a time when the child plays capture games, wants a bow and arrow or perhaps a spear or other weapon. By acting out those early years of mankind's history, children put that history behind them. Most violent criminals are cases of arrested development where, for one reason or another, they never grow out of that period.

24   A girl, of course, will play with dolls, playing at being a mother, making a home, and what goes with it. All this is an essential part of growing up, of learning to be a human.

25   Much of this early violence can be sublimated through reading. In my own stories, there is no violence for the sake of violence. I tell it as it happened and, my books are all thoroughly grounded in history. What so many of us who abhor violence often forget is that we have peace and civilized lives because there were men and women who went before us who were willing to fight for our freedom to live in peace.

26   It is always well to remember that many of us sleep safe at night because there are people out there cruising the streets and on call to keep it so. As many have discovered, violence is with us still, and no one is immune to a sudden strike in the night.

27   One of the questions a writer is most often asked is "Where do you get your ideas?" If a person does not have ideas, he had better not even think of becoming a writer. But ideas are everywhere. There are ideas enough in any daily newspaper to keep a man writing for years. Ideas are all about us, in the people we meet, the way we live, the way we travel, and how we think about things. It's important to remember that we are writing about people. Ideas are important only as they affect people. And we are writing about emotion. A few people reason, but all people feel.

28   The raw material is not important. It is what the writer does with the material. One writer will make you laugh, another can make you cry, and a third might write a horror story.

29   At least once a week I get a letter from someone who has material he wants me to shape into a story (wanting, of course, a piece of the action). But a writer builds a readership because those readers like what he does with a story, not because of the material.

30   There are only a certain number of plots, and they are, very basic. When Ray Long was editor of *Cosmopolitan* years ago, he gave the same plot to six different writers, and they came up with six vastly different stories.

31   Plots are nothing devious. I have heard some literary or dramatic critics talk of plot in ways that indicated they had no grasp of the idea at all. A plot is nothing but a normal human situation that keeps arising again and again. Shakespeare's work has lived as long as it has because he dealt with normal human emotions—envy, ambition, rivalry, love, hate, greed, and so on. These are basic drives among us humans and are with us forever.

32   Because I have traveled widely it is often suspected I traveled for the purpose of gathering material. That was not the reason. Material is wherever you find it, or can see it. Some of the greatest novels have been written about small areas. Thomas Hardy and William Faulkner, for example, wrote about country districts they knew well. The Brontë sisters (whose name was originally Prunty) wrote about the part of England in which they lived.

33   It is not necessary to travel in order to write good stories; it is only necessary to see, to understand, to reveal.

34   What few realize is that no writer is free to write exactly as he might wish. He is guided, to a great extent, by the tastes of readers and by the choices of

editors. Of course, one can write whatever one wishes, but unless it conforms to the tastes of the public at the time, it will stay right on the author's shelf.

35 All manner of weird conjectures have grown up around Edgar Allan Poe, for example, but few have ever understood that he was writing what the public wanted to buy. In the first half of the nineteenth century, over in Europe, Mary Shelley was writing *Frankenstein* and Baudelaire was writing his macabre poetry and prose, while in this country Hawthorne was writing "Rappaccini's Daughter," and Washington Irving was writing *The Legend of Sleepy Hollow.* And this has been true in every age and time.

36 For a while I worked in the big timber but could not bear to see the big ones come down. I topped trees for a time, cleared brush, did whatever was available, but the times were growing worse. When the crash came in '29, we who were on the road hardly noticed the difference.

37 Yet it was a time for decision and I had made mine. If I was ever to get an education beyond my haphazard reading, it must be now.

∼

VOCABULARY

pedantic (7)	succession (15)	agile (17)
sublimated (25)	abhor (25)	conjectures (35)
macabre (35)	haphazard (37)	

QUESTIONS FOR CRITICAL READING

1. Paragraphs 2 and 3 consist of a series of questions that L'amour asked himself. What do these questions tell you about the man?

2. What lesson is L'amour teaching in relating the episode with the professor? Why do you think the professor was so surprised? What does his reaction to L'amour tell you about this unnamed person?

3. What question would a diligent reader ask about paragraph 13?

4. What accusation could a modern reader make about L'amour's attitude toward women?

5. What theory about criminality does L'amour espouse in paragraphs 21 through 23?

6. L'amour claims that there are only so many plots available to a writer and what is important is what the writer does with them. Name two of these basic plots that different writers seem to use over and over again.

7. Read paragraph 32. Based on what you've learned in this chapter, what would a critical reader do after reading this paragraph?

8. How would you characterize the author's attitude toward the land?

2

What is Rhetoric?

EDITORS' COUNSEL

Rhetoric is the art of putting one's case in the strongest and best possible way. All of the strategies of communicating in speech and writing that we use daily in an attempt to sway each other come under its heading, with practical effects so lasting and widespread that we take them for granted. For instance, when we open a popular cookbook, we expect it to be written clearly, with ordinary words framed into speakable sentences. We do not expect it to be dense and wordy like a piece of legislation. Because of rhetoric, cookbooks are not written like legal contracts; insurance policies do not read like a comic's jokes; and love letters do not sound like State of the Union speeches. Yet, there is no law requiring that this should be so. It is merely the effect of rhetoric—a combination of audience expectation and writers' desire to please that operates like a force of nature. No doubt there are badly written cookbooks, but few are either published or read; flippant insurance companies go bankrupt; and pompous lovers have trouble finding mates. This desire of writers to please—to communicate with their audiences—is the basic law of rhetoric.

Grammar and Rhetoric

In the minds of some students, grammar and rhetoric are often confused, but they are significantly different. Grammar tells a writer how words should be used and sentences framed. Just as drivers obey the rules of the road, writers follow the rules of grammar. They know that they should not begin a sentence with "one" and then suddenly switch to "you," as in "One must try to do well or you will be embarrassed." That is called a shift in point of view and, like most grammatical lapses, tends to muddy meaning.

While grammar speaks in terms of rules, rhetoric speaks only in terms of effectiveness—and effectiveness is always a relative judgment. If you are writing to a child, for example, you must use simple words and short sentences if you wish to be understood. However, simple words and short sentences may be entirely inappropriate in a paper explaining a complex process to an audience of specialists. When you know the rules of grammar, it is easy

to compare two versions of a writing assignment and say if one is more con-
ventionally grammatical than the other. It is far harder to say whether one
version is more effectively written than the other.

Judging the effectiveness of a work is, in fact, the chief business of rhetoric. For example, consider this student paragraph:

> During high school, my favorite English course was English literature. Lit-
> erature was not only interesting, but it was also fun. Learning about writers and
> poets of the past was enjoyable because of the teachers I had and the activities
> they scheduled. Teachers made past literature interesting because they could re-
> late the writers back to the time in which they lived. This way I not only learned
> about English writers but also about English history.

Grammatically, this paragraph is correct; rhetorically, it is empty. It cries
out for examples and supporting details. Which writers and poets did the student find so interesting? What activities did the teacher schedule to make
them seem so? Without such details, the paragraph is shallow and monotonous. Here is a paragraph on the same subject, written by a student with a
strong sense of rhetoric:

> Picture a shy small-town girl of eighteen, attending college for the first time
> in a large city. She is terrified of the huge campus with its crowds of bustling stu-
> dents, but she is magnetically drawn to a course entitled "Survey of English Lit-
> erature," for this awkward girl has always been an avid reader. College for me,
> this alien creature on campus, was the sudden revelation of a magical new
> world. I now could read the great English literary masterpieces—Milton's *Par-
> adise Lost,* Shakespeare's *Othello,* Jane Austen's *Pride and Prejudice.* Then I could
> discuss them in class under the watchful eye of my professor, who encouraged
> me to dig for ideas and interpret them on my own. As the teacher asked ques-
> tions, and the students responded to them, I received exciting flashes of insight
> into the human condition: I understood the loneliness of *Jude the Obscure,* the
> hardness of life in *Oliver Twist,* and the extravagant beauty of nature as detailed
> by the Romantic poets. English literature also led me into the mazy paths of his-
> tory. I learned about the greed for political power as I read about the War of the
> Roses. I saw how the *Magna Carta,* so reluctantly signed by King John, influ-
> enced our present democracy. And Chaucer's tales convinced me that the
> pageantry of people has not changed much since medieval times. English liter-
> ature educated me without my being aware of the act of acquiring knowledge.
> I learned through falling in love with English literature.

The second paragraph is rhetorically more effective than the first because
it tells us in richer detail exactly how the author was affected by her English
classes.

Audience and Purpose

To write well, you must bear in mind two truths about writing: It has an audience and it is done for a purpose. Many students think that the audience of
their writing is a single instructor whose tastes must be satisfied, but this view-

point is too narrow. The instructor is your audience only in a symbolic sense. The instructor's real job is to be a stand-in for the educated reader. In this capacity, the instructor represents universal standards of today's writing. An English instructor knows writing, good and bad, and can tell you what is good about your work and what is not so good. In this capacity, your instructor can be compared to the working editor of a newspaper, and you, to a reporter.

Purpose, on the other hand, refers to what you hope to accomplish with your writing—the influence you calculate your work will exert on your reader. Contrary to what you might think, earning a grade is not the purpose of an essay. That might be its result, but it cannot be its purpose. A freelance writer who sits down to do an article has expectations of earning money for the effort, but that is not the writer's primary purpose. Instead, purpose refers to the intention—be it grand or simple—the writer had in mind when he or she first put pen to paper. If you are writing an essay about the funniest summer vacation you have ever had, your purpose is to amuse. If you are writing an essay about how amino acids are necessary for life, your purpose is to inform. If you are writing an essay urging mandatory jail terms for sellers of child pornography, your purpose is to persuade.

It follows from this discussion that you must understand the audience and purpose of an assignment if you are to have a context for judging the effectiveness of your words and sentences. Context hints at what might work and what might flop; it warns of perils and points to possible breakthroughs. Anyone knows that a love letter should not be written in the dense sentences of a bank report and that a note of sympathy to a grieving friend should not tell jokes—anyone, that is, who thinks about the audience and the purpose of the written words. As the English writer W. Somerset Maugham put it, "To write good prose is an affair of good manners." Like good manners, good prose is always appropriate. It fits the audience; it suits the purpose. This fitting and suiting of one's writing to audience and purpose are among the chief concerns of rhetoric.

The Internal Reader/Editor

The basic aim of any instruction in rhetoric is to teach you how to distinguish between what is appropriate and inappropriate for different audiences and purposes. You develop a sixth sense of what you should say in an essay for an English instructor, a note addressed to your mother, or an ad seeking a new roommate. We call this sixth sense the *internal reader/editor.* One writer defined it this way: " . . . as it is for any writer, there are two characters in my head: the Writer (me) and a Reader/Editor (also me), who represents anyone who reads what I write. These two talk to each other."

Your internal reader/editor is your sense for judging aptness and effectiveness in writing. This sense improves with practice and exposure to assignments intended for different audiences and purposes. Whether you are penning an essay for a psychology instructor or a letter to a creditor asking for more time to repay a debt, the same internal reader/editor judges the rhetorical and grammatical appropriateness of what you have written.

By the time you are old enough to read this book, your internal reader/ editor is already in place and functioning with some sophistication. For example, your reader/editor surely knows that obscenities have no place in an essay, that "ain't" is not appropriate in a formal exam paper, and that a wealth of personal jokes and anecdotes do not belong in an objective paper on science.

Levels of English

Virtually all writing can be subdivided into three levels of English: formal, informal, and technical. Each has its place in the various assignments you will be asked to do. It is your internal reader/editor that must decide on the appropriateness of each for a specific assignment.

Formal English   is characterized by full, complex sentences and the use of standard and consistent grammar. It states ideas in an orderly fashion and with an educated vocabulary. It avoids the "I" point of view and does not use contractions such as "can't," "don't," "he'd," or "wouldn't." Here is an example of formal English:

> As the sun rose higher that morning swarms of canoes, or *canoas* as they were called in the Arawak language, were pushed out to sea through the surf breaking over the glistening white sands of Long Bay. They were all full of excited, painted Indians carrying balls of cotton thread, spears and vividly colored parrots to trade with the vessels lying a short distance off-shore. The Indian craft, probably painted as colorfully as their occupants, must have given the atmosphere of a festive regatta, and trading was brisk and lasted all day until nightfall.
>
> —D. J. R. Walker, *Columbus and the Golden World of the Island Arawaks*

The aim of formal writing is to make a case or present an argument impartially rather than to relate the writer's own views on a subject. The writer takes special care to eliminate the "I" reference and to remain discreetly in the background. Examples are either generalized or in the third person, but never personal. The facts are allowed to speak for themselves; the writer's task is to present them with objectivity.

Formal English is the staple of college writing. You should use it in research papers, scholarly papers, written examinations, and serious letters. Unless instructed to do otherwise, you should also use it in your essays.

Informal English   is based on the familiar grammatical patterns and constructions of everyday speech. It uses short sentences, contractions, the "I" point of view, and colloquial expressions. Informal English is commonly found in much journalistic writing and in personal letters, diaries, and light essays. The following student essay is a typical example:

> I drive a truck for a living, and every other week I'm assigned to a senior driver called Harry. Now, Harry is the dirtiest person I've ever met. Let's start

with the fact that he never takes a bath or shower. Sitting in the closed cab of a diesel truck on a hot August day with Harry is like being shut up in a rendering plant; in fact, the smell he emanates has, on many occasions, made my eyes water and my stomach turn. I always thought Harry was just dark complexioned until it rained one day and his arms started to streak—I mean this guy is a self-inflicted mud slide. In fact, I could've sworn that once or twice I saw Harry scratch his head and a cloud of dust whirled up above him.

The legitimate topics of informal writing are what the writer thinks or has experienced. It makes free use of the pronoun "I" and draws its material mainly from the writer's personal stock of opinions or memories. Because most of us are thoroughly fascinated with ourselves and have no trouble setting down what we think, informal English is the first kind of writing we are taught. Some assignments, given mainly in English departments, demand its use. For example, you could not write that old standby on your most memorable summer vacation without being subjective, nor should you even try.

Use informal English only in your personal writing and in those special circumstances where you are free to express yourself in your own individualistic style.

Technical English   is formal English that uses the vocabulary of a specialized field. It is written most often by engineers, technicians, and scientists. It commonly suffers from wordiness, overuse of abstract nouns, misuse of the passive voice, and improper subordination. Nevertheless, some technical writers are experts at their craft. Here is an example of technical writing:

Installing the ViaVoice software
1. Insert the ViaVoice CD in your CD-ROM drive to start the installation program. If it does not start automatically, do the following:
    a. Click **Start > Run** from the Windows taskbar.
    b. Type d;setup (where *d* is your CD-ROM drive).
    c. Click OK.
2. Follow the instructions on the screen.
    —*IBM ViaVoice for Windows User's Guide. First edition (August 2002)*

If you enter into a specialized field and have to write about your work, most of your writing will be technical writing.

The level of English you should use in any specific essay will depend on its audience and purpose; that is a judgment your internal reader/editor must make. Let us take an example. Your English teacher asks you to write an essay on the most unforgettable date you've ever had. One student wrote this paragraph:

My most unforgettable date was with Carolyn, whom I took to a drive-in movie. I chose the drive-in movie as the site of our date because Carolyn was nearly a foot taller than I, and I was embarrassed to be seen out in the open with her. What I did not expect was that my car would break down and I would not only have to get out and try to fix it, but that we would end up walking home side by side like Mutt and Jeff.

The tale that followed was a funny one about the writer's mishaps at the drive-in with Carolyn. He wrote the paragraph and the essay in an informal style because that is exactly what this assignment called for.

If, however, your sociology teacher asks you to write an essay on dating as a courtship ritual in America, you must write a formal essay. Instead of saying what happened to you personally on a date, you must say what is likely to happen on a date. Instead of airing your personal views, you must express the researched ideas and opinions of others. You should not use the pronoun "I" to refer to yourself nor attempt to impose your personality on the material. This does not mean that you should have no opinions of your own—quite the opposite—but you should base your expressed opinions on grounds more substantial than personal experience or unsupported belief. Here is an example of a student paper that follows the rules of objectivity:

> Dating is a universal courtship experience in the life of most American adolescents. The ritual goes back to the earliest chaperoned drawing-room meetings between eligible couples and has evolved to the present-day social outing. But the greatest impact on the ritual, so far as its American practice goes, has been the introduction and popularization of the automobile.

The writer supported her thesis—that the automobile has had a drastic impact on the dating ritual in America—throughout the paper and amply supported it with statistics, facts, and the testimony of experts. Her examples are also generalized rather than personal. Instead of writing that so-and-so happened to me on a date, she wrote that so-and-so is likely to happen to an American couple dating.

All writers will similarly adapt their language to suit the audience and purpose of their writing, using the principles that spring from common sense and the ancient discipline of rhetoric. While much of this adapting may be done unconsciously, it still must be done by all who sincerely wish to communicate with an audience.

Writing as a Process

Learning to write well cannot be mastered by rote the way you might absorb facts about the anatomy of a fish or the chemistry of a nebula. It involves learning a process, and that is always harder to do than memorizing a set of facts. The parts of a bicycle can be memorized from a manual, but no one can learn to ride a bicycle merely by reading a book about it. *Scribendo disces scribere* says the Latin proverb: "You learn to write by writing." Here, then, are some truths about the writing process uncovered by laboratory research:

1. Composing Is a Difficult, Back-and-Forth Process.   Many writers compose in a halting, lurching way. A writer will pen a few sentences, pause to go back and revise them, compose several new sentences, and then pause again to reread and further edit before continuing with the paragraph. "In their thinking and writing," says one researcher, "writers 'go back' in order to push thought forward."

Any professional writer will recognize the truth of this observation, but often it comes as a revelation to students who tend to worry when their own compositions emerge by similar fits and starts. Be assured that this back-and-forth movement is a healthy and normal part of composing. The research even suggests that writers who accept the halting, stumbling nature of composing actually have an easier time with this necessary process of "waiting, looking, and discovering" than those who fight against it.

Because of this circularity in composing, writing is often described as a *recursive process,* meaning that results are achieved by a roundabout rather than a straight-line path. Often it is necessary to retrace one's trail, to go back to the beginning of a work, to revise earlier sentences and paragraphs before writing new ones. If you find yourself doing something similar in your own writing, be heartened by this truth: That is how the vast majority of writers work. You are merely going through the normal cycle of composing.

2. The Topic Can Make a Difference in Your Writing.   Professional or amateur, few writers are entirely free to choose their own topics. Most are assigned topics by employers, professors, circumstances. Yet, when choice does exist, the lesson from common sense and research is that you should always pick the topic you like best. The fact is that most people write better when they write about a subject that appeals to them.

It is no mystery why this should be so. We all try harder when we are engaged in a labor of love—whether building our dream house or writing an essay. Unfortunately, in a classroom setting, many students are content to settle for a topic that seems simplest to research or easiest to write about, regardless of whether or not they find it appealing. This is a mistake. When you write for your own enjoyment, you will behave more like an experienced writer than when you force yourself to write about a subject you find boring.

3. Your Writing Will Not Automatically Improve with Each Essay.   Writing does not automatically get better with every paper. It is realistic to compare writing to, say, archery. The first arrow might hit the bull's-eye, while the tenth might entirely miss the target. An archer's overall accuracy will gradually improve with practice, but never to the point of absolute certainty for any one arrow. In practical terms, this simply means that you shouldn't brood if you find a later essay turning out worse than an earlier one. Your overall writing skills are bound to improve with experience, even if the improvement isn't reflected in any single essay.

The gist of this chapter may be summed up thus: You can learn to write well, and rhetoric can teach you how. Writing well means doing more than simply scribbling down the first idea that pops into your head. It involves thinking about your audience and purpose and choosing between this level of language or that. It means developing a rhetorical sense about what techniques are likely to work for a particular assignment. All of these skills can be learned from a study of rhetoric.

Writing about Visual Images

Visual images range from works of art found only in museums to photographs published in daily newspapers. They include television images, line drawings, sketches, computer graphics, and a bewitching gallery of exotic scenes and pictures of beautiful people from advertising. So widespread and influential are visual images that many instructors use them as essay topics.

If you've never done this kind of writing before, don't worry. Writing about an image is not that different than writing about a pig, a poem, or an adventure. Here are some techniques for writing about (1) art works, (2) news photographs, (3) cartoons, (4) and advertising images.

1. Writing About Artworks.   You do not have to be an art critic to write about a work of art, and you do not have to try to write like one. As in all kinds of writing, it is better for a writer to write from an honest self than to pretend to be someone else. In other words, be yourself always, whether you're writing about a real plum or one in a still-life painting. Here are some steps you can take to write about a work of art:

- Study the work carefully. Is it realistic or is it an abstract work with a distorted and imaginary vision? If it is a realistic work—say, the painting of a rural scene—take note of the colors and the way the paint is applied. An artist, by using drab colors and bold strokes of the brush, can suggest a negative feeling about a scene. On the other hand, a scene can be idealized with the use of bright colors and fine brushstrokes. After studying the work carefully, sum up in a single sentence your overall impression of it. This single sentence will be your thesis.

- Pay attention to the title of the work. Many Expressionist painters create images that are purely imaginary and have no equivalent in reality. It often takes a title to help us understand what the images mean. Figure 2–1 is a dramatic example of the importance of title. The painting shows a sinister assembly of men, two of whom have half a skull crammed with what looks like excrement and miscellaneous garbage. In the background is an ugly priest and a Nazi soldier with a bloody sword. It is only after we know the title of the painting, "Pillars of Society," that we grasp who these revolting men are meant to be—the emerging Nazi rulers whom the artist was satirizing. Another example can be found in Figure 2–2, a lithograph by Kathe Kollwitz of a woman whose hand is raised in a gesture explained by the work's title, *Never Again War.*

Figure 2–1. © *Estate of George Grosz/Licensed by VAGA, New York, NY.* The Pillars of Society, *1926.* © *VAGA Nationalgallerie, Staatliche Museen; Berlin, Germany* © *Foto Marburg/Art Resource, NY. Oil on Canvas, 78 3/4 × 42 1/2.*

■ Use the Internet to research background about the artist and the work. For example, before writing the paragraph about "Pillars of Society," we entered the name of the artist George Grosz and the title of his painting in the search engine *Google,* which gave us the information we needed about the work and its creator. Another example is the lithograph of the anti-war woman. Through the Internet we learned that losing a son in World War I and a grandson in World War II made the artist, German Expressionist Kathe Kollwitz (1867–1945), into a committed pacifist and explains much of her work.

■ Check your response to the work of art against the responses of art critics. We all have a unique eye. If beauty is in the eye of the beholder, so is much of art. Some modernists argue that one reaction to a work of art is as valid as another. Traditionalists take just the opposite point of view, arguing that it is possible for one reaction to be "right" and another "wrong." Most likely the truth lies somewhere in between. It is possible for an interpretation of an artwork to be so far-fetched and unprovable as to come entirely from the viewer's mind rather than from the art work itself. It is also possible for two contrary interpretations of the same artwork to exist side by side, one no more "right" than the other. In situations like this one, art critics can be helpful. They have the

Figure 2–2. Kathe Kollwitz, Never Again War! *Nie Wieder Kreig. 1924. © 2003 Artists Rights Society (ARS), New York/VG Bild-Kunst, Bonn. Lithograph, 39 × 26.*

experience and background in evaluating artistic works that enable them to spot what is unique about an artwork and what is imitative.

- Support your opinions or interpretations of the artwork. Any opinion you have about an artwork should be supported by details drawn from the work itself. If you say that the portrait of a certain person reflects an air of gloom, you should say why you think that. In support of this opinion, you can point to background colors, a grim facial expression, or perhaps the way the figure slumps.

- Say how the work made you feel. An artwork is meant to appeal both to the mind and to the heart. Don't be afraid to express how the work made you feel or to say why you think it affected you as it did. That kind of admission will help a reader better understand your opinions of the work. It is also perfectly allowable to use "I" in an essay interpreting a visual image. As a matter of fact, writing on such a personal topic without the use of "I" would be very difficult to do. You are, after all, expected to say how the work affected *you* and how *you* feel about it. You should not necessarily feel any obligation to like the artwork just because you're writing an essay about it. You may find that you heartily dislike the work. In such a case, what you have to do is to say why. If you did like the work, you should also say why.

Summary

1. State your overall impression of the work in a single sentence.
2. Ground your opinions and impressions of the artwork in details drawn from it.
3. Say how the work affected you.

WRITING ASSIGNMENT   Find and make a copy of a work of art that you like. Write three paragraphs about it, interpreting the work of art and saying what about it you especially appreciate. Include a copy of the work of art with your essay.

2. Writing about News Photographs.

■ News photographs, a staple of newspapers and magazines, range from the serene to the horrific. In the hands of a good photographer, the camera can seem to totally capture a subject. That uncanny ability, to seemingly x-ray the human soul, coupled with the spontaneity missing in more formal artworks such as paintings, has made photography into a universal language. A photograph of people leaping to their death from a burning skyscraper is globally understandable and universally wrenching, no matter what language we speak. Here are some tips on how to approach writing about a news photo:

1. Begin by researching and describing the context of the photograph. When was it taken and by whom? Under what circumstances was it shot? Knowing its context puts a photograph in historical perspective and affects your interpretation of it.

2. Describe the news photograph, clearly stating its details. Sum up, as well as you can, the facial expressions of people in the shot. The photo in Figure 2–3, for example, taken on July 28, 2002, depicts a jubilant moment in mining history. After being trapped 100 feet beneath the earth in a water-filled cave for more than three days, nine miners were, one by one, lifted to safety. The photo shows the rescue of the third miner. How would you describe the expression on the rescued miner's face?

3. Sum up your interpretation of the meaning of the photograph in one sentence. This sentence, placed in the opening paragraph, will serve as the thesis of the essay. Many variations are possible, but one summation might be, "The relief of being rescued is visibly etched on the weary face of a miner on July 28, 2002, as he was finally hoisted to the surface after spending more than 78 hours trapped underground in a water-filled cave."

Figure 2–3. Third trapped coal miner being rescued. Copyright © Reuters New Media, Inc./ CORBIS

4. Elaborate on the thesis based on evidence from the photo. You are now ready to write the body of the essay. Focusing on the photograph, you could mention the narrow rescue cage that was rigged to extract the men one at a time from their place of entrapment. You could mention the rescuers' hands reaching protectively for the trapped man and the dark and cramped confines in which the rescue seems to take place. You could describe the weariness reflected in the eyes of the miner who spent the last three days huddled underground without food in a small cave threatened by rising water. All of these details will come from the picture. You can get whatever else you need from studying its context. Again, the Internet is an ideal tool for establishing the context of a photograph.

In review, here are the steps involved in writing about a news photo:

1. Establish the context of the photograph, when and where it was taken, and why.

2. Describe the photo in detail.

3. Compose a thesis for the photo.

4. Develop evidence from the photo and its context to support your thesis.

WRITING ASSIGNMENT. Write a couple of paragraphs about a news photograph, explaining its context and giving your interpretation of it. Include a copy of the photo with your written work.

3. Writing about Cartoons. Nothing captures the spirit of an age better than a collection of its best cartoons. They seem to sum up in shorthand the idiosyncrasies of the time. The political cartoon, particularly the caricature—which is a cartoon that exaggerates physical appearance—is actually a good measure of how a particular person is regarded at a particular time. To get an idea of how Teddy Roosevelt was perceived in his day, for example, you need only go to the collection of cartoons that depict him. Here are some tips about writing about cartoons:

- Make sure you understand the message of the cartoon. Some cartoons, of course, are merely intended to amuse and have no particular message. Many cartoons mix sugar (humor) with medicine (a message). Look at Figure 2–4, for example. Here, a mother vulture is scolding her chick for complaining about being fed regurgitated yak carcass. On one level, this is a funny line from a vulture. But on a deeper level, the cartoon voices a variation on the universal complaint all parents occasionally make—that their kids are ungrateful. Another example of this subtlety is in a cartoon that depicts an English teacher standing angrily in front of her class. Behind her on the chalkboard is scrawled, "Homework due today." In front of the teacher stands a young boy who is saying, "I did my homework, but the dog pressed control-alt-delete." What makes this line funny is that it is the computer-age equivalent of "the dog ate my homework."

- Be aware of the topsy-turvy world of cartoons. Many cartoons spoof the accepted and habitual views of society, often by turning the world upside down. For example, one cartoon shows the seats of a movie theater filled with an audience of winged bugs waiting for the feature to begin. On the screen is the name of the upcoming movie: "Return of the Killer Windshield." Another—one of our favorites—shows a horrible monster scrambling to get dressed. Looking at his watch worriedly, he is complaining to his wife that he's late and should have already been in a certain boy's closet. The caption of the cartoon? "Monster jobs." The humor of both cartoons comes mainly from the inversion of normalcy, giving us an unusual slant on a familiar situation.

- State what lesson the cartoon teaches. Many cartoons teach a lesson. Sometimes the lesson can be obvious, as in the cartoon showing an enormous, savage dog turning to bare its teeth at a tiny cowboy,

"Listen, buster, I didn't sit on your hard little egg in the blazing sun for six weeks just to hear you say, 'Ewww, I don't like regurgitated yak carcass.'"

Figure 2–4. Tom Cheney. The New Yorker, *August 19 & 26, 2002.*

President Bush, who is tweaking the dog's tail. Painted in a sinister scrawl on the back of the dog is its name: War. The lesson is rather obvious. If you provoke war, it is likely to savagely turn on you. Sometimes the lesson is less obvious. For example, a cartoon featuring two forlorn-looking people standing side-by-side in the aisle of a library and looking at two different books, one entitled "Self-Improvement," the other "Self-Involvement" is teaching a subtle lesson about narcissism. In any case, part of your interpretation of the cartoon is to say what lesson it teaches—if it, indeed, teaches any. Study the cartoon until you get its meaning.

Summary

1. Make sure you understand the message of the cartoon, if it has one.
2. Be aware of the topsy-turvy world of cartoons.
3. Study the lesson of the cartoon.

WRITING ASSIGNMENT.   Write a few paragraphs about any cartoon that you particularly like. Be sure to include a copy of the cartoon with your work.

Figure 2–5. Two white androgynous looking young men pose on billboard advertising Gucci designer clothing. Copyright © Bill Aron / Photo Edit, Inc. All rights reserved.

4. Writing about Advertisements. Advertising images, although sometimes bewitching, often have an air of unreality. They glamorize persons, settings, and objects. See Figure 2–5. Many of the graphic messages are either exaggerated or outright lies. We know that it is impossible for any one to turn a rainy day into a sunny one just by swallowing a pill; that all our worries will not vanish if we take a certain laxative, and that rubbing our faces with a cream will not make wrinkles disappear overnight. Buying a certain mattress will not turn the insomniac into another Rip Van Winkle, nor will driving a new car make you into an overnight sensation with the opposite sex.

Anyone who writes about advertising images has to exercise both common sense and logic. Common sense will enable you to see through the pitch. Logic will help you to sift through the exaggerated claims made by the hype. To write about an advertising image requires you to take the following steps:

■ Be sure you know the audience at whom the ad is aimed and the product that is being advertised. An ad directed at women—for a perfume fragrance, for example—often comes with a feminized image. On the other hand, masculine images are typically found in a beer advertisement aimed mainly at men. Strange as it may seem, a few advertisements have been oblique rather than blunt in their hype of a product. Probably the most famous example of this is the advertising campaign for a certain, new Japanese car. The ads show scenes of pastures and mountain brooks—to the accompaniment of philosophical babble that have little to do with a car. Ask yourself what the product is, who uses it, and what it does. Sum up this information in a single sentence and you have your thesis.

■ Pay attention to the language that accompanies the image. Advertising copy is often written in fragments rather than whole sentences. For example, an ad for a trip to Wales uses the following copy: "Suggested itinerary: London-Nirvana-London. It's a stopover in serenity. A side trip to paradise. Where the wonders of nature and the comforts of home live side by side. Wales. Just two hours from London." One sentence and five fragments make up this copy. Notice any poetic touch used to highlight the image. For example, the most successful advertising slogan of all time consists of two rhyming words: "Think Mink." Advertising copy is also often openly romantic, as in this example: "Somewhere she went from the girl of your dreams to the love of your life. A diamond is forever."

■ Notice any inversion of reality. Advertisers are notorious for turning reality on its head. If a product is bad for you, the advertising may tout it as a health remedy. For example, cigarette advertisements used to always show smokers as specimens of perfect, robust health. The typical image associated with Marlboro cigarettes was a rugged cowboy shown on the range herding cattle and occasionally pausing for a "healthful" smoke.

■ Watch out for buzzwords or euphemisms. A buzzword is a slogan or saying that is associated with the product. The slogan of a certain underarm deodorant was, "Strong enough for a man. But made for a woman." A euphemism is a gentler way of saying something. For example, saying "he passed away" is a euphemism for "he died." Advertisers often combine images with euphemisms as part of their pitch. For example, an advertisement for insurance will talk about sparing your family the heartbreak of final decisions—meaning, finding a place to bury you and a way to pay for it. Personal hygiene products for women are always euphemistic in their claims. Sometimes, even an image can be euphemistic, as is often the case in some advertisements for laxatives.

■ Use logic to evaluate the extravagant claims of an advertising image. It is no exaggeration to say that advertisements often tell outright lies. Ad people would probably claim that they do not lie, but merely stress the positives about their product. Yet, anyone with common sense can't help but wonder what to make of a claim like "X toothpaste is used by two out of three dentists." How many dentists were surveyed to come to this conclusion? It might have been three. And what does this claim mean: "Degree antiperspirant deodorant is body-heat activated. Your body heat turns it on." And when an insect repellent advertises that it makes "you invisible to bugs," is that claim meant literally or figuratively?

- Mention any humor associated with image. An ad for Toshiba copy machines features a speaking copier: "I print 80 pages per minute and sit near the men's room. She types 40 words per minute and gets the corner office. Is there no balance in the universe?" To discuss this particular image you would have to touch on the humor of the talking copier.

Summary

1. Be sure you know what's being advertised and to whom.
2. Pay attention to the language that accompanies the image.
3. Notice any inversion of reality.
4. Watch out for buzzwords or euphemisms.
5. Use logic to evaluate the extravagant claims of an advertising image.
6. Mention any humor associated with the image.

WRITING ASSIGNMENT.   Write two paragraphs on a magazine or newspaper ad that you particularly dislike. Include a copy of the ad with your work.

EXERCISES

1. After studying the following passages, suggest the purpose of each and the audience for which it is intended. Give specific examples of language suitable to that audience.

    a. At first our Greg was a model child. Healthy, happy, unfailingly sweet-tempered, he was a total joy as a baby. When he was one year old, he thought that everything mother and father wanted him to do was wonderful. His second birthday passed, and he remained cooperative and adorable. Aha, I thought, the "terrible twos" that everyone complains about must result from inadequate attention and discipline.

    Then Greg turned 2¾ years old. Suddenly we had an obnoxious monster in the house. His favorite word was "No!" and he used it constantly. At the simplest request he would stamp his feet and cry. It took a battle to get him to put on clothing he had previously worn happily. Favorite foods were thrown on the floor. It became almost impossible to take him shopping because he would lie down in the store and refuse to move. There was constant tension in the house, and my husband and I became irritable, too. We felt as if we were living on the slopes of a volcano, and we found ourselves giving in to Greg too much in order to avoid the threatened eruptions.

    b. Others will debate the controversial issues, national and international, which divide men's minds. But serene, calm, aloof, you stand as the nation's war guardians, as its lifeguards from the raging tides of international conflict, as its gladiators in the arena of battle. For a century-and-a-half you have defended, guarded, and protected its hallowed traditions of liberty and freedom, of right and justice.

Let civilian voices argue the merits or demerits of our processes of government: whether our strength is being sapped by deficit financing indulged in too long; by federal paternalism grown too mighty; by power groups grown too arrogant; by politics grown too corrupt; by crime grown too rampant; by morals grown too low; by taxes grown too high; by extremists grown too violent; whether our personal liberties are as firm and complete as they should be.

These great national problems are not for your professional participation or military solution. Your guidepost stands out like a tenfold beacon in the night: duty, honor, country.

c. To give Eleanor her due, any suspicion as to the slightest inclination on her part toward Mr. Slope was a wrong to her. She had no more idea of marrying Mr. Slope than she had of marrying the bishop, and the idea that Mr. Slope would present himself as a suitor had never occurred to her. Indeed, to give her her due again, she had never thought about suitors since her husband's death. But nevertheless it was true that she had overcome all that repugnance to the man which was so strongly felt for him by the rest of the Grantly faction. She had forgiven him his sermon. She had forgiven him his low church tendencies, his Sabbath schools, and puritanical observances. She had forgiven his pharisaical arrogance, and even his greasy face and oily vulgar manners. Having agreed to overlook such offences as these, why should she not in time be taught to regard Mr. Slope as a suitor?

d. Earthquakes are often accompanied by a roaring noise that comes from the bowels of the earth. This phenomenon was known to early geographers. Pliny wrote that earthquakes are "preceded or accompanied by a terrible sound." Vaults supporting the ground give way and it seems as though the earth heaves deep sighs. The sound was attributed to the gods and called theophany.

The eruptions of volcanoes are also accompanied by loud noises. The sound produced by Krakatoa in the East Indies, during the eruption of 1883, was so loud that it was heard as far as Japan, 3,000 miles away, the farthest distance travelled by sound recorded in modern annals.

e. I beg you to excuse a father who dares to approach you in the interests of his son.

I wish to mention first that my son is 22 years old, has studied for four years at the Zurich Polytechnic and last summer brilliantly passed his diploma examinations in mathematics and physics. Since then he has tried unsuccessfully to find a position as assistant, which would enable him to continue his education in theoretical and experimental physics. Everybody who is able to judge, praises his talent, and in any case I can assure you that he is exceedingly assiduous and industrious and is attached to his science with a great love.

    f. Letters written by a potential customer asking suppliers for free materials, information, or routine services are among the easiest to write. The customer will usually receive what he or she is asking for since it is to the supplier's advantage to provide it. The potential customer need only be clear and courteous. In writing routine request letters, give all the information the supplier will need in order to be really helpful, keep your request as brief as possible without omitting important *details,* and express your wishes courteously and tactfully.

2. Write two, one-page essays explaining the reasons why you wish to pursue a certain career. Address the first to the personnel manager of an organization that might hire you and the second to your father. Contrast the language and phrasing of each essay and explain the differences between them.

3. Both of the following letters refuse credit to a potential customer. How does the second differ in purpose from the first?

    a. Please accept our regrets that we cannot offer you a 60-day credit for the meeting of your organization here at Pine Lodge in July of 1987. When you held your meeting here last year, we had the embarrassing experience of having to wait six months before you made full payment on your bill. I am sure that you will understand that we cannot take chances on such bad credit risks.

    b. Thank you for choosing Pine Lodge again for your 1987 meeting. We consider it a pleasure to have you, although we must ask you to send us a 25% deposit and to make a full settlement when you check out. This is now our standard arrangement with organizations similar to yours. If these arrangements are satisfactory, we shall do our best to make sure that your group is extended every courtesy and service during its stay.

4. A restaurant owner has sent the following memorandum to the waiters and waitresses working for him. Rewrite the memo to create a more positive tone, without destroying its purpose.

To: All waiters and waitresses

I've had it with you lazy clowns! This month's profits fell 20% below last year's at this same time. Now, any fool can tell that the problem is your sloppy service to the customers, your excessive breaking of china and glassware, and your horsing around instead of paying attention to such details as keeping the food warm, setting the tables properly, and getting the customer's order straight. So, I'm warning you: either start doing your job right, or you'll find yourselves fired.

5. Assuming an educated audience, label the purpose of each of the following passages: (1) to inspire, (2) to get action, (3) to amuse, or (4) to inform.

   a. Please send us either a check within the next week or an explanation if some problem has arisen. We are eager to cooperate with you.

   b. Conscience is a sacred sanctuary where God alone may enter as judge.

   c. In great straits, and when hope is small, the boldest counsels are the safest.

   d. Men seldom make passes at girls who wear glasses.

   e. The more one comes to know men, the more one admires the dog.

   f. "Gavelkind" is the custom of having all of the sons of an estate holder share equally in the estate upon the death of the father. Most of the lands in England were held in gavelkind tenure prior to the Norman Conquest.

   g. Seek not the favor of the multitude; it is seldom got by honest and lawful means. But seek the testimony of few; and number not voices, but weigh them.

   h. Botticelli isn't a wine, you dunce! Botticelli is a cheese.

   i. The Indus River is approximately 1,900 miles long. It rises in the Kailas range of Tibet, flows west across Kashmir, India, and then moves southwest to the Arabian Sea.

   j. Flaming manifestoes and prophecies of doom are no longer much help, and a search for scapegoats can only make matters worse. The time for sensations and manifestoes is about over. Now we need rigorous analysis, united effort, and very hard work

6. Label each of the following passages according to its level of English: formal, informal, or technical. In each case, describe the characteristics that identify the level of writing.

   a. Sometimes I wish I were a mountain stream. If I were a mountain stream, I'd flow down a beautiful green, woodsy, snow-capped mountain. I'd be fed by the cool, melting snow, and I'd shimmer and glisten as the sun warmed my flowing presence. Being a mountain stream, I'd attract only a few select people—those with enough courage and stamina to climb through thickets, across ravines, and up steep paths to my cool, ethereal banks. Those special people could enjoy sitting on my banks to search my clear depths for the solitude, serenity, and peace they're longing to find.

b. The bony remains of Peking Man all came from a single limestone cave at Chou-k'ou-tien. The bones consist of fifteen crania, six facial bones, twelve mandibles, a miscellaneous collection of postcranial bones, and 147 teeth. Studies of the physical characters of these bones by Davidson Black and Franz Weidenreich disclose that Peking Man was still in an early stage of human development, comparable to the *Homo erectus* of Java. The limbs were highly developed and quite modern, indicating that he stood upright and walked on two feet, but the cranium is characterized by low vault, heavy bony features, thick wall, and small cranial capacity (914–1,225 cc., with an average of 1,043 cc., as against Java Man's 860 cc. and modern man's 1,350 cc.).

—John T. Meskill

c. Unlike in nature, where the root feeds the plant, in art, the pinnacle makes possible the base. Drama did not begin with a lot of hacks gradually evolving into Aeschylus and Sophocles; the novel did not start with a slew of James Micheners and Leon Urises building up to Dickens and Joyce. Richardson, Fielding, Sterne, and Smollett started things on a pretty high level; it is they who made the Jacqueline Susanns possible, not the other way around. Public funds for the dissemination of culture are necessary, but unless the most difficult and demanding creations on the individual level are subsidized, no amount of grants to public television to put on The Adams Chronicles will prevent culture and art from withering away or becoming debased, which is the same thing.

—John Simon

7. Remember your last significant writing assignment and answer the following questions:
   a. Who was your audience?
   b. What was your purpose?
   c. What level of English did you use?

8. Assuming that choice of topic affects the quality of your writing, choose the topic that most interests you from the following list. In two or three sentences, state why the topic appeals to you. Describe the audience for whom you would like to write about your chosen topic.
   a. The future of working women
   b. Care for the elderly
   c. The cost of owning a house

   d. The pleasures associated with a particular hobby

   e. Preserving our environment

   f. Some aspect of working with computers

   g. Handicapped children

   h. Some aspect of primitive civilization

   i. A favorite painter, sculptor, dancer, or musician

   j. Business ethics

   k. Political reform

———— ADVICE ————

WHAT—AND HOW—TO WRITE WHEN YOU HAVE NO TIME TO WRITE

Donald Murray

Donald Murray (b. 1924) is a Pulitzer Prize–winning journalist who has made it part of his life's work to teach others how to write. He writes a much-read weekly column for The Boston Globe *as well as feature articles for a variety of magazines. Many teachers of composition rely on Murray's books for teaching strategies. Among his most influential books are* Shoptalk: Learning to Write with Writers *(1991);* Expecting the Unexpected: Teaching Myself and Others to Read and Write *(1989);* The Craft of Revision *(1997); and* Crafting a Life in Essay, Story, Poem *(1996). Murray is Professor Emeritus of English at the University of New Hampshire.*

Murray, who is known for his practical approach to writing, dispenses some sensible advice, which he summarizes into "ten little habits of mind and craft." While his ideas apply particularly to the full-time writer, they are also practical enough to help the student.

∼

1 The less time I have for writing, the more important it is that I write. Writing gives me a necessary calm, what Robert Frost called "a momentary stay against confusion." Writing slows down the rush of life, forcing awareness and reflection. As writing increases my awareness, language clarifies that vision. What is vague and general becomes concrete and specific as I find the words. These words connect with other words in phrase and sentence, placing the immediate experience in the context of my life. I read the story of my life by writing it. I also receive the gift of concentration and escape the swirling problems of my life as I follow paragraph and page toward meaning.

2   I write fragments in slivers of time, always with interruptions, and yet, when I look back, I am surprised that the writing caught on the fly has produced a lifetime of productivity. I have come to realize that very little published writing is produced during sustained periods of composition without interruption. You have to arrange a life in which part of your mind is writing all the time; that's when the seeds of writing are sown and then cultivated. The writing is harvested in short periods of time between the busy chores that crowd the day.

3   Graham Greene said, "If one wants to write, one simply has to organize one's life in a mass of little habits." Here are ten little habits of mind and craft that I realize, looking back, made me a productive writer—without long writing days free of interruption.

4   1. Don't wait for an idea.

5   If you know what you want to say, you've probably said it before, or it's not worth saying. Writing is thinking, and thought begins not with a conclusion but with an itch, a hint, a clue, a question, a doubt, a wonder, a problem, an answer without a question, an image that refuses to be forgotten. Such fragments are caught on the wing, when I think my mind is somewhere else.

6   My four-year-old grandson told his mother, "I know Grandpa is a writer because he's always writing in his wallet." It is not a wallet, but a container for the 3 × 5 cards that are always in my shirt pocket with three pens. In a shoulder case that is not far from me night and day is the spiral daybook in which I talk to myself, capturing and playing with fragments of language that may become a draft.

7   2. Listen to your own difference.

8   People who want to write look at what is being published, but the writers who are published have looked within themselves, found their own vision of the world, heard their own voices. Sandra Cisneros said, "Write about what makes you different."

9   As I look back, I realize that what made me strange to my family, classmates and teachers, friends and neighbors, colleagues and editors, is what has produced the writing that has been read. In the wonderful way of art, what is most personal, eccentric, individual, becomes most universal. When I have tried to become someone else I have failed; when I have been myself I have succeeded.

10   3. Avoid long writing sessions.

11   Most people believe, as I once did, that it is necessary to have long, uninterrupted days in which to write. But there are no such days. Life intrudes. I try to follow the counsel of Horace, Pliny, and so many others through the centuries: nulla dies sine linea—never a day without a line.

12   How long does it take me to write? My weekly columns take 71 years of living and about forty-five minutes of writing. I write in bursts of twenty minutes, five, fifteen, thirty, sixty; ninety minutes is the maximum amount of writing time that is effective for me.

13   And how much writing do I produce? I've finished a book averaging 300 words a day. These days I try to average 500 words a day. The important thing is not the time or the words, but the habit, that dailiness of the writing.

14   4. Break long writing projects into brief daily tasks.

15   Books are written a page at a time, and I find it helpful—essential—to break a book into units that can be finished in a short morning's writing: lead for Ch. 3, scene in court, description of experiment, interview with source, column on writing time.

16   5. Write in the morning.

17   Most writers write in the early morning before the world intrudes. They harvest the product of their subconscious. Each hour of the day becomes less efficient as the writer is not only interrupted, but increasingly aware of all the professional and family concerns that crowd the mind. An 800-word column I can write in 45 minutes in the morning takes me three hours in the afternoon.

18   6. Know tomorrow's task today.

19   I set myself a single writing task and know what it is the night before. I don't know what I am going to write, but I assign the writing problem to my subconscious at the end of the morning writing session or before I go to bed, and part of my mind works on it as I go about my living.

20   7. Seek instructive failure.

21   Effective writing is the product of instructive failure. You try to say what you cannot yet say, but in the attempt you discover—draft by draft—what you have to say and how you can say it. Failure is essential. Failure occurs when the words race ahead of thought, producing insights that may be developed through revision. The writer should seek to fail, not to say what has been said before, but what has not yet been said and is worth saying.

22   8. Focus on what works.

23   Once failure has revealed what you want to say, you should develop the topic by concentrating on what works, rather than focusing on correcting errors. Most errors will not occur if you develop what works and, at the end of the drafting process, you can solve any problems that remain. I revise mostly by layering, writing over—and over—what has been written.

24   9. Keep score.

25   As you write, it is important to suspend critical judgment until after a draft is finished. It's helpful to count words—or pages or hours—so that you can tell yourself that you have written without assessing how well you have written until the piece is finished.

26   10. Let it go.

27   Hardest of all is to let it go. The draft never equals the dream. The draft will expose your private thoughts and feelings to the world, but when you are published, what you most feared would appear foolish, your readers often find most profound. You have given words to their private thoughts and feelings.

28   Writing produces writing. When writing you are more aware of the world and your own reaction to it. As a writer, you relive your life hundreds of times, and when you are in your seventies, as I am, you'll come to your writing desk and discover you have even more to say than you imagined when you were 17 years old and dreaming of a writing life.

～

(1,289 words)

VOCABULARY

sustained (2) daybook (6) eccentric (9)
suspend (25) assessing (25)

——————— **EXAMPLES** ———————

I HAVE A DREAM

Martin Luther King, Jr.

Martin Luther King, Jr. (1929–1968), American clergyman and black civil rights leader, was born in Atlanta and educated at Morehouse College, Crozer Theological Seminary, and Boston University (Ph.D., 1955). Dr. King, a lifelong advocate of nonviolent resistance to segregation, led a boycott of blacks in Montgomery, Alabama (1955–1956) against the city's segregated bus system and organized a massive march on Washington, D.C. in 1963, during which he delivered his famous "I Have a Dream" speech. In 1964, he was awarded the Nobel Peace Prize. Dr. King was assassinated on April 4, 1968 on a motel balcony in Memphis, Tennessee, where he had journeyed in support of the city's striking sanitation workers.

In August 1963, more than 200 thousand blacks and whites gathered peacefully in Washington, D.C., to focus attention on black demands for civil rights. The marchers gathered at the Lincoln Memorial, where Dr. King delivered this impassioned speech.

∼

1   Five score years ago, a great American, in whose symbolic shadow we stand today, signed the Emancipation Proclamation. This momentous decree came as a great beacon light of hope to millions of Negro slaves who had been seared in the flames of withering injustice. It came as a joyous daybreak to end the long night of their captivity.

2   But one hundred years later, the Negro still is not free. One hundred years later, the life of the Negro is still sadly crippled by the manacles of segregation and the chains of discrimination.

3   One hundred years later, the Negro lives on a lonely island of poverty in the midst of a vast ocean of material prosperity. One hundred years later, the Negro is still languished in the corners of American society and finds himself an exile in his own land. So we have come here today to dramatize a shameful condition.

4   In a sense we have come to our nation's capital to cash a check. When the architects of our republic wrote the magnificent words of the Constitution and the Declaration of Independence, they were signing a promissory note to which every American was to fall heir. This note was a promise that all men,

yes, black men as well as white men, would be granted the unalienable rights of life, liberty, and the pursuit of happiness.

5   It is obvious today that America has defaulted on this promissory note insofar as her citizens of color are concerned. Instead of honoring this sacred obligation, America has given the Negro people a bad check, which has come back marked "insufficient funds."

6   But we refuse to believe that the bank of justice is bankrupt. We refuse to believe that there are insufficient funds in the great vaults of opportunity of this nation. So we have come to cash this check—a check that will give us upon demand the riches of freedom and the security of justice.

7   We have also come to this hallowed spot to remind America of the fierce urgency of now. This is no time to engage in the luxury of cooling off or to take the tranquilizing drug of gradualism. Now is the time to make real the promises of democracy. Now is the time to rise from the dark and desolate valley of segregation to the sunlit path of racial justice. Now is the time to lift our nation from the quick sands of racial injustice to the solid rock of brotherhood. Now is the time to make justice a reality for all of God's children.

8   It would be fatal for the nation to overlook the urgency of the movement and to underestimate the determination of the Negro. This sweltering summer of the Negro's legitimate discontent will not pass until there is an invigorating autumn of freedom and equality. 1963 is not an end but a beginning. Those who hope that the Negro needed to blow off steam and will now be content will have a rude awakening if the nation returns to business as usual.

9   There will be neither rest nor tranquility in America until the Negro is granted his citizenship rights. The whirlwinds of revolt will continue to shake the foundations of our nation until the bright day of justice emerges.

10   But there is something that I must say to my people who stand on the warm threshold which leads into the palace of justice. In the process of gaining our rightful place we must not be guilty of wrongful deeds.

11   Let us not seek to satisfy our thirst for freedom by drinking from the cup of bitterness and hatred. We must forever conduct our struggle on the high plane of dignity and discipline. We must not allow our creative protest to degenerate into physical violence. Again and again we must rise to the majestic heights of meeting physical force with soul force.

12   The marvelous new militancy which has engulfed the Negro community must not lead us to a distrust of all white people, for many of our white brothers, as evidenced by their presence here today, have come to realize that their destiny is tied up with our destiny and they have come to realize that their freedom is inextricably bound to our freedom. This offense we share mounted to storm the battlements of injustice must be carried forth by a biracial army. We cannot walk alone.

13   And as we walk, we must make the pledge that we shall always march ahead. We cannot turn back. There are those who are asking the devotees of civil rights, "When will you be satisfied?" We can never be satisfied as long as the Negro is the victim of the unspeakable horrors of police brutality.

14   We can never be satisfied as long as our bodies, heavy with the fatigue of travel, cannot gain lodging in the motels of the highways and the hotels of the cities. We cannot be satisfied as long as the Negro's basic mobility is from a smaller ghetto to a larger one.

15   We can never be satisfied as long as our children are stripped of their self-hood and robbed of their dignity by signs stating "for whites only." We cannot be satisfied as long as a Negro in Mississippi cannot vote and a Negro in New York believes he has nothing for which to vote. No, we are not satisfied, and we will not be satisfied until justice rolls down like waters and righteousness like a mighty stream.

16   I am not unmindful that some of you have come here out of excessive trials and tribulation. Some of you have come fresh from narrow jail cells. Some of you have come from areas where your quest for freedom left you battered by the storms of persecution and staggered by the winds of police brutality. You have been the veterans of creative suffering. Continue to work with the faith that unearned suffering is redemptive.

17   Go back to Mississippi; go back to Alabama; go back to South Carolina; go back to Georgia; go back to Louisiana; go back to the slums and ghettos of the Northern cities, knowing that somehow this situation can, and will be changed. Let us not wallow in the valley of despair.

18   So I say to you, my friends, that even though we must face the difficulties of today and tomorrow, I still have a dream. It is a dream deeply rooted in the American dream that one day this nation will rise up and live out the true meaning of its creed—we hold these truths to be self evident, that all men are created equal.

19   I have a dream that one day on the red hills of Georgia, sons of former slaves and sons of former slave-owners will be able to sit down together at the table of brotherhood.

20   I have a dream that one day, even the state of Mississippi, a state sweltering with the heat of injustice, sweltering with the heat of oppression, will be transformed into an oasis of freedom and justice.

21   I have a dream my four little children will one day live in a nation where they will not be judged by the color of their skin but by the content of their character. I have a dream today!

22   I have a dream that one day, down in Alabama, with its vicious racists, with its governor having his lips dripping with the words of interposition and nullification, that one day, right there in Alabama, little black boys and black girls will be able to join hands with little white boys and white girls as sisters and brothers. I have a dream today!

23   I have a dream that one day every valley shall be exalted, every hill and mountain shall be made low, the rough places shall be made plain, and the crooked places shall be made straight and the glory of the Lord will be revealed and all flesh shall see it together.

24   This is our hope. This is the faith that I go back to the South with.

25   With this faith we will be able to hew out of the mountain of despair a stone of hope. With this faith we will be able to transform the jangling discords of our nation into a beautiful symphony of brotherhood.

26   With this faith we will be able to work together, to pray together, to struggle together, to go to jail together, to stand up for freedom together, knowing
that we will be free one day. This will be the day when all of God's children
will be able to sing with new meaning—"my country 'tis of thee; sweet land
of liberty; of thee I sing; land where my fathers died, land of the pilgrim's
pride; from every mountain side, let freedom ring"—and if America is to be
a great nation, this must become true.

27   So let freedom ring from the prodigious hilltops of New Hampshire.

28   Let freedom ring from the mighty mountains of New York.

29   Let freedom ring from the heightening Alleghenies of Pennsylvania.

30   Let freedom ring from the snow-capped Rockies of Colorado.

31   Let freedom ring from the curvaceous slopes of California.

32   But not only that.

33   Let freedom ring from Stone Mountain of Georgia.

34   Let freedom ring from Lookout Mountain of Tennessee.

35   Let freedom ring from every hill and molehill of Mississippi, from every
mountainside, let freedom ring.

36   And when we allow freedom to ring, when we let it ring from every village and hamlet, from every state and city, we will be able to speed up that
day when all of God's children—black men and white men, Jews and Gen-
tiles, Catholics and Protestants—will be able to join hands and to sing in the
words of the old Negro spiritual, "Free at last, free at last; thank God
Almighty, we are free at last."

～

(1,643 words)

VOCABULARY

momentous (1)	manacles (2)	languished (3)
unalienable (4)	hallowed (7)	gradualism (7)
invigorating (8)	degenerate (11)	militancy (12)
inextricably (12)	tribulation (16)	redemptive (16)
sweltering (20)	interposition (22)	nullification (22)
exalted (23)	prodigious (27)	curvaceous (31)

THE FACTS

1. The speech begins "Five score years ago . . ." Why was this beginning
   especially appropriate?

2. What grievances of black Americans does Dr. King summarize in
   paragraphs 2 and 3 of this speech?

3. What does Dr. King caution his listeners against in paragraph 11?

4. What attitude toward white people does the speaker urge upon his
   audience?

5. Although Dr. King speaks out mainly against injustices committed against blacks in the South, he is also critical of the North. What can be inferred from this speech about the living conditions of blacks in the North during the early 1960s?

THE STRATEGIES

1. One critic of this speech has written that its purpose was to intensify the values of the black movement. What characteristic of its style can you point to that might be said to have served this purpose?
2. Paragraphs 4 through 6 of the speech are linked through the use of an extended analogy. What is this analogy?
3. What common rhetorical device does the speech frequently use to emphasize its points?
4. It is often said that speakers and writers use paragraphs differently. How are the paragraphs of this speech especially adapted for oral delivery? What is the most obvious difference between these paragraphs and those a writer might use?
5. What is the function of the brief paragraph 32?

THE ISSUES

1. "Black" is a term widely used in the United States to designate people whose skin color may range from dark brown to sepia; however, what definition of blackness does our society seem implicitly to use?
2. In your opinion, what is the basis of racial prejudice?
3. Will the United States ever have a black president? Defend your answer.
4. Does prejudice in the United States against black men exceed or equal the prejudice against black women? Explain the difference, if there is one, and justify your answer.
5. What stereotypes do you hold about people of other races? Write them down along with an explanation of how you arrived at them. Share them with your classmates.

SUGGESTIONS FOR WRITING

1. Write an essay analyzing the extensive use of metaphors in this speech. Comment on their effectiveness, bearing in mind the audience for whom the speech was intended.
2. Write an essay analyzing the oral style of this speech. Point out specific techniques of phrasing, sentence construction, paragraphing,

and so on that identify this composition as a speech. Suggest how a writer might have phrased some passages if this work had been written to be read rather than heard.

LETTER TO THE REV. J. PAGE HOPPS

Oscar Wilde

Oscar Wilde (1854–1900) is considered one of Ireland's greatest authors and wits. Born in Dublin, he is known for his sophisticated and witty dramas that expose the manners of the middle and upper classes in Eng- land. He studied at Trinity College in Dublin as well as at Magdalen Col- lege in Oxford, where he distinguished himself for both his scholarship and his ability to debate. Following the revelation of his love affair with a young aristocrat, Lord Alfred Douglas, Wilde was arrested—at the height of his acclaim in London—tried, convicted, and sent to prison for homosexuality, then considered a crime. After his release from jail, his health failed and he never regained his literary creativity. Among his best-known works are the plays Lady Windermere's Fan *(1892),* A Woman of No Importance *(1893),* An Ideal Husband *(1895), and* The Importance of Being Earnest *(1895). Wilde also wrote a tragedy,* Salome *(1893), which was used for the opera by that title. While in jail, Wilde wrote his moving poem "The Ballad of Reading Gaol," and a long apology for his behavior, "De Profundis" (1905), addressed to Lord Douglas. Wilde died in France, lonely and isolated from a once-admiring English public.*

The Reverend Hopps, to whom the following letter is addressed, was a clergy- man, religious author, and editor. Wilde had been one of the speakers invited to address a meeting of a civic group trying to reform funeral services and mourning traditions. Hopps read the letter aloud at the meeting because Wilde had canceled his appearance due to a severe cold. Although Wilde's letter was written in 1885, his ideas are still appropriate and thought provoking.

~

January 1885

1   Dear Mr. Hopps, I am very sorry to say that I am confined to the house with a severe cold, caught by lecturing in a Lincolnshire snowstorm, and am not allowed *by my* doctor to travel. It is with much regret that I find myself un- able to join in the meeting tomorrow, as I sympathise most strongly with the object in question. The present style of burying and sorrowing for the dead seems to me to make grief grotesque, and to turn mourning to a mockery. Any reform you can bring about in these customs would be of value quite ines- timable. The present ostentation and extravagance of burial rites seems to me

to harmonise but ill with the real feeling of those at the doors of whose house the Angel of Death has knocked. The ceremony by which we part from those whom we have loved should not merely be noble in its meaning, but simple in its sincerity. The funeral of Ophelia does not seem to me "a maimed rite" when one thinks of the flowers strewn on her grave. I regret exceedingly that I cannot hear the actual suggestions on the matter which will be made at your meeting. I have always been of the opinion that the coffin should be privately conveyed at night-time to the churchyard chapel, and that there the mourners should next day meet. By these means the public procession through the streets would be avoided; and the publicity of funerals is surely the real cause of their expense. As regards dress, I consider that white and violet should be recognised as mourning, and not black merely, particularly in the case of children. The habit of bringing flowers to the grave is now almost universal, and is a custom beautiful in its symbolism; but I cannot help thinking that the elaborate and expensive designs made by the florist are often far less lovely than a few flowers held loose in the hand. There are many other points on which I should have liked to listen, and one point on which I had hoped to have the privilege of speaking. I mean the expression of sorrow in art. The urns, pyramids and sham sarcophagi—ugly legacies from the eighteenth century to us—are meaningless as long as we do not burn or embalm our dead. If we are to have funeral memorials at all, far better models are to be found in the beautiful crosses of Ireland, such as the cross at Monasterboice, or in the delicate bas-reliefs on Greek tombs. Above all, such art, if we are to have it, should concern itself more with the living than the dead—should be rather a noble symbol for the guiding of life than an idle panegyric on those who are gone. If a man needs an elaborate tombstone in order to remain in the memory of his country, it is clear that his living at all was an act of absolute superfluity. Keats's grave is a hillock of green grass with a plain headstone, and is to me the holiest place in Rome. There is in Westminster Abbey a periwigged admiral in a nightgown hurried off to heaven by two howling cherubs, which is one of the best examples I know of ostentatious obscurity.

2   Pray offer to the committee of the society my sincere regrets at my inability to be present, and my sincere wishes for the success of your movement.

Believe me, sincerely yours
Oscar Wilde

~

(577 words)

VOCABULARY

grotesque	inestimable	sarcophagi
bas-relief	panegyric	superfluity
hillock	periwigged	ostentatious
obscurity		

THE FACTS

1. What is the subject of Wilde's letter? When was it written, and what importance does the date have?
2. What attitude toward funerals does Wilde's letter reveal?
3. Why does Wilde use Keats's grave as an example? Where is Keats's grave?
4. On what particular point would Wilde have liked to speak if his illness had not prevented him from attending the meeting?
5. According to Wilde, with what should cemetery art concern itself?

THE STRATEGIES

1. Is Wilde's style in this letter appropriate to his purpose? Why or why not?
2. What figurative language does Wilde use in describing death? What is your interpretation of this image? What effect does it have on the reader?
3. What concrete suggestions does the author make to improve funerals? Indicate the reason for each specific suggestion.
4. What example of a hideous and meaningless tombstone does the author give? What is your response to the example?
5. Oscar Wilde's letter was read at the meeting he could not attend. What effect do you think it had on the listeners? If you had been in the audience, how would you have reacted?

THE ISSUES

1. Societies throughout history have followed a variety of customs and traditions when it comes to burying their dead. What is your idea of an appropriate funeral? Give examples from your personal experience or that of others.
2. What, if any, are your objections to the way funerals are typically handled in our country today? Cite examples to strengthen your view.
3. Most funeral eulogies exaggerate the deceased person's virtues while totally ignoring any bad character traits. Do you agree with this approach? Why or why not?
4. What kind of art do you like best on a gravestone? Give reasons for your choice.
5. What kind of epitaph would you place on your best friend's gravestone if you had a choice? What about on your own tombstone?

SUGGESTIONS FOR WRITING

1. Write a letter to your congressman or congresswoman expressing your displeasure with some aspect of government or your neighborhood. Make sure your style fits your purpose and your audience.

2. Using your imagination, describe the kind of funeral you would like to have.

HAVE A CIGAR

James Herriot

James Herriot, pseudonym of James Alfred Wight (1916–1995), was a Scottish-born veterinary surgeon and writer. His books about his veterinary practice in the Dales of England were enormously popular and led to feature films and a television series. His many books include All Creatures Great and Small *(1972),* All Things Bright and Beautiful *(1974), and* All Things Wise and Wonderful *(1977).*

This poignant story, *Have a Cigar*, is typical of Herriot's writing in its sharp observations and simple but evocative prose. Herriot is a master at pacing a story and at drawing a powerful and appealing scene with a minimum of words.

～

1   I looked again at the slip of paper where I had written my visits. "Dean, 3 Thompson's Yard. Old dog ill." There were a lot of these "yards" in Darrowby. They were, in fact, tiny streets, like pictures from a Dickens novel. Some of them opened off the market-place and many more were scattered behind the main thoroughfares in the old part of the town. From the outside you could see only an archway, and it was always a surprise to me to go down a narrow passage and come suddenly upon the uneven rows of little houses with no two alike, looking into each other's windows across eight feet of cobbles.

2   In front of some of the houses a strip of garden had been dug out and marigolds and nasturtium straggled over the rough stones; but at the far end the houses were in a tumbledown condition and some were abandoned with their windows boarded up.

3   Number three was down at this end and looked as though it wouldn't be able to hold out much longer.

4   The flakes of paint quivered on the rotten wood of the door as I knocked; above, the outer wall bulged dangerously on either side of a long crack in the masonry.

5   A small, white-haired man answered. His face, pinched and lined, was enlivened by a pair of cheerful eyes; he wore a much-darned woollen cardigan, patched trousers and slippers.

6   "I've come to see your dog," I said, and the old man smiled.

7   "Oh, I'm so glad you've come, sir,"he said. "I'm getting a bit worried about the old chap. Come inside, please."

8   He led me into the tiny living-room. "I'm alone now, sir. Lost my missus over a year ago. She used to think the world of the old dog."

9   The grim evidence of poverty was everywhere. In the worn out lino, the fireless hearth, the dank, musty smell of the place. The wallpaper hung away from the damp patches and on the table the old man's solitary dinner was laid: a fragment of bacon, a few fried potatoes and a cup of tea. This was life on the old age pension.

10   In the corner, on a blanket, lay my patient, a cross-bred Labrador. He must have been a big, powerful dog in his time, but the signs of age showed in the white hairs round his muzzle and the pale opacity in the depth of his eyes. He lay quietly and looked at me without hostility.

11   "Getting on a bit, isn't he, Mr. Dean?"

12   "Aye he is that. Nearly fourteen, but he's been like a pup galloping about until these last few weeks. Wonderful dog for his age is old Bob, and he's never offered to bite anybody in his life. Children can do anything with him. He's my only friend now—I hope you'll soon be able to put him right."

13   "Is he off his food, Mr. Dean?"

14   "Yes, clean off, and that's a strange thing because by gum, he could eat. He always sat by me and put his head on my knee at meal times, but he hasn't been doing it lately."

15   When his master spoke, the tail thumped twice on the blankets and a momentary interest showed in the white old eyes; but it quickly disappeared and the blank, inward look returned.

16   I passed my hand carefully over the dog's abdomen. Ascites was pronounced and the dropsical fluid had gathered till the pressure was intense. "Come on, old chap," I said, "let's see if we can roll you over." The dog made no resistance as I eased him slowly on to his other side, but, just as the movement was completed, he whimpered and looked round. The cause of the trouble was now only too easy to find.

17   I palpated gently. Through the thin muscle of the flank I could feel a hard, corrugated mass; certainly a splenic or hepatic carcinoma, enormous and completely inoperable. I stroked the old dog's head as I tried to collect my thoughts. This wasn't going to be easy.

18   "Is he going to be ill for long?" the old man asked, and came the thump, thump of the tail at the sound of the loved voice. "It's miserable when Bob isn't following me round the house when I'm doing my little jobs."

19   "I'm sorry, Mr. Dean, but I'm afraid this is something very serious. You see this large swelling. It is caused by an internal growth."

20   "You mean . . . cancer?" the little man said faintly.

21   "I'm afraid so, and it has progressed too far for anything to be done. I wish there was something I could do to help him, but there isn't."

22   The old man looked bewildered and his lips trembled. "Then he's going to die?"

23   I swallowed hard. "We really can't just leave him to die, can we? He's in some distress now, but it will soon be an awful lot worse. Don't you think it would be kindest to put him to sleep? After all he's had a good, long innings." I always aimed at a brisk, matter-of-fact approach, but the old clichés had an empty ring.

24   The old man was silent, then he said, "Just a minute," and slowly and painfully knelt down by the side of the dog. He did not speak, but ran his hand again and again over the grey muzzle and the ears, while the tail thump, thump, thumped on the floor.

25   He knelt there a long time while I stood in the cheerless room, my eyes taking in the faded pictures on the walls, the frayed, grimy curtains, the broken-springed armchair.

26   I filled the syringe and said the things I always said. "You needn't worry, this is absolutely painless. Just an overdose of an anaesthetic. It is really an easy way out for the old fellow."

27   The dog did not move as the needle was inserted, and, as the barbiturate began to flow into the vein, the anxious expression left his face and the muscles began to relax. By the time the injection was finished, the breathing had stopped.

28   "Is that it?" the old man whispered.

29   "Yes, that's it," I said. "He is out of his pain now."

30   The old man stood motionless except for the clasping and unclasping of his hands. When he turned to face me his eyes were bright. "That's right, we couldn't let him suffer, and I'm grateful for what you've done. And now, what do I owe you for your services, sir?"

31   "Oh that's all right, Mr. Dean," I said quickly. "It's nothing—nothing at all. I was passing right by here—it was no trouble."

32   The old man was astonished. "But you can't do that for nothing."

33   "Now please say no more about it, Mr. Dean. As I told you, I was passing right by your door." I said goodbye and went out of the house, through the passage and into the street. In the bustle of people and the bright sunshine, I could still see only the stark, little room, the old man and his dead dog.

34   As I walked towards my car, I heard a shout behind me. The old man was shuffling excitedly towards me in his slippers. His cheeks were streaked and wet, but he was smiling. In his hand he held a small, brown object.

35   "You've been very kind, sir. I've got something for you." He held out the object and I looked at it. It was tattered but just recognisable as a precious relic of a bygone celebration.

36   "Go on, it's for you," said the old man. "Have a cigar."

$\sim$

(1,269 words)

VOCABULARY

dank (9)	opacity (10)	ascites (16)
dropsical (16)	palpated (17)	corrugated (17)
hepatic (17)	carcinoma (17)	clichés (23)
stark (33)		

THE FACTS

1. What was the name of the old man's dog?
2. Where was the old man's wife?
3. What was wrong with the dog?
4. What kind of dog did the old man own?
5. How much did the veterinarian charge the old man for the visit?

THE STRATEGIES

1. In paragraph 3, the author writes about the old man's house that it looked "as though it wouldn't be able to hold out much longer." Aside from its descriptive effect, what does this observation add to the story?
2. Examine paragraph 9. How does the author drive home to us the stark reality of the old man's poverty?
3. In paragraphs 16 and 17, Herriot uses terms such as "ascites" and "splenic or hepatic carcinoma," which ordinary readers are unlikely to understand. What does he accomplish by using this specialized vocabulary?
4. What is Herriot's attitude toward the old man? How can you tell how Herriot really feels?
5. What is ironic about the old man's offering the veterinarian a cigar?

THE ISSUES

1. Some critics have accused Herriot of being "a Disney veterinarian." What is your opinion of this accusation? What justification do you think critics have for making it?
2. What is your opinion of the euthanasia of terminally ill animals? Why should not a similar mercy be applied to humans in the same situation?
3. How should dead animals be disposed of? What is your opinion of pet cemeteries that offer formal burial sites with headstones for dead pets?

4. Why do you think Herriot has been such a popular writer? What explanation for his popularity can you infer from this story?

5. This particular story is about the relationship between an old man and his dog. Why do you think the dog has become such a popular pet worldwide?

SUGGESTIONS FOR WRITING

1. Write about any incident that occurred between you and an animal.

2. Write about your favorite pet.

CHAPTER WRITING ASSIGNMENTS

1. Select any two paragraphs, one from an article in *Reader's Digest* and another from an article in *The New Yorker*. Analyze the differences in the language (diction, phrasing, sentence style, and paragraph length) and speculate on the intended audience of each magazine.

2. Write an essay on the meaning and practice of rhetoric as exemplified in this chapter.

3. Rewrite the Oscar Wilde letter in the type of English style that someone might use in a similar letter today.

WRITING ASSIGNMENTS FOR A SPECIFIC AUDIENCE

1. To an audience of African American readers, write an essay arguing for or against the idea that race relations in America have gotten better since Dr. King delivered his "I Have a Dream" speech.

2. Write an essay aimed at an audience of eighth graders explaining to them what they can expect to encounter later in high school and college writing courses.

COLLABORATIVE WRITING PROJECT

Dividing a group of students into two teams, have each team poll its members for the writing techniques, tips, and practices they have successfully used over the years to write their essays. Make a list of these after appropriate discussion and explanation. Get together as two groups to compare and discuss the findings. Finally, have each group team-write an essay that summarizes what the team has found about the writing process and the way it has been practiced by its members.

──────── REAL-LIFE ────────
STUDENT WRITING
E-MAIL FROM SOMOA

The following excerpt is from an actual e-mail written by one student to another. The sender, Mark, is writing from the South Pacific island of Samoa, where he had gone two months before as a Peace Corps volunteer. He was on the island only a month when he and another volunteer fell afoul of local authorities and were expelled from the Peace Corps—in their opinion, unfairly. To appeal their expulsion would have required a trip to Washington, D.C., which neither could afford. Instead of returning home like his friend did, Mark decided to stay on the island for as long as he could. He took a job teaching English at a local school while he applied for his visa, which would allow him to remain in Samoa for at least another year. Mark sent this e-mail to his friend, Adam. The two had been classmates in a cross-cultural program in British and American studies.

Mark

From:	Mark Smith
Sent:	Wednesday, January 15, 2004 4:14PM
To:	Adam Johnson
Subject:	Hey What's Up

So things got a little out of hand last night. My friend Taui fire danced at this club last night and we made quite an event of the whole thing. I guess I got a little wasted and then found myself in the Peace Corps office and for the first time in weeks I had access to email and just figured I should send something, anything. I guess my typing fluency was a bit shattered with the excessive alcohol abuse.

I still haven't heard about this work permit. My stamp on my passport runs out soon. Tomorrow actually. I probably should have prepared better for this, but I didn't. I just went to the immigration office. Maybe they'll deport me. It's hard to say.

1

This school year ends in a couple of weeks, and after that I've got a couple of months off to do absoluetely nothing I don't feel like doing. I'll have no money, so I can't really go anywhere, but I've got plenty of free places to stay in Samoa.

If I get my work permit I'm going to buy a spear for spear fishing. Basically, you just put on your snorkel gear and carry around this 4-pronged spear with a rubber band on the end of it that wraps around your wrist. It'll be a fun thing to do when I take my boat out everyday.

My Samoan language skills are going to hell. I haven't been learning that much because I don't want to spend my precious time (that is, maybe my last month or so here) learning new words that I'll never ever use again. It's more fun to swim in the ocean, drink recklessly, and use the language I'm used to. But if I stay I'll get my butt back in gear.

A new Peace Corps group just showed up. They've heard many stories about me and my fellow, fallen comrade. They're scared. When we arrived I was told by some friends the only way to get kicked out was to ride up to the Country director's house with a spliff in your mouth on a motorcycle naked with no helmet.

That was true for a while there; now, with the new administration, they're cracking down on this wild summer camp in Samoa called the Peace Corps. I'm not really to bothered by it. I'm still doing it my own way without that childish organization.

Anyway. . .

Post me some literature if you've got any—writing of any sort. I'm reading like a madman, and writing even more. I've started my book. I like where it's going so far. It's time to stop talking about being a writer and actually piece this thing together.

2

If people like us aren't going to do it, who will?

Well, let me know what you're doing back home?

You've quit the carpet cleaning job, right? What sort of job does a guy with a degree in British and American cultures get?

Well, take care man. Give me a buzz too if you get a phone card and some time.

Rock on,Mark

Oh yeah, for Halloween I grew a moustache. It was absolutely repulsive.

3

3

What Is a Writer's Voice?

EDITORS' COUNSEL

Most writers do not sit down to write consciously in a certain style. They do, however, try to project a certain voice onto the page. Sometimes the writer assumes this voice deliberately, but often it is chosen for the writer by the psychology of audience and material—by the need and occasion that make the writing necessary.

Here is an example. You are the boss. You sit down to write a memo to your employees, but being the boss goes to your head, and you write:

> Illumination of the overhead fixtures must be extinguished by the final person exiting the premises.

This notice tells the reader two things: First, it tells the reader to turn off the lights before leaving the room; second, it tells the reader that you are the boss and you say so. That is not the only kind of notice you could have written. You might, for example, have written this equivalent:

> The last person to leave this room must turn out the overhead lights.

This makes the point, but you think it also makes you sound awfully humble.

The difference between these two is not one of content, but of tone or style. It is tone of voice when you are composing the memo, for what you tried to do was not write in a certain style but to sound like the boss; to the reader, however, it is your style.

Many writing teachers, with some justification, approach voice and style as if they were always related to the writer's psychology. If you had confidence in your authority as the boss, if you really felt comfortable with your power, you wouldn't think it necessary to sound like God in your every memo. So if you must sound like the Almighty in your memos, perhaps it is because you really don't feel at ease with the idea of being the boss. Many similar mishaps of voice or style in student papers can be traced to a psychological uncertainty about the material, to an unconfident attitude, or even to the writer's feelings about the assignment.

The relationship between feelings and tone is slippery but makes sense. It is only natural that our feelings about a subject or person should spill out onto the page and affect our tone. Here is an example:

> Dear Monty,
>
> I'm really sick and tired of your mess. It's embarrassing to walk into our room with a visitor and see your bed unmade, your clothes scattered all over the floor, and your beer cans making sticky rings on the table. I've told you before about this, but now I want you to know that if you don't shape up, I'm moving out.
>
> Bob

Do you hear the angry tone in that note? On the other hand, listen to the difference in the tone of this e-mail:

> Hi, Everyone,
>
> I have just returned from my backpacking trip through Europe. You won't believe the wonderful experiences I had. At one point I even lost my passport, but the American consulate was very helpful in getting me a temporary one. I met some exciting new friends, who, like me, were camping out or riding the second class compartments of the trains. The world is really a great place. Anyway, I'll wait until I see you to fill in the details. I sure missed you. A bunch.
>
> Irene

The practical effect of tone on our writing is sometimes plainly evident and sometimes not. We would expect, for example, that if we write a letter to a roommate we're mad at, our tone will reflect that anger. Less evident is the effect a feeling of boredom about an assignment might have on our tone. It is only logical to assume that if we're bored with the topic and think it a waste of our time, our tone will be affected for the worse. That is why instructors always urge students to write about topics they like.

Another piece of traditional advice related to tone is the ancient warning instructors often give to student writers to be themselves—and it is genuinely good advice. Don't try to write in a voice that is not truly your own; don't try to put on airs in your writing. If you do, your tone is bound to be affected by the pretense. You will discover, if you have not already, that you do your best writing when you simply sound like your true self.

VOICE

WHY DID THE CHICKEN CROSS THE ROAD?

Evangelical minister (preachy)

Because the chicken was gay! Oh what a sin it is to go "to the other side"!

Conservative Republican politician (self-righteous)

My fellow Republicans, the chicken crossed to steal a job from a decent, hard-working American. That is what these reckless left-wing chickens do.

Children's book writer (nonsensical)

Did the chicken cross the road? Did he cross it with a toad? Yes, the chicken crossed the road, but why it crossed, I've not been told!

Ernest Hemingway (straightforward)

To die. In the rain. Alone. From an *idée fixe.*

Grandpa (self-important)

In my day, we didn't ask why the chicken crossed the road. Someone told us that the chicken crossed the road, and that was good enough for us.

Karl Marx (philosophical)

It was a historical inevitability.

Freud (psychological)

All chickens cross the road for the same reason: sex.

Einstein: (ambiguous)

Did the chicken really cross the road or did the road cross under the chicken?

Colonel Sanders (miffed)

Darn! I missed one!

These psychological considerations aside, we do know—on a more practical level—that voice in writing is influenced by three factors under the writer's control: (1) vocabulary, (2) syntax, and (3) attitude.

Vocabulary

The English language is a treasure trove of words. It is bursting with synonyms— words that have the same meaning. As you write, you can express the same idea any number of different ways. Often, the choice seems to boil down to expressing yourself either simply or complexly. You can give the facts without frills while remaining quietly in the background or you can mount the pulpit, take on the grandeur of a bishop, and posture.

The second choice is one that we do not recommend. You will do your reader a kindness if you write without putting on airs or pretending to be a know-it-all. Choose your words to inform, not to impress. Faced with a choice between a big, little-known word and a smaller, better-known equivalent, choose the smaller one because more people will understand it. Your overriding aim is to tell your reader what you know about the subject, not to impress. (Yet, oddly enough, sophisticated readers are generally impressed by writing that is plain and to the point.)

Here's an example of a style of writing that even for its day was pompous:

> It is the fate of those who toil at the lower employments of life, to be rather driven by the fear of evil, than attracted by the prospect of good; to be exposed to censure, without hope of praise; to be disgraced by miscarriage, or punished for neglect, where success would have been without applause, and diligence without reward.

Samuel Johnson, *Preface to the Dictionary of the English Language* (1755)

Johnson was a noted scholar and conversationalist who had a definite flair for spoken and written pompousness. If we replace some of the words with their more common equivalents, the passage takes on a different tone:

> It is the lot of those who work at the lower jobs of life, to be rather driven by the fear of evil, than drawn by the likelihood of good; to be open to criticism, without hope of praise; to be shamed by mistakes, or punished for neglect, where success would have been without recognition, and hard work without reward.

Even with the changes in vocabulary, this passage is still hard to follow because it suffers from a second problem—knotty syntax.

Syntax

The arrangement of words in a sentence is known as *syntax*. Because English is so flexible, the same idea can be said in many different ways and in many different kinds of sentences. The considerate writer uses only as many sentences as are needed to get the job done. Most of these sentences will be simple subject-verb-object combinations. For the sake of variety, a few will have a different construction, but mainly, the sentences will be short and easy to read and understand.

In constructing a sentence, your aim should be to express your ideas clearly. It should not be to show off your learning or scholarship. The Johnson passage quoted earlier consists of a single sentence punctuated by commas and semicolons. A little alteration in the syntax—mainly in the use of simpler sentences—makes the ideas in the quotation much easier to understand:

> Those who work at the lower jobs of life are driven by the fear of doing wrong, rather than drawn by the likelihood of doing good. They are open to criticism yet have no hope of praise. They are both shamed by their mistakes and punished for their neglect; yet their success wins no recognition, and their hard work no reward.

Now we have a better idea of what Johnson is trying to say. We may agree or disagree with it, but at least we share a common understanding.

Why, then, did Johnson express himself the way he did if he could have written the same idea more clearly? The answer is because of his *attitude*—the third factor affecting a writer's voice.

Attitude

Your attitude toward yourself and your work is bound to affect your voice. If you regard writing as a means of communication, you will work hard to make your meaning clear. If you regard writing as a reflection of your inner self, you might behave as some people do when they stand in front of a mirror: preen and strut.

The problem with the Johnson passage is that what he says he does not believe because he knows it is not true. He is, in fact, pretending to feel a humility and modesty he does not have. It is his attitude toward the work that makes his style so self-inflated and pompous. Here are the next two paragraphs from the preface:

> Among these unhappy mortals is the writer of dictionaries; whom mankind have considered, not as the pupil, but the slave of science, the pioneer of literature, doomed only to remove rubbish and clear obstructions from the paths of Learning and Genius, who press forward to conquest and glory, without bestowing a smile on the humble drudge that facilitates their progress. Every other author may aspire to praise; the lexicographer can only hope to escape reproach, and even this negative recompence has been yet granted to very few.
>
> I have, notwithstanding this discouragement, attempted a dictionary of the *English* language, which, while it was employed in the cultivation of every species of literature, has itself been hitherto neglected, suffered to spread, under the direction of chance, into wild exuberance, resigned to the tyranny of time and fashion, and exposed to the corruptions of ignorance, and caprices of *innovation*.

Does Johnson really believe that he is a "drudge," a "slave of science," a garbageman "doomed only to remove rubbish and clear obstructions from the paths of Learning and Genius"? Nothing about the man or his life tells us that he saw himself in such lowly terms. He had just completed, after a massive labor of nine years, a dictionary that defined 43,000 words supported by 114,000 quotations from literature. His was not the first dictionary of the English language, but even today it is ranked as the most important. Part of the problem with his preface is that he uses it to show off his learning and scholarship rather than to communicate facts about his dictionary. His attitude affects his voice.

Vocabulary, syntax, and attitude—these are all factors the writer can control. They are important in developing the voice you can use in factual writing. Naturally, they're less important in some other kinds of writing—poetry and fiction, for example—that aim to do more than merely communicate an idea. The lessons we are teaching are meant only for factual writing, which is to prose what the camel is to the desert. For that kind of writing, you must strive for clarity and readability if you wish to please your reader.

EXERCISES

1. How would you characterize the tone of the following paragraph that came from a letter a tenant sent to a landlord?

> If you want your rent this month, you'd better do something about the leaky kitchen faucet. I've told you about this at least five times and still you have done nothing. The dripping at night is driving me mad. I don't know what ever possessed me to rent such a pigsty. But if you don't do something about it, I'm going

to go to the city and complain and tell them what a roach infested dump you're renting to innocent people.

2. Change the voice of the preceding paragraph by rewriting it to reflect a softer tone.

3. How would you characterize the voice in the following excerpts? Describe the vocabulary, syntax, and attitude evident in each passage:

    a. I am 20 years of age today. The past year has been an eventful one to me, and I thank God for all his mercies to me. I trust my life in the future may be spent in His service.

    b. The Internet is a treasure chest of data, facts, statistics, opinions, speculations, and viewpoints—all that comes under the general heading of information.

    c. In clinical psychiatry and psychoanalytical work there are few such heroes, men and women whose intelligence, compassion, and above all, candor, illuminate their deeds, their words, and the failures they inevitably suffer.

4. Write two, brief letters on any event that occurred in your school and in which you took part: one to a parent or an authority figure and the other to your best friend.

5. Write a paragraph or two analyzing the differences in the voices you used in the letters you just wrote.

6. What attitude toward medical doctors does the following paragraph reveal? What kind of person might write such a paragraph?

    If I had cancer, I would not submit to chemotherapy. I watched my mom have chemotherapy, and it made her so nauseated and so weak that she often said, "I can't take this anymore." I can't see why it would be beneficial to put what is obviously a strong poison into any human body. Surely, nature has better ways of curing cancer than chemotherapy. Doctors are just too tunnel-visioned to use natural herbs to help cure cancer. They think that only pre-scriptions you get through pharmaceutical companies can possibly be effective; yet, I know someone who was cured of breast cancer by drinking a quart of carrot juice every day.

7. Which of the two statements that follow reflects the more rational and objective tone toward a photographic exhibit? Identify the vocabulary that makes the difference.

    a. This photographic exhibit is a wonderful gallery of varied portraits—politician, seamstress, drifter, ballet dancer, mother, and much more. Each portrait has been shot against a starkly white background, which seems to allow no place for the subject to hide and therefore suggests a confrontational intimacy between the photographer and the subject. Because of the backlighting involved, each head appears to sprout a halo that contrasts paradoxically with the shadows on the face, lending a beguiling mystery to the facial features in each frame.

b. After staring at this portrait gallery for almost an hour, I decided that it was all meaningless trash. Who wants to waste time looking at this sort of nightmare? This is not art; it is the revelation of a sick mind. All I could see were men and women photographed against a white wall. Some kind of weird circle of light surrounded their heads, but their faces were dark and wrinkled. The ugliness of these faces really bugged me. I felt depressed to think that this Halloween-type exhibit was considered great modern art and was shown at the local museum.

——————— ADVICE ———————

HOW TO SAY NOTHING IN FIVE HUNDRED WORDS

Paul Roberts

Paul McHenry Roberts (1917–1967) taught college English for over twenty years, first at San Jose State College and later at Cornell University. He wrote several books on linguistics, including Understanding Grammar *(1954),* Patterns of English *(1956), and* Understanding English *(1958).*

Freshman composition, like everything else, has its share of fashions. In the 1950s, when this article was written, the most popular argument raging among student essayists was the proposed abolition of college football. With the greater social consciousness of the early 1960s, the topic of the day became the morality of capital punishment. Topics may change, but the core principles of good writing remain constant, and this essay has become something of a minor classic in explaining them. Be concrete, says Roberts; get to the point; express your opinions colorfully. Refreshingly, he even practices what he preaches. His essay is humorous, direct, and almost salty in summarizing the working habits that all good prose writers must cultivate.

～

1 It's Friday afternoon, and you have almost survived another week of classes. You are just looking forward dreamily to the weekend when the English instructor says: "For Monday you will turn in a five-hundred-word composition on college football."

2   Well, that puts a good hole in the weekend. You don't have any strong views on college football one way or the other. You get rather excited during the season and go to all the home games and find it rather more fun than not. On the other hand, the class has been reading Robert Hutchins in the anthology and

perhaps Shaw's "Eighty-Yard Run," and from the class discussion you have got the idea that the instructor thinks college football is for the birds. You are no fool. You can figure out what side to take.

3   After dinner you get out the portable typewriter that you got for high school graduation. You might as well get it over with and enjoy Saturday and Sunday. Five hundred words is about two double-spaced pages with normal margins. You put in a sheet of paper, think up a title, and you're off:

Why College Football Should Be Abolished

College football should be abolished because it's bad for the school and also for the players. The players are so busy practicing that they don't have any time for their studies.

This, you feel, is a mighty good start. The only trouble is that it's only thirty-two words. You still have four hundred and sixty-eight to go, and you've pretty well exhausted the subject. It comes to you that you do your best thinking in the morning, so you put away the typewriter and go to the movies. But the next morning you have to do your washing and some math problems, and in the afternoon you go to the game. The English instructor turns up too, and you wonder if you've taken the right side after all. Saturday night you have a date, and Sunday morning you have to go to church. (You can't let English assignments interfere with your religion.) What with one thing and another, it's ten o'clock Sunday night before you get out the typewriter again. You make a pot of coffee and start to fill out your views on college football. Put a little meat on the bones.

Why College Football Should Be Abolished

In my opinion, it seems to me that college football should be abolished. The reason why I think this to be true is because I feel that football is bad for the colleges in nearly every respect. As Robert Hutchins says in his article in our anthology in which he discusses college football, it would be better if the colleges had race horses and had races with one another, because then the horses would not have to attend classes. I firmly agree with Mr. Hutchins on this point, and I am sure that many other students would agree too.

One reason why it seems to me that college football is bad is that it has become too commercial. In the olden times when people played football just for the fun of it, maybe college football was all right, but they do not play college football just for the fun of it now as they used to in the old days. Nowadays college football is what you might call a big business. Maybe this is not true at all schools, and I don't think it is especially true here at State, but certainly this is the case at most colleges and universities in America nowadays, as Mr. Hutchins points out in his very interesting article. Actually the coaches and alumni go around to the high schools and offer the high school stars large salaries to come to their colleges and play football for them. There was one case where a high school star was offered a convertible if he would play football for a certain college.

Another reason for abolishing college football is that it is bad for the players. They do not have time to get a college education, because they are so busy playing football. A football player has to practice every afternoon from three to six and then he is so tired that he can't concentrate on his studies. He just feels like dropping off to sleep after dinner, and then the next day he goes to his classes without having studied and maybe he fails the test.

(Good ripe stuff so far, but you're still a hundred and fifty-one words from home. One more push.)

Also I think college football is bad for the colleges and the universities because not very many students get to participate in it. Out of a college of ten thousand students only seventy-five or a hundred play football, if that many. Football is what you might call a spectator sport. That means that most people go to watch it but do not play it themselves.

(Four hundred and fifteen. Well, you still have the conclusion, and when you retype it, you can make the margins a little wider.)

These are the reasons why I agree with Mr. Hutchins that college football should be abolished in American colleges and universities.

4 On Monday you turn it in, moderately hopeful, and on Friday it comes back marked "weak in content" and sporting a big "D."

5   This essay is exaggerated a little, not much. The English instructor will recognize it as reasonably typical of what an assignment on college football will bring in. He knows that nearly half of the class will contrive in five hundred words to say that college football is too commercial and bad for the players. Most of the other half will inform him that college football builds character and prepares one for life and brings prestige to the school. As he reads paper after paper all saying the same thing in almost the same words, all bloodless, five hundred words dripping out of nothing, he wonders how he allowed himself to get trapped into teaching English when he might have had a happy and interesting life as an electrician or a confidence man.

6   Well, you may ask, what can you do about it? The subject is one on which you have few convictions and little information. Can you be expected to make a dull subject interesting? As a matter of fact, this is precisely what you are expected to do. This is the writer's essential task. All subjects, except sex, are dull until somebody makes them interesting. The writer's job is to find the argument, the approach, the angle, the wording that will take the reader with him. This is seldom easy, and it is particularly hard in subjects that have been much discussed: College Football, Fraternities, Popular Music, Is Chivalry Dead?, and the like. You will feel that there is nothing you can do with such subjects except repeat the old bromides. But there are some things you can do which will make your papers, if not throbbingly alive, at least less insufferably tedious than they might otherwise be.

Avoid the Obvious Content

7 Say the assignment is college football. Say that you've decided to be against it. Begin by putting down the arguments that come to your mind: it is too commercial, it takes the students' minds off their studies, it is hard on the

players, it makes the university a kind of circus instead of an intellectual center, for most schools it is financially ruinous. Can you think of any more arguments, just offhand? All right. Now when you write your paper, make sure that you don't use any of the material on this list. If these are the points that leap to your mind, they will leap to everyone else's too, and whether you get a "C" or a "D" may depend on whether the instructor reads your paper early when he is fresh and tolerant or late, when the sentence "In my opinion, college football has become too commercial," inexorably repeated, has brought him to the brink of lunacy.

8   Be against college football for some reason or reasons of your own. If they are keen and perceptive ones, that's splendid. But even if they are trivial or foolish or indefensible, you are still ahead so long as they are not everybody else's reasons too. Be against it because the colleges don't spend enough money on it to make it worthwhile, because it is bad for the characters of the spectators, because the players are forced to attend classes, because the football stars hog all the beautiful women, because it competes with baseball and is therefore unAmerican and possibly Communist-inspired. There are lots of more or less unused reasons for being against college football.

9   Sometimes it is a good idea to sum up and dispose of the trite and conventional pots before going on to your own. This has the advantage of indicating to the reader that you are going to be neither trite nor conventional. Something like this:

We are often told that college football should be abolished because it has become too commercial or because it is bad for the players. These arguments are no doubt very cogent, but they don't really go to the heart of the matter.

Then you go to the heart of the matter.

Take the Less Usual Side

10   One rather simple way of getting into your paper is to take the side of the argument that most of the citizens will want to avoid. If the assignment is an essay on dogs, you can, if you choose, explain that dogs are faithful and lovable companions, intelligent, useful as guardians of the house and protectors of children, indispensable in police work—in short, when all is said and done, man's best friends. Or you can suggest that those big brown eyes conceal, more often than not, a vacuity of mind and an inconstancy of purpose; that the dogs you have known most intimately have been mangy, ill-tempered brutes, incapable of instruction; and that only your nobility of mind and fear of arrest prevent you from kicking the flea-ridden animals when you pass them on the street.

11   Naturally personal convictions will sometimes dictate your approach. If the assigned subject is "Is Methodism Rewarding to the Individual?" and you are a pious Methodist, you have really no choice. But few assigned subjects, if any, will fall in this category. Most of them will lie in broad areas of discussion with much to be said on both sides. They are intellectual exercises, and it is legitimate to argue now one way and now another, as debaters do in sim-

ilar circumstances. Always take the side that looks to you hardest, least defensible. It will almost always turn out to be easier to write interestingly on that side.

12   This general advice applies where you have a choice of subjects. If you are to choose among "The Value of Fraternities" and "My Favorite High School Teacher" and "What I Think About Beetles," by all means plump for the beetles. By the time the instructor gets to your paper, he will be up to his ears in tedious tales about a French teacher at Bloombury High and assertions about how fraternities build character and prepare one for life. Your views on beetles, whatever they are, are bound to be a refreshing change.

13   Don't worry too much about figuring out what the instructor thinks about the subject so that you can cuddle up with him. Chances are his views are no stronger than yours. If he does have convictions and you oppose him, his problem is to keep from grading you higher than you deserve in order to show he is not biased. This doesn't mean that you should always cantankerously dissent from what the instructor says; that gets tiresome too. And if the subject assigned is "My Pet Peeve," do not begin, "My pet peeve is the English instructor who assigns papers on 'my pet peeve.' " This was still funny during the War of 1812, but it has sort of lost its edge since then. It is in general good manners to avoid personalities.

Slip Out of Abstraction

14   If you will study the essay on college football [near the beginning of this essay], you will perceive that one reason for its appalling dullness is that it never gets down to particulars. It is just a series of not very glittering generalities: "football is bad for the colleges," "it has become too commercial," "football is big business," "it is bad for the players," and so on. Such round phrases thudding against the reader's brain are unlikely to convince him, though they may well render him unconscious.

15   If you want the reader to believe that college football is bad for the players, you have to do more than say so. You have to display the evil. Take your roommate, Alfred Simkins, the second-string center. Picture poor old Alfy coming home from football practice every evening, bruised and aching, agonizingly tired, scarcely able to shovel the mashed potatoes into his mouth. Let us see him staggering up to the room, getting out his econ textbook, peering desperately at it with his good eye, falling asleep and failing the test in the morning. Let us share his unbearable tension as Saturday draws near. Will he fail, be demoted, lose his monthly allowance, be forced to return to the coal mines? And if he succeeds, what will be his reward? Perhaps a slight ripple of applause when the third-string center replaces him, a moment of elation in the locker room if the team wins, of despair if it loses. What will he look back on when he graduates from college? Toil and torn ligaments. And what will be his future? He is not good enough for pro football, and he is too obscure and weak in econ to succeed in stocks and bonds. College football is tearing the heart from Alfy Simkins and, when it finishes with him, will callously toss aside the shattered hulk.

16   This is no doubt a weak enough argument for the abolition of college football, but it is sight better than saying, in three or four variations, that college football (in your opinion) is bad for the players.

17   Look at the work of any professional writer and notice how constantly he is moving from the generality, the abstract statement, to the concrete example, the facts and figures, the illustrations. If he is writing on juvenile delinquency, he does not just tell you that juveniles are (it seems to him) delinquent and that (in his opinion) something should be done about it. He shows you juveniles being delinquent, tearing up movie theatres in Buffalo, stabbing high school principals in Dallas, smoking marijuana in Palo Alto. And more than likely he is moving toward some specific remedy, not just a general wringing of the hands.

18   It is no doubt possible to be too concrete, too illustrative or anecdotal, but few inexperienced writers err this way. For most the soundest advice is to be seeking always for the picture, to be always turning general remarks into seeable examples. Don't say, "Sororities teach girls the social graces." Say, "Sorority life teaches a girl how to carry on a conversation while pouring tea, without sloshing the tea into the saucer." Don't say, "I like certain kinds of popular music very much." Say, "Whenever I hear Gerber Sprinklittle play 'Mississippi Man' on the trombone, my socks creep up my ankles."

Get Rid of Obvious Padding

19   The student toiling away at his weekly English theme is too often tormented by a figure: five hundred words. How, he asks himself, is he to achieve this staggering total? Obviously by never using one word when he can somehow work in ten.

20   He is therefore seldom content with a plain statement like "Fast driving is dangerous." This has only four words in it. He takes thought, and the sentence becomes:

In my opinion, fast driving is dangerous.

Better, but he can do better still:

In my opinion, fast driving would seem to be rather dangerous.

If he is really adept, it may come out:

In my humble opinion, though I do not claim to be an expert on this complicated subject, fast driving, in most circumstances, would seem to be rather dangerous in many respects, or at least so it would seem to me.

Thus four words have been turned into forty, and not an iota of content has been added.

21   Now this is a way to go about reaching five hundred words, and if you are content with a " grade, it is as good a way as any. But if you aim higher, you must work differently. Instead of stuffing your sentences with straw, you must try steadily to get rid of the padding, to make your sentences lean and tough. If you are really working at it, your first draft will greatly exceed the required total, and then you will work it down, thus:

It is thought in some quarters that fraternities do not contribute as much as might be expected to campus life.

Some people think that fraternities contribute little to campus life.

The average doctor who practices in small towns or in the country must toil night and day to heal the sick.

Most country doctors work long hours.

When I was a little girl, I suffered from shyness and embarrassment in the presence of others.

I was a shy little girl.

It is absolutely necessary for the person employed as a marine fireman to give the matter of steam pressure his undivided attention at all times.

The fireman has to keep his eye on the steam gauge.

22 You may ask how you can arrive at five hundred words at this rate. Simple. You dig up more real content. Instead of taking a couple of obvious points off the surface of the topic and then circling warily around them for six paragraphs, you work in and explore, figure out the details. You illustrate. You say that fast driving is dangerous, and then you prove it. How long does it take to stop a car at forty and at eighty? How far can you see at night? What happens when a tire blows? What happens in a head-on collision at fifty miles an hour? Pretty soon your paper will be full of broken glass and blood and headless torsos, and reaching five hundred words will not really be a problem.

Call a Fool a Fool

23 Some of the padding in freshman themes is to be blamed not on anxiety about the word minimum but on excessive timidity. The student writes, "In my opinion, the principal of my high school acted in ways that I believe every un-biased person would have to call foolish." This isn't exactly what he means. What he means is, "My high school principal was a fool." If he was a fool, call him a fool. Hedging the thing about with "in-my-opinion's" and "it-seems-to-me's" and "as-I-see-it's" and "at-least-from-my-point-of-view's" gains you nothing. Delete these phrases whenever they creep into your paper.

24 The student's tendency to hedge stems from a modesty that in other circumstances would be commendable. He is, he realizes, young and inexperienced, and he half suspects that he is dopey and fuzzy-minded beyond the average. Probably only too true. But it doesn't help to announce your incompetence six times in every paragraph. Decide what you want to say and say it as vigorously as possible, without apology and in plain words.

25 Linguistic diffidence can take various forms. One is what we call euphemism. This is the tendency to call a spade "a certain garden implement" or women's underwear "unmentionables." It is stronger in some eras than others and in some people than others but it always operates more or less in subjects that are touchy or taboo: death, sex, madness, and so on. Thus we shrink from saying "He died last night" but say instead "passed away," "left us," "joined his Maker," "went to his reward." Or we try to take off the tension with a lighter cliché: "kicked the bucket," "cashed in his chips," "handed in his dinner pail." We have found all sorts of ways to avoid saying mad: "mentally ill," "touched," "not quite right upstairs," "feebleminded," "innocent,"

"simple," "off his trolley," "not in his right mind." Even such a now plain word as insane began as a euphemism with the meaning "not healthy."

26   Modern science, particularly psychology, contributes many polysyllables in which we can wrap our thoughts and blunt their force. To many writers there is no such thing as a bad schoolboy. Schoolboys are maladjusted or un-oriented or misunderstood or in the need of guidance or lacking in continued success toward satisfactory integration of the personality as a social unit, but they are never bad. Psychology no doubt makes us better men and women, more sympathetic and tolerant, but it doesn't make writing any easier. Had Shakespeare been confronted with psychology, "To be or not to be" might have come out, "To continue as a social unit or not to do so. That is the per-sonality problem. Whether 'tis a better sign of integration at the conscious level to display a psychic tolerance toward the maladjustments and repres-sions induced by one's lack of orientation in one's environment or—" But Hamlet would never have finished the soliloquy.

27   Writing in the modern world, you cannot altogether avoid modern jargon. Nor, in an effort to get away from euphemism, should you salt your paper with four-letter words. But you can do much if you will mount guard against those roundabout phrases, those echoing polysyllables that tend to slip into your writing to rob it of its crispness and force.

Beware of Pat Expressions

28 Other things being equal, avoid phrases like "other things being equal." Those sentences that come to you whole, or in two or three doughy lumps, are sure to be bad sentences. They are no creation of yours but pieces of com-mon thought floating in the community soup.

29   Pat expressions are hard, often impossible, to avoid, because they come too easily to be noticed and seem too necessary to be dispensed with. No writer avoids them altogether, but good writers avoid them more often than poor writers.

30   By "pat expressions" we mean such tags as "to all practical intents and purposes," "the pure and simple truth," "from where I sit," "the time of his life," "to the ends of the earth," "in the twinkling of an eye," "as sure as you're born," "over my dead body," "under cover of darkness," "took the easy way out," "when all is said and done," "told him time and time again," "parted the best of friends," "stand up and be counted," "gave him the best years of her life," "worked her fingers to the bone." Like other clichés, these expres-sions were once forceful. Now we should use them only when we can't pos-sibly think of anything else.

31   Some pat expressions stand like a wall between the writer and thought. Such a one is "the American way of life." Many student writers feel that when they have said that something accords with the American way of life or does not they have exhausted the subject. Actually, they have stopped at the highest level of abstraction. The American way of life is the complicated set of bonds between a hundred and eighty million ways. All of us know this when we think about it, but the tag phrase too often keeps us from thinking about it.

32   So with many another phrase dear to the politician: "this great land of ours," "the man in the street," "our national heritage." These may prove our patriotism or give a clue to our political beliefs, but otherwise they add nothing to the paper except words.

Colorful Words

33   The writer builds with words, and no builder uses a raw material more slippery and elusive and treacherous. A writer's work is a constant struggle to get the right word in the right place, to find that particular word that will convey his meaning exactly, that will persuade the reader or soothe him or startle or amuse him. He never succeeds altogether—sometimes he feels that he scarcely succeeds at all—but such successes as he has are what make the thing worth doing.

34   There is no book of rules for this game. One progresses through everlasting experiment on the basis of ever-widening experience. There are few useful generalizations that one can make about words as words, but there are perhaps a few.

35   Some words are what we call "colorful." By this we mean that they are calculated to produce a picture or induce an emotion. They are dressy instead of plain, specific instead of general, loud instead of soft. Thus, in place of "Her heart beat," we may write, "her heart pounded, throbbed, fluttered, danced." Instead of "He sat in his chair," we may say, "he lounged, sprawled, coiled." Instead of "It was hot," we may say, "It was blistering, sultry, muggy, suffocating, steamy, wilting."

36   However, it should not be supposed that the fancy word is always better. Often it is as well to write "Her heart beat" or "It was hot" if that is all it did or all it was. Ages differ in how they like their prose. The nineteenth century liked it rich and smoky. The twentieth has usually preferred it lean and cool. The twentieth century writer, like all writers, is forever seeking the exact word, but he is wary of sounding feverish. He tends to pitch it low, to understate it, to throw it away. He knows that if he gets too colorful, the audience is likely to giggle.

37   See how this strikes you: "As the rich, golden glow of the sunset died away along the eternal western hills, Angela's limpid blue eyes looked softly and trustingly into Montague's flashing brown ones, and her heart pounded like a drum in time with the joyous song surging in her soul." Some people like that sort of thing, but most modern readers would say, "Good grief," and turn on the television.

Colored Words

38   Some words we would call not so much colorful as colored—that is, loaded with associations, good or bad. All words—except perhaps structure words—have associations of some sort. We have said that the meaning of a word is the sum of the contexts in which it occurs. When we hear a word, we hear with it an echo of all the situations in which we have heard it before.

39   In some words, these echoes are obvious and discussible. The word *mother,* for example, has, for most people, agreeable associations. When you hear *mother* you probably think of home, safety, love, food, and various other pleasant things. If one writes, "She was like a mother to me," he gets an effect which he would not get in "She was like an aunt to me." The advertiser makes use of the associations of *mother* by working it in when he talks about his product. The politician works it in when he talks about himself.

40   So also with such words as *home, liberty, fireside, contentment, patriot, tenderness, sacrifice, childlike, manly, bluff, limpid.* All of these words are loaded with associations that would be rather hard to indicate in a straightforward definition. There is more than a literal difference between "They sat around the fireside" and "They sat around the stove." They might have been equally warm and happy around the stove, but fireside suggests leisure, grace, quiet tradition, congenial company, and stove does not.

41   Conversely, some words have bad associations. *Mother* suggests pleasant things, but *mother-in-law* does not. Many mothers-in-law are heroically lovable and some mothers drink gin all day and beat their children insensible, but these facts of life are beside the point. The point is that mother sounds good and mother-in-law does not.

42   Or consider the word *intellectual.* This would seem to be a complimentary term, but in point of fact it is not, for it has picked up associations of impracticality and ineffectuality and general dopiness. So also such words as *liberal, reactionary, Communist, socialist, capitalist, radical, schoolteacher, truck driver, undertaker, operator, salesman, huckster, speculator.* These convey meaning on the literal level, but beyond that—sometimes, in some places—they convey contempt on the part of the speaker.

43   The question of whether to use loaded words or not depends on what is being written. The scientist, the scholar, try to avoid them; for the poet, the advertising writer, the public speaker, they are standard equipment. But every writer should take care that they do not substitute for thought. If you write, "Anyone who thinks that is nothing but a Socialist (or Communist or capitalist)" you have said nothing except that you don't like people who think that, and such remarks are effective only with the most naive readers. It is always a bad mistake to think your readers more naive than they really are.

Colorless Words

44 But probably most student writers come to grief not with words that are colorful or those that are colored but with those that have no color at all. A pet example is *nice,* a word we would find it hard to dispense with in casual conversation but which is no longer capable of adding much to a description. Colorless words are those of such general meaning that in a particular sentence they mean nothing. Slang adjectives like *cool* ("That's real cool") tend to explode all over the language. They are applied to everything, lose their original force, and quickly die.

45   Beware also of nouns of very general meaning, like *circumstances, cases, instances, aspects, factors, relationships, attitudes, eventualities,* etc. In most circumstances you will find that those cases of writing which contain too many instances of words like these will in this and other aspects have factors leading to unsatisfactory relationships with the reader resulting in unfavorable attitudes on his part and perhaps other eventualities, like a grade of "D." Notice also what *etc.* means. It means "I'd like to make this list longer, but I can't think of any more examples."

～

(5,080 words)

VOCABULARY

contrive (5)	bromides (6)	inexorably (7)
cogent (9)	vacuity (10)	warily (22)
diffidence (25)	euphemism (25)	jargon (27)
polysyllables (27)	elusive (33)	induce (35)

———— EXAMPLES ————

TONE: THE WRITER'S VOICE IN THE READER'S MIND

Mort Castle

Mort Castle (b. 1946) is a dedicated teacher and fiction writer. He has 350 short stories and a dozen books to his credit, including Cursed Be the Child *(1994),* The Strangers *(1984), and* Moon on the Water *(2000). Castle takes particular pride in the fact that 2,000 of his students, ranging in age from six to ninety-three, have seen their work in print. He is a frequent keynote speaker at writing conferences or workshops. His book,* Writing Horror *(1997), for which he served as editor, has become the "bible" for aspiring horror authors. He is also the executive editor of Thorby Comics, which publishes the popular comic books* Night City, Death Asylum, The Skuler, Blythe: Nightvision, *and* Johnny Cosmic.

Novice writers often think that tone is used only in speaking, not in writing. By using numerous examples and taking on a humorous tone, Castle convinces us that tone is a key ingredient in the relationship between reader and writer.

～

1 Johnny, the new kid, walks into third grade, casually waves to his teacher, Ms. Cruth, and says, "How's it goin', Butthead?"

2   "We do not talk that way in this class, Johnny," says Ms. Cruth. Opting for educational strategy #101: neo-traditional negative reinforcement, but not allowed to hit, she sends Johnny to the corner.

3   The next day, Johnny steps into the classroom, with "Hey, what's up, Ms. Bimbo?"

4   "Corner, Johnny," says Ms. Cruth.

5   The day after, Johnny comes into the classroom. He says, "Good morning, Ms. Cruth."

6   "Go to the corner, Johnny," says Ms. Cruth.

7   "Huh?" Johnny's inquiring mind wants to know, "Why are you sending me to the corner? I did not call you 'Butthead' and I did not call you 'Ms. Bimbo', and I didn't say one word that might be considered pejorative!"

8   "No," says Ms Cruth, "but I don't like your tone."

9   When we speak to others, our tone of voice is no less important than our actual words. Call your faithful friend, Fido, into the room, for our experiment in tone. Granted, with the difference in the communicative arts as practiced by human being and canine being, the following analogy is not fully apropos, yet 'twill serve:

10   Talk to your dog. Though your tone is a warm one, you know, "praise the pup, I love my wonderful companionate animal, etc.," don't use real words of praise. Try: "Fido, you double ugly moron, you stinky poo puppy, you drecky wretched doggy dastard!"

11   Fido wags his tail. All is well. I may not get the words, but I know what you mean.

12   In speaking, stressed sounds, vocal cadences, pronunciation, rhythm and pauses, repetition, voice pitch, timbre, and volume, etc. help the listener get the message. The "sincere" tone tells the listener "I'm sorry" truly indicates . . . "I am sorry." Yet, with a sneering, sarcastic tone, those same two words can implicitly say, "I am sorry I did not cause you half the grief, misery, agony, and woe I could have had I only been a trace more imaginative."

13   The "Listen up" tone is for when the mechanic needs to hear that this time, damn it, he'd better find the oil leak.

14   The "cooing selected little nothings" tone can be well suited for the prelude to the proposal moment, whether that be a major commitment proposal or a suggestion of serious messing around.

15   Most kids know the tone that signals, "You'd really better cut it out and this time I mean it!"

16   The conspiratorial tone signals it's "True dirt dishing time."

17   The "ha ha ha ready to happen" tone is for the joke . . .

18   The writer putting words on the page (or computer screen or out there in cyberville) also has a tone of voice. The writer, of course, does not have a speaker's unique tone tools: vocal cords, sinus cavities, lip, tongue, and palette, etc. Nor does the writer have a raised eyebrow to provide a hint, nor a smile, nor a broad hand wave. Instead, tone is achieved by choice and arrangement of our prime building blocks: words.

19   The reader hears—and responds to—that tone of voice as he is reading.

20   That voice, that tone, must be suited to the material so that reader clearly understands what is said, understands on both the literal and the figurative levels.

21   "Let us go then, you and I," T. S. Eliot begins "The Love Song of J. Alfred Prufrock." The tone is somber and formal, made more so, perhaps, by the deliberate grammar fluff of the nominative "I" used instead of the objective "me," an error often made by those hoping to sound "educated": the reader is invited to undertake a desolate and wearying journey. The tone helps to establish the mood of the poem, gives the reader a feeling. But if Eliot had begun, with (or without an apology to The Ramones): "Hey ho! Let's go!"

22   Or had he whined in classic Jerry Lewis style, "Look, would you please come on, already? Aw, just come on, okay?"

23   Or in keeping with contemporary "dirty words currently acceptable on Prime Time Network TV": "Let's haul ass!"

24   Well, we would not exactly be anticipating gloom and soul dread as we walk with J. Alfred, would we?

25   Consider the opening of Edgar Alan Poe's familiar "The Tell-Tale Heart":

26   "True!—nervous—very very dreadfully nervous I had been and am, but why will you say that I am mad?"

27   There's an immediate rush of energy with that very first word and exclamation point: A frantic energy. A crazed madman's energy. You hear the protagonist protesting way, way more than a "bit too much" the idea that he is insane. To use today's pseudo-artistic term, the "edgy tone" of the story is established: a barely-in-control-and-soon-to-wig-out tone.

28   The right tone, the proper voice in the reader's mind, lets you say what you want to say the way you want to say it.

29   And the wrong tone . . .

30   In the scene that follows from a deservedly unpublished short story, Mike is visited by his psychopathic brother, Arnold. Mike believes Arnold intends to kill him—and Mike is right.

31   Arnold stepped in. "How are you doing, Mike?" he asked.

32   "I've been doing all right," Mike responded promptly.

33   "That's good," Arnold said.

34   "How about you?" Mike asked.

35   "Well, I guess I have been doing okay," Arnold calmly said.

36   "I'm glad to hear it. It certainly is a snowy day."

37   "I guess everyone talks about the weather but no one does anything about it," Arnold said. "That is my opinion, anyway."

38   "I agree," Mike said.

39   Then Arnold shouted, "It's a perfect day for you to die, you dirty rat!"

40   Except for Arnold's closing outburst, the tone of this passage is mundane, prosaic, no more tense (or interesting) than that of an ordinary, everyday conversation you might overhear in the dentist's waiting room. It is totally unsuited for what is meant to be a moment of high drama.

41   Here's another cutting from a different "wrong tone" story. The protagonist is attempting to get up the nerve to stand before an Alcoholics Anonymous meeting and say for the first time: "My name is Sharon and I am an alcoholic." She sits, biting her nails, and then shakily gets to her feet,

     . . . flinging her hair back like a galloping filly tossing its mane . . .

42   Uh-uh. That "mane tossing filly" gives the scene an inappropriate tone. My Girl Friend Flicka. Light-hearted Retro-Range-Romance: Up rides Dale Evans on Buttermilk, meeting her spunky niece from out East, Manda Llewellyn Travis . . . This light hearted tone and the upbeat optimism one feels make for what most critics would judge wrong.

43   That is not to say, of course, that only the "comic tone" can be employed for comic writing, that the "romantic tone" must be used for romance writing, that a horrific tone must be used for horror writing.

44   Let's spend a tone moment with the late Charles Beaumont, one of my all time literary heroes and the writer of many classic short short stories that came to typify what is thought of as "Playboy Magazine horror" in the late 1950s and 1960s.

45   Beaumont's short story is called "Free Dirt":

46   It opens:
"No fowl had ever looked so posthumous."

47   Seven words—and the tone is established. "Posthumous" gives the sentence an overly formal, almost pompous tone. "Fowl," rather than chicken, is likewise formal. The voice that reads this sentence inside the reader's mind is wryly sardonic, not unlike the voice of the late Alfred Hitchcock. There's humor here, but it's dark humor, the laughter we can hear as we stand by the grave site, and it's perfect for a brief and utterly chilling story, a work of "moral fiction" in the best sense: It teaches in a non-didactic way.

48   The right tone, then, is the one that allows the writer to speak clearly to the reader. The goal, of course, is the essence of the writer-reader relationship: "I get it," the reader implicitly says.

49   You don't want your home builder cracking up with laughter, telling you that you should be swapping one liners with Leno, when you demand he put the front door in front, just as the blueprints have it, instead of on the roof—and you don't want your reader snickering, giggling, guffawing, and hoo-ha-ing because your voice in his mind cues him to laugh at your sequel to A Christmas Carol, in which Tiny Tim dies of consumption, Bob Cratchit is run over by a hansom cab, and Scrooge gets murdered by Marley's ghost!

∼

(5,080 words)

VOCABULARY

neo-traditional (2)	pejorative (7)	apropos (9)
cadences (12)	pitch (12)	timbre (12)
conspiratorial (16)	figurative (20)	desolate (21)
pseudo-artistic (27)	mundane (40)	prosaic (40)
posthumous (46)	sardonic (47)	non-didactic (47)

THE FACTS

1. What kind of student is the author portraying through Johnny? How would you react to having such a student in your class?

2. What was wrong with Johnny's third greeting?

3. What analogy does the author use to illustrate the importance of tone over words in speech? What other analogy can you cite?

4. What elements, not used in writing, can a person use to communicate in speech?

5. What is the only arsenal available to writers to establish tone? Does this limited arsenal curtail good writers? Give examples that support your opinion.

THE STRATEGIES

1. What rhetorical strategy does the author use to persuade us that his view of tone is correct? Are you convinced? Give reasons for your answer.

2. In what paragraph does the author switch from vocal tone to writing tone? Were you able to follow his shift? If no, why not? If yes, why?

3. Why do you think the author uses the opening line of T. S. Eliot's "J Alfred Prufrock" as an example of setting a definite tone? Do you think this was a good choice? Why or why not?

4. In paragraph 29, the author does not finish his sentence, but leaves you hanging with ellipsis points. How would you finish this sentence?

5. In what paragraph does the author tell you what the right tone is? What will the reader implicitly say if the author has established the right tone?

THE ISSUES

1. Are there kinds of writing in which no tone is necessary? If you think there are, give examples of this kind of writing.

2. How can mastery of tone help your writing?

3. How can voice and tone be suited to the material on the figurative level? (See paragraph 20.) Explain this idea by using an example.

4. The author assures us that tone does not always need to match the writing genre. For instance, a comic tone might be used for a romance and a romantic tone for a comedy. Cite an example from literature that mixes tone and genre.

5. What tone would most likely suit the following situations:

    a. A mother writes goodbye to her son leaving for war

    b. A college student thanks her sorority sisters for giving her a wild bachelorette party the week before her wedding

    c. A minister encourages his congregation to donate money for some new hymn books

SUGGESTIONS FOR WRITING

1. Write a letter to one of the following people, using an appropriate tone:

   a. To your boss, announcing that you are quitting the company for a new assignment

   b. To your father, asking for money to pay your car insurance

   c. To your best friend, describing a recent camping trip

   d. To an acquaintance who borrowed money from you and refuses to pay you back

2. Write an essay in which you define tone as you now understand it.

THE POLITICS OF HOUSEWORK

Pat Mainardi

Though women do not complain of the power of husbands, each complains of her own husband, or of the husbands of her friends. It is the same in all other cases of servitude; at least in the commencement of the emancipatory movement. The serfs did not at first complain of the power of the lords, but only of their tyranny.
—*John Stuart Mill*, **On the Subjection of Women**

Pat Mainardi is a professor of art history at the City College of New York. In 1969, when she wrote this article, she was a member of a radical feminist group, the Redstockings of New York City. This article is considered a pivotal document in the feminist movement of the 1960s and 1970s.

This essay is an excellent example of how a writer can create voice and tone with the use of words. Pay particular attention to the dialogue between the writer and her husband. The tone assigned to the husband is meant to portray him as a man who uses every trick to get out of doing his share of the housework. As you read, ask yourself whether the portrayal of the husband is representative of most modern men or whether the writer is exaggerating to make a point.

~

1 Liberated women—very different from Women's Liberation! The first signals all kinds of goodies, to warm the hearts (not to mention other parts) of the most radical men. The other signals-HOUSEWORK. The first brings sex without marriage, sex before marriage, cozy housekeeping arrangements ("I'm living with this chick") and the self-content of knowing that you're not the kind of man who wants a doormat instead of a woman. That will come later. After all, who wants that old commodity anymore, the Standard Amer-

ican Housewife, all husband, home and kids? The New Commodity—the Liberated Woman—has sex a lot and has a Career, preferably something that can be fitted in with the household chores—like dancing, pottery, or painting.

2   On the other hand is Women's Liberation—and housework. What? You say this is all trivial? Wonderful! That's what I thought. It seemed perfectly reasonable. We both had careers, both had to work a couple of days a week to earn enough to live on, so why shouldn't we share the housework? So I suggested it to my mate and he agreed—most men are too hip to turn you down flat. You're right, he said. It's only fair. Then an interesting thing happened. I can only explain it by stating that we women have been brainwashed more than even we can imagine, Probably too many years of seeing television women in ecstasy over their shiny waxed floors or breaking down over their dirty shirt collars. Men have no such conditioning. They recognize the essential fact of housework right from the very beginning. Which is that it stinks.

3   Here's my list of dirty chores: buying groceries, carting them home and putting them away; cooking meals and washing dishes and pots; doing the laundry; digging out the place when things get out of control; washing floors. The list could go on but the sheer necessities are bad enough. All of us have to do these things, or get someone else to do them for us. The longer my husband contemplated these chores, the more repulsed he became, and so proceeded the change from the normally sweet, considerate Dr. Jekyll into the crafty Mr. Hyde, who would stop at nothing to avoid the horrors of housework. As he felt himself backed into a corner laden with dirty dishes, brooms, mops and reeking garbage, his front teeth grew longer and pointier, his fingernails haggled and his eyes grew wild. Housework trivial? Not on your life! Just try to share the burden.

4   So ensued a dialogue that's been going on for several years. Here are some of the high points: "I don't mind sharing the housework, but I don't do it very well. We should each do the things we're best at." MEANING: Unfortunately I'm no good at things like washing dishes or cooking. What I do best is a little light carpentry, changing light bulbs, moving furniture (how often do you move furniture?). ALSO MEANING: Historically the lower classes (black men and us) have had hundreds of years experience doing menial jobs. It would be a waste of manpower to train someone else to do them now. ALSO MEANING: I don't like the dull, stupid, boring jobs, so you should do them. "I don' t mind sharing the work, but you'll have to show me how to do it." MEANING: I ask a lot of questions and you'll have to show me everything every time I do it because I don't remember so good. Also don' t try to sit down and read while I'm doing my jobs because I'm going to annoy hell out of you until it's easier to do them yourself."

5   "We used to be so happy!" (Said whenever it was his turn to do something.) MEANING: I used to be so happy. MEANING: Life without housework is bliss. No quarrel here. Perfect agreement.

6   "We have different standards, and why should I have to work to your standards? That's unfair." MEANING: If I begin to get bugged by the dirt and

crap, I will say, "This place sure is a sty" or "How can anyone live like this?" and wait for your reaction. I know that all women have a sore called "Guilt over a messy house" or "Household work is ultimately my responsibility." I know that men have caused that sore. If anyone visits and the place is a sty— they're not going to leave and say, "He sure is a lousy housekeeper." You'll take the rap in any case. I can outwait you. ALSO MEANING: I can provoke innumerable scenes over the housework issue. Eventually doing all the housework yourself will be less painful to you than trying to get me to do half. Or I'll suggest we get a maid. She will do my share of the work. You will do yours. It's women's work.

7   "I've got nothing against sharing the housework, but you can' t make me do it on your schedule." MEANING: Passive resistance. I'll do it when I damned well please, if at all. If my job is doing dishes, it's easier to do them once a week. If taking out laundry, once a month. If washing the floors, once a year. If you don't like it, do it yourself oftener, and then I won't do it at all.

8   "I hate it more than you. You don't mind it so much." MEANING: Housework is garbage work. It's the worst crap I've ever done. It's degrading and humiliating for someone of my intelligence to do it. But for someone of your intelligence. . . .

9   "Housework is too trivial to even talk about." MEANING: It's even more trivial to do. Housework is beneath my status. My purpose in life is to deal with matters of significance. Yours is to deal with matters of insignificance. You should do the housework.

10   "This problem of housework is not a man-woman problem. In any relationship between two people one is going to have a stronger personality and dominate." MEANING: That stronger personality had better be me.

11   "In animal societies, wolves, for example, the top animal is usually a male even where he is not chosen for brute strength but on the basis of cunning and intelligence. Isn't that interesting?" MEANING: I have historical, psychological, anthropological and biological justification for keeping you down. How can you ask the top wolf to be equal?

12   "Women's liberation isn't really a political movement." MEANING: The revolution is coming too close to home. ALSO MEANING: I am only interested in how I am oppressed, not how I oppress others. Therefore the war, the draft, and the university are political. Women's liberation is not.

13   "Man's accomplishments have always depended on getting help from other people, mostly women. What great man would have accomplished what he did if he had to do his own housework?" MEANING: Oppression is built into the system and I, as the white American male, receive the benefits of this system. I don't want to give them up.

14   Participatory democracy begins at home. If you are planning to implement your politics, there are certain things to remember.

> **1.** He is feeling it more than you. He's losing some leisure, and you're gaining it. The measure of your oppression is his resistance.

2. A great many American men are not accustomed to doing monotonous, repetitive work which never issues in any lasting, let alone important, achievement. This is why they would rather repair a cabinet than wash dishes. If human endeavors are like a pyramid with man's highest achievements at the top, then keeping oneself alive is at the bottom. Men have always had servants (us) to take care of this bottom stratum of life while they have confined their efforts to the rarefied upper regions. It is thus ironic when they ask of women "Where are your great painters, statesmen, etc."? Mme. Matisse ran a military shop so he could paint. Mrs. Martin Luther King kept his house and raised his babies.

3. It is a traumatizing experience for someone who has always thought of himself as being against any oppression or exploitation of one human being by another to realize that in his daily life he has been accepting and implementing (and benefiting from) this exploitation; that his rationalization is little different from that of the racist who says, "Black people don' t feel pain." (women don't mind doing the crap work); and that the oldest form of oppression in history has been the oppression of 50 percent of the population by the other 50 percent.

4. Arm yourself with some knowledge of the psychology of oppressed peoples everywhere, and a few facts about the animal kingdom. I admit playing top wolf or who runs the gorillas is silly but as a last resort men bring it up all the time. Talk about bees. If you feel really hostile bring up the sex life of spiders. They have sex. She bites off his head. The psychology of oppressed peoples is not silly. Jews, immigrants, black men, and all women have employed the same psychological mechanisms to survive—admiring the oppressor, glorifying the oppressor, wanting to be like the oppressor, wanting the oppressor to like them, mostly because the oppressor held all the power.

5. In a sense, all men everywhere are slightly schizoid—divorced from the reality of maintaining life. This makes it easier for them to play games with it. It is almost a cliche that women feel greater grief at sending a son off to a war or losing him to that war because they bore him, suckled him, and raised him. The men who foment those wars did none of those things and have a more superficial estimate of the worth of human life. One hour a day is a low estimate of the amount of time one has to spend "keeping" oneself. By foisting this off on others, man has seven hours a week—one working day more to play with his mind and not his human needs. Over the course of generations it is easy to see whence evolved the horrifying abstractions of modern life.

6. With the death of each form of oppression, life changes and new forms evolve. English aristocrats at the turn of the century were horrified at the idea of enfranchising working men—were sure that it

signaled the death of civilization and a return to barbarism. Some working men were even deceived by this line. Similarly with the minimum wage, abolition of slavery, and female suffrage. Life changes but it goes on. Don't fall for any line about the death of everything if men take a turn at the dishes. They will imply that you are holding back the revolution (their revolution). But you are advancing it (your revolution).

7. Keep checking up. Periodically consider who's actually doing the jobs. These things have a way of backsliding so that a year later once again the woman is doing everything. After a year, make a list of jobs the man has rarely if ever done. You will find cleaning pots, toilets, refrigerators and ovens high on the list. Use time sheets if necessary. He will accuse you of being petty. He is above that sort of thing (housework). Bear in mind what the worst jobs are, namely the ones that have to be done every day or several times a day. Also the ones that are dirty—it's more pleasant to pick up books, newspapers, etc., than to wash dishes. Alternate the bad jobs. It's the daily grind that gets you down. Also make sure that you don' t have the responsibility for the housework with occasional help from him. "I'll cook dinner for you tonight" implies it's really your job and isn't he a nice guy to do some of it for you.

8. Most men had a rich and rewarding bachelor life during which they did not starve or become encrusted with crud or buried under the linen. There is a taboo that says women mustn't strain themselves in the presence of men—we haul around 50 pounds of groceries if we have to, but aren't allowed to open a jar if there is someone around to do it for us. The reverse side of the coin is that men aren't supposed to be able to take care of themselves without a woman. Both are excuses for making women do the housework.

9. Beware of the double whammy. He won't do the little things he always did because you're now a "Liberated Woman," right? Of course he won't do anything else either. . . .

I was just finishing this when my husband came in and asked what I was doing. Writing a paper on housework. Housework? he said. Housework? Oh my god how trivial can you get? A paper on housework.

∽

(2,526 words)

VOCABULARY

commodity (1)   haggled (3)   ensued (4)
innumerable (6)   anthropological (11)   participatory (14)
stratum (14, #2)   rarefied (14, #2)   schizoid (14, #5)
foment (14, #5)   enfranchising (14, #6)

THE FACTS

1. What, according to the author, is the difference between liberated women and women's liberation? Do you agree or disagree with her distinction? Explain your answer.

2. Much of the author's essay is taken up by a dialogue. Who are the two people taking part in this dialogue? How can the reader distinguish between the two?

3. At which point in the dialogue does the wife completely agree with her husband? Does the agreement help the couple to get along better as husband and wife? Why or why not?

4. How does the husband pull rank by referring to animal society? How do you feel about his assessment? How does the wife eventually counter this argument? Who do you think has the better argument, the wife or the husband? Explain your answer.

5. How many points does the author want women to remember if they intend to implement participatory democracy regarding housework? Which of these points is the most important to her argument? Explain your choice.

THE STRATEGIES

1. Why does the author end her ninth admonishment to women with an ellipsis? What point is she trying to make?

2. What attitude does the wife take throughout the essay? Do you like her? Why or why not? Do you think her attitude represents the majority of women? Explain your answer.

3. What difference, if any, do you see between the voice and tone of the writer and the voice and tone of the husband? Point to passages that support your view. Who ultimately controls the voices represented? How important is it for the reader to understand this?

4. What does the author want the women's liberation movement to become? Is this purpose openly stated or simply implied? Point to the appropriate passage in the text.

5. What relationship exists between the title and content of the essay? Does the title help the reader to guess the subject of the essay?

THE ISSUES

1. How is housework related to the author's ultimate goal? Do you agree with her view of the role of housework as it is connected to her goal?

2. What is the first male attitude listed by the author? Evaluate this point in terms of its fairness to women and society.

3. What is your opinion of the idea that in every society, including those of animals, the strongest and fittest should dominate? Who, in your society, is the strongest and fittest?

4. According to the idea attributed to the husband, what aspect of society is built into the social systems to support male dominance? What is your reaction to this view?

5. What is the purpose of the nine points women must remember as they try to revolutionize the present political system by insisting on participatory democracy, which, according to the author, begins at home? Has the author overlooked any major point? If so, what is it?

SUGGESTIONS FOR WRITING

1. Write an essay in which you propose your own strategy for dealing with housework in a marriage.

2. In 500 words or so, write an essay in which you either agree or disagree with Mainardi's argument. Try to use a consistent voice and tone in your essay.

REMARKS ON THE LIFE OF SACCO AND ON HIS OWN LIFE AND EXECUTION

Bartolomeo Vanzetti

Bartolomeo Vanzetti (1888–1927) was born of peasant stock in northern Italy, where he worked as a baker's apprentice. He migrated to the United States in 1908, where he worked as a laborer and became an avowed anarchist. In 1920, along with Nicolo Sacco, another Italian immigrant, Vanzetti was arrested for the murder of a guard during a payroll robbery. While in prison awaiting execution, he wrote his autobiography. Maintaining their innocence to the end, and despite the worldwide public protest mounted in their behalf, Sacco and Vanzetti were executed on August 22, 1927.

These four paragraphs are assembled from Vanzetti's writings and sayings. The first three paragraphs are notes from a speech. Vanzetti intended to deliver them in court before his sentencing but the judge barred him from doing so. The final paragraph is a transcription from an interview that Vanzetti gave to Philip D. Strong, a reporter for the North American Newspaper Alliance, in April 1927. The entire excerpt illustrates the lyricism and elegance of simple words cast in idiomatic sentences.

～

1   I have talk a great deal of myself but I even forgot to name Sacco. Sacco too is a worker from his boyhood, a skilled worker lover of work, with a good job and pay, a good and lovely wife, two beautiful children and a neat little home at the verge of a wood, near a brook. Sacco is a heart, a faith, a character, a man; a man lover of nature and of mankind. A man who gave all, who sacrifice all to the cause of Liberty and to his love for mankind; money, rest, mundane ambitions, his own wife, his children, himself and his own life. Sacco has never dreamt to steal, never to assassinate. He and I have never brought a morsel of bread to our mouths, from our childhood to today—which has not been gained by the sweat of our brows. Never. His people also are in good position and of good reputation.

2   Oh, yes, I may be more witful, as some have put it, I am a better babbler than he is, but many, many times in hearing his heartful voice ringing a faith sublime, in considering his supreme sacrifice, remembering his heroism I felt small small at the presence of his greatness and found myself compelled to fight back from my throat to not weep before him—this man called thief and assassin and doomed. But Sacco's name will live in the hearts of the people and in their gratitude when Katzmann's[1] and your bones will be dispersed by time, when your name, his name, your laws, institutions, and your false god are but a deem rememoring of a cursed past in which man was wolf to the man. . . .

3   If it had not been for these thing . . . I might have live out my life talking at street corners to scorning men. I might have die, unmarked, unknown, a failure. Now we are not a failure. This is our career and our triumph. Never in our full life could we hope to do such work for tolerance, for joostice, for man's onderstanding of man as now we do by accident.

4   Our words—our lives—our pains—nothing! The taking of our lives—lives of a good shoemaker and a poor fish-peddler—all! That last moment belongs to us—that agony is our triumph.

~

(390 words)

VOCABULARY

mundane (1)   sublime (2)

THE FACTS

1. What kind of man does the excerpt make Sacco out to be?
2. What does Vanzetti claim to be better at than Sacco?
3. According to Vanzetti, how might his life have turned out were it not for his trial and conviction?

---

[1]Frederick G. Katzmann was the district attorney who prosecuted the case.—Ed.

THE STRATEGIES

1. The author was an Italian with a frail grasp of the American speech idiom. What is the effect of his grammatical errors on the way he expresses himself?

2. How would you characterize the diction of this excerpt? Is it lofty? Plain?

3. Why do some editors include this excerpt in poetry anthologies? What is poetic about it?

THE ISSUES

1. Because of his beliefs, Vanzetti was labeled a philosophical anarchist. What is a philosophical anarchist?

2. In the final paragraph, Vanzetti calls his impending execution with Sacco "our triumph." What do you think he meant by that?

3. The Sacco and Vanzetti trial was made famous mainly because of the intense media attention it drew. What restrictions, if any, do you think should be imposed on media coverage of sensational criminals and trials? Why? Justify your answer.

SUGGESTIONS FOR WRITING

1. Copy this excerpt, correcting its grammatical and spelling errors as you go. Add any words that are necessary to make it grammatical. Write a paragraph on which version you think is more effective—the original or the corrected one—giving your reasons.

2. Without doing any further research into Vanzetti, and using this excerpt as your only evidence, write an impressionistic description of the kind of man you think he was. Be specific in your references to passages in the excerpt.

TERM PAPER SUGGESTION

Write a term paper on the Sacco-Vanzetti trial. Reach your own conclusion as to whether or not it was a fair trial, and support your belief.

SALVATION

Langston Hughes

Langston Hughes (1902–1967) was born in Joplin, Missouri, and edu-cated at Columbia University, New York, and Lincoln University, Penn-sylvania. He worked at odd jobs in this country and in France before becoming established as a writer. His lifelong interest was the promotion of black art, history, and causes. In addition to many collections of poetry, Hughes wrote a novel, Not Without Laughter *(1930), and an autobiography,* The Big Sea *(1940).*

In this selection from *The Big Sea*, Hughes recounts a dramatic incident from his childhood. The incident is narrated from the perspective of a twelve-year-old boy and demonstrates a skillful writer's use of language to re-create the innocent voice of childhood.

~

1 I was saved from sin when I was going on thirteen. But not really saved. It happened like this. There was a big revival at my Auntie Reed's church. Every night for weeks there had been much preaching, singing, praying, and shouting, and some very hardened sinners had been brought to Christ, and the membership of the church had grown by leaps and bounds. Then just before the revival ended, they held a special meeting for children, "to bring the young lambs to the fold." My aunt spoke of it for days ahead. That night I was escorted to the front row and placed on the mourners' bench with all the other young sinners, who had not yet been brought to Jesus.

2 My aunt told me that when you were saved you saw a light, and something happened to you inside! And Jesus came into your life! And God was with you from then on! She said you could see and hear and feel Jesus in your soul. I believed her. I had heard a great many old people say the same thing and it seemed to me they ought to know. So I sat there calmly in the hot, crowded church, waiting for Jesus to come to me.

3 The preacher preached a wonderful rhythmical sermon, all moans and shouts and lonely cries and dire pictures of hell, and then he sang a song about the ninety and nine safe in the fold, but one little lamb was left out in the cold. Then he said: "Won't you come? Won't you come to Jesus? Young lambs, won't you come?" And he held out his arms to all us young sinners there on the mourners' bench. And the little girls cried. And some of them jumped up and went to Jesus right away. But most of us just sat there.

4 A great many old people came and knelt around us and prayed, old women with jet-black faces and braided hair, old men with work-gnarled hands. And the church sang a song about the lower lights are burning, some poor sinners to be saved. And the whole building rocked with prayer and song.

5 Still I keep waiting to see Jesus.

6 Finally all the young people had gone to the altar and were saved, but one boy and me. He was a rounder's son named Westley. Westley and I were surrounded by sisters and deacons praying. It was very hot in the church, and getting late now. Finally Westley said to me in a whisper: "God damn! I'm tired o' sitting here. Let's get up and be saved." So he got up and was saved.

7 Then I was left all alone on the mourners' bench. My aunt came and knelt at my knees and cried, while prayers and songs swirled all around me in the little church. The whole congregation prayed for me alone, in a mighty wail of

moans and voices. And I kept waiting serenely for Jesus, waiting, waiting—but he didn't come. I wanted to see him, but nothing happened to me. Nothing! I wanted something to happen to me, but nothing happened.

8   I heard the songs and the minister saying: "Why don't you come? My dear child, why don'you come to Jesus? Jesus is waiting for you. He wants you. Why don't you come? Sister Reed, what is this child's name?"

9   "Langston," my aunt sobbed.

10   "Langston, why don't you come? Why don't you come and be saved? Oh, Lamb of God! W don't you come?"

11   Now it was really getting late. I began to be ashamed of myself, holding everything up so long. I began to wonder what God thought about Westley, who certainly hadn't seen Jesus either, but who was now sitting proudly on the platform, swinging his knickerbockered legs and grinning down at me, surrounded by deacons and old women on their knees praying. God had not struck Westley dead for taking his name in vain or for lying in the temple. So I decided that maybe to save further trouble, I'd better lie, too, and say that Jesus had come, and get up and be saved.

12   So I got up.

13   Suddenly the whole room broke into a sea of shouting, as they saw me rise. Waves of rejoicing swept the place. Women leaped in the air. My aunt threw her arms around me. The minister took me by the hand and led me to the platform.

14   When things quieted down, in a hushed silence, punctuated by a few ecstatic "Amens," all the new young lambs were blessed in the name of God. Then joyous singing filled the room.

15   That night, for the last time in my life but one—for I was a big boy twelve years old—I cried. I cried, in bed alone, and couldn't stop. I buried my head under the quilts, but my aunt heard me. She woke up and told my uncle I was crying because the Holy Ghost had come into my life, and because I had seen Jesus. But I was really crying because I couldn't bear to tell her that I had lied, that I had deceived everybody in the church, and I hadn't seen Jesus, and that now I didn't believe there was a Jesus any more, since he didn't come to help me.

~

(889 words)

VOCABULARY

gnarled (4)   punctuated (14)   ecstatic (14)

THE FACTS

1. How does Westley's attitude differ from the narrator's? Is Westley more realistic and less gullible, or is he simply more callous and less sensitive than the narrator?

2. The narrator holds out to the last minute and finally submits to being saved. What is his motive for finally giving in?

3. Who has been deceived in the story? The aunt by the narrator? The narrator by the aunt? Both the narrator and the aunt by the minister? Everybody by the demands of religion?

4. What insight does the narrator reach at the end of the story? What has he learned?

5. The story is told as a flashback to Hughes's boyhood. What is his attitude toward the experience as he retells it?

THE STRATEGIES

1. The story is narrated from the point of view of a twelve-year-old boy. What techniques of language are used in the story to create the perspective of a boy? How is the vocabulary appropriate to a boy?

2. In his article "How to Say Nothing in Five Hundred Words," Paul Roberts urges the use of specific details in writing. How does Hughes make use of such details?

3. The description in paragraph 4 is vivid but compressed. How does Hughes achieve this effect?

THE ISSUES

1. Marx wrote that "religion . . . is the opium of the people." What is your view of this sentiment? How does it apply or not apply to this excerpt?

2. The little girls were the first to break down and offer themselves to be saved. The last two holdouts were boys. How do you explain this different reaction of the two sexes?

3. What do you think would have likely happened if the narrator had not gone up to be saved?

4. Religions often use ovine terms (sheep, lamb, flock) to refer to their congregations. What do you think is the origin of this usage? What does this usage imply about the members?

SUGGESTIONS FOR WRITING

1. Describe an experience of your own in which group pressure forced you into doing something you did not believe in.

2. Write a brief biographical sketch of Westley, fantasizing on the kind of man you believe he grew into and the kind of life he eventually led.

WHEN BECKY LEFT HOME

Anthony C. Winkler

Anthony C. Winkler (b. 1942) is a novelist and writer of English text-books. Winkler's novels, mostly set in Jamaica, where he was born and reared, depict realistically, but always with wit and gentle humor, the lives of ordinary Jamaicans. Two of his works have been turned into films that reaped praise from reviewers who admired the mixture of comedy and seriousness. Winkler, with his co-author, Jo Ray McCuen, has written fifteen textbooks for college writing classes.

Among the most emotional moments of a father's life is the day his daughter packs up and leaves home. It is the day when the little girl who sat on his lap on so many occasions is now a grown woman who will begin her journey into adulthood with all of its responsibilities. The past seems a nostalgic blur while the future leaves an empty spot in the father's heart.

~

1   When Becky left home
    the old drought did not break
    the ungainly dragonflies
    did not abandon us
5   the mosquitoes
    did not lay aside their chopsticks
    and not even a single rose
    shed a single petal
    like a crystallized tear
10 of sorrow or longing.
    The world around us was unchanged.
    There was no easing
    in the intemperance of summer
    and the heat battered our heads
15 with the same routine
    unconscionable indifference.
    But inside my heart
    where no eye sees
    no palpation can ever touch
20 and no shadow ever falls
    I heard a seismic crack
    as the tectonic plates
    in the subterranean
    continent that is me shifted.
    No one else on this whole earth
25 but I, her father, felt it.

(118 words)

VOCABULARY

unconscionable (15)   palpation (18)   seismic (20)
tectonic (21)

THE FACTS

1. What line reveals the relationship between the speaker and Becky? What advantage does this placement have?
2. To what aspect of nature does the speaker keep referring throughout the poem?
3. Why do you think Becky left home and where did she go? Speculate on the answer to this question and give reasons for your choice.
4. What is the "seismic crack" referred to in line 20?
5. According to the poem, how many people heard the earth crack?

THE STRATEGIES

1. What is the effect of having only five periods and two commas throughout the entire poem? Did you have difficulty following the line of thought? Why or why not?
2. What is the purpose of the rose reference in lines 6–9?
3. What is the meaning of lines 20–23? Explain this passage by unraveling the metaphor used.
4. Why does the speaker insist that no one else on this whole earth, besides him, felt the shift in tectonic plates?
5. How important is the title to understanding the poem? Suggest another title that might work just as well.

THE ISSUES

1. If Becky is leaving home to enrich her life or further her career, does the father's anguish seem justified? How did your parents react to your departure for college?
2. Why does the speaker mention the fact that nature seems indifferent to the suffering he is experiencing? How do you think he expected nature to react? Is his attitude sane or abnormal?
3. What lesson, if any, does the indifference of nature teach us?
4. What advice would you give someone who expects nature to respond to human sorrow?
5. What is the meaning of lines 24 and 25? Explain their meaning in your own words.

SUGGESTIONS FOR WRITING

1. Write an essay narrating the experience of leaving home for college.

2. Choosing an incident from your life that made you angry, sad, happy, or bitter, write an essay in which your voice reflects your mood.

CHAPTER WRITING ASSIGNMENTS

1. Contrast the voice of the writer of *The Politics of Housework* with that of the writer of *Salvation.*

2. When you write, do you find yourself deliberately altering your voice for a particular audience? In a paragraph or two, describe how you use your writing voice in different contexts.

WRITING ASSIGNMENTS FOR A SPECIFIC AUDIENCE

1. Assuming an audience of junior high students, write a couple of paragraphs explaining the concept of voice in a writer's work.

2. Write a letter to the editor of your local newspaper complaining about a problem in your neighborhood.

COLLABORATIVE WRITING PROJECTS

1. About style, the Reverend Samuel Wesley (1662–1735) said, "Style is the dress of thought." On the other hand, the Comte de Buffon (1707–1788) said something that sounds just the opposite: "Style is the man." Taking these two views as opposing opinions about style, research what critics and scholars have said about style and write a paper summarizing their findings and giving the opinions of the members of your group.

2. After dividing your group into teams of two or three, each team should collaborate on writing a short piece imitating the voice used by one of the writers in this section. Meet as a group to discuss and critique whether each imitation successfully captured the voice of the particular writer.

———— REAL-LIFE ————
STUDENT WRITING

A THANK-YOU NOTE TO AN AUNT

The thank-you note continues to flourish even in these days of e-mail and instant communication by telephone. Nothing can replace the personal touch found in a handwritten note. Here, for example, is a student's note thanking her aunt for a graduation present.

Thank You...

Dear Auntie Jo-Jo:

Thanks tons for the $50.00 graduation present. I didn't place it in a savings account because you said to spend it on something personal. Well, I thought you might want to know how prudently I spent the money. I went to T.J. Max, my favorite discount store, where I always get amazing deals. Believe it or not, for $50.00 I bought a smart-looking DKNY argyle sweater and a pair of navy corduroy pants. I'm sure my friends think I have been spending profligately at Neiman Marcus. I wish every college student had an adorable aunt like you. You have been far better than Auntie Mame.

Much love,

Trudi

P.S. I painted this card myself, hope you like it.

4

What Is a Thesis?

EDITORS' COUNSEL

The thesis is a single sentence that announces to your reader exactly what you intend to argue, to prove, to refute, to describe, to tell, or to explain. By convention, it is usually the final sentence of the first paragraph. Of course, this is not the only place a thesis can appear; but the final sentence of the first paragraph has evolved in classroom compositions as the most effective niche for the thesis, especially in the 500-word essay, which students are usually asked to write.

The idea of the thesis is an old one that has survived for the simple reason that it works. Writers generally write better when they know exactly what they have to say, and readers usually are better able to follow a writer's chain of thought when they know the main point of a written work. For example, consider this thesis statement from an actual student essay:

> Our government must assume the responsibility of caring for the thousands of homeless mentally ill people who are now forced to roam the streets because of changes in governmental policy.

This thesis tells us, in a nutshell, what the student intends to argue. We expect her to show us how changes in governmental policy have caused thousands of the mentally ill to become homeless. We also expect her to argue the moral rightness of helping them.

The thesis, then, is the main point of your essay summed up in a single sentence. In it, you tell the reader where you stand on the issue, what subtopics you intend to cover, and in what order.

Finding Your Thesis

Let us say, for example, your assignment is to write an essay about a sport or recreation you enjoy. You muse and think and finally decide to write about sailing. That is your topic. It is a usable topic because it falls under a general subject. If you had decided to do an essay on the composition of mosaic tile or on the Roman technique of road building, you would have strayed from the subject, because neither is a sport or recreation.

So sailing will be your topic. You think some more and decide to write an essay on the joys of sailing. Note, by the way, that you could have chosen to write about the boredom and work of sailing; you could also have slanted your essay any number of other ways. But you love sailing and think it a wonderful sport, so you decide to sing its praises in your essay. The joy of sailing will be your main point.

Next you must express this main point in a thesis. One way to do this is to write down the main point on the top of a page either as a sentence or a fragment—sailing is a wonderful sport; sailing is a joy; sailing is a relaxing recreation—and then ask yourself questions about it. Write down the questions as they occur to you. Perhaps you will come up with a list of questions such as these:

Main Point: Sailing is a wonderful sport.

Why do I love sailing as much as I do?

What are the benefits of sailing?

Why is sailing such a popular sport?

Why is sailing so relaxing?

What does sailing teach?

To find your thesis, choose the question that seems most appropriate to your main point, audience, and assignment, and answer it in a single, detailed sentence. This means you must make a decision about whether the instructor wants a personal essay—one heavy with "I" pronouns and emphasizing your own experiences with sailing—or an impersonal essay that presents its ideas in an objective style. For example, you might answer the last question this way:

Sailing is a delightful sport that teaches independence, balance, and navigation.

Now you have a thesis. You also have a sketch of your essay's subtopics. First, you will explain how sailing teaches independence; next, how it teaches balance; finally, how it teaches navigation. You will draw on your personal experiences and anecdotes as a sailor to amplify on these points.

Answering a different question will obviously give you another thesis. For example, if your instructor makes it clear that the essay may be based on your own experiences, answering the first question would give you a thesis suitable for a personal essay:

I love the exhilaration, the freedom, and the adventure of sailing.

You now have a thesis that emphasizes your personal views of sailing.

When you do have your thesis, write it on a post-it note and stick it on your word processor or typewriter. It is a promise you make to your reader, and you must be faithful to it in the essay by covering the subtopics in the exact order of occurrence in your thesis. This means, for example, that in writing an essay on the joy of sailing, you must first discuss the exhilaration, and then the freedom, and finally the adventure of sailing. And you should discuss nothing else but these three points.

Key Words in the Thesis

Every thesis contains one or more key words that represent ideas on which the essay will focus. In effect, these key words are ideas that the essay must amplify with definitions, examples, and explanations. The following theses, for example, contain a single key word, which is underlined:

Pheasant hunting is a <u>tiring</u> sport.

I am a <u>jealous</u> person.

Investing in the stock market is <u>risky</u>.

Most of the time, however, theses will contain several key words:

Good English is <u>clear</u>, <u>appropriate</u>, and <u>vivid</u>.

Studies show that as children the real achievers in our society were <u>independent</u> and <u>spirited</u>.

Riding a bicycle to work has <u>several</u> <u>advantages</u> over driving a car.

Soviet children are members of collectives—nurseries, schools, camps, youth programs—that emphasize <u>obedience</u>, <u>self-discipline</u>, and <u>subordination</u>.

Occasionally, the thesis will contain a proposition that is inseparable from its individual words. The essay will have to amplify the whole statement:

<u>Students should be advised against majoring in subjects in which job prospects are limited</u>.

<u>If the United States is to survive, Americans will have to learn to conserve their country's resources</u>.

Characteristics of a Good Thesis

The precision with which you word your thesis will help determine the quality of your essay. At a minimum, a good thesis predicts, controls, and obligates.

The Thesis Predicts A good thesis will contain a discussible idea while also suggesting to the writer a method of developing it. (For more on methods of development, see part II of this book.) Some propositions, however, such as the following, are so self-evident that they warrant no further discussion:

A relationship exists between excessive eating and gaining weight.

Rich people usually live in big houses.

In our country, movie stars are greatly admired.

None of these statements contains a discussible idea that one might enlarge on in a whole essay; their wording suggests no method of development. They would, therefore, not make good theses. In contrast, the following thesis not only contains discussible assertions, but also predicts a likely method of development:

> Being a student reporter for the local paper means conducting interviews at odd hours and in strange places.

At what odd hours and in which strange places, one immediately wonders. The most obvious method of development for such a thesis is by illustration/exemplification (see chapter 10). The reader expects more particulars about interviews at odd hours and in strange places; and the writer knows that he or she must find examples of these and work them into the essay. This sentence makes a good thesis.

Consider another example of how a properly worded thesis can predict the development of an essay:

> Because of the computer revolution and the premium it places on educational skills, many people over the age of twenty-one are enrolling in colleges today.

This is a "reason why" thesis, one that predicts the development of the essay primarily by an analysis of cause (see chapter 14).

Common sense tells us that it is easier to write the essay whose method of development is predicted in the wording of its thesis than the one for which some developmental pattern must be found during the actual writing. Wording the thesis so that it predicts not only what you will say, but the pattern of development in which you will say it, can help you write a better essay.

The Thesis Controls   The thesis controls the essay by restricting you to a specific order of topics or by presenting an obvious organizing principle for the essay (for more on patterns of organization, see chapter 5 and the introduction to chapter 7). Consider this term paper thesis, for example:

> Today, religion is no longer the uncontested center and ruler of human life, because Protestantism, science, and capitalism have brought about a secularized world.

Implicit in this thesis are a certain number and order of subtopics:

1. A description of medieval society when religion was the center of human existence

2. An explanation of how Protestantism secularized the world
3. An explanation of how science secularized the world
4. An explanation of how capitalism secularized the world

The advantage of this thesis is obvious. You do not have to cast around wondering what you should say next, for you know what your subtopics are and in what order they should occur. Moreover, the wording of the thesis tells you the kind of information you need to look up in the library.

Sometimes a thesis will control an essay by presenting the writer with a ready-made scheme for organization. Consider, for example, this thesis:

> My religious outlook has been shaped by three distinct phases of belief and disbelief in my life.

This thesis requires a chronological organization, with the writer detailing her religious beliefs from the earliest to the present. Note, however, that this thesis is suitable only for a personal essay; you could not write an objective essay on it without some drastic rewording.

Consider, on the other hand, this thesis:

> A winning tennis strategy requires a player to have a grasp of the geometry of the playing surface and to work to cut off the angle of an opponent's shots.

This thesis cries out for an essay organized by a spatial pattern. You could divide the playing surface into three zones—backcourt, midcourt, and net—and show how a player might win by maneuvering within them to cut off the angle of an opponent's shots.

The Thesis Obligates   When a writer strays from the thesis, the result is often vague, unfocused writing. If the thesis is "Police officers spend more time controlling traffic and providing information than they spend enforcing the law," then you must prove this point in your essay. You should not rhapsodize about the heroism of the police or complain about police brutality. Likewise, if your thesis is "California college students are sexually more liberated than their New York counterparts," then that is the only point you should discuss. You should not write about the disputed intellectual superiority of New York college students or weave in facts about vegetarianism in California unless these issues are somehow related to the sexual behavior of college students in New York and California.

However, it follows that in a focused essay the wording of the thesis must obligate the writer to discuss a single issue. Consider this thesis, for example:

> Definitions of obscenity change as society changes, and the courts' decisions on censorship reflect the legal profession's confusion on the issue.

This thesis is pulling in two directions. The first part of it requires a discussion of how definitions of obscenity reflect changes in society, while the second part leads to a discussion of the legal profession's confusion on obscenity. An essay based on this thesis would fall into two mismatched parts. The student should rewrite the thesis until it discusses a single issue. Here is a suggested revision of the thesis, which unifies its two parts and commits the writer to a single idea:

> Because definitions of obscenity change as society changes, the courts have handed down some contradictory decisions on censorship.

Although many students worry about making their theses too restrictive, this fault is found only rarely in the essays of beginners. Far more common is the overly broad thesis that cannot be adequately developed in a brief essay. For example, none of the following actual student theses is restrictive enough to be dealt with in a short paper:

Parachuting is unbelievable!

The Gulf War against Iraq was stupid.

Evaluating college teachers is an interesting idea.

Admittedly, these examples are vaguely worded and overly terse, but they are also not restrictive enough to guide a writer's hand. Ambiguous key words like *unbelievable, stupid,* and *interesting* need to be replaced. To predict, control, and obligate the course of an essay, a thesis must be unambiguous, structured, and restrictive. Common sense also tells us that the scope of the thesis must be in proportion to the length of the essay. A broad thesis is not suited to a short essay, nor a narrow thesis to a long essay.

Nine Errors to Avoid in Composing a Thesis

1. A thesis cannot be a fragment; it must be expressed as a complete sentence. A fragment is a phrase or dependent clause that is punctuated as if it were a complete sentence. Our objection to using a fragment as a thesis, however, is based neither on punctuation nor on grammar, but on the fact that it is usually too limited or sketchy for a writer to elaborate on in an essay. A fragment simply cannot adequately sum up what your essay will cover, which is what the thesis should do. Here is an example:

   Poor: How life is in a racial ghetto.

   Better: Residents of a racial ghetto tend to have a higher death rate, a higher infant mortality rate, and a higher unemployment rate than do residents of the suburbs.

2. A thesis must not be worded as a question (usually, the answer to the question could be the thesis). The purpose of the thesis is to spell out the main idea of the essay, which is difficult, if not impossible, to do in a question:

> Poor: Do Americans really need large refrigerators?

> Better: If Americans did their marketing daily, as do most Europeans, they could save energy by using smaller refrigerators.

3. A thesis should not be too broad. An overly broad thesis will commit you to write on an idea you may be unable to adequately cover in a short essay. The solution in that case is to rewrite your thesis and begin again, for no matter how hard you work, your essay will otherwise seem labored and abstract:

> Poor: The literature of mythology contains many resurrection stories.

> Better: One of the oldest resurrection myths is the story of the Egyptian god Osiris.

4. A thesis should not contain unrelated elements. The expression of a single and unified purpose should be your overriding aim in drafting your thesis. You are trying to prove one point, make one case, dramatize one situation. Veteran writers can, of course, do more than one task in an essay, but this is a skill acquired only with much practice. The beginner is better off framing the thesis to commit the essay to making one point or performing one function. One way to do this is to avoid using a compound sentence as a thesis statement.

    A compound sentence is two independent clauses joined by a conjunction. An independent clause is a grammatical construction that can be punctuated to make sense on its own. Two independent clauses automatically imply two different ideas, which may be hard for the writer to keep separate or treat fairly in a single essay without making a muddle of both. Here is an example:

> Poor: All novelists seek the truth, and some novelists are good psychologists.

Properly punctuated, each clause expresses a different idea and can stand on its own. "All novelists seek the truth" is one idea. "Some novelists are good psychologists" is the other. Writing an essay on this thesis will require the writer to prove two unrelated points.

> Better: In their attempt to probe human nature, many novelists become excellent psychologists.

5. A thesis should not contain phrases like "I think" or "in my opinion" because they weaken a writer's argument. Use the thesis to tell your reader plainly where you stand, what you think, or what you intend to prove in the essay. This is no place to be wishy-washy or uncertain as if you were not quite sure about your opinion or viewpoint. Indeed, if you are not sure about the opinion expressed in your thesis, you should rethink it until you are.

> Poor: In my opinion, public buildings should be required by law to have no-smoking zones because of the adverse health effects of "passive smoking."

Better: Public buildings should be required by law to have no-smoking zones because of the adverse health effects of "passive smoking."

6. A thesis should not be expressed in vague language. With only rare exceptions, it is a general truth that the vague thesis will lead to a vague essay. If the thesis is vaguely worded, it is usually because the writer is uncertain of what to say or has not sufficiently thought through the controlling idea. Should that happen to you, rethink your views on the topic.

> Poor: Religion as part of the school curriculum should be avoided because it can cause trouble.

> Better: Religion as part of the school curriculum should be avoided because it is a highly personal commitment.

7. A thesis must not be expressed in muddled or incoherent language. If the thesis is incoherent or muddled, the essay is likely to follow suit. Work on your thesis until it expresses exactly the opinion or viewpoint you intend to cover in the essay.

> Poor: The benefits of clarity and easy communication of a unified language compel a state to adopt codes to the effect that make bilingualism possible but preserving a single official language for transacting business and social intercourse.

> Better: The benefits of clarity and easy communication offered by a single official language in a state are compelling and persuasive.

8. A thesis should not be expressed in figurative language. Figurative language has a place in factual writing, but not in a thesis statement. As we have stressed, the thesis is where you plainly state the main point of your essay. Figurative language tends to weaken this healthy plainness and should, therefore, never be used in a thesis.

> Poor: The Amazons of today are trying to purge all the stag words from our language.

> Better: Today's feminists are trying to eliminate the use of sex-biased words from public documents and publications.

9. A thesis must not be nonsensical. Above all else, your thesis statement must make sense. You cannot defend the indefensible or argue the unarguable, nor should you waste ink on behalf of a thesis that is absurd. For example, consider this sentence:

> Poor: A good university education is one that is useful, fulfilling, and doesn't require study.

As a thesis, it is virtually useless, even though it does predict, control, and obligate. The problem is that its proposition is plainly nonsense. We cannot conceive of a good university education that doesn't require study. Only a frivolous essay could be written on such a thesis.

> Better: A good university education is one that is useful, fulfilling, and challenging.

We are not suggesting that your theses should always advance narrowly orthodox or boringly conventional ideas, but the ideas they contain should be sensible enough to merit discussion by reasonable people.

The Explicit versus the Implicit Thesis

Anyone who has ever listened to a speaker ramble or read a piece of aimless writing can readily appreciate the usefulness of a thesis statement that sets down clearly the writer's main point. However, not all writers find it necessary to be explicit about their main points. Veteran writers know how to make a main point and stick faithfully to it without broadcasting it in a thesis statement. A conspicuous example of this is the essay *Once More to the Lake* reprinted in chapter 16. In that essay, the writer sticks to the point without ever expressing it in a single thesis sentence.

As a matter of fact, many veteran writers do not need or use a thesis. Yet, they always write with a built-in sense of structure, do not stray from the point, or lose their train of thought. The explicit thesis admittedly has become a requirement of classroom writing, but while it is useful device for the inexperienced, it can be too simplistic for the professional writer—too much of a formula. Later, as you become a more experienced writer, you too might abandon the use of the explicit thesis. But for now, it is a convention that will help you write better essays.

EXERCISES

1. Formulate a thesis for one of the following topics. Use the step-by-step method outlined in the chapter.
    a. Adolescence
    b. Women and the draft
    c. Obligation of parents
    d. The entertainment world
    e. Spectator sports
2. Find a picture that expresses some aspect of today's society, such as violence, youthful idealism, sexual cautiousness, or religious piety; then write a thesis that could serve as an appropriate caption.
3. Underline the key words of the following theses:
    a. Memory entails recall, recognition, and revival.
    b. An argument must present both sides of the question being debated.
    c. The Amish people resist public education because they believe that a simple farm life is best and that formal education will corrupt their young people.
    d. A good farmer cooperates with weather, soil, and seed.

    e. Laura in "Flowering Judas" by Katherine Anne Porter is tortured by doubt, guilt, and disappointment.

    f. The racetracks, the ballparks, the fight rings, and the gridirons draw crowds in increasing numbers.

4. Which of the following theses is the best? Support your choice.

    a. Forest fires are enormously destructive because they ravage the land, create problems for flood control, and destroy useful lumber.

    b. Installment buying is of great benefit to the economy, having in mind the consumer to use a product while paying for it and being like forced savings.

    c. Television is a handicap.

5. The following theses are poorly worded. Analyze their weaknesses in terms of the nine errors discussed earlier, and rewrite each to make it clear and effective.

    a. In my opinion, birth control is the most urgent need in today's world.

    b. Just how far should the law go in its tolerance of pornography?

    c. How Christian missionaries were sent to the Ivory Coast of Africa to introduce Western civilization.

    d. The history of psychology had its inception with Plato and came to full term with Freud.

    e. Strip mining is an environmentally destructive solution to the problem of fuel shortage, and the fuel shortage is caused by our government's foreign policy.

    f. In the United States, the press is the watchdog of society.

    g. Three factors may be singled out as militating against the optimum adjustment that partners in the marriage relationship should experience as money, culture, and education.

    h. Homemaking is the most meaningful work a woman can perform.

    i. The problem with sound pollution is, How much longer can our ears bear the noise?

    j. The noteworthy relaxation of language taboos both in conversation and in print today.

    k. My feeling is that educationalists are just as infatuated with jargon as are sociologists.

    l. Retirement homes need not be depressing places which commercial activities can bring residents together in shared experiences.

    m. The city of New York is in bad shape.

6. From the following pairs of theses, pick out the thesis with the discussable issue. Explain your choice.

   a. (1) The Eiffel Tower is located near the center of Paris.

   (2) Three spectacular crimes have been committed near the Eiffel Tower in Paris.

   b. (1) Michelangelo's "David" symbolizes the best qualities of youthful manhood.

   (2) Michelangelo's "David" is carved out of white marble from Carara.

   c. (1) The Model-A Ford became popular because it was dependable and uncomplicated.

   (2) Close to a million people still own Model-A Fords today.

   d. (1) In Hemingway's *Farewell to Arms,* the knee injury suffered by Frederick Henry symbolizes man's wounded spirit.

   (2) In Hemingway's novel *Farewell to Arms,* Frederick Henry is shot in the knee while driving an ambulance truck.

   e. (1) The Greek historian Herodotus claimed that the city of Troy was destroyed in 1250 B.C.

   (2) Troy was an important city because any fortress built on its site could control all shipping traffic through the Dardanelles.

   f. (1) Good grammar is the equivalent of good manners.

   (2) According to the rules of grammar, "he don't" is a barbarism.

——————— ADVICE ———————

THE THESIS

Sheridan Baker

Sheridan Baker (b. 1918) is Emeritus Professor of English at the University of Michigan and has been a Fulbright lecturer. He has edited several works by the 18th-century novelist Henry Fielding, including Joseph Andrews, Shamela, *and* Tom Jones. *Baker's two rhetorics,* The Practical Stylist *(1962) and* The Complete Stylist *(1976) have been widely used in colleges throughout the United States.*

In this excerpt from *The Complete Stylist,* Baker advises the student to state clearly, in a sharp-edged thesis, the controlling purpose of the essay.

∼

1   You can usually blame a bad essay on a bad beginning. If your essay falls apart, it probably has no primary idea to hold it together. "What's the big

idea?" we used to ask. The phrase will serve as a reminder that you must find the "big idea" behind your several smaller thoughts and musings before you start to write. In the beginning was the logos, says the Bible—the idea, the plan, caught in a flash as if in a single word. Find your logos, and you are ready to round out your essay and set it spinning.

2   The big idea behind our ride in the speeding car[1] was that in adolescence, especially, the group can have a very deadly influence on the individual. If you had not focused your big idea in a thesis, you might have begun by picking up thoughts at random, something like this:

> Everyone thinks he is a good driver. There are more accidents caused by young drivers than any other group. Driver education is a good beginning, but further practice is very necessary. People who object to driver education do not realize that modern society, with its suburban pattern of growth, is built around the automobile. The car becomes a way of life and a status symbol. When a teenager goes too fast he is probably only copying his own father.

3   A little reconsideration, aimed at a good thesis-sentence, could turn this into a reasonably good beginning:

> Modern society is built on the automobile. Every child looks forward to the time when he can drive; every teen-ager, to the day when his father lets him take out the car alone. Soon he is testing his skill at higher and higher speeds, especially with a group of friends along. One final test at extreme speeds usually suffices. The teen-ager's high-speed ride, if it does not kill him, will probably open his eyes to the deadly dynamics of the group.

4   Thus the central idea, or thesis, is your essay's life and spirit. If your thesis is sufficiently firm and clear, it may tell you immediately how to organize your supporting material and so obviate elaborate planning. If you do not find a thesis, your essay will be a tour through the miscellaneous. An essay replete with scaffolds and catwalks—"We have just seen this; now let us turn to this"—is an essay in which the inherent idea is weak or nonexistent. A purely expository and descriptive essay, one simply about "Cats," for instance, will have to rely on outer scaffolding alone (some orderly progression from Persia to Siam) since it really has no idea at all. It is all subject, all cats, instead of being based on an idea about cats.

THE ARGUMENTATIVE EDGE
Find Your Thesis

5   The about-ness puts an argumentative edge on the subject. When you have something to say about cats, you have found your underlying idea. You have something to defend, something to fight about: not just "Cats," but "The cat

---

[1]The example to which the paragraph refers occurred earlier in material that was not printed here.

is really man's best friend." Now the hackles on all dog men are rising, and you have an argument on your hands. You have something to prove. You have a thesis.

6   "What's the big idea, Mac?" Let the impudence in that time-honored demand remind you that the best thesis is a kind of affront to somebody. No one will be very much interested in listening to you deplete the thesis "The dog is man's best friend." Everyone knows that already. Even the dog lovers will be uninterested, convinced that they know better than you. But the cat. . . .

7   So it is with any unpopular idea. The more unpopular the viewpoint and the stronger the push against convention, the stronger the thesis and the more energetic the essay. Compare the energy in "Democracy is good" with that in "Communism is good," for instance. The first is filled with platitudes, the second with plutonium. By the same token, if you can find the real energy in "Democracy is good," if you can get down through the sand to where the roots and water are, you will have a real essay, because the opposition against which you generate your energy is the heaviest in the world: boredom. Probably the most energetic thesis of all, the greatest inner organizer, is some tired old truth that you cause to jet with new life, making the old ground green again.

8   To find a thesis and put it into one sentence is to narrow and define your subject to a workable size. Under "Cats" you must deal with all felinity from the jungle up, carefully partitioning the eons and areas, the tigers and tabbies, the sizes and shapes. The minute you proclaim the cat the friend of man, you have pared away whole categories and chapters, and need only think up the arguments sufficient to overwhelm the opposition. So, put an argumentative edge on your subject—and you will have found your thesis.

9   Simple exposition, to be sure, has its uses. You may want to tell someone how to build a doghouse, how to can asparagus, how to follow the outlines of relativity, or even how to write an essay. Performing a few exercises in simple exposition will no doubt sharpen your insight into the problems of finding orderly sequences, of considering how best to lead your readers through the hoops, of writing clearly and accurately. It will also illustrate how much finer and surer an argument is.

10   You will see that picking an argument immediately simplifies the problems so troublesome in straight exposition: the defining, the partitioning, the narrowing of the subject. Actually, you can put an argumentative edge on the flattest of expository subjects. "How to build a doghouse" might become "Building a doghouse is a thorough introduction to the building trades, including architecture and mechanical engineering." "Canning asparagus" might become "An asparagus patch is a course in economics." "Relativity" might become "Relativity is not so inscrutable as many suppose." You have simply assumed that you have a loyal opposition consisting of the uninformed, the scornful, or both. You have given your subject its edge; you have limited and organized it at a single stroke. Pick an argument, then, and you will automatically be defining and narrowing your subject,

and all the partitions you don't need will fold up. Instead of dealing with things, subjects, and pieces of subjects, you will be dealing with an idea and its consequences.

Sharpen Your Thesis

11   Come out with your subject pointed. Take a stand, make a judgment of value. Be reasonable, but don't be timid. It is helpful to think of your thesis, your main idea, as a debating question—"Resolved: Old age pensions must go"—taking out the "Resolved" when you actually write the subject down. But your resolution will be even stronger, your essay clearer and tighter, if you can sharpen your thesis even further "Resolved: Old age pensions must go because—." Fill in that blank and your worries are practically over. The main idea is to put your whole argument into one sentence.

12   Try for instance: "Old age pensions must go because they are making people irresponsible." I don't know at all if that is true, and neither will you until you write your way into it, considering probabilities and alternatives and objections, and especially the underlying assumptions. In fact, no one, no master sociologist or future historian, can tell absolutely if it is true, so multiplex are the causes in human affairs, so endless and tangled the consequences. The basic assumption—that irresponsibility is growing—may be entirely false. No one, I repeat, can tell absolutely. But by the same token, your guess may be as good as another's. At any rate, you are now ready to write. You have found your logos.

13   Now you can put your well-pointed thesis-sentence on a card on the wall in front of you to keep from drifting off target. But you will now want to dress it for the public, to burnish it, and make it comely. Suppose you try:

> Old age pensions, perhaps more than anything else, are eroding our heritage of personal and familial responsibility.

But is this true? Perhaps you had better try something like:

> Despite their many advantages, old age pensions may actually be eroding our heritage of personal and familial responsibility.

This is really your thesis, and you can write that down on a scrap of paper too.

~

(1,415 words)

VOCABULARY

obviate (4)	replete (4)	inherent (4)
affront (6)	platitudes (7)	multiplex (12)

—————— EXAMPLES ——————

THE GRIEVING NEVER ENDS

Roxanne Roberts

Roxanne Roberts is an American journalist who occasionally writes for the Los Angeles Times.

This essay alerts us to the painful truth about suicide: Often, it can cause life-long scars that linger to torment those left behind. As the author tells us, twenty years after her father's suicide, she still finds herself cleaning up the emotional debris from that tragic act.

~

1   The blood was like Jell-O. That is what blood gets like, after you die, before they tidy up. Somehow, I had expected it would be gone. The police and coroner spent more than an hour behind the closed door; surely it was someone's job to clean it up. But when they left, it still covered the kitchen floor like the glazing on a candy apple.

2   You couldn't mop it. You needed a dustpan and a bucket.

3   I got on my knees, slid the pan against the linoleum and lifted chunks to the bucket. It took hours to clean it all up.

4   It wasn't until I finally stood up that I noticed the pictures from his wallet. The wooden breadboard had been pulled out slightly, and four photographs were spilled across it. "Now what?" I thought with annoyance. "What were the police looking for?"

5   But then it hit me. The police hadn't done it. These snapshots—one of my mother, one of our dog and two of my brother and me—had been carefully set out in a row by my father.

6   It was his penultimate act, just before he knelt on the floor, put the barrel of a .22 rifle in his mouth, and squeezed the trigger.

7   He was 46 years old. I was 21. It has been 20 years since his death and I am still cleaning up.

8   By the time you finish this article, another person in the United States will have killed himself. More than 30,000 people do it every year, one every 15 minutes. My father's was a textbook case: Depressed white male with gun offs himself in May. December may be the loneliest month, April the cruelest, but May is the peak time for suicide. No one knows why, but I can guess: You've made it through another winter, but your world is no warmer.

9   This year, thousands of families will begin the process that ours began that night 20 years ago. Studies show that their grief will be more complicated, more intense and longer lasting than for any other form of death in the family. They will receive less support and more blame from others. Some will

never really get over it: Children of suicides become a higher risk for suicide themselves.

10   These are the legacies of suicide: guilt, anger, doubt, blame, fear, rejection, abandonment and profound grieving.

11   Shortly after he died, I remember thinking, "I wonder how I'll feel about this in 20 years?"

12   Twenty years later, my father's suicide is, simply, a part of me. Think of your life as a can of white paint. Each significant experience adds a tiny drop of color: pink for a birthday, yellow for a good report card. Worries are brown; setbacks, gray. Lavender—my favorite color when I was a little girl—is for a pretty new dress. Over time, a color begins to emerge. Your personality.

13   When a suicide happens, someone hurls in a huge glob of red. You can't get it out. You can't start over. The red will always be there, no matter how many drops of yellow you add.

14   The call came about 9 P.M. It was a Friday night in suburban Minneapolis; the restaurant was packed. I was racing from the bar with a tray of drinks for my customers when the manager gestured me to the phone. It's your mother, she said.

15   "Roxanne, he's got a gun. He's in the garage with a gun. You have to come."

16   There had been many, many threats. This was different. There had never been a weapon before.

17   I made many choices that night; some were smart, some stupid, some crazy. I believed my father would indeed kill himself, sooner or later. Looking back, I feel lucky to have survived the night.

18   I drove past the house. He was standing in the shadows of the front yard; I couldn't see if he had the gun. I sped to a phone booth two blocks away and dialed.

19   She answered. "He's in the front yard," I said. "Can you get out?"

20   Five minutes later, she walked up to the car. He was quiet now, she said. She told him she was going to talk to me but would be back. Then she dropped the bombshell: He had held her at gunpoint for two hours before she called me.

21   We attempted rational conversation. We came to what seemed, at the time, a rational decision. We pulled up to the house, and my father came out the front door without the gun. He wanted to talk.

22   Give me the gun, I said. He refused. We can't talk until the gun is gone, we said. He shook his head. Come inside, he asked my mother. She shook her head.

23   He went back in, we drove to a coffee shop nearby. Frantic, we debated what to do next. To this day, I am still astonished that it never occurred to us to get help.

24   It was almost midnight; exhausted, my mother wanted to go home. She would stay the night if he let her take the gun away.

25   The house was silent; the door to the kitchen was shut. Ominous. My mother reached it first. Opened it.

26   "He did it," she whispered and slumped against the wall.

27 There was a time when suicide was considered a noble act of noble men. There was a time when corpses of suicides were dragged through the streets, refused Christian burial, and all the family's worldly goods were seized by the state. There was a time when romantics embraced suicide as a sign of their sensitivity.

28 Now we have long, impassioned debates about "assisted suicide," which pales beside the much larger issue: How do we feel about suicides when there isn't a terminal disease and a supportive family on hand? How do we feel about suicide if a 46-year-old guy just doesn't want to live anymore?

29 How do we feel about someone who's depressed but won't get help? Who blames all his problems on someone else? Who emotionally terrorizes and blackmails the people he loves? Is that OK too?

30 This is what I will tell you: Suicide is the last word in an argument, maybe an argument you never knew you were having. It is meant to be the last scene of the last act of life. Curtain down. End of story.

31 Except it isn't.

32 Tosca jumps off the parapet and I wonder who finds the shattered body. Romeo and Juliet die with a kiss, and I grieve for their parents.

33 The calls began: first to my father's only brother, who lived three blocks away, then to the police. Officers arrived, then detectives and someone from the coroner's office. Someone came into the living room to ask questions. I answered. Yes, he was depressed. Yes, he had threatened suicide. No, there wasn't a note.

34 This was the night of my brother Mike's high school senior prom. The dance was on a boat—we didn't know where—then there was an all-night party and a picnic the next day.

35 The detectives were still in the kitchen when Mike's car turned slowly onto the street and found a sea of police cars, lights flashing.

36 I watched from the front step as my mother ran to him. "Your father shot himself and he's dead," she said, guiding him to the neighbor's house. I watched as the police took the body out, dripping thick drops of blood. I watched my uncle stare blankly when I asked him to help clean up the kitchen.

37 White-lipped, he watched as I scooped up buckets of blood and flushed them down the toilet. I threw him an old sheet and told him to start wiping.

38 Years later, I learned how angry I made him, how he never forgave me for making him do that.

39 I was alone in the kitchen again when I noticed the pictures from my father's wallet. There were two portraits of his children. He loved both pictures. Everybody knew Mike Roberts loved his kids. So why ruin his son's prom night?

40 "You selfish bastard," I thought.

41 "You couldn't have waited one more night?"

42 My mother was never well liked by my father's sisters, and so they concluded that what had happened was my mother's fault. She was having an affair. That's what my father had told them before he died. The fact that she

wore an aqua suit to the funeral was proof, wasn't it? (My mother swears there was no affair.)

43   And I? I was on her side. So it was my fault too.

44   After the funeral, we were simply abandoned by my father's family. My mother was still numb, but I was confused and angry. No calls, no help, no kindness. There were no invitations to dinner, not even Thanksgiving or Christmas.

45   Two years later, I found out why: They thought my mother and I killed him.

46   At one of those little get-togethers just after he died, my father's family decided that perhaps my mother and I had cleverly managed to murder my father and make it look like a suicide.

47   A cousin was so skeptical he went to the coroner and asked to see police photos. It was a suicide, the coroner assured him.

48   I vowed never, ever to speak to any of them again. When a distant member of the family—a devoted wife and mother—found her husband dead, sucking the end of an exhaust pipe, I was almost glad.

49   "Good," I thought fiercely. "Now they'll understand that suicide happens in nice families too."

50   Second-guessing is the devil's game, for there are no answers and infinite questions. But it is an inevitable, inescapable refrain, like a bad song you can't get out of your mind. What if, what if, what if. What if we had forced him to get help? Had him committed? What if we had called the police that night? Why didn't we?

51   Part of it was the natural tendency toward privacy. Part of it was arrogance, believing that we knew father best, or at least we could handle whatever he threw at us. I think I knew my father would have charmed the police, sent them away, leaving him furious with me, furious with my mother, dangerous, armed.

52   Maybe that's why. Maybe it was fear. Maybe not. Maybe I wanted him to die.

53   The police were puzzled by a wand of black mascara they found in my father's pocket. Another woman? Proof of an affair? The answer was simple: He used it to touch up the gray on his temples.

54   I don't think he ever really expected to get old. He was the baby, the youngest of five children. He was a very happy child; it was adulthood that he could never quite grasp.

55   He was charming enough to talk his way into job after job. There was the real estate phase, the radio phase, the political hanger-on phase. (In one photo, he is shaking hands with Hubert Humphrey.) No job lasted long; it never occurred to him to do heavy lifting.

56   Things started out well enough: a beautiful teenage bride, two kids and—after his mother died—his childhood home, a little bungalow, to raise his family in.

57   When did things start falling apart? Or were they ever really together?

58   I remember a night when I was 11. One of our cats streaked across the living room. In his mouth was a hamster that had somehow escaped from its cage. We all jumped to the rescue; my father caught the cat at the top of the

basement stairs. He was suddenly, unaccountably livid. He shook the cat, and the hamster fell to the floor and scampered free.

59   I will never forget what came next: With all his might, he threw the cat down the stairs.

60   There was a moment of stunned silence, then tears and regret and an emergency trip to the vet. The cat lived. But I think I never fully trusted my father again.

61   The 10 years that followed were filled with sudden rages, explosions. I found out later that he first hit my mother when she was pregnant with me, and continued on and off for two decades.

62   We begged him to get help. We asked his brother and sisters to talk to him. And when, ultimately, I told my mother I thought she needed to leave for her own safety, my father saw that as a betrayal. He didn't speak to me for two months, until the night he died.

63   I lied to the police.

64   I told them there was no suicide note. In fact, there were three. Two were waiting in the living room as we walked into the house.

65   The note to my mother begged for forgiveness but said he simply could not go on the way things were. She has, to this day, no memory of reading it.

66   The note addressed to me opened with a rapprochement. "All is forgiven," read the first line. My eyes filled. No, I said silently, all is not forgiven.

67   The rest of the note instructed me to take care of things.

68   When I went to call the police, I found the third note, addressed to my brother. I cannot recall the specific words, but the short message to an 18-year-old boy was this: Son, you can't trust women.

69   My father had asked me to take care of things. And I was going to take care of things.

70   I stuffed all three notes in my purse and went back out to the living room. A week later, I ripped them to pieces and flushed them down the toilet.

71   When I recently told my brother about this, he was angry and hurt. He asked, quietly, "What made you think you could take something Dad left for me?" Fair question.

72   Here is the answer, Mike. It is simple. I hope you can live with it: I had to. The wishes of the dead do not take precedence over the needs of the living.

73   About a year after my father died, I left Minneapolis. I stumbled through my 20s, met a terrific man and got married, and spent a lot of time thinking about what I wanted to be when I grew up.

74   Nine months after the funeral, my brother moved to California. He was reckless, strong, adrift and almost died three times—once in a motorcycle accident, once in a stabbing and once in a heedless dive into a pool that split open his skull. He returned to Minnesota, subdued and gentle, and went on to a successful computer career. He was, surprisingly, never angry at my father or his family.

75   But he cannot bring himself to marry his girlfriend of 16 years. They live together, in a home they bought together, but he simply does not trust marriage.

76   Two years after the suicide, my mother remarried, changing her friends, her religion, even her first name. She was widowed again—a heart attack—and announced a year later that she was getting married again. Her fiancé was my cousin—her nephew by marriage. He was the son of the aunt who had accused us of murder.

77   "I expect you to be civil to her," my mother told me.

78   We had an ugly fight, and my mother didn't speak to me for months. I went to her wedding but fled the other side of the room when my aunt approached me.

79   My mother tells me my aunt is very hurt by all this. The cycle continues, in ways I will never fully understand.

80   Four years ago, when my son was a month old, I took him to Minnesota to meet my family.

81   "Take me to Father's grave," I told my brother.

82   It's the first time I'd been there since the funeral. I introduced my beautiful new baby to his grandfather, and my father to his only grandchild.

83   Today, when I stare at the boy who takes my breath away, I think about how much my father missed over the past 20 years, and how much more he will miss. I've more sorrow than anger now.

84   A lot of wonderful things have happened in those years, hundreds of shimmering droplets added to the mix. When I stir the paint now, it is a soft dusky rose. A grownup's color, with a touch of sweetness and a touch of melancholy.

~

(3,013 words)

VOCABULARY

coroner (1)	penultimate (6)	legacies (10)
ominous (25)	wand (53)	rapprochement (66)

THE FACTS

1. What did the author discover in her father's wallet?
2. According to the author, how many people commit suicide annually in the United States?
3. When the author drove past the house after her mother called, what did she see?
4. Where was the author's brother, Mike, when the father committed suicide?
5. Whom did the father's relatives blame for the suicide?

THE STRATEGIES

1. What is the thesis of the essay? Write it in one sentence in your own words.

2. Every once in a while the author interrupts the story of the father's suicide with commentary about suicide in general. Why do you think she does this? Does the technique appeal to you? Why or why not?

3. How important is the reference to "assisted suicide" in paragraph 28? What, if anything, does it add to the development of the author's thesis?

4. What figurative language does the author use in her essay? Point out at least one simile and one metaphor. Do you consider these images effective? Give reasons for your answer.

5. How effective is the author's strategy of relating her father's suicide from her own "I" point of view? What does it add to the essay?

THE ISSUES

1. What is the purpose of this essay on the gloomy subject of suicide? Do you agree or disagree with its purpose?

2. What does the author mean when she says, "He was 46 years old. I was 21. It has been 20 years since his death and I am still cleaning up"?

3. The author refers to the fact that in the past, suicide was considered a noble act, a sinful act, or a romantic act (see paragraph 27). How do you view suicide today? Should everyone embrace your view? Give reasons for your answer.

4. In your opinion, what consequences of the father's suicide seem the worst?

5. What do you think was the basic cause of the father's suicide?

SUGGESTIONS FOR WRITING

1. Choose one of the following topics and develop a thesis-oriented essay:

   a. Suicide as an act of desperation

   b. Suicide as an act of selfishness

2. Write an essay about the steps recommended by mental-health professionals to help avert suicide.

A GOOD MAN IS HARD TO FIND

Flannery O'Connor

Flannery O'Connor (1925–1964) was a Christian humanist writer and a member of the so-called "southern renaissance" in American literature. She was born in Savannah, Georgia, and educated at the Woman's College of Georgia and the State University of Iowa. Her best-known stories,

written from an orthodox Catholic perspective, are contained in A Good
Man Is Hard to Find and Other Stories *(1953) and* Everything That
Rises Must Converge *(1956).*

We do not usually think of a story as having a thesis, but we almost always
think of a story as having a point. The point of this story—its thesis—is hinted
at in its title, from which it proceeds with grim, irresistible logic.

～

1   The grandmother didn't want to go to Florida. She wanted to visit some of
her connections in east Tennessee and she was seizing at every chance to
change Bailey's mind. Bailey was the son she lived with, her only boy. He was
sitting on the edge of his chair at the table, bent over the orange sports section of the *Journal*. "Now look here, Bailey," she said, "see here, read this,"
and she stood with one hand on her thin hip and the other rattling the newspaper at his bald head. "Here this fellow that calls himself The Misfit is aloose
from the Federal Pen and headed toward Florida and you read here what it
says he did to these people. Just you read it. I wouldn't take my children in
any direction with a criminal like that aloose in it. I couldn't answer to my
conscience if I did."

2   Bailey didn't look up from his reading so she wheeled around then and
faced the children's mother, a young woman in slacks, whose face was as
broad and innocent as a cabbage and was tied around with a green headker-
chief that had two points on the top like a rabbit's ears. She was sitting on the
sofa, feeding the baby his apricots out of a jar. "The children have been to
Florida before," the old lady said. "You all ought to take them somewhere
else for a change so they would see different parts of the world and be broad.
They never have been to east Tennessee."

3   The children's mother didn't seem to hear her but the eight-year-old boy,
John Wesley, a stocky child with glasses, said, "If you don't want to go to
Florida, why dontcha stay at home?" He and the little girl, June Star, were
reading the funny papers on the floor.

4   "She wouldn't stay at home to be queen for a day," June Star said without
raising her yellow head.

5   "Yes and what would you do if this fellow, The Misfit, caught you?" the
grandmother asked.

6   "I'd smack his face," John Wesley said.

7   "She wouldn't stay at home for a million bucks," June Star said. "Afraid
she'd miss something. She has to go everywhere we go."

8   "All right, Miss," the grandmother said. "Just remember that the next time
you want me to curl your hair."

9   June Star said her hair was naturally curly.

10   The next morning the grandmother was the first one in the car, ready to go.
She had her big black valise that looked like the head of a hippopotamus in
one corner, and underneath it she was hiding a basket with Pitty Sing, the cat,
in it. She didn't intend for the cat to be left alone in the house for three days

because he would miss her too much and she was afraid he might brush against one of the gas burners and accidentally asphyxiate himself. Her son, Bailey, didn't like to arrive at a motel with a cat.

11   She sat in the middle of the back seat with John Wesley and June Star on either side of her. Bailey and the children's mother and the baby sat in front and they left Atlanta at eight forty-five with the mileage on the car at 55890. The grandmother wrote this down because she thought it would be interesting to say how many miles they had been when they got back. It took them twenty minutes to reach the outskirts of the city.

12   The old lady settled herself comfortably, removing her white cotton gloves and putting them up with her purse on the shelf in front of the back window. The children's mother still had on slacks and still had her head tied up in a green kerchief, but the grandmother had on a navy blue straw sailor hat with a bunch of white violets on the brim and a navy blue dress with a small white dot in the print. Her collars and cuffs were white organdy trimmed with lace and at her neckline she had pinned a purple spray of cloth violets containing a sachet. In case of an accident, anyone seeing her dead on the highway would know at once that she was a lady.

13   She said she thought it was going to be a good day for driving, neither too hot nor too cold, and she cautioned Bailey that the speed limit was fifty-five miles an hour and that the patrolmen hid themselves behind billboards and small clumps of trees and sped out after you before you had a chance to slow down. She pointed out interesting details of the scenery: Stone Mountain; the blue granite that in some places came up to both sides of the highway; the brilliant red clay banks slightly streaked with purple; and the various crops that made rows of green lace-work on the ground. The trees were full of silver-white sunlight and the meanest of them sparkled. The children were reading comic magazines and their mother had gone back to sleep.

14   "Let's go through Georgia fast so we won't have to look at it much," John Wesley said.

15   "If I were a little boy," said the grandmother, "I wouldn't talk about my native state that way. Tennessee has the mountains and Georgia has the hills."

16   "Tennessee is just a hillbilly dumping ground," John Wesley said, "and Georgia is a lousy state too."

17   "You said it," June Star said.

18   "In my time," said the grandmother, folding her thin veined fingers, "children were more respectful of their native states and their parents and everything else. People did right then. Oh look at the cute little pickaninny!" she said and pointed to a Negro child standing in the door of a shack. "Wouldn't that make a picture, now?" she asked and they all turned and looked at the little Negro out of the back window. He waved.

19   "He didn't have any britches on," June Star said.

20   "He probably didn't have any," the grandmother explained. "Little niggers in the country don't have things like we do. If I could paint, I'd paint that picture," she said.

21   The children exchanged comic books.

22   The grandmother offered to hold the baby and the children's mother passed him over the front seat to her. She sat him on her knee and bounced him and told him about the things they were passing. She rolled her eyes and screwed up her mouth and stuck her leathery thin face into his smooth bland one. Occasionally he gave her a faraway smile. They passed a large cotton field with five or six graves fenced in the middle of it, like a small island. "Look at the graveyard!" the grandmother said, pointing it out. "That was the old family burying ground. That belonged to the plantation."

23   "Where's the plantation?" John Wesley asked.

24   "Gone With the Wind," said the grandmother. "Ha. Ha."

25   When the children finished all the comic books they had brought, they opened the lunch and ate it. The grandmother ate a peanut butter sandwich and an olive and would not let the children throw the box and the paper napkins out the window. When there was nothing else to do they played a game by choosing a cloud and making the other two guess what shape it suggested. John Wesley took one the shape of a cow and June Star guessed a cow and John Wesley said, no, an automobile, and June Star said he didn't play fair, and they began to slap each other over the grandmother.

26   The grandmother said she would tell them a story if they would keep quiet. When she told a story, she rolled her eyes and waved her head and was very dramatic. She said once when she was a maiden lady she had been courted by a Mr. Edgar Atkins Teagarden from Jasper, Georgia. She said he was a very good-looking man and a gentleman and that he brought her a watermelon every Saturday afternoon with his initials cut in it, E. A. T. Well, one Saturday, she said, Mr. Teagarden brought the watermelon and there was nobody at home and he left it on the front porch and returned in his buggy to Jasper, but she never got the watermelon, she said, because a nigger boy ate it when he saw the initials, E. A. T.! This story tickled John Wesley's funny bone and he giggled and giggled but June Star didn't think it was any good. She said she wouldn't marry a man that just brought her a watermelon on Saturday. The grandmother said she would have done well to marry Mr. Teagarden because he was a gentleman and had bought Coca-Cola stock when it first came out and that he had died only a few years ago, a very wealthy man.

27   They stopped at The Tower for barbecued sandwiches. The Tower was a part stucco and part wood filling station and dance hall set in a clearing outside of Timothy. A fat man named Red Sammy Butts ran it and there were signs stuck here and there on the building and for miles up and down the highway saying, TRY RED SAMMY'S FAMOUS BARBECUE. NONE LIKE FAMOUS RED SAMMY'S! RED SAM! THE FAT BOY WITH THE HAPPY LAUGH! A VETERAN! RED SAMMY'S YOUR MAN!

28   Red Sammy was lying on the bare ground outside The Tower with his head under a truck while a gray monkey about a foot high, chained to a small chinaberry tree, chattered nearby. The monkey sprang back into the tree and got on the highest limb as soon as he saw the children jump out of the car and run toward him.

29   Inside, The Tower was a long dark room with a counter at one end and tables at the other and dancing space in the middle. They all sat down at a
board table next to the nickelodeon and Red Sam's wife, a tall burnt-brown
woman with hair and eyes lighter than her skin, came and took their order.
The children's mother put a dime in the machine and played "The Tennessee
Waltz," and the grandmother said that tune always made her want to dance.
She asked Bailey if he would like to dance but he only glared at her. He didn't
have a naturally sunny disposition like she did and trips made him nervous.
The grandmother's brown eyes were very bright. She swayed her head from
side to side and pretended she was dancing in her chair. June Star said play
something she could tap to so the children's mother put in another dime and
played a fast number and June Star stepped out onto the dance floor and did
her tap routine.

30   "Ain't she cute?" Red Sam's wife said, leaning over the counter. "Would
you like to come be my little girl?"

31   "No I certainly wouldn't," June Star said. "I wouldn't live in a broken-
down place like this for a million bucks!" and she ran back to the table.

32   "Ain't she cute?" the woman repeated, stretching her mouth politely.

33   "Aren't you ashamed?" hissed the grandmother.

34   Red Sam came in and told his wife to quit lounging on the counter and
hurry up with these people's order. His khaki trousers reached just to his hip
bones and his stomach hung over them like a sack of meal swaying under his
shirt. He came over and sat down at a table nearby and let out a combination
sigh and yodel. "You can't win," he said. "You can't win," and he wiped his
sweating red face off with a gray handkerchief. "These days you don't know
who to trust," he said. "Ain't that the truth?"

35   "People are certainly not nice like they used to be," said the grandmother.

36   "Two fellers come in here last week," Red Sammy said, "driving a
Chrysler. It was a old beat-up car but it was a good one and these boys looked
all right to me. Said they worked at the mill and you know I let them fellers
charge the gas they bought? Now why did I do that?"

37   "Because you're a good man!" the grandmother said at once.

38   "Yes'm, I suppose so," Red Sam said as if he were struck with this answer.

39   His wife brought the orders, carrying the five plates all at once without a
tray, two in each hand and one balanced on her arm. "It isn't a soul in this
green world of God's that you can trust," she said. "And I don't count nobody
out of that, not nobody," she repeated, looking at Red Sammy.

40   "Did you read about that criminal, The Misfit, that's escaped?" asked the
grandmother.

41   "I wouldn't be a bit surprised if he didn't attact this place right here," said
the woman. "If he hears about it being here, I wouldn't be none surprised to
see him. If he hears it's two cent in the cash register, I wouldn't be a tall surprised if he . . .

42   "That'll do," Red Sam said, "Go bring these people their Co'-Colas," and
the woman went off to get the rest of the order.

43   "A good man is hard to find," Red Sammy said. "Everything is getting terrible. I remember the day you could go off and leave your screen door un-
latched. Not no more."

44   He and the grandmother discussed better times. The old lady said that in
her opinion Europe was entirely to blame for the way things were now. She
said the way Europe acted you would think we were made of money and Red
Sam said it was no use talking about it, she was exactly right. The children
ran outside into the white sunlight and looked at the monkey in the lacy chinaberry tree. He was busy catching fleas on himself and biting each one carefully between his teeth as if it were a delicacy.

45   They drove off again into the hot afternoon. The grandmother took cat
naps and woke up every few minutes with her own snoring. Outside of
Toombsboro she woke up and recalled an old plantation that she had visited
in this neighborhood once when she was a young lady. She said the house
had six white columns across the front and that there was an avenue of oaks
leading up to it and two little wooden trellis arbors on each side in front
where you sat down with your suitor after a stroll in the garden. She recalled
exactly which road to turn off to get to it. She knew that Bailey would not be
willing to lose any time looking at an old house, but the more she talked
about it, the more she wanted to see it once again and find out if the little twin
arbors were still standing. "There was a secret panel in this house," she said
craftily, not telling the truth but wishing that she were, "and the story went
that all the family silver was hidden in it when Sherman came through but it
was never found . . ."

46   "Hey!" John Wesley said. "Let's go see it! We'll find it! We'll poke all the
woodwork and find it! Who lives there? Where do you turn off at? Hey Pop,
can't we turn off there?"

47   "We never have seen a house with a secret panel!" June Star shrieked.
"Let's go to the house with the secret panel! Hey Pop, can't we go see the
house with the secret panel!"

48   "It's not far from here, I know," the grandmother said. "It wouldn't take
over twenty minutes."

49   Bailey was looking straight ahead. His jaw was as rigid as a horseshoe.
"No," he said.

50   The children began to yell and scream that they wanted to see the house
with the secret panel. John Wesley kicked the back of the front seat and June
Star hung over her mother's shoulder and whined desperately into her ear
that they never had any fun even on their vacation, that they could never do
what THEY wanted to do. The baby began to scream and John Wesley kicked
the back of the seat so hard that his father could feel the blows in his kidney.

51   "All right!" he shouted and drew the car to a stop at the side of the road.
"Will you all shut up? Will you all just shut up for one second? If you don't
shut up, we won't go anywhere."

52   "It would be very educational for them," the grandmother murmured.

53   "All right," Bailey said, "but get this: This is the only time we're going to
stop for anything like this. This is the one and only time."

54   "The dirt road that you have to turn down is about a mile back," the grand-mother directed. "I marked it when we passed."

55   "A dirt road," Bailey groaned.

56   After they had turned around and were headed toward the dirt road, the grandmother recalled other points about the house, the beautiful glass over the front doorway and the candle-lamp in the hall. John Wesley said that the secret panel was probably in the fireplace.

57   "You can't go inside this house," Bailey said. "You don't know who lives there."

58   "While you all talk to the people in front, I'll run around behind and get in a window," John Wesley suggested.

59   "We'll all stay in the car," his mother said.

60   They turned onto the dirt road and the car raced roughly along in a swirl of pink dust. The grandmother recalled the times when there were no paved roads and thirty miles was a day's journey. The dirt road was hilly and there were sudden washes in it and sharp curves on dangerous embankments. All at once they would be on a hill, looking down over the blue tops of trees for miles around, then the next minute, they would be in a red depression with the dust-coated trees looking down on them.

61   "This place had better turn up in a minute," Bailey said, "or I'm going to turn around."

62   The road looked as if no one had traveled on it in months.

63   "It's not much farther," the grandmother said and just as she said it, a hor-rible thought came to her. The thought was so embarrassing that she turned red in the face and her eyes dilated and her feet jumped up, upsetting her valise in the corner. The instant the valise moved, the newspaper top she had over the basket under it rose with a snarl and Pitty Sing, the cat, sprang onto Bailey's shoulder.

64   The children were thrown to the floor and their mother, clutching the baby, was thrown out the door onto the ground; the old lady was thrown into the front seat. The car turned over once and landed right-side-up in a gulch off the side of the road. Bailey remained in the driver's seat with the cat—gray-striped with a broad white face and an orange nose—clinging to his neck like a caterpillar.

65   As soon as the children saw they could move their arms and legs, they scrambled out of the car, shouting, "We've had an ACCIDENT!" The grand-mother was curled up under the dashboard, hoping she was injured so that Bailey's wrath would not come down on her all at once. The horrible thought she had had before the accident was that the house she had remembered so vividly was not in Georgia but in Tennessee.

66   Bailey removed the cat from his neck with both hands and flung it out the window against the side of a pine tree. Then he got out of the car and started looking for the children's mother. She was sitting against the side of the red gutted ditch, holding the screaming baby, but she only had a cut down her face and a broken shoulder. "We've had an ACCIDENT!" the children screamed in a frenzy of delight.

67   "But nobody's killed," June Star said with disappointment as the grand-mother limped out of the car, her hat still pinned to her head but the broken front brim standing up at a jaunty angle and the violet spray hanging off the side. They all sat down in the ditch, except the children, to recover from the shock. They were all shaking.

68   "Maybe a car will come along," said the children's mother hoarsely.

69   "I believe I have injured an organ," said the grandmother, pressing her side, but no one answered her. Bailey's teeth were clattering. He had on a yellow sport shirt with bright blue parrots designed in it and his face was as yellow as the shirt. The grandmother decided that she would not mention that the house was in Tennessee.

70   The road was about ten feet above and they could see only the tops of the trees on the other side of it. Behind the ditch they were sitting in there were more woods, tall and dark and deep. In a few minutes they saw a car some distance away on top of a hill, coming slowly as if the occupants were watching them. The grandmother stood up and waved both arms dramatically to attract their attention. The car continued to come on slowly, disappeared around a bend and appeared again, moving even slower, on top of the hill they had gone over. It was a big black battered hearselike automobile. There were three men in it.

71   It came to a stop just over them and for some minutes, the driver looked down with a steady expressionless gaze to where they were sitting, and didn't speak. Then he turned his head and muttered something to the other two and they got out. One was a fat boy in black trousers and a red sweat shirt with a silver stallion embossed on the front of it. He moved around on the right side of them and stood staring, his mouth partly open in a kind of loose grin. The other had on khaki pants and a blue striped coat and a gray hat pulled down very low, hiding most of his face. He came around slowly on the left side. Neither spoke.

72   The driver got out of the car and stood by the side of it, looking down at them. He was an older man than the other two. His hair was just beginning to gray and he wore silver-rimmed spectacles that gave him a scholarly look. He had a long creased face and didn't have on any shirt or undershirt. He had on blue jeans that were too tight for him and was holding a black hat and a gun. The two boys also had guns.

73   "We've had an ACCIDENT!" the children screamed.

74   The grandmother had the peculiar feeling that the bespectacled man was someone she knew. His face was as familiar to her as if she had known him all her life but she could not recall who he was. He moved away from the car and began to come down the embankment, placing his feet carefully so that he wouldn't slip. He had on tan and white shoes and no socks, and his ankles were red and thin. "Good afternoon," he said. "I see you all had you a little spill."

75   "We turned over twice!" said the grandmother.

76   "Oncet," he corrected. "We seen it happen. Try their car and see will it run, Hiram," he said quietly to the boy with the gray hat.

77   "What you got that gun for?" John Wesley asked. "Whatcha gonna do with that gun?"

78   "Lady," the man said to the children's mother, "would you mind calling them children to sit down by you? Children make me nervous. I want all you all to sit down right together there where you're at."

79   "What are you telling us what to do for?" June Star asked.

80   Behind them the line of woods gaped like a dark open mouth. "Come here," said their mother.

81   "Look here now," Bailey began suddenly, "we're in a predicament! We're in. . . ."

82   The grandmother shrieked. She scrambled to her feet and stood staring. "You're The Misfit!" she said, "I recognized you at once!"

83   "Yes'm," the man said, smiling slightly as if he were pleased in spite of himself to be known, "but it would have been better for all of you, lady, if you hadn't of reckernized me."

84   Bailey turned his head sharply and said something to his mother that shocked even the children. The old lady began to cry and The Misfit reddened.

85   "Lady," he said, "don't you get upset. Sometimes a man says things he don't mean. I don't reckon he meant to talk to you thataway."

86   "You wouldn't shoot a lady, would you?" the grandmother said and removed a clean handkerchief from her cuff and began to slap at her eyes with it.

87   The Misfit pointed the toe of his shoe into the ground and made a little hole and then covered it up again. "I would hate to have to," he said.

88   "Listen," the grandmother almost screamed, "I know you're a good man. You don't look a bit like you have common blood. I know you must come from nice people!"

89   "Yes mam," he said, "finest people in the world." When he smiled he showed a row of strong white teeth. "God never made a finer woman than my mother and my daddy's heart was pure gold," he said. The boy with the red sweat shirt had come around behind them and was standing with his gun at his hip. The Misfit squatted down on the ground. "Watch them children, Bobby Lee," he said. "You know they make me nervous." He looked at the six of them huddled together in front of him and he seemed to be embarrassed as if he couldn't think of anything to say. "Ain't a cloud in the sky," he remarked, looking up at it. "Don't see no sun but don't see no cloud neither."

90   "Yes, it's a beautiful day," said the grandmother. "Listen," she said, "you shouldn't call yourself The Misfit because I know you're a good man at heart. I can just look at you and tell."

91   "Hush!" Bailey yelled. "Hush! Everybody shut up and let me handle this!" He was squatting in the position of a runner about to sprint forward but he didn't move.

92   "I pre-chate that, lady," The Misfit said and drew a little circle in the ground with the butt of his gun.

93   "It'll take a half a hour to fix this here car," Hiram called, looking over the raised hood of it.

94   "Well, first you and Bobby Lee get him and that little boy to step over yonder with you," The Misfit said, pointing to Bailey and John Wesley. "The boys want to ast you something," he said to Bailey. "Would you mind stepping back in them woods there with them?"

95   "Listen," Bailey began, "we're in a terrible predicament! Nobody realizes what this is," and his ice cracked. His eyes were as blue and intense as the parrots in his shirt and he remained perfectly still.

96   The grandmother reached up to adjust her hat brim as if she were going to the woods with him but it came off in her hand. She stood staring at it and after a second she let it fall on the ground. Hiram pulled Bailey up by the arm as if he were assisting an old man. John Wesley caught hold of his father's hand and Bobby Lee followed. They went off toward the woods and just as they reached the dark edge, Bailey turned and supporting himself against a gray naked pine trunk, he shouted, "I'll be back in a minute, Mamma, wait on me!"

97   "Come back this instant!" his mother shrilled but they all disappeared into the woods.

98   "Bailey Boy!" the grandmother called in a tragic voice but she found she was looking at The Misfit squatting on the ground in front of her. "I just know you're a good man," she said desperately. "You're not a bit common!"

99   "Nome, I ain't a good man," The Misfit said after a second as if he had considered her statement carefully. "But I ain't the worst in the world neither. My daddy said I was a different breed of dog from my brothers and sisters. 'You know,' Daddy said, 'it's some that can live their whole life out without asking about it and it's others has to know why it is, and this boy is one of the latters. He's going to be into everything!' " He put on his black hat and looked up suddenly and then away deep into the woods as if he were embarrassed again. "I'm sorry I don't have on a shirt before you ladies," he said, hunching his shoulders slightly. "We buried our clothes that we had on when we escaped and we're just making do until we can get better. We borrowed these from some folks we met," he explained.

100   "That's perfectly all right," the grandmother said. "Maybe Bailey has an extra shirt in his suitcase."

101   "I'll look and see terrectly," The Misfit said.

102   "Where are they taking him?" the children's mother screamed.

103   "Daddy was a card himself," The Misfit said. "You couldn't put anything over on him. He never got in trouble with the Authorities though. Just had the knack of handling them."

104   "You could be honest too if you'd only try," said the grandmother. "Think how wonderful it would be to settle down and live a comfortable life and not have to think about somebody chasing you all the time."

105   The Misfit kept scratching in the ground with the butt of his gun as if he were thinking about it. "Yes'm, somebody is always after you," he murmured.

106   The grandmother noticed how thin his shoulder blades were just behind his hat because she was standing up looking down on him. "Do you ever pray?" she asked.

107   He shook his head. All she saw was the black hat wiggle between his shoulder blades. "Nome," he said.

108   There was a pistol shot from the woods, followed closely by another. Then silence. The old lady's head jerked around. She could hear the wind move through the tree tops like a long satisfied insuck of breath. "Bailey Boy!" she called.

109   "I was a gospel singer for a while," The Misfit said. "I been most everything. Been in the arm service, both land and sea, at home and abroad, been twicet married, been an undertaker, been with the railroads, plowed Mother Earth, been in a tornado, seen a man burnt alive oncet," and looked up at the children's mother and the little girl who were sitting close together, their faces white and their eyes glassy; "I even seen a woman flogged," he said.

110   "Pray, pray," the grandmother began, "pray, pray . . ."

111   "I never was a bad boy that I remember of," The Misfit said in an almost dreamy voice, "but somewheres along the line I done something wrong and got sent to the penitentiary. I was buried alive," and he looked up and held her attention to him by a steady stare.

112   "That's when you should have started to pray," she said. "What did you do to get sent to the penitentiary that first time?"

113   "Turn to the right, it was a wall," The Misfit said, looking up again at the cloudless sky. "Turn to the left, it was a wall. Look up it was a ceiling, look down it was a floor. I forget what I done, lady. I set there and set there, trying to remember what it was I done and I ain't recalled it to this day. Oncet in a while, I would think it was coming to me, but it never come."

114   "Maybe they put you in by mistake," the old lady said vaguely.

115   "Nome," he said. "It wasn't no mistake. They had papers on me."

116   "You must have stolen something," she said.

117   The Misfit sneered slightly. "Nobody had nothing I wanted," he said. "It was a head-doctor at the penitentiary said what I had done was kill my daddy but I known that for a lie. My daddy died in nineteen ought nineteen of the epidemic flu and I never had a thing to do with it. He was buried in the Mount Hopewell Baptist churchyard and you can go there and see for yourself."

118   "If you would pray," the old lady said, "Jesus would help you."

119   "That's right," The Misfit said.

120   "Well then, why don't you pray?" she asked trembling with delight suddenly.

121   "I don't want no hep," he said, "I'm doing all right by myself."

122   Bobby Lee and Hiram came ambling back from the woods. Bobby Lee was dragging a yellow shirt with bright blue parrots in it.

123   "Throw me that shirt, Bobby Lee," The Misfit said. The shirt came flying at him and landed on his shoulder and he put it on. The grandmother couldn't name what the shirt reminded her of. "No, lady," The Misfit said while he was

buttoning it up, "I found out the crime don't matter. You can do one thing or you can do another, kill a man or take a tire off his car, because sooner or later you're going to forget what it was you done and just be punished for it."

124 The children's mother had begun to make heaving noises as if she couldn't get her breath. "Lady," he asked, "would you and that little girl like to step off yonder with Bobby Lee and Hiram and join your husband?"

125 "Yes, thank you," the mother said faintly. Her left arm dangled helplessly and she was holding the baby, who had gone to sleep, in the other. "Hep that lady up, Hiram," The Misfit said as she struggled to climb out of the ditch, "and Bobby Lee, you hold onto that little girl's hand."

126 "I don't want to hold hands with him," June Star said. "He reminds me of a pig."

127 The fat boy blushed and laughed and caught her by the arm and pulled her off into the woods after Hiram and her mother.

128 Alone with The Misfit, the grandmother found that she had lost her voice. There was not a cloud in the sky nor any sun. There was nothing around her but woods. She wanted to tell him that he must pray. She opened and closed her mouth several times before anything came out. Finally she found herself saying, "Jesus, Jesus," meaning, Jesus will help you, but the way she was saying it, it sounded as if she might be cursing.

129 "Yes'm," The Misfit said as if he agreed, "Jesus thrown everything off balance. It was the same case with Him as with me except He hadn't committed any crime and they could prove I had committed one because they had the papers on me. Of course," he said, "they never shown me my papers. That's why I sign myself now. I said long ago, you get you a signature and sign everything you do and keep a copy of it. Then you'll know what you done and you can hold up the crime to the punishment and see do they match and in the end you'll have something to prove you ain't been treated right. I call myself The Misfit," he said, "because I can't make what all I done wrong fit what all I gone through in punishment."

130 There was a piercing scream from the woods, followed closely by a pistol report. "Does it seem right to you, lady, that one is punished a heap and another ain't punished at all?"

131 "Jesus!" the old lady cried. "You've got good blood! I know you wouldn't shoot a lady! I know you come from nice people! Pray! Jesus, you ought not to shoot a lady, I'll give you all the money I've got!"

132 "Lady," The Misfit said, looking beyond her far into the woods, "there never was a body that give the undertaker a tip."

133 There were two more pistol reports and the grandmother raised her head like a parched old turkey hen crying for water and called, "Bailey Boy, Bailey Boy!" as if her heart would break.

134 "Jesus was the only One that ever raised the dead." The Misfit continued, "and He shouldn't have done it. He thrown everything off balance. If He did what He said, then it's nothing for you to do but throw away everything and follow Him, and if He didn't, then it's nothing for you to do but enjoy the few

minutes you got left the best way you can—by killing somebody or burning down his house or doing some other meanness to him. No pleasure but meanness," he said and his voice had become almost a snarl.

135   "Maybe He didn't raise the dead," the old lady mumbled, not knowing what she was saying and feeling so dizzy that she sank down in the ditch with her legs twisted under her.

136   "I wasn't there so I can't say He didn't," The Misfit said. "I wisht I had of been there," he said, hitting the ground with his fist. "It ain't right I wasn't there because if I had of been there I would of known. Listen lady," he said in a high voice, "if I had of been there I would of known and I wouldn't be like I am now." His voice seemed about to crack and the grandmother's head cleared for an instant. She saw the man's face twisted close to her own as if he were going to cry and she murmured, "Why you're one of my babies. You're one of my own children!" She reached out and touched him on the shoulder. The Misfit sprang back as if a snake had bitten him and shot her three times through the chest. Then he put his gun down on the ground and took off his glasses and began to clean them.

137   Hiram and Bobby Lee returned from the woods and stood over the ditch, looking down at the grandmother who half sat and half lay in a puddle of blood with her legs crossed under her like a child's and her face smiling up at the cloudless sky.

138   Without his glasses, The Misfit's eyes were red-rimmed and pale and defenseless-looking. "Take her off and throw her where you thrown the others," he said, picking up the cat that was rubbing itself against his leg.

139   "She was a talker, wasn't she?" Bobby Lee said, sliding down the ditch with a yodel.

140   "She would of been a good woman," The Misfit said, "if it had been somebody ere to shoot her every minute of her life."

141   "Some fun!" Bobby Lee said.

142   "Shut up, Bobby Lee," The Misfit said. "It's no real pleasure in life."

⁓

(6,471 words)

VOCABULARY

asphyxiate (10)	sachet (12)	bland (22)
dilated (63)	jaunty (67)	embossed (71)
ambling (122)	parched (133)	

THE FACTS

1. Why didn't the grandmother want to go to Florida? Where did she want to go instead?

2. Why does the family turn off onto the lonely dirt road?

3. What caused the accident?

4. For what crime was The Misfit sent to the penitentiary?

5. Why does he call himself "The Misfit"?

THE STRATEGIES

1. The Misfit is mentioned in the first paragraph. Why does O'Connor introduce him so early?

2. What does the initial dialogue between the grandmother and the children accomplish?

3. In paragraph 70, The Misfit's automobile is described as "a big black battered hearselike automobile." What is O'Connor doing in this description?

4. At a climactic part of the story, the grandmother has a sudden, dramatic recognition of responsibility. When does it occur? Whom does it involve?

5. In paragraph 80, O'Connor writes: "Behind them the line of woods gaped like a dark open mouth." What does this description accomplish? What does it signal to the reader?

THE ISSUES

1. The Misfit and his cronies commit cold-blooded murder on a family of six. What prerequisite, if any, do you think must exist before a person is capable of murder? If you think there is no prerequisite, do you also think anyone is capable of cold-blooded murder? Justify your answer.

2. What punishment would you regard as just and fitting for The Misfit and his henchmen?

3. Some commentators have said that the children are brats, pure and simple, whereas others have argued that they are rather typical. What is your opinion of the children and their behavior?

4. One interpretation argues that The Misfit is the devil and the grandmother a Christian who confronts him. What is your opinion of this interpretation?

5. What do you think the grandmother meant when she said to The Misfit, "Why you're one of my babies. You're one of my own children!" Why do you think The Misfit killed her when she said that?

SUGGESTIONS FOR WRITING

1. Write an essay analyzing the techniques used by the author to foreshadow the family's fatal encounter with The Misfit. Make specific references to scenes and images and include as many quoted passages as necessary to prove your case.

2. Write an essay interpreting this story. You might begin by asking yourself, "What does the story teach about life?"

SPRING

Edna St. Vincent Millay

Edna St. Vincent Millay (1892–1950), a graduate of Vassar and one of the most popular poets of her day, lived a Bohemian life during the 1920s in Greenwich Village, New York, writing satirical columns for Vanity Fair *under a pseudonym. Her first volume of poetry,* Renascence, *was published in 1917 to glowing praise for its vitality. Subsequent volumes include* A Few Figs from Thistle *(1920) and* The Ballad of the Hat Weaver and Other Poems *(1923; Pulitzer Prize). She also wrote verse dramas, many of which were produced by the Provincetown Players. Later volumes of her work include* Fatal Interview *(1931),* Conversation at Midnight *(1937), and* Make Bright the Arrows *(1940). Her former home, "Steepletop" in Austerlitz, New York, which she shared with husband Eugan Jan Boissevain, is a Registered Historic Landmark and the center of the Edna St. Vincent Millay National Society, founded in 1978.*

In many poems, the opening sentence presents a theme around which the rest of the poem is organized. In a way, this opening sentence, although strictly speaking not a thesis, fulfills the function of one. This poem is a classic example of what we mean.

~

To what purpose, April, do you return again?
Beauty is not enough.
You can no longer quiet me with the redness
Of little leaves opening stickily.
5 I know what I know.
The sun is hot on my neck as I observe
The spikes of the crocus.
The smell of the earth is good.
It is apparent that there is no death.
But what does that signify?
Not only under ground are the brains of men
Eaten by maggots.
Life in itself
Is nothing,
15 An empty cup, a flight of uncarpeted stairs,
It is not enough that yearly, down this hill,
April
Comes like an idiot, babbling and strewing flowers.

~

(109 words)

VOCABULARY

crocus (7)   strewing (18)

THE FACTS

1. What quality does April bring with it?
2. In what way do little red leaves open "stickily"?
3. According to the author, what is just as obvious as the fact that at death, the human body is eaten by maggots?
4. What keeps the author dissatisfied with spring?

THE STRATEGIES

1. The poem begins with a question. Is the question ever answered? If so, what is the answer?
2. A sharp contrast underlies the poem. What is that contrast?
3. In what way, according to Millay, is the line "brains of men eaten by maggots" symbolic?
4. What metaphors and similes are used in the poem? Explain what they mean.
5. What is the tone of the poem? Is the tone appropriate for the theme?

THE ISSUES

1. What is the theme (thesis) of Millay's poem? State it in one sentence. What do you think has caused the poet to take such a position? Do you agree with it? Why or why not?
2. What is the meaning of the expression "no longer" in line 3?
3. What concrete aspects of spring please the poet? What do these aspects have in common?
4. Why does the author stress the beautiful aspects of spring?
5. Why is it not enough to experience a beautiful spring? What is your personal answer to this poem?

SUGGESTIONS FOR WRITING

1. Write an essay on spring and what it means to you.
2. Write an essay refuting Millay's comment that "Life in itself is nothing."

CHAPTER WRITING ASSIGNMENTS

1. Convert one of the following general subjects into a suitable thesis:
    a. college life
    b. parental behavior
    c. unprotected sex
    d. television coverage of crime or war
    e. meaningful versus meaningless work
    f. youth and age
    g. nostalgia
    h. flag burning
2. Select any issue covered in your local news reports, formulate your position on it in a thesis, and then explain and defend your thesis in an essay.

WRITING ASSIGNMENTS FOR A SPECIFIC AUDIENCE

1. For an audience of third graders, explain in an essay the concept of a thesis and how you make use of it in your own writing.
2. Explain to an audience of business executives how the English education you are presently receiving will make you a better employee.

COLLABORATIVE WRITING PROJECT

Divide your group into at least three teams, each of which should research the retirement policies of some specific profession or institution of its choice. Conduct whatever interviews are necessary to learn more about any specific retirement policy. After completing the research, the teams should meet to discuss and debate the fairness of the retirement policies. Finally, each team should write a group essay outlining what it learned about the researched retirement policy as well as its impact on elderly employees.

——————— REAL-LIFE ———————
STUDENT WRITING

A EULOGY TO A FRIEND KILLED IN A CAR WRECK

Students sometimes have the unenviable duty of saying a few last words at a funeral or memorial service of friends, relatives, and classmates. Here is a brief eulogy, given by a young man whose best friend was killed in an automobile crash.

He was my best friend. We went to elementary school together, where we drove our teachers crazy. We grew up in North Hollywood, both loving the Giants, the 49ers, and the Lakers. We never missed a Rose Bowl game on TV. We weathered a thunderstorm in our pup tents in the Sierra Nevadas; we played Blind Man's Bluff in my parent's swimming pool; we TP'd our girlfriends' homes; we learned to play the guitar; and we read a lot of science fiction books together. When I was angry at my parents, Brett would calm me down. When I felt nervous about some final exam, Brett encouraged me.

What evil force is this that has taken Brett away without warning? Yes, I am angry at the driver who mowed him down; I am angry that God didn't save him. But I am also aware that anger won't bring him back. So, I guess we must all live with the knowledge that Brett was a one-of-a-kind friend—loyal, upbeat, and generous. We'll all remember the good times we had with him. And for those of us who believe in life after death—we look forward to someday meeting him again and hearing him say, "Hey man, how's it goin'?"

5

How Do I Organize?

EDITORS' COUNSEL

Writers and the way they work fall mainly into two major camps: the organic and the mechanical. The organic writer writes from the subconscious. Such writers often go to sleep thinking about an assignment and wake up the next morning knowing exactly what they intend to write. The mechanical writer, like a carpenter building a house, works from a blueprint or plan. These writers organize their thoughts before writing and plot out their ideas and topics before committing a single word to paper.

We raise this distinction to point out that organizing is not for everyone. It is a technique better suited to the working habits of the mechanical writer. For the organic writer whose subconscious does most of the work, organizing offers little benefit and might even interfere with the process of composing.

Organizing the Short Essay

Short essays (about 300 words long) are usually written in class under the pressure of a time limit. An instructor may assign you to write three paragraphs on some topic you have been studying in class, or you may be asked to write an informal essay on a topic such as why an uninformed person should or should not vote. Obviously, you cannot spend a great deal of time planning what to say in such an essay. Yet, you think some preliminary sketch would be helpful. What can you do?

Make a Jot List   A jot list is exactly as it says: a list of those points you mean to cover in the essay. You begin your jot list by scribbling down your main point or thesis. In this case, you think it is better for an ignorant voter to abstain than to cast a vote that amounts to a guess. You express this position in a thesis sentence:

> Thesis: To vote for someone whose record you don't know is worse than not voting at all.

Then you add the points you think you ought to cover:

1. If I don't vote, at least the people who know what the candidates stand for will make the decision for me.
2. Uncle John picks candidates by closing his eyes and poking at the ballot with his finger.
3. Voting from ignorance is disrespectful of the democratic process.
4. If I don't know anything about a candidate or an issue, I won't vote. At least that way, I leave the decision up to people who do know.

The jot list has no conventional form. You do not hand it in to your instructor. You can number its entries or arrange them in any other way you please. When you're done writing the essay, you can make a paper plane of the jot list if you like. It is nothing more than a thumbnail sketch of what you want to do.

Sketch Out Your Paragraphs   This method of organizing is as simple as a jot list. Sketch out the paragraphs that you intend to write. Most in-class essays require no more than five paragraphs—and usually around three. Here's an example. You have been given the essay topic to write on any aspect of modern popular culture. You choose to write about the movies and why you like them.

Begin by writing down a rough draft of your thesis:

> Thesis: The most interesting and entertaining products of modern popular culture are movies.

Next, write down the topics of your beginning paragraphs:

> First paragraph: interesting movies. *The African Queen. The Two of Us. The Apartment.* Why these movies are interesting to me.
>
> Second paragraph: entertaining movies. *Life is Beautiful. Chicago. The Gods Must Be Crazy.* Why I find these movies entertaining.
>
> Third paragraph: Our movies are a global influence. They spread our culture and way of life better than literature does.

You don't want to make this list too long because you still have the actual essay to write. But at least you know what topics you have to cover in upcoming paragraphs.

Make a Flowchart   This is a more graphic variation of the jot list. Simply make a plan of your entire essay, using specially shaped boxes for supporting ideas and main points. In the example given (Figure 5–1), the triangular shapes indicate supporting details. The rectangular shapes indicate main points, and the diamond shapes indicate where transitions need to be inserted.

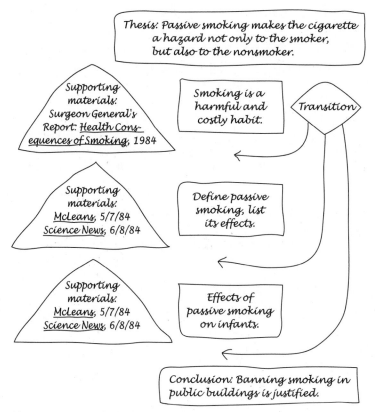

Figure 5–1. Example of Flowchart Essay

Organizing the Long Essay

The long essay might be a weekend assignment or a research paper completed over the course of several weeks. You might be expected to write an essay five to ten pages long with appropriate and accurate documentation on topics such as the following: "Why the Shark Is Such a Successful Predator"; "Art Therapy"; or "Initial Critical Reactions to Henry Miller's Novels." Such subjects involve both library and Internet research as well as outside reading.

The plan of such an essay should function as a guide not only to its writing but also to the research you need to do before you are ready to write. You should consult the plan both as you do the research—modifying it if necessary as you accumulate more supporting materials and possibly change your mind—and as you do the writing. If you go off in a different direction from the plan during the actual writing, never mind. Follow the lead of inspiration. When you are finished, go back over the rough draft and compare what you actually have with your original plan. Be sure that you can justify the switch.

Planning by Listing Supporting Materials

If you have a topic, you can often generate a crude outline of the essay by making a list of the supporting materials you will need for reference. How can you know what supporting materials you need? You find out by asking commonsense questions about the topic. These questions are those that any interested reader would likewise ask.

Here is an example: A student who accompanied her parents on a summer trip to Stonehenge, England, decided to do a paper on the area's mysterious monoliths. Her own tourist pamphlets, bolstered by some preliminary background reading in the college library, led her to this thesis:

> Thesis: A visit to Stonehenge, England, taught me that some civilizations of the past have left us some challenging mysteries we can't seem to solve.

These are the questions that naturally occurred to her as she thought about what supporting materials she would need.

Where is Stonehenge? Give its geographical location.

What is Stonehenge? Describe the stones so that the reader can visualize their size and arrangement. Try to get across the awesome nature of the stones.

What was Stonehenge used for? What are the theories of its use? Summarize the most popular legends surrounding the history of Stonehenge:

1. Stonehenge as a sanctuary of the Druids. Look up "Druids" in the encyclopedia. See what role they played in the early history of England (probably Celtic).
2. The Devil's confrontation with a friar. Find out how this exotic legend got started.
3. A memorial to the slain knights of King Arthur.
4. An observatory for tracking the heavens, especially the rising of the moon. This seems to be a realistic explanation. Find out if many sources mention this theory.

Why is Stonehenge so popular even today? Explain the reasons for its popularity.

These rather straightforward questions gave the writer an idea of the supporting materials she needed to complete the assignment. Asking these questions also resulted in a rough outline of the paper.

Organizing with a Formal Outline

The outline is a summary of what you plan to say in your essay. The outline tells you what you have to do, where you have to go, and when you have gotten there. If you tend to get sidetracked by details or bogged down in vast quantities of information, outlining is a handy way of imposing structure on a long essay.

A convention has evolved for the formal outline, based mainly on the desire to make it readable at a glance. The title of the essay is centered at the top of the page, with the thesis below it. Main ideas are designated by Roman numerals. Subideas branching off the main ideas are indented and designated by capital letters. Examples of these subideas are further indented and designated by Arabic numerals. Indented beneath the examples are supporting details, designated by lowercase letters. In theory, this subdividing could go on forever; in practice, it rarely extends beyond the fourth level. Here is the framework for the formal outline:

TITLE

Thesis

   I. Main idea

      A. Subidea

         1. Division of subidea

            a. Part of division of subidea

An outline omits introductory materials, transitions, examples, illustrations, and details; it lists only the major ideas and subideas of the essay. This practice makes sense when you remember that the prime purpose of an outline is to condense the major divisions of a long essay into a form that can be read at a glance. To make the outline as long and complex as the essay itself is self-defeating and pointless labor.

To make an outline, begin with the thesis of your essay and divide it into smaller ideas. It is an axiom of division that nothing can be divided into fewer than two parts. From this, it follows that under every main idea that has been divided, at least two subideas must appear. In other words, for every *I* there must be at least a *II*; for every *A*, at least a *B*. Consider this example:

    Thesis: Extremes in temperatures can have dangerous effects on mountain climbers.

   I. The dangerous effects of excessive heat

      A. Heat exhaustion

      B. Heat stroke

  II. The dangerous effects of excessive cold

      A. Surface frostbite

      B. Bodily numbness

The logic of division will always produce an outline characterized by symmetry. A by-product of this symmetry is evenness in the treatment of all topics. Notice also that each entry is worded in more or less parallel language. This wording underscores the equal importance of the entries and emphasizes the major divisions in the outline.

Creating the Outline   Outlining is systematic thinking about your thesis. You examine the essay as a reader might and try to decide what points you need to present, and in what order, to make the topic understandable. For example, let us suppose that you were planning to write an essay on this thesis:

> Thesis: Listening is such an important and badly practiced communicative skill that schools should begin offering courses in how to do it better.

The first question a reader is likely to ask is, "Why is listening so important?" The answer should be the development of your first major point.

I. Listening is an important communicative skill.

What do you mean by "listening is badly practiced"? Common sense suggests that this is the second question likely to occur to an interested reader. The answer could be the development of your second major point.

II. Listening is a badly practiced communicative skill.

Fill out these two major headings with some secondary points that serve as answers, and you have completed the first part of your outline.

I. Listening is an important communicative skill.
  A. We spend most of our communicating time listening.
  B. We get most of our political information from radio and television.
II. Listening is a badly practiced communicative skill.
  A. We typically understand only one-half of what we hear.
  B. We typically recall only one-quarter of what we hear.

Following this line of thinking, we can deduce some other questions that common sense tells us are likely to occur to a reader: What do you mean by listening? Are all types of listening alike? Answers to these questions can provide us with two more headings:

III. Listening is an active communicative skill that is divisible into four components.
  A. Receiving entails decoding the message.
  B. Attending entails analyzing the message.

    C. Assigning meaning entails interpreting the message.

    D. Remembering entails information storage and retrieval.

IV. Listening is grouped into five major types.

    A. Appreciative listening involves acceptance.

    B. Discriminative listening involves selection.

    C. Comprehensive listening involves generalizing.

    D. Therapeutic listening involves relaxation.

    E. Critical listening involves judgment.

Think about the purpose of the assignment and the questions your thesis is likely to evoke in a reader and you will likewise discover the logical divisions of your essay.

Guidelines for Outlining   You should observe the following guidelines in making your outline:

1. *Don't make the outline too long.* One page of an outline is the basis for five pages of developed writing. Your aim is to produce a model of the essay that you can inspect for flaws at a glance.

2. *Don't clutter the sentences of your outline.* Make your entries brief. The idea is to make the outline instantly readable.

3. *Use parallel wording for subordinate entries whenever possible.* Parallel entries are easier to read than nonparallel ones.

4. *Align the entries properly.* Do not allow the second line of an entry to go farther toward the left margin than the line above it.

If you observe these simple guidelines, the outline that results should be easy to read. You should be able to glance at its major entries and immediately spot any flaws in the structure of the essay.

Outlining by Topic/Outlining by Sentence   Some outlines are topic outlines in which the entries are not complete sentences, but fragments that sum up the topic. Other outlines are sentence outlines in which the entries are complete sentences. Your decision on whether to use a topic or a sentence outline depends on how complete a breakdown you need. If your subject is simple and all you need are key words to serve as guideposts so that you will not get sidetracked, or if you merely wish to set down some major trends, categories, or stages, then you should use a topic outline. If your subject is a difficult one or in an area that is new to you, you should use a sentence outline. Consider the following topic outline:

THE FUTURE OF OUR CITIES

Thesis: An assessment of the future of our cities reveals two emerging trends.

I. The megalopolis
  A. Definition
    1. Cluster
    2. System
  B. Two major organizational problems
    1. Transcendence
    2. Coordination

II. Shift in decision making
  A. Local decisions
    1. Facts not known
    2. Outside agencies
  B. Federal government
    1. Increase in power
    2. Local restrictions

This topic outline is of no value to a person who is not thoroughly familiar with the problems of city government. A student writing a paper based on such a cryptic outline is bound to have difficulty. Now consider the following sentence outline of the same subject:

THE FUTURE OF OUR CITIES

Thesis: An assessment of the future of our cities reveals two emerging trends.

I. The megalopolis is replacing the city.
  A. Megalopolis can be defined in two ways.
    1. A megalopolis is a cluster of cities.
    2. A megalopolis is a system of interwoven urban and suburban areas.
  B. Two major organizational problems of the megalopolis will need to be solved.
    1. One problem is how to handle questions that transcend individual metropolitan areas.
    2. Another problem is how to coordinate the numerous activities in the megalopolis.

II. Decision making is shifting from local control to higher echelons of public and private authority.
  A. The growing scale of the urban world often makes local decisions irrelevant.
    1. Local agencies may not know all of the facts.
    2. National policies may supersede local decisions.

B. The federal government moves into the picture.
1. The extent of federal involvement increases as the city grows.
    a. Federal long-range improvement plans are used.
    b. Grant-in-aid programs become necessary.
2. Federal assistance imposes restrictions.
    a. Federal policies make sure that no discrimination takes place in the areas of housing, employment, and education.
    b. Federal representatives check on local installations to make sure that they are up to federal standards.

A good sentence outline supplies all of the basic information you need to write your paper. Without an outline, you run the risk of treating major ideas like details and details like major ideas; furthermore, you may find yourself moving forward, then backtracking, and then moving forward again, resulting in an incoherent paper. Because a careful outline takes into account the relationships among ideas and their degrees of importance, it keeps a novice from muddled writing.

We do not wish to mislead you into thinking that every essay you write will be just as easily and neatly outlined as our examples may suggest. In fact, you will most likely find it necessary to revise the outline heavily. You might even end up with three or four scratched-up versions before you are satisfied with the result. As you outline, new ideas will occur to you and clamor to be fitted in somewhere. Old headings will strike you as too obvious to be included. Whether you make a formal outline or simply draw up a sketch of your essay, you are still likely to revise heavily before you are happy with your plan.

EXERCISES

1. Write a paragraph outline for one of the following theses:
    a. Inflation has had a deteriorating effect on the purchasing power of the dollar.
    b. The essay exam has several advantages over the objective test.
    c. The first three months of an infant's life are crucial to the development of his or her personality.
2. Create a flowchart for one of the following theses:
    a. Society often uses language to favor one sex over the other.
    b. Economic inflation has political consequences.
    c. Teachers deserve higher salaries.
    d. English should be made the official language of the United States.

3. List the supporting materials you might use for an essay on one of the following topics:

   a. Why people often don't help in a crisis

   b. Multiple choice versus essay exams as tools of education

   c. Comic strips that have social value

   d. Why modern products are often shoddy

4. Identify the key words in the following theses, specifying two or three subtopics into which they may be divided:

   a. Strong diplomatic ties with China would have several advantages for the United States.

   b. An electrical blackout in any major city of the United States would have disastrous results.

   c. The words *disinterested, inflammable,* and *fortuitous* are often misunderstood.

5. Delete the entry that destroys the logical order in the following outlines:

   a. Thesis: Because of their cultural traits, the Dobuans are different from other primitive tribes.

      I. The location and environment of Dobuan Island make it difficult for the Dobuans to find sufficient food.

      II. The rituals of marriage set the Dobuans apart from other primitive tribes.

      III. The Dobuans' reliance on magic makes them more superstitious than other primitive tribes.

      IV. The fact that the Dobuans value treachery and ill will sets them apart from other primitive tribes.

   b. Thesis: The purpose of the California missions was to Christianize the Indians and to strengthen Spain's claim to California.

      I. The mission padres taught the Indians Christian virtues.

      II. The padres were concerned with saving the souls of the Indians.

      III. The missions were constructed in the form of small cities.

      IV. Without its colonists in California, Spain's claim to this territory was weak.

      V. Spain was competing with Russia and England for territory in California.

   c. Thesis: American political assassins have acted on nonpolitical impulses.

      I. They are pathetic loners.

      II. Their reality is a fantasy world.

   III. The victim is usually a surrogate parent image.

   IV. The assassin is seeking the same "fame" that the victim has.

   V. European assassinations, unlike ours, have been the results of elaborate plots.

6. Scrutinize the following outline for errors of form as well as content. Correct the errors by producing two improved versions—a sentence outline and a topic outline.

   a. Thesis: The adult Moses is one of the most commanding and inspirational figures of the Old Testament.

      I. Moses was a God-intoxicated man.

        A. Moses' faith in God.

        B. He created in the Hebrews a religious faith that was to endure after their life as a nation had died.

          1. The Babylonian and Persian conquests.

          2. The faith endured during the Greek conquest.

          3. The faith endured during the Roman conquest.

          4. Despite their faith, the Hebrews often worshiped foreign gods.

          5. The faith endured during the various diasporas.

      II. Moses was a peerless travel guide.

        A. During the long sojourn in the wilderness, Moses showed endless patience.

          1. Enduring constant grumbling on the part of the tribes.

          2. This period of desert wandering symbolizes the age of innocence of any developing nation.

          3. He settled quarrels with great patience.

        B. His earlier flight in order to escape punishment for having killed an Egyptian made him fully acquainted with the Sinai desert.

          1. He knew where to find water.

          2. He knew how to avoid dangerous enemy territory.

          3. He always followed a magical cloud by day and a pillar of fire by night.

      III. Moses was the founder of a complex legal system.

        A. He gave the Hebrews the Torah.

          1. Parts of the Torah dealt with man's relationship to God.

          2. Parts of the Torah dealt with man's relationship to man.

        B. He gave the Hebrews the ordinances.

          1. Some of the ordinances dealt with matters of social justice.

          2. According to one ordinance, a man who knocks out his slave's tooth must let that slave go free.

          3. Others of the ordinances dealt with religious ceremonies.

          4. Some of the ordinances dealt with plans for building a temple.

———— ADVICE ————

HOW TO WRITE CLEARLY

Edward T. Thompson

Edward Thorwald Thompson (b. 1928) was born in Milwaukee and educated at MIT. Between 1976 and 1984, he was editor-in-chief of Reader's Digest. *He is currently a consultant in publications.*

Whatever you may think of the *Reader's Digest*—there are those who love it and those who hate it—you cannot say that its hodgepodge of self-help, optimistic, and heartwarming articles is written in a disorganized way. In fact, the *Digest* is known above all else for its clear (some would say simplistic) style of writing. In the article that follows, a former editor of this venerable, popular publication offers some specific advice on how to organize ideas and express them on paper.

~

1   If you are afraid to write, don't be.

2   If you think you've got to string together big fancy words and high-flying phrases, forget it.

3   To write well, unless you aspire to be a professional poet or novelist, you only need to get your ideas across simply and clearly.

4   It's not easy. But it is easier than you might imagine.

5   There are only three basic requirements:

6   First, you must want to write clearly. And I believe you really do, if you've stayed this far with me.

7   Second, you must be willing to work hard. Thinking means work—and that's what it takes to do anything well.

8   Third, you must know and follow some basic guidelines.

9   If, while you're writing for clarity, some lovely, dramatic or inspired phrases or sentences come to you, fine. Put them in.

10   But then with cold, objective eyes and mind ask yourself "Do they detract from clarity?" If they do, grit your teeth and cut the frills.

Follow Some Basic Guidelines

11   I can't give you a complete list of "do's and don'ts" for every writing problem you'll ever face.

12   But I can give you some fundamental guidelines that cover the most common problems.

1. Outline What You Want to Say

13   I know that sounds grade-schoolish. But you can't write clearly until, before you start, you know where you will stop.

14   Ironically, that's even a problem in writing an outline (i.e., knowing the ending before you begin).

15   So try this method:

- On 3 × 5 cards, write—one point to a card—all the points you need to make.

- Divide the cards into piles—one pile for each group of points closely related to each other. (If you were describing an automobile, you'd put all the points about mileage in one pile, all the points about safety in another, and so on.)

- Arrange your piles of points in a sequence. Which are most important and should be given first or saved for last? Which must you present before others in order to make the others understandable?

- Now, within each pile, do the same thing—arrange the points in logical, understandable order.

16   There you have your outline, needing only an introduction and conclusion.

17   This is a practical way to outline. It's also flexible. You can add, delete or change the location of points easily.

2. Start Where Your Readers Are

18   How much do they know about the subject? Don't write to a level higher than your readers' knowledge of it.

19   CAUTION: Forget that old—and wrong—advice about writing to a 12-year-old mentality. That's insulting. But do remember that your prime purpose is to explain something, not prove that you're smarter than your readers.

3. Avoid Jargon

20   Don't use words, expressions, phrases known only to people with specific knowledge or interests.

21   Example: A scientist, using scientific jargon, wrote, "The biota exhibited a one hundred percent mortality response." He could have written: "All the fish died."

4. Use Familiar Combinations of Words

22   A speech writer for President Franklin D. Roosevelt wrote, "We are endeavoring to construct a more inclusive society." F.D.R. changed it to, "We're going to make a country in which no one is left out."

23   CAUTION: By familiar combinations of words, I do not mean incorrect grammar. That can be unclear. Example: John's father says he can't go out Friday. (Who can't go out? John or his father?)

5. Use "First-Degree" Words

24   These words immediately bring an image to your mind. Other words must be "translated" through the first-degree word before you see the image. Those are second/third-degree words.

First-degree words	Second/Third-degree words
face	visage, countenance
stay	abide, remain, reside
book	volume, tome, publication

25   First-degree words are usually the most precise words, too.

6. Stick to the Point

26   Your outline—which was more work in the beginning—now saves you work. Because now you can ask about any sentence you write: "Does it relate to a point in the outline? If it doesn't, should I add it to the outline? If not, I'm getting off the track." Then, full steam ahead—on the main line.

7. Be as Brief as Possible

27   Whatever you write, shortening—condensing—almost always makes it tighter, straighter, easier to read and understand.

28   Condensing, as *Reader's Digest* does it, is in large part artistry. But it involves techniques that anyone can learn and use.

- Present your points in logical ABC order: Here again, your outline should save you work because, if you did it right, your points already stand in logical ABC order—A makes B understandable, B makes C understandable and so on. To write in a straight line is to say something clearly in the fewest possible words.

- Don't waste words telling people what they already know: Notice how we edited this: "Have you ever wondered how banks rate you as a credit risk? ~~You know, of course, that it's some combination of facts about your income, your job, and so on. But actally,~~ many banks have a scoring system. . . ."

- Cut out excess evidence and unnecessary anecdotes: Usually, one fact or example (at most, two) will support a point. More just belabor it.

- And while writing about something may remind you of a good story, ask yourself: "Does it really help to tell the story, or does it slow me down?"

29   (Many people think *Reader's Digest* articles are filled with anecdotes. Actually, we use them sparingly and usually for one of two reasons: either the subject is so dry it needs some "humanity" to give it life; or the subject is so hard to grasp, it needs anecdotes to help readers understand. If the subject is both lively and easy to grasp, we move right along.)

■ Look for the most common word wasters: windy phrases.

Windy phrases	Cut to ...
at the present time _____	now
in the event of _____	of
in the majority of instances _____	usually

■ Look for passive verbs you can make active: Invariably, this produces a shorter sentence. "The cherry tree was chopped down by George Washington." (Passive verb and nine words.) "George Washington chopped down the cherry tree." (Active verb and seven words.)

■ Look for positive/negative sections from which you can cut the negative: See how we did it here: "The answer ~~does not rest with carelessness or incompetence~~ it lies ~~largely~~ in having enough people to do the job."

■ Finally, to write more clearly by saying it in fewer words: when you've finished, stop.

∼

(1,078 words)

———— EXAMPLES ————

MY WOOD

E. M. Forster

E. M. Forster (1879–1969) was a British novelist, essayist, and short-story writer whose work first won wide recognition in 1924, with the publication of his Passage to India. *In 1946, Forster was made an honorary fellow of King's College, Cambridge, where he lived until his death. Among his many other works are* Howard's End *(1910) and* Two Cheers for Democracy *(1951), a collection of his essays.*

My Wood, a superbly organized short essay, investigates the effect of property ownership on the individual and society.

∼

1 A few years ago I wrote a book which dealt in part with the difficulties of the English in India. Feeling that they would have had no difficulties in India

themselves, the Americans read the book freely. The more they read it the better it made them feel, and a cheque to the author was the result. I bought a wood with the cheque. It is not a large wood—it contains scarcely any trees, and it is intersected, blast it, by a public footpath. Still, it is the first property that I have owned, so it is right that other people should participate in my shame, and should ask themselves, in accents that will vary in horror, this very important question: What is the effect of property upon the character? Don't let's touch economics; the effect of private ownership upon the community as a whole is another question—a more important question, perhaps, but another one. Let's keep to psychology. If you own things, what's their effect on you? What's the effect on me of my wood?

2   In the first place, it makes me feel heavy. Property does have this effect. Property produces men of weight, and it was a man of weight who failed to get into the Kingdom of Heaven. He was not wicked, that unfortunate millionaire in the parable, he was only stout; he stuck out in front, not to mention behind, and as he wedged himself this way and that in the crystalline entrance and bruised his well-fed flanks, he saw beneath him a comparatively slim camel passing through the eye of a needle and being woven into the robe of God. The Gospels all through couple stoutness and slowness. They point out what is perfectly obvious, yet seldom realized: that if you have a lot of things you cannot move about a lot, that furniture requires dusting, dusters require servants, servants require insurance stamps,[1] and the whole tangle of them makes you think twice before you accept an invitation to dinner or go for a bathe in the Jordan. Sometimes the Gospels proceed further and say with Tolstoy that property is sinful; they approach the difficult ground of asceticism here, where I cannot follow them. But as to the immediate effects of property on people, they just show straightforward logic. It produces men of weight. Men of weight cannot, by definition, move like the lightning from the East unto the West, and the ascent of a fourteen-stone bishop into a pulpit is thus the exact antithesis of the coming of the Son of Man. My wood makes me feel heavy.

3   In the second place, it makes me feel it ought to be larger.

4   The other day I heard a twig snap in it. I was annoyed at first, for I thought that someone was blackberrying, and depreciating the value of the undergrowth. On coming nearer, I saw it was not a man who had trodden on the twig and snapped it, but a bird, and I felt pleased. My bird. The bird was not equally pleased. Ignoring the relation between us, it took fright as soon as it saw the shape of my face, and flew straight over the boundary hedge into a field, the property of Mrs. Henessy, where it sat down with a loud squawk. It had become Mrs. Henessy's bird. Something seemed grossly amiss here, something that would not have occurred had the wood been larger. I could not afford to buy Mrs. Henessy out, I dared not murder her, and limitations of this sort beset me on every side. Ahab did not want that vineyard—he only

---

[1]In England—eds.

needed it to round off his property, preparatory to plotting a new curve—and all the land around my wood has become necessary to me in order to round off the wood. A boundary protects. But—poor little thing—the boundary ought in its turn to be protected. Noises on the edge of it. Children throw stones. A little more, and then a little more, until we reach the sea. Happy Canute! Happier Alexander! And after all, why should even the world be the limit of possession? A rocket containing a Union Jack, will, it is hoped, be shortly fired at the moon. Mars. Sirius. Beyond which . . . . But these immensities ended by saddening me. I could not suppose that my wood was the destined nucleus of universal dominion—it is so very small and contains no mineral wealth beyond the blackberries. Nor was I comforted when Mrs. Henessy's bird took alarm for the second time and flew clean away from us all, under the belief that it belonged to itself.

5   In the third place, property makes its owner feel that he ought to do something to it. Yet he isn't sure what. A restlessness comes over him, a vague sense that he has a personality to express—the same sense which, without any vagueness, leads the artist to an act of creation. Sometimes I think I will cut down such trees as remain in the wood, at other times I want to fill up the gaps between them with new trees. Both impulses are pretentious and empty. They are not honest movements towards money-making or beauty. They spring from a foolish desire to express myself and from an inability to enjoy what I have got. Creation, property, enjoyment form a sinister trinity in the human mind. Creation and enjoyment are both very good, yet they are often unattainable without a material basis, and at such moments property pushes itself in as a substitute, saying, "Accept me instead—I'm good enough for all three." It is not enough. It is, as Shakespeare said of lust, "The expense of spirit in a waste of shame": it is "Before, a joy proposed; behind, a dream." Yet we don't know how to shun it. It is forced on us by our economic system as the alternative to starvation. It is also forced on us by an internal defect in the soul, by the feeling that in property may lie the germs of self-development and of exquisite or heroic deeds. Our life on earth is, and ought to be, material and carnal. But we have not yet learned to manage our materialism and carnality properly; they are still entangled with the desire for ownership, where (in the words of Dante) "Possession is one with loss."

6   And this brings us to our fourth and final point: the blackberries.

7   Blackberries are not plentiful in this meagre grove, but they are easily seen from the public footpath which traverses it, and all too easily gathered. Foxgloves, too—people will pull up the foxgloves, and ladies of an educational tendency even grub for toad stools to show them on the Monday in class. Other ladies, less educated, roll down the bracken in the arms of their gentlemen friends. There is a paper, there are tins. Pray, does my wood belong to me or doesn't it? And, if it does, should I not own it best by allowing no one else to walk there? There is a wood near Lyme Regis, also cursed by a public footpath, where the owner has not hesitated on this point. He has built high stone walls on each side of the path, and has spanned it by bridges, so that the public circulate like termites while he gorges on the blackberries unseen.

He really does own his wood, this able chap. Dives in Hell did pretty well, but the gulf dividing him from Lazarus could be traversed by vision, and nothing traverses it here. And perhaps I shall come to this in time. I shall wall in and fence out until I really taste the sweets of property. Enormously stout, endlessly avaricious, pseudo-creative, intensely selfish, I shall weave upon my forehead the quadruple crown of possession until those nasty Bolshies come and take it off again and thrust me aside into the outer darkness.

∼

(1,333 words)

THE FACTS

1. What intersects Forster's wood and is a source of annoyance to him?
2. What is the first effect Forster's wood had on him?
3. What or whom did Forster discover on his property when he heard a twig snap?
4. According to Forster, what is the effect of property on its owner?
5. What does Forster think he will eventually do with his wood?

THE STRATEGIES

1. What are the obvious divisions in the topics and subtopics of this essay? Make an outline showing the thesis, main points, and subtopics of the essay.
2. Read the last sentence of paragraph 2. What is the purpose of this sentence?
3. What is the purpose of paragraph 3?
4. What tone does Forster use throughout this essay? Do you regard his tone as mocking, serious, or ironic? Justify your answer.
5. In paragraph 4, Forster writes: "Happy Canute! Happier Alexander!" What is this figure of speech called? Why is Alexander happier than Canute?

THE ISSUES

1. What point does Forster make obliquely in his discussion about the bird?
2. What effect does ownership have on you? Is Forster exaggerating here, or have you experienced the same effects that he describes?
3. What benefits, if any, do you think society gains from ownership of private property?

4. What do you think Dante meant by "Possession is one with loss"? Interpret this statement.

5. "Our life on earth is, and ought to be, material and carnal." What is your opinion of this statement? How do you think our life on earth ought to be?

SUGGESTIONS FOR WRITING

1. Write an analysis of the tone of this essay, carefully supporting your points with quotations from the work itself.

2. Write an essay on the benefits of property ownership.

RULES FOR AGING

Roger Rosenblatt

Roger Rosenblatt (b. 1940) is one of Time's *most venerated editorial writers. His astute insights into politics and society, as well as his wonderful sense of humor, have delighted his readers for close to two decades. Rosenblatt graduated from Harvard, where he earned a Ph.D. and briefly taught English. He has been featured on television reading his eloquent* Time *essays.*

~

1 Since older people are as close to perfection as human beings get, I thought it would be generous, from time to time, to use this space to offer guidelines for living to those less old to help them age successfully, or at all. The art of aging requires not doing things more than taking positive action, so this is essentially a list of "nots" and "don'ts."

2   1. *It doesn't matter.* Whatever you think matters, doesn't. This guideline is absolutely reliable and adhering to it will add decades to your life. It does not matter if you are late for anything; if you're having a bad hair day, or a no hair day; if your car won't start; if your boss looks at you cockeyed; if your girlfriend or boyfriend looks at you cockeyed; if you are cockeyed; if you don't get the promotion; if you do; if you have spinach in your teeth or if you lose your teeth in your spinach. It doesn't matter.

3   2. *Nobody is thinking about you.* Yes, I know. You are certain that your friends are becoming your enemies; that your enemies are acquiring nuclear weapons; that your grocer, garbage man, clergyman, sister-in-law, and dog are all of the opinion that you have put on weight; furthermore, that everyone spends two thirds of every day commenting on your disintegration, denigrating your work, plotting your murder. I promise you: Nobody is thinking about you. They are thinking about themselves, just like you.

4   *3. Do not go to your left.* Going to one's left, or working on going to one's left, is a basketball term for strengthening one's weakness. A right-handed player will improve his game considerably if he learns to dribble and shoot with his left hand, and to move to his left on the court. But this is true only for basketball, not for living. In life, if you attempt to strengthen a weakness, you will grow weaker. If, on the other hand (the right), you keep playing to your strength, people will not notice that you have weaknesses. Of course, you do not believe me. You will go ahead and take singing lessons or write that novel anyway. Trust me.

5   *4. Give honest, frank, and open criticism to nobody, never.* The following situation will present itself to you over and over: There is a friend, a relative, an employee, an employer, a colleague, whose behavior flaws are so evident to everyone but themselves, you just know that a straightforward, no-punches-pulled conversation with them will show them the error of their ways. They will see the light at once, and forever be grateful that only as good and candid a person as yourself would have sufficient kindness and courage to confront them.

6   Better still: From the moment you inform them about their bad table manners, their poor choices in clothing, their hygiene, their loudness, their deafness, their paranoia, they will reform on the spot. Their lives will be redeemed, and they will owe their renewed selves and all future happiness to you—honest, frank, and open you.

7   I implore you: forget about it. When the muse of candor whispers in your ear, swat it, take a long walk, a cold shower, and clear your head. This guideline relates to guideline number two. Nobody is thinking about you, unless you tell them about their faults. Then you can be sure they are thinking of you. They are thinking of killing you.

8   That's enough wisdom for now. I know younger people will not heed my advice anyway. So the guideline I offer them is: Don't. Go ahead and stay awake worrying what people are thinking about you, work on your weaknesses, and criticize your friends. It doesn't matter.

～

(620 words)

VOCABULARY

adhering (2)	disintegration (3)	denigrating (3)
paranoia (6)	muse (7)	candor (7)

THE FACTS

1. How many rules for aging does Rosenblatt offer? What form do these rules follow?

2. The first rule is pronounced with great authority—"It doesn't matter." What is the author telling us with this rule?

3. In what way is rule #2 related to rule #1?

4. What does the author mean by the image of going "to your left"?

5. What is the implication behind rule #4?

THE STRATEGIES

1. How would you describe the tone of this essay? How does the tone affect the purpose of the essay? Does the essay have a thesis? If so, where is it stated?

2. What is your reaction to the opening sentence of the essay? How did it strike you? Consider such matters as the author's voice, his tone, and his purpose.

3. What is the effect of the "Yes, I know" sentence at the beginning of paragraph 3?

4. Where does the author use parallelism to achieve balance and euphony? Point to specific passages in the essay.

5. Why does the author refer to "the muse of candor" in paragraph 7?

THE ISSUES

1. What is your personal understanding of the author's statement, "It doesn't matter"? Elaborate on his meaning.

2. Assuming that most human beings are concerned with their own problems more than those of other people, why do they often persist in feeling that their neighbors are plotting against them or making disparaging remarks behind their backs?

3. People say that getting old gracefully is an art. What does that popular saying mean? Do you agree? Give an example of someone you know who has grown old gracefully.

4. Which of Rosenblatt's rules do you think is the most difficult to follow? Why?

5. In giving us rule #3, do you think the author is discouraging forays into new and exciting territories? Might he be keeping older people from trying new hobbies or taking on new responsibilities that might enrich the final years of their lives? Explain your answer.

SUGGESTIONS FOR WRITING

1. Write an essay in which you propose your own rules for aging. You can be humorous like Rosenblatt or dead serious, but use a clear method of organization.

2. Choose one of the following comments as your thesis for a 500-word essay:

    a. Don't let the opinions of others control your life.

    b. Be sensitive to the advice of wise people.

Use a clear pattern of organization for this essay.

THE CATBIRD SEAT

James Thurber

James Thurber (1894–1963) was an American humorist, cartoonist, and social commentator. His contributions to The New Yorker *made him immensely popular. Among his best-known works are* My Life and Hard Times *(1933),* Fables for Our Time *(1940), and* The Thurber Carnival *(1945), from which this selection was taken.*

A conventional, well-behaved office clerk suddenly finds his job threatened by an aggressive, loud-mouthed "special adviser to the president." To protect his job, this unobtrusive, little man resorts to a most unusual crime.

~

1 Mr. Martin bought the pack of Camels on Monday night in the most crowded cigar store on Broadway. It was theatre time and seven or eight men were buying cigarettes. The clerk didn't even glance at Mr. Martin, who put the pack in his overcoat pocket and went out. If any of the staff at F & S had seen him buy the cigarettes, they would have been astonished, for it was generally known that Mr. Martin did not smoke, and never had. No one saw him.

2   It was just a week to the day since Mr. Martin had decided to rub out Mrs. Ulgine Barrows. The term "rub out" pleased him because it suggested nothing more than the correction of an error—in this case an error of Mr. Fitweiler. Mr. Martin had spent each night of the past week working out his plan and examining it. As he walked home now he went over it again. For the hundredth time he resented the element of imprecision, the margin of guesswork that entered into the business. The project as he had worked it out was casual and bold, the risks were considerable. Something might go wrong anywhere along the line. And therein lay the cunning of his scheme. No one would ever see in it the cautious, painstaking hand of Erwin Martin, head of the filing department at F & S, of whom Mr. Fitweiler had once said, "Man is fallible but Martin isn't." No one would see his hand, that is, unless it were caught in the act.

3   Sitting in his apartment, drinking a glass of milk, Mr. Martin reviewed his case against Mrs. Ulgine Barrows, as he had every night for seven nights. He began at the beginning. Her quacking voice and braying laugh had first profaned the halls of F & S on March 7, 1941 (Mr. Martin had a head for dates). Old Roberts, the personnel chief, had introduced her as the newly appointed special adviser to the president of the firm, Mr. Fitweiler. The woman had appalled Mr. Martin instantly, but he hadn't shown it. He had given her his dry

hand, a look of studious concentration, and a faint smile. "Well," she had said, looking at the papers on his desk, "are you lifting the oxcart out of the ditch?" As Mr. Martin recalled that moment, over his milk, he squirmed slightly. He must keep his mind on her crimes as a special adviser, not on her peccadilloes as a personality. This he found difficult to do, in spite of entering an objection and sustaining it. The faults of the woman as a woman kept chattering on in his mind like an unruly witness. She had, for almost two years now, baited him. In the halls, in the elevator, even in his own office, into which she romped now and then like a circus horse, she was constantly shouting these silly questions at him. "Are you lifting the oxcart out of the ditch? Are you tearing up the pea patch? Are you hollering down the rain barrel? Are you scraping around the bottom of the pickle barrel? Are you sitting in the catbird seat?"

4   It was Joey Hart, one of Mr. Martin's two assistants, who had explained what the gibberish meant. "She must be a Dodger fan," he had said. "Red Barber announces the Dodger games over the radio and he uses those expressions—picked 'em up down South." Joey had gone on to explain one or two. "Tearing up the pea patch" meant going on a rampage; "sitting in the catbird seat" meant sitting pretty, like a batter with three balls and no strikes on him. Mr. Martin dismissed all this with an effort. It had been annoying, it had driven him near to distraction, but he was too solid a man to be moved to murder by anything so childish. It was fortunate, he reflected as he passed on to the important charges against Mrs. Barrows, that he had stood up under it so well. He had maintained always an outward appearance of polite tolerance. "Why, I even believe you like the woman," Miss Paird, his other assistant, had once said to him. He had simply smiled.

5   A gavel rapped in Mr. Martin's mind and the case proper was resumed. Mrs. Ulgine Barrows stood charged with willful, blatant, and persistent attempts to destroy the efficiency and system of F & S. It was competent, material, and relevant to review her advent and rise to power. Mr. Martin had got the story from Miss Paird, who seemed always able to find things out. According to her, Mrs. Barrows had met Mr. Fitweiler at a party, where she had rescued him from the embraces of a powerfully built drunken man who had mistaken the president of F & S for a famous retired Middle Western football coach. She had led him to a sofa and somehow worked upon him a monstrous magic. The aging gentleman had jumped to the conclusion there and then that this was a woman of singular attainments, equipped to bring out the best in him and in the firm. A week later he had introduced her into F & S as his special adviser. On that day confusion got its foot in the door. After Miss Tyson, Mr. Brundage, and Mr. Bartlett had been fired and Mr. Munson had taken his hat and stalked out, mailing in his resignation later, old Roberts had been emboldened to speak to Mr. Fitweiler. He mentioned that Mr. Munson's department had been "a little disrupted" and hadn't they perhaps better resume the old system there? Mr. Fitweiler had said certainly not. He had the greatest faith in Mrs. Barrows' ideas. "They require a little seasoning, a little seasoning, is all," he had added. Mr. Roberts had given it up. Mr. Martin

reviewed in detail all the changes wrought by Mrs. Barrows. She had begun chipping at the cornices of the firm's edifice and now she was swinging at the foundation stones with a pickaxe.

6   Mr. Martin came now, in his summing up, to the afternoon of Monday, November 2, 1942—just one week ago. On that day, at 3 P. M., Mrs. Barrows had bounced into his office. "Boo!" she had yelled. "Are you scraping around the bottom of the pickle barrel?" Mr. Martin had looked at her from under his green eyeshade, saying nothing. She had begun to wander about the office, taking it in with her great, popping eyes. "Do you really need all these filing cabinets?" she had demanded suddenly. Mr. Martin's heart had jumped. "Each of these files," he had said, keeping his voice even, "plays an indispensable part in the system of F & S." She had brayed at him, "Well, don't tear up the pea patch!" and gone to the door. From there she had bawled, "But you sure have got a lot of fine scrap in here!" Mr. Martin could no longer doubt that the finger was on his beloved department. Her pickaxe was on the upswing, poised for the first blow. It had not come yet; he had received no blue memo from the enchanted Mr. Fitweiler bearing nonsensical instructions deriving from the obscene woman. But there was no doubt in Mr. Martin's mind that one would be forthcoming. He must act quickly. Already a precious week had gone by. Mr. Martin stood up in his living room, still holding his milk glass. "Gentlemen of the jury" he said to himself, "I demand the death penalty for this horrible person."

7   The next day Mr. Martin followed his routine, as usual. He polished his glasses more often and once sharpened an already sharp pencil, but not even Miss Paird noticed. Only once did he catch sight of his victim; she swept past him in the hall with a patronizing "Hi!" At five-thirty he walked home, as usual, and had a glass of milk, as usual. He had never drunk anything stronger in his life—unless you could count ginger ale. The late Sam Schlosser, the S of F & S, had praised Mr. Martin at a staff meeting several years before for his temperate habits. "Our most efficient worker neither drinks nor smokes," he had said. "The results speak for themselves." Mr. Fitweiler had sat by, nodding approval.

8   Mr. Martin was still thinking about that red-letter day as he walked over to the Schrafft's on Fifth Avenue near Forty-sixth Street. He got there, as he always did, at eight o'clock. He finished his dinner and the financial page of the Sun at a quarter to nine, as he always did. It was his custom after dinner to take a walk. This time he walked down Fifth Avenue at a casual pace. His gloved hands felt moist and warm, his forehead cold. He transferred the Camels from his overcoat to a jacket pocket. He wondered, as he did so, if they did not represent an unnecessary note of strain. Mrs. Barrows smoked only Luckies. It was his idea to puff a few puffs on a Camel (after the rubbing-out), stub it out in the ashtray holding her lipstick-stained Luckies, and thus drag a small red herring across the trail. Perhaps it was not a good idea. It would take time. He might even choke, too loudly.

9   Mr. Martin had never seen the house on West Twelfth Street where Mrs. Barrows lived, but he had a clear enough picture of it. Fortunately, she had

bragged to everybody about her ducky first-floor apartment in the perfectly darling three-story red-brick. There would be no doorman or other attendants; just the tenants of the second and third floors. As he walked along, Mr. Martin realized that he would get there before nine-thirty. He had considered walking north on Fifth Avenue from Schrafft's to a point from which it would take him until ten o'clock to reach the house. At that hour people were less likely to be coming in or going out. But the procedure would have made an awkward loop in the straight thread of his casualness, and he had abandoned it. It was impossible to figure when people would be entering or leaving the house, anyway. There was a great risk at any hour. If he ran into anybody, he would simply have to place the rubbing-out of Ulgine Barrows in the inactive file forever. The same thing would hold true if there were someone in her apartment. In that case he would just say that he had been passing by, recognized her charming house, and thought to drop in.

10   It was eighteen minutes after nine when Mr. Martin turned into Twelfth Street. A man passed him, and a man and a woman, talking. There was no one within fifty paces when he came to the house, halfway down the block. He was up the steps and in the small vestibule in no time, pressing the bell under the card that said "Mrs. Ulgine Barrows." When the clicking in the lock started, he jumped forward against the door. He got inside fast, closing the door behind him. A bulb in a lantern hung from the hall ceiling on a chain seemed to give a monstrously bright light. There was nobody on the stair, which went up ahead of him along the left wall. A door opened down the hall in the wall on the right. He went toward it swiftly, on tiptoe.

11   "Well, for God's sake, look who's here!" bawled Mrs. Barrows, and her braying laugh rang out like the report of a shotgun. He rushed past her like a football tackle, bumping her. "Hey, quit shoving!" she said, closing the door behind them. They were in her living room, which seemed to Mr. Martin to be lighted by a hundred lamps. "What's after you?" she said. "You're as jumpy as a goat." He found he was unable to speak. His heart was wheezing in his throat. "I—yes," he finally brought out. She was jabbering and laughing as she started to help him off with his coat. "No, no," he said. "I'll put it here." He took it off and put it on a chair near the door. "Your hat and gloves, too," she said. "You're in a lady's house." He put his hat on top of the coat. Mrs. Barrows seemed larger than he had thought. He kept his gloves on. "I was passing by," he said. "I recognized—is there anyone here?" She laughed louder than ever. "No," she said, "we're all alone. You're as white as a sheet, you funny man. Whatever has come over you? I'll mix you a toddy." She started toward a door across the room. "Scotch-and-soda be all right? But say, you don't drink, do you?" She turned and gave him her amused look. Mr. Martin pulled himself together. "Scotch-and-soda will be all right," he heard himself say. He could hear her laughing in the kitchen.

12   Mr. Martin looked quickly around the living room for the weapon. He had counted on finding one there. There were andirons and a poker and something in a corner that looked like an Indian club. None of them would do. It couldn't be that way. He began to pace around. He came to a desk. On it lay a metal

paper knife with an ornate handle. Would it be sharp enough? He reached for it and knocked over a small brass jar. Stamps spilled out of it and it fell to the floor with a clatter. "Hey," Mrs. Barrows yelled from the kitchen, "are you tearing up the pea patch?" Mr. Martin gave a strange laugh. Picking up the knife, he tried its point against his left wrist. It was blunt. It wouldn't do.

13   When Mrs. Barrows reappeared, carrying two highballs, Mr. Martin, standing there with his gloves on, became acutely conscious of the fantasy he had wrought. Cigarettes in his pocket, a drink prepared for him—it was all too grossly improbable. It was more than that; it was impossible. Somewhere in the back of his mind a vague idea stirred, sprouted. "For heaven's sake, take off those gloves," said Mrs. Barrows. "I always wear them in the house," said Mr. Martin. The idea began to bloom, strange and wonderful. She put the glasses on a coffee table in front of a sofa and sat on the sofa. "Come over here, you odd little man," she said. Mr. Martin went over and sat beside her. It was difficult getting a cigarette out of the pack of Camels, but he managed it. She held a match for him, laughing. "Well," she said, handing him a drink, "this is perfectly marvelous. You with a drink and a cigarette."

14   Martin puffed, not too awkwardly, and took a gulp of the highball. "I drink and smoke all the time," he said. He clinked his glass against hers. "Here's nuts to that old windbag, Fitweiler," he said, and gulped again. The stuff tasted awful, but he made no grimace. "Really, Mr. Martin," she said, her voice and posture changing, "you are insulting our employer." Mrs. Barrows was now all special adviser to the president. "I am preparing a bomb," said Mr. Martin, "which will blow the old goat higher than hell." He had only had a little of the drink, which was not strong. It couldn't be that. "Do you take dope or something?" Mrs. Barrows asked coldly. "Heroin," said Mr. Martin. "I'll be coked to the gills when I bump that old buzzard off." "Mr. Martin!" she shouted, getting to her feet. "That will be all of that. You must go at once." Mr. Martin took another swallow of his drink. He tapped his cigarette out in the ashtray and put the pack of Camels on the coffee table. Then he got up. She stood glaring at him. He walked over and put on his hat and coat. "Not a word about this," he said, and laid an index finger against his lips. All Mrs. Barrows could bring out was "Really!" Mr. Martin put his hand on the doorknob. "I'm sitting in the catbird seat," he said. He stuck his tongue out at her and left. Nobody saw him go.

15   Mr. Martin got to his apartment, walking, well before eleven. No one saw him go in. He had two glasses of milk after brushing his teeth, and he felt elated. It wasn't tipsiness, because he hadn't been tipsy. Anyway, the walk had worn off all effects of the whiskey. He got in bed and read a magazine for a while. He was asleep before midnight.

16   Mr. Martin got to the office at eight-thirty the next morning, as usual. At a quarter to nine, Ulgine Barrows, who had never before arrived at work before ten, swept into his office. "I'm reporting to Mr. Fitweiler now!" she shouted. "If he turns you over to the police, it's no more than you deserve!" Mr. Martin gave her a look of shocked surprise. "I beg your pardon?" he said. Mrs. Barrows snorted and bounced out of the room, leaving Miss Paird and Joey

Hart staring after her. "What's the matter with that old devil now?" asked Miss Paird. "I have no idea," said Mr. Martin, resuming his work. The other two looked at him and then at each other. Miss Paird got up and went out. She walked slowly past the closed door of Mr. Fitweiler's office. Mrs. Barrows was yelling inside, but she was not braying. Miss Paird could not hear what the woman was saying. She went back to her desk.

17   Forty-five minutes later, Mrs. Barrows left the president's office and went into her own, shutting the door. It wasn't until half an hour later that Mr. Fitweiler sent for Mr. Martin. The head of the filing department, neat, quiet, attentive, stood in front of the old man's desk. Mr. Fitweiler was pale and nervous. He took his glasses off and twiddled them. He made a small, bruffing sound in his throat. "Martin," he said, "you have been with us more than twenty years." "Twenty-two, sir," said Mr. Martin. "In that time," pursued the president, "your work and your—uh—manner have been exemplary." "I trust so, sir," said Mr. Martin. "I have understood, Martin," said Mr. Fitweiler, "that you have never taken a drink or smoked." "That is correct, sir," said Mr. Martin. "Ah, yes." Mr. Fitweiler polished his glasses. "You may describe what you did after leaving the office yesterday, Martin," he said. Mr. Martin allowed less than a second for his bewildered pause. "Certainly, sir," he said. "I walked home. Then I went to Schrafft's for dinner. Afterward I walked home again. I went to bed early, sir, and read a magazine for a while. I was asleep before eleven." "Ah, yes," said Mr. Fitweiler again. He was silent for a moment, searching for the proper words to say to the head of the filing department. "Mrs. Barrows," he said finally, "Mrs. Barrows has worked hard, Martin, very hard. It grieves me to report that she has suffered a severe breakdown. It has taken the form of a persecution complex accompanied by distressing hallucinations." "I am very sorry, sir," said Mr. Martin. "Mrs. Barrows is under the delusion," continued Mr. Fitweiler, "that you visited her last evening and behaved yourself in an—uh—unseemly manner." He raised his hand to silence Mr. Martin's little pained outcry. "It is the nature of these psychological diseases," Mr. Fitweiler said, "to fix upon the least likely and most innocent party as the—uh—source of persecution. These matters are not for the lay mind to grasp, Martin. I've just had my psychiatrist, Dr. Fitch, on the phone. He would not, of course, commit himself, but he made enough generalizations to substantiate my suspicions. I suggested to Mrs. Barrows, when she had completed her—uh—story to me this morning, that she visit Dr. Fitch, for I suspected a condition at once. She flew, I regret to say, into a rage, and demanded—uh—requested that I call you on the carpet. You may not know, Martin, but Mrs. Barrows had planned a reorganization of your department—subject to my approval, of course, subject to my approval. This brought you, rather than anyone else, to her mind—but again that is a phenomenon for Dr. Fitch and not for us. So, Martin, I am afraid Mrs. Barrows' usefulness here is at an end." "I am dreadfully sorry, sir," said Mr. Martin.

18   It was at this point that the door to the office blew open with the suddenness of a gas-main explosion and Mrs. Barrows catapulted through it. "Is the little rat denying it?" she screamed. "He can't get away with that!" Mr. Martin

got up and moved discreetly to a point beside Mr. Fitweiler's chair. "You drank and smoked at my apartment," she bawled at Mr. Martin, "and you know it! You called Mr. Fitweiler an old windbag and said you were going to blow him up when you got coked to the gills on your heroin!" She stopped yelling to catch her breath and a new glint came into her popping eyes. "If you weren't such a drab, ordinary little man," she said, "I'd think you'd planned it all. Sticking your tongue out, saying you were sitting in the catbird seat, because you thought no one would believe me when I told it! My God, it's really too perfect!" She glared at Mr. Fitweiler. "Can't you see how he has tricked us, you old fool? Can't you see his little game?" But Mr. Fitweiler had been surreptitiously pressing all the buttons under the top of his desk and employees of F & S began pouring into the room. "Stockton," said Mr. Fitweiler, "you and Fishbein will take Mrs. Barrows to her home. Mrs. Powell, you will go with them." Stockton, who had played a little football in high school, blocked Mrs. Barrows as she made for Mr. Martin. It took him and Fishbein together to force her out of the door into the hall, crowded with stenographers and office boys. She was still screaming imprecations at Mr. Martin, tangled and contradictory imprecations. The hubbub finally died out down the corridor.

19   "I regret that this has happened," said Mr. Fitweiler. "I shall ask you to dismiss it from your mind, Martin." "Yes, sir," said Mr. Martin, anticipating his chief's "That will be all" by moving to the door. "I will dismiss it." He went out and shut the door, and his step was light and quick in the hall. When he entered his department he had slowed down to his customary gait, and he walked quietly across the room to the W20 file, wearing a look of studious concentration.

∼

(3,827 words)

VOCABULARY

fallible (2)	appalled (3)	peccadilloes (3)
romped (3)	gibberish (4)	edifice (5)
indispensable (6)	obscene (6)	patronizing (7)
temperate (7)	red herring (8)	ducky (9)
monstrously (10)	wheezing (11)	grossly (13)
bruffing (17)	exemplary (17)	hallucinations (17)
unseemly (17)	catapulted (18)	surreptitiously (18)
imprecations (18)		

THE FACTS

1. What is the origin of the colorful expressions that Mrs. Barrows constantly uses?

2. What is Mrs. Barrow's title in the firm of F & S?

3. Why does Mr. Martin finally decide to "rub out" Mrs. Barrows?

4. What shocking disclosures does Mr. Martin reveal to Mrs. Barrows on his surprise visit to her apartment?

5. What is the outcome of Mrs. Barrows's accusations against Mr. Martin?

THE STRATEGIES

1. The organization of the story falls naturally into four divisions: (a) the trial and verdict of Mrs. Barrows, (b) preparation for the crime, (c) change of plan and perpetration of the crime, and (d) result of the crime. Summarize what happens in each of these segments.

2. Early in the story, the author tells us that Mr. Martin plans to kill Mrs. Barrows. Why does this announcement not eliminate suspense from the story?

3. What is the emotional climax of the story?

4. How does Thurber prepare us for Mr. Fitweiler's incredulous reaction to Mrs. Barrows's story about Mr. Martin? Why are we amused but not surprised at Mr. Fitweiler's reaction?

THE ISSUES

1. What obvious contrasts between Mr. Martin and Mrs. Barrows does Thurber draw?

2. What is your view of the morality of Mr. Martin's actions? Was he justified in his extreme steps or not?

3. How does Mrs. Barrows's character reinforce an ancient sexual stereotype about women? How would you characterize this stereotype?

4. If this story were set in an office today rather than in the 1940s, would it be as believable? Why or why not?

5. Reverse the characters of Mrs. Barrows and Mr. Martin: She is now the fastidious head of the filing department; he the brassy opportunist who has ingratiated himself in the good graces of the boss, Fitweiler. Does the story still work? Why or why not?

SUGGESTIONS FOR WRITING

1. Write a short caricature about one of your close friends and exaggerate his or her traits.

2. Write an essay analyzing the humorous devices used by Thurber in the story *The Catbird Seat*. Pay attention to such factors as character, plot reversal, and style.

THAT TIME OF YEAR (SONNET 73)

William Shakespeare

William Shakespeare (1564–1616) is generally acknowledged as the great-est literary genius of the English language. Born in Stratford-on-Avon, Eng-land, he was the son of a prosperous businessman, and probably attended grammar schools in his native town. In 1582, Shakespeare married Anne Hathaway, who was eight years his senior, and who bore him three children. The legacy of his writing includes 36 plays, 154 sonnets, and 5 long poems.

The English or Shakespearean sonnet is composed of three quatrains of four lines each and a concluding couplet of two, rhyming abab cdcd efef gg. There is usually a correspondence between the units marked off by the rhymes and the develop-ment of the thought. The three quatrains, for instance, may represent three differ-ent images or three questions from which a conclusion is drawn in the final couplet. As a result, the sonnet is one of the most tightly organized poetic forms used.

~

     That time of year thou mayst in me behold
     When yellow leaves, or none, or few, do hang
     Upon those boughs which shake against the cold,
     Bare ruined choirs where late the sweet birds sang.
     In me thou see'st the twilight of such day
5   As after sunset fadeth in the west,
     Which by and by black night doth take away,
     Death's second self, that seals up all in rest.
     In me thou see'st the glowing of such fire,
     That on the ashes of his youth doth lie
10 As the deathbed whereon it must expire,
     Consumed with that which it was nourished by.
     This thou perceivest, which makes thy love more strong,
     To love that well which thou must leave ere long.

~

(121 words)

THE FACTS

1. What image does the poet focus on in the first quatrain? What relationship does this image have to the speaker?
2. The speaker shifts to another image in the second quatrain. What is it, and what relationship does it bear to him?
3. Yet another image is introduced in the third quatrain. What is the image, and how does it relate to the speaker? What rather complex philosophical paradox is involved?
4. The final couplet states the poet's thesis (or theme). What is that thesis? State it in your own words.

THE STRATEGIES

1. The entire poem is organized around three analogies. State them in three succinct sentences.

2. The three images in the poem are presented in a particular order. Do you see any reason for this order?

3. In lines 3 and 4, what effect do the words "cold,/Bare ruined choirs" have on the rhythm and meter?

4. In line 2, what would be the result of substituting "hang" for "do hang"?

5. What is the antecedent of "this" in line 13?

THE ISSUES

1. What can you deduce from this poem about the speaker and his frame of mind?

2. Someone once said, "Youth is wasted on the young." How might that witticism be applied to this poem?

3. Why should a student whose major is, say, business and who has no interest whatsoever in literature be forced to take classes in which poems such as this one are studied?

4. Shakespeare has been called surprisingly modern in his outlook. What about this poem would seem to justify that observation?

SUGGESTIONS FOR WRITING

1. In two or three well-developed paragraphs, answer the question, "What is the single worst aspect of old age?"

2. Write an essay in which you outline the way you plan to make your own old age as pleasant and fulfilling as possible.

CHAPTER WRITING ASSIGNMENTS

1. Write a well-organized essay describing your study habits and methods.

2. Write a well-organized chronological autobiography.

3. Write an essay detailing the steps you follow when you have to complete a writing assignment.

4. Detail in a tightly organized essay any particular procedure or process (e.g., how to tune a car engine) with which you are intimately familiar.

WRITING ASSIGNMENTS FOR A SPECIFIC AUDIENCE

1. Write an essay of appreciation directed at your favorite teacher— from any grade—telling how he or she affected your life.

2. Write an essay, after doing the necessary research, telling an audience of high-school drop-outs the opportunities available to them for continuing their education.

COLLABORATIVE WRITING PROJECT

In teams of three, survey the incidence of drug use among a separate and specific segment of your college population. (For example, one team can focus on business majors, another on sociology majors, and so on.) After meeting with the three teams to compare the results, each team should write an essay on its findings.

———— REAL-LIFE ————
STUDENT WRITING
NOTE FROM A GRADUATE STUDENT
TO A DEPARTMENT SECRETARY

The following note was written by a student named Jennifer, who is in the graduate school program of a well-known Catholic university. Katie is the department secretary of the business school. Jennifer is writing to Katie to ask for her help in getting registered in a statistics class. Notice the polite social remarks Jennifer makes before saying what she really wants. Jeff is Katie's new husband. Bailey is Jennifer's boyfriend.

Hi Katie!

Welcome back from your honeymoon! Hope married life is treating you well. Bailey said he ran into ya'll last night, and Jeff's wig was realistically scary. Wish I could have seen it.

Lucinda sent me to you on an issue I'm having. I keep trying to register for classes in the business school for next quarter, but the system won't let me in! Lucinda said something about how they've changed their criteria. I wonder if I could be using the wrong password. I heard it was due to be changed, but I haven't seen any memo telling us that it had been. Meantime, I need to register for business statistics ASAP! As department secretary, you're my last hope.

Can you help me?

Thanks!
Jennifer

6

Developing Paragraphs

EDITORS' COUNSEL

From ancient times, the primary use of the paragraph has been to signal the introduction of a new idea or the further development of an old one. Here is an example of a paragraph signaling a new idea:

> In the modern formal bullfight or "corrida de toros" there are usually six bulls that are killed by three different men. Each man kills two bulls. The bulls by law are required to be from four to five years old, free from physical defects, and well armed with sharp-pointed horns. They are inspected by a municipal veterinary surgeon before the fight. The veterinary is supposed to reject bulls that are under age, insufficiently armed or with anything wrong with their eyes, their horns or any apparent disease or visible bodily defects such as lameness.
>
> The men who are to kill them are called matadors and which of the six bulls they are to kill is determined by lot. Each matador, or killer, has a caudrilla, or team, of from five to six men who are paid by him and work under his orders. Three of these men, who aid him on foot with capes and at his orders place the banderillas, three-foot wooden sharps with harpoon points, are called peones or banderilleros. The other two, who are mounted on horses when they appear in the ring, are called picadors.
>
> —Ernest Hemingway, *The Bullfight*

The shift in discussion between the first and second paragraph is obvious: Paragraph 1 is about the bulls; paragraph 2 is about the men who will fight and kill them.

A second use of the paragraph is to add significantly to or elaborate on what has been said in a preceding paragraph. Here is an example:

> The oxen in Africa have carried the heavy load of the advance of European civilization. Wherever new land has been broken they have broken it, panting and pulling knee-deep in the soil before the ploughs, the long whips in the air over them. Where a road has been made they have made it; and they have trudged the iron and tools through the land, to the yelling and shouting of the drivers, by tracks in the dust and the long grass of the plains, before there ever were any roads. They have been inspanned before daybreak, and have sweated up and down the long hills, and across dungas and riverbeds, through the burning hours

of the day. The whips have marked their sides, and you will often see oxen that have had an eye, or both of them, taken away by the long cutting whip-lashes. The waggon-oxen of many Indian and white contractors worked every day, all their lives through, and did not know of the Sabbath.

It is a strange thing that we have done to the oxen. The bull is in a constant stage of fury, rolling his eyes, shovelling up the earth, upset by everything that gets within his range of vision—still he has got a life of his own, fire comes from his nostrils, and new life from his loins; his days are filled with his vital cravings and satisfactions. All of that we have taken away from the oxen, and in reward we have claimed their existence for ourselves. The oxen walk along within our own daily life, pulling hard all the time, creatures without a life, things made for our use. They have moist, limpid, violet eyes, soft muzzles, silky ears, they are patient and dull in all their ways; sometimes they look as if they were thinking about things.

—Isak Dinesen, *Out of Africa*

In the first paragraph the author points out that oxen have played a key role in civilizing the African continent. In the second paragraph she elaborates on the first by reminding us that the oxen's patient subservience has come at a price.

Parts of the Paragraph

A paragraph generally consists of two main parts: a topic sentence and specific details that support it.

The Topic Sentence   This is the sentence that tells us what the writer intends to propose, argue, or demonstrate. Here's an example:

<u>To all English-speaking peoples the Bible is a national as well as a noble monument, for much of their history is securely rooted and anchored within it.</u> In 17th century England it nurtured the Puritan revolt and paved the way for the Bill of Rights. In 17th and 18th century America it supplied not only the names of our ancestors but the stout precepts by which they lived. They walked by its guidance; their rough places were made plain by their trust in its compassionate promises. It was a lamp to their feet and a light to their path, a pillar of cloud by day and of fire by night. It was the source of the convictions that shaped the building of this country, of the faith that endured the first New England winters and later opened up the Great West. It laid the foundations of our educational system, built our earliest colleges, and dictated the training within our homes. In the words alike of Jefferson and Patrick Henry, John Quincy Adams and Franklin it made better and more useful citizens to their country by reminding a man of his individual responsibility, his own dignity, and his equality with his fellow man. The Bible is, indeed, so imbedded in our American heritage that not to recognize its place there becomes a kind of national apostasy, and not to know and understand it, in these days when we give all for its principles of human worth and human freedom, an act unworthy of us as a people.

—Mary Ellen Chase, *The Bible and the Common Reader*

The topic sentence of this paragraph is underlined.

Implied Topic Sentences   Some paragraphs have an *implied topic sentence*, also known as a *controlling idea*. Here is an example:

> At graveside, the casket is lowered into the earth. This office, once the prerogative of friends of the deceased, is now performed by a patented mechanical lowering device. A "Lifetime Green" artificial grass mat is at the ready to conceal the sere earth, and overhead, to conceal the sky, is a portable Steril Chapel Tent ("resists the intense heat and humidity of summer and the terrific storms of winter. . . . available in Silver Grey, Rose or Evergreen"). Now is the time for the ritual scattering of earth over the coffin, as the solemn words "earth to earth, ashes to ashes, dust to dust" are pronounced by the officiating cleric. This can be accomplished "with a mere flick of the wrist with the Gordon Leak-proof Earth Dispenser. No grasping of a handful of dirt, no soiled fingers. Simple, dignified, beautiful, reverent! The modern way!" The Gordon Earth Dispenser (at $5) is of nickel-plated brass construction. It is not only "attractive to the eye and long wearing"; it is also "one of the 'tools' for building better public relations" if presented as "an appropriate noncommercial gift" to the clergyman. It is shaped something like a saltshaker.
>
> —Jessica Mitford, *The American Way of Death*

The controlling idea of this paragraph is that the funeral industry is guilty of vulgar commercialism. The details amply support that point, and the writer's focus is clear even though she uses no topic sentence. A writer does not have to telegraph a paragraph's meaning in an explicit topic sentence so long as all its details are linked by some organizing theme or focus.

Supporting Details

Good paragraphs are filled with supporting facts, instances, examples, and details. They make a point and then adequately support it. They do not circle the subject, nor do they repeat at the same level of generality what the writer has already said. Here are two examples. We made up the first example as a dramatic illustration of the repetitive writing we often find in bad paragraphs, where the main point is restated over and over at the same level of generality:

> Rotten writing is scarcely a new problem. People have always had bad handwriting. Some old manuscripts are difficult to read because they are so badly written. Old letters are also indecipherable. Some writing from the past looks as if a drunken chicken had walked over it. Strain as much as you might, you just can't tell what the writer meant. Inscriptions of various kinds are just as impossible to read.

Has the point of this paragraph—that "rotten writing is scarcely a new problem"—been proved? It has not. The paragraph simply says that people have always written badly but gives no concrete instances or facts to make this assertion believable.

Here, on the other hand, is a paragraph that begins with the same generalization and then proves it with examples drawn from history:

> Rotten writing is scarcely a new problem. Napoleon's script was so miserable that one of his generals once mistook a letter of his for battle orders. Charles Hamilton, a Manhattan dealer in autographs and manuscripts, contends that Gertrude Stein's oblique prose style may be explained by the fact that compositors often misread her cryptic script. Poet William Butler Yeats often could not read his own work. Horace Greeley, the editor of the old New York *Tribune*, had a notoriously illegible scrawl. He once scribbled a note to a reporter telling him that he was fired for incompetence; so indecipherable was the missive that for years afterwards the man was able to pass it off as a letter of recommendation.
>
> —"Nowadays, Writing Is Off the Wall," *Time*, January 1, 1980

Paragraphs with a Final Summing Up Sentence   Some paragraphs begin and end with a generalization. The first generalization is the topic sentence; the second is a summary. Here is an example:

> A language changes because things happen to people. If we could imagine the impossible-a society in which nothing happened—there would be no changes in language. But except possibly in a cemetery, things are constantly happening to people: they eat, drink, sleep, talk, make love, meet strangers, struggle against natural perils, and fight against one another. They slowly adapt their language to meet the changing conditions of their lives. Although the changes made in one generation may be small, those made in a dozen generations may enormously affect the language. The big and little phases of history-fashions, fads, inventions, the influence of a leader, a war or two, an invasion or two, travel to a foreign land, the demands of business intercourse-may alter a language so much that a Rip Van Winkle who slept two or three hundred years might have trouble making himself understood when he awoke. Even in a relatively quiet society, linguistic change proceeds inexorably.
>
> —J. N. Hook and E. G. Mathews, *Modern American Grammar and Usage*

Topic Sentence Developed Over More Than One Paragraph

A single topic sentence can also be developed over the course of two or more paragraphs. This development usually occurs when the topic sentence is too broad or complex to be adequately covered in a single paragraph or when the presentation of supporting details in several paragraphs is more emphatic. The following is an example of a topic sentence developed over two paragraphs. The topic sentence is underlined:

> There has always been something so fascinating about the mere fact of fatness that men of all nations and of many degrees of wisdom or lack of it have

formulated opinions on its state, its origins, and its correction. Shakespeare's characters are at their most eloquent when the topic is obesity. "Make less thy body and hence more thy grace. Leave gormandizing. Know the grave cloth gape for thee thrice wider than for other men." And, of course, to Julius Caesar, the Bard attributed the notion of the harmlessness of fat companions in warning against "the lean and hungry look" of "yon Cassius."

In *Coming Up for Air,* George Orwell has the narrator, himself a fat man, sum it up: "They all think a fat man isn't quite like other men. He goes through life on a light-comedy plane . . . as low farce." Sometimes the situation is just as sad and much less tolerable. When W. D. Howells was consul at Venice, he was told by a tall, lanky man, "If I were as fat as you, I would hang myself." And Osborn in his otherwise lightly satirical picture-essay, *The Vulgarians,* pontificates, "The fat and the fatuous are interchangeable."

—Jean Mayer, *Overweight: Causes, Cost, and Control*

Covering a topic sentence in more than one paragraph allows for a fuller development of the general idea, but it also tempts the writer to stray from the point. Beginning writers will find it safer to use a separate topic sentence for each paragraph.

Position of the Topic Sentence

As the sum of what a paragraph is about, the topic sentence should naturally occupy a prominent position, and in all of our examples so far, the topic sentence has come first. Such a paragraph is said to be organized from the general to the particular: the idea first followed by the particulars. The reverse of this arrangement is the paragraph organized from the particular to the general: The supporting details come first and the topic sentence last. Here is an example:

The human population already stands at over 4 billion, and at current growth rates that number will double within thirty-eight years. If the growth rate were to continue unchecked, in fact, the global population would reach about 150 billion within two centuries. Yet nearly two-thirds of the existing inhabitants of the earth are undernourished or malnourished, and they are dying of starvation at the rate of more than 10 million every year. There can be little question that unchecked population growth is the most critical social problem in the modern world, with potential consequences in terms of sheer human misery that are almost unimaginable.

—Ian Robertson, *Sociology*

This arrangement is an uncommon one and somewhat mannered. Before you can cite details in support of an idea, you must first know the idea. Consequently, it has become traditional for writers to first state the general idea of a paragraph and then cite details in support of it—this pattern conforms to the way people usually think. The paragraph in which the topic sentence appears after the supporting details should be used only as a change of pace, not as a matter of course.

Finally, some paragraphs have topic sentences that come not first or last, but second or third. Paragraphs of this kind are usually found in the middle of an essay. The initial sentences are used to ensure a smooth transition from the preceding paragraph, and then the topic sentence makes its appearance. Here is an example:

> In our own *way*, we conform as best as we can to the rest of nature. <u>The obit-</u><u>uary pages tell us of the news that we are dying off, while the birth announce-</u><u>ments in finer print, off at the side of the page, inform us of our replacements,</u><u>but we get no grasp from this of the enormity of scale.</u> There are 3 billion of us on the earth, and all 3 billion must be dead, on schedule, within this lifetime. The vast mortality, involving something over 50 million of us each year, takes place in relative secrecy. We can only really know of the deaths in our house-holds, or among our friends. These, detached in our minds from the rest, we take to be unnatural events, anomalies, outrages. We speak of our own dead in low voices; struck down, we say, as though visible death can only occur for cause, by disease, or violence, avoidably. We send off flowers, grieve, make cer-emonies, scatter bones, unaware of the rest of the 3 billion on the same sched-ule. All that immense mass of flesh and bone and consciousness will disappear by absorption into the earth, without recognition by the transient survivors.
>
> —Lewis Thomas, *Death in the Open*

The first sentence is for transition—to connect this paragraph with the one before. The second sentence is the topic sentence. It contains the assertion that the supporting details prove.

Paragraph Patterns

Paragraphs are often written to conform to certain abstract patterns that are partly rhetorical and partly based on some common operations of thinking. You might, for example, write a paragraph drawing a contrast between two animals, two objects, or two people. Or, you might write a paragraph ex-plaining why an incident occurred or predicting what is likely to happen if something is done or left undone. In the first case, you would develop the paragraph by a pattern of comparison and contrast; in the second, by one of causal analysis.

In part II of this book, we will focus extensively on how to write para-graphs by these common patterns. We will explain the paragraph-writing techniques used to compare and contrast, analyze cause, narrate, describe, il-lustrate, define, classify, and explain process. But for now, we mention these patterns to emphasize this point: No matter what its developmental pattern, any paragraph you write must support its main idea with specific details.

Characteristics of a Well-Designed Paragraph

The characteristics of the well-designed paragraph are *unity, coherence,* and *completeness.*

Unity   A paragraph is said to have *unity* when its sentences stick to the topic and do not stray to secondary issues or deal with irrelevancies. Here's an example of a paragraph that lacks unity:

> (1) A fairy tale is a serious story with a human hero and a happy ending. (2) The hero in a fairy tale is different from the hero in a tragedy in that his progression is from bad to good fortune, rather than the reverse. (3) <u>In the Greek tragedy "Oedipus Rex," for example, the hero goes from highest fortune to lowest misery, but in the end he recognizes his error in judgment and maintains a noble posture despite profound suffering. (4) The audience watching him is purged of pity and fear through what Aristotle labeled a "catharsis."</u> (5) The hero in a fairy tale usually has a miserable beginning. (6) He is either socially obscure or despised as being stupid and lacking in heroic virtues. (7) But in the end, he has surprised everyone by demonstrating his courage, consequently winning fame, riches, and love. (8) We clearly see this bad-to-good-fortune progress in stories like "Cinderella," "Sleeping Beauty," and "The Frog Prince."

The topic sentence of the paragraph promises to give a definition of a fairy tale, but part of the paragraph drifts away from the definition. Sentences 3 and 4 are entirely beside the point. With the fifth sentence, the writer resumes the announced intent of the paragraph—to define a fairy tale.

The possible causes of this fault are several. Some digressions can be traced to a writer's daydreaming; some to boredom with the topic on hand; some to a desire to impress the reader by introducing an interesting but irrelevant point. The cure is not easy to prescribe. The inexperienced writer needs to remember that the purpose of the paragraph is announced in the topic sentence, and it is this purpose that the other sentences of the paragraph must carry out.

Coherence   A paragraph has *coherence* when its sentences are logically connected. However, sentences are not automatically linked simply because they follow one after another on the page. Four devices can be used to ensure paragraph coherence:

1. Transitional words and phrases
2. Pronoun reference
3. Repeated key terms
4. Parallelism

Transitional words and phrases, which point out the direction of the paragraph, are used to link sentences. Here are examples, underlined;

> In addition to the academic traditionalism in schools, there are other problems. First, there is the problem of coordinating education with the realities of the work. Second, there is the question of how long the schooling period should be. Despite evidence to the contrary, a case can be made for the notion that we not only overeducate our children, but also take too long to do it.

The underlined words and phrases add coherence to the passage. They join sentences and, consequently, ideas in clear and logical relationships. Without the use of transitional words and phrases, the writing would seem choppy and the relationships between sentences unclear.

Coherence can also be achieved by *pronoun reference.* A noun is used in one sentence or clause and a pronoun that refers to it is used in the next sentence or clause. In the following paragraph the pronouns so used are underlined:

> Twenty years ago women were a majority of the population, but they were treated like a minority group. The prejudice against them was so deep-rooted that, paradoxically, most people pretended that it did not exist. Indeed, most women preferred to ignore the situation than to rock the boat. They accepted being paid less for doing the same work as a man. They were as quick as any male to condemn a woman who ventured outside the limits of the roles men had assigned to females: those of toy and drudge.

Key terms may be repeated throughout the paragraph to link sentences. The key terms in the following paragraph are underlined:

> Fantasy is not restricted to one sector of the southern California way of life; it is all pervasive. Los Angeles restaurants and their parking lots are such million-dollar structures because they are palaces of fantasy in which the upward-moving individual comes to act out a self-mythology he or she has learned from a hero of the mass media. Often enough, the establishments of La Cienega Boulevard's Restaurant Row are fantasies of history in their very architecture.

Parallelism is also used to ensure coherence, although not nearly so often as any of the other three devices. The principle behind parallelism is that similar ideas are expressed in structurally similar sentences. Here is a paragraph that uses parallelism to ensure coherence:

> Now, I will not for a moment deny that getting ahead of your neighbor is delightful, but it is not the only delight of which human beings are capable. There are innumerable things which are not competitive. It is possible to enjoy food and drink without having to reflect that you have a better cook and a better wine merchant than your former friends whom you are learning to cold-shoulder. It is possible to be fond of your wife and children without reflecting how much better she dresses than Mrs. So-and-So and how much better they are at athletics than the children of that old stick-in-the-mud Mr. Such-and-Such. There are

those who can enjoy music without thinking how cultured the other ladies in their women's club will be thinking them. There are even people who enjoy a fine day in spite of the fact that the sun shines on everybody. All these simple pleasures are destroyed as soon as competitiveness gets the upper hand.

—Bertrand Russell, *The Unhappy American Way*

The repetition of "It is possible" and "There are" add bridges that smoothly connect one thought with another.

Completeness   A paragraph is complete when it has provided enough details to support its topic sentence. A paragraph is incomplete when the topic sentence is not developed or when it is merely extended through repetition. In either case, the reader is burdened with useless generalizations. The following paragraph is incomplete:

> Withholding tax is a bad way to go about collecting taxes from the people in our country because this system assumes that the American people are incompetent.

This paragraph hints at an argument but then comes to a dead stop. The reader will automatically ask, "In what way or by what means does tax withholding assume that the American people are incompetent?" Without further evidence, the paragraph goes nowhere. Now read the following paragraph:

> Withholding is a bad way to go about collecting tax money, even though the figures may show that it gets results. It is bad because it implies that the individual is incapable of handling his own affairs. The government as much as says, We know that, if left to your own devices, you will fritter away your worldly goods, and tax *day* will catch you without cash. Or it says, We're not sure you'll come clean in your return, so we will just take the money before it reaches you, and you will be saved the trouble and fuss of being honest. This implication is an unhealthy thing to spread around, being contrary to the old American theory that the individual is a very competent little guy indeed. The whole setup of our democratic government assumes that the citizen is bright, honest, and at least as fundamentally sound as a common stock. If you start treating him as something less than that, you are going to get into deep water. The device of withholding tax money, which is clearly confiscatory, since the individual is not allowed to see, taste, or touch a certain percentage of his wages, tacitly brands him as negligent or unthrifty or immature or incompetent or dishonest, or all of those things at once. There is, furthermore, a bad psychological effect in earning money that you never get your paws on. We believe this effect to be much stronger than the government realizes. At any rate, if the American individual is in truth incapable of paying his tax all by himself, then he should certainly be regarded as incapable of voting all by himself, and the Secretary of the Treasury should accompany him into the booth to show him where to put the X.

—E. B. White, *Withholding*

While the reader may not agree with these ideas, the writer has fulfilled his promise to show why he does not like withholding tax. He has provided clear examples and has moved from the general to the specific, keeping in mind the direction of his topic sentence. His paragraph is complete. Make your own paragraphs complete by providing enough detail to support their topic sentences.

It is an essential part of a writer's job to dig up the details necessary to make an essay complete. One source of such details, of course, is the library. Another is the Internet and its various electronic databases. A particularly useful database is *Infotrac College Edition,* offered in a free four-month trial to anyone who purchases this text book. *Infotrac College Edition* gives the student 24-hour access to thousands of articles stored electronically through the magic of computers. See the offer that comes with this book.

Writing Your Own Paragraphs

There is no mystery to writing good paragraphs. Begin with a topic sentence that states your opinion or proposes an idea. Back up this sentence with ample supporting details. Stick to the point of the topic sentence. Insert transitions as necessary to keep the text coherent. That, in a nutshell, is all there is to it.

The problems that arise with paragraph writing are usually problems of content rather than of technique. In other words, the writing is affected by the fact that the writer has not done the necessary research and does not understand the topic. Even gifted writers have difficulty writing on topics they know little about. Writing does not begin when you first sit down behind a keyboard. It actually begins when you begin to research your topic. If you are thoroughly grounded in the details of your topic, you'll find that writing paragraphs about it will be surprisingly easy.

EXERCISES

1. Write a suitable topic sentence for a paragraph that would contain the following supporting details:

   a. (1) Cultivate only the best writers.

      (2) You needn't assume that just because something is in print, it is well written.

      (3) If you fall into the habit of reading hacks or writers that have only a dulled sense for the right word, then you are not helping yourself to become a writer who is fresh and original.

      (4) Read those authors who appear in *The New Yorker,* who get good reviews in magazines like *Time,* and who haven't faded after writing one book or one play.

   b. (1) In primitive tribes this concern was limited to members of the tribe. If a man was not a member, one need not worry about whether one was behaving ethically or unethically toward him.

(2) But as man started reflecting on his own behavior and how it affected others, he slowly began to realize that his social concerns—his ethics—must include all human beings with whom he came in contact.

(3) Thus it can be said that a system of ethics evolved in order to ensure that man would be at peace with himself.

  c. (1) Vaccination for German measles has practically eradicated the incidence of birth defects and other complications resulting from that disease.

(2) Smallpox vaccination has been so effective that the virus lingers only in special labs.

(3) In the last thirty years, vaccines have all but wiped out polio in our country.

(4) While a few people fear that some new and terrible disease will crop up for which no vaccine will be powerful enough, we can rejoice in the fact that at least the major child killers of the past have been vanquished.

2. Provide four sentences of supporting details for each of the following topic sentences. (Make sure that the details are on a more specific level than is the topic sentence.)

  a. Many people treat their pets with a lack of respect.

  b. Buying items "on sale" often means buying lower quality.

  c. Advertising in good periodicals is a workable, dignified way to attract a mate. Or advertising for a mate, even in good periodicals, is unsafe and degrading.

  d. A long commute to work can have some advantages.

  e. Today's newspaper cartoons get to the heart of social concerns.

3. Choose one of the following topics and write a paragraph about it based on a controlling idea rather than on a topic sentence (see p. 165.)

  a. Summer camp for disabled children

  b. Typical class reunions

  c. Advantages of coming from a poor family or disadvantages of coming from an affluent family

  d. Stereotyping as revealed in movies

  e. Stopping pollution on an individual level

4. Select one sentence from the following pairs that more clearly consists of supporting details:

  a. (1) Much has been written about the afflictions of growing old.

    (2) The worst aspect of growing old is losing hearing and eyesight.

  b. (1) The average outfit for snow skiing costs $1,000.

(2) Some popular sports are so expensive that few people can afford to compete in them.

  c. (1) In Little Red Riding Hood the wolf pounces on the innocent little girl, devouring her.

(2) Children's fairy tales are filled with horrible violence.

  d. (1) Some women feel more comfortable being treated by a female rather than a male gynecologist.

(2) For many women who are modest to begin with, to be checked for such problems as uterine or breast cancer is less traumatic when the physician is also female.

  e. (1) Too many cooks today have no idea how to prepare homemade corn bread, meat casseroles from scratch, or freshly cooked garden peas.

(2) The market of "prepared" or "frozen" foods is replacing food that really tastes good with food that is barely appealing to the gourmet's taste buds.

5. In the following paragraphs, draw a line through any sentence that weakens paragraph unity.

  a. I agree with Thomas Jefferson that there is a natural aristocracy among human beings, based on virtue and talent. A natural aristocrat is a person who shows genuine concern for his fellow human beings and has the wisdom as well as ability to help them improve the quality of their lives. He is the kind of person to whom you would entrust your most important concerns because his decisions would be honest rather than self-serving. A natural aristocrat cannot be bought or manipulated. He will not promise what he cannot deliver. But when he makes a promise, he has virtue backed up by talent to fulfill it. Unfortunately, few political leaders today are natural aristocrats, because early in their ambitious careers they get beholden to those powers that helped them up the political ladder.

  b. In medieval society physical strength and animal cunning were the most admired characteristics of human beings, but since the invention of gunpowder, we have come to value other qualities more highly. Now that even a physically weak person can be made strong by carrying a gun, other ingenuities have become the marks of heroic people. Of course, boxing requires physical strength and animal cunning; yet many people today admire good boxers. The qualities most admired today are intellectual acumen, leadership ability, artistic talent, and social adjustment. I find it distressing that we do not prize goodness as much as we should. After all, Lincoln's outstanding feature was goodness. If a person is not good, he is not admirable. The tournament and personal combat have been replaced by the university, the political arena, the stage, and the personality inventory as testing grounds for heroes.

6. Identify the most obvious means used to establish coherence in the following paragraphs:

a. In general, relevancy is a facet of training rather than of education. What is taught at law school is the present law of the land, not the Napoleonic Code or even the archaic laws that have been scratched from the statute books. And at medical school, too, it is modern medical practice that is taught, that which is relevant to conditions today. And the plumber and the carpenter and the electrician and the mason learn only what is relevant to the practice of their respective trades in this day with the tools and materials that are presently available and that conform to the building code.

—Harry Kemelman, *Common Sense in Education*

b. The extent of personal privacy varies, but there are four degrees that can be identified. Sometimes the individual wants to be completely out of the sight and hearing of anyone else, in solitude; alone, he is in the most relaxed state of privacy. In a second situation the individual seeks the intimacy of his confidants—his family, friends, or trusted associates with whom he chooses to share his ideas and emotions. But there are still some things that he does not want to disclose, whether he is with intimates or in public. Either by personal explanation or by social convention, the individual may indicate that he does not wish certain aspects of himself discussed or noticed, at least at that particular moment. When his claim is respected by those around him, he achieves a third degree of privacy, the state of reserve. Finally, an individual sometimes goes out in public to seek privacy, for by joining groups of people who do not recognize him, he achieves anonymity, being seen but not known. Such relaxation on the street, in bars or movies or in the park constitutes still another dimension of the individual's quest for privacy.

—Alan F. Westin, *Privacy*

c. The motor car is, more than any other object, the expression of the nation's character and the nation's dream. In the free billowing fender, in the blinding chromium grills, in the fluid control, in the everwidening front seat, we see the flowering of the America that we know. It is of some interest to scholars and historians that the same autumn that saw the abandonment of the window crank and the adoption of the push button (removing the motorist's last necessity for physical exertion) saw also the registration of sixteen million young men of fighting age and symphonic styling. It is of deep interest to me that in the same week Japan joined the Axis, De Soto moved its clutch pedal two inches to the left—and that the announcements caused equal flurries among the people.

—E. B. White, *The Motor Car*

7. Write a provocative introductory paragraph for an essay on one of the following topics:
   a. Admitting women to military schools
   b. Rationing water or gasoline
   c. Automatic capital punishment for terrorists who take hostages
   d. Purging our language of all words with a sexist bias ("he" as a general pronoun—chairman, congressman, businessman, insurance man)
   e. Job prospects for college seniors
   f. One of today's most serious urban problems

8. Write a brief paragraph that would function as a smooth transition from one to the other of the following pairs of paragraphs:
   a. (1) The first paragraph lists activities of a male executive that are the same as activities for which the homemaker is chided (long phone conversations, coffee klatches with colleagues, unnecessary fancy luncheons).

   (2) The second paragraph indicates the differences between the two sets of activities.
   b. (1) The first paragraph provides statistics to demonstrate that thousands of poor people in America live on pet food.

   (2) The second paragraph argues that we must do something in order to solve the problem of hunger and malnutrition in America.
   c. (1) The first paragraph makes the point that many foreign countries consider Americans wasteful, extravagant, and selfish in their insistence on driving big cars.

   (2) The second paragraph holds the automobile industry responsible for shaping America's taste in cars.

ADVICE

WRITING SUCCESSFUL PARAGRAPHS

A. M. Tibbetts
Charlene Tibbetts

Arnold M. Tibbetts (b. 1927) has taught English at the University of Iowa, Western Illinois University, Vanderbilt University, and the University of Illinois, Urbana. His wife, Charlene Tibbetts (b. 1921), has also taught part-time at the University of Illinois, Urbana. The Tibbettses are coauthors of Strategies of Rhetoric *(1969), from which this excerpt was taken.*

The proverbial warning "Don't promise more than you can give" applies to writing as well as to everyday life. The basis of a good paragraph, say the authors, is a promise that is made in the topic sentence and then carried out in the specific details. In this excerpt, the authors demonstrate with examples how to make and keep your "paragraph promises."

~

1 A paragraph is a collection of sentences that helps you fulfill your thesis (theme promise). Itself a small "theme," a paragraph should be clearly written and specific; and it should not wander or make irrelevant remarks. Each paragraph should be related in some way to the theme promise. Here are suggestions for writing successful paragraphs:

1. Get to the Point of Your Paragraph Quickly and Specifically

2 Don't waste time or words in stating your paragraph promise. Consider this good example of getting to the point—the writer is explaining the ancient Romans' technique for conquering their world:

The technique of expansion was simple. Divide et impera [divide and conquer]: enter into solemn treaty with a neighbouring country, foment internal disorder, intervene in support of the weaker side on the pretense that Roman honour was involved, replace the legitimate ruler with a puppet, giving him the status of a subject ally; later, goad him into rebellion, seize and sack the country, burn down the temples, and carry off the captive gods to adorn a triumph. Conquered territories were placed under the control of a provincial governor-general, an ex-commander-in-chief who garrisoned it, levied taxes, set up courts of summary justice, and linked the new frontiers with the old by so called Roman roads—usually built by Greek engineers and native forced labour. Established social and religious practices were permitted so long as they did not threaten Roman administration or offend against the broad-minded Roman standards of good taste. The new province presently became a springboard for further aggression.

—Robert Graves, *It Was a Stable World*

3   Graves makes his promise in the first nine words, in which he mentions the "simple" technique the Romans had for "dividing" and "conquering" in order to expand their empire. Suppose Graves had started his paragraph with these words:

The technique of expansion was interesting. It was based upon a theory about human nature that the Romans practically invented. This theory had to do with how people reacted to certain political and military devices which . . .

4   Do you see what is wrong? Since the beginning sentences are so vague, the paragraph never gets going. The writer can't fulfill a promise because he hasn't made one. Another example of a poor paragraph beginning:

The first step involves part of the golf club head. The club head has removable parts, some of which are metal. You must consider these parts when deciding how to repair the club.

5   Specify the beginning of this paragraph and get to the point quicker:

Your first step in repairing the club head is to remove the metal plate held on by Phillips screws.

6   This solid, specific paragraph beginning gives your reader a clear promise which you can fulfill easily without wasting words. (Observe, by the way, that specifying a writer's stance—as we did in the last example—can help you write clearer paragraph beginnings.)

2. Fulfill Your Reader's Expectation Established by the Paragraph Promise

7   Do this with specific details and examples—explain as fully as you can. Example:

The next thing is to devise a form for your essay. This, which ought to be obvious, is not. I learned it for the first time from an experienced newspaperman. When I was at college I earned extra pocket- and book-money by writing several weekly columns for a newspaper. They were usually topical, they were always carefully varied, they tried hard to be witty, and (an essential) they never missed a deadline. But once, when I brought in the product, a copy editor stopped me. He said, "Our readers seem to like your stuff all right; but we think it's a bit amateurish." With due humility I replied, "Well I am an amateur. What should I do with it?" He said, "Your pieces are not coherent; they are only sentences and epigrams strung together; they look like a heap of clothespins in a basket. Every article ought to have a shape. Like this" (and he drew a big letter S on his page) "or this" (he drew a descending line which turned abruptly upward again) "or this" (and he sketched a solid central core with five or six lines pushing outward from it) "or even this" (and he outlined two big arrows coming into collision). I never saw the man again, but I have never ceased to be grateful to him for his wisdom and for his kindness. Every essay must have a shape. You can ask a question in the first paragraph, discussing several different answers to it till you reach one you think is convincing. You can give a curious fact and offer an explanation of it: a man's character (as Hazlitt did with his fives champion), a building, a book, a striking adventure, a peculiar custom. There are many other shapes which essays can take; but the principle laid down by the copy editor was right. Before you start you must have a form in your mind; and it ought to be a form felt in paragraphs or sections, not in words or sentences—so that, if necessary, you could summarize each paragraph in a single line and put the entire essay on a postcard.

—Gilbert Highet, *How to Write an Essay*

8   Highet makes a promise in the first three sentences, and in the remaining sentences he specifically fulfills it.

3. Avoid Fragmentary Paragraphs

9   A fragmentary paragraph does not develop its topic or fulfill its promise. A series of fragmentary paragraphs jumps from idea to idea in a jerky and unconvincing fashion:

> My freshman rhetoric class is similar in some ways to my senior English class in high school, but it is also very different.
>
> In my English class we usually had daily homework assignments that were discussed during the class period. If we were studying grammar, the assignments were to correct grammatical errors in the text. If we were studying literature, we were supposed to read the material and understand its ideas.
>
> In rhetoric class, we do basically the same things, except that in the readings we are assigned, we look much deeper into the purpose of the author.
>
> In my English class . . .

10   Fragmentary paragraphs are often the result of a weak writer's stance.

4. Avoid Irrelevancies in Your Paragraphs

11   The italicized sentence does not fit the development of this paragraph:

> We need a better working atmosphere at Restik Tool Company. The workers must feel that they are a working team instead of just individuals. If the men felt they were part of a team, they would not misuse the special machine tools, which now need to be resharpened twice as often as they used to be. *Management's attitude toward the union could be improved too.* The team effort is also being damaged by introduction of new products before their bugs have been worked out. Just when the men are getting used to one routine, a new one is installed, and their carefully created team effort is seriously damaged.

12   As with the fragmentary paragraph, the problem of irrelevancies in a paragraph is often the result of a vague writer's stance. The paragraph above does not seem to be written for any particular reader.

∿

(1,271 words)

VOCABULARY

foment (2)   topical (7)

———————— EXAMPLES ————————

FROM THE LESSONS OF THE PAST

Edith Hamilton

Edith Hamilton (1867–1963) was an American classicist, educator, and writer. Her writing career began after retirement, and at the age of eighty, she started giving public addresses and lectures. When she was ninety, she was made an honorary citizen of Greece. Among her books are The Greek Way *(1942),* The Roman Way *(1932), and* Witness to the Truth: Christ and His Interpreters *(1948).*

∼

Basic to all the Greek achievement was freedom. The Athenians were the only free people in the world. In the great empires of antiquity—Egypt, Babylon, Assyria, Persia—splendid though they were, with riches beyond reckoning and immense power, freedom was unknown. The idea of it never dawned in any of them. It was born in Greece, a poor little country, but with it able to remain unconquered no matter what manpower and what wealth were arrayed against her. At Marathon and at Salamis overwhelming numbers of Persians had been defeated by small Greek forces. It had been proved that one free man was superior to many submissively obedient subjects of a tyrant. Athens was the leader in that amazing victory, and to the Athenians freedom was their dearest possession. Demosthenes said that they would not think it worth their while to live if they could not do so as free men, and years later a great teacher said, "Athenians, if you deprive them of their liberty, will die."

∼

(169 words)

VOCABULARY

reckoning   arrayed   Marathon
Salamis   submissively   tyrant
Demosthenes

THE FACTS

1. Were you convinced of the truth of the topic sentence after reading the paragraph? If so, what convinced you?

2. In what way are free men superior to those who are submissively obedient to a tyrant?

THE STRATEGIES

1. What is the topic sentence of the paragraph?

2. Who is the "great teacher" alluded to?

THE ISSUES

1. Hamilton writes that freedom was basic to the Greek achievement. What does freedom mean to you in a political context?

2. According to Hamilton, it has "been proved that one free man [is] superior to many submissively obedient subjects." Why do you think this is so?

PAIN

William Somerset Maugham

English author William Somerset Maugham (1874–1965) wrote short stories, novels, plays, and books of criticism. His most popular plays include The Circle *(1921),* Our Betters *(1923), and* The Constant Wife *(1927). His best-known novel is his semiautobiographical account of a young physician with a clubfoot,* Of Human Bondage *(1919).*

～

No more stupid apology for pain has ever been devised than that it elevates. It is an explanation due to the necessity of justifying pain from the Christian point of view. Pain is nothing more than the signal given by the nerves that the organism is in circumstances hurtful to it; it would be as reasonable to assert that a danger signal elevates a train. But one would have thought that the ordinary observation of life was enough to show that in the great majority of cases, pain, far from refining, has an effect which is merely brutalising. An example in point is the case of hospital in-patients: physical pain makes them self-absorbed, selfish, querulous, impatient, unjust and greedy; I could name a score of petty vices that it generates, but not one virtue. Poverty also is pain. I have known well men who suffered from that grinding agony of poverty which befalls persons who have to live among those richer than themselves; it makes them grasping and mean, dishonest and untruthful. It teaches them all sorts of detestable tricks. With moderate means they would have been honourable men, but ground down by poverty they have lost all sense of decency.

～

(282 words)

VOCABULARY

querulous

THE FACTS

1. According to Maugham, why do some people think it necessary to justify pain?
2. What is Maugham's view of pain?
3. Aside from the pain of physical illness, what is another cause of pain?

THE STRATEGIES

1. What analogy does Maugham use in refuting the view that pain elevates?
2. What example does Maugham give to support his view of pain?
3. The paragraph discusses two causes of pain. What transitional word does Maugham use to move the discussion from the one cause to the other?

THE ISSUES

1. Maugham says that he cannot name a single virtue that pain produces. What virtue is pain generally thought to produce?
2. What is the distinction between pain and suffering?
3. Maugham writes that to say pain elevates is as reasonable as asserting that "a danger signal elevates a train." What is fundamentally false about this analogy?

I AM TIRED OF FIGHTING (SURRENDER SPEECH)

Chief Joseph of the Nez Percé

Chief Joseph (1840?–1904) was the leader of the Nez Percé tribe of the Sahaptin Indians, who lived along the Snake River in Idaho and Oregon. In 1877, under Chief Joseph, the tribe fought the United States government in a desperate attempt to preserve its land. Eventually, the Indians lost their struggle and were forced to retreat to the border of Canada.

~

I am tired of fighting. Our chiefs are killed. Looking Glass is dead. Toohulsote is dead. The old men are all dead. It is the young men who say no and yes. He who led the young men is dead. It is cold and we have no blankets. The little children are freezing to death. My people, some of them, have run away to the hills and have no blankets, no food. No one knows where they are— perhaps they are freezing to death. I want to have time to look for my children and see how many of them I can find. Maybe I shall find them among the dead. Hear me, my chiefs, I am tired. My heart is sad and sick. From where the sun stands I will fight no more forever.

～

(135 words)

THE FACTS

1. According to this speech, what nonmilitary factor contributed most to Chief Joseph's decision to surrender?
2. Who was left among the Nez Percé to say no and yes?

THE STRATEGIES

1. On what word do most of the sentences of this paragraph end? What is the effect of this repeated ending?
2. How would you characterize the language used in this speech? Formal? Informal? Colloquial? What effect do you think the speaker achieves in his diction?
3. What are some examples of poetic constructions that add to the stateliness and dignity of this speech? Translate them literally and say what is lost in the translation.

THE ISSUES

1. How are American Indians portrayed in popular literature and films? How has this portrayal affected your impression of them?
2. Historians agree that the Indians got short shrift at the hands of the encroaching white settlers. What responsibility, if any, do the descendants of the victors have to the descendants of the vanquished Indians?

Paragraphs with the Topic Sentence at the End

MAN AGAINST DARKNESS

W. T. Stace

Walter Terrence Stace (1886–1967) was an English naturalist and philosopher known for his ability to translate complex theories into terms that appealed to a general reader. An authority on Hegel, Stace was the author of numerous books, among them A Critical History of Greek Philosophy *(1920) and* The Philosophy of Hegel *(1924).*

~

The picture of a meaningless world, and a meaningless human life, is, I think, the basic theme of much modern art and literature. Certainly it is the basic theme of modern philosophy. According to the most characteristic philosophies of the modern period from Hume in the eighteenth century to the so-called positivists of today, the world is just what it is, and that is the end of all inquiry. There is no reason for its being what it is. Everything might just as well have been quite different, and there would have been no reason for that either. When you have stated what things are, what things the world contains, there is nothing more which could be said, even by an omniscient being. To ask any question about why things are thus, or what purpose their being so serves, is to ask a senseless question, because they serve no purpose at all. For instance, there is for modern philosophy no such thing as the ancient problem of evil. For this once famous question pre-supposes that pain and misery, though they seem so inexplicable and irrational to us, must ultimately subserve some rational purpose, must have their places in the cosmic plan. But this is nonsense. There is no such overruling rationality in the universe. Belief in the ultimate irrationality of everything is the quintessence of what is called the modern mind.

~

(233 words)

VOCABULARY

positivists   omniscient   subserve
quintessence

THE FACTS

1. What is the basic theme of much modern art and literature?
2. How do the most characteristic philosophies of the modern era view the world?
3. Why is there no such thing in modern philosophy as the ancient problem of evil?

THE STRATEGIES

1. Stace is known for expressing complex ideas with clarity. In this example, how does he make clear the complex views of modern philosophy?
2. From which point of view is this paragraph mainly written? How can you tell?
3. "Begging the question" is the logical name given to an argument that assumes as proven the very thing that is in dispute. Is the attitude of

modern philosophy toward evil an example of begging the question? Why or why not?

THE ISSUES

1. What is your opinion of modern philosophy, as Stace summarizes it, that ascribes everything to irrationality? How does this philosophy square with your own beliefs?
2. What is the ancient problem of evil?
3. What imaginable purpose can evil possibly serve? If evil did not exist, would it have to be invented?

WHAT IS A POET?

Mark Van Doren

Mark Van Doren (1894–1973), American poet and critic, was born in Illinois and educated at Columbia University, where he later won renown as a dedicated teacher. He was the author of many books, among them American and British Literature Since 1890 *(1939, written with his brother Carl),* Collected Poems, 1922–1938 *(1939, Pulitzer Prize), and* The Last Days of Lincoln *(1959).*

~

Here is the figure we have set up. A pale, lost man with long, soft hair. Tapering fingers at the ends of furtively fluttering arms. An air of abstraction in the delicate face, but more often a look of shy pain as some aspect of reality—a real man or woman, a grocer's bill, a train, a load of bricks, a newspaper, a noise from the street—makes itself manifest. He is generally incompetent. He cannot find his way in a city, he forgets where he is going, he has no aptitude for business, he is childishly gullible and so the prey of human sharks, he cares nothing for money, he is probably poor, he will sacrifice his welfare for a whim, he stops to pet homeless cats, he is especially knowing where children are concerned (being a child himself), he sighs, he sleeps, he wakes to sigh again. The one great assumption from which the foregoing portrait is drawn is an assumption which thousands of otherwise intelligent citizens go on. It is the assumption that the poet is more sensitive than any other kind of man, that he feels more than the rest of us and is more definitely the victim of his feeling.

~

(205 words)

VOCABULARY

gullible

THE FACTS

1. What do we expect a poet to look like?
2. What kind of personality do we expect a poet to have?
3. What one great assumption do we make about poets?

THE STRATEGIES

1. What is Van Doren attempting to do in this paragraph? What single word could you use to describe the type of portrait he is sketching?
2. Van Doren writes: "A pale, lost man with long, soft hair. Tapering fingers at the ends of furtively fluttering arms." Grammatically, what do these two assertions have in common? What effect do they contribute to the description?
3. A catalogue is a list of things or attributes. Where in this paragraph does the author obviously use a catalogue?

THE ISSUES

1. Given the characteristics traditionally identified as masculine and feminine, which would you expect a poet to be—more masculine than feminine or vice versa? Why?
2. What, in your mind, is a poet? Does your definition of a poet differ substantially from Van Doren's description? In what way?
3. Of what use is poetry in the modern world?

ON DISEASE

Lewis Thomas, M. D.

Lewis Thomas (b. 1913–1993) was born in New York and educated at Princeton and Harvard. Dr. Thomas was a medical administrator of the Memorial Sloan-Kettering Cancer Center in New York and an essayist who has been praised for his lucid style. His essays have been published in collections such as The Lives of a Cell *(1974, National Book Award),* The Medusa and the Snail *(1979),* Late Night Thoughts on Listening to Mahler's Ninth Symphony *(1983), and* Etcetera Etcetera *(1990).*

~

We were all reassured, when the first moon landing was ready to be made, that the greatest precautions would be taken to protect the life of the earth, especially human life, against infection by whatever there might be alive on the moon. And, in fact, the elaborate ceremony of lunar asepsis was performed after each of the early landings; the voyagers were masked and kept behind plate glass, quarantined away from contact with the earth until it was a certainty that we wouldn't catch something from them. The idea that germs are all around us, trying to get at us, to devour and destroy us, is so firmly rooted in modern consciousness that it made sense to think that strange germs, from the moon, would be even scarier and harder to handle.

∽

(132 words)

VOCABULARY

asepsis   quarantined

THE FACTS

1. What were we all reassured about before the first moon landing was made?

2. What idea about germs is firmly rooted in our consciousness?

THE STRATEGIES

1. What specific detail does the author use to support his assertion that an elaborate ceremony of asepsis was performed after each of the lunar landings?

2. Assuming that the paragraph is representative of the style of the whole essay, for what kind of audience do you think the essay was written?

THE ISSUES

1. Do you trust medical doctors to the extent that you implicitly follow their advice? Why or why not?

2. Which disease do you fear the most? Why?

THE FLOOD

Robert Frost

Robert Frost (1874–1963) was a lecturer, poet, and teacher. When he was nineteen and working in a mill in Lawrence, Massachusetts, the Independent accepted and published My Butterfly, An Elegy—*the poem that began Frost's career as one of America's great poets. Rugged New England farm life was the inspiration for many of his poems.*

∼

Blood has been harder to dam back than water.
Just when we think we have it impounded safe
Behind new barrier walls (and let it chafe!),
It breaks away in some new kind of slaughter.
5   We choose to say it is let loose by the devil;
But power of blood itself releases blood.
It goes by might of being such a flood
Held high at so unnatural a level.
10 It will have outlet, brave and not so brave.
Weapons of war and implements of peace
Are but the points at which it finds release.
And now it is once more the tidal wave
That when it has swept by leaves summits stained.
Oh, blood will out. It cannot be contained.

∼

(122 words)

VOCABULARY

chafe   impounded

THE FACTS

1. What interpretation can be given to Frost's mention of a flood of blood?
2. What is meant by the statement "power of blood itself releases blood"?
3. What is the "tidal wave" Frost refers to? Why does it leave summits stained?

THE STRATEGIES

1. In poetry, the stanza serves a purpose similar to that of the paragraph. That being the case, what do you consider the topic sentence of this poem? Is it stated more than once?
2. Both water and blood are mentioned in this poem. Which of these words is used literally and which symbolically?

THE ISSUES

1. What is the theme of this poem?
2. In writing about blood, Frost says: ". . . Implements of peace / Are but the points at which it finds release." What can this line possibly mean?

CHAPTER WRITING ASSIGNMENTS

1. Select one of the following topics and develop it into a unified, coherent, and complete paragraph:

    a. Carelessness can do more harm than lack of knowledge.

    b. Today the prevailing mood on the campus is one of . . . (fill in the words you think apply).

    c. Many cars are still not designed for safety.

    d. Kissing is an odd, overromanticized act.

    e. A plagiarized paper has several bad effects.

    f. Buying term papers from a commercial source is unethical.

2. List the particular details that you would use to write a convincing paragraph on the following topic sentences:

    a. Sarcastic people are unpleasant to be around.

    b. I like the security of dating the same person (or, I like the freedom of dating different people).

    c. Yuppies have gotten bad press and a bad name.

    d. Children and fools speak the truth.

    e. Common sense is _____ (define it).

WRITING ASSIGNMENTS FOR A SPECIFIC AUDIENCE

1. Write an essay aimed at an audience of unemployed loggers arguing the importance of preserving the habitat of the spotted owl even at the cost of logging jobs.

or

2. Write an essay aimed at an audience of environmentalists arguing the importance of preserving jobs even at the cost of the spotted owls' habitat.

COLLABORATIVE WRITING PROJECT

Divide your group into four teams. Assign each team to investigate and report on the paragraph-writing techniques practiced by such publications as *Reader's Digest, Atlantic, Consumer Reports,* and the editorial page of your local newspaper. Consider the relationship between the audience of the publication and the kinds of paragraphs it uses. Meet to discuss your findings and then team-write an essay outlining what you have learned.

——— REAL-LIFE ——— STUDENT WRITING

LETTER OF APPLICATION TO AN HONORS PROGRAM

Students who apply to gain entrance to colleges, honor programs, and graduate schools or for scholarship grants are usually required to submit a personal essay telling about their goals, motivation, special interests, and the like. The following essay was written as part of an application to a community college honors program. If the tone seems a tad formal and stiff, remember the student was under pressure to look angelic.

THE ASSIGNMENT In a brief essay, state your educational goals and why you want to be in the Honors Program.

Some day I want to be a labor lawyer like my father and his father before him. To achieve this goal will require dedication and focus. I realize that I will have to give up the more frivolus activities of fraternity life, such as beer busts, poker games, and hanging out. I have already tried to get into the habit of getting top grades not only to gain entrance to a good law school, but also because I would really like to know the details of important historical events, such as how Lincoln won the Civil War, what the Watergate Scandal was all about, and why labor unions have become so weak. I also want to read a few more Shakespeare plays and even learn to read and write in French. My short-term educational goal is to receive a B.A. in history with a minor in business administration. Two reasons drive me to join the Honors Program: First, in honors classes I shall be surrounded by students who are highly motivated and serious about their studies. Consequently, it seems to me that the classroom debates and discussions would be on a more challenging level than in regular classes. Second, I know that the top universities in the country give preference to honor students in their acceptance rankings. While some of my college friends think honors programs are elitist, I think they stimulate students to value learning and scholarship. Thank you for considering my application.

Phil Anderson

PART II
Patterns of Development

INTRODUCTION: THE RHETORICAL MODES

Chances are good that you have already heard of the rhetorical modes or perhaps even practiced them in another class. Part II of this book is devoted to teaching all eight rhetorical modes as well as argumentation.

Behind the rhetorical modes or patterns in composition is this simple idea: To write about a subject, you must first have thought about it, and this systematic thinking can be translated into an idealized pattern for writing. For example, you might choose to tell a story about your subject (narration); to describe it (description); to say how it happened (process analysis); to give examples of it (example); to define it (definition); to compare it to something else (comparison and contrast); to break it down into its constituent parts (division and classification); or to list its known causes or effects (causal analysis). Superimposing one of these seven abstract modes or patterns on your subject will make writing about it easier.

Each of these rhetorical modes is a composite of specific writing and organizing techniques that can be isolated and taught. All narrations are alike, whether they tell a story about aliens from Mars or about facing up to a bully. All descriptions draw on common organizing and focusing techniques, no matter what they describe. If you are writing a comparison and contrast, for example, you know that you must alternate back and forth between the compared items and that you must insert suitable transitions so your reader can follow this movement. If you are defining, you know that there are specific techniques to be used in a definition. Knowing that a subject is to be approached a certain way also endows a writer's purpose with a refreshing narrowness, for what is especially bedeviling to the writer is not necessarily the complexity of a subject, but the infinity of possible approaches suggested by the blank sheet of paper.

The advice that instructors often give beginning writers is, "Narrow your subject." Writing by rhetorical modes allows you to limit and narrow your approach to a subject. You say, "I'm going to divide and classify this subject," and you have an abstract pattern in mind that you can follow. You say, "I'm going to analyze cause," and you also have an abstract pattern to follow. In either case, you are not left dangling between "What shall I say?" and "How shall I say it?" You know how to say it in the abstract. What's left is the application of the ideal pattern to your particular subject.

Here is an example—the subject of guilt as developed in the eight, most widely used rhetorical patterns. Notice how the writer's focus shifts with the use of each new pattern.

THE EDITORS

Patterns of Development for the Subject "Guilt"

1. Narration

I was seven years old when I first became aware of the terrible power of guilt. For piling our toys into the toy box, Mother had rewarded my brother and me with five shiny pennies each. If I had had ten pennies instead of just five, I could have bought a gingerbread man with raisin eyes and sugar-frosted hair. The image danced in my head all day, until, finally, I crept into my brother's room and stole his five pennies. The next morning, as my brother and I were dressing to go to school, I hid all ten pennies in the pocket of my coat, cramming one of my father's handkerchiefs on top of them. As my brother and I lined up in front of Mother to be kissed goodbye, she looked at my bulging pocket with amazement. "What on earth do you have in your pocket?" she asked. "It's nothing," I said as offhandedly as I could. "It's nothing at all." Bewildered, but too busy to investigate any further, Mother kissed me goodbye. I ran out the door and down our gravel path as fast as my feet could carry me. But the farther from home I got, the more miserable I became. The shiny pennies in my pocket felt oppressively like one-ton boulders. And I was haunted by the idea that I had become a thief. Forgotten was the gingerbread man, for whose sake I had stolen my brother's pennies. Finally, unable to bear my horrible feeling of guilt, I ran back home to blurt out my crime to my mother.

2. Description

Never before had Pedro experienced such a depth of despair and such a sense of isolation. He began to avoid those nearest to him, returning their friendly greetings with rough and indifferent replies. Often he sat in his room staring vacantly into space with hollow eyes. His hands were cold and clammy most of the time; yet his forehead burned hot with a mysterious fever. Terrible nightmares haunted his sleep, causing him to rise out of bed in the middle of the night, overcome with terror. When strangers at the store asked him a simple question such as "Where is the thread?" or "Have you any molasses?" he would read silent accusations in their eyes and his hands would tremble. He had become a man tormented by guilt.

3. Process Analysis

Do you know the most effective way to handle a friend turned a debtor? Make the person feel guilty. Let us say that you lent your friend Tom $500.00 to buy a motorcycle, but he refuses to repay the loan. Your first step is to place him in a category of bogus moral superiority. Say, "Tom, you have always been a person of honor. Why do you refuse to pay what you owe me?" If that doesn't work, your second step is to take the behavior personally, indicating that it is causing you emotional pain. Say, "I can't tell you how disappointed I am that you are treating me worse than a total stranger. You would pay back your bank, your credit cards, but you ignore me, your best friend, who needs the money." Unless your present debtor and former friend is a sociopath, he will feel bad about hurting you. Finally, you can threaten to cut off the relationship, making the threat look as if it were the debtor's doing. Say, "Look, Tom, unless I get the money you owe me within a week, I will take your refusal to repay me as a sign that you don't care any more about our friendship." With that, you have really turned up the guilt barometer. Indeed, inducing guilt can be a powerful tool in the process of debt collection.

4. Illustration/Exemplification

Seneca once said, "Every guilty person is his own hangman." The truth of this observation can be illustrated by the lives of countless villains. One such is Macbeth, from Shakespeare's tragedy of the same name. At the instigation of his wife, Macbeth kills the king of Scotland and usurps his throne—an act of treachery for which Macbeth and his wife suffer torments of guilt. Lady Macbeth develops an obsession that her hands are stained with blood, and she wanders somnambulistically through the castle trying vainly to cleanse them. Before he murders the king, Macbeth hallucinates a dagger floating in the air. Later, after his assassins murder Banquo, Macbeth is tormented by hallucinations of Banquo's ghost. Eventually, Lady Macbeth commits suicide. Macbeth is killed during a rebellion of his noblemen, which is brought about—in the main—by the excesses to which his guilt has driven him.

5. Definition

Guilt is the remorse that comes from an awareness of having done something wrong. The origin of guilt is psychological. From childhood, we have all been conditioned by family and society to act within defined standards of reasonableness and decency. Gradually, over a period of years, these standards are internalized and modified to become the core of what is called "conscience." When we do something that violates these internalized standards, we feel guilty. If we have been brought up in a religious environment, we feel an added measure of guilt when we break what we think is a divine commandment. Whenever we don't play according to our internalized rules, we feel miserable, and this misery is what guilt is all about.

6. COMPARISON AND CONTRAST

Although the two words may seem to share some connotations, guilt is not a synonym for blame. Guilt must be felt; blame must be assessed. Guilt implies self-reproach that comes from an internal consciousness of wrong. Blame hints at fault that has been externally assessed. A man may suffer guilt yet be entirely exonerated of blame; conversely, he may be blamed and yet feel no guilt. In short, while guilt is a feeling, blame is a judgment—and that is the chief distinction between the two.

7. DIVISION AND CLASSIFICATION

The Bible identifies three kinds of guilt: guilt of the unpardonable sin, redeemable guilt, and guilt of innocence. First, the guilt of the unpardonable sin belongs to any being who has become so steeped in evil that a change for good is no longer possible. Lucifer is said to have committed this sin by which he cut himself off eternally from Yahweh, the source of all good. Second, redeemable guilt is guilt that can be erased because it belongs to one whose heart is not incorrigibly corrupt, but which has weakened temporarily under the pressure of temptation. King David, for instance, murdered Uriah in order to marry Bathsheba, Uriah's wife. But despite this sin, David was a noble king with a thirst for righteousness; he was redeemable. Finally, the guilt of innocence is the guilt that Jesus bore when he decided to be crucified for the collective wrong of mankind even though he was, of all men, most innocent. In other words, Jesus died as if he were guilty when, in fact, his character was free from any trace of evil.

8. CAUSAL ANALYSIS

Guilt is caused by the failure of the will. The human mind, according to Freudian theory, is delicately balanced between the drive for instant gratification that comes from the id, and the desire for regulation and postponement that originates in the superego, which is sometimes identified with what we call the conscience. The function of the will is to mediate between these two desires. When the individual succumbs to temptation, the forces of the id have triumphed over the repression of the superego. But the superego fights back by tormenting the self with regret—in short, by evoking feelings of guilt. The stricter the superego, or conscience, the harsher the toll in guilt and the greater the person suffers. Whoever allows the will to fail must therefore pay for the gratification of the libido's urges in the coin of guilt.

These eight rhetorical modes allow us to teach idealized writing forms and techniques. You will not always use them, and you will most likely use them less and less consciously as your writing skills mature. But, in the beginning, you will find it easier to approach a writing assignment from the viewpoint of a specific mode rather than to invent a wholly original form for every essay.

7

Narration

EDITORS' COUNSEL

What Narration Does

To narrate means to tell a story. It does not necessarily have to be a made-up story. Narration, in fact, is a relating of events in some climactic sequence. Whether the events you relate are imaginary or real, the narrative technique is more or less the same. The preceding paragraph on guilt is an example of narration.

If there is a rhetorical mode that can be said to be inborn in some people, it is narration. Most of us think we can tell a good story, and almost all of us have tried our hand at narration. Granted, our stories may have been oral and we told them on the front porch to family and friends, but a story is a story and the techniques for telling one orally or in writing are essentially the same.

When to Use Narration

The most widespread use of narration occurs in fiction, whether in the short story or novel. Narration is also used in essays, minutes of business meetings, reports of scientific experiments, news releases, and case histories. Brief narratives, called *anecdotes,* are often used to effectively enliven or illustrate a point. Use narration whenever you need to relate an experience or present information in dramatic or purposeful sequence.

How to Write a Narration

Narratives differ in content, length, and point, but the techniques they all use are remarkably similar. To write an engaging narration, you need to do the following:

Have a Point The point of a story is what gives it movement—a beginning, a middle, and an end. If your story has no point, it will also seem to have no movement, to go nowhere, to become bogged down and stagnant. Good storytellers always begin with a point in mind. They want to show how absentminded Uncle Mickey has become; they wish to prove that "haste makes waste." From this beginning, the story should proceed without pause or slip. Sometimes a storyteller will even begin by revealing the point of the story, an admission that is often helpful to both writer and reader. A classic example of a story that begins by revealing its point is George Orwell's *Shooting an Elephant.*

> One day something happened which in a roundabout way was enlightening. It was a tiny incident in itself, but it gave me a better glimpse than I had had before of the real nature of imperialism—the real motives for which despotic governments act.

This tells us what to expect. As we read on, we expect Orwell to deliver what he has advertised.

Have a point and stick to it—that age-old advice often given by writing teachers definitely applies to narration.

Pace the Story   Fiction tells lies about time—it has to. Real time is not always action-packed, does not always carry us to the dizzying brink, or make us feel the throb of life. In fact, time is usually humdrum and dull in real life. But no reader wants a story to trudge through uneventful hours. What the reader wants is for the dull and humdrum to disappear in the puff of a sentence, and for the focus of the story always to be on time—that is, eventful and exciting. The technique of doing this is known as pacing.

All storytellers pace their materials to focus only on eventful periods and to ignore all inconsequential stretches in between. In the following example, taken from a story entitled *We're Poor,* an entire season disappears in a single paragraph:

> I didn't go back to school that fall. My mother said it was because I was sick. I did have a cold the week that school opened; I had been playing in the gutters and had got my feet wet, because there were holes in my shoes. . . . As long as I had to stay in the house anyway, they were all right.
>
> I stayed cooped up in the house, without any companionship. . . .

In *We're Poor,* the author, Floyd Dell, learns from a Christmas experience that his family is destitute. The story consequently spends a good deal of time and attention on that climactic Christmas Eve during which the narrator makes this discovery, but the inconsequential months of the preceding fall are quickly dismissed in a paragraph.

Tell the Story from a Consistent Point of View   The point of view of a story is the angle from which it is told. This angle can be personal and intimate, referring to the narrator with the pronoun I, or it can be from an omniscient point of view. In this view, the narrator is like a video camera sweeping over the scene and pausing briefly to focus on selected characters—describing how they look, what they say, and how they feel. Often this omniscient observer will select one central character, setting the person in relief so that he or she will catch the reader's intense and undivided attention. In any case, the writer must always stay in character when telling a story and must always remain consistent to the viewpoint from which he or she is telling it.

Here is an example of the omniscient point of view in a narration. Telling the story of a troubled teacher-student relationship as an omniscient narrator, Joyce Carol Oates, the writer, moves skillfully from character to character as if seeing everything clearly and truthfully. About the main female character, the narrator observes:

> Sister Irene was a tall, deft woman in her early thirties. What one could see of her face made a striking impression—serious, hard gray eyes, a long slender nose, a face waxen with thought. Seen at the right time, from the right angle, she was almost handsome. In her past teaching positions she had drawn a little upon the fact of her being young and brilliant and also a nun, but she was beginning to grow out of that.

A little further into the story, the narrator moves from Sister Irene to the male lead character, a student, seeing him just as clearly as she sees Sister Irene:

> About two weeks after the semester began, Sister Irene noticed a new student in her class. He was slight and fair-haired, and his face was blank, but not blank by accident, blank on purpose, suppressed and restricted into a dumbness that looked hysterical.

The story continues to develop both characters, the teacher and the student. Although Sister Irene is the central consciousness of the story, Allen Weinstein, the student, becomes a crucial part of the total narrative conflict—with the author recording faithfully all he does, says, and feels, just as she also records the comings and goings of Sister Irene. In fact, in this story, the narrator records even the actions and words of minor characters, which makes her a typical omniscient narrator.

Now consider the following excerpt from a vivid childhood memory by Beryl Markham in *Praise God for the Blood of the Bull:*

> I lean for a moment on my spear peering outward at what is nothing, and then turn toward my thorn tree.
>
> "Are you here, Lakwani?"
>
> Arap Maina's voice is cool as water on shaded rocks.
>
> "I am here, Maina."
>
> He is tall and naked and very dark beside me. His shuka is tied around his left forearm to allow his body freedom to run.
>
> "You are alone, and you have suffered, my child."
>
> "I am all right, Maina, but I fear for Buller. I think he may die."
>
> Arap Maina kneels on the earth and runs his hand over Buller's body.

> *"He has been seriously and perhaps mortally wounded, Lakwani, but do not permit your mind to be too obsessed with any imaginary deficiencies or self-recriminations on your part. I conjecture that your lance has rescued him from a certain death, and God will recompense you for that. . . ."*

If the final paragraph sounds bizarre to you in the context of the excerpt, it should. We have altered the dialogue (and added italics to clearly distinguish it from Markham's words) to dramatize what we mean by a lapse in consistency. In the final paragraph, Maina suddenly and inexplicably shifts from the simple speech of a native African to the pompous, long-winded speech of a British magistrate. A character in a narrative must always speak more or less the same way throughout and cannot lurch from one style of talk to another, as we have made Maina do. Make your characters consistent and your narrative will seem believable.

Insert Appropriate Details   Details are indispensable to narrative writing and can make the difference between boredom and delight in a reader. No one can teach you the art of including captivating details, but common sense tells us that you are more likely to include the right details if you write your narrations about what you truly know. Here, for example, in Beryl Markham's description of a warthog, we get the feeling that the writer has had personal experience with the animal:

> I know animals more gallant than the African warthog, but none more courageous. He is the peasant of the plains—the drab and dowdy digger in the earth. He is the uncomely but intrepid defender of family, home, and bourgeois convention, and he will fight anything of any size that intrudes upon his smug existence. Even his weapons are plebeian—curved tusks, sharp, deadly, but not beautiful, used inelegantly for rooting as well as for fighting.

If you cannot write about what you know, the next best thing is to know about what you write. The advice to always research your subject before writing about it cannot be given too strongly. Even veteran fiction writers do not simply plunge into their narrations without doing the spadework necessary to make their scenes authentic. Although personal experience is probably the best basis for a narration, adequate and detailed research can be every bit as good.

Warming Up to Write a Narration

1. Choose one of the most interesting people whom you know well and sketch out a conflict you have had with him or her. List the events that led up to the conflict and also indicate how it was resolved. Before actually narrating the conflict, delete from your list all items that would slow down your narration with tedious or irrelevant material. Next, jot down the theme of your narration—that is, the

point it made or the lesson you learned about life and human relationships.

2. Try to recall five moments in your life that somehow defined who you are. It could be the time you lost an important contest, stood up to a bully, or first realized the importance of parents. List each moment as it occurs to you. Now, select from the list the moment that could best be turned into a good narration. Don't forget to write down how the moment defined who you are today.

3. What is the most exciting and unusual experience that you've ever had? Try to recall it with a richness of detail. Jot down on a notepad, without paying any attention to sequence, all the incidents and events that made up the experience. Write down everything that you remember about it. Later, after leaving the list to sink in, take the out-of-sequence memories and try to assemble them in some climactic order. If this is not the way you usually work, how did this method of recalling an experience and writing about it work for you?

—————— EXAMPLES ——————

SHOOTING AN ELEPHANT

George Orwell

George Orwell (1903–1950) was the pseudonym of Eric Arthur Blair. Born in India and educated at Eton, he served with the imperial police in Burma and fought on the republican side in the Spanish civil war. Orwell published two influential novels, Animal Farm *(1945) and* Nineteen Eighty-four *(1949). He is widely admired for the crisp, lucid prose style of his essays.*

George Orwell writes in a style that has been described as having "singular directness and honesty." In this selection, he relates an incident that occurred while he was with the imperial police in Burma from 1921 to 1927.

⁓

1 In Moulmein, in Lower Burma, I was hated by large numbers of people—the only time in my life that I have been important enough for this to happen to me. I was sub-divisional police officer of the town, and in an aimless, petty kind of way anti-European feeling was very bitter. No one had the guts to raise a riot, but if a European woman went through the bazaars alone somebody would probably spit betel juice over her dress. As a police officer I was an obvious target and was baited whenever it seemed safe to do so. When a nimble Burman tripped me up on the football field and the referee (another

Burman) looked the other way, the crowd yelled with hideous laughter. This happened more than once. In the end the sneering yellow faces of young men that met me everywhere, the insults hooted after me when I was at a safe distance, got badly on my nerves. The young Buddhist priests were the worst of all. There were several thousand of them in the town and none of them seemed to have anything to do except stand on the street corners and jeer at Europeans.

2   All this was perplexing and upsetting. For at that time I had already made up my mind that imperialism was an evil thing and the sooner I chucked up my job and got out of it the better. Theoretically—and secretly, of course—I was all for the Burmese and all against their oppressors, the British. As for the job I was doing, I hated it more bitterly than I can perhaps make clear. In a job like that you see the dirty work of Empire at close quarters. The wretched prisoners huddling in the stinking cages of the lock-ups, the grey, cowed faces of the long-term convicts, the scarred buttocks of the men who had been flogged with bamboos—all these oppressed me with an intolerable sense of guilt. But I could get nothing into perspective. I was young and ill-educated and I had had to think out my problems in the utter silence that is imposed on every Englishman in the East. I did not even know that the British Empire is dying, still less did I know that it is a great deal better than the younger empires that are going to supplant it. All I knew was that I was stuck between my hatred of the empire I served and my rage against the evil-spirited little beasts who tried to make my job impossible. With one part of my mind I thought of the British Raj as an unbreakable tyranny, as something clamped down, in saecula saeculorum,[1] upon the will of prostrate peoples; with another part I thought that the greatest joy in the world would be to drive a bayonet into a Buddhist priest's guts. Feelings like these are the normal by-products of imperialism; ask any Anglo-Indian official, if you can catch him off duty.

3   One day something happened which in a roundabout way was enlightening. It was a tiny incident in itself, but it gave me a better glimpse than I had had before of the real nature of imperialism—the real motives for which despotic governments act. Early one morning the sub-inspector at a police station the other end of the town rang me up on the 'phone and said that an elephant was ravaging the bazaar. Would I please come and do something about it? I did not know what I could do, but I wanted to see what was happening and I got on to a pony and started out. I took my rifle, an old .44 Winchester and much too small to kill an elephant, but I thought the noise might be useful in terrorem.[2] Various Burmans stopped me on the way and told me about the elephant's doings. It was not, of course, a wild elephant, but a tame one which had gone "must." It had been chained up, as tame elephants always are when their attack of "must" is due, but on the previous night it had broken its chain and escaped. Its mahout, the only person who could manage

---

[1]Latin meaning for ever and ever.

[2]Latin meaning as a warning.

it when it was in that state, had set out in pursuit, but had taken the wrong direction and was now twelve hours' journey away, and in the morning the elephant had suddenly reappeared in the town. The Burmese population had no weapons and were quite helpless against it. It had already destroyed somebody's bamboo hut, killed a cow and raided some fruit-stalls and devoured the stock; also it had met the municipal rubbish van and, when the driver jumped out and took to his heels, had turned the van over and inflicted violences upon it.

4   The Burmese sub-inspector and some Indian constables were waiting for me in the quarter where the elephant had been seen. It was a very poor quarter, a labyrinth of squalid bamboo huts, thatched with palm-leaf, winding all over a steep hillside. I remember that it was a cloudy, stuffy morning at the beginning of the rains. We began questioning the people as to where the elephant had gone and, as usual, failed to get any definite information. That is invariably the case in the East; a story always sounds clear enough at a distance, but the nearer you get to the scene of events the vaguer it becomes. Some of the people said that the elephant had gone in one direction, some said that he had gone in another, some professed not even to have heard of any elephant. I had almost made up my mind that the whole story was a pack of lies, when we heard yells a little distance away. There was a loud, scandalized cry of "Go away, child! Go away this instant!" and an old woman with a switch in her hand came round the corner of a hut, violently shooing away a crowd of naked children. Some more women followed, clicking their tongues and exclaiming; evidently there was something that the children ought not to have seen. I rounded the hut and saw a man's dead body sprawling in the mud. He was an Indian, a black Dravidian coolie, almost naked, and he could not have been dead many minutes. The people said that the elephant had come suddenly upon him round the corner of the hut, caught him with its trunk, put its foot on his back and ground him into the earth. This was the rainy season and the ground was soft, and his face had scored a trench a foot deep and a couple of yards long. He was lying on his belly with arms crucified and head sharply twisted to one side. His face was coated with mud, the eyes wide open, the teeth bared and grinning with an expression of unendurable agony. (Never tell me, by the way, that the dead look peaceful. Most of the corpses I have seen looked devilish.) The friction of the great beast's foot had stripped the skin from his back as neatly as one skins a rabbit. As soon as I saw the dead man I sent an orderly to a friend's house nearby to borrow an elephant rifle. I had already sent back the pony, not wanting it to go mad with fright and throw me if it smelt the elephant.

5   The orderly came back in a few minutes with a rifle and five cartridges, and meanwhile some Burmans had arrived and told us that the elephant was in the paddy fields below, only a few hundred yards away. As I started forward practically the whole population of the quarter flocked out of the houses and followed me. They had seen the rifle and were all shouting excitedly that I was going to shoot the elephant. They had not shown much interest in the elephant when he was merely ravaging their homes, but it was

different now that he was going to be shot. It was a bit of fun to them, as it would be to an English crowd; besides they wanted the meat. It made me vaguely uneasy. I had no intention of shooting the elephant—I had merely sent for the rifle to defend myself if necessary—and it is always unnerving to have a crowd following you. I marched down the hill, looking and feeling a fool, with the rifle over my shoulder and an ever-growing army of people jostling at my heels. At the bottom, when you got away from the huts, there was a metalled road and beyond that a miry waste of paddy fields a thousand yards across, not yet ploughed but soggy from the first rains and dotted with coarse grass. The elephant was standing eight yards from the road, his left side towards us. He took not the slightest notice of the crowd's approach. He was tearing up bunches of grass, beating them against his knees to clean them and stuffing them into his mouth.

6   I had halted on the road. As soon as I saw the elephant I knew with perfect certainty that I ought not to shoot him. It is a serious matter to shoot a working elephant—it is comparable to destroying a huge and costly piece of machinery—and obviously one ought not to do it if it can possibly be avoided. And at that distance, peacefully eating, the elephant looked no more dangerous than a cow. I thought then and I think now that his attack of "must" was already passing off; in which case he would merely wander harmlessly about until the mahout came back and caught him. Moreover, I did not in the least want to shoot him. I decided that I would watch him for a little while to make sure that he did not turn savage again, and then go home.

7   But at that moment I glanced round at the crowd that had followed me. It was an immense crowd, two thousand at the least and growing every minute. It blocked the road for a long distance on either side. I looked at the sea of yellow faces above the garish clothes—faces all happy and excited over this bit of fun, all certain that the elephant was going to be shot. They were watching me as they would watch a conjurer about to perform a trick. They did not like me, but with the magical rifle in my hands I was momentarily worth watching. And suddenly I realized that I should have to shoot the elephant after all. The people expected it of me and I had got to do it; I could feel their two thousand wills pressing me forward, irresistibly. And it was at this moment, as I stood there with the rifle in my hands, that I first grasped the hollowness, the futility of the white man's dominion in the East. Here was I, the white man with his gun, standing in front of the unarmed native crowd—seemingly the leading actor of the piece; but in reality I was only an absurd puppet pushed to and fro by the will of those yellow faces behind. I perceived in this moment that when the white man turns tyrant it is his own freedom that he destroys. He becomes a sort of hollow, posing dummy, the conventionalized figure of a sahib. For it is the condition of his rule that he shall spend his life in trying to impress the "natives," and so in every crisis he has got to do what the "natives" expect of him. He wears a mask, and his face grows to fit it. I had got to shoot the elephant. I had committed myself to doing it when I sent for the rifle. A sahib has got to act like a sahib; he has got to appear resolute, to know his own mind and do definite things. To come all that way, rifle in hand, with

two thousand people marching at my heels, and then to trail feebly away, having done nothing—no, that was impossible. The crowd would laugh at me. And my whole life, every white man's life in the East, was one long struggle not to be laughed at.

8   But I did not want to shoot the elephant. I watched him beating his bunch of grass against his knees, with that preoccupied grandmotherly air that elephants have. It seemed to me that it would be murder to shoot him. At that age I was not squeamish about killing animals, but I had never shot an elephant and never wanted to. (Somehow it always seems worse to kill a large animal.) Besides, there was the beast's owner to be considered. Alive, the elephant was worth at least a hundred pounds; dead, he would only be worth the value of his tusks, five pounds, possibly. But I had got to act quickly. I turned to some experienced-looking Burmans who had been there when we arrived, and asked them how the elephant had been behaving. They all said the same thing: he took no notice of you if you left him alone, but he might charge if you went too close to him.

9   It was perfectly clear to me what I ought to do. I ought to walk up to within, say, twenty-five yards of the elephant and test his behavior. If he charged, I could shoot; if he took no notice of me, it would be safe to leave him until the mahout came back. But also I knew that I was going to do no such thing. I was a poor shot with a rifle and the ground was soft mud into which one would sink at every step. If the elephant charged and I missed him, I should have about as much chance as a toad under a steam-roller. But even then I was not thinking particularly of my own skin, only of the watchful yellow faces behind. For at that moment, with the crowd watching me, I was not afraid in the ordinary sense, as I would have been if I had been alone. A white man mustn't be frightened in front of "natives"; and so, in general, he isn't frightened. The sole thought in my mind was that if anything went wrong those two thousand Burmans would see me pursued, caught, trampled on and reduced to a grinning corpse like that Indian up the hill. And if that happened it was quite probable that some of them would laugh. That would never do. There was only one alternative. I shoved the cartridges into the magazine and lay down on the road to get a better aim.

10   The crowd grew very still, and a deep, low, happy sigh, as of people who see the theatre curtain go up at last, breathed from innumerable throats. They were going to have their bit of fun after all. The rifle was a beautiful German thing with cross-hair sights. I did not then know that in shooting an elephant one would shoot to cut an imaginary bar running from ear-hole to ear-hole. I ought, therefore, as the elephant was sideway on, to have aimed straight at his ear-hole; actually I aimed several inches in front of this, thinking the brain would be further forward.

11   When I pulled the trigger I did not hear the bang or feel the kick—one never does when a shot goes home—but I heard the devilish roar of glee that went up from the crowd. In that instant, in too short a time, one would have thought, even for the bullet to get there, a mysterious, terrible change had come over the elephant. He neither stirred nor fell, but every line of his body

had altered. He looked suddenly stricken, shrunken, immensely old, as though the frightful impact of the bullet had paralyzed him without knocking him down. At last, after what seemed a long time—it might have been five seconds, I dare say he sagged flabbily to his knees. His mouth slobbered. An enormous senility seemed to have settled upon him. One could have imagined him thousands of years old. I fired again into the same spot. At the second shot he did not collapse but climbed with desperate slowness to his feet and stood weakly upright, with legs sagging and head drooping. I fired a third time. That was the shot that did for him. You could see the agony of it jolt his whole body and knock the last remnant of strength from his legs. But in falling he seemed for a moment to rise, for as his hind legs collapsed beneath him he seemed to tower upward like a huge rock toppling, his trunk reaching skywards like a tree. He trumpeted, for the first and only time. And then down he came, his belly towards me, with a crash that seemed to shake the ground even where I lay.

12   I got up. The Burmans were already racing past me across the mud. It was obvious that the elephant would never rise again, but he was not dead. He was breathing very rhythmically with long rattling gasps, his great mound of a side painfully rising and falling. His mouth was wide open—I could see far down into caverns of pale pink throat. I waited for a long time for him to die, but his breathing did not weaken. Finally I fired my two remaining shots into the spot where I thought his heart must be. The thick blood welled out of him like red velvet, but still he did not die. His body did not even jerk when the shots hit him, the tortured breathing continued without a pause. He was dying, very slowly and in great agony, but in some world remote from me where not even a bullet could damage him further. I felt that I had got to put an end to that dreadful noise. It seemed dreadful to see the great beast lying there, powerless to move and yet powerless to die, and not even to be able to finish him. I sent back for my small rifle and poured shot after shot into his heart and down his throat. They seemed to make no impression. The tortured gasps continued as steadily as the ticking of a clock.

13   In the end I could not stand it any longer and went away. I heard later that it took him half an hour to die. Burmans were bringing dahs and baskets even before I left, and I was told they had stripped his body almost to the bones by the afternoon.

14   Afterwards, of course, there were endless discussions about the shooting of the elephant. The owner was furious, but he was only an Indian and could do nothing. Besides, legally I had done the right thing, for a mad elephant has to be killed, like a mad dog, if its owner fails to control it. Among the Europeans opinion was divided. The older men said I was right, the younger men said it was a damn shame to shoot an elephant for killing a coolie, because an elephant was worth more than any damn Coringhee coolie. And afterwards I was very glad that the coolie had been killed; it put me legally in the right and it gave me a sufficient pretext for shooting the elephant. I often wondered

whether any of the others grasped that I had done it solely to avoid looking a fool.

~

(3,305 words)

VOCABULARY

supplant (2)	prostrate (2)	despotic (3)
labyrinth (4)	squalid (4)	garish (7)
conventionalized (7)	resolute (7)	pretext (14)

THE FACTS

1. Which class of Burmese did Orwell despise most of all?
2. What would likely happen to a white woman who went through the bazaars alone?
3. What is Orwell's opinion of the younger empires that were going to supplant the British Empire?
4. What is invariably the case with stories set in the East?
5. According to Orwell, what is a condition of white rule over the empire?

THE STRATEGIES

1. Orwell writes: "They had not shown much interest in the elephant when he was merely ravaging their homes, but it was different now that he was going to be shot." What tone is he using here?
2. Why does Orwell use Latin phrases? What purpose do they have in the story?
3. The story is told in two tenses: the past and the present. What effect does this have on its telling?
4. Orwell encloses some remarks in parentheses in paragraphs 4 and 8. Why are these remarks set off in this way?
5. What analogy does Orwell use in paragraph 10 to describe his feelings about the crowd gathered to see him kill the elephant? Is this an appropriate analogy? Explain.

THE ISSUES

1. What is the value of a role and of role-playing in the relationships of everyday life?

2. What are the obvious disadvantages of role-playing?

3. How would you characterize Orwell's attitude toward the empire he serves?

4. How do you think the author might have behaved, and what do you think he might have done, if other Europeans had been with him when he met the elephant?

5. What circumstances of today's life might similarly make someone, say a student, feel impelled to behave in a way contrary to his or her better judgment?

SUGGESTIONS FOR WRITING

1. Analyze and discuss *Shooting an Elephant* as a story about the abstract versus the concrete, the general versus the particular.

2. Write an essay entitled "I Wore a Mask, and My Face Grew to Fit It."

MY NAME IS MARGARET

Maya Angelou

Maya Angelou (b. 1928) is novelist, poet, playwright, actress, composer, and singer. Her varied accomplishments have thrown her into the public limelight, where she is greatly admired as a speaker and reader of her own works. She is best known for her single-minded devotion to the cause of tolerance. Many of her novels recount incidents in which her characters must fight ardently to maintain their identity in a world of prejudice. Among her best-known works are I Know Why the Caged Bird Sings *(1970), from which the selection that follows is taken,* Gather Together in My Name *(1974),* Singin' and Swingin' and Gettin' Merry Like Christmas *(1976),* Heart of a Woman *(1981), and* All God's Children Need Traveling Shoes *(1986). Angelou has also written volumes of poetry, including* Oh Pray My Wings Are Gonna Fit Me Well *(1975) and* I Shall Not Be Moved *(1990). She has become a role model for aspiring female writers of various minority backgrounds.*

In this reading, a black author, admired for her stories dealing with affronts to a black person's pride and sense of dignity, tells of an incident in which a white woman arrogantly attempts to change the name of a young black girl who is working for her.

⁓

1 Recently a white woman from Texas, who would quickly describe herself as a liberal, asked me about my hometown. When I told her that in Stamps my

grandmother had owned the only Negro general merchandise store since the turn of the century, she exclaimed "Why, you were a debutante." Ridiculous and even ludicrous. But Negro girls in small Southern towns, whether poverty-stricken or just munching along on a few of life's necessities, were given as extensive and irrelevant preparations for adulthood as rich white girls shown in magazines. Admittedly the training was not the same. While white girls learned to waltz and sit gracefully with a tea cup balanced on their knees, we were lagging behind, learning the mid-Victorian values with very little money to indulge them. (Come and see Edna Lomax spending the money she made picking cotton on five balls of ecru tatting thread. Her fingers are bound to snag the work and she'll have to repeat the stitches time and time again. But she knows that when she buys the thread.)

2   We were required to embroider and I had trunkfuls of colorful dishtowels, pillowcases, runners and handkerchiefs to my credit. I mastered the art of crocheting and tatting, and there was a lifetime's supply of dainty doilies that would never be used in sacheted dresser drawers. It went without saying that all girls could iron and wash, but the finer touches around the home, like setting a table with real silver, baking roasts and cooking vegetables without meat, had to be learned elsewhere. Usually at the source of those habits. During my tenth year, a white woman's kitchen became my finishing school.

3   Mrs. Viola Cullinan was a plump woman who lived in a three-bedroom house somewhere behind the post office. She was singularly unattractive until she smiled, and then the lines around her eyes and mouth which made her look perpetually dirty disappeared, and her face looked like the mask of an impish elf. She usually rested her smile until late afternoon when her women friends dropped in and Miss Glory, the cook, served them cold drinks on the closed-in porch.

4   The exactness of her house was inhuman. This glass went here and only here. That cup had its place and it was an act of impudent rebellion to place it anywhere else. At twelve o'clock the table was set. At 12:15 Mrs. Cullinan sat down to dinner (whether her husband had arrived or not). At 12:16 Miss Glory brought out the food.

5   It took me a week to learn the difference between a salad plate, a bread plate and a dessert plate.

6   Mrs. Cullinan kept up the tradition of her wealthy parents. She was from Virginia. Miss Glory, who was a descendant of slaves that had worked for the Cullinans, told me her history. She had married beneath her (according to Miss Glory). Her husband's family hadn't had their money very long and what they had "didn't 'mount to much."

7   As ugly as she was, I thought privately, she was lucky to get a husband above or beneath her station. But Miss Glory wouldn't let me say a thing against her mistress. She was very patient with me, however, over the housework. She explained the dishware, silverware and servants' bells. The large round bowl in which soup was served wasn't a soup bowl, it was a tureen. There were goblets, sherbet glasses, ice-cream glasses, wine glasses, green glass coffee cups with matching saucers, and water glasses. I had a

glass to drink from, and it sat with Miss Glory's on a separate shelf from the others. Soup spoons, gravy boat, butter knives, salad forks and carving platter were additions to my vocabulary and in fact almost represented a new language. I was fascinated with the novelty, with the fluttering Mrs. Cullinan and her Alice-in-Wonderland house.

8   Her husband remains, in my memory, undefined. I lumped him with all the other white men that I had ever seen and tried not to see.

9   On our way home one evening, Miss Glory told me that Mrs. Cullinan couldn't have children. She said that she was too delicate-boned. It was hard to imagine bones at all under those layers of fat. Miss Glory went on to say that the doctor had taken out all her lady organs. I reasoned that a pig's organs included the lungs, heart and liver, so if Mrs. Cullinan was walking around without those essentials, it explained why she drank alcohol out of unmarked bottles. She was keeping herself embalmed.

10   When I spoke to Bailey about it, he agreed that I was right, but he also informed me that Mr. Cullinan had two daughters by a colored lady and that I knew them very well. He added that the girls were the spitting image of their father. I was unable to remember what he looked like, although I had just left him a few hours before, but I thought of the Coleman girls. They were very light-skinned and certainly didn't look very much like their mother (no one ever mentioned Mr. Coleman).

11   My pity for Mrs. Cullinan preceded me the next morning like the Cheshire cat's smile. Those girls, who could have been her daughters, were beautiful. They didn't have to straighten their hair. Even when they were caught in the rain, their braids still hung down straight like tamed snakes. Their mouths were pouty little cupid's bows. Mrs. Cullinan didn't know what she missed. Or maybe she did. Poor Mrs. Cullinan.

12   For weeks after, I arrived early, left late and tried very hard to make up for her barrenness. If she had had her own children, she wouldn't have had to ask me to run a thousand errands from her back door to the back door of her friends. Poor old Mrs. Cullinan.

13   Then one evening Miss Glory told me to serve the ladies on the porch. After I set the tray down and turned toward the kitchen, one of the women asked, "What's your name, girl?" It was the speckled-faced one. Mrs. Cullinan said, "She doesn't talk much. Her name's Margaret."

14   "Is she dumb?"

15   "No. As I understand it, she can talk when she wants to but she's usually quiet as a little mouse. Aren't you, Margaret?"

16   I smiled at her. Poor thing. No organs and couldn't even pronounce my name correctly.

17   "She's a sweet little thing, though."

18   "Well, that may be, but the name's too long. I'd never bother myself. I'd call her Mary if I was you."

19   I fumed into the kitchen. That horrible woman would never have the chance to call me Mary because if I was starving I'd never work for her. I decided I wouldn't pee on her if her heart was on fire. Giggles drifted in off the

porch and into Miss Glory's pots. I wondered what they could be laughing about.

20   Whitefolks were so strange. Could they be talking about me? Everybody knew that they stuck together better than the Negroes did. It was possible that Mrs. Cullinan had friends in St. Louis who heard about a girl from Stamps being in court and wrote to tell her. Maybe she knew about Mr. Freeman.

21   My lunch was in my mouth a second time and I went outside and relieved myself on the bed of four-o'clocks. Miss Glory thought I might be coming down with something and told me to go on home, that Momma would give me some herb tea, and she'd explain to her mistress.

22   I realized how foolish I was being before I reached the pond. Of course Mrs. Cullinan didn't know. Otherwise she wouldn't have given me two nice dresses that Momma cut down, and she certainly wouldn't have called me a "sweet little thing." My stomach felt fine, and I didn't mention anything to Momma.

23   That evening I decided to write a poem on being white, fat, old and without children. It was going to be a tragic ballad. I would have to watch her carefully to capture the essence of her loneliness and pain.

24   The very next day, she called me by the wrong name. Miss Glory and I were washing up the lunch dishes when Mrs. Cullinan came to the doorway. "Mary?"

25   Miss Glory asked, "Who?"

26   Mrs. Cullinan, sagging a little, knew and I knew. "I want Mary to go down to Mrs. Randall's and take her some soup. She's not been feeling well for a few days."

27   Miss Glory's face was a wonder to see. "You mean Margaret, ma'am. Her name's Margaret."

28   "That's too long. She's Mary from now on. Heat that soup from last night and put it in the china tureen and, Mary, I want you to carry it carefully."

29   Every person I knew had a hellish horror of being "called out of his name." It was a dangerous practice to call a Negro anything that could be loosely construed as insulting because of the centuries of their having been called niggers, jigs, dinges, blackbirds, crows, boots and spooks.

30   Miss Glory had a fleeting second of feeling sorry for me. Then as she handed me the hot tureen she said, "Don't mind, don't pay that no mind. Sticks and stones may break your bones, but words . . .You know, I been working for her for twenty years."

31   She held the back door open for me. "Twenty years. I wasn't much older than you. My name used to be Hallelujah. That's what Ma named me, but my mistress give me 'Glory,' and it stuck. I likes it better too."

32   I was in the little path that ran behind the houses when Miss Glory shouted, "It's shorter too."

33   For a few seconds it was a tossup over whether I would laugh (imagine being named Hallelujah) or cry (imagine letting some white woman rename you for her convenience). My anger saved me from either outburst. I had to

quit the job, but the problem was going to be how to do it. Momma wouldn't allow me to quit for just any reason.

34   "She's a peach. That woman is a real peach." Mrs. Randall's maid was talking as she took the soup from me, and I wondered what her name used to be and what she answered to now.

35   For a week I looked into Mrs. Cullinan's face as she called me Mary. She ignored my coming late and leaving early. Miss Glory was a little annoyed because I had begun to leave egg yolk on the dishes and wasn't putting much heart in polishing the silver. I hoped that she would complain to our boss, but she didn't.

36   Then Bailey solved my dilemma. He had me describe the contents of the cupboard and the particular plates she liked best. Her favorite piece was a casserole shaped like a fish and the green glass coffee cups. I kept his instructions in mind, so on the next day when Miss Glory was hanging out clothes and I had again been told to serve the old biddies on the porch, I dropped the empty serving tray. When I heard Mrs. Cullinan scream, "Mary!" I picked up the casserole and two of the green glass cups in readiness. As she rounded the kitchen door I let them fall on the tiled floor.

37   I could never absolutely describe to Bailey what happened next, because each time I got to the part where she fell on the floor and screwed up her ugly face to cry, we burst out laughing. She actually wobbled around on the floor and picked up shards of the cups and cried, "Oh, Momma. Oh, dear Gawd. It's Momma's china from Virginia. Oh, Momma, I sorry."

38   Miss Glory came running in from the yard and the women from the porch crowded around. Miss Glory was almost as broken up as her mistress. "You mean to say she broke our Virginia dishes? What we gone do?"

39   Miss Cullinan cried louder, "That clumsy nigger. Clumsy little black nigger."

40   Old speckled-face leaned down and asked, "Who did it, Viola? Was it Mary? Who did it?"

41   Everything was happening so fast I can't remember whether her action preceded her words, but I know that Mrs. Cullinan said, "Her name's Margaret, goddamn it, her name's Margaret." And she threw a wedge of the broken plate at me. It could have been the hysteria which put her aim off, but the flying crockery caught Miss Glory right over the ear and she started screaming.

42   I left the front door wide open so all the neighbors could hear.

43   Mrs. Cullinan was right about one thing. My name wasn't Mary.

~

(2,101 words)

VOCABULARY

debutante (1)	ludicrous (1)	tatting (2)
sacheted (2)	impudent (4)	barrenness (12)
ballad (23)	shards (37)	crockery (41)

THE FACTS

1. In their preparations for adulthood, what did both white girls and Negro girls have in common?
2. Where did Negro girls learn to set the table and cook?
3. What kind of housekeeper was Mrs. Viola Cullinan? How does the narrator view her habits?
4. Why does the narrator feel pity for Mrs. Cullinan?
5. Why did the narrator get furious at Mrs. Cullinan? What did the narrator do to vent her anger?

THE STRATEGIES

1. From whose point of view is this story told? How does the point of view affect the narration? How is the narration paced?
2. The narrator calls Mrs. Cullinan's house an "Alice-in-Wonderland house." What kind of image does this label conjure up? Where else in the story does the narrator use an image from Lewis Carroll's *Adventures of Alice in Wonderland*? To what purpose?
3. Although the tale about Margaret's name is essentially a serious matter, there are nevertheless some humorous elements in the narrative. What humorous incidents can you point out? Refer to specific passages.
4. What examples of figurative language does the narrator use in paragraph 11? How effective are they?
5. Why does the narrator never explain who Bailey and Mr. Freeman are? From the context of the story, who do you think they are?

THE ISSUES

1. The narrator is extremely sensitive about her name. Why is this so? How do you feel about your own name? Does it bother you when someone mispronounces or misspells it?
2. The narrator leaves the ending wide open. What do you think will happen to Margaret following this incident?
3. What does Margaret's decision to write a poem about Mrs. Cullinan indicate?
4. What is the relationship between Glory and Mrs. Cullinan?
5. Describe Glory. Do you think Margaret will ever be like her?
6. What do you think of Glory's attempt to calm down Margaret after Mrs. Cullinan called her "Mary" from the doorway? (See paragraphs 30–32.) How does her reaction differ from Bailey's? Which reaction seems more appropriate to you?

WRITING ASSIGNMENTS

1. Narrate an incident in which you reacted to someone who treated
    you with arrogance or meanness. Make your narration come to life
    by using dialogue and vivid details.

2. Narrate an incident from your youth that taught you a lesson in
    tolerance concerning race, religion, sex, social status, or some other
    aspect of society. Pace the narration properly and use vivid details.

SHAME

Dick Gregory

*Dick Gregory (b. 1932) is a political activist, comedian, and writer. He
attended Southern Illinois University, where he was named Outstanding
Athlete in 1953. Gregory has been much admired for his interest in social
issues, such as world famine, and for his outstanding ability as a stand-
up comedian. In 1966, he ran for Mayor of Chicago, and in 1968, he was
the presidential candidate of the Freedom and Peace Party. Gregory has
written several books, including* From the Back of the Bus *(1962),*
What's Happening? *(1965),* The Shadow That Scares Me *(1968),*
Dick Gregory's Bible Tales *(1974), and his autobiography,* Up from
Nigger *(1976). Gregory was one of the first black comedians to break the
"color barrier" and perform for white audiences. His popularity is based
on his ability to satirize race relations without being derogatory.*

Even if you have never felt the poverty described by the narrator in the story
that follows, you can probably remember someone from your childhood or adolescence who somehow represented all the romance and beauty you longed
for. Ponder the details that make the narrator's experience so heartbreaking.

~

1   I never learned hate at home, or shame. I had to go to school for that. I was
about seven years old when I got my first big lesson. I was in love with a little girl named Helene Tucker, a light-complected little girl with pigtails and
nice manners. She was always clean and she was smart in school. I think I
went to school mostly to look at her. I brushed my hair and even got me a little old handkerchief. It was a lady's handkerchief, but I didn't want Helene
to see me wipe my nose on my hand. The pipes were frozen again, there was
no water in the house, but I washed my socks and shirt every night. I'd get a
pot, and go over to Mr. Ben's grocery store, and stick my pot down into his
soda machine. Scoop out some chopped ice. By evening the ice melted to water for washing. I got sick a lot that winter because the fire would go out at
night before the clothes were dry. In the morning I'd put them on, wet or dry,
because they were the only clothes I had.

2   Everybody's got a Helene Tucker, a symbol of everything you want. I loved her for her goodness, her cleanliness, her popularity. She'd walk down my street and my brothers and sisters would yell, "Here comes Helene," and I'd rub my tennis sneakers on the back of my pants and wish my hair wasn't so nappy and the white folks' shirt fit me better. I'd run out on the street. If I knew my place and didn't come too close, she'd wink at me and say hello. That was a good feeling. Sometimes I'd follow her all the way home, and shovel the snow off her walk and try to make friends with her Momma and her aunts. I'd drop money on her stoop late at night on my way back from shining shoes in the taverns. And she had a Daddy, and he had a good job. He was a paper hanger.

3   I guess I would have gotten over Helene by summertime, but something happened in that classroom that made her face hang in front of me for the next twenty-two years. When I played the drums in high school it was for Helene and when I broke track records in college it was for Helene and when I started standing behind microphones and heard applause I wished Helene could hear it, too. It wasn't until I was twenty-nine years old and married and making money that I really got her out of my system. Helene was sitting in that classroom when I learned to be ashamed of myself.

4   It was on a Thursday. I was sitting in the back of the room, in a seat with a chalk circle drawn around it. The idiot's seat, the troublemaker's seat.

5   The teacher thought I was stupid. Couldn't spell, couldn't read, couldn't do arithmetic. Just stupid. Teachers were never interested in finding out that you couldn't concentrate because you were so hungry, because you hadn't had any breakfast. All you could think about was noontime, would it ever come? Maybe you could sneak into the cloakroom and steal a bit of some kid's lunch out of a coat pocket. A bit of something. Paste. You can't really make a meal out of paste, or put it on bread for a sandwich, but sometimes I'd scoop a few spoonfuls out of the paste jar in the back of the room. Pregnant people get strange tastes. I was pregnant with poverty. Pregnant with dirt and pregnant with smells that made people turn away, pregnant with cold and pregnant with shoes that were never bought for me, pregnant with five other people in my bed and no Daddy in the next room, and pregnant with hunger. Paste doesn't taste too bad when you're hungry.

6   The teacher thought I was a troublemaker. All she saw from the front of the room was a little black boy who squirmed in his idiot's seat and made noises and poked the kids around him. I guess she couldn't see a kid who made noises because he wanted someone to know he was there.

7   It was on a Thursday, the day before the Negro payday. The eagle always flew on Friday. The teacher was asking each student how much his father would give to the Community Chest. On Friday night, each kid would get the money from his father, and on Monday he would bring it to the school. I decided I was going to buy me a Daddy right then. I had money in my pocket from shining shoes and selling papers and whatever Helene Tucker pledged for her Daddy I was going to top it. And I'd hand the money right in. I wasn't going to wait until Monday to buy me a Daddy.

8   I was shaking, scared to death. The teacher opened her book and started calling our names alphabetically.

9   "Helene Tucker?"

10   "My Daddy said he'd give two dollars and fifty cents."

11   "That's very nice, Helene. Very, very nice indeed."

12   That made me feel pretty good. It wouldn't take too much to top that. I had almost three dollars in dimes and quarters in my pocket. I stuck my hand in my pocket and held onto the money, waiting for her to call my name. But the teacher closed her book after she called everybody else in the class.

13   I stood up and raised my hand.

14   "What is it now?"

15   "You forgot me."

16   "She turned toward the blackboard. "I don't have time to be playing with you, Richard."

17   "My Daddy said he'd . . ."

18   "Sit down, Richard, you're disturbing the class."

19   "My Daddy said he'd give . . . fifteen dollars."

20   She turned around and looked mad. "We are collecting this money for you and your kind, Richard Gregory. If your Daddy can give fifteen dollars you have no business being on relief."

21   "I got it right now, I got it right now, my Daddy gave it to me to turn in to-day, my Daddy said . . ."

22   "And furthermore," she said, looking right at me, her nostrils getting big and her lips getting thin and her eyes opening wide, "we know you don't have a Daddy."

23   Helene Tucker turned around, her eyes full of tears. She felt sorry for me. Then I couldn't see her too well because I was crying, too.

24   "Sit down, Richard."

25   And I always thought the teacher kind of liked me. She always picked me to wash the blackboard on Friday, after school. That was a big thrill, it made me feel important. If I didn't wash it, come Monday the school might not function right.

26   "Where are you going, Richard?"

27   I walked out of school that day, and for a long time I didn't go back very often. There was shame there.

28   Now there was shame everywhere. It seemed like the whole world had been inside that classroom, everyone had heard what the teacher had said, everyone had turned around and felt sorry for me. There was shame in going to the Worthy Boys Annual Christmas Dinner for you and your kind, because everybody knew what a worthy boy was. Why couldn't they just call it the Boys Annual Dinner, why'd they have to give it a name? There was shame in wearing the brown and orange and white plaid mackinaw the welfare gave to 3,000 boys. Why'd it have to be the same for everybody so when you walked down the street the people could see you were on relief? It was a nice

warm mackinaw and it had a hood, and my Momma beat me and called me a little rat when she found out I stuffed it in the bottom of a pail full of garbage way over on Cottage Street. There was shame in running over to Mister Ben's at the end of the day and asking for his rotten peaches, there was shame in asking Mrs. Simmons for a spoonful of sugar, there was shame in running out to meet the relief truck. I hated that truck, full of food for you and your kind. I ran into the house and hid when it came. And then I started to sneak through alleys, to take the long way home so people going into White's Eat Shop wouldn't see me. Yeah, the whole world heard the teacher that day, we all know you don't have a Daddy.   ∼

(1,423 words)

VOCABULARY

mackinaw (28)

THE FACTS

1. Where did the narrator learn shame?
2. What did the narrator do for Helene Tucker? How important was she in his life?
3. According to the narrator, why could he not do well in school? What did the teachers think?
4. What event at school caused shame to control the narrator's life for a long time? Summarize what happened.
5. What did the author dislike about the Worthy Boys Annual Christmas Dinner?

THE STRATEGIES

1. The narration begins in paragraph 3, following two paragraphs of commentary about Helene Tucker, a girl on whom the narrator had a crush. What is the purpose of the preliminary paragraphs?
2. What dominant impression is always in the background of the narration? Why?
3. Beginning with paragraph 9, the narrator adds conversation to the narration. What is the effect of this technique?
4. What is the main theme (lesson about life) revealed in this story? Is it implied or stated?
5. In paragraph 5, what is the purpose of repeating the word "pregnant"? What does the author mean?

THE ISSUES

1. Do you agree with the narrator's comment that "everybody's got a Helene Tucker"? What does Helene Tucker symbolize? Give an example of a Helene Tucker from your own experience.

2. The teacher thought the narrator was a troublemaker. Was he really, or was there another reason for drawing attention to himself?

3. Why did the teacher humiliate the narrator when he announced that his father would donate fifteen dollars? Do you think the teacher should have handled the situation differently? If so, how should she have reacted?

4. The narrator states that he thought the teacher liked him because she always picked him to clean the blackboard on Friday. Why do you think she picked him?

5. Did the narrator do the right thing by not going back to the school often after the shame incident? What kept him away? Do you empathize or do you think the narrator was oversensitive?

SUGGESTIONS FOR WRITING

1. Write about an incident in which you or someone you love experienced shame. Use the techniques of pacing, using vivid details, and making a point.

2. Write an essay in which you examine the psychological effects of poverty on children in elementary school.

THE ODOUR OF CHEESE

Jerome K. Jerome

Jerome Klapka Jerome (1859–1927) was an English writer known for his genial humor. Among his works are Idle Thoughts of an Idle Fellow *(1886), his best known and still read* Three Men in a Boat *(1889), and a morality play,* The Passing of the Third Floor Back *(1907).*

In 1889, when the author was only thirty, *Three Men in a Boat* was published to overnight success. It has been translated into every European language and several Asian ones as well. This excerpt, a hilarious narrative about the author's misadventures with smelly cheese, contains one of its funniest stories.

∾

1   Cheese, like oil, makes too much of itself. It wants the whole boat to itself. It goes through the hamper, and gives a cheesy flavour to everything else there.

You can't tell whether you are eating apple-pie or German sausage, or straw-berries and cream. It all seems cheese. There is too much odour about cheese.

2   I remember a friend of mine buying a couple of cheeses at Liverpool. Splendid cheeses they were, ripe and mellow, and with a two hundred horse-power scent about them that might have been warranted to carry three miles, and knock a man over at two hundred yards. I was in Liverpool at the time, and my friend said that if I didn't mind he would get me to take them back with me to London, as he should not be coming up for a day or two himself, and he did not think the cheeses ought to be kept much longer.

3   "Oh, with pleasure, dear boy," I replied, "with pleasure."

4   I called for the cheeses, and took them away in a cab. It was a ramshackle affair, dragged along by a knock-kneed, broken-winded somnambulist, which his owner, in a moment of enthusiasm, during conversation, referred to as a horse. I put the cheeses on the top, and we started off at a shamble that would have done credit to the swiftest steam-roller ever built, and all went merry as a funeral bell, until we turned the corner. There, the wind carried a whiff from the cheeses full on to our steed. It woke him up, and, with a snort of terror, he dashed off at three miles an hour. The wind still blew in his di-rection, and before we reached the end of the street he was laying himself out at the rate of nearly four miles an hour, leaving the cripples and stout old ladies simply nowhere.

5   It took two porters as well as the driver to hold him in at the station; and I do not think they would have done it, even then, had not one of the men had the presence of mind to put a handkerchief over his nose, and to light a bit of brown paper.

6   I took my ticket, and marched proudly up the platform, with my cheeses, the people falling back respectfully on either side. The train was crowded, and I had to get into a carriage where there were already seven other people. One crusty old gentleman objected, but I got in, notwithstanding; and put-ting my cheeses upon the rack, squeezed down with a pleasant smile, and said it was a warm day. A few moments passed, and then the old gentleman began to fidget.

7   "Very close in here," he said.

"Quite oppressive," said the man next him.

8   And then they both began sniffing, and, at the third sniff, they caught it right on the chest, and rose up without another word and went out. And then a stout lady got up, and said it was disgraceful that a respectable married woman should be harried about in this way, and gathered up a bag and eight parcels and went. The remaining four passengers sat on for a while, until a solemn-looking man in the corner who, from his dress and general appear-ance, seemed to belong to the undertaker class, said it put him in mind of a dead baby; and the other three passengers tried to get out of the door at the same time, and hurt themselves.

9   I smiled at the black gentleman, and said I thought we were going to have the carriage to ourselves; and he laughed pleasantly and said that some peo-ple made such a fuss over a little thing. But even he grew strangely depressed

after we had started, and so, when we reached Crewe, I asked him to come and have a drink. He accepted, and we forced our way into the buffet, where we yelled, and stamped, and waved our umbrellas for a quarter of an hour; and then a young lady came and asked us if we wanted anything.

10   "What's yours?" I said, turning to my friend.

"I'll have a half a crown's worth of brandy, neat, if you please, miss," he responded.

11   And he went off quietly after he had drunk it and got into another carriage, which I thought mean.

12   From Crewe I had the compartment to myself, though the train was crowded. As we drew up at the different stations, the people, seeing my empty carriage, would rush for it. "Here y'are, Maria; come along, plenty of room." "All right, Tom; we'll get in here," they would shout. And they would run along, carrying heavy bags, and fight around the door to get in first. And one would open the door and mount the steps and stagger back into the arms of the man behind him; and they would all come and have a sniff, and then droop off and squeeze into other carriages, or pay the difference and go first.

13   From Euston I took the cheeses down to my friend's house. When his wife came into the room she smelt round for an instant. Then she said:

14   "What is it? Tell me the worst."

I said: "It's cheeses. Tom bought them in Liverpool, and asked me to bring them up with me."

15   And I added that I hoped she understood that it had nothing to do with me; and she said that she was sure of that, but that she would speak to Tom about it when he came back.

16   My friend was detained in Liverpool longer than he expected; and three days later, as he hadn't returned home, his wife called on me. She said:

17   "What did Tom say about those cheeses?"

I replied that he had directed they were to be kept in a moist place, and that nobody was to touch them.

She said: "Nobody's likely to touch them. Had he smelt them?"

I thought he had, and added that he seemed greatly attached to them.

"You think he would be upset," she queried, "if I gave a man a sovereign to take them away and bury them?"

I answered that I thought he would never smile again.

An idea struck her. She said:

18   "Do you mind keeping them for him? Let me send them round to you."

19   "Madam," I replied, "for myself I like the smell of cheese, and the journey the other day with them from Liverpool I shall ever look back upon as a happy ending to a pleasant holiday. But, in this world, we must consider others. The lady under whose roof I have the honour of residing is a widow, and, for all I know, possibly an orphan too. She has a strong, I may say an eloquent, objection to being what she terms 'put upon.' The presence of your husband's cheeses in her house she would, I instinctively feel, regard as a 'put upon'; and it shall never be said that I put upon the widow and the orphan."

20   "Very well, then," said my friend's wife, rising, "all I have to say is, that I shall take the children and go to an hotel until those cheeses are eaten. I decline to live any longer in the same house with them."

21   She kept her word, leaving the place in charge of the charwoman, who, when asked if she could stand the smell, replied, "What smell?" and who, when taken close to the cheeses and told to sniff hard, said she could detect a faint odour of melons. It was argued from this that little injury could result to the woman from the atmosphere, and she was left.

22   The hotel bill came to fifteen guineas; and my friend, after reckoning everything up, found that the cheeses had cost him eight-and-sixpence a pound. He said he dearly loved a bit of cheese, but it was beyond his means; so he determined to get rid of them. He threw them into the canal; but had to fish them out again, as the bargemen complained. They said it made them feel quite faint. And, after that, he took them one dark night and left them in the parish mortuary. But the coroner discovered them, and made a fearful fuss.

23   He said it was a plot to deprive him of his living by waking up the corpses.

24   My friend got rid of them, at last, by taking them down to a seaside town, and burying them on the beach. It gained the place quite a reputation. Visitors said they have never noticed before how strong the air was, and weak-chested and consumptive people used to throng there for years afterwards.

~

(1,460 words)

VOCABULARY

ramshackle (4)   somnambulist (4)   harried (8)

THE FACTS

1. What happened when the horse drawing the cab caught a whiff of the cheese?
2. What effect did the odor of the cheese have on the passengers in the train compartment?
3. What did the wife do when the cheeses were delivered to her?
4. Upon whom did the cheeses have no effect at all? What did the smell remind that person of?
5. How were the cheeses finally disposed of?

THE STRATEGIES

1. What is the thesis of this short piece and where is it stated?
2. What is the author's main technique for achieving humor?

3. The excerpt comes from an immensely successful Victorian book. What characteristics of its writing tell you that it was intended for a popular audience?

4. Paragraphs 21 and 22 contain an example of how this narrative is paced. In what way is the narrative paced in these paragraphs?

5. The author writes: "I took my ticket, and marched proudly up the platform, with my cheeses, and people falling respectfully on either side." What word in that sentence gives rise to subtle humor?

THE ISSUES

1. How does the humor of this piece differ from the humor we are likely to read today?

2. Deducing the narrator's lifestyle from this piece, what social type would we likely call him today?

3. What modern convenience is obviously missing from the author's life, and how did it seem to affect him and his relationship with others around him?

4. What did the people aboard the train not do in response to the stink of the cheeses that they would likely do in America today?

5. How do you think people today would react to a similar situation of a conspicuous stink in public transportation?

SUGGESTIONS FOR WRITING

1. Narrate a humorous incident that happened to you or that you witnessed in a public place.

2. Rewrite this story in a modern time and setting, placing it in a large urban area. Be sure your characters are drawn realistically to conform to modern types.

THOSE WINTER SUNDAYS

Robert Hayden

Robert Hayden (1913–1980) was born in Detroit, attended the University of Michigan, and taught at Fisk University. His Ballad of Remembrance *was awarded a prize at the 1966 World Festival of Negro Arts held in Dakar, Senegal.*

The following poem recounts a childhood memory.

~

Sundays too my father got up early
and put his clothes on in the blueblack cold,

then with cracked hands that ached
from labor in the weekday weather made
5   banked fires blaze. No one ever thanked him.
I'd wake and hear the cold splintering, breaking.
When the rooms were warm, he'd call,
and slowly I would rise and dress,
fearing the chronic angers of that house,
10 Speaking indifferently to him,
who had driven out the cold
and polished my good shoes as well.
What did I know, what did I know
of love's austere and lonely offices?

~

(100 words)

VOCABULARY

banked (5)   chronic (9)   austere (14)

THE FACTS

1. What did the narrator's father do on Sundays?
2. How did the narrator react to his father in the morning?
3. How would you characterize the narrator's attitude as he looks back on this time with his father?

THE STRATEGIES

1. In what poetic form is this narration framed? (Hint: Count the number of lines.)
2. The author writes about his father: "No one ever thanked him." Why do you think he chose to put it this way? Why not simply say "I never thanked him"?
3. The poet writes: "I'd wake and hear the cold splintering, breaking." What kind of figure of speech is this?
4. Examine the sentences in the poem. How many are there? What is the technique of running a sentence across several lines without an end-stop or break?

THE ISSUES

1. What kind of work do you suppose the speaker's father did? How can his probable occupation be deduced from the poem?
2. What are "love's austere and lonely offices"? What other examples can you give of them?

SUGGESTIONS FOR WRITING

1. Write an analysis of this poem.
2. Narrate an incident from your own childhood that involved your relationship with a parent or other significant adult.

——————— ISSUE FOR CRITICAL ——————— THINKING AND DEBATE
TERRORISM

The September 11, 2001 suicide bombing of the World Trade Center in New York and the Pentagon in Washington D.C. was, to most of the horrified Western world, an act of unspeakable wickedness and evil. To many in the Islamic world, it was a deed of heroic martyrdom done in the name of God and one that guaranteed heaven to the self-sacrificing souls responsible for it. After the attack, as the rescuers sifted through the physical rubble, and the talking heads on television combed through the shreds of whys and whats, the irreconcilable divide between the terrorists and us became sharply clear. While we mourned for the victims and prayed for their families, elsewhere in the world people rejoiced at our sorrow. Even now, when we think about the murderers' coldbloodedness, their diabolical planning, and their fanatical sacrifice, many of us cannot comprehend the depth of the hate that drove them to invest so much time and energy into slaughtering so many innocents.

Why do they hate us so? We're used to being admired—our material wealth and lifestyle the envy of the world. Our history has repeatedly shown us to be a generous people, donating billions of dollars to help less fortunate nations in the grip of war, famine, pestilence, or economic ruin. When we have won wars, we have always tried to help our former enemies rebuild rather than occupy their territory. Yet, there are millions of people—some Islamic, some not—who hate us with such passion that they are willing, even eager, to sacrifice themselves in murderous and indiscriminate attacks aimed at our destruction. Al-Qaeda, the terrorist organization headed by Osama bin Laden, even now reportedly continues to train assassins and saboteurs, all willing to blow themselves up in an attempt to hurt us. What stuns most Americans is that these people believe that their terroristic attacks are the will of God. Few of us associate God with mass slaughter; even fewer can comprehend the belief that the rewards of paradise will be lavished on such murderers.

Neither of the two writers whose opinions are given here has any doubt about the wickedness of terrorism. Where they differ is in how they would respond to the terrorist. Peter Worthington, a Canadian conservative, sides outright with President Bush, telling us plainly that we're lucky to have a president who is prepared to fight fire with fire. Salman Rushdie, who went into hiding on February 14, 1989, after his novel, *The Satanic Verses*, was de-

Terrorism: Firefighter watches smoke from remains of the World Trade Center. Copyright © Mark M. Lawrence/ CORBIS.

clared blasphemous by the Ayatollah Khomeini of Iran and a fatwa or death sentence was issued against him, warns us against cockiness. Although the fatwa was lifted by the government of Iran in 1998, in February 1999 Ayatollah Hassan Sanei promised a reward of $2.8 million to anyone who would kill Rushdie, who still remains elusive.

We're not used to people trying to kill us. To many Americans, that kind of despicable plotting is a fact of life abroad, not life at home. The horror of 9-11 etched forever in our memories, many of us still remain jumpy, for we now know that there are people out there who hate us more than they love life. What we should do about them is the fundamental question.

IT'S AMERICA'S GOOD FORTUNE THAT THEY HAVE A PRESIDENT WILLING TO DECLARE WAR ON TERRORISM

Peter Worthington

Peter Worthington, a conservative columnist for the Toronto Sun, *is also the founding editor of that Canadian newspaper.*

~

1   Prime Minister Jean Chretien thinks poverty is a cause of terrorism; Transport Minister David Collenette regrets the Soviet Union isn't still around to check what he calls American "bullying"; Foreign Minister Bill Graham thinks just because Saddam Hussein is nasty is insufficient reason to take him out.

2   Good grief. These are guys who guide Canada!

3   First of all, poverty and terror are unrelated. The terrorism the civilized world (i.e., America and Britain) is at war against mostly comes from countries that have oodles of oil money, little of which trickles down to the people. Really poor countries are mostly passive.

4   If Collenette thinks the U.S. is a "bully," he's never met a real bully—which is what the U.S.S.R. was in its quest to dominate the world. The U.S. seeks to save the world, and by its example dictatorships have virtually been eliminated in the Western Hemisphere, except for Cuba.

5   Terrorism is the flavor of our times, but often misunderstood. For starters, our above-mentioned "leaders" might peruse a new book that's an excellent primer as to why Sept. 11 happened, who is to blame, and what to do about it. *The War Against the Terror Masters* is by Michael Ledeen, a scholarly "expert" who has worked in the State Department, Pentagon, National Security Council, and is now with the American Enterprise Institute.

6   Ledeen punctures many myths and shibboleths about terrorism, and how to thwart it. Everyone now acknowledges that Sept. 11 was a failure, in part, of intelligence. But it was a greater failure of political will. Starting in the 1970s, the CIA was told that assassination of presumed enemies was taboo. CIA agents were forbidden to deal with unsavory characters as sources.

7   The FBI wasn't even allowed to keep news clippings of groups proclaiming their intent to destroy America. Little in the way of intelligence analysis and documentation was done, nor was there cooperation or exchange of information among various U.S. security agencies.

8   When Jimmy Carter became president, the quality of intelligence deteriorated, and by the time of Bill Clinton, the U.S. had no agents in places like Iran, Iraq, Syria. All terror states.

9   Under Clinton, the U.S. decided there was no such thing as "state-sponsored terrorism." Terrorism was viewed as a criminal act, not a strategy of war. Even though every president since Gerald Ford has declared "war" on terrorism, none linked it directly to a particular state.

10   As for Sept. 11, there were all sorts of warnings and hints about Osama bin Laden which were ignored. The Italians had hard information—disregarded. Several times Sudan, of all places, warned the U.S. about the impending attack on embassies in Kenya and Tanzania, hoping to return to America's good graces. Sudan offered to turn over bin Laden who, even then, was on the U.S. wanted list. The State Department shrugged—and Clinton bombed a Sudanese aspirin factory.

11   By the 1993 bombing of the World Trade Center, neither the CIA nor the FBI were communicating, and neither followed evidence that indicated this was not a "crime" by individuals, but a sponsored act of war. Signs pointed

Some in U.S. Intelligence insisted (still do) that Sunni, Shiite, and secular to
12 Iraq's involvement, as well as Iran's and bin Laden's.

Muslims are so mutually hostile that they cannot cooperate in terror—
which is transparent rubbish.

13 Secular Iraq, fanatic Sunnis, and Shiites in Saudi Arabia, Syria, Iraq, Iran,
Afghanistan and Egypt cooperate against Israel and the U.S. when conditions
dictate.

14 If the Iraqi connection had been pursued in 1993, maybe 9/11 would have
been short-circuited. It now turns out that Mohammed Atta, a key figure in
Sept. 11, met Iraq's intelligence chief in Prague prior to the attack.

15 Terrorism is a cancer that requires surgery. Faint hearts who deplore military action against Saddam Hussein (on behalf of Iraqi people) resemble
those who warned going to war in Afghanistan would unite Afghan people
against America, would unite the Muslim world, would be a graveyard for
the U.S. army, would mean victory for Russia and so on.

16 All wrong. The opposite happened. As for Russians controlling
Afghanistan, U.S military bases are now solid in what used to be southern regions of the old U.S.S.R.

17 If Saddam is eliminated, the Middle East spawning grounds for international terror will be diminished.

18 The Iranian regime is vulnerable and could topple to a fairly substantial
opposition that's ready and waiting. Syria will be isolated, and the U.S. will
be able to get tougher with Saudi Arabia, where the disgraceful Saudi royal
family plays both sides for its own self-interest.

19 Contrary to some views, the world seems safer today than it was prior to
9/11. Bush sees it as his destiny to make the world safer, and since Sept. 11, U.S.
intelligence agencies have been revived and coordinated, so little happens anywhere that the Americans don't know about. Another state-sponsored sneak
attack is unlikely, as the security network spreads and becomes more vigilant.

20 No longer are warning signs ignored.

21 Ledeen itemizes Machiavelli's five rules for successful political and military
action, which are as pertinent today as they were in 1532 when he defined them:
1. Evil constantly wars against the good, and those who want peace—an ab-
normality—must win wars; peace is ensured by the gun barrel. 2. Winning is
the only important thing, and by winning it is the right thing; 3. If unpleasant
things must be done—do them all at once, decisively, quickly and ignore diplomats who always advise going slowly; 4. Being feared (respected) is safer than
being loved. People are fickle with those they love, consistent with those they
respect; 5. Never underestimate "luck," which can be good or bad and is un-
controllable; 50% good luck is sufficient if other factors fall into place.

22 Unlike his father, this President Bush is decisive, driven, has convictions
and has people around him who don't vacillate, as his dad did when he urged
Ukraine not to become independent, and Boris Yeltsin not to replace Mikhail
Gorbachev.

∿

(999 words)

VOCABULARY

shibboleths (6)	unsavory (6)	short-circuited (14)
spawning (17)	vigilant (19)	pertinent (21)
vacillate (22)		

THE FACTS

1. What do the men referred to in paragraph 1 have in common? Why are their opinions of concern to the United States?

2. What is the author's response to the accusation that the U.S. is a "bully"?

3. Why, according to the essay, was September 11 a failure? List the major reasons.

4. According to the author, what will happen if Saddam Hussein is eliminated?

5. What distinctions does the writer draw between George Bush and his father? Why are these distinctions important?

THE STRATEGIES

1. What tone does the author use throughout the essay? Point to specific passages that reveal the tone. Does the tone add or detract from the point being made? Give reasons for your answer.

2. In paragraph 15, what metaphor does the author use to clarify his point? Explain the metaphor. How does it help to explain the author's meaning? How would you rate its effectiveness?

3. What is the purpose of paragraph 21? Who is Machiavelli? What possible relationship can exist between him and today's politicians? Which of Machiavellian's rules, if any, might be of use today?

4. What is the meaning of the image "Terrorism is the flavor of our times"? Rewrite this literary allusion into plain prose.

5. In paragraph 10, why does the author refer to Clinton bombing a Sudanese aspirin factory?

THE ISSUES

1. In your opinion, is there a relationship between poverty and terror? If there is, what is the relationship?

2. The author's position is based mainly on a book by someone named Michael Ledeen who is affiliated with an organization identified as the American Enterprise Institute. Look up information on the Internet about this organization. What does Ledeen's affiliation with this institution tell you about him and his views?

3. On whom does the writer blame the decline in American intelligence over the decades? Do you find any significance in the fact that he singles out and names two particular presidents as being responsible? What do his choices for blame have in common?

4. How should the free world react to a tyrant like Hitler in Germany, Milosovic in Yugoslavia, bin Laden in Afghanistan, and Saddam Hussein in Iraq? More specifically, how should the United States react? Is it our duty to police the world?

5. Where does the world now stand with respect to terrorism? Are we in a safer position than we were before September 11, 2001? What still needs to be accomplished before we can breathe comfortably and without fear?

SUGGESTIONS FOR WRITING

1. Read Michael Ledeen's *The War Against the Terror Masters.* Do a critical analysis of the book, indicating its strengths and weaknesses. State your overall opinion of the book in your thesis.

2. Write an essay in which you suggest what students can do to help fight terrorism in the United States. Try to come up with some practical proposals.

AMERICA AND ANTI-AMERICANS

Salman Rushdie

Salman Rushdie (b. 1947, Bombay, India) is the well-known author of The Satanic Verses *(1989). Ayatollah Ruhollah Khomeini declared the book blasphemous and placed a death sentence on Rushdie's head. Rushdie, who attended Rugby School in England and read history at King's College, Cambridge University, has remained elusive ever since. He continues to write and publish books, however, among them* The Moors Last Sight *(1995), and* The Ground Beneath her Feet *(1999).*

∼

1 They told us it would be a long, ugly struggle, and so it is. America's war against terror has entered its second phase, a phase characterized by the storm over the status and human rights of the prisoners held at Camp X-Ray and by the frustrating failure of the United States to find Osama bin Laden and Mullah Omar. Additionally, if America now attacks other countries suspected of harboring terrorists it will almost certainly do so alone. In spite of the military successes, America finds itself facing a broader ideological adversary that may turn out to be as hard to defeat as militant Islam: anti-Americanism, which is presently becoming more evident everywhere.

Israel: aftermath of a suicide bomber. Copyright © AFP/CORBIS.

2   The good news is that these post-Taliban days are bad times for Islamic fanatics. Dead or alive, Osama bin Laden and Mullah Omar look like yesterday's men, unholy warriors who forced martyrdom on others while running for the hills themselves. Also, if the persistent rumors are to be believed, the fall of the terrorist axis in Afghanistan may well have prevented an Islamic coup against President Pervez Musharraf in Pakistan, led by the more Taliban-like elements in the armed forces and intelligence services—people like the terrifying General Hamid Gul. And President Musharraf, no angel himself, has been pushed into arresting the leaders of the Kashmiri terrorist groups he used to encourage.

3   Around the world, the lessons of the American action in Afghanistan are being learned. Jihad is no longer quite as cool an idea as it was last fall.

4   States under suspicion of giving succor to terrorism have suddenly been trying to make nice, even going so far as to round up a few bad guys. Iran has accepted the legitimacy of the new Afghan government. Even Britain, a state which has been more tolerant of Islamic fanaticism than most, is beginning to distinguish between resisting "Islamophobia" and providing a safe haven for some of the worst people in the world.

5   America did, in Afghanistan, what had to be done, and did it well. The bad news, however, is that these successes have not won new friends for the United States outside Afghanistan. In fact, the effectiveness of the American campaign may have made some parts of the world hate America more than they did before. Critics of the Afghan campaign in the West are enraged because they have been shown to be wrong at every step: no, American forces weren't humiliated the way the Russians had been; and yes, the air strikes did work; and no, the Northern Alliance didn't massacre people in Kabul; and yes, the Taliban did crumble away like the hated tyrants they were, even in

their southern strongholds; and no, it wasn't that difficult to get the militants out of their cave fortresses; and yes, the various factions succeeded in putting together a new government that seems to have broad support among the people.

6   Meanwhile, those elements in the Arab and Muslim world who blame America for their own feelings of political impotence are feeling more impotent than ever. As always, anti-American radicalism feeds off widespread anger over the plight of the Palestinians, and it remains true that nothing would undermine the fanatics' propaganda more completely than an acceptable settlement in the Middle East.

7   However, even if that settlement were arrived at tomorrow, anti-Americanism would probably not abate. It has become too useful a smokescreen for Muslim nations' many defects—their corruption, their incompetence, their oppression of their citizens, their economic, scientific and cultural stagnation. America-hating has become a badge of identity, making possible a chest-beating, flag-burning rhetoric of word and deed that makes men feel good. It contains a strong streak of hypocrisy, hating most what it desires most, and elements of self-loathing. ("We hate America because it has made of itself what we cannot make of ourselves.") What America is accused of—closed-mindedness, stereotyping, ignorance—is also what its accusers would see if they looked into a mirror.

8   These days there seem to be as many of these accusers outside the Muslim world as inside it. Anybody who has visited Britain and Europe, or followed the public conversation there during the past five months, will have been struck, even shocked, by the depth of anti-American feeling among large segments of the population. Western anti-Americanism is an altogether more petulant phenomenon than its Islamic counterpart and far more personalized. Muslim countries don't like America's power, its "arrogance," its success; but in the non-American West, the main objection seems to be to American people. Night after night, I have found myself listening to Londoners' diatribes against the sheer weirdness of the American citizenry. The attacks on America are routinely discounted. ("Americans only care about their own dead.") American patriotism, obesity, emotionality, self-centeredness: these are the crucial issues.

9   It would be easy for America, in the present climate of hostility, to fail to respond to constructive criticism, or worse: to start acting like the overwhelming superpower it is, making decisions and throwing its weight around without regard for the concerns of what it perceives as an already hostile world. The treatment of the Camp X-Ray detainees is a worrying sign. Secretary of State Colin Powell's reported desire to determine whether, under the Geneva Convention, these persons should be considered prisoners of war was a statesmanlike response to global pressure—but Mr. Powell has apparently failed to persuade President Bush and Donald Rumsfeld.

10   The Bush administration has come a long way from its treaty-smashing beginnings. It should not abandon consensus-building now. Great power and great wealth are perhaps never popular, yet, more than ever, we need the

United States to exercise its power and economic might responsibly. This is not the time to ignore the rest of the world and decide to go it alone. To do so would be to risk losing after you've won.

⁓

(972 words)

VOCABULARY

ideological (1)	axis (2)	succor (4)
impotence (6)	radicalism (6)	abate (7)
petulant (8)	diatribes (8)	detainees (9)
consensus-building (10)		

THE FACTS

1. Who is the "They" mentioned at the start of the essay? After September 11, 2001, did you believe that the struggle against terrorism would be a painfully long one? Give reasons for your answer.

2. According to the author, why are "these post-Taliban days" bad times for Islam fanatics? Do you agree with his reasoning? Why or why not?

3. Why, according to the author, has the United States enraged so many people with its successful Afghan campaign? What sense can you make of this passionate animosity? Explain your answer.

4. According to Rushdie, what cause keeps gaining support in the Middle East? What do you think should be done to solve this problem?

5. Of what faults is the United States accused by its critics? How does the author feel about these faults? Which of these faults, if any, seem justified? What faults do you see in our country?

THE STRATEGIES

1. What is the author's overall approach to the problem of terrorism in the United States? What effect does his approach have?

2. According to the author, what new adversary is the United States facing since its military success in Afghanistan? Where does the author first mention this adversary? What importance, if any, does this placement have? Do you consider this a threatening adversary or

merely a temporary show of peevishness on the part of countries that are jealous? Support your answer with evidence.

3. In paragraph 2, the author announces "good news." Does he follow this announcement with bad news as well? If so, where is the bad news mentioned? What is the bad news?

4. What is the meaning of the term "petulant phenomenon" in paragraph 8? Why do you think the author used this term?

5. How does the author end his essay? What rhetorical effect does the ending have?

THE ISSUES

1. What in your view is the present status of terrorism in the world—especially terrorism aimed at the United States? Do you believe terrorism is gaining strength or is it being weakened?

2. What important advice does Rushdie give the United States concerning its faults? Do you think his advice is wise? How should the United States handle this advice?

3. According to Rushdie, what is the "strong streak of hypocrisy" contained in the hostility toward Americans? What is your response to this kind of hostility?

4. How do you think the work of terrorists would be affected if a permanent peace was brokered between Israel and Palestine? Would this sound the death knell for terrorism because it would lose its cause, or are terrorists psychologically so encased by hatred that they would continue to browbeat the world?

5. What do you think Rushdie means when he indicates that it would be a mistake for the United States to act "like the overwhelming superpower it is"? Give an example of what the United States might do to throw its weight around without regard for the concerns of other nations. What would be the result of such an action?

SUGGESTIONS FOR WRITING

1. Write a critical analysis of Rushdie's opinions, following his essay point by point, from beginning to end. State each major point; then respond to it.

2. Write an essay in which you analyze why hating America has become such a badge of identity in many parts of the world. Develop your thesis with logic and evidence.

──────── STUDENT CORNER ────────
────────────────■────────────────

THE RIGHT MOVES AGAINST TERRORISM

Sion Arakelian, Glendale Community College

Terrorism is nothing new to the world. But it is relatively new to us who live in the United States. The 911 attack of 2001 is still fresh enough in our memories to draw strong opinions from almost anyone you ask. With the frequent emphasis on security, particularly airport security, we're reminded almost daily that the United States is now in the front lines of the battle against terrorism. Uppermost in everyone's mind is how we're doing and whether what we're doing is right. I believe firmly that the United States must continue its aggressive leadership in the war against terrorism.

As an emigrant from Iran, I know that it is my tendency to hold conservative political views. Many newly arrived immigrants often find themselves siding with the status quo, if only because they also want a piece of the pie. Yet if I look dispassionately on the policies of the government and the steps we're taking to combat terrorism to date, I cannot help but be encouraged and to think that we're on the right road.

The first thing we did right was to proclaim from the beginning that anyone or any country who harbors terrorists we would regard as terrorists themselves. This is an entirely sensible point of view. What our doctrine says is that you do not have to actually throw the bomb yourself to be guilty in a bombing. If you bought the bomb, if you contributed to those who actually acquired the bomb, if you gave comfort and safe haven to the bombers or to those who made the bomb or bought the bomb, you were, in our eyes, equally guilty of an act of terrorism as the bombers themselves. This point of view draws a line in the sand. On one side stand the terrorists and their abettors; on the other side stand the free world and the United Nations. There can be no fudging about which side a country belongs to. You're either for terrorism or against terrorism.

The second thing we did right was taking the war to the enemy, which strangely enough, was of our own creation. As far back as 1978, before the Russians occupied Afghanistan, the United States was secretly sending arms to the rebel forces in Afghanistan known as the mujahedeen. This practice, in turn, created a war that lasted ten years between the Russians and the people of Afghanistan. At the end of this war, the fundamentalists, whom the United States supported, took power and established their own regime. One of their first acts was to establish the rule of the harshest Islamic fundamentalism that removed women from the workplace and wrapped them in the chador. Then they turned against their benefactors—us.

When we went into Afghanistan there was a great outcry about how we were doomed to failure. But that, too, turned out to be the right move. Yes, it is true that Afghanistan has always been a wasteland to invaders. Alexander the Great failed in his invasion of 330 B.C. The Arabs tried in 700 A.D. and failed. The British Empire tried in 1838 and 1878, losing 5,000 men in the first attempt and partly succeeding in the second. Russia sent 115,000 troops in 1979, along with armor and air support. The campaign was going well until we armed the mujahedeen. But in spite of opposition we faced at home and the gloom of the naysayers, we soon had the Taliban, the Al-Qaida and Osama bin Laden on the run. Modern weaponry and air power proved to be more than a match for rugged terrain and inhospitable climate.

Finally, our next right move was involving the world's great peacekeeping organization—the United Nations—from the outset. This alliance made it clear that the United States was not alone in wanting to keep the world a safe, hospitable place. Having the United Nations cooperate with the United States is important in garnering the support of western nations, and it is also an underlying factor in the scheme of safely yet secretly destroying all terrorist forces. These forces are out there, and the United States, as well as the United Nations, knows that. Knowing exactly what to do and how to cut short any harm it may bring to the rest of the world is one of the key problems right now.

Yes, innocent lives may be sacrificed in the battle against terrorism, but were there not thousands who died that tragic day on September 11? People forget that the lives lost were not only American lives but also lives of other nationalities that pledged their allegiance to the United States by way of citizenship. The issue of human rights is at stake here, and if nothing is done by the United States to ensure the safety and security of its citizens, there will be additional harm caused by terrorist forces all over the world. This great country, whose priority is to ensure that its citizens are free to pursue their own individual goals and desires, makes its case known to the rest of the world that world peace will be in grave jeopardy should terrorism continue to rear its ugly head.

~

How I Write

I tend to wander and wonder before I print out any words on paper. I can do this kind of pre-writing in any environment—in my car, at the breakfast table, or just anywhere I happened to be. Once I start writing at my computer, I need a quiet place without interruptions so that I can concentrate. Since I am from Iran, and English is my second language, I need to concentrate on my writing, and then I also need to spend time revising, editing, and proofreading.

How I Wrote This Paper

I wrote this paper with the intent of getting the message across that this war must take place and also that the United States must prevail in order to uphold world peace and human rights. I wrote this paper after watching several TV programs whose news pundits offered opinions on the war against terrorism. I also consulted several websites that had already formed opinions of why the war was taking place and exactly how it would continue to develop. While many of these websites led to opinion pieces, some articles to which I referred contained actual facts as to how the United States has dealt with wars in the past. After researching these articles online, I started to form my own opinions about the war and decided to write my paper in favor of the war against terrorism. I created an outline in which I listed my major ideas. Once I thought about these major ideas, the details occurred to me rapidly so that I could develop my essay.

My Writing Tip

If I were to give advice to anyone interested in writing a similar essay, it would be this: Be sure to hold at least a minimal level of interest in the work you are about to write, because success will be difficult to achieve without it. Also, don't leave the paper until you get a measure of pleasure from reading it to yourself. If you don't like it, probably your reader won't like it either.

CHAPTER WRITING ASSIGNMENTS

1. Write an essay in which you narrate an incident that proves one of the following:
   a. People are often bigoted.
   b. Having good neighbors is important.
   c. Pets are often astoundingly loyal.
   d. Difficulties can be stepping stones to success.

WRITING ASSIGNMENTS FOR A SPECIFIC AUDIENCE

1. Write a diary entry, listing chronologically the major events of your day. Treat your diary as a confidential, intimate friend to whom you can trust your innermost feelings.
2. Write to your parents, describing to them your college living quarters.

COLLABORATIVE WRITING PROJECT

Joining three other students in the class, as a group edit a long paper that one of you wrote in a previous semester and for a different class. Each member of the group should have a copy of the paper on which to scribble editing remarks and criticism. Make at least three passes through the manuscript, giving each member of the group an opportunity not only to edit the paper but also to critique it orally. When you're finished, submit the paper to your instructor and request a grade. Was the grade on the edited paper higher than the paper's original grade?

8

Description

EDITOR'S COUNSEL

What Description Does

A description is a word picture. It is the writer's attempt to capture with words the essence and flavor of a scene, person, or thing. No matter what you've heard to the contrary, a sharply drawn description can be every bit as moving as a picture. Focus and concentration contribute more to a vivid description than either the size of the writer's vocabulary or the heedless splattering of adjectives on a page. Here is an example of what we mean. The author, Charles Reade, in this excerpt from *The Cloister and the Hearth*, is describing a medieval inn partly through the eyes, but mainly through the nose, of a weary traveler:

> In one corner was a travelling family, a large one; thence flowed into the common stock the peculiar sickly smell of neglected brats. Garlic filled up the interstices of the air. And all this with closed window, and intense heat of the central furnace, and the breath of at least forty persons.
>
> They had just supped.
>
> Now Gerard, like most artists, had sensitive organs, and the potent effluvia struck dismay into him. But the rain lashed him outside, and the light and the fire tempted him in.
>
> He could not force his way all at once through the palpable perfumes, but he returned to the light again and again like a singed moth. At last he discovered that the various smells did not entirely mix, no fiend being there to stir them around. Odor of family predominated in two corners; stewed rustic reigned supreme in the center; and garlic in the noisy group by the window. He found, too, by hasty analysis, that of these the garlic described the smallest aerial orbit, and the scent of reeking rustic darted farthest—a flavor as if ancient goats, or the fathers of all foxes, had been drawn through a river, and were here dried by Nebuchadnezzar.

What is characteristic about this vivid description is its focus. Instead of trying to give us a sweeping view of the dingy inn, the writer zooms in on how bad it smells. The stink of the inn is the dominant impression of this description, and the writer's every word, image, and metaphor aims only to serve up this stench to our nostrils.

When to Use Description

Next to narration, description is probably the most widely used of all the rhetorical modes. In letters, journal entries, reports, and memos we describe places we have visited, people we have met, and adventures that we have had. Over the course of any given week, it is likely that we have painted a word picture, if not in writing, then certainly in speech.

How to Write a Description

There are some well-known techniques of description that all writers use. We recommend that you practice them in your own writing.

Focus on a Dominant Impression   Vivid descriptions invariably focus on a single, dominant impression and unremittingly deliver it. Nothing distracts from the dominant impression; every word and image is devoted to rendering it keener and sharper. By *dominant impression,* we mean a feature of the scene that is characteristic of it. Not all scenes have strikingly characteristic features, and writers must often absorb the atmosphere of a place before they can sum it up in a dominant impression. Some scenes, however, will give off a dominant impression that leaps out at you. For example, a freeway at rush hour is anything but a scene of placidity; usually it is a tangled skein of cars jockeying for position or trying to nose from one lane into another. To describe a freeway scene at rush hour, you should word your dominant impression to take in the antics of the drivers, the fumes of the cars, the background grind and roar of traffic. You might write, as your dominant impression, "The San Diego Freeway at rush hour is a bedlam of traffic noise, choking fumes, and aggressive drivers." Then you would support that dominant impression with specific images and details.

Here is a description of the Spanish night that uses this technique:

> The Spanish night is so deep and pompous as quite to browbeat the noisier light of day. The buildings, which always look clear-cut and newly built, become, against the dark stress of evening, brilliantly crisp and more brittle than glass. A long line of white buildings will tower up to threaten you with its proud, wave-like bulwarks. At every corner, behind the dark trees that are deep, still areas of water, there will rise up another of those strutting waves out of the depth. In its turn it will draw up, holding itself to full height before it launches a leonine assault on your puny presence. Then it will hold itself back from you before the superior strength of the next glittering wave that you meet, as you walk through the brittle moonlight. In this way the slowest progress through a town will be running the gauntlet of a whole pack of hungry shadows.

—Sacheverell Sitwell, Southern Baroque Art

The paragraph vividly captures the sights and sensations associated with *nightfall* over a Spanish town. At its core is a single, overwhelming impression of night "so deep and pompous as quite to browbeat the noisier light of day." All of the details in the paragraph support this dominant impression.

The dominant impression of your description should be the heart of the person, place, or scene you are attempting to describe. If you are describing an elderly aunt who is dull, use her dullness as your dominant impression. If you are writing a description of a Christmas shopping scene, word your dominant impression to show the frazzled and weary shoppers, the harried salesclerks, the dazzling Christmas lights.

However, you should not account for every speck in the scene you are describing in your dominant impression. For example, among the streaming throngs in the department store at Christmas, there are bound to be a few souls who are calm and composed and seemingly immune to the shopping frenzy. Because these lucky few are not at all representative of the overall scene, you should leave them out lest they water down the description. Similarly, if your sister is mainly a bundle of nerves, that is how you should paint her on the page, even if you have glimpsed her in rare moments of serenity.

Use Images in Your Descriptions   Most of us know the basics of imagery, especially the simile and the metaphor. We know that the simile is an image based on an explicit comparison. For example, in *The King of the Birds*, Flannery O'Connor describes the crest of a peabiddy with this simile: "This looks at first like a bug's antennae and later like the head feathers of an Indian." We also know that the metaphor is an image based on an indirect comparison with no obvious linking word such as "as" or "like" used to cement it. For example, in *Once More to the Lake*, E. B. White uses metaphors to describe a thunderstorm: "Then the kettle drum, then the snare, then the bass drum and cymbals, then crackling light against the dark, and the gods grinning and licking their chops in the hills." This is how a thunderstorm seems to the writer—it makes noises like many drums and flashes wicked lights against the hills that look like gods licking their chops. Even though the writer omits the "like" that might have made the comparison explicit, we still get the picture.

In addition to these basic images, which every writer occasionally uses, there are some hard-won lessons about descriptive imagery that can be imparted. The first is this: Vivid images do not miraculously drip off the pen but are usually the result of the writer reworking the material repeatedly. If nothing original or fresh occurs to you after you've sat at your desk for a scant few minutes trying to write a description, all it means is that you did not sit long enough or work hard enough. Reread what you have written. Try to picture in your mind the person, place, or thing you are struggling to describe. Cut a word here; replace another there; persistently scratch away at what you have written and you'll soon be astonished at how much better it gets.

The second lesson about writing vivid images is summed up in the adage "Less is more." Overdoing a descriptive passage is not only possible, it is very likely. If you are unhappy with a description you have written, instead of stuffing it with more adjectives, try taking some out. Here is an example of a bloated and overdone description, from *Delina Delaney* by Amanda McKittrick Ros. The speaker is trying his utmost to describe his feelings as he says goodbye to his sweetheart:

> I am just in time to hear the toll of a parting bell strike its heavy weight of appalling softness against the weakest fibers of a heart of love, arousing and tickling its dormant action, thrusting the dart of evident separation deeper into its tubes of tenderness, and fanning the flame, already unextinguishable, into volumes of blaze.

This is wretched stuff, of course. One can see the writer huffing and puffing at the pen as she tries desperately to infuse her hero's words with passion. She fails awfully from too much effort.

Appeal to All of Your Reader's Senses   Most of us are so unabashedly visual that we are tempted to deliver only looks in our descriptions. There is usually much more to a scene than its looks; you could also write about how it sounds, smells, or feels. The best descriptions draw on all kinds of images and appeal to as many senses as are appropriate. Here is an example from Elspeth Huxley's *The Flame Trees of Thika*. The writer is describing a World War I troop train as it leaves an African station at night carrying soldiers to the front:

> The men began to sing the jingle then that was so popular then—"Marching to Tabora"; and the shouts and cheers, the whistles, the hissing and chugging of the engine, filled the station as a kettle fills with steam. Everything seemed to bubble over; men waved from windows; Dick gave a hunting cry; the red hair of Pioneer Mary flared under a lamp; the guard jumped into his moving van; and we watched the rear light of the last coach vanish, and heard the chugging die away. A plume of sparks, a long coil of dancing fireflies, spread across the black ancient shoulder of the crater Menegai; and gradually the vast digesting dark of Africa swallowed up all traces of that audacious grub, the hurrying train.

This description is a mixture of appeals to our senses of sight and hearing. The men sing and cheer, and the engine chugs and hisses. We see Pioneer Mary's red hair and the sparks from the train's engine. We are regaled with a clever simile, "filled the station as a kettle fills with steam," and treated to a riveting image, "the vast digesting dark of Africa swallowed up all traces of that audacious grub, the hurrying train." Did the author really just sit down and calmly mine this rich descriptive vein without effort? We do not know, but most likely not. If her experience is at all typical, she hit this mother lode of imagery only after persistent and labored digging.

Warming Up to Write a Description

1. Train yourself to be observant. Withdraw to your room or some other familiar place with a note pad and pencil in hand and place yourself at an angle where you have a sweeping view. Jot down details of what the place looks like. After you have absorbed the details, formulate a dominant impression of the place and write it down on your note pad. An example might be, "My room always makes me feel cozy because it is filled with mementos from my childhood." Or, "The Hometown Buffet, a restaurant five blocks away from where I live, is a spot where one can breathe in all kinds of smells, hear all kinds of noises, and observe all kinds of people." Next, write down on your note pad only those details that support the dominant impression.

2. Drive through your town or neighborhood, focusing on eyesores that you think the local authorities should correct. Examples might be a huge refuse bin sitting outside a popular coffee house, withered flowers in a planter at the side of a real estate office, or broken-down cars and car parts littering someone's front yard. Take notes that describe the eyesore with sensory details of sight, sound, smell, and touch.

3. Rewrite these undescriptive and dull sentences to make them vivid. Use figurative language whenever possible.
   a. The convalescent hospital spelled unappetizing.
   b. His face bore many wrinkles, indicating his old age.
   c. The protesters were quite loud and active.
   d. The snow falling on the creek is lovely.

   As an added exercise, complete the following sentences to make them vividly descriptive:
   e. The squirrels chased each other up and down the trees as if. . . .
   f. Jasmine's eyes were so deeply green, they looked like. . . .
   g. The suitcase fell off the rack of our car and crashed on the highway, causing. . . .
   h. A cold wind blew from the north, shaking up the trees and bending their trunks back and forth so that from a distance the aspen grove looked like. . . .

———— EXAMPLES ————

THE LIBIDO FOR THE UGLY

H. L. Mencken

Henry Louis Mencken (1880–1956) was an editor, author, and critic. He begin his journalism career at the Baltimore Morning Herald *and later became editor of the* Baltimore Evening Herald. *From 1906 until his death, he was on the staff of the* Baltimore Sun (*or* Evening Sun). *In 1924, with George Jean Nathan, Mencken founded the* American Mercury *and served as its editor from 1925 to 1933. Mencken's writing was chiefly devoted to lambasting the smug, conventional attitudes of the middle class. Among his numerous works is* The American Language, *a monumental study of the American idiom, first published in 1919.*

Few writers have such an eye for colorful detail as the incomparable Mencken, at his best when he's railing against physical ugliness or storming against a tradition he dislikes. In the essay that follows, Mencken turns his literary wrath against the ugliness of the industrial heartland of America in the 1920s.

~

1   On a Winter day some years ago, coming out of Pittsburgh on one of the expresses of the Pennsylvania Railroad, I rolled eastward for an hour through the coal and steel towns of Westmoreland county. It was familiar ground; boy and man, I had been through it often before. But somehow I had never quite sensed its appalling desolation. Here was the very heart of industrial America, the center of its most lucrative and characteristic activity, the boast and pride of the richest and grandest nation ever seen on earth—and here was a scene so dreadfully hideous, so intolerably bleak and forlorn that it reduced the whole aspiration of man to a macabre and depressing joke. Here was wealth beyond computation, almost beyond imagination—and here were human habitations so abominable that they would have disgraced a race of alley cats.

2   I am not speaking of mere filth. One expects steel towns to be dirty. What I allude to is the unbroken and agonizing ugliness, the sheer revolting monstrousness, of every house in sight. From East Liberty to Greensburg, a distance of twenty-five miles, there was not one in sight from the train that did not insult and lacerate the eye. Some were so bad, and they were among the most pretentious—churches, stores, warehouses, and the like—that they were downright startling; one blinked before them as one blinks before a man with his face shot away. A few linger in memory, horrible even there: a crazy little church just west of Jeannette, set like a dormer-window on the side of a bare, leprous hill; the headquarters of the Veterans of Foreign Wars at another forlorn town, a steel stadium like a huge rat-trap somewhere further down the line. But most of all I recall the general effect—of hideousness without a

break. There was not a single decent house within eye-range from the Pittsburgh suburbs to the Greensburg yards. There was not one that was not misshapen, and there was not one that was not shabby.

3   The country itself is not uncomely, despite the grime of the endless mills. It is, in form, a narrow river valley, with deep gullies running up into the hills. It is thickly settled, but not noticeably overcrowded. There is still plenty of room for building, even in the larger towns, and there are very few solid blocks. Nearly every house, big and little, has space on all four sides. Obviously, if there were architects of any professional sense or dignity in the region, they would have perfected a chalet to hug the hillsides—a chalet with a high-pitched roof, to throw off the heavy Winter snows, but still essentially a low and clinging building, wider than it was tall. But what have they done? They have taken as their model a brick set on end. This they have converted into a thing of dingy clapboards, with a narrow, low-pitched roof. And the whole they have set upon thin, preposterous brick piers. By the hundreds and thousands these abominable houses cover the bare hillsides, like gravestones in some gigantic and decaying cemetery. On their deep sides they are three, four and even five stories high; on their low sides they bury themselves swinishly in the mud. Not a fifth of them are perpendicular. They lean this way and that, hanging on to their bases precariously. And one and all they are streaked in grime, with dead and eczematous patches of paint peeping through the streaks.

4   Now and then there is a house of brick. But what brick! When it is new it is the color of a fried egg. When it has taken on the patina of the mills it is the color of an egg long past all hope or caring. Was it necessary to adopt that shocking color? No more than it was necessary to set all of the houses on end. Red brick, even in a steel town, ages with some dignity. Let it become downright black, and it is still sightly, especially if its trimmings are of white stone, with soot in the depths and the high spots washed by the rain. But in Westmoreland they prefer that uremic yellow, and so they have the most loathsome towns and villages ever seen by mortal eye.

5   I award this championship only after laborious research and incessant prayer. I have seen, I believe, all of the most unlovely towns of the world; they are all to be found in the United States. I have seen the mill towns of decomposing New England and the desert towns of Utah, Arizona and Texas. I am familiar with the back streets of Newark, Brooklyn and Chicago, and have made scientific explorations to Camden, N. J., and Newport News, Va. Safe in a Pullman, I have whirled through the gloomy, God-forsaken villages of Iowa and Kansas, and the malarious tide-water hamlets of Georgia. I have been to Bridgeport, Conn., and to Los Angeles. But nowhere on this earth, at home or abroad, have I seen anything to compare to the villages that huddle along the line of the Pennsylvania from the Pittsburgh yards to Greensburg. They are incomparable in color, and they are incomparable in design. It is as if some titanic and aberrant genius, uncompromisingly inimical to man, had devoted all the ingenuity of Hell to the making of them. They show grotesqueries of

ugliness that, in retrospect, become almost diabolical. One cannot imagine mere human beings concocting such dreadful things, and one can scarcely imagine human beings bearing life in them.

6   Are they so frightful because the valley is full of foreigners—dull, insensate brutes, with no love of beauty in them? Then why didn't these foreigners set up similar abominations in the countries that they came from? You will, in fact, find nothing of the sort in Europe—save perhaps in the more putrid parts of England. There is scarcely an ugly village on the whole Continent. The peasants, however poor, somehow manage to make themselves graceful and charming habitations, even in Spain. But in the American village and small town the pull is always toward ugliness, and in that Westmoreland valley it has been yielded to with an eagerness bordering upon passion. It is incredible that mere ignorance should have achieved such masterpieces of horror.

7   On certain levels of the American race, indeed, there seems to be a positive libido for the ugly, as on other and less Christian levels there is a libido for the beautiful. It is impossible to put down the wallpaper that defaces the average American home of the lower middle class to mere inadvertence, or to the obscene humor of the manufacturers. Such ghastly designs, it must be obvious, give a genuine delight to a certain type of mind. They meet, in some unfathomable way, its obscure and unintelligible demands. They caress it as "The Palms" caresses it, or the art of the movie, or jazz. The taste for them is as enigmatical and yet as common as the taste for dogmatic theology and the poetry of Edgar A. Guest.

8   Thus I suspect (though confessedly without knowing) that the vast majority of the honest folk of Westmoreland county, and especially the 100% Americans among them, actually admire the houses they live in, and are proud of them. For the same money they could get vastly better ones, but they prefer what they have got. Certainly there was no pressure upon the Veterans of Foreign Wars to choose the dreadful edifice that bears their banner, for there are plenty of vacant buildings along the track-side, and some of them are appreciably better. They might, indeed, have built a better one of their own. But they chose that clapboarded horror with their eyes open, and having chosen it, they let it mellow into its present shocking depravity. They like it as it is: beside it, the Parthenon would no doubt offend them. In precisely the same way the authors of the rat-trap stadium that I have mentioned made a deliberate choice. After painfully designing and erecting it, they made it perfect in their own sight by putting a completely impossible pent-house, painted a staring yellow, on top of it. The effect is that of a fat woman with a black eye. It is that of a Presbyterian grinning. But they like it.

9   Here is something that the psychologists have so far neglected: the love of ugliness for its own sake, the lust to make the world intolerable. Its habitat is the United States. Out of the melting pot emerges a race which hates beauty as it hates truth. The etiology of this madness deserves a great deal more study than it has got. There must be causes behind it; it arises and flourishes

in obedience to biological laws, and not as a mere act of God. What, precisely, are the terms of those laws? And why do they run stronger in America than elsewhere? Let some honest Privat Dozent in pathological sociology apply himself to the problem.

∼

(1,531 words)

VOCABULARY

lucrative (1)	aspiration (1)	macabre (1)
lacerate (2)	dormer-window (2)	clapboards (3)
eczematous (3)	patina (4)	uremic (4)
malarious (5)	aberrant (5)	inimical (5)
grotesqueries (5)	insensate (6)	libido (7)
inadvertence (7)	enigmatical (7)	dogmatic (7)
Parthenon (8)	etiology (9)	Privat Dozent (9)
pathological (9)		

THE FACTS

1. What area of the country does this essay describe?
2. What is the principal occupation of the region?
3. Mencken not only criticizes the architecture of the region, he also suggests an alternative. What sort of architecture does he think is suited to this region?
4. On what does Mencken blame the ugliness he describes?
5. What are Mencken's views of the villages in Europe? In his view, how do they compare with American towns?

THE STRATEGIES

1. A good description focuses on and develops a dominant impression. Examine the second paragraph. What is the dominant impression here?
2. Examine the third paragraph. What dominant impression does Mencken focus on in his description of the buildings?
3. What aspect of the ugliness does paragraph 4 deal with?
4. "I have seen, I believe, all of the most unlovely towns of the world; they are all to be found in the United States." Why does he say unlovely rather than ugly? Which is more effective? Why?
5. "And one and all they are streaked in grime, with dead and eczematous patches of paint peeping through the streaks." What comparison is implied in this metaphor?

THE ISSUES

1. One of the most vigilant civic groups in the United States today is the environmentalists—men and women determined to preserve historical buildings, wilderness areas, seacoasts, and public parks. What importance do you attribute to the efforts of these people? What do you think would happen if they no longer cared?

2. Mencken seems to feel that although architectural ugliness on any scale is lamentable, it is especially insulting when the edifice is pretentious. Do you agree with Mencken's view? Why or why not?

3. What stretch of highway in the United States is charmingly beautiful and stands in total contrast to Mencken's description of the houses in Westmoreland County? Describe this stretch in detail, focusing on architectural characteristics.

4. Do you agree with Mencken that Americans are psychologically obsessed with ugliness? If you agree, try to find reasons for this obsession. If you disagree, prove that Mencken is wrong by citing instances in which typical Americans have promoted beauty and good taste.

5. If you were to oversee a development of beautiful homes, what aesthetic requirements would you insist on? Describe the development in concrete terms.

SUGGESTIONS FOR WRITING

1. Write an essay describing the town or city where you live.

2. Write an analysis of Mencken's diction in this essay, paying particular attention to his use of adjectives.

HELL

James Joyce

James Joyce (1882–1941) is considered by many to be among the most significant novelists of the 20th century. He was born in Dublin, Ireland, and educated at University College, Dublin. Joyce, a writer who pushed language to its outer limit of comprehensibility, wrote poetry, short stories, and novels. His major novels include A Portrait of the Artist as a Young Man *(1916),* Ulysses *(written between 1914 and 1921 and published in the United States in 1933), and* Finnegan's Wake *(1939).*

Joyce, in this selection from *A Portrait of the Artist as a Young Man*, shows us the wreathing fires of hell and persuades us to smell its stench of brimstone and sin. The description that follows is so graphic, so detailed, and so filled with such shuddering imagery, that we almost believe that someone has returned from this dreadful place to tell the tale.

~

1   Hell is a strait and dark and foulsmelling prison, an abode of demons and lost souls, filled with fire and smoke. The straitness of this prisonhouse is expressly designed by God to punish those who refused to be bound by His laws. In earthly prisons the poor captive has at least some liberty of movement, were it only within the four walls of his cell or in the gloomy yard of his prison. Not so in hell. There, by reason of the great number of the damned, the prisoners are heaped together in their awful prison, the walls of which are said to be four thousand miles thick: and the damned are so utterly bound and helpless that, as a blessed saint, saint Anselm, writes in his book on similitudes, they are not even able to remove from the eye a worm that gnaws it.

2   —They lie in exterior darkness. For, remember, the fire of hell gives forth no light. As, at the command of God, the fire of the Babylonian furnace lost its heat but not its light so, at the command of God, the fire of hell, while retaining the intensity of its heat, burns eternally in darkness. It is a neverending storm of darkness, dark flames and dark smoke of burning brimstone, amid which the bodies are heaped one upon another without even a glimpse of air. Of all the plagues with which the land of the Pharaohs was smitten one plague alone, that of darkness, was called horrible. What name, then, shall we give to the darkness of hell which is to last not for three days alone but for all eternity?

3   —The horror of this strait and dark prison is increased by its awful stench. All the filth of the world, all the offal and scum of the world, we are told, shall run there as to a vast reeking sewer when the terrible conflagration of the last day has purged the world. The brimstone too which burns there in such prodigious quantity fills all hell with its intolerable stench; and the bodies of the damned themselves exhale such a pestilential odour that as saint Bonaventure says, one of them alone would suffice to infect the whole world. The very air of this world, that pure element, becomes foul and unbreathable when it has been long enclosed. Consider then what must be the foulness of the air of hell. Imagine some foul and putrid corpse that has lain rotting and decomposing in the grave, a jellylike mass of liquid corruption. Imagine such a corpse a prey to flames, devoured by the fire of burning brimstone and giving off dense choking fumes of nauseous loathsome decomposition. And then imagine this sickening stench, multiplied a millionfold and a millionfold again from the millions upon millions of fetid carcasses massed together in the reeking darkness, a huge and rotting human fungus. Imagine all this and you will have some idea of the horror of the stench of hell.

4   —But this stench is not, horrible though it is, the greatest physical torment to which the damned are subjected. The torment of fire is the greatest torment to which the tyrant has ever subjected his fellow creatures. Place your finger for a moment in the flame of a candle and you will feel the pain of fire. But

our earthly fire was created by God for the benefit of man, to maintain in him the spark of life and to help him in the useful arts whereas the fire of hell is of another quality and was created by God to torture and punish the unrepentant sinner. Our earthly fire also consumes more or less rapidly according as the object which it attacks is more or less combustible so that human ingenuity has even succeeded in inventing chemical preparations to check or frustrate its action. But the sulphurous brimstone which burns in hell is a substance which is specially designed to burn for ever and for ever with unspeakable fury. Moreover our earthly fire destroys at the same time as it burns so that the more intense it is the shorter is its duration: but the fire of hell has this property that it preserves that which it burns and though it rages with incredible intensity it rages for ever.

5   —Our earthly fire again, no matter how fierce or widespread it may be, is always of a limited extent: but the lake of fire in hell is boundless, shoreless and bottomless. It is on record that the devil himself, when asked the question by a certain soldier, was obliged to confess that if a whole mountain were thrown into the burning ocean of hell it would be burned up in an instant like a piece of wax. And this terrible fire will not afflict the bodies of the damned only from without but each lost soul will be a hell unto itself, the boundless fire raging in its very vitals. O, how terrible is the lot of those wretched beings! The blood seethes and boils in the veins, the brains are boiling in the skull, the heart in the breast glowing and bursting, the bowels a redhot mass of burning pulp, the tender eyes flaming like molten balls.

6   —And yet what I have said as to the strength and quality and boundlessness of this fire is as nothing when compared to its intensity, an intensity which it has as being the instrument chosen by divine design for the punishment of soul and body alike. It is a fire which proceeds directly from the ire of God, working not of its own activity but as an instrument of divine vengeance. As the waters of baptism cleanse the soul with the body so do the fires of punishment torture the spirit with the flesh. Every sense of the flesh is tortured and every faculty of the soul therewith: the eyes with impenetrable utter darkness, the nose with noisome odours, the ears with yells and howls and execrations, the taste with foul matter, leprous corruption, nameless suffocating filth, the touch with redhot goads and spikes, with cruel tongues of flame. And through the several torments of the senses the immortal soul is tortured eternally in its very essence amid the leagues upon leagues of glowing fires kindled in the abyss by the offended majesty of the Omnipotent God and fanned into everlasting and ever increasing fury by the breath of the anger of the Godhead.

7   Consider finally that the torment of this infernal prison is increased by the company of the damned themselves. Evil company on earth is so noxious that even the plants, as if by instinct, withdraw from the company of whatsoever is deadly or hurtful to them. In hell all laws are overturned: there is no thought of family or country, of ties, of relationships. The damned howl and scream at one another, their torture and rage intensified by the presence of beings tortured and raging like themselves. All sense of humanity is forgotten.

The yells of the suffering sinners fill the remotest corners of the vast abyss. The mouths of the damned are full of blasphemies against God and of hatred for their fellow sufferers and of curses against those souls which were their accomplices in sin. In olden times it was the custom to punish the parricide, the man who had raised his murderous hand against his father, by casting him into the depths of the sea in a sack in which were placed a cock, a monkey and a serpent. The intention of those lawgivers who framed such a law, which seems cruel in our times, was to punish the criminal by the company of hateful and hurtful beasts. But what is the fury of those dumb beasts compared with the fury of execration which bursts from the parched lips and aching throats of the damned in hell when they behold in their companions in misery those who aided and abetted them in sin, those whose words sowed the first seeds of evil thinking and evil living in their minds, those whose immodest suggestions led them on to sin, those whose eyes tempted and allured them from the path of virtue. They turn upon those accomplices and upbraid them and curse them. But they are helpless and hopeless: it is too late now for repentance.

~

(1,406 words)

VOCABULARY

strait (1)	similitudes (1)	offal (3)
conflagration (3)	prodigious (3)	pestilential (3)
fetid (3)	noisome (6)	execrations (6)
parricide (7)	allured (7)	upbraid (7)

THE FACTS

1. How thick are the walls of hell?
2. What peculiar characteristics does the fire of hell have?
3. What is the greatest physical torment that the damned of hell suffer?
4. What is the source of the fire in hell?
5. How were parricides punished in olden times?

THE STRATEGIES

1. Examine carefully this description of hell. What is its overall structure? How are its paragraphs deployed?
2. Examine paragraph 4. How is it developed? What is its purpose?
3. What is the purpose of mentioning the "earthly prisons" in paragraph 1?
4. Examine paragraph 5. How is this paragraph structured? What technique does the writer use to make his description so vivid?

5. In the novel *A Portrait of the Artist as a Young Man,* the preacher delivers this description of hell in a sermon. Identify at least one technique that the preacher uses to involve his listeners in the description.

THE ISSUES

1. For the most part, modern minds have rejected the medieval view of a physical hell, where the damned suffer such tortures as heat, cold, foul smell, laceration, and persecution from demons. What, if anything, has replaced this notion of hell?

2. In your view, why do many people believe in paradise and hell? What disadvantage or advantage does the lack of belief in these places provide?

3. What effect do you think this sermon on hell might have on young boys listening to it? What is your opinion of the technique used?

4. Is torture as a means of punishment ever justified in a civilized society? Why or why not?

5. A portion of Dante's hell was reserved for those who encouraged others to sin. Where in this excerpt does Joyce express a similar idea? Why do both Dante and Joyce call down a harsh judgment on those who aid and abet evil?

SUGGESTIONS FOR WRITING

1. Write an essay on hell as it is described here, arguing for or against a belief in its existence.

2. Write a brief description of heaven following the example of this selection.

A WORN PATH

Eudora Welty

Eudora Welty (b. 1909) is an American novelist and short-story writer whose tales about eccentric but charming characters from small Mississippi towns have won her a large audience. The best known of her stories have been collected in A Curtain of Green *(1941),* The Wide Net *(1943), and* The Golden Apples *(1949). Among her novels are* Delta Wedding *(1946),* The Ponder Heart *(1954), and* The Optimist's Daughter *(1972). In 1983, she delivered the* William E. Massey Sr. Lectures in American Civilization *at Harvard, which were published as* One Writer's Beginnings *(1984).*

In this story, a woman, undaunted by age and hardships, presses on toward her goal—to get the medicine her sick grandchild must have in order to survive.

~

1 It was December—a bright frozen day in the early morning. Far out in the country there was an old Negro woman with her head tied in a red rag, coming along a path through the pinewoods. Her name was Phoenix Jackson. She was very old and small and she walked slowly in the dark pine shadows, moving a little from side to side in her steps, with the balanced heaviness and lightness of a pendulum in a grandfather clock. She carried a thin, small cane made from an umbrella, and with this she kept tagging the frozen earth in front of her. This made a grave and persistent noise in the still air, that seemed meditative, like the chirping of a solitary little bird.

2 She wore a dark striped dress reaching down to her shoetops, and an equally long apron of bleached sugar sacks, with a full pocket; all neat and tidy, but every time she took a step she might have fallen over her shoelaces, which dragged from her unlaced shoes. She looked straight ahead. Her eyes were blue with age. Her skin had a pattern all its own of numberless branching wrinkles and as though a whole little tree stood in the middle of her forehead, but a golden color ran underneath, and the two knobs of her cheeks were illuminated by a yellow burning under the dark. Under the red rag her hair came down on her neck in the frailest of ringlets, still black, and with an odor like copper.

3 Now and then there was a quivering in the thicket. Old Phoenix said, "Out of my way, all you foxes, owls, beetles, jack rabbits, coons, and wild animals!. . .Keep out from under these feet, little bobwhites. . . . Keep the big wild hogs out of my path. Don't let none of those come running my direction. I got a long way." Under her small black-freckled hand her cane, limber as a buggy whip, would switch at the brush as if to rouse up any hiding things.

4 On she went. The woods were deep and still. The sun made the pine needles almost too bright to look at, up where the wind rocked. The cones dropped as light as feathers. Down in the hollow was the mourning dove— it was not too late for him.

5 The path ran up a hill. "Seem like there is chains about my feet, time I get this far," she said, in the voice of argument old people keep to use with themselves. "Something always take a hold on this hill—pleads I should stay."

6 After she got to the top she turned and gave a full, severe look behind where she had come. "Up through pines," she said at length. "Now down through oaks."

7 Her eyes opened their widest and she started down gently. But before she got to the bottom of the hill a bush caught her dress.

8 Her fingers were busy and intent, but her skirts were full and long, so that before she could pull them free in one place they were caught in another. It was not possible to allow the dress to tear. "I in the thorny bush," she said.

"Thorns, you doing your appointed work. Never want to let folks past—no sir. Old eyes thought you was a pretty little green bush."

9   Finally, trembling all over, she stood free, and after a moment dared to stoop for her cane.

10   "Sun so high!" she cried, leaning back and looking, while the thick tears went over her eyes. "The time getting all gone here."

11   At the foot of this hill was a place where a log was laid across the creek.

12   "Now comes the trial," said Phoenix.

13   Putting her right foot out, she mounted the log and shut her eyes. Lifting her skirt, leveling her cane fiercely before her, like a festival figure in some parade, she began to march across. Then she opened her eyes and she was safe on the other side.

14   "I wasn't as old as I thought," she said.

15   But she sat down to rest. She spread her skirts on the bank around her and folded her hands over her knees. Up above her was a tree in a pearly cloud of mistletoe. She did not dare to close her eyes, and when a little boy brought her a little plate with a slice of marble-cake on it she spoke to him. "That would be acceptable," she said. But when she went to take it there was just her own hand in the air.

16   So she left that tree, and had to go through a barbed-wire fence. There she had to creep and crawl, spreading her knees and stretching her fingers like a baby trying to climb the steps. But she talked loudly to herself: she could not let her dress be torn now, so late in the day, and she could not pay for having her arm or her leg sawed off if she got caught fast where she was.

17   At last she was safe through the fence and risen up out in the clearing. Big dead trees, like black men with one arm, were standing in the purple stalks of the withered cotton field. There sat a buzzard.

18   "Who you watching?"

19   In the furrow she made her way along.

20   "Glad this not the season for bulls," she said, looking sideways, "and the good Lord made his snakes to curl up and sleep in the winter. A pleasure I don't see no two-headed snake coming around that tree, where it come once. It took a while to get by him, back in the summer."

21   She passed through the old cotton and went into a field of dead corn. It whispered and shook, and was taller than her head. "Through the maze now," she said, for there was no path.

22   Then there was something tall, black, and skinny there, moving before her.

23   At first she took it for a man. It could have been a man dancing in the field. But she stood still and listened, and it did not make a sound. It was as silent as a ghost.

24   "Ghost," she said sharply, "who be you the ghost of? For I have heard of nary death close by."

25   But there was no answer, only the ragged dancing in the wind.

26   She shut her eyes, reached out her hand, and touched a sleeve. She found a coat and inside that an emptiness, cold as ice.

27 "You scarecrow," she said. Her face lighted. "I ought to be shut up for good," she said with laughter. "My senses is gone. I too old. I the oldest people I ever know. Dance, old scarecrow," she said, "while I dancing with you."

28 She kicked her foot over the furrow, and with mouth drawn down shook her head once or twice in a little strutting way. Some husks blew down and whirled in streamers about her skirts.

29 Then she went on, parting her way from side to side with the cane, through the whispering field. At last she came to the end, to a wagon track, where the silver grass blew between the red ruts. The quail were walking around like pullets, seeming all dainty and unseen.

30 "Walk pretty," she said. "This is the easy place. This is the easy going."

31 She followed the track, swaying through the quiet bare fields, through the little strings of trees silver in their dead leaves, past cabins silver from weather, with the doors and windows boarded shut, all like old women under a spell sitting there. "I walking in their sleep," she said, nodding her head vigorously.

32 In a ravine she went where a spring was silently flowing through a hollow log. Old Phoenix bent and drank. "Sweetgum makes the water sweet," she said, and drank more. "Nobody know who made this well, for it was here when I was born."

33 The track crossed a swampy part where the moss hung as white as lace from every limb. "Sleep on, alligators, and blow your bubbles." Then the track went into the road.

34 Deep, deep the road went down between the high green-colored banks. Overhead the live-oaks met, and it was as dark as a cave.

35 A black dog with a lolling tongue came up out of the weeds by the ditch. She was meditating, and not ready, and when he came at her she only hit him a little with her cane. Over she went in the ditch, like a little puff of milkweed.

36 Down there, her senses drifted away. A dream visited her, and she reached her hand up, but nothing reached down and gave her a pull. So she lay there and presently went to talking. "Old woman," she said to herself, "that black dog come up out of the weeds to stall you off, and now there he sitting on his fine tail, smiling at you."

37 A white man finally came along and found her—a hunter, a young man, with his dog on a chain.

38 "Well, Granny!" he laughed. "What are you doing there?"

39 "Lying on my back like a June-bug waiting to be turned over, mister," she said, reaching up her hand.

40 He lifted her up, gave her a swing in the air, and set her down, "Anything broken, Granny?"

41 "No sir, them old dead weeds is springy enough," said Phoenix, when she had got her breath. "I thank you for your trouble."

42 "Where do you live, Granny?" he asked, while the two dogs were growling at each other.

43 "Away back yonder, sir, behind the ridge. You can't even see it from here."

44 "On your way home?"

45   "No sir, I going to town."

46   "Why, that's too far! That's as far as I walk when I come out myself, and I get something for my trouble." He patted the stuffed bag he carried, and there hung down a little closed claw. It was one of the bobwhites, with its beak hooked bitterly to show it was dead. "Now you go on home, Granny!"

47   "I bound to go to town, mister," said Phoenix. "The time come around."

48   He gave another laugh, filling the whole landscape. "I know you colored people! Wouldn't miss going to town to see Santa Claus!"

49   But something held Old Phoenix very still. The deep lines in her face went into a fierce and different radiation. Without warning she had seen with her own eyes a flashing nickel fall out of the man's pocket on to the ground.

50   "How old are you, Granny?" he was saying.

51   "There is no telling, mister," she said, "no telling."

52   Then she gave a little cry and clapped her hands, and said, "Git on away from here, dog! Look! Look at that dog!" She laughed as if in admiration. "He ain't scared of nobody. He a big black dog." She whispered, "Sick him!"

53   "Watch me get rid of that cur," said the man. "Sick him, Pete! Sick him!"

54   Phoenix heard the dogs fighting and heard the man running and throwing sticks. She even heard a gunshot. But she was slowly bending forward by that time, further and further forward, the lids stretched down over her eyes, as if she were doing this in her sleep. Her chin was lowered almost to her knees. The yellow palm of her hand came out from the fold of her apron. Her fingers slid down and along the ground under the piece of money with the grace and care they would have in lifting an egg from under a sitting hen. Then she slowly straightened up, she stood erect, and the nickel was in her apron pocket. A bird flew by. Her lips moved. "God watching me the whole time. I come to stealing."

55   The man came back, and his own dog panted about them. "Well, I scared him off that time," he said, and then he laughed and lifted his gun and pointed it at Phoenix.

56   She stood straight and faced him.

57   "Doesn't the gun scare you?" he said, still pointing it.

58   "No sir, I seen plenty go off closer by, in my day, and for less than what I done," she said, holding utterly still.

59   He smiled, and shouldered the gun. "Well, Granny," he said, "you must be a hundred years old, and scared of nothing. I'd give you a dime if I had any money with me. But you take my advice and stay home, and nothing will happen to you."

60   "I bound to go on my way, mister," said Phoenix. She inclined her head in the red rag. Then they went in different directions, but she could hear the gun shooting again and again over the hill.

61   She walked on. The shadows hung from the oak trees to the road like curtains. Then she smelled wood-smoke, and smelled the river, and she saw a steeple and the cabins on their steep steps. Dozens of little black children whirled around her. There ahead was Natchez shining. Bells were ringing. She walked on.

62   In the paved city it was Christmas time. There were red and green electric lights strung and crisscrossed everywhere, and all turned on in the day time. Old Phoenix would have been lost if she had not distrusted her eyesight and depended on her feet to know where to take her.

63   She paused quietly on the sidewalk, where people were passing by. A lady came along in the crowd, carrying an armful of red-, green-, and silver-wrapped presents; she gave off perfume like the red roses in hot summer, and Phoenix stopped her.

64   "Please, missy, will you lace up my shoe?" She held up her foot.

65   "What do you want, Grandma?"

66   "See my shoe," said Phoenix. "Do all right for out in the country, but wouldn't look right to go in a big building."

67   "Stand still then, Grandma," said the lady. She put her packages down carefully on the sidewalk beside her and laced and tied both shoes tightly.

68   "Can't lace 'em with a cane," said Phoenix. "Thank you, missy. I doesn't mind asking a nice lady to tie up my shoes when I gets out on the street."

69   Moving slowly and from side to side, she went into the stone building and into a tower of steps, where she walked up and around and around until her feet knew to stop.

70   She entered a door, and there she saw nailed up on the wall the document that had been stamped with the gold seal and framed in the gold frame which matched the dream that was hung up in her head.

71   "Here I be," she said. There was a fixed and ceremonial stiffness over her body.

72   "A charity case, I suppose," said an attendant who sat at the desk before her.

73   But Phoenix only looked above her head. There was sweat on her face; the wrinkles shone like a bright net.

74   "Speak, up, Grandma," the woman said. "What's your name? We must have your history, you know. Have you been here before? What seems to be the trouble with you?"

75   Old Phoenix only gave a twitch to her face as if a fly were bothering her.

76   "Are you deaf?" cried the attendant.

77   But then the nurse came in.

78   "Oh, that's just old Aunt Phoenix," she said. "She doesn't come for herself—she has a little grandson. She makes these trips just as regular as clockwork. She lives away back off the Old Natchez Trace." She bent down. "Well, Aunt Phoenix, why don't you just take a seat? We won't keep you standing after your long trip." She pointed.

79   The old woman sat down, bolt upright in the chair.

80   "Now how is the boy?" asked the nurse.

81   Old Phoenix did not speak.

82   "I said, how is the boy?"

83   But Phoenix only waited and stared straight ahead, her face very solemn and withdrawn into rigidity.

84   "Is his throat any better?" asked the nurse. "Aunt Phoenix, don't you hear me? Is your grandson's throat any better since the last time you came for the medicine?"

85   With her hand on her knees, the old woman waited, silent, erect and motionless, just as if she were in armor.

86   "You mustn't take up our time this way, Aunt Phoenix," the nurse said. "Tell us quickly about your grandson, and get it over. He isn't dead, is he?"

87   At last there came a flicker and then a flame of comprehension across her face, and she spoke.

88   "My grandson. It was my memory had left me. There I sat and forgot why I made my long trip."

89   "Forgot?" The nurse frowned. "After you came so far?"

90   Then Phoenix was like an old woman begging a dignified forgiveness for waking up frightened in the night. "I never did go to school—I was too old at the Surrender," she said in a soft voice. "I'm an old woman without an education. It was my memory fail me. My little grandson, he is just the same, and I forgot it in the coming."

91   "Throat never heals, does it?" said the nurse, speaking in a loud, sure voice to Old Phoenix. By now she had a card with something written on it, a little list. "Yes. Swallowed lye. When was it—January—two—three years ago—"

92   Phoenix spoke unasked now. "No, missy, he not dead, he just the same. Every little while his throat begin to close up again, and he not able to swallow. He not get his breath. He not able to help himself. So the time come around, and I go on another trip for the soothing medicine."

93   "All right. The doctor said as long as you came to get it you could have it," said the nurse. "But it's an obstinate case."

94   "My little grandson, he sit up there in the house all wrapped up, waiting by himself," Phoenix went on. "We is the only two left in the world. He suffer and it don't seem to put him back at all. He got a sweet look. He going to last. He wear a little patch quilt and peep out, holding his mouth open like a little bird. I remembers so plain now. I not going to forget him again, no, the whole enduring time. I could tell him from all the others in creation."

95   "All right." The nurse was trying to hush her now. She brought her a bottle of medicine. "Charity," she said, making a check mark in a book.

96   Old Phoenix held the bottle close to her eyes and then carefully put it into her pocket.

97   "I thank you," she said.

98   "It's Christmas time, Grandma," said the attendant. "Could I give you a few pennies out of my purse?"

99   "Five pennies is a nickel," said Phoenix stiffly.

100   "Here's a nickel," said the attendant.

101   Phoenix rose carefully and held out her hand. She received the nickel and then fished the other nickel out of her pocket and laid it beside the new one. She stared at her palm closely, with her head on one side.

102   Then she gave a tap with her cane on the floor.

103   "This is what come to me to do," she said. "I going to the store and buy my child a little windmill they sells, made out of paper. He going to find it hard to believe there such a thing in the world. I'll march myself back where he waiting, holding it straight up in this hand."

104   She lifted her free hand, gave a little nod, turned round, and walked out of the doctor's office. Then her slow step began on the stairs, going down.

~

(3,382 words)

VOCABULARY

meditative (1)	illuminated (2)	bobwhites (3)
limber (3)	appointed (8)	furrow (19)
maze (21)	nary (24)	strutting (28)
husks (28)	pullets (29)	sweetgum (32)
lolling (35)	radiation (49)	ceremonial (71)
lye (91)		

THE FACTS

1. In paragraph 1, to what piece of antique furniture is Phoenix Jackson's walk compared? What characteristic is Welty trying to get across? Later on in the narrative, where is the same piece of furniture alluded to again? Why?

2. What is the purpose of the old woman's journey?

3. Essentially this is the story of a courageous woman. What part of the trip is especially difficult for her? How does she manage this obstacle?

4. What details indicate that Phoenix Jackson is slightly senile and therefore not always in touch with reality?

5. What excuse does the old woman offer for not remembering what errand she is on?

THE STRATEGIES

1. What is the plot structure of the story? What is the conflict in the plot? When is the conflict resolved?

2. Analyze Phoenix's language. What is conveyed through her speech?

3. Point out some instances of humor. What kind of humor is used?

4. During what decade would you judge this story to have taken place? What clues to your answer are given in the story?

5. In paragraph 85, we read: "With her hand on her knees, the old woman waited, silent, erect and motionless, just as if she were in armor." What meaning do you attribute to this passage?

THE ISSUES

1. In Egyptian mythology, the phoenix was a bird of great splendor that consumed itself by fire every 500 years and rose renewed from its own ashes. In what way is Phoenix Jackson like this bird?

2. The narrative abounds in descriptive passages. What is the dominant impression in paragraph 2? Are any details included that do not support this impression? What other descriptive passages can you identify?

3. Why does Phoenix keep talking to herself? What do her monologues add to the total portrait of her?

4. What is the meaning of the episode in which Phoenix steals the nickel? Does the act offend our sense of honesty? Explain your answer.

5. What significance can you attribute to the fact that the journey takes place at Christmas time?

6. Phoenix Jackson's journey is in the literary tradition of the mythological quest. What aspects of the story place it in that tradition?

SUGGESTIONS FOR WRITING

1. Using your imagination, describe Phoenix's journey home. Make your scenes descriptive by providing details that support a dominant impression.

2. Write an essay in which you describe a loving relationship between a grandparent and a grandchild or between a person and a pet.

PIGEON WOMAN

May Swenson

May Swenson (1919–1989) poet, playwright, and lecturer, was born in Logan, Utah, and educated at Utah State University. She resided in New York City until her death. She published a number of collections of poetry including her last volume, New and Selected Things Taking Place *(1978).*

The meaning of *Pigeon Woman* emerges from the irony contained in a strange old lady's fantasy.

～

Slate, or dirty-marble-colored,
or rusty-iron-colored, the pigeons
on the flagstones in front of the
Public Library make a sharp lake

5 into which the pigeon woman wades
at exactly 1:30. She wears a
plastic pink raincoat with a round
collar (looking like a little
girl, so gay) and flat gym shoes,

10   her hair square-cut, orange.
      Wide-apart feet carefully enter
      the spinning, crooning waves
      (as if she'd just learned how
      to walk, each step conscious,

15   an accomplishment); blue knots in the
      calves of her bare legs (uglied marble),
      age in angled cords of jaw
      and neck, her pimento-colored hair,
      hanging in thin tassels, is gray

20   around a balding crown.
      The day-old bread drops down
      from her veined hand dipping out
      of a paper sack. Choppy, shadowy ripples
      the pigeons strike around her legs.

25   Sack empty, she squats and seems to rinse
      her hands in them—the rainy greens and
      oily purples of their necks. Almost
      they let her wet her thirsty fingertips—
      but drain away in an untouchable tide.

30   A make-believe trade
      she has come to, in her lostness
      or illness or age—to treat the motley
      city pigeons at 1:30 every day, in all
      weathers. It is for them she colors

35   her own feathers. Ruddy-footed
      on the lime-stained paving,
      purling to meet her when she comes,
      they are a lake of love. Retreating
      from her hands as soon as empty,

40   they are the flints of love.

                              ～

(266 words)

VOCABULARY

crooning	pimento	motley
purling	flints	

THE FACTS

1. What is the dominant impression conveyed by this "pigeon woman"?
    In terms of her looks, what role could she play in a fairy tale?

2. As the poem develops, how do our feelings change about the
    woman?

3. Describe the fantasy that gives purpose to the woman's life.

4. What is the meaning of the final stanza?

5. Is this woman an impossible figment of the poet's imagination or does she represent a kind of reality? Comment.

THE STRATEGIES

1. How does the level of language used contribute to the description of the woman?

2. How do you explain the image of the pigeons as a lake?

3. What are the "blue knots in the / calves of her bare legs"? Comment on the effectiveness of this image.

4. What is the meaning of the metaphor "her own feathers" in the next-to-last stanza?

5. Interpret the metaphor "the flints of love" in the final line.

THE ISSUES

1. Various public, as well as private, agencies have been concerned with the plight of the poor, especially women who have been labeled "bag ladies," "crazy drifters," or "old female transients." What suggestions do you have for dealing with this alienated group of our population? Are we doing enough, or should we do more?

2. What is it that keeps this woman from giving up on life? What do you consider the driving force that keeps most people who lead desperate lives from committing suicide?

3. The woman in the poem chooses to feed a flock of pigeons. What other activities could give meaning to such a person's life?

4. How would you describe the male counterpart of the pigeon woman? Include the details of his appearance.

5. What measures do you suggest for reducing the number of street vagrants in our major cities?

SUGGESTIONS FOR WRITING

1. Write an essay comparing the pigeon woman with Phoenix Jackson from the previous story.

2. Imagine the loneliness that comes from being old and alone. Describe this loneliness in terms of specific, concrete details.

——— ISSUE FOR CRITICAL ——— THINKING AND DEBATE
SPANKING CHILDREN

To spank or not to spank—that is the question many parents ask today. It is a question that has lately acquired increased urgency and caused some nostalgic souls to look back with longing to the days when the reigning principle in most households was derived from the blunt biblical warning, "Spare the rod and spoil the child."

Today the issue is not that simple. We now understand more about the effects of a traumatic childhood on the adult—or, at least, we think we do—and many parents worry not about the immediate reaction of the child, but about the long-term damage to the psyche that the spanking might do.

Corporeal punishment has lately gotten bad press. Gone forever are the days when a school principal could physically punish any student at his or her discretion. Now corporal punishment, in schools where it is still practiced, must follow rigid rules: An eyewitness must be present during the punishment; the instrument of punishment must be a paddle with holes in it; and the strokes must not exceed three. In some jurisdictions, corporeal punishment without the parents' approval is likely to draw a lawsuit or, worse even, physical retaliation.

The debate over spanking was sparked by the research findings of a well-known child psychologist, Elizabeth Gershoff, who claims to have found links between spanking in early childhood and negative behavior in adulthood, including aggression, antisocial conduct, and mental problems. Her claim is a controversial one and the cause of much furor. Many parents who are in the trenches every day with their children know only too well the dangers posed even in a normal household to the child who is willful or disobedient and does not immediately react to a warning. A child, for example, who insists on sticking a finger down an electrical outlet, will grasp the urgency imparted by a quick slap on the bottom more quickly than that of a timeout in the corner. It is the same with children who have the bad habit of dashing across the street. The terrified parent is likely to react by slapping the child on the bottom. Of course, the intent is not to be abusive but simply to teach the child an urgent lesson about never doing that again.

Nevertheless, nowadays we're more respectful of research and less likely to be dismissive of findings we do not like. In this particular case, the researcher adds fuel to the fire by asking Americans to re-evaluate "why we believe it is reasonable to hit young, vulnerable children, when it is against the law to hit other adults, prisoners, and even animals."

Not every psychologist agrees with her, however, and certainly, neither does every mother. Both points of view are represented in the following debate.

Until the practicalities of child-rearing are entirely reconciled with the findings of psychology, every parent will simply have to follow the dictates of common sense in disciplining children. The photos on pages 263 and 266 represent opposite approaches in the parent-child relationship—the first shouting angrily to dominate, the second kissing affectionately to show closeness.

THE NEED FOR SPANKING

Betsy Hart

Betsy Hart is a freelance writer. This article was reprinted from the July 23, 2002, issue of New Jersey's Bergen County Record.

～

1   HERE WE GO AGAIN. Another "independent study" purports to show that parents who spank their kids should have their hands slapped.

2   This debate has been around for decades and the latest research is hardly about to settle it, despite glaring headlines in last week's newspapers.

3   Elizabeth Gershoff is a psychologist and a researcher with a well-known liberal advocacy group, Columbia University's National Center for Children in Poverty. But in fact she did not do a study. She assessed dozens of old ones on spanking children, and, she says, she found that while spanking often produced "immediate compliance," it could also lead to negative effects on many other behaviors like aggression and delinquency.

4   Her findings are reported in the latest edition of the American Psychological Association Journal, alongside critiques by other psychologists who don't necessarily advocate spanking, but who argue that Gershoff failed to find any evidence that spanking causes behavioral problems. They say it could just as well be behavioral problems that lead to the spankings.

5   But it didn't take the other psychologists to point that out. Gershoff herself does.

6   As one newspaper put it, "Gershoff said her research had not provided data that showed causative links between spanking and bad behaviors, but said everything she had studied indicated that the effects of spanking were mostly harmful."

7   Back up. Where's the science? How could Gershoff be so sure that the effects of spanking are "mostly harmful" if she admits finding no causative evidence that they are?

8   Gershoff's own writing gives us a clue:

9   "Americans need to re-evaluate why we believe it is reasonable to hit young, vulnerable children, when it is against the law to hit other adults, prisoners, and even animals," she wrote in the journal.

10   This is the emotional and value-laden language of advocacy, not science.

11   Even putting aside for a moment her over-wrought misperception of what a spanking is, the truth remains that if I put my children in the car to go visit

Mother and Son Shouting. Copyright © Tim Pannell/CORBIS

grandma in Vermont, it's called a family vacation. If I put my neighbor's children in my car to go visit grandma in Vermont, it's called kidnapping. Nor do I tell the neighbor children's parents to do their homework, to "share," or when to go to bed at night.

12   My husband and I have a unique responsibility to and an authority over our children that we have with no one else. To argue, as Gershoff does, that the same "rules" that adhere to our relationships with adults and other children adhere to our relationships with our kids is silly at best, anarchy at worst.

13   But where Gershoff shows her true colors is when she said she could not think of a single situation when a spanking would ever be appropriate. Really? What if her child were drawn to running into streets with speeding cars? Sure, she might try to keep him away from busy streets. But in the meantime would her politics really keep her from administering a controlled, open-handed swat on the bottom or fatty thigh (the proper definition of "spanking"), which even Gershoff admits is good at ensuring "immediate compliance?"

14   There are times when "immediate compliance" might mean life or death.

15   On too many occasions I've seen frustrated parents who were reluctant to spank resort to what are really crueler forms of "discipline." "Fine, if you won't come, I'm leaving you here alone" to a little 5-year-old in a crowded mall, or what amounts to banishment from Mom or Dad as in "go to your room/go to time-out."

16   And abuse? It's a good bet that it often comes at the hands of such parents, afraid to check bad behavior early on with an appropriate spanking, who later lash out in frustration and anger instead.

17   We often hear that actions speak louder than words. If I told my kids all day long that I loved them like crazy, but never touched them, never hugged, kissed, or held them, would they believe me? Of course not.

18   So then something as important as "no" and "right and wrong" sometimes need a physical touch, too—a controlled, appropriately administered spanking—in order to mean something.

19   Delivered with love, it's part of the same package that tells kids how precious, cared for, and protected they really are.

~

(732 words)

VOCABULARY

purports (1)   assessed (3)   compliance (3)
causative (6)   advocacy (10)   adhere (12)

THE FACTS

1. To whom is the author responding in her essay? Why does she write this response?

2. What are Gershoff's credentials? Do you consider them intellectually solid? Explain your answer.

3. How did a few other psychologists receive Gershoff's report? What is their point?

4. What does Hart say in Paragraph 18? What is the main idea of this passage? Rephrase it in your own words.

5. According to Hart, what is Gershoff's most egregious logical error? With what tone of voice does Hart treat this error?

THE STRATEGIES

1. What is the effect of Hart's opening paragraph? Pay special attention to tone and voice.

2. In paragraph 5, what damning evidence against Gershoff does Hart use? What is your view of this approach? Is it fair or unfair? Give reasons for your answer.

3. What tactic does Hart use repeatedly to discredit Gershoff? How effective do you find this tactic?

4. Where in the essay does Hart become personal in her attitude? Does this approach help or hinder her argument? Give reasons for your answer.

5. What analogy does Hart use to make her point about spanking? What purpose do analogies serve in an argument?

THE ISSUES

1. How important is the problem of whether or not to spank children? Does the issue deserve a federal or state law? Or should it be left up to the individual parents to decide?
2. Why do you think Gershoff is so opposed to spanking? Try to see her point of view and frame it in words.
3. Where do you think Gershoff and Hart might agree on spanking?
4. Have you ever witnessed an incident when a child's immediate compliance with a parent's command saved a life? What were the specific circumstances of the incident?
5. What is your view of the modern punishment of "time out" for children? What are the pros and cons of this disciplinary method?

SUGGESTIONS FOR WRITING

1. Write an essay in which you either attack or defend punishment by spanking. Be sure to indicate your definition of spanking and who may or may not administer this form of punishment.
2. In 500 words or less, write how you feel about today's approach to child discipline. To remain concrete rather than abstract, use specific examples to support your view.

CHILDREN DON'T NEED TO BE SPANKED TO LEARN A LESSON

Geoff Axford

Geoff Axford is a freelance writer who resides in London.

~

1 I know this comes as a blow to some lazy people. Aside from a quick and easy solution and some minimal exercise for the punisher, there is an underlying greater challenge for all involved when the option to spank is eliminated.

2 My wife and I believe there are more creative ways for a child to "learn a lesson" by carefully dealing one-on-one with the offender, pointing out the effects of his/her actions and using the situation as the cure to the problem. We then are able to take away certain privileges, such as television, video games, playtime—in effect, "grounding" the child.

3 Here's an example.

4 Recently we received a call from a teacher who said our normally shy eight-year-old was disrupting her computer class by being silly with her friends. Instead of reacting in a frenzy, my wife and I decided bedtime would

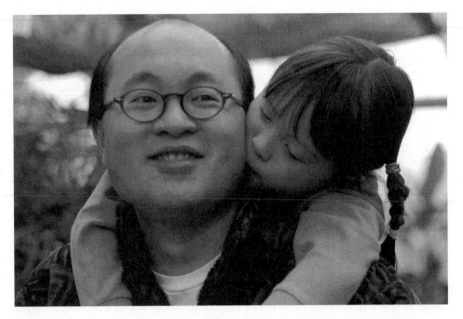

Little girl kissing father on the cheek. Copyright © Barbara Haynor/Index Stock Imagery

come an hour earlier and there would be no playing with friends after the supper hour for the remainder of the week.

5   The real kicker was this shy, usually quiet kid had to apologize to her computer teacher and make a heartfelt pledge before him she would not disrupt the class again.

6   Her home room teacher gasped and thought this to be a "fate worse than death" for this tenderhearted butterfly.

7   I called the computer teacher and told him to be prepared for this, as a way for me to ensure the apology would be delivered and for him to prepare, as I knew he would, a response that would acknowledge her for her braveness and her commitment.

8   She came home on the day she apologized and appeared quite happy with her results.

9   Lessons learned: remorse, respect, forgiveness, courage, self-esteem. Hardly any of what a "good spanking" would have achieved.

10   The results of this type of discipline are obvious and positive for all, but spanking can have confusing results.

11   How can a child rationalize that someone who is hurting them is still truly loving them?

12   In conservative and traditional cultures, I'm sure there are as many creative ways available to bring the message home.

13   I trust most parents can spank and keep love in their hearts. Usually after the punishment, the message has been sent and most all is forgiven.

14   But how can the rest of society be assured all parents will not abuse the right to spank? It's a dangerous balancing act for many adults to keep their own emotions in check when striking out in force. One solution is to delay punishment until all calm down and cooler heads prevail.

15   By teaching our children to deal thoughtfully with a situation, we can show them there are alternatives to striking another being.

16   We can encourage them to create their own solutions by allowing them time to think long and hard about the result of their actions.

~

(488 words)

VOCABULARY

frenzy (4)   prevail (14)

THE FACTS

1. Which does the author consider more challenging—spanking or eliminating spanking? Do you agree with his assumption? Explain your answer.

2. How does the author propose to deal creatively with a child who needs to learn a lesson? Name some specific methods he mentions. Have you ever seen anyone use these methods? If so, what did you think of them?

3. What was the most important part of teaching the author's eight-year-old daughter a lesson? Do you agree that this was the "kicker" of the entire process? Explain your answer.

4. How did the author's daughter feel after she had atoned for her misbehavior? Does this reaction seem normal and realistic? Why or why not?

5. According to the author, what should parents encourage their children to do when they have misbehaved? How can this goal be accomplished?

THE STRATEGIES

1. What style does the author use in writing this essay? Where does this style best fit? What are the characteristics of the style?

2. In the opening paragraph, how does the author get his reader's attention?

3. How does the author make sure that the reader knows when the author is using an example? Do you think the example really represents the author's view? Why or why not?

4. Why do you suppose the homeroom teacher gasped at the thought of this "tenderhearted butterfly" having to apologize? What is the purpose of using this metaphor?

5. What are the only two questions asked in the essay? How important are they to the point being argued? What is the author's answer to each question? What is your answer?

THE ISSUES

1. Why do you think the issue of spanking or not spanking children has lately surfaced as a debatable issue in our society?

2. Do you think there are some times when spanking is the only reasonable response to a child's disobedience? Give an example to support your answer.

3. What personality quality will be required from a parent who refuses ever to spank his or her children? Is this quality an asset worth developing in all parents? Why or why not?

4. Not long ago we observed a child in the supermarket kicking his mother because she would not buy him a miniature car. How would you have handled that moment if this had been your child?

5. What is your answer to the question posed in paragraph 14: "How can the rest of society be assured all parents will not abuse the right to spank?"

SUGGESTIONS FOR WRITING

1. Write an essay in which you suggest creative alternatives to spanking children. Begin with a thesis that states why you think spanking should be eliminated.

2. In 500 words or less, describe an event in your childhood when you learned an important lesson about proper social behavior.

—————— STUDENT CORNER ——————

|

Spanking—So What Is the Fuss About?
Shelley Taylor, State University of New York, Oswego

He stood there in the grocery store, looking defiantly at his mother. "I want *that*," he said in a loud voice, pointing at a package of fruit-flavored candy. "No, Nathan," she said in her best contemporary parenting-book voice, "I told you that we were not going to buy any more candy today." He began to stamp his feet. "But I *want* some," he shrieked. The mother appeared to visibly cower in front of this four-year-old "giant." "It's time to go," she coaxed. "Here, why don't you ride in the grocery cart?" She reached out and started to pick him up. "No! Put me down!" he yelled, wriggling out of her grasp. Now normally, I don't stare, but I stood there transfixed, unable to keep my eyes off the unfolding drama. The mother looked around helplessly, with an embarrassed look on her face. "Nathan," she said desperately, "if you don't stop that right now, you'll have to have a time-out when we get home." (By this time, the young prince was on the floor writhing and crying at the top of his lungs, totally blocking traffic in the aisle.) His mother's face was crimson. "Please, Nathan," she pleaded. "If you are a good boy, I'll give you a special treat tonight." A crowd of onlookers had begun to gather, and I could tell by their expressions that they were all itching to walk over to that child, give him a good swat, and tell him to knock it off and to mind his mother.

Taylor 2

In all fairness to her, how many parents would do that today with people watching? During the last 15 years or so, the anti-spanking movement has gained such momentum that a parent swatting a child in public might well be accused of child abuse on the spot. And parents are truly afraid that if they ever spank their children, their offspring will turn out to be maladjusted adolescents and permanently damaged adults. Almost all of the experts say confidently that this is the case.

Recently, as I was sitting in one of my psychology classes, this very topic came up while we were discussing Skinner's Behaviorist Theory. I was amazed that students on both sides of the issue were so vocal. I didn't think that anyone was in favor of spanking these days, especially young students. Books and articles on child psychology cite all of the recent research that proves how harmful this practice can be. I listened in disbelief as person after person told how they were spanked occasionally as children and how they now realized that it had been good for them and that their parents had done this out of love and concern for them.

Just for interest sake, I decided to look for others' opinions on the subject, and I found that even today, the controversy regarding spanking is still alive and well. Of course, the vast majority of child psychologists are adamantly against it. And they have very good reasons for taking this position. Many claim that even one spanking can leave an emotional scar on the child that lasts a lifetime. They say that spanking confuses children, making it difficult for them to learn the lessons that adults are trying to teach them. It is asserted that the spanked child learns to fear his or her parents and loses the ability to trust them.

Taylor 3

Another argument against spanking is that it teaches the child that force is the way to deal with problems. If it is okay for mom or dad to hit their children, then the children grow up feeling that they have the right to hit others who treat them shabbily or even disagree with them. It is also more likely that these children will become adults who abuse their own children and spouses. It has even been strongly suggested that some of these children become violent criminals because of the physical punishment they suffered when they were young.

Again, many feel that spanking has sexual consequences. The child who is spanked is considered to be more vulnerable to child molesters. And it has been found that in some cases spanking can stimulate immature sexual feelings in some children. Tragically, they can form a connection between pain, humiliation, and sexual arousal that can haunt them the rest of their lives.

The final thing that I will mention here (although I am sure there are other considerations) is the possibility of actual physical injury to parts of the body, including the legs, the tailbone, and sexual organs. Even hitting the hands of younger children is said to occasionally cause bone or joint damage or premature osteoarthritis.

It is hard to imagine that there could even be another side to this issue today, and yet there are people who dispute some of the above arguments. Diana Baumrind, a Ph.D. from the Institute of Human Development of the University of California at Berkeley, gave an address at the Annual Convention of the American Psychological Association on August 24, 2001. Here she questioned whether current research provides a causal argument supporting a blanket injunction against disciplinary spanking by parents. In order to do this, the research would have to distinguish between physical abuse and normative discipline, contain a control for baseline child misbehavior, account for parental rejection or other related variables that would cause a variance in the results, contrast the impact of physical punishment with the impact of other disciplinary interventions, and contain comprehensive information about parents and children in a variety of naturalistic settings.

Okey Chigbo (1998), a freelance magazine writer and editor from Toronto, goes as far as to say that the anti-spanking movement has used weak, and in some cases, non-existent evidence in defending its views. He specifically mentions the claims that spanking increases violence in society. Though parents spanked much more in the '50's and '60's than now, the crime rate today is three times higher than it was then. He cites other findings that contradict other points made by the other side. He is most concerned with the push to make spanking illegal and tells of a man who was actually locked up in jail in London, Ontario for spanking his five-year-old daughter. I think it is also important to mention that these opponents of the anti-spanking movement do not believe in spanking as a primary method of discipline. But they do think that rarely it is warranted and effective.

So there you have it—the bare nuts and bolts of two widely different views on this obviously relevant and provocative subject. We cannot ignore the arguments of either side if we want to assess the question fairly. So where do we go from here?

As I have thought about this issue, I have come to some of my own opinions that could very well change over time. Before

Taylor 5

getting into the actual practice of spanking, I would like to postulate a theory. I really think that this controversy has stemmed from the much more basic issue of child management in general. It seems to me that parents in our society have become much more permissive and less involved with their children. And that has had tragic results. Many kids are left to do pretty much what they want. Gangs have increased, crime is on the rise, and adolescent pregnancy, drug use, and suicide are rampant. I think that children need and want boundaries. I consider this lack of responsibility on the parents' part constitutes a form of child neglect and even rejection. It HAS been shown that authoritative discipline (not authoritarian) is essential is raising healthy, happy, well-adjusted children and building strong family relationships.

As to the practice of spanking, per se, I definitely see it as a last resort. And I feel that it should not be used with children after the age of six. I am generally opposed to the idea of physical punishment of any kind, but if it must be used, it must be done in the right way and spirit. Punishment of any kind should never be administered in anger. A parent should not simply react to a child's behavior, but respond in a loving way. And parents must always be clear with their children about why they are being punished. It is very important that children do not grow up thinking that force is the only way to confront problems and feeling that they cannot express their own anger in acceptable ways. Communication should always be stressed. The important question for parents should always be "What is the lesson learned?"

Actually I agree with B. F. Skinner, who stated that punishment is usually far less effective than reinforcement. If children received more positive reinforcement for the good, kind, and loving behavior and attitudes that they exhibit, the need for punishment would greatly diminish. Children have a natural need to be accepted and respected. And they need to feel a sense of security and belonging.

Personally, I like the idea of *consequences* related to individual choice. I think that children are not always being taught that they are responsible for the choices they make and the consequences that follow. And the more natural the consequences, the better. A parent can let a child know that a job must be done, and that he or she can decide to do it right away or to put it off and then have to complete it while the rest of the family is involved in some pleasurable activity. A music teacher I knew always told the choir at the beginning of class that certain goals (i.e. songs learned, etc.) must be accomplished that day. The choir members could choose to work hard and to get out early, or they could choose to act up and stay late during part of their lunch period. (Needless to say, the peer pressure for staying on task was quite strong.) I think that one of the problems today is that people have not learned to take responsibility for their own actions.

The subject of discipline is a complex one. There are no easy answers. Most of us will have to grapple with these issues at some time in our lives. And we will make mistakes, just as our parents did before us. Because, after all, we are only human, and we will not always make the right decisions. But we must always strive to learn and to grow and to help our children do the same. We must be willing to confront ourselves, our motives and attitudes, and our own self-discipline. And most importantly, we must always see our children, and every child, as a precious gift who must be affirmed, cared for, and loved.

How I Write

Before I actually write, I do a lot of reflective thinking and organizing in my head. I decide what information and material I am going to include and try to get a rough idea of the order and format I want to use. Sometimes I even write an outline that I can follow. When doing the actual writing of the piece, I sit down at my computer and just start typing—editing and making changes as I go along until I am satisfied with the result.

How I Wrote This Essay

While working on this piece, I used the Internet to look up a few sites on the subject of spanking, just to get an idea about current research, others' opinions, etc. Then I searched my memory for incidents in my own experience that were relevant to the issue. Finally, I synthesized and integrated all of this information so as to formulate my own feelings and insights.

My Writing Tip

- Start your writing with something that will capture the attention of your reader—such as an interesting story, an amazing fact, or simply a dynamic statement.
- Be imaginative and descriptive in your illustrations.
- Prune redundant words and phrases from your writing.
- Be sincere. Be sure that you are present in your work. Anyone can write down a bunch of facts, but your own insights can make them come to life.
- Make sure your conclusion leaves your reader with something to think about. (I personally think the introduction and conclusion are the crucial parts of an essay.)

CHAPTER WRITING ASSIGNMENTS

1. Write an essay in which you describe one of the following places:
   a. The most peaceful place you know
   b. The most disturbing place you have ever been to
   c. The most boring place you know
2. Write an essay describing a particularly vivid dream. Begin by thinking of and writing down a dominant impression for the scenes you saw in your dream. Using that dominant impression as your thesis, write a description that is supported by specific details.

WRITING ASSIGNMENTS FOR A SPECIFIC AUDIENCE

1. Write a diary entry, describing the major events of your day. Treat your diary as a confidential, intimate friend to whom you can trust your innermost feelings.
2. Write to your parents, describing to them your college living quarters.

COLLABORATIVE WRITING PROJECT

Joining three other students in the class, go—pen and notebook in hand—to a place on campus. Sit and observe your environment for five minutes, trying to absorb details you normally would not notice. Then spend another ten to fifteen minutes writing a list of these details in your notebook. Exchange your list with those of the other students in your group. Because we can assume that four pairs of eyes are better than one, you should now have enough details to develop an essay vividly describing the spot you observed, beginning with a dominant impression and supporting that impression with the details you observed. Once you have completed your essay, compare it with the essays of the other members in your group.

9

Process Analysis

EDITORS' COUNSEL

What Process Analysis Does

An essay that gives instructions on how to do something or describes how something was done is developed by *process analysis*. Many best-sellers have been written in this mode, all bearing such telltale how-to titles as *How to Make a Million in Real Estate* or *How to Learn Spanish the Easy Way*. Historians such as Will Durant use process analysis to tell us how Spartan warriors were trained, how Christianity became the dominant religion of Western civilization, and how the Battle of Normandy was won. Like narration, process presents information in chronological order, commonly in the form of instructions. Here, a student explains the process of cooking vegetables in a microwave oven:

> If you follow these seven easy steps, you will have the pleasure of eating vegetables cooked al dente the way they are done in the finest restaurants where nouvelle cuisine is the rage:
>
> First, choose three vegetables that normally take approximately the same time to cook (for instance, carrots, broccoli, and summer squash). For aesthetic purposes it is a good idea to choose vegetables of different colors.
>
> Second, slice the vegetables into bite-size pieces or slices, depending on which is easier.
>
> Third, arrange the pieces in alternating circles on a ceramic quiche plate.
>
> Fourth, add butter, salt, and pepper to taste.
>
> Fifth, pour one-half cup of water over the vegetables.
>
> Sixth, place a piece of saran wrap over the plate and seal the sides.
>
> Last, cook the vegetables in the microwave oven for four minutes on "high." The vegetables will be crisply delicious and ready to serve the most discriminating of palates. Best of all, the vitamins will be preserved.

Although process analysis is a simple rhetorical mode and is fairly straightforward to write, it is often done badly and with irksome consequences. Anyone who has ever struggled to understand an inept manual meant to explain some necessary but practical chore can attest to the importance of clear process writing.

When to use process analysis

Although found in all kinds of writing, process explanations are common in science and technology, where they vary from instructions on how to perform a simple test for acidity to how to diagnose a high-risk pregnancy with ultrasound. Many of your classes will require you to write various process explanations: A political-science teacher may ask you to describe how a bill is passed in Congress; a geology teacher, how glaciers are formed; a botany teacher, how flowers are reproduced. Process explanations can range from a historical blow-by-blow account of Custer's Last Stand to an anthropological explanation of how ancient tribes buried their dead.

How to write a process analysis

The first and most important step in writing a process essay is to select an appropriate subject. Decide whether your overall purpose is to give instructions or to inform. If you intend, say, to instruct readers in how to organize a volunteer team to nab graffiti writers or how to study for the SAT, your purpose is to give instructions. On the other hand, if you want to list the steps that led to the collapse of the dot com companies in 2001 or the sequence of events that led to the resignation of President Richard Nixon, your purpose is to inform. In writing either kind of essay, you must know and be able to cite appropriate details.

State Your Purpose in a Clear Thesis The second step in writing your process essay is to begin with a thesis that plainly states your overall aim. "It is possible for you to acquire a competitive spirit" is an example of a thesis that leaves your reader in the dark and is singularly unhelpful to you, the writer. On the other hand, the thesis "You can acquire a competitive spirit by practicing five personality traits" establishes an agenda for the writer and tells the reader what to expect—a recital and description of the traits. Similarly, "I want to inform you how juveniles are imprisoned," tells your reader practically nothing. Contrast it with this more helpful thesis: "Juveniles face four legal steps before they can be imprisoned."

A convenient and simple way to make the steps of your explanation stand out is to number them 1, 2, 3, etc. For example, in an explanation to a nonswimmer of *how* to become drownproof, the logical sequence of steps is as follows:

1. Take a deep breath.
2. Float vertically in the water.

3. Lift the arms to shoulder height and give scissors kicks while flapping the arms down in a winging motion.
4. Raise the head out of the water and exhale.

This sequence of steps is the only one that works, so your explanation must cover it accurately.

Organize the Sequence of Steps Logically   Next, you should arrange the steps in the most logical order. Essays that cover simple how-to tasks such as changing a tire or baking a cake are best organized chronologically. On the other hand, essays on broader topics, such as how to build self-esteem in a child, how to make a marriage work, or how Stalin rose to power, are best organized in order of importance.

Regardless of which arrangement you use, you should single out and explain each step clearly. It often helps to sketch out the steps exactly as they will occur in your chosen order. For example, let us say that your parents won a court case against a landlord for discriminating against them because of their ethnic origin. Using your familiarity with their case, combined with further research, you decide to write a paper on how to file an antidiscrimination housing suit. Here are your steps, outlined chronologically:

1. File the complaint with the local Fair Housing Council.
2. Explain your reasons for filing to the investigator who hears your complaint.
3. If the investigation uncovers evidence of discrimination, state or federal authorities will formally accuse the landlord of discrimination. (If your case has no merit, the matter will probably fizzle out here.)
4. Choose between appearing before an administrative hearing officer or hiring an attorney to file a lawsuit in civil court.
5. Either the case will be solved through a settlement or the state will impose a punitive fine to compensate for damages.

Once you have outlined these steps clearly, all you have to do is flesh out the essay with necessary facts and details.

Explain Everything   The devil is said to be in the details, and that is clearly the case in process essays. Always assume that your reader is uninformed about your subject. Explain everything. Don't be vague, as maddeningly unhelpful manuals often are. If your essay is giving specific directions about how to do something, simply address the reader directly, as in a command: "Next, [you] fold the paper along the dotted line. . . . Then, [you] write your personal number in the upper left-hand corner," and so on.

It also helps to carefully signal the succession of described steps with words such as "first," "second," "next," "then," and "finally." Within each step, using words such as "before," "after," and "while" can help the reader keep track of the discussion. It might even be helpful to mention a previous step before going on to the next. For example, in a process essay about how juveniles are imprisoned, the first step might be for the police to bring the youth to a screening office. If so, you might introduce the second step this way, "If after the screening has taken place the case still cannot be informally resolved, the second step is to arrange a date for a court hearing."

As we said, process essays are usually straightforward and relatively simple to write. Most require no poetic or metaphoric language—a manual so written would drive consumers over the brink—and generally demand nothing more of a writer than a sensible grasp of facts and the ability to explain them in understandable sequence.

Warming Up to Write a Process Analysis

1. Choosing one of the following how-to processes, write down in chronological order or in order of importance the steps involved in completing the task. Do not omit a step.

    a. How to trim a Christmas tree

    b. How to intelligently read a newspaper

    c. How to make your college professors like you

    d. How to get ready for a long-distance bicycle race

    e. How to ask for a dinner date, or how to turn down a dinner date

2. Choosing one of the following how-it-happened processes, write down the major steps that led up to it.

    a. How a friend of yours got hooked on an illegal drug such as cocaine or ecstasy

    b. How a serious accident that involved you or a loved one occurred

    c. How John Muhamad and John Lee Malvo were finally caught and brought to justice for being serial killers

    d. The stages of AIDS

3. From each group, choose the best topic for a process essay.

    a. 1. How to fly a commercial airplane

        2. How to wash a car

        3. How to write a novel

        4. How to speak Chinese

    b. 1. How the world came into being

        2. How my great grandfather became a millionaire

        3. The stages of international economic bankruptcy

        4. How the United Nations functions

——————— EXAMPLES ———————

HOW TO BUY A NEW CAR

Clark Howard

Clark Howard is the popular host of a syndicated consumer advocate show that originates from WSB in Atlanta and is heard nationwide over more than 150 radio stations. A regular contributor to many magazines and newspapers, Howard is also the author of several books including Clark Howard's Consumer Survival Kit III *(1998) and* Get Clark Smart *(2001).*

For most young people, buying a first car is one of life's important milestones—like baptism, graduation, or getting a driver's license—but that was when buying a car was actually fun and not the annoying experience it has become lately. It was also before the car had been transformed from a simple convenience to how it is seen in some quarters—as a symbolic reflection of both our taste and character. The essay that follows reminds us of the simple truths about car ownership and offers practical advice on how to use our brains while remembering our wallets when we buy a car.

~

1   There are a lot of tools available today to help you buy a car. Unfortunately, most people don't take advantage of them, because they get caught up in the emotion of buying. If money matters to you, put that emotion aside and be smart about your car purchase.

2   First, go to your bank or credit union and prequalify for a car loan, or apply online. Once you prequalify, you'll know how much car you can afford and what type of monthly payment you will have to budget. It also means your purchase won't collapse because you can't get financing.

3   Once your financing is set up, decide what kind of car you want. One of the best times to go look at cars is when a dealership is closed. If the dealership isn't open, there's no salesperson there to pressure you. You're free to look around the lot at vehicles. It may sound strange, but a shopping mall parking lot also is a good place to look at a lot of different vehicles.

4   Everyone wants a car that will run dependably and stay out of the repair shop. The best way to improve your odds of getting a trouble-free car is to check out the repair records of the models you like. *Consumer Reports* magazine is the best place to find repair data on cars. Each year, the magazine's April issue is devoted to car buying, and it contains detailed ratings and data on a variety of models.

5   For several model years, Consumers Union, which publishes *Consumer Reports,* also publishes a car-buying guide that is available year-round in bookstores. *Consumer Reports* is available online for a monthly fee at www.consumerreports.com.

6   Of course, no repair data is available on newly introduced car models. I don't recommend buying a new or radically redesigned model, because if you do, you are the guinea pig for any problems the vehicle might have. After a few model years, you have a better idea if a car is well-made and worth purchasing.

7   Once you've narrowed your search to a couple of different models, call your insurance agent to find out how much it would cost to insure those vehicles. There may be a significant difference between your choices, even between two versions of the same model. The size of the cars' engines, for example, could be one reason for a cost difference.

8   Become familiar with the various versions of a car. The Honda Accord, for example, might come in a DX, LX, EX, and SE version. Each version comes with a different package of options and standard equipment. You'll find that the most expensive version of the car will cost several thousand dollars more than the least expensive version. It's to your advantage to buy the least expensive version of the model that meets your needs. That's because, over time, the value of those two vehicles converges. An initial gap of $8,000 between the cheapest and most expensive versions might dwindle to $1,000 in the resale value of the two cars after a few years of ownership. if you buy the most expensive version, you pay a higher price both up-front and at resale time.

9   I don't recommend test-driving a car at a dealership. You'll only have a short time to check out the car, and the salesperson will be right there. The best way to test-drive a car is to rent it for a day or two. Car rental companies make most of their money on business rentals, so they offer great specials on the weekends, when volume is light. I actually check out cars this way on business, since I travel so much. I've rented cars I thought I might want to buy and changed my mind after driving them for a few days. It's the ultimate test drive and it's not expensive. After all, considering that you might spend $25,000 to buy a car, spending $25 to $40 to rent it is rather inexpensive.

10   If you do a test-drive at a dealership, a representative may ask for your driver's license. If you turn it over, make the dealership give you a signed release saying they will not pull a credit report on you. Dealerships like to check your credit while you're on a test drive, and if you visit several dealerships, the number of credit inquiries could damage your credit rating.

11   The Internet has put consumers completely in control of the car-buying process. To get the best deal, you have to have Internet access. If you're not online, find a friend who is and enlist their help, or go to a local library. It's that important. In fact, using the Internet will save you so much on the car purchase that, even if you don't have a computer or an Internet-only appliance, spending a few hundred dollars to buy one would be a bargain.

12   First, go to www.edmunds.com and look up the actual dealer cost on the base vehicle and options you're interested in. Add the dealer cost for air conditioning, automatic transmission, whatever you want, and calculate the total dealer cost for the car. Any negotiating you do with the dealer should start

from the dealer's cost, not the manufacturer's suggested retail price. The price you pay will depend upon the popularity of a particular model, and it could range from thousands of dollars above dealer cost for the most popular cars to below dealer cost for unpopular models.

13   You can get an instant price quote for the model you want to buy at a number of Web sites. Some of the biggest are *www.carorder.com*, *www.carsdirect.com* and *www.greenlight.com*. There will be many others. With these sites, you enter the model, equipment and color you want, interior and exterior, and within 15 seconds, they give you a guaranteed price for which they will sell you the car. It's amazing. If you wish, you can then go through that process, as I have, and buy a car online. I did it at www.carorder.com for my mom, and I was able to buy her car at $6,000 less than she had been quoted from two dealers.

14   The process was so easy it was startling. There's no delivery charge, and you have the option of picking the car up at a nearby dealer, or having it delivered to your home or office. You sign the papers and hand them the money and they hand you the keys. Buying a car via the Internet is so superior to the traditional process that dealer groups in state after state are trying to outlaw Internet car shopping. If they're successful, you may have to accept delivery at the home of a friend or relative in another state.

15   If you decide not to buy online, you still can use the Web sites to get a feel for fair market value. Use the online price as a guideline when you call local dealers. See if they'll match or beat the price you found on the Internet. If the dealer agrees and then reneges, walk out.

16   You'll find big differences in price at different Web sites, just as you would from different dealers. So don't assume any one Web site will be the cheapest for any car. It will depend on their sources of supply.

17   However, beware of the many supposed Internet car-buying services that actually are glorified referral services paid for by the dealers. These simply are a form of advertising for the dealers, and you won't benefit by using them.

18   If you choose to buy a car the old-fashioned way, by walking into a dealership and talking with a salesperson, be prepared for a difficult process. Some dealers still use a variety of tactics to snare you. They know you're excited about buying a new car and will use that to their advantage. One strategy they'll employ is delay. Dealers know that the longer they can keep you at the dealership, the more likely you are to buy a car, So they'll try to keep you there for several hours.

19   One common tactic to delay you is to make your car unavailable. When you show up at a dealership, they ask to have the used-car manager check out your car, to evaluate its trade-in value. While you're test-driving a new car, they send somebody to look over your car and make sure you don't get it back too quickly.

20   I recommend that you discuss any trade-in only after you've negotiated the purchase of the new car. I'll talk more about why in the next section. But

if you keep the transactions separate and stay close to your car, you won't be kept in the dealership any longer than you want to be there.

21   One of the most despicable practices in the industry is "roofing," in which the used-car people literally throw the keys to your car onto the dealership roof, then report that they somehow can't find the keys. The purpose is to get you to drive home in the new car while they look for the keys. The best way to protect yourself in a dealership is to be willing to walk out.

∼

(1,648 words)

VOCABULARY

converges (8)   via (14)   snare (18)
despicable (21)

THE FACTS

1. According to the author, what should you set aside when you begin the process of buying a car? Why do you think he makes this suggestion before offering any other guidelines?

2. How many steps in buying a car does the author list? What are these steps?

3. What is the purpose of reading *Consumer Reports* magazine? What other source might provide the same information?

4. What is the purpose of pre-qualifying for a loan? If you have ever pre-qualified for any kind of loan, what was your experience? Was it difficult or easy?

5. What are the advantages of buying a car on-line? If you were to buy a car soon, would you buy it on-line? Why or why not?

THE STRATEGIES

1. How does the author indicate the first step in the process of buying a car? What about subsequent steps? Is the process simple to follow and clear? Explain your answer.

2. How does the author facilitate your use of the Internet to buy a car? How usable do you consider his advice?

3. What verb mood does the author use throughout the essay? What is his purpose in using this mood?

4. Why doesn't the author recommend test driving a car at a dealership? Do you agree with his reasoning?

5. What does the second sentence of paragraph 20 announce? How necessary is this sentence?

THE ISSUES

1. What do you consider the most important advice in this essay? Support your answer with reasons.

2. Do you agree that the number of inquiries about your credit could damage your credit rating? How would this happen?

3. Re-read paragraph 18. Do you agree with the author that buying a car at a dealership is the "old-fashioned way"? What advantages can you list for buying at a dealership in our modern world?

4. If you've ever bought a car before, what steps did you take and how did they differ from those recommended by the author?

5. Did you find out anything you didn't already know by reading this essay? If so, what was it? If you did not learn anything new, how do you feel about the information the author has provided?

WRITING ASSIGNMENTS

1. Write a process essay in which you list the steps you plan to take the next time you buy a car.

2. Describe some kind of medical process with which you are familiar. List the steps in the order in which they occur. Examples: Having a tooth filled or braces placed on your teeth, donating blood, getting a flu shot, having a cut cleaned and stitched up, having your throat swabbed, having your eyes checked.

HUNTING OCTOPUS IN THE GILBERT ISLANDS

Sir Arthur Grimble

Sir Arthur Grimble (1888–1956) was a British colonial government official and writer. After receiving an education from Magdalene College at Cambridge, he joined the colonial service in the Pacific and was posted to the Gilbert and Ellice islands, where he remained in various positions from 1914 until 1933. From 1933 to 1948, he worked as administrator and then governor of the Windward Islands, retiring from the colonial service in 1948. In retirement, Grimble developed a talent for narrating his island experiences on radio for the British Broadcasting Corporation. The result was a series of talks that became so popular that they were published under the title of A Pattern of Islands *(1952), from which the following excerpt was taken.*

Grimble relates an amusing story of watching two young boys hunting just off a reef in the Gilbert Islands. His curiosity about what the boys were doing got him into a predicament from which he could not escape without taking part in their sport. In the course of telling this riveting story, Grimble gives us a process explanation of how the Gilbertese hunt and kill octopus.

~

1   The Gilbertese happen to value certain parts of the octopus as food, and their method of fighting it is coolly based upon the one fact that its arms never change their grip. They hunt for it in pairs. One man acts as the bait, his partner as the killer. First, they swim eyes-under at low tide just off the reef, and search the crannies of the submarine cliff for sight of any tentacle that may flicker out for a catch. When they have placed their quarry, they land on the reef for the next stage. The human bait starts the real game. He dives and tempts the lurking brute by swimming a few strokes in front of its cranny, at first a little beyond striking range. Then he turns and makes straight for the cranny, to give himself into the embrace of those waiting arms. Sometimes nothing happens. The beast will not always respond to the lure. But usually it strikes.

2   The partner on the reef above stares down through the pellucid water, waiting for his moment. His teeth are his only weapon. His killing efficiency depends on his avoiding every one of those strangling arms. He must wait until his partner's body has been drawn right up to the entrance of the cleft. The monster inside is groping then with its horny mouth against the victim's flesh, and sees nothing beyond it. That point is reached in a matter of no more than thirty seconds after the decoy has plunged. The killer dives, lays hold of his pinioned friend at arms' length, and jerks him away from the cleft; the octopus is torn from the anchorage of its proximal suckers, and clamps itself the more fiercely to its prey. In the same second, the human bait gives a kick which brings him, with quarry annexed, to the surface. He turns on his back, still holding his breath for better buoyancy, and this exposes the body of the beast for the kill. The killer closes in, grasps the evil head from behind, and wrenches it away from its meal. Turning the face up towards himself, he plunges his teeth between the bulging eyes, and bites down and in with all his strength. That is the end of it. It dies on the instant; the suckers release their hold; the arms fall away; the two fishers paddle with whoops of delighted laughter to the reef, where they string the catch to a pole before going to rout out the next one.

3   Any two boys of seventeen, any day of the week, will go out and get you half a dozen octopus like that for the mere fun of it. Here lies the whole point of this story. The hunt is, in the most literal sense, nothing but child's play to the Gilbertese.

4   As I was standing one day at the end of a jetty in Tarawa lagoon, I saw two boys from the near village shouldering a string of octopus slung on a pole between them. I started to wade out in their direction, but before I hailed them they had stopped, planted the carrying-pole upright in a fissure and, leaving it there, swum off the edge for a while with faces submerged evidently searching for something under water. I had been only a few months at Tarawa, and that was my first near view of an octopus-hunt. I watched every

stage of it from the dive of the human bait to the landing of the dead catch. When it was over, I went up to them. I could hardly believe that in those few seconds, with no more than a frivolous-looking splash or two on the surface, they could have found, caught and killed the creature they were now stringing up before my eyes. They explained the amusing simplicity of the thing.

5   "There's only one trick the decoy-man must never forget," they said, "and that's not difficult to remember. If he is not wearing the water-spectacles of the Men of Matang,[1] he must cover his eyes with a hand as he comes close to the kika (octopus), or the sucker might blind him." It appeared that the ultimate fate of the eyes was not the thing to worry about; the immediate point was that the sudden pain of a sucker clamping itself to an eyeball might cause the bait to expel his breath and inhale sea-water; that would spoil his buoyancy, and he would fail then to give his friend the best chance of a kill.

6   Then they began whispering together. I knew in a curdling flash what they were saying to each other. Before they turned to speak to me again, a horrified conviction was upon me. My damnable curiosity had led me into a trap from which there was no escape. They were going to propose that I should take a turn at being the bait myself, just to see how delightfully easy it was.

7   And that is what they did. It did not even occur to them that I might not leap at the offer. I was already known as a young Man of Matang who liked swimming, and fishing, and laughing with the villagers; I had just shown an interest in this particular form of hunting; naturally, I should enjoy the fun of it as much as they did. Without even waiting for my answer, they gleefully ducked off the edge of the reef to look for another octopus—a fine fat one— mine. Left standing there alone, I had another of those visions . . .

8   It was dusk in the village. The fishers were home, I saw the cooking-fires glowing orange-red between the brown lodges. There was laughter and shouted talk as the women prepared the evening meal. But the laughter was hard with scorn. "What?" they were saying, "Afraid of a kika? The young Man of Matang? Why, even the boys are not afraid of a kika!" A curtain went down and rose again on the Residency; the Old Man was talking: "A leader? You? The man who funked a schoolboy game? We don't leave your sort in charge of Districts." The scene flashed to my uncles: "Returned empty," they said. "We always knew you hadn't got it in you. Returned empty. . ."

9   Of course it was all overdrawn, but one fact was beyond doubt; the Gilbertese reserved all their most ribald humour for physical cowardice. No man gets himself passed for a leader anywhere by becoming the butt of that kind of wit. I decided I would rather face the octopus.

10   I was dressed in khaki slacks, canvas shoes and a short-sleeved singlet. I took off the shoes and made up my mind to shed the singlet if told to do so; but I was wildly determined to stick to my trousers throughout. Dead or alive, said a voice within me, an official minus his pants is a preposterous object, and I felt I could not face that extra horror. However, nobody asked me to remove anything.

---

[1]"Men of Matang" is the Gilbertese phrase for white foreigners.

11   I hope I did not look as yellow as I felt when I stood to take the plunge; I have never been so sick with funk before or since. "Remember, one hand for your eyes," said someone from a thousand miles off, and I dived.

12   I do not suppose it is really true that the eyes of an octopus shine in the dark; besides, it was clear daylight only six feet down in the limpid water; but I could have sworn the brute's eyes burned at me as I turned in towards his cranny. That dark glow—whatever may have been its origin—was the last thing I saw as I blacked out with my left hand and rose into his clutches. Then, I remember chiefly a dreadful sliminess with a herculean power behind it. Something whipped round my left forearm and the back of my neck, binding the two together. In the same flash, another something slapped itself high on my forehead, and I felt it crawling down inside the back of my singlet. My impulse was to tear at it with my right hand, but I felt the whole of that arm pinioned to my ribs. In most emergencies the mind works with crystal-clear impersonality. This was not even an emergency, for I knew myself perfectly safe. But my boyhood's nightmare was upon me. When I felt the swift constriction of those disgusting arms jerk my head and shoulders in towards the reef, my mind went blank of every thought save the beastliness of contact with that squat head. A mouth began to nuzzle below my throat, at the junction of the collar-bones. I forgot there was anyone to save me. Yet something still directed me to hold my breath.

13   I was awakened from my cowardly trance by a quick, strong pull on my shoulders, back from the cranny. The cables around me tightened painfully, but I knew I was adrift from the reef. I gave a kick, rose to the surface and turned on my back with the brute sticking out of my chest like a tumour. My mouth was smothered by some flabby moving horror. The suckers felt like hot rings pulling at my skin. It was only two seconds, I suppose, from then to the attack of my deliverer, but it seemed like a century of nausea.

14   My friend came up between me and the reef. He pounced, pulled, bit down, and the thing was over—for everyone but me. At the sudden relaxation of the tentacles, I let out a great breath, sank, and drew in the next under water. It took the united help of both boys to get me, coughing, heaving and pretending to join in their delighted laughter, back to the reef. I had to submit there to a kind of war-dance round me, in which the dead beast was slung whizzing past my head from one to the other. I had a chance to observe then that it was not by any stretch of fancy a giant, but just plain average. That took the bulge out of my budding self-esteem. I left hurriedly for the cover of the jetty, and was sick.

～

(1,707 words)

VOCABULARY

quarry (1)	pellucid (2)	pinioned (2)
proximal (2)	annexed (2)	ribald (9)

singlet (10)   funk (11)   limpid (12)
herculean (12)   constriction (12)

THE FACTS

1. What two roles in hunting octopus do the hunting partners separately play?
2. What weapon do the Gilbertese use to kill the octopus?
3. What danger does the decoy man face in the octopus hunt?
4. Why did the author consent to take part in the sport of octopus hunting?
5. After the hunt was over, what did the author do?

THE STRATEGIES

1. What do you think is the most prominent feature of the style of this piece?
2. What can you infer about Grimble's attitude toward octopuses from the words he uses to describe them?
3. In describing the reaction (see, particularly, paragraph 8) that might follow his refusal to take part in the octopus hunt, what simple device does Grimble use to make the scene humorous?
4. In paragraph 13, Grimble writes that he was awakened from his "cowardly trance." What is your opinion of this characterization? What effect does it and other self-deprecatory remarks have on the tone of the story?
5. This process explanation of how the Gilbertese hunt octopus consists of two major parts. What are they, and how effective do you find them?

THE ISSUES

1. In spite of the deprecating remarks Grimble makes about his lack of courage, what picture of him emerges from this tale?
2. How does the portrait that Grimble draws of the octopus match your own knowledge of that creature?
3. Had Grimble not been a colonial official assigned to the Gilbert Islands, what do you think his reaction would have been to the invitation from the boys to join the octopus hunt?
4. Based on this story, what can you infer about the Gilbertese and their culture?
5. Imagine yourself in Grimble's place. What would you have done when the Gilbertese boys invited you to take part in the octopus hunt?

WRITING ASSIGNMENTS

1. Write a process essay depicting the steps involved in any sporting event you've experienced.

2. Write an essay showing how you got entangled in doing something you did not really want to do.

HITLER'S WORKDAY

William Shirer

William Shirer (1904–1993) was a journalist and author who covered the Third Reich for CBS radio during the 1930s and 1940s. Between 1942 and 1948, he wrote a syndicated column for the New York Herald Tribune *and worked for the Mutual Broadcasting System before becoming a full-time writer. His monumental* The Rise and Fall of the Third Reich *(1960) won the National Book Award and became a controversial best-seller, with some critics accusing him of oversensationalizing his subject. Among his many other books are* Berlin Diary: The Journal of a Foreign Correspondent *(1941) and a two-volume memoir,* Twentieth-Century Journey *(1976 and 1984).*

Taken from *Berlin Diary*, this process excerpt, dated November 5, 1939, gives a step-by-step recounting of a typical workday in the life of Nazi dictator Adolf Hitler. Shirer was then a correspondent for CBS and relied on information provided by unnamed informants.

～

Berlin, November 5

1   CBS wants me to broadcast a picture of Hitler at work during war-time. I've been inquiring around among my spies. They say: He rises early, eats his first breakfast at seven A.M. This consists usually of either a glass of milk or fruit-juice and two or three rolls, on which he spreads marmalade liberally. Like most Germans, he eats a second breakfast, this one at nine A.M. It's like the first except that he also eats a little fruit. He begins his working day by wading into state papers (a job he detests, since he hates detail work) and discussing the day's program with his adjutants, chiefly S. A. Leader Wilhelm Brückner and especially with his deputy, Rudolf Hess, who was once his private secretary and is one of the few men he trusts with his innermost thoughts. During the forenoon he usually receives the chiefs of the three armed services, listens to their reports and dictates decisions. With Göring he talks about not only air-force matters but general economic problems, or rather results, since he's not interested in details or even theories on this subject.

2   Hitler eats a simple lunch, usually a vegetable stew or a vegetable omelet. He is of course a vegetarian, teetotaler, and non-smoker. He usually invites a small circle to lunch, three or four adjutants, Hess, Dr. Diettrich, his press chief, and sometimes Göring. A one-percent beer, brewed specially for him, is served at this meal, or sometimes a drink made out of kraut called "Herve," flavoured with a little Mosel wine.

3   After lunch he returns to his study and work. More state papers, more conferences, often with his Foreign Minister, occasionally with a returned German ambassador, invariably with some party chieftain such as Dr. Ley or Max Amann, his old top sergeant of the World War and now head of the lucrative Nazi publishing house Eher Verlag, which gets out the Völkische Beobachter and in which Hitler is a stockholder. Late in the afternoon Hitler takes a stroll in the gardens back of the Chancellery, continuing his talk during the walk with whoever had an appointment at the time. Hitler is a fiend for films, and on evenings when no important conferences are on or he is not overrunning a country, he spends a couple of hours seeing the latest movies in his private cinema room at the Chancellery. News-reels are a great favourite with him, and in the last weeks he has seen all those taken in the Polish war, including hundreds of thousands of feet which were filmed for the army archives and will never be seen by the public. He likes American films and many never publicly exhibited in Germany are shown him. A few years ago he insisted on having *It Happened One Night* run several times. Though he is supposed to have a passion for Wagnerian opera, he almost never attends the Opera here in Berlin. He likes the Metropol, which puts on tolerable musical comedies with emphasis on pretty dancing girls. Recently he had one of the girls who struck his fancy to tea. But only to tea. In the evening, too, he likes to have in Dr. Todt, an imaginative engineer who built the great Autobahn network of two-lane motor roads and later the fortifications of the Westwall. Hitler, rushing to compensate what he thinks is an artistic side that was frustrated by non-recognition in his youthful days in Vienna, has a passion for architects' models and will spend hours fingering them with Dr. Todt. Lately, they say, he has even taken to designing new uniforms. Hitler stays up late, and sleeps badly, which I fear is the world's misfortune.

⌒

(616 words)

VOCABULARY

teetotaler (2)   lucrative (3)

THE FACTS

1.   What time does Hitler eat his breakfast?

2.   How many breakfasts does Hitler eat?

3. With whom does Hitler usually eat lunch? What is he likely to have for lunch?

4. What kind of entertainment is Hitler particularly fond of?

5. What particular movie did Hitler run several times a few years ago?

THE STRATEGIES

1. What logical method of organization does Shirer use in recounting Hitler's workday?

2. In writing a process, a writer will often use some common words and phrases to indicate steps in the process. What are some of these words and phrases that Shirer uses?

3. Shirer was a lifelong journalist. What characteristic of this piece reveals his journalistic training?

4. In paragraph 3, Shirer writes that when Hitler is "not overrunning a country" he likes to watch movies. How would you characterize the tone of that observation?

5. In paragraph 2, Shirer says of Hitler that he is "of course a vegetarian, a teetotaler, and non-smoker." What do you think Shirer implies by writing "of course"?

THE ISSUES

1. Shirer says that he has been inquiring among his spies. How would you characterize the kind of information his spies uncovered?

2. Based on this entry, what can you infer about Shirer's personal attitude toward Hitler?

3. What do you think of the ethics of the request made to Shirer—to find out the personal details of a world leader's daily life?

4. Shirer says that "Hitler stays up late, and sleeps badly." Why do you think he fears this as "the world's misfortune"?

5. What picture of Hitler and his work habits emerges from this journal entry?

WRITING ASSIGNMENTS

1. Write a journal entry that chronicles in step-by-step sequence how you spend a typical day.

2. Write a process essay showing the steps involved in keeping a journal.

HOW TO BE AN ARMY

Kenneth Patchen

Kenneth Patchen (1911–1972) was an American poet and graphic artist who became famous in poetry circles for pioneering the technique of reading poetry to the accompaniment of jazz music. During his career as a poet, he received many literary awards, including a Guggenheim fellowship in 1936 and a National Foundation on Arts and Humanities Award in 1967. Collections of his works include Poems of Humor and Protest *(1960) and* The Collected Poems of Kenneth Patchen *(1969). He also wrote a novel,* Sleepers Awake *(1946). His paintings have been exhibited in various cities and at university galleries.*

82

The unusual amalgamation of figures on page 295 is a concrete poem. Concrete poetry emerged as a form during the 1950s to protest against the aridness of a tradition demanding that poets follow certain stanza, meter, and rhyme forms. Concrete poetry depends on visual effects instead of mere words to deliver its message, suggesting meaning through iconographic pictures and word arrangements.

~

THE FACTS

1. How would you summarize the content of this poem in one sentence?

2. Why does the poet choose shoes as the first element necessary to the process of waging war?

3. What is the meaning of the equation presented?

THE STRATEGIES

1. The artwork in the poem resembles the drawings of elementary school children. Why do you suppose the author did not choose more sophisticated drawings?

2. What irony exists between the words "and a faith in the right" and the drawings that follow those words?

3. What technique does the author use to stress certain concepts more than others? How effective is this technique?

THE ISSUES

1. Under what circumstances would you be willing to go to war and possibly lose your life in battle?

2. Of all the ingredients listed in the poem, which one do you consider the most important to waging a successful war?

3. What ingredient for dealing with a third world war seems to be missing from the poem?

SUGGESTIONS FOR WRITING

1. Write an essay detailing the steps involved in any kind of military or job training in which you have been involved.

2. Write a process analysis of how an army leader could boost troop morale before heading into combat.

Henry Koerner, My Parents. *Oil on masonite, 25 x 30 inches. Courtesy of Myron Kunin. The Regis Foundation.* © *The Curtis Galleries, Inc.*

———— ISSUE FOR CRITICAL ————
THINKING AND DEBATE
AGEISM

The painting *My Parents*, by Henry Koerner, symbolically sums up the issue of ageism in its portrayal of two elderly people deep in a woods. Lost in thought, the man is walking on a separate path away from the woman, who sits near a tree and stares down the narrow trail that unwinds and ominously ends ahead of her. The painting—actually a portrait of Koerner's parents who were exterminated by the Nazis—reminds us that aging also brings infirmity and befuddlement, which intensify the separations that occur naturally at the end of life. Koerner wrote that he spent many days walking with his parents peacefully through the woods of Vienna before World War II and that the painting was meant to commemorate that experience. Yet, in this portrayal, the painting is unrepresentative of growing old today because many of our elderly spend their last days not in an idyllic woodland, but in a grimy apartment or a cheap room. The photograph of pensioners protesting (see page 299) illustrates this point.

The essayists in this section address ageism from quite different perspectives. As the title of Malcolm Cowley's essay reminds us, he was past eighty when he wrote the book from which this excerpt comes, and he finds philosophical consolations in growing old. He is not embittered, but a stoical, observant elder. Food tastes wonderful when you are old, he tells us; napping drowsily in the sun is blissful. On the other hand, the view from Mayra Mannes is sharp-edged and petulant. When she wrote this essay, she was facing old age, not immersed in it, and from this perspective, she rails against the pressures of growing old and the futility of trying to smother the years under creams and lotions. She is right, too, when she reminds us that a dignified beauty awaits those who gracefully accept the battle scars of aging.

Ageism, unlike other issues, will ultimately and personally affect every reader of this book who achieves life expectancy. It is an issue that is progressively becoming not only more common, but more pressing. Unprecedented numbers of baby boomers are aging, making America inevitably older and grayer. According to the 2000 census, 37.7 millions Americans were between the ages of forty-five and fifty-four. The median age (the most common age of the population) in 1820 was 16.7 years; by 1980, it had jumped to 30; in the 1990 census, it was 32.9 years. In the 2000 census it was 35.3 years, the highest it has ever been.

If you die young or in your middle years, you will escape the consequences of ageism. Otherwise, ageism will surely and eventually affect your life. Indeed, how you treat the elderly today when you are young might well foreshadow how the young will treat you when you yourself are numbered among the elderly.

THE VIEW FROM EIGHTY

Malcolm Cowley

Malcolm Cowley (1898–1989), American critic and poet, was born in Belsano, Pennsylvania and educated at Harvard. After World War I, Cowley lived abroad for many years among the so-called "lost generation" of writers, eventually writing about them in Exile's Return *(1934) and* Second Flowering *(1973). He was the literary editor of* The New Republic *from 1930 to 1940 and numbers among his published works* A Dry Season *(poems, 1942),* Blue Juanita: Collected Poems *(1964), and* The View from Eighty *(1981), from which this excerpt was taken.*

The View from Eighty is a heartening and refreshing reminder that old age does not necessarily entail the loss of literary style, vigor, and wit. Using examples to show how the aged see the world, Cowley writes with the same freshness and liveliness that have characterized all of his works.

~

1   Even before he or she is 80, the aging person may undergo another identity crisis like that of adolescence. Perhaps there had also been a middle-aged cri-

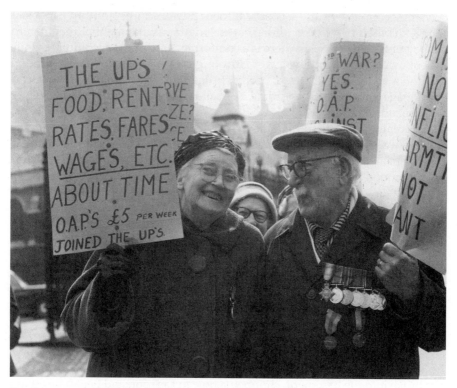

Pensions protest. Copyright © Hulton Archive/CORBIS.

sis, the male or the female menopause, but for the rest of adult life he had taken himself for granted, with his capabilities and failings. Now, when he looks in the mirror, he asks himself, "Is this really me?"—or he avoids the mirror out of distress at what it reveals, those bags and wrinkles. In his new makeup he is called upon to play a new role in a play that must be improvised. André Gide, that long-lived man of letters, wrote in his journal, "My heart has remained so young that I have the continual feeling of playing a part, the part of the 70-year-old that I certainly am; and the infirmities and weaknesses that remind me of my age act like a prompter, reminding me of my lines when I tend to stray. Then, like the good actor I want to be, I go back into my role, and I pride myself on playing it well."

2   In his new role the old person will find that he is tempted by new vices, that he receives new compensations (not so widely known), and that he may possibly achieve new virtues. Chief among these is the heroic or merely obstinate refusal to surrender in the face of time. One admires the ships that go down with all flags flying and the captain on the bridge.

3   Among the vices of age are avarice, untidiness, and vanity, which last takes the form of a craving to be loved or simply admired. Avarice is the worst of those three. Why do so many old persons, men and women alike, insist on hoarding money when they have no prospect of using it and even when they

have no heirs? They eat the cheapest food, buy no clothes, and live in a single room when they could afford better lodging. It may be that they regard money as a form of power; there is a comfort in watching it accumulate while other powers are dwindling away. How often we read of an old person found dead in a hovel, on a mattress partly stuffed with bankbooks and stock certificates! The bankbook syndrome, we call it in our family, which has never succumbed.

4   Untidiness we call the Langley Collyer syndrome. To explain, Langley Collyer was a former concert pianist who lived alone with his 70-year-old brother in a brownstone house on upper Fifth Avenue. The once fashionable neighborhood had become part of Harlem. Homer, the brother, had been an admiralty lawyer, but was now blind and partly paralyzed; Langley played for him and fed him on buns and oranges, which he thought would restore Homer's sight. He never threw away a daily paper because Homer, he said, might want to read them all. He saved other things as well and the house became filled with rubbish from roof to basement. The halls were lined on both sides with bundled newspapers, leaving narrow passageways in which Langley had devised booby traps to catch intruders.

5   On March 21, 1947, some unnamed person telephoned the police to report that there was a dead body in the Collyer house. The police broke down the front door and found the hall impassable, then they hoisted a ladder to a second-story window. Behind it Homer was lying on the floor in a bathrobe; he had starved to death. Langley had disappeared. After some delay, the police broke into the basement, chopped a hole in the roof, and began throwing junk out of the house, top and bottom. It was 18 days before they found Langley's body, gnawed by rats. Caught in one of his own booby traps, he had died in a hallway just outside Homer's door. By that time the police had collected, and the Department of Sanitation had hauled away, 120 tons of rubbish, including besides the newspapers, 14 grand pianos and the parts of a dismantled Model T Ford.

6   Why do so many old people accumulate junk, not on the scale of Langley Collyer, but still in a dismaying fashion? Their tables are piled high with it, their bureau drawers are stuffed with it, their closet rods bend with the weight of clothes not worn for years. I suppose that the piling up is partly from lethargy and partly from the feeling that everything once useful, including their own bodies, should be preserved. Others, though not so many, have such a fear of becoming Langley Collyers that they strive to be painfully neat. Every tool they own is in its place, though it will never be used again; every scrap of paper is filed away in alphabetical order. At last their immoderate neatness becomes another vice of age, if a milder one.

7   The vanity of older people is an easier weakness to explain, and to condone. With less to look forward to, they yearn for recognition of what they have been: the reigning beauty, the athlete, the soldier, the scholar. It is the beauties who have the hardest time. A portrait of themselves at twenty hangs on the wall, and they try to resemble it by making an extravagant use of creams, powders, and dyes. Being young at heart, they think they are merely

revealing their essential persons. The athletes find shelves for their silver trophies, which are polished once a year. Perhaps a letter sweater lies wrapped in a bureau drawer. I remember one evening when a no-longer athlete had guests for dinner and tried to find his sweater. "Oh, that old thing," his wife said. "The moths got into it and I threw it away." The athlete sulked and his guests went home early.

8   Often the yearning to be recognized appears in conversation as an innocent boast. Thus, a distinguished physician, retired at 94, remarks casually that a disease was named after him. A former judge bursts into chuckles as he repeats bright things that he said on the bench. Aging scholars complain in letters (or one of them does), "As I approach 70 I'm becoming avid of honors, and such things—medals, honorary degrees, etc.—are only passed around among academics on a quid pro quo basis (one hood capping another)." Or they say querulously, "Bill Underwood has ten honorary doctorates and I have only three. Why didn't they elect me to. . .?" and they mention the name of some learned society. That search for honors is a harmless passion, though it may lead to jealousies and deformations of character, as with Robert Frost in his later years. Still, honors cost little. Why shouldn't the very old have more than their share of them?

9   To be admired and praised, especially by the young, is an autumnal pleasure enjoyed by the lucky ones (who are not always the most deserving). "What is more charming," Cicero observes in his famous essay *De Senectute*, "than old age surrounded by the enthusiasm of youth!. . . Attentions which seem trivial and conventional are marks of honor—the morning call, being sought after, precedence, having people rise for you, being escorted to and from the forum. . . . What pleasures of the body can be compared to the prerogatives of influence?" But there are also pleasures of the body, or the mind, that are enjoyed by a greater number of older persons.

10   Those pleasures include some that younger people find hard to appreciate. One of them is simply sitting still, like a snake on a sunwarmed stone, with a delicious feeling of indolence that was seldom attained in earlier years. A leaf flutters down; a cloud moves by inches across the horizon. At such moments the older person, completely relaxed, has become a part of nature—and a living part, with blood coursing through his veins. The future does not exist for him. He thinks, if he thinks at all, that life for younger persons is still a battle royal of each against each, but that now he has nothing more to win or lose. He is not so much above as outside the battle, as if he had assumed the uniform of some neutral country, perhaps Liechtenstein or Andorra. From a distance he notes that some of the combatants, men or women, are jostling ahead—but why do they fight so hard when the most they can hope for is a longer obituary? He can watch the scrounging and gouging, he can hear the shouts of exultation, the moans of the gravely wounded, and meanwhile he feels secure; nobody will attack him from ambush.

11   Age has other physical compensations besides the nirvana of dozing in the sun. A few of the simplest needs become a pleasure to satisfy. When an old woman in a nursing home was asked what she really liked to do, she answered

in one word: "Eat." She might have been speaking for many of her fellows. Meals in a nursing home, however badly cooked, serve as climactic moments of the day. The physical essence of the pensioners is being renewed at an appointed hour; now they can go back to meditating or to watching TV while looking forward to the next meal. They can also look forward to sleep, which has become a definite pleasure, not the mere interruption it once had been.

12   Here I am thinking of old persons under nursing care. Others ferociously guard their independence, and some of them suffer less than one might expect from being lonely and impoverished. They can be rejoiced by visits and meetings, but they also have company inside their heads. Some of them are busiest when their hands are still. What passes through the minds of many is a stream of persons, images, phrases, and familiar tunes. For some that stream has continued since childhood, but now it is deeper; it is their present and their past combined. At times they conduct silent dialogues with a vanished friend, and these are less tiring—often more rewarding—than spoken conversations. If inner resources are lacking, old persons living alone may seek comfort and a kind of companionship in the bottle. I should judge from the gossip of various neighborhoods that the outer suburbs from Boston to San Diego are full of secretly alcoholic widows. One of those widows, an old friend, was moved from her apartment into a retirement home. She left behind her a closet in which the floor was covered wall to wall with whiskey bottles. "Oh, those empty bottles!" she explained. "They were left by a former tenant."

13   Not whiskey or cooking sherry but simply giving up is the greatest temptation of age. It is something different from a stoical acceptance of infirmities, which is something to be admired. At 63, when he first recognized that his powers were failing, Emerson wrote one of his best poems, "Terminus":

> It is time to be old,
> To take in sail:
> The god of bounds,
> Who sets to seas a shore,
> Came to me in his fatal rounds,
> And said: "No more!
> No farther shoot
> Thy broad ambitious branches, and thy root.
> Fancy departs: no more invent;
> Contract thy firmament
> To compass of a tent."

14   Emerson lived in good health to the age of 79. Within his narrowed firmament, he continued working until his memory failed; then he consented to having younger editors and collaborators. The givers-up see no reason for working. Sometimes they lie in bed all day when moving about would still be possible, if difficult. I had a friend, a distinguished poet, who surrendered in that fashion. The doctors tried to stir him to action, but he refused to leave his room. Another friend, once a successful artist, stopped painting when his eyes began to fail. His doctor made the mistake of telling him that he suffered

from a fatal disease. He then lost interest in everything except the splendid Rolls-Royce, acquired in his prosperous days, that stood in the garage. Daily he wiped the dust from its hood. He couldn't drive it on the road any longer, but he used to sit in the driver's seat, start the motor, then back the Rolls out of the garage and drive it in again, back twenty feet and forward twenty feet; that was his only distraction.

15   I haven't the right to blame those who surrender, not being able to put myself inside their minds or bodies. Often they must have compelling reasons, physical or moral. Not only do they suffer from a variety of ailments, but also they are made to feel that they no longer have a function in the community. Their families and neighbors don't ask them for advice, don't really listen when they speak, don't call on them for efforts. One notes that there are not a few recoveries from apparent senility when that situation changes. If it doesn't change, old persons may decide that efforts are useless. I sympathize with their problems, but the men and women I envy are those who accept old age as a series of challenges.

16   For such persons, every new infirmity is an enemy to be outwitted, an obstacle to be overcome by force of will. They enjoy each little victory over themselves, and sometimes they win a major success. Renoir was one of them. He continued painting, and magnificently, for years after he was crippled by arthritis; the brush had to be strapped to his arm. "You don't need your hand to paint," he said. Goya was another of the unvanquished. At 72 he retired as an official painter of the Spanish court and decided to work only for himself. His later years were those of the famous "black paintings" in which he let his imagination run (and also of the lithographs, then a new technique). At 78 he escaped a reign of terror in Spain by fleeing to Bordeaux. He was deaf and his eyes were failing; in order to work he had to wear several pairs of spectacles, one over another, and then use a magnifying glass; but he was producing splendid work in a totally new style. At 80 he drew an ancient man propped on two sticks, with a mass of white hair and beard hiding his face and with the inscription "I am still learning."

17   Giovanni Papini said when he was nearly blind, "I prefer martyrdom to imbecility." After writing sixty books, including his famous Life of Christ, he was at work on two huge projects when he was stricken with a form of muscular atrophy. He lost the use of his left leg, then of his fingers, so that he couldn't hold a pen. The two big books, though never to be finished, moved forward slowly by dictation; that in itself was a triumph. Toward the end, when his voice had become incomprehensible, he spelled out a word, tapping on the table to indicate letters of the alphabet. One hopes never to be faced with the need for such heroic measures.

18   "Eighty years old!" the great Catholic poet Paul Claudel wrote in his journal. "No eyes left, no ears, no teeth, no legs, no wind! And when all is said and done, how astonishingly well one does without them!"

～

(2,552 words)

VOCABULARY

improvised (1)	infirmities (1)	avarice (3)
succumbed (3)	lethargy (6)	immoderate (6)
condone (7)	querulously (8)	deformations (8)
prerogatives (9)	indolence (10)	exultation (10)
nirvana (11)	climactic (11)	

THE FACTS

1. What kind of crisis does the aging person undergo?
2. What are the virtues of old age? What are its main vices?
3. What is the Langley Collyer syndrome? Why do old people suffer so often from it? What part does society's treatment of the elderly have to play in this syndrome?
4. Why are some old people so vain?
5. What pleasures do the old revel in?

THE STRATEGIES

1. Aside from examples that illustrate what it is like to be old, what kind of supporting detail does Cowley use? What does its use add to the essay?
2. What is the function of the question in paragraph 6?
3. Old people, says Cowley, suffer chronically from avarice, untidiness, and vanity. He gives extended examples of the second and third of these, but not of the first. How does he support his view that the old are often avaricious? What rhetorical logic lies behind this omission of examples?
4. What extended analogy does Cowley use to describe how the young appear to the old? How effective is this analogy?
5. In this excerpt, Cowley gives anecdotes about aging in others, rather than in himself. Do you think this a better tactic than focusing on his own experiences? Why or why not?

THE ISSUES

1. Has Cowley overlooked any vices or virtues associated with old age? Make a written list of the characteristics of old age you wish to avoid and then a second list of characteristics you wish to develop.
2. What is your answer to the question posed in paragraph 3: "Why do so many old persons, men and women alike, insist on hoarding money when they have no prospect of using it and even when they

have no heirs?" Do you agree with Cowley's suggestion that perhaps they regard money as a form of power, or are there other reasons for the avarice?

3. What about old age do you fear most? What do you plan to do in order to alleviate your fear?

4. In "Rabbi Ben Ezra," the famous Victorian poet Robert Browning wrote these lines:

> Grow old along with me!
> The best is yet to be,
> The last of life, for which the first was made:
> Our times are in His hand
> Who saith, "A whole I planned,
> Youth shows but half, trust God: see all, nor be afraid."

5. What kind of person do you imagine yourself to be at age eighty? Describe in detail what kinds of clothes you will wear, how you will spend your time, and what philosophy will guide your existence.

SUGGESTIONS FOR WRITING

1. Some sociologists have suggested that because women generally outlive men, marriage laws should be relaxed to allow the elderly to practice polygyny (wherein a man has more than one wife or mate) as a way of reducing the many lonely widows. Express your views on this issue in an essay in which you use examples to support your thesis.

2. Write an essay giving examples of the way age has affected an elderly friend or relative.

STAY YOUNG

Marya Mannes

Marya Mannes (1904–1990) was an American novelist, poet, and essayist who worked as a staff writer for Reporter *magazine. Her books include* The New York I Know *(1961),* But Will It Sell *(1964),* Subverse *(poems, 1964), and* Out of My Time *(1971).*

~

1 Like all people in the middle span, I am aware of death and saddened by its advance forces of disintegration. I do not like the signs in flesh and muscle and bone of slow decline, even if they are yet unaccompanied by pain. To one in love with physical beauty, its inevitable blurring by years is a source of melancholy.

2   Yet I feel sure that while the flesh may retreat before age, the man or woman can advance if he goes towards death rather than away from it, if he understands the excitement implicit in this progression from the part to the whole. For that is, really, what it should be: a steady ascent from personal involvement—the paths and rocks and valleys and rises of the foothills—to the ultimate height where they fuse into one grand and complex pattern, remote and yet rewarding. It is like coming into clearer air. And if that air becomes in course too rare to breathe, the final breath is one of total purity.

3   It is because of these convictions that I protest against the American tyranny of youth. There is beauty and freshness in youth (if there is less and less innocence), but it is an accident of time and therefore ephemeral. There is no "trick" in being young: it happens to you. But the process of maturing is an art to be learned, an effort to be sustained. By the age of fifty you have made yourself what you are, and if it is good, it is better than your youth. If it is bad, it is not because you are older but because you have not grown.

4   Yet all this is obscured, daily, hourly, by the selling barrage of youth: perhaps the greatest campaign for the arrested development of the human being ever waged anywhere. Look young, be young, stay young, they call from every page and on every air wave. You must be young to be loved. And with this mandate, this threat, this pressure, millions of goods are sold and millions of hours are spent in pursuit of a youth which no longer exists and which cannot be recaptured.

5   The result of this effort is, in women, obscene; in men, pathetic. For the American woman of middle age thinks of youth only in terms of appearance and the American man of middle age thinks of youth only in terms of virility.

6   If obscene seems a strong word to use for old women who try to look young, I will be more explicit. It is quite true and quite proper that better eating habits, better care and less drudgery have made American women look ten years younger than their mothers did at the same age. One of the pleasing phenomena of our life is the naturally young and pretty grandmother, almost as lithe and active as her daughter. But I am talking of the still older woman, past her middle fifties, often alone, often idle, who has the means to spend the greater part of her leisure in beauty salons and shops and weight-reducing parlors, resisting age with desperate intensity. They do not know it, but the fact of this resistance nullifies the effects of the effort. The streets of American cities are full of these thin, massaged, made-up, corseted, tinted, overdressed women with faces that are repellent masks of frustration; hard, empty, avid. Although their ankles are slender and their feet perched on backless high-heeled slippers, they fool no one, and certainly no man. They are old legs and old feet. Although their flesh is clear and fairly firm in the visible areas, it is kneaded flesh, and fools no one. The hips are small indeed, but the girdle only emphasizes their stiff aridity. And the uplift bra, the platinum hair, the tight dress? Whom do they fool? The woman herself, alone. And the obscenity in all this is that she uses the outward techniques of sexual allure to maintain her youth when she is no longer wanted by men. And she does it

because she has been told to do it by the advertising media. She has been sold a bill of goods.

7   Let me hastily say at this point that it is the solemn duty of all women to look as well as they can and to maintain through life the grooming that makes them pleasing to others. Towards this end, the advertisers have performed a signal service to Americans. But they have over-reached themselves, and us. Instead of saying "Be Yourself," they say, "Be Young." Instead of saying "Relax," they say "Compete!" In doing this, they deprive the maturing woman of a great joy, an astounding relief: the end, not of sex, heaven knows, but of sexual competition. By the time a woman is fifty she is either wanted as a woman of fifty or not really wanted at all. She does not have to fool her husband or her lover, and she knows that competition with women far younger than she is not only degrading but futile.

8   It is also an axiom that the more time a woman spends on herself, the less she has for others and the less desirable she is to others. If this goes for young women—and I believe it does—it goes doubly for older women, who have— if they knew it—more to give.

9   When I go to Europe and see the old people in villages in France or Italy, for instance, I am struck at once by the age of all women who are no longer young, pitying their premature withering; and at the same time startled by the occasional beauty of their old faces. Lined and grooved and puckered as they may be, their hair grizzled or lank, there is something in their eyes and in their bones that gives age austerity and makes their glossy contemporaries at a bridge table here seem parodies of women. They show that they have lived and they have not yet found the means to hide it.

10   I remember also that as a child and a young girl I never thought of my mother in terms of age. Whatever it was at any time, she looked it; and nobody then told her to lose weight or do something about her hair because she was far too interesting a human being to need such "ameliorations." It would, indeed, have been an impertinence. My mother had no illusions of beauty: she was too concerned with music and her husband and her children to be concerned, in detail, with herself. I don't doubt that, given today's aids, she could have looked younger and smarter than she did. But she would have lost something. The time and effort spent in improving her looks would have been taken from music and from love. With her unruly eyebrows plucked to a thin line, her face made-up, her plump, small body moulded into girdles, an important part of her would have vanished: her identity.

11   It is this that the older women of America are losing. At club gatherings, at hotels, at resorts, they look identical. What lives they have led have been erased from their faces along with the more obvious marks of age. They have smoothed and hardened into a mould. Their lotions have done well.

12   It could be said that if they maintain the illusion of youth to themselves only, no harm is done and some good. But I wonder if all self-deceptions do not harm, and if their price is not loss of self.

13   I wonder too whether one of the reasons for wild, intemperate, destructive youth might not be this same hard finish, this self-absorption, of the women to whom they might otherwise turn. I cannot imagine going for counsel and comfort to a mother or aunt or grandmother tightly buttressed by latex and heavily masked by makeup. Where is the soft wide lap, the old kind hands, the tender face of age?

14   None of us with any pride in person and any sense of aesthetics can allow ourselves to crumble into decay without trying to slow the process or at least veil its inroads. But that is not the major battle. The fight is not for what is gone but for what is coming; and for this the fortification of the spirit is paramount, the preservation of the flesh a trivial second.

15   Let the queen bee keep her royal jelly. Or so I keep telling myself.

~

(1,422 words)

VOCABULARY

ephemeral (3)	nullifies (6)	repellent (6)
allure (6)	axiom (8)	austerity (9)
ameliorations (10)	intemperate (13)	aesthetics (14)
inroads (14)	paramount (14)	

THE FACTS

1. According to the author, what must a man or woman do to advance with old age?

2. In what terms do American women think of youth? In what contrasting terms do American men think of youth?

3. What does the author think advertisers should be saying to women? Instead, what are they actually saying?

4. In what countries is the author often struck by the natural beauty of older women who do not try to hide their ages?

5. What price do women pay for their attempts at deceiving themselves and the world about how old they are?

THE STRATEGIES

1. The author opens her essay with a frank admission about her sadness in the face of aging. What does this admission add to the essay?

2. What evidence does the author offer to support her assertions about the obscene efforts women make to avoid looking their age? How convincing do you find this evidence?

3. Given what the author has written in paragraph 6 about American women who desperately labor to look younger, what rhetorical strategy is implicit in her description of European women in paragraph 9?

4. Why do you think the author included the anecdote about her mother in paragraph 10?

5. What does the final sentence of the essay imply about the author? Why is this an apt implication on which to end this essay?

THE ISSUES

1. What do you think is entailed in the author's advice that a person should go "towards death rather than away from it"?

2. What difference, if any, do you think the feminist movement has made in easing the unrealistic pressures on aging women?

3. From this essay, what can you infer are the causes behind what the author calls "the American tyranny of youth"?

4. What pressures, if any, are exerted upon the young by the culture of youth? Or are the young exempt from such pressures? Explain.

5. Why does it necessarily follow, as the author alleges, that there is scant comfort available from aging aunts, mothers, and grandmothers who try hard to avoid looking their age?

SUGGESTIONS FOR WRITING

1. Write an essay discussing how you would like to be treated when you are old.

2. In an essay, explore the potential benefits a successful feminist revolution could have on the present tyranny of youth.

—————————— **STUDENT CORNER** ——————————

1

Final Draft

Aging

Kimberly Caitlin Wheeler, Yale University

There is a general perception in our society that once you reach middle age, you are "Over the hill and going down." As people get older, their value, unlike that of wine, is perceived to decrease. Thus the elderly are "worthless" members of society: They contribute nothing, but take much. This prejudice against the elderly and even the middle aged, ageism, is a big problem in our youth-oriented culture. Ageism does not end with mere perceptions, but also begets action. There are problems with age discrimination both in the entertainment industry and the workplace, but neither problem can be solved without a change in attitude towards the elderly.

Ageism is extremely noticeable within the entertainment industry. Most television programs and movies cater to the younger members of society. The shows portray young characters who are usually facing age-specific problems, such as starting a career or raising a family. Those who have reached retirement and have raised their families are often ignored or are peripheral characters. There are virtually no shows that sympathetically portray the interests of the elderly. One consequence of this is that people begin to perceive the elderly through the eyes of the media—as valueless members of society.

Wheeler 2

The entertainment industry has some economic justifications in producing only shows geared towards a younger audience. Research has shown that the 18–44 age group has more spending money than members of older age groups. Older age groups are actually wealthier, but they are less likely to spend money frivolously. They are not as receptive to advertisements and product trends. Because members of the 18–44 age group are more likely to spend their money, advertisers who pay for television shows want shows that members of this age group are watching, and support "younger" shows. Likewise, film studios, eager to make box office money, tend to produce shows designed for a more youthful audience.

Age discrimination also appears in the workplace. Employers are often unwilling to hire or keep workers that have reached a certain age. They perceive these workers as incompetent and lacking ambition. For example, the European Union recently implemented a policy of not hiring workers over the age of 35. This policy is unjustified. For most jobs, mature employees bring added skill and experience that can actually improve their performance. The one exception to this rule is in the area of technological advances. In today's workplace, where computers are an essential means of performing tasks, and the Internet forms the hub of office communication, those trained in a less technological age may find themselves at a disadvantage. In a survey done by Great Britain's Motorola Company, 22% of people ages 16–24 had had no Internet training, compared to 78% of people over the age of 65. Those over 65 were also less enthusiastic about technology or comfortable using high-tech equipment or online services. Thus many older workers lack skills that are essential in a high-tech work environment. This often offsets their advantages of experience and dedication.

Solutions to the problems that create age discrimination do exist, but before they can be implemented, it is necessary to overcome the prejudice against older people in this country. The general perception of the elderly as worthless and burdensome members of the society needs to change. Older people should be valued for their knowledge, experience, and successes. Once the attitude has changed, it is possible to effect the solutions for the entertainment industry and the workplace. If older people are perceived as valued customers and quality shows are created for them, they are more likely to watch them and spend their money. Likewise, if mature workers were trained in the use of advanced technology, this skill would add to their other resources of experience and knowledge. Life doesn't have to go downhill at age 40; it should become a time to reap the rewards of previous successes, a time to enjoy maturity.

How I Write

When I first get a topic, I like to take a few days and think about it. I may do some preliminary research, but what I usually do is just think, and jot down any ideas that come to me. This is a technique known to some as "procrastination" but it really is useful. When I have thought for a few days, I do some research, to find facts and figures to support my ideas, or to derive ideas. I usually go to the library for books or periodicals. For a contemporary topic such as this, I like to turn to the Internet. Once I get books, I skim them for discussions of my topic, then take notes at my computer. I print out these notes, then sit down, away from the computer with a pencil, my notes, and a notebook, and plan my paper. My first step is to come up with a rough outline—usually two or three points to talk about. I then read through my material and find information that directly relates to the points that I may use in my paper later. I cut out my notes, divide them into piles that relate to each point, then tape them together in the order I want to use them. Once this is accomplished, I can begin writing the paper.

I always write the paper from scratch at the computer, because I type faster than I write and it is easier to make changes later. I like to listen to music while I write for several reasons. I usually listen to classical music, which is supposed to boost your IQ and focus. Music also helps when you're writing in a crowded dorm room. With headphones on, it is easier to block out the distracting conversations of my roommates. I also use earplugs sometimes. When I am typing and my fingers or brain cramp up, I take a short break and literally run around the room. Or I get a drink of water or have a short conversation with someone. When I return to writing, my brain is refreshed and ready to go. After I've finished writing, I look at the paper. If it is too short, I look for things I could explain more fully; and if it is too long, I look for things to cut. Then I print the paper out to proofread for obvious errors. At this point, I like to put it down for a while and do something else. Then I can come back to it and see what really needs to be revised and changed. Sometimes it is a few sentences, and sometimes it is the entire focus of the paper. After revising, I spell check and proofread again before printing it out and turning it in. Then I stop thinking about it until I get it back from the professor.

How I Wrote this Essay

For this paper, because I was writing at home, I used a slightly different approach. Because this topic was such a contemporary one, I turned first to the Internet for research. I typed "ageism" into several different search engines, then browsed the pages offered to see what looked interesting or relevant. I printed out the pages that appeared to be most useful, then sat down on the couch with my pencil, my notebook, and my Web pages. I came up with main points, found some statistics to use in my paper, then began writing. I stopped a few times in the middle—for dinner, and to check my e-mail—but I eventually finished it. Then I printed it out to proofread. I marked my revisions, then went back to the computer and changed them.

My Writing Tip

Always write your body paragraphs first. I often don't know exactly what my thesis is until I'm done with the paper, so I always write an introduction and conclusion last. This also makes it easier to begin to write—usually the most difficult thing about writing a paper!

CHAPTER WRITING ASSIGNMENTS

Write a process analysis about one of the following topics:

1. How to cook your favorite dish
2. How you celebrate a favorite holiday
3. How you reconciled two friends who were not speaking to each other
4. How you study for a big test

WRITING ASSIGNMENTS FOR A SPECIFIC AUDIENCE

1. Explain to an audience of third graders how to write a process analysis.
2. Explain to an audience of business executives how the English education you are presently receiving will make you a better employee.

COLLABORATIVE WRITING PROJECT

Divide your group into at least three teams, each of which should research the retirement policies of some specific profession or institution of its choice. Conduct whatever interviews are necessary to learn more about any specific retirement policy. After the research is completed, the teams should meet to discuss and debate the fairness of the retirement policies. Finally, each team should write a group essay outlining what it has learned about the researched retirement policy as well as its impact on elderly employees.

10

Illustration/Exemplification

EDITORS' COUNSEL

What Illustration/Exemplification Does

To illustrate means to give examples that clarify what you are trying to say. Short or long, illustrations are especially useful for sharpening abstract ideas or ambiguous generalizations. They might consist of one item or a list of items that exemplify something, as in this paragraph, which illustrates what the author means by the "Discipline of Nature or of Reality":

> A child, in growing up, may meet and learn from three different kinds of discipline. The first and most important is what we might call the Discipline of Nature or of Reality. When he is trying to do something real, if he does the wrong thing or doesn't do the right one, he doesn't get the result he wants. If he doesn't pile one block right on top of another, or tries to build on a slanting surface, his tower falls down. If he hits the wrong key, he hears the wrong note. If he doesn't hit the nail squarely on the head, it bends, and he has to pull it out and start with another. If he doesn't measure properly when he is trying to build, it won't open, close, fit, stand up, fly, float, whistle, or do whatever he wants it to do. If he closes his eyes when he swings, he misses the ball. A child meets this kind of discipline every time he tries to do something, which is why it is so important in school to give children more chances to do things, instead of just reading or listening to someone talk (or pretending to). . . .
>
> —John Holt, "Kinds of Discipline"

On the other hand, an illustration might consist of one extended example rather than a list. Here is an example:

> Even the shrewdest of men cannot always judge what is useful and what is not. There never was a man so ingeniously practical as Thomas Alva Edison, surely the greatest inventor who ever lived, and we can take him as our example.
>
> In 1896 he patented his first invention. It was a device to record votes mechanically. By using it, congressmen could press a button and all their votes would be instantly recorded and totaled. There was no question but that the invention worked; it remained only to sell it. A congressman whom Edison con-

sulted, however, told him, with mingled amusement and horror, that there wasn't a chance of the invention's being accepted, however unfailingly it might work.

A slow vote, it seemed, was sometimes a political necessity. Some congressmen might have their opinions changed in the course of a slow vote where a quick vote might, in a moment of emotion, commit Congress to something undesirable.

Edison, chagrined, learned his lesson. After that, he decided never to invent anything unless he was sure that it would be needed and wanted and not merely because it worked.

—Isaac Asimov, *Of What Use?*

When to Use Illustration

The illustration is typically used in support of an assertion or point. On every page, in almost every paragraph, writers who wish to communicate their meaning must back up their assertions with appropriate examples. It is not enough to generalize that such and such is the case, as you might do in a casual chat. To make your assertions believable, you must back them up with specific instances. Illustration is often practiced in combination with other modes of development, such as definition, description, classification, causal analysis, and so forth. In the following paragraph, for instance, two examples are used to define "romantic recognition":

Romantic recognition. Two examples will do. When we were flying from Erivan, the capital of Armenia, to Sukhum, on the Black Sea, a Soviet scientist, who spoke English, tapped me on the shoulder and then pointed to a fearsome rock face, an immeasurable slab bound in the iron of eternal winter. "That," he announced, "is where Prometheus was chained." And then all my secret terror-for a journey among the mountains of the Caucasus in a Russian plane is to my unheroic soul an ordeal-gave way for a moment to wonder and delight, as if an illuminated fountain had shot up in the dark. And then, years earlier, in the autumn of 1914, when we were on a route march in Surrey, I happened to be keeping step with the company commander, an intelligent Regular lent to us for a month or two. We were passing a little old woman who was watching us from an open carriage, drawn up near the entrance to a mansion. "Do you know who that is?" the captain asked; and of course I didn't. "It's the Empress Eugenie," he told me; and young and loutish as I was in those days, nevertheless there flared about me then, most delightfully, all the splendor and idiocy of the Second Empire, and I knew that we, every man Jack of us, were in history, and knew it once and for all.

—J. B. Priestly, *Romantic Recognition*

Here, an illustration is used to help describe the humility of John Masefield, the English poet:

This quality of his can best be illustrated by his behavior that night. When the time came for him to read his poems, he would not stand up in any position of pre-eminence but sheltered himself behind the sofa, in the shade of an old lamp, and from there he delivered passages from "The Everlasting Mercy," "Dauber," "The Tragedy of Nan," and "Pompey the Great." He talked, too, melodiously, and with the ghost of a question mark after each of his sentences as though he were saying, "Is that right? Who am I to lay down the law?" And when it was all over, and we began to discuss what he had said, all talking at the top of our voices, very superficially, no doubt, but certainly with a great deal of enthusiasm, it was with a sudden shock that I realized that Masefield had retired into his shell, and was sitting on the floor, almost in the dark, reading a volume of poems by a young and quite unknown writer.

—Beverley Nichols, *Twenty-five*

Illustration is especially effective as support for a persuasive argument. For example, the bland assertion that animal experimentation is necessary to the advancement of science will persuade more forcefully when coupled with an example of how an infant's life was saved by a surgical procedure learned in practice on laboratory animals.

An illustration can also be visual: a picture, chart, map, line drawing, graph, or spread sheet. Such visual illustrations are used widely in scientific and technical writing.

How to Use Illustration

1. An illustration must be real and specific. It must not consist simply of a restatement of what you've already said. Here is an example of a paragraph whose "illustration" is merely a rewording of a preceding statement:

> Before being sold to the American colonies, many slaves had acquired a knowledge of Wolof and Mandingo, the creolized English that had come into use along the Guinea coast as a trade language. For example, many slaves were conversant in both of these languages.

Although the writer uses "for example," what follows is not an authentic illustration but only further commentary. Here is an improvement:

> Before being sold to the American colonies, many slaves had acquired a knowledge of Wolof and Mandingo, the creolized English that had come into use along the Guinea coast as a trade language. For example, when a runaway slave who could speak no English was arrested in Pennsylvania in 1731, his white interrogators had no difficulty in finding another Wolof-speaking slave to act as an interpreter.

The illustration now supports the assertion that many slaves came to America already knowing creolized English.

2. An illustration should be clearly introduced and contextually linked to the point it is intended to support.   If you reread the preceding paragraphs in this section, you will notice that the writers generally use some introductory phrases such as "take him as our example," "two examples will do," or "for example." Such phrases are needed when the context of the paragraph does not alert the reader that an illustration is to follow. On the other hand, if it is clear from the context that an illustration is to follow, no introductory phrase is necessary:

> While viruses and bacteria cause most of the common diseases suffered by people who live in the developed world, protozoa are the major cause of disease in undeveloped tropical zones. Of these diseases, the most widespread are malaria, amoebic dysentery, and African sleeping sickness.

The first sentence makes it plain that malaria, amoebic dysentery, and African sleeping sickness are examples of diseases caused by protozoa in the tropical zones.

Beware, however, of plunging too abruptly into an illustration:

> The idea that art does not exist among the lower animals is a primitive notion. The bower birds of Australia decorate their bowers with shells, colored glass, and shining objects. Some paint their walls with fruit pulp, wet powdered charcoal, or paste of chewed-up grass mixed with saliva. One kind of bower bird even makes a paintbrush from a wad of bark to apply the paint.

Notice how this passage is improved with a transition:

> The idea that art does not exist among the lower animals is a primitive notion. <u>A perfect illustration of art in the animal kingdom is the art of the amazing bower birds of Australia.</u> These birds decorate their bowers with shells, colored glass, and shining objects. Some paint their walls with fruit pulp, wet powdered charcoal, or paste of chewed-up grass mixed with saliva. One kind of bower bird even makes a paintbrush from a wad of bark to apply the paint.

Some illustrations need to be followed by commentary that interprets them for the reader. Here is an example:

> In 1796 Edward Jenner observed that people who came down with cowpox were protected against the far more serious infection of smallpox; therefore, he decided to infect people with cowpox to keep them from getting smallpox. In 1881 Louis Pasteur accidentally left a culture of chicken cholera out on a shelf. Two weeks later, having returned from a vacation, he injected the culture into some laboratory animals and found to his surprise that the animals, instead of getting cholera, had become immune to the disease. These two experiences illustrate the beginnings of genetic engineering, a science that is now on the verge of splicing out from a virulent microbe the genes that cause disease. Millions of seriously ill people hope to be cured from deadly viruses through the miracles of genetic engineering.

The last two sentences of the paragraph interpret by telling us that the examples cited were illustrations of early genetic engineering. Whether or not you should use an introductory phrase, a concluding phrase, or simply imbed your illustration within the context of the paragraph is mainly a matter of common sense. Use phrases to introduce your illustrations only if they are necessary. In every case, you should ask yourself whether you have made your point clearly enough to be instantly understood. If the answer is no, then you should add whatever sentence or phrase is necessary to complete your illustration.

3. An illustration should always be relevant to the point you are making. If it is not, you should leave it out. Again, much of this judgment is a matter of common sense. But sometimes we get paragraphs that read like this:

> My stepfather is a stodgy person. For example, he contributes money every year to the Audubon fund. He serves as an usher in church and is a Scoutmaster for my half brother's troop. He is active in a club that devotes its time to restoring old buildings in our town.

Not being instances of "stodginess," the examples given do not support the writer's assertion. It is better to avoid illustrations entirely than to cite irrelevant ones that do not support your point.

Warming Up to Write an Illustration

1. Following are five different theses that could well be developed through examples. Sketch out three examples for two theses of your choice. Be sure that each example supports the thesis.
   a. If you shop wisely, you can save large amounts of money.
   b. My mom and dad hear and see things differently.
   c. Sometimes imperfections are beautiful.
   d. Not being covered by medical insurance can be disastrous.
   e. My boyfriend (or girlfriend) always thinks of romantic things to do.

2. Answer the following questions by listing an example that clarifies the answer to the question.
   a. What makes a snowy landscape beautiful?
   b. What are some typical elements of authority against which teenagers rebel?
   c. Why do most people admire firefighters?
   d. What makes our national parks so valuable?
   e. What are the worst aspects of homelessness?

3. Provide an appropriate example to illustrate each of the following facts.

a. Being a dentist requires ultimate patience.

b. The President of the United States is not always a role model.

c. E-mail is one of the great inventions of the last decade.

d. Modern medicine has created miracle cures.

e. Saying goodbye can be heart wrenching.

———————— **EXAMPLES** ————————

WHAT IS STYLE?

F. L. Lucas

F. L. Lucas (1894–1967) was, for many years, a distinguished scholar and lecturer at Cambridge. In his teaching, he placed particular emphasis on the classics and on good writing. Lucas tried his hand at virtually every literary form; yet, his best work was in the field of literary criticism, where he was prolific. Among his principal works are The Decline and Fall of the Romantic Ideal *(1934),* Greek Poetry for Everyman *(1951),* Greek Drama for Everyman *(1954), and* The Art of Living *(1959).*

Style belongs to that category of things about which people commonly say: I don't know what it is but I know what I like. We all think that we can recognize and appreciate style when we see it, but few of us would undertake defining it. In this essay, originally published in March 1960, F. L. Lucas tackles the concept of style, drawing many examples from what some famous people have written and said about it. He also suggests that writers who have good style write for their readers with honesty, courtesy, and brevity.

～

1   When it was suggested to Walt Whitman that one of his works should be bound in vellum, he was outraged—"Pshaw!" he snorted, "—hangings, curtains, finger bowls, chinaware, Matthew Arnold!" And he might have been equally irritated by talk of style; for he boasted of "my barbaric yawp"—he would not be literary; his readers should touch not a book but a man. Yet Whitman took the pains to rewrite *Leaves of Grass* four times, and his style is unmistakable. Samuel Butler maintained that writers who bothered about their style became unreadable but he bothered about his own. "Style" has got a bad name by growing associated with precious and superior persons who, like Oscar Wilde, spend a morning putting in a comma, and the afternoon (so he said) taking it out again. But such abuse of "style" is misuse of English. For the word means merely "a way of expressing oneself, in language, manner, or appearance"; or, secondly, "a good way of so expressing oneself"—as when one says, "Her behavior never lacked style."

2   Now there is no crime in expressing oneself (though to try to impress oneself on others easily grows revolting or ridiculous). Indeed one cannot help
expressing oneself, unless one passes one's life in a cupboard. Even the most
rigid Communist, or Organization-man, is compelled by Nature to have a
unique voice, unique fingerprints, unique handwriting. Even the signatures
of the letters on your breakfast table may reveal more than their writers
guess. There are blustering signatures that swish across the page like corn-
stalks bowed before a tempest. There are cryptic signatures, like a scrabble of
lightning across a cloud, suggesting that behind is a lofty divinity whom all
must know, or an aloof divinity whom none is worthy to know (though, as
this might be highly inconvenient, a docile typist sometimes interprets the
mystery in a bracket underneath). There are impetuous squiggles implying
that the author is a sort of strenuous Sputnik streaking around the globe
every eighty minutes. There are florid signatures, all curlicues and dangle-
ments and flamboyance, like the youthful Disraeli (though these seem rather
out of fashion). There are humble, humdrum signatures. And there are also,
sometimes, signatures that are courteously clear, yet mindful of a certain simple grace and artistic economy—in short, of style.

3   Since, then, not one of us can put pen to paper, or even open his mouth,
without giving something of himself away to shrewd observers, it seems
mere common sense to give the matter a little thought. Yet it does not seem
very common. Ladies may take infinite pains about having style in their
clothes, but many of us remain curiously indifferent about having it in our
words. How many women would dream of polishing not only their nails but
also their tongues? They may play freely on that perilous little organ, but they
cannot often be bothered to tune it. And how many men think of improving
their talk as well as their golf handicap?

4   No doubt strong silent men, speaking only in gruff monosyllables, may despise "mere words." No doubt the world does suffer from an endemic plague
of verbal dysentery. But that, precisely, is bad style. And consider the amazing power of mere words. Adolf Hitler was a bad artist, bad statesman, bad
general, and bad man. But largely because he could tune his rant, with psychological nicety, to the exact wave length of his audiences and make millions
quarrelsome-drunk all at the same time by his command of windy nonsense,
skilled statesmen, soldiers, scientists were blown away like chaff, and he came
near to rule the world. If Sir Winston Churchill had been a mere speechifier,
we might well have lost the war; yet his speeches did quite a lot to win it.

5   No man was less of a literary aesthete than Benjamin Franklin; yet this tal-
low-chandler's son, who changed world history, regarded as "a principal
means of my advancement" that pungent style which he acquired partly by
working in youth over old Spectators; but mainly by being Benjamin
Franklin. The squinting demagogue, John Wilkes, as ugly as his many sins,
had yet a tongue so winning that he asked only half an hour's start (to coun-
teract his face) against any rival for a woman's favor. "Vote for you!" growled
a surly elector in his constituency. "I'd sooner vote for the devil!" "But in case

your friend should not stand. . .?" Cleopatra, the ensnarer of world conquerors, owed less to the shape of her nose than to the charm of her tongue. Shakespeare himself has often poor plots and thin ideas; even his mastery of character has been questioned; what does remain unchallenged is his verbal magic. Men are often taken, like rabbits, by the ears. And though the tongue has no bones, it can sometimes break millions of them.

6   "But," the reader may grumble, "I am neither Hitler, Cleopatra, nor Shakespeare. What is all this to me?" Yet we all talk—often too much; we all have to write letters—often too many. We live not by bread alone but also by words. And not always with remarkable efficiency. Strikes, lawsuits, divorces, all sorts of public nuisance and private misery, often come just from the gaggling incompetence with which we express ourselves. Americans and British get at cross-purposes because they use the same words with different meanings. Men have been hanged on a comma in a statute. And in the valley of Balaclava a mere verbal ambiguity, about which guns were to be captured, sent the whole Light Brigade to futile annihilation.

7   Words can be more powerful, and more treacherous, than we sometimes suspect; communication more difficult than we may think. We are all serving life sentences of solitary confinement within our own bodies; like prisoners, we have, as it were, to tap in awkward code to our fellow men in their neighboring cells. Further, when A and B converse, there take part in their dialogue not two characters, as they suppose, but six. For there is A's real self—call it A_1; there is also A's picture of himself—A_2; there is also B's picture of A—A_3. And there are three corresponding personalities of B. With six characters involved even in a simple tête-à-tête, no wonder we fall into muddles and misunderstandings.

8   Perhaps, then, there are five main reasons for trying to gain some mastery of language:

> We have no other way of understanding, informing, misinforming, or persuading one another.
>
> Even alone, we think mainly in words; if our language is muddy, so will our thinking be.
>
> By our handling of words we are often revealed and judged. "Has he written anything?" said Napoleon of a candidate for an appointment. "Let me see his style."
>
> Without a feeling for language one remains half-blind and deaf to literature.
>
> Our mother tongue is bettered or worsened by the way each generation uses it. Languages evolve like species. They can degenerate; just as oysters and barnacles have lost their heads. Compare ancient Greek with modern. A heavy responsibility, though often forgotten.

9   Why and how did I become interested in style? The main answer, I suppose, is that I was born that way. Then I was, till ten, an only child running loose in a house packed with books, and in a world (thank goodness) still

undistracted by radio and television. So at three I groaned to my mother, "Oh, I *wish* I could read," and at four I read. Now travel among books is the best travel of all, and the easiest, and the cheapest. (Not that I belittle ordinary travel—which I regard as one of the three main pleasures in life.) One learns to write by reading good books, as one learns to talk by hearing good talkers. And if I have learned anything in writing, it is largely from writers like Montaigne, Dorothy Osborne, Horace Walpole, Johnson, Goldsmith, Montesquieu, Voltaire, Flaubert and Anatole France. Again, I was reared on Greek and Latin, and one can learn much from translating Homer or the Greek Anthology, Horace or Tacitus, if one is thrilled by the originals and tries, however vainly, to recapture some of that thrill in English.

10   But at Rugby I could not write English essays. I believe it stupid to torment boys to write on topics that they know and care nothing about. I used to rush to the school library and cram the subject, like a python swallowing rabbits; then, still replete as a postprandial python, I would tie myself in clumsy knots to embrace those accursed themes. Bacon was wise in saying that reading makes a full man; talking, a ready one; writing, an exact one. But writing from an empty head is futile anguish.

11   At Cambridge, my head having grown a little fuller, I suddenly found I *could* write—not with enjoyment (it is always tearing oneself in pieces)—but fairly fluently. Then came the War of 1914–18; and though soldiers have other things than pens to handle, they learn painfully to be clear and brief. Then the late Sir Desmond MacCarthy invited me to review for the New Statesman: it was a useful apprenticeship, and he was delightful to work for. But I think it was well after a few years to stop; reviewers remain essential, but there are too many books one cannot praise, and only the pugnacious enjoy amassing enemies. By then I was an ink-addict—not because writing is much pleasure, but because not to write is pain; just as some smokers do not so much enjoy tobacco as suffer without it. The positive happiness of writing comes, I think, from work when done—decently, one hopes, and not without use—and from the letters of readers which help to reassure, or delude, one that so it is.

12   But one of my most vivid lessons came, I think, from service in a war department during the Second World War. Then, if the matter one sent out was too wordy, the communication channels might choke; yet if it was not absolutely clear, the results might be serious. So I emerged, after six years of it, with more passion than ever for clarity and brevity, more loathing than ever for the obscure and the verbose.

13   For forty years at Cambridge I have tried to teach young men to write well, and have come to think it impossible. To write really well is a gift inborn; those who have it teach themselves; one can only try to help and hasten the process. After all, the uneducated sometimes express themselves far better than their "betters." In language, as in life, it is possible to be perfectly correct—and yet perfectly tedious, or odious. The literate last letter of the doomed Vanzetti[1] was more moving than most professional orators; 18th

---

[1]See p. 82—Ed.

Century ladies, who should have been spanked for their spelling, could yet write far better letters than most professors of English; and the talk of Synge's Irish peasants seems to me vastly more vivid than the latter styles of Henry James. Yet Synge averred that his characters owed far less of their eloquence to what he invented for them than to what he had overheard in the cottages of Wicklow and Kerry.

> CHRISTY: It's little you'll think if my love's a poacher's, or an earl's itself, when you'll feel my two hands stretched around you, and I squeezing kisses on your puckered lips, till I'd feel a kind of pity for the Lord God in all ages sitting lonesome in His golden chair.
>
> PEGEEN: That'll be right fun, Christy Mahon, and any girl would walk her heart out before she'd meet a young man was your like for eloquence, or talk at all.

14   Well she might! It's not like that they talk in universities—more's the pity.

15   But though one cannot teach people to write well, one can sometimes teach them to write rather better. One can give a certain number of hints, which often seem boringly obvious—only experience shows they are not.

16   One can say: Beware of pronouns—they are devils. Look at even Addison, describing the type of pedant who chatters of style without having any:

> Upon enquiry I found my learned friend had dined that day with Mr. Swan, the famous punster; and desiring him to give me some account of Mr. Swan's conversation, he told me that he generally talked in the Paronomasia, that he sometimes gave it to the Ploce, but that in his humble opinion he shone most in the Antanaclasis.

17   What a sluttish muddle of *he* and *him* and *his!* It all needs rewording. Far better repeat a noun, or a name, than puzzle the reader, even for a moment, with ambiguous pronouns. Thou shalt not puzzle thy reader.

18   Or one can say: Avoid jingles. The B.B.C. news bulletins seem compiled by earless persons, capable of crying around the globe: "The enemy is *reported* to have seized this *important port,* and reinforcements are hurrying up in *support.*" Any fool, once told, can hear such things to be insupportable.

19   Or one can say: Be sparing with relative clauses. Don't string them together like sausages, or jam them inside one another like Chinese boxes or the receptacles of Buddha's tooth. Or one can say: Don't flaunt jargon, like Addison's Mr. Swan, or the type of modern critic who gurgles more technical terms in a page than Johnson used in all his Lives or Sainte-Beuve in thirty volumes. But dozens of such snippety precepts, though they may sometimes save people from writing badly, will help them little toward writing well. Are there no general rules of a more positive kind, and of more positive use?

20   Perhaps. There *are* certain basic principles which seem to me observed by many authors I admire, which I think have served me and which may serve others. I am not talking of geniuses, who are a law to themselves (and do not

always write a very good style, either); nor of poetry, which has different laws from prose; nor of poetic prose, like Sir Thomas Browne's or De Quincey's which is often more akin to poetry; but of the plain prose of ordinary books and documents, letters and talk.

21 The writer should respect truth and himself; therefore honesty. He should respect his readers; therefore courtesy. These are two of the cornerstones of style. Confucius saw it, twenty-five centuries ago: "The Master said, The gentleman is courteous, but not pliable: common men are pliable, but not courteous."

22 First, honesty. In literature, as in life, one of the fundamentals is to find, and be, one's true self. One's true self may indeed be unpleasant (though one can try to better it); but a false self, sooner or later, becomes disgusting—just as a nice plain woman, painted to the eyebrows, can become horrid. In writing, in the long run, pretense does not work. As the police put it, anything you say may be used as evidence against you. If handwriting reveals character, writing reveals it still more. You cannot fool all your judges all the time.

23 Most style is not honest enough. Easy to say, but hard to practice. A writer may take to long words, as young men to beards—to impress. But long words, like beards, are often the badge of charlatans. Or a writer may cultivate the obscure, to seem profound. But even carefully muddied puddles are soon fathomed. Or he may cultivate eccentricity, to seem original. But really original people do not have to think about being original—they can no more help it than they can help breathing. They do not need to dye their hair green. The fame of Meredith, Wilde or Bernard Shaw might now shine brighter, had they struggled less to be brilliant; whereas Johnson remains great, not merely because his gifts were formidable but also because, with all his prejudice and passion, he fought no less passionately to "clear his mind of cant."

24 Secondly, courtesy—respect for the reader. From this follow several other basic principles of style. Clarity is one. For it is boorish to make your reader rack his brains to understand. One should aim at being impossible to misunderstand—though men's capacity for misunderstanding approaches infinity. Hence Molière and Po Chu-i tried their work on their cooks; and Swift his on his men-servants—"which, if they did not comprehend, he would alter and amend, until they understood it perfectly." Our bureaucrats and pundits, unfortunately, are less considerate.

25 Brevity is another basic principle. For it is boorish to waste your reader's time. People who would not dream of stealing a penny of one's money turn not a hair at stealing hours of one's life. But that does not make them less exasperating. Therefore there is no excuse for the sort of writer who takes as long as a marching army corps to pass a given point. Besides, brevity is often more effective; the half can say more than the whole, and to imply things may strike far deeper than to state them at length. And because one is particularly apt to waste words on preambles before coming to the substance, there was sense in the Scots professor who always asked his pupils—"Did ye remember to tear up that fir-r-st page?"

26 Here are some instances that would only lose by lengthening.

It is useless to go to bed to save the light, if the result is twins. (Chinese proverb.)

My barn is burnt down—

Nothing hides the moon. (Complete Japanese poem.)

Je me regrette.[2] (Dying words of the gay Vicomtesse d'Houdetot.)

I have seen their backs before. (Wellington, when French marshals turned their backs on him at a reception.)

Continue until the tanks stop, then get out and walk. (Patton to the Twelfth Corps, halted for fuel supplies at St. Dizier, 8/30/44.)

27   Or there is the most laconic diplomatic note on record: when Philip of Macedon wrote to the Spartans that, if he came within their borders, he would leave not one stone of their city, they wrote back the one word—"If."

28   Clarity comes before even brevity. But it is a fallacy that wordiness is necessarily clearer. Metternich when he thought something he had written was obscure would simply go through it crossing out everything irrelevant. What remained, he found, often became clear. Wellington, asked to recommend three names for the post of Commander-in-Chief, India, took a piece of paper and wrote three times—"Napier." Pages could not have been clearer—or as forcible. On the other hand the lectures, and the sentences, of Coleridge became at times bewildering because his mind was often "wiggle-waggle"; just as he could not even walk straight on a path.

29   But clarity and brevity, though a good beginning, are only a beginning. By themselves, they may remain bare and bleak. When Calvin Coolidge, asked by his wife what the preacher had preached on, replied "Sin," and, asked what the preacher had said, replied, "He was against it," he was brief enough. But one hardly envies Mrs. Coolidge.

30   An attractive style requires, of course, all kinds of further gifts—such as variety, good humor, good sense, vitality, imagination. Variety means avoiding monotony of rhythm, of language, of mood. One needs to vary one's sentence length (this present article has too many short sentences; but so vast a subject grows here as cramped as a djin in a bottle); to amplify one's vocabulary; to diversify one's tone. There are books that petrify one throughout, with the rigidly pompous solemnity of an owl perched on a leafless tree. But ceaseless facetiousness can be as bad; or perpetual irony. Even the smile of Voltaire can seem at times a fixed grin, a disagreeable wrinkle. Constant peevishness is far worse, as often in Swift; even on the stage too much irritable dialogue may irritate an audience, without its knowing why.

31   Still more are vitality, energy, imagination gifts that must be inborn before they can be cultivated. But under the head of imagination two common devices may be mentioned that have been the making of many a style—metaphor and simile. Why such magic power should reside in simply saying,

---

[2]"I shall miss myself."—Ed.

or implying, that A is like B remains a little mysterious. But even our unconscious seems to love symbols; again, language often tends to lose itself in
clouds of vaporous abstraction, and simile or metaphor can bring it back to
concrete solidity; and, again, such imagery can gild the gray flats of prose
with sudden sun-glints of poetry.

32   If a foreigner may for a moment be impertinent, I admire the native gift of
Americans for imagery as much as I wince at their fondness for slang. (Slang
seems to me a kind of linguistic fungus; as poisonous, and as short-lived, as
toadstools.) When Matthew Arnold lectured in the United States, he was
likened by one newspaper to "an elderly macaw pecking at a trellis of
grapes"; he observed, very justly, "How lively journalistic fancy is among the
Americans!" General Grant, again, unable to hear him, remarked: "Well,
wife, we've paid to see the British lion, but as we can't hear him roar, we'd
better go home." By simile and metaphor, these two quotations bring before
us the slightly pompous, fastidious, inaudible Arnold as no direct description
could have done.

33   Or consider how language comes alive in the Chinese saying that lending
to the feckless is "like pelting a stray dog with dumplings," or in the Arab
proverb: "They came to shoe the pasha's horse, and the beetle stretched forth
his leg"; in the Greek phrase for a perilous cape—"stepmother of ships"; or
the Hebrew adage that "as the climbing up a sandy way is to the feet of the
aged, so is a wife full of words to a quiet man"; in Shakespeare's phrase for a
little England lost in the world's vastness—"in a great Poole, a Swan's nest";
or Fuller's libel on tall men—"Ofttimes such who are built four stories high
are observed to have little in their cockloft"; in Chateaubriand's "I go yawn-
ing my life"; or in Jules Renard's portrait of a cat, "well buttoned in her fur."
Or, to take a modern instance, there is Churchill on dealing with Russia:

> Trying to maintain good relations with a Communist is like wooing a croco-
> dile. You do not know whether to tickle it under the chin or beat it over the head.
> When it opens its mouth, you cannot tell whether it is trying to smile or prepar-
> ing to eat you up.

34   What a miracle human speech can be, and how dull is most that one hears!
Would one hold one's hearers, it is far less help, I suspect, to read manuals on
style than to cultivate one's own imagination and imagery.

35   I will end with two remarks by two wise old women of the civilized 18th
Century.

36   The first is from the blind Mme. du Deffand (the friend of Horace Walpole)
to that Mlle. de Lespinasse with whom, alas, she was to quarrel so unwisely:
"You must make up your mind, my queen, to live with me in the greatest truth
and sincerity. You will be charming so long as you let yourself be natural, and
remain without pretension and without artifice." The second is from Mme.
de Charrière, the Zélide whom Boswell had once loved at Utrecht in vain, to
a Swiss girl friend: "Lucinde, my clever Lucinde, while you wait for the
Romeos to arrive, you have nothing better to do than become perfect. Have

ideas that are clear, and expressions that are simple." ("Ayez des idées nettes et des expressions simples.") More than half the bad writing in the world, I believe, comes from neglecting those two very simple pieces of advice.

37   In many ways, no doubt, our world grows more and more complex; sputniks cannot be simple; yet how many of our complexities remain futile, how many of our artificialities false. Simplicity too can be subtle—as the straight lines of a Greek temple, like the Parthenon at Athens, are delicately curved, in order to look straighter still.

~

(4,043 words)

VOCABULARY

curlicues (2)	endemic (4)	aesthete (5)
tallow-chandler (5)	demagogue (5)	gaggling (6)
annihilation (6)	tête-à-tête (7)	degenerate (8)
replete (10)	postprandial (10)	pugnacious (11)
verbose (12)	odious (13)	averred (13)
pedant (16)		

THE FACTS

1. According to the author, why did "style" get a bad name?
2. What are the two basic principles of good writing style? What other principles follow from the second?
3. What are some other gifts of an attractive style listed in paragraph 30?
4. What are two common literary devices that have made many a style? According to paragraph 32, who has a particular gift for these devices?
5. Lucas ends his essay with some pertinent advice from two women. Who are they, and what is their advice?

THE STRATEGIES

1. What is the difference between "expressing" and "impressing" as discussed in paragraph 2?
2. In paragraph 4, Lucas states that skilled statesmen, soldiers, and scientists were "blown away like chaff" by Adolf Hitler's "windy nonsense." What would happen to Lucas's style if you substituted "drowned" for "blown away"?
3. Paragraph 5 alludes to Benjamin Franklin, John Wilkes, Cleopatra, and Shakespeare as people who owed their charm or success to their verbal style. Whom else can you add to the list? Give reasons for your choices.

4. In paragraph 9, Lucas suggests that people learn to write by reading good books. What purpose is served by the list of nine authors that follows?

5. What is the rhetorical function of paragraph 34?

THE ISSUES

1. What is the difference, if any, between "class" and "style" when each word is used to designate an individual's personal conduct and mode of living?

2. The author says that we all express a self no matter how hard we may try to efface it. Does it not follow, then, that we all have "style"? Why or why not?

3. Lucas comes from a highly elitist background in which privilege and status dictated advancement and social preferment. How does his definition of style implicitly reflect this background? Or does it?

4. What is your opinion of the adage "Style is the man"? How does it apply or not apply to Lucas's idea of style?

5. Lucas implies that growing up in a world undistracted by radio and television helped him to develop early as a writer and reader. What effect, if any, have radio and television had on your own development as a reader and writer?

SUGGESTIONS FOR WRITING

1. Lucas's essay was first published as a magazine article in March 1960. Write an essay quoting and evaluating particular passages and opinions to which a modern reader, especially a feminist, might take offense.

2. Write an essay explaining the effect you think the media have had on your own development as a reader and writer. Say how this effect might have been overcome or lessened.

THE BUCK STOPS WHERE?

Barry Parr

Barry Parr is a freelance journalist who lives and writes in the San Francisco Bay area.

You will enjoy the humor in Parr's recital of anecdotes involving many of our best-loved presidents. One way to approach this essay is to note what past leaders of our nation got away with compared to the more recent occupants of the White House. Have we become more scrutinizing, or have the media become more invasive? This essay was reprinted from the October 1996 issue of *America West*.

~

1   "It's been my experience," observed Honest Abe, "that people who have no vices have very few virtues."

2   Such a wise and tolerant perception would make a fine sound bite in an election year. But rest assured, no one will touch it, for the sad truth is that a little dab of vice makes for a more interesting campaign than a whole vat of virtue. An unflattering image, a well-delivered sound bite, a silly gaffe or a youthful indiscretion raked through the muck all attract far more attention than a lifetime of honest public service.

3   Doubtless, voters in the early days of the republic were no less hungry for all the sottish details—and, indeed, our public leaders were no less inclined to provide them. But for better or worse—probably for better—our forefathers (and foremothers) simply didn't have the technology that we have today for efficiently disseminating a public figure's flaws, shenanigans and peccadilloes to an eager and expectant nation.

4   Could George Washington—who was totally toothless by age 57—have weathered the merciless barrage of jokes on late-night TV? Would daytime television talk-show hosts have ever allowed Lincoln to get beyond his early career as a stripped-down, frontier wrestler?

5   And what would the news media—which have shown more than a passing interest in Bill Clinton's jogging shorts and pale thighs—have made of John Quincy Adams's daily constitutional of skinny-dipping in the Potomac River? When on one occasion a rascal stole his clothes, our sixth president was forced to hail a passing boy, requesting him to ring at the White House to obtain a change of clothes from the first lady.

6   The news media have not played the game on an equal footing with all the presidents. They could tiptoe around the White House with utmost discretion during the sometimes ribald Kennedy tenure, and yet quail with shock when Jimmy Carter fessed up, with boy-like candor, that he had known lust in his heart.

7   Protest trumpeted mightily across the land when Lyndon Johnson lifted his pet beagle by the ears, but the gentlemen of the press were more bemused than outraged when visitors plucked bald spots on Zachary Taylor's old war horse, Whitey, in an effort to collect souvenirs. (Taylor had pastured poor Whitey on the White House lawn.)

8   No one batted an eye while President Grant smoked up the Oval Office with his daily allotment of 20 cigars, and yet, Andrew Jackson's wife, Rachel, was driven to despair (and Old Hickory believed even unto death) by gleefully mean-spirited rumors that she smoked a pipe.

9   We are all too familiar with hullabaloos that arise over completely trivial matters—the hole in presidential candidate Adlai Stevenson's shoe, for in-

stance, or Richard Nixon's 5 o'clock shadow in his famous Kennedy debate (both of which have been blamed for costing their election bids). But the reverse is also true: The most stupendous of presidential stunts has sometimes gone almost totally unnoticed. Somewhat less than obscure is the tale of when Harry S. Truman buzzed the White House. After taking off from Washington, D.C., in May 1946, Truman reportedly bid his pilot to detour through the no-fly zone that surrounds the presidential mansion. After spotting his family and friends gathered on the roof—where he'd apparently summoned them for a surprise—"Give em Hell" Harry ordered his pilot to dive. As the plane nosed down and accelerated into a steep descent, Truman was delighted to see their excited waves of recognition suddenly dissolve into a wild scramble for cover. Truman apparently enjoyed the prank so much that he ordered a second round, before proceeding onward to Independence, Missouri.

10   Decidedly less spectacular are some of the incidental diversions of Thomas Jefferson, probably our most intellectually accomplished president. A cultured violinist, superb architect and successful lawyer, Jefferson spoke six languages and held his own with the best philosophers of his day, but he still found time for puttering around with other pursuits of a more practical nature. Not only did he invent the chaise lounge, the swivel chair and a successful prototype of an indoor toilet—all considered essential fixtures in the White House to this day—but he also introduced his country to waffles and ice cream, and was reputed to be the first man in America to grow a tomato. (JFK once remarked at one of his famous state dinners—glittering events that garnered cultivated crowds of poets, novelists, musicians, Nobel laureates, Harvard lecturers and heads of states—that the last time so much brilliance had gathered in the White House was when Jefferson ate his supper there, alone.)

11   "Public opinion in this country is everything," Abe Lincoln once noted, indicating that the primal force we now know as "spin" was operating full tilt even in the 19th century. Spin doctors made hay out of Lincoln's humble birth by celebrating him as "The Log Cabin President." Yet, the same "Washington insiders" dealt a dirty hand to his successor, Andrew Johnson, and for much the same humble origins. A tailor and the son of a tailor, Johnson never received a formal education, and first learned to write as a young man, tutored by his patient and sterling wife, Eliza McArdle Johnson. The contempt that fueled his impeachment charges was to no small degree inspired by the vicious snobbery rampant in Washington's higher society. (It bears noting, too, that the egalitarian 1960s never did warm up to Richard Nixon, even after it was revealed that the supreme commander of the United States of America, when a youth, had taken a summer job at the Slippery Gulch Rodeo in Prescott, Arizona, where he worked as a barker for the wheel of chance.)

12   Spin doctors are an ingenious bunch, and even can score points—or deduct them—from something so trivial as a presidential snack. The public was charmed by Gerald Ford's habit of toasting his own muffin for breakfast. We feel somewhat closer to Grover Cleveland to learn that his favorite meal was a plate of corned beef and cabbage. Ronald Reagan's fondness for jelly

beans sparked a nationwide run on that commodity. And who can resist smiling with benign indulgence upon learning that U. S. Grant enjoyed nothing better for breakfast than a cucumber in vinegar? On the other hand, Nixon seems to have inspired almost universal condemnation for enjoying a luncheon of cottage cheese with ketchup. Nixon's advisers seem to have been particularly inept at the science of managing spin. The nation expressed almost universal shock and displeasure at the saltiness of his language on the Watergate tapes. Yet, we are almost universally inclined to view the "oaths" of the Jackson era as, well, something rather quaint. (At Jackson's funeral, his pet parrot had to be removed from the room for peppering the solemnities with a barrage of fine 19th century cusses.) And, of course, "Give 'em Hell" Harry Truman is actually venerated for the pungency of his discourse. ("I never did give anybody hell," Truman once snapped. "I just told the truth, and they thought it was hell.")

13   Some presidents have survived public-relations disasters that would ring the death knell with today's voters. Warren Harding routinely parted with pieces of White House china, which he used as chips in friendly poker games. Probably the second most famous act of William Howard Taft—who stood 6 feet 2 inches and weighed up to 350 pounds during his presidential tenure— was becoming stuck in the White House bathtub. (His most famous act? Starting the presidential custom of throwing out the first pitch of the baseball season.) And, of course, we could never stand for a modern president to be as cavalier as Andrew Jackson over matters of security. At his inaugural reception, a rowdy crowd of thousands poured into the White House on open invitation, gobbling and drinking the refreshments in record speed and heatedly demanding more, while Old Hickory himself was forced to escape to a local hotel for the night. On another occasion, the Hero of New Orleans invited the public to enjoy a gigantic cheese, which measured 4 feet in diameter and 2 feet thick, and weighed 1,400 pounds. Milling throngs pressed with knives through the White House entry and ravenously hacked it to pieces, devouring some on the spot and carrying away hunks wrapped in newspapers. The hallowed halls stunk of cheese for weeks thereafter.

14   Despite the all-too-human behavior of many of our leaders, there is indeed something almost shiningly virtuous in any man or woman who has the courage to survive the toss and gore of a presidential campaign amid the fickle court of public opinion. Our next president, whoever that might be, could do worse than take heart from the wry, but wise, observations of Harry Truman, who knew firsthand the glory, and the thankless strain, of life at the top.

15   "A politician," said he, "is a man who understands government, and it takes a politician to run a government. A statesman is a politician who's been dead 10 or 15 years."

16   I believe it also was Truman who noted, "If you want a friend in this life, get a dog."

∼

(1,541 words)

VOCABULARY

sound bite (2)	dab (2)	vat (2)
gaffe (2)	sottish (3)	peccadilloes (3)
pungency (12)		

THE FACTS

1. Who made the following observation: "It's been my experience that people who have no vices have very few virtues"?
2. What kept our forebears from hearing about the indiscretions of their leaders?
3. Which American president had his clothes stolen while skinny dipping in the Potomac?
4. What prank did President Truman organize while his friends and family gathered on the roof of the White House, where he had summoned them?
5. Which president spoke six languages, played the violin, and was an architect as well as a lawyer?
6. Who said, "A statesman is a politician who's been dead 10 or 15 years"?

THE STRATEGIES

1. What pre-writing strategy do you think the author used to develop this essay?
2. In addition to comparing contemporary presidents with those of the past, what rhetorical strategy does the author use? How important is it to his subject?
3. The author seems to poke fun at U.S. presidents. Does his attitude make you respect these presidents less? Why or why not?
4. How does the author portray the presidents he mentions? Are they well-rounded, three-dimensional people? Is the author's description superficial? State how his descriptions relate to the purpose of the essay.
5. What is the meaning of the title? Explain how it fits the essay.

THE ISSUES

1. What kind of president would you prefer—one who is exemplary and virtuous in every respect or one who has a few vices? Describe the morality of your ideal president.
2. Why are people intrigued by the vices of public figures?

3. Are the news media excessive in their quest for scandalous news about public figures? Why should Americans have the right to know all the details of the lives of important people, especially those who lead our country?

4. Do public figures have a duty to curb their tongues and to behave like gentlemen or gentlewomen so long as they hold public office?

5. What does the author mean when he states that "spin doctors are an ingenious bunch, and even can score points—or deduct them—from something so trivial as a presidential snack"? Give an example from recent news in which this kind of spin was created.

SUGGESTIONS FOR WRITING

1. Write an essay describing an important trait you admire in your favorite American president. Give examples of the trait you have chosen.

2. Write an essay in which you deplore the way the news media intrude into the private lives of public figures. Give examples of this kind of intrusion.

"MIRROR, MIRROR, ON THE WALL . . ."

John Leo

John Leo (b. 1935), associate editor of Time, *was born in Hoboken, New Jersey, and educated at the University of Toronto. He has been associated with* Commonweal, The New York Times, *the* Village Voice, *and more recently as editor and columnist for* U.S. News and World Report.

In the following brief essay from *Time,* Leo discusses and gives examples of the relativity of beauty.

~

1 The poet may insist that beauty is in the eye of the beholder; the historian might argue that societies create the image of female perfection that they want. There has always been plenty of evidence to support both views. Martin Luther thought long, beautiful hair was essential. Edmund Burke recommended delicate, fragile women. Goethe insisted on "the proper breadth of the pelvis and the necessary fullness of the breasts." Hottentot men look for sharply projecting buttocks. Rubens favored a full posterior, and Papuans require a big nose. The Mangaians of Polynesia care nothing of fat or thin and never seem to notice face, breasts or buttocks. To the tribesmen, the only standard of sexiness is well-shaped female genitals.

2   An anthropologized world now knows that notions of what is most attractive do vary with each age and culture. One era's flower is another's frump. Primitive man, understandably concerned with fertility, idealized ample women. One of the earliest surviving sculptures, the Stone Age Venus of Willendorf, depicts a squat woman whose vital statistics—in inches— would amount to 96–89–96. This adipose standard stubbornly recurs in later eras. A 14th-century treatise on beauty calls for "narrow shoulders, small breasts, large belly, broad hips, fat thighs, short legs and a small head." Some Oriental cultures today are turned on by what Simone de Beauvoir calls the "unnecessary, gratuitous blooming" of wrap-around fat.

3   The Greeks were so concerned with working out precise proportions for beauty that the sculptor Praxiteles insisted that the female navel be exactly midway between the breasts and genitals. The dark-haired Greeks considered fair-haired women exotic, perhaps the start of the notion that blondes have more fun. They also offered early evidence of the rewards that go to magnificent mammaries. When Phryne, Praxiteles' famous model and mistress, was on trial for treason, the orator defending her pulled aside her veil, baring her legendary breasts. The awed judges acquitted her on the spot.

4   Romans favored more independent, articulate women than the Greeks. Still, there were limits. Juvenal complains of ladies who "discourse on poets and poetry, comparing Vergil with Homer. . . . Wives shouldn't read all the classics—there ought to be some things women don't understand."

5   In ancient Egypt, women spent hours primping: fixing hair, applying lipstick, eye shadow and fingernail polish, grinding away body and genital hair with pumice stones. It worked: Nefertiti could make the cover of Vogue any month she wanted. For Cleopatra, the most famous bombshell of the ancient world, eroticism was plain hard work. Not a natural beauty, she labored diligently to learn coquettishness and flattery and reportedly polished her amatory techniques by practicing on slaves.

6   If Cleopatra had to work so hard at being desirable, can the average woman do less? Apparently not. In the long history of images of beauty, one staple is the male tendency to spot new flaws in women, and the female tendency to work and suffer to remedy them. In the Middle Ages, large women rubbed themselves with cow dung dissolved in wine. When whiter skin was demanded, women applied leeches to take the red out. Breasts have been strapped down, cantilevered up, pushed together or apart, oiled and siliconed and, in 16th-century Venice, fitted with wool or hair padding for a sexy "duck breast" look, curving from bodice to groin. In the long run, argues feminist Elizabeth Gould Davis, flat-chested women are evolutionary losers. Says she: "The female of the species owes her modern mammary magnificence to male sexual preference."

7   Still, a well-endowed woman can suddenly find herself out of favor when cultural winds change. The flapper era in America is one example. So is Europe's Romantic Age, which favored the wan, cadaverous look. In the 1820s, women sometimes drank vinegar or stayed up all night to look pale

and interesting. Fragility was all. Wrote Keats: "God! she is like a milkwhite lamb that bleats/For man's protection."

8   Victorians took this ideal of the shy, clinging vine, decorously desexed it, and assigned it to the wife. According to one well-known Victorian doctor, it was a "vile aspersion" to suggest that women were capable of sexual impulses. Inevitably that straitlaced era controlled women's shapes by severe compression of the waistline, without accenting breasts or hips.

9   Those womanly curves reasserted themselves at the turn of the century. During the hourglass craze, Lillie Langtry seemed perfection incarnate at 38–18–38. Since then, the ideal woman in Western culture has gradually slimmed down. Psyche, the White Rock girl,[3] was 5 ft. 4 in. tall and weighed in at a hippy 140 lbs. when she first appeared on beverage bottles in 1893. Now, *sans* cellulite, she is 4 in. taller and 22 lbs. lighter.

10   In psychological terms, the current slim-hipped look amounts to a rebellion against male domination: waist-trimming corsets are associated with male control of the female body, and narrow hips with a reluctance to bear children. Says Madge Garland, a former editor of *British Vogue*: "The natural shape of the female body has not been revealed and free as it is today for 1,500 years." W. H. Auden once complained that for most of Western history, the sexy beautiful women have seemed "fictionalized," set apart from real life. In the age of the natural look, a beauty now has to seem as though she just strolled in from the beach at Malibu. Like Cheryl Tiegs.

⌒

(918 words)

VOCABULARY

frump (2)	adipose (2)	gratuitous (2)
coquettishness (5)	amatory (5)	cantilevered (6)
decorously (8)	aspersion (8)	incarnate (9)
cellulite (9)		

THE FACTS

1. What kinds of women did primitive man idealize?
2. What was the Greeks' standard of beauty?
3. According to feminist Elizabeth Gould Davis, to what do women owe their "modern mammary magnificence"?
4. What kind of feminine beauty was favored during Europe's Romantic Age?
5. What does the modern, slim-hipped look signify in psychological terms?

---

[3]Psyche has been the emblem of White Rock brand soft drinks and mixes since the nineteenth century.—Ed.

THE STRATEGIES

1. What notion do most of the examples in this essay support? Where is this notion stated?

2. Much of the detail about beauty is given not in full-blown examples, but in sketchy references to the opinions of famous people. What are such references called?

3. In paragraph 3, what does the anecdote about Phryne exemplify?

4. The author quotes Goethe, Simone de Beauvoir, Juvenal, Elizabeth Gould Davis, John Keats, Madge Garland, and W. H. Auden. What effect does all this opinion sampling have on the tone of the essay?

5. In paragraph 6, the author writes: "In the long history of images of beauty, one staple is the male tendency to spot new flaws in women, and the female tendency to work and suffer to remedy them." How does the author proceed to support and document this view?

THE ISSUES

1. Paragraph 2 alludes to an "anthropologized world." How would you define this world? What significance lies in this label?

2. What, for you, constitutes a beautiful female? A beautiful male? Refer to specific examples from history, from the current scene, or from your personal encounters.

3. How do you feel about the present emphasis on an athletic female body? Is it justified, or does it diminish some other innately feminine characteristic? Give reasons for your answer.

4. Even if you agree with the poet that beauty is in the eye of the beholder, argue that true beauty must follow certain standards. Suggest what these standards might be when applied to, say, a painting or a sculpture.

5. In paragraph 8, the author describes the typical Victorian wife as a woman who must never be perceived as having sexual impulses. How does the typical Victorian wife compare with the women we observe in the movies or on TV today? Give examples to support your view.

SUGGESTIONS FOR WRITING

1. Write an essay that specifies your idea of human beauty. Give convincing examples to illustrate your point.

2. Write an essay in which you argue that human beauty is in the eye of the beholder.

LIVING IN SIN

Adrienne Rich

Adrienne Rich (b. 1929) is an award-winning poet, critic, and translator. She graduated from Radcliffe College in 1951 and has since held many academic positions, including Adjunct Professor teaching writing at Columbia University, and Visiting Poet at Swarthmore College. She won the National Institute of Arts and Letters Award for poetry in 1961. Her works are represented in many anthologies, such as New Poets of England and America *(1961) and* A Little Treasure of Modern Poetry, English and American *(1970). Rich's other works include* Diving into the Wreck *(1973) and* The Dream of a Common Language *(1979).*

The poem that follows points out the unrealistic outlook of lovers caught in the grip of sexual passion, providing graphic examples of what these lovers do not foresee.

~

She had thought the studio would keep itself;
no dust upon the furniture of love.
Half heresy, to wish the taps less vocal,
the panes relieved of grime. A plate of pears,

5 a piano with a Persian shawl, a cat
stalking the picturesque amusing mouse
had risen at his urging.
Not that at five each separate stair would writhe
under the milkman's tramp; that morning light

10 so coldly would delineate the scraps
of last night's cheese and three sepulchral bottles;
that on the kitchen shelf among the saucers
a pair of beetle-eyes would fix her own—
envoy from some black village in the mouldings . . .

15 Meanwhile, he, with a yawn,
sounded a dozen notes upon the keyboard,
declared it out of tune, shrugged at the mirror,
rubbed at his beard, went out for cigarettes;
while she, jeered by the minor demons,

20 pulled back the sheets and made the bed and found
a towel to dust the table-top,
and let the coffee-pot boil over on the stove.
By evening she was back in love again,
though not so wholly but throughout the night

25　she woke sometimes to feel the daylight coming
　　like a relentless milkman up the stairs.

　　　　　　　　　　　　　～

(205 words)

VOCABULARY

heresy (3)　　　　　　picturesque (6)　　　　　delineate (10)
sepulchral (11)　　　　envoy (14)

THE FACTS

1. What is the meaning of the first line?
2. What happens at five in the morning?
3. What difference is there between the activity of the male and the activity of the female in the poem?

THE STRATEGIES

1. What words are omitted in front of the "Not" of line 8? What effect is created by the omission?
2. Whose point of view dominates the poem? Why?
3. What two roles does the milkman play in the poem?
4. What does the word "sepulchral" in line 11 contribute?

THE ISSUES

1. What is the theme (the lesson about life) of this poem? Try to express it in one sentence.
2. What contrast is clearly drawn through the many vivid examples?
3. What does the author mean by the lines "By evening she was back in love again, / though not so wholly. . ."?
4. How does this poem relate to real love?

SUGGESTIONS FOR WRITING

1. Write an essay using examples to describe a feeling of disappointment you have experienced or observed.
2. Write an essay about the dangers of a relationship based purely on romance and passion. Supply vivid examples to support your thesis.

──────── ISSUE FOR CRITICAL ──────── THINKING AND DEBATE
DRUG ABUSE

The faces portrayed in *The Subway*, by George Tooker, are gaunt, stark, and rigidly gripped with a palpable terror. In the foreground, a woman frozen in a robotic pose stares emptily into the distance. Behind her lurk men caught in the act of shuffling along with a grim, isolated detachment. Off to the side, we see a man peering timorously from around a cubicle, his visible, peeping eye wary and fearful. We have selected this painting, in spite of its title, as the pictorial equivalent of the devastation of drugs—of their brutal power to wall off the individual into a private world of tormented addiction.

Ours is a society awash in a transcontinental tidal surge of drugs. We awake to the kick of caffeine, soothe our nerves with tobacco, ease our tension headaches with aspirin, wind down the day with alcohol, and swallow an antihistamine to help us sleep—all perfectly legal, respectable, and even expected. But there is a dark side to this epidemic of drug use as illustrated by the woman in the photo on page 347. Over 400 thousand of us perish annually from the effects of tobacco. Some 23 million of us regularly take illegal drugs, ranging from marijuana to cocaine to heroin. A causal relationship exists between drug addiction and criminal wrongdoing, with a significant proportion of those arrested for felonies—in some cities as much as sixty to seventy percent—testing positive for drug use (Skolnick, Jerome H., "Making Sense of the Crime Decline," *Newsday*, 2 Feb. 1997: Electric Library. 27 Nov. 1999. http://www.elibrary.com). The exact incidence of drug usage and addiction among the general population is unknown, although the National Household Survey on Drug Abuse (NHSDA) found that in 2001 an estimated 15.9 million Americans were illicit drugs users (Office of Applied Studies, National Household "Illicit Drug Use." Available online at http://www.samhsa.gov/oas/NHSDA/2k1NHSDA/vol1/Chapter2.htm).

The political response to the spreading tide of illegal drugs has been predictable: Conservatives urge heightened efforts at the interdiction of illegal drugs, mandatory drug testing, stiffer prison terms for pushers, and a crackdown on recreational users. Liberals and libertarians advocate an agenda of education and rehabilitation and, probably the most controversial measure of all, the legalization of drug use. It is this last proposal that has set off the latest and most vehement round of debate.

Making the case for legalization, and doing so in his usual caustic style, is the novelist and writer Gore Vidal. His argument is not new, but it is refreshingly presented. Prohibition increases the allure of drugs, argues Vidal, and it is only because our society is so devoted to the concepts of sin and punishment that we reject out of hand this simple solution. Equally emphatic in his refutation of the case of legalization is editorial writer Morton Kondracke. He makes his case with an array of statistics from which he infers the direst possible consequences of legalization. The student corner argues that only early education about the dangers can stem the tide of drug abuse.

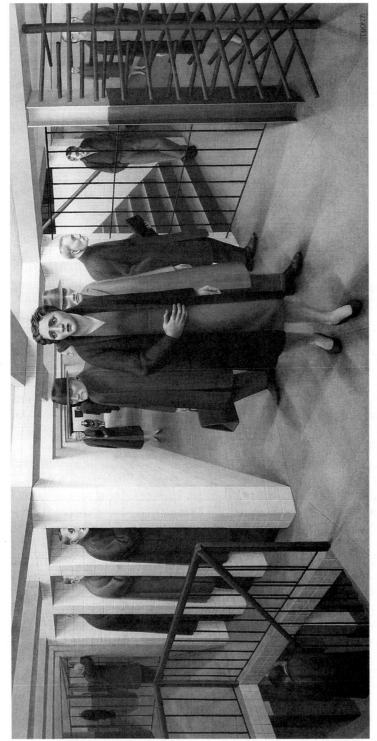

George Tooker, The Subway. 1950. Egg tempera on composition board. Sight: 18⅛ 3 36⅛ inches (46 cm 3 91.8 cm). Whitney Museum of American Art, New York. Purchased with funds from the Juliana Force Purchase Award. 50.23. Photo by Geoffrey Clements. Photograph copyright © 1997 Whitney Museum of American Art.

England and a few other European countries have experimented with the legalization of drugs, and with some success, but no society as complex and variegated as ours has ever attempted to legalize drugs on such a vast scale as would be involved if the liberals win this argument. The consequences of legalization might ultimately be anyone's guess. Given the strong moral strain that permeates American political thinking, however, we think Vidal is right, and that unless drug abuse becomes incalculably worse than it is today, legalization will likely remain a topic for academic debate rather than be adopted as national policy by any present or future administration.

DRUGS

Gore Vidal

Gore Vidal (b. 1925), is a writer of novels, plays, short stories, book reviews, and essays. His major novels include The City and the Pillar *(1948),* Julian *(1964),* Myra Breckenridge *(1968),* 1876 *(1976),* Burr *(1980),* Creation *(1981),* Lincoln *(1984), and* Eighteen Seventy-Six *(1988).*

∼

1 It is possible to stop most drug addiction in the United States within a very short time. Simply make all drugs available and sell them at cost. Label each drug with a precise description of what effect—good and bad—the drug will have on the taker. This will require heroic honesty. Don't say that marijuana is addictive or dangerous when it is neither, as millions of people know—unlike "speed," which kills most unpleasantly, or heroin, which is addictive and difficult to kick.

2 For the record, I have tried—once—almost every drug and liked none, disproving the popular Fu Manchu theory that a single whiff of opium will enslave the mind. Nevertheless many drugs are bad for certain people to take and they should be told why in a sensible way.

3 Along with exhortation and warning, it might be good for our citizens to recall (or learn for the first time) that the United States was the creation of men who believed that each man has the right to do what he wants with his own life as long as he does not interfere with his neighbor's pursuit of happiness (that his neighbor's idea of happiness is persecuting others does confuse matters a bit).

4 This is a startling notion to the current generation of Americans. They reflect a system of public education which has made the Bill of Rights, literally, unacceptable to a majority of high school graduates (see the annual Purdue reports) who now form the "silent majority"—a phrase which that underestimated wit Richard Nixon took from Homer who used it to describe the dead.

5 Now one can hear the warning rumble begin: if everyone is allowed to take drugs everyone will and the GNP will decrease, the Commies will stop

us from making everyone free, and we shall end up a race of Zombies, passively murmuring "groovie" to one another. Alarming thought. Yet it seems most unlikely that any reasonably sane person will become a drug addict if he knows in advance what addiction is going to be like.

6　Is everyone reasonably sane? No. Some people will always become drug addicts just as some people will always become alcoholics, and it is just too bad. Every man, however, has the power (and should have the legal right) to kill himself if he chooses. But since most men don't, they won't be mainliners either. Nevertheless, forbidding people things they like or think they might enjoy only makes them want those things all the more. This psychological insight is, for some mysterious reason, perennially denied our governors.

7　It is a lucky thing for the American moralist that our country has always existed in a kind of time-vacuum: we have no public memory of anything that happened before last Tuesday. No one in Washington today recalls what happened during the years alcohol was forbidden to the people by a Congress that thought it had a divine mission to stamp out Demon Rum—launching, in the process, the greatest crime wave in the country's history, causing thousands of deaths from bad alcohol, and creating a general (and persisting) contempt among the citizenry for the laws of the United States.

8　The same thing is happening today. But the government has learned nothing from past attempts at prohibition, not to mention repression.

9　Last year when the supply of Mexican marijuana was slightly curtailed by the Feds, the pushers got the kids hooked on heroin and deaths increased dramatically, particularly in New York. Whose fault? Evil men like the Mafiosi? Permissive Dr. Spock? Wild-eyed Dr. Leary? No.

10　The Government of the United States was responsible for those deaths. The bureaucratic machine has a vested interest in playing cops and robbers. Both the Bureau of Narcotics and the Mafia want strong laws against the sale and use of drugs because if drugs are sold at cost there would be no money in it for anyone.

11　If there was no money in it for the Mafia, there would be no friendly playground pushers, and addicts would not commit crimes to pay for the next fix. Finally, if there was no money in it, the Bureau of Narcotics would wither away, something they are not about to do without a struggle.

12　Will anything sensible be done? Of course not. The American people are as devoted to the idea of sin and its punishment as they are to making money—and fighting drugs is nearly as big a business as pushing them. Since the combination of sin and money is irresistible (particularly to the professional politician), the situation will only grow worse.

～

(768 words)

VOCABULARY

exhortation (3)　　　　　perennially (6)　　　　　repression (8)

THE FACTS

1. What specific proposal does Vidal make for selling drugs?
2. According to Vidal, to whom is the Bill of Rights unacceptable?
3. What lesson about repression does Vidal say the government has largely forgotten?
4. Which two groups, according to Vidal, have a vested interest in prolonging the ban against drugs?
5. What dismal prophecy does Vidal make at the conclusion of his argument? How has his prophecy stood the test of time?

THE STRATEGIES

1. Vidal opens his argument with a blunt declaration of his position and without any softening up of the opposition with statistics or background material. What do you think the reaction to this opening would be if this were an essay written by a student? Why?
2. Vidal admits to having used almost every drug and having liked none. How does this frank admission affect his argument?
3. What one word in paragraph 5 dates this essay as from another era?
4. What is the rhetorical purpose of paragraphs 5 and 6?
5. Aside from its blunt tone, what characteristic of this essay would make it unsuitable as a student submission in a writing class?

THE ISSUES

1. What do you think is the likely effect of a governmental attitude that says all drugs are bad for you?
2. What do you think would happen if all drugs were legalized?
3. Vidal says that "forbidding people things they like or think they might enjoy only makes them want those things all the more." Do you think this a truth or a cliché? Why?
4. If the government of the United States sprays marijuana crops with a herbicide that then poisons an unknowing user, who is morally responsible?
5. Do you agree with Vidal that the American people are hooked on the idea of sin and punishment? Why or why not?

SUGGESTIONS FOR WRITING

1. Write an essay relating any encounter you have had with, or have heard someone else tell about, drugs.
2. Attack or defend Vidal's opinions in an essay.

Woman with pills. Copyright © Zefa Visual Media-Germany/Index Stock Imagery.

DON'T LEGALIZE DRUGS

Morton M. Kondracke

Morton Kondracke (b. 1939) is an American journalist who has worked for Newsweek *and the* New Republic. *Kondracke is a regular commentator on the National Public Radio program "All Things Considered" and writes a monthly column for* The Wall Street Journal. *He is the author of* Gerald R. Ford (1976), *one in a series of short biographies.*

~

1   The next time you hear that a drunk driver has slammed into a school bus full of children or that a stoned railroad engineer has killed 16 people in a train wreck, think about this: if the advocates of legalized drugs have their way, there will be more of this, a lot more. There will also be more unpublicized fatal and maiming crashes, more job accidents, more child neglect, more of almost everything associated with substance abuse: babies born addicted or retarded, teenagers zonked out of their chance for an education, careers destroyed, families wrecked, and people dead of overdoses.

2   The proponents of drug legalization are right to say that some things will get better. Organized crime will be driven out of the drug business, and there will be a sharp drop in the amount of money (currently about $10 billion per year) that society spends to enforce the drug laws. There will be some reduction in the cost in theft and injury (now about $20 billion) by addicts to get the money to buy prohibited drugs. Internationally, Latin American governments presumably will stop being menaced by drug cartels and will peaceably export cocaine as they now do coffee.

3   However, this is virtually the limit of the social benefits to be derived from legalization, and they are far outweighed by the costs, which are always underplayed by legalization advocates such as the Economist, Princeton scholar Ethan A. Nadelmann, economist Milton Friedman and other libertarians, columnists William F. Buckley and Richard Cohen, and Mayors Keith Schmoke of Baltimore and Marion Barry of Washington, D.C. In lives, money, and human woe, the costs are so high, in fact, that society has no alternative but to conduct a real war on the drug trade, although perhaps a smarter one than is currently being waged.

4   Advocates of legalization love to draw parallels between the drug war and Prohibition. Their point, of course, is that this crusade is as doomed to failure as the last one was, and that we ought to surrender now to the inevitable and stop wasting resources. But there are some important differences between drugs and alcohol. Alcohol has been part of Western culture for thousands of years; drugs have been the rage in America only since about 1962. Of the 115 million Americans who consume alcohol, 85 percent rarely become intoxicated; with drugs, intoxication is the whole idea. Alcohol is consistent chemically, even though it's dispensed in different strengths and forms as beer, wine, and "hard" liquor; with drugs there's no limit to the variations. Do we legalize crack along with snortable cocaine, PCPs as well as marijuana, and LSD and "Ecstasy" as well as heroin? If we don't—and almost certainly we won't—we have a black market, and some continued crime.

5   But Prohibition is a useful historical parallel for measuring the costs of legalization. Almost certainly doctors are not going to want to write prescriptions for recreational use of harmful substances, so if drugs even are legalized they will be dispensed as alcohol now is—in government-regulated stores with restrictions on the age of buyers, warnings against abuse (and, probably, with added restrictions on amounts, though this also will create a black market).

6   In the decade before Prohibition went into effect in 1920, alcohol consumption in the United States averaged 2.6 gallons per person per year. It fell to 0.73 gallons during the Prohibition decade, then doubled to 1.5 gallons in the decade after repeal, and is now back to 2.6 gallons. So illegality suppressed usage to a third or a fourth of its former level. At the same time, incidence of cirrhosis of the liver fell by half.

7   So it seems fair to estimate that use of drugs will at least double, and possibly triple, if the price is cut, supplies are readily available, and society's sanction is lifted. It's widely accepted that there are now 16 million regular

users of marijuana, six million of cocaine, a half million of heroin, and another half million of other drugs, totaling 23 million. Dr. Robert DuPont, former director of the National Institutes of Drug Abuse and an anti-legalization crusader, says that the instant pleasure afforded by drugs—superior to that available with alcohol—will increase the number of regular users of marijuana and cocaine to about 50 or 60 million and heroin users to ten million.

8   Between ten percent and 15 percent of all drinkers turn into alcoholics (ten million to 17 million), and these drinkers cost the economy an estimated $117 billion in 1983 ($15 billion for treatment, $89 billion in lost productivity, and $13 billion in accident-related costs). About 200,000 people died last year as a result of alcohol abuse, about 25,000 in auto accidents. How many drug users will turn into addicts, and what will this cost? According to President Reagan's drug abuse policy adviser, Dr. David I. McDonald, studies indicate that marijuana is about as habit-forming as alcohol, but for cocaine, 70 percent of users become addicted, as many as with nicotine.

9   So it seems reasonable to conclude that at least four to six million people will become potheads if marijuana is legal, and that coke addicts will number somewhere between 8.5 million (if regular usage doubles and 70 percent become addicted) and 42 million (if DuPont's high estimate of use is correct). An optimist would have to conclude that the number of people abusing legalized drugs will come close to those hooked on alcohol. A pessimist would figure the human damage as much greater.

10   Another way of figuring costs is this: the same study (by the Research Triangle Institute of North Carolina) that put the price of alcoholism at $117 billion in 1983 figured the cost of drug abuse then at $60 billion—$15 billion for law enforcement and crime, and $45 billion in lost productivity, damaged health, and other costs. The updated estimate for 1988 drug abuse is $100 billion. If legalizing drugs would save $30 billion now being spent on law enforcement and crime, a doubling of use and abuse means that other costs will rise to $140 billion or $210 billion. This is no bargain for society.

11   If 200,000 people die every year from alcohol abuse and 320,000 from tobacco smoking, how many will die from legal drugs? Government estimates are that 4,000 to 5,000 people a year are killed in drug-related auto crashes, but this is surely low because accident victims are not as routinely blood-tested for drugs as for alcohol. Legalization advocates frequently cite figures of 3,600 or 4,100 as the number of drug deaths each year reported by hospitals, but this number too is certainly an understatement, based on reports from only 75 big hospitals in 27 metropolitan areas.

12   If legalization pushed the total number of drug addicts to only half the number of alcoholics, 100,000 people a year would die. That's the figure cited by McDonald. DuPont guesses that, given the potency of drugs, the debilitating effects of cocaine, the carcinogenic effects of marijuana, and the AIDS potential of injecting legalized heroin, the number of deaths actually could go as high as 500,000 a year. That's a wide range, but it's clear that legalization of drugs will not benefit human life.

13   All studies show that those most likely to try drugs, get hooked, and die—as opposed to those who suffer from cirrhosis and lung cancer—are young people, who are susceptible to the lure of quick thrills and are terribly adaptable to messages provided by adult society. Under pressure of the current prohibition, the number of kids who use illegal drugs at least once a month has fallen from 39 percent in the late 1970s to 25 percent in 1987, according to the annual survey of high school seniors conducted by the University of Michigan. The same survey shows that attitudes toward drug use have turned sharply negative. But use of legal drugs is still strong. Thirty-eight percent of high school seniors reported getting drunk within the past two weeks, and 27 percent said they smoke cigarettes every day. Drug prohibition is working with kids; legalization would do them harm.

14   And, even though legalization would lower direct costs for drug law enforcement, it's unlikely that organized crime would disappear. It might well shift to other fields—prostitution, pornography, gambling or burglaries, extortion, and murders-for-hire—much as it did in the period between the end of Prohibition and the beginning of the drug era. As DuPont puts it, "Organized crime is in the business of giving people the things that society decides in its own interest to prohibit. The only way to get rid of organized crime is to make everything legal." Even legalization advocates such as Ethan Nadelmann admit that some street crimes will continue to occur as a result of drug abuse—especially cocaine paranoia, PCP insanity, and the need of unemployable addicts to get money for drugs. Domestic crime, child abuse and neglect surely would increase.

15   Some legalization advocates suggest merely decriminalizing marijuana and retaining sanctions against other drugs. This would certainly be less costly than total legalization, but it would still be no favor to young people, would increase traffic accidents and productivity losses—and would do nothing to curtail the major drug cartels, which make most of their money trafficking in cocaine.

16   Legalizers also argue that the government could tax legal drug sales and use the money to pay for anti-drug education programs and treatment centers. But total taxes collected right now from alcohol sales at the local, state, and federal levels come to only $13.1 billion per year—which is a pittance compared with the damage done to society as a result of alcohol abuse. The same would have to be true for drugs—and any tax that resulted in an official drug price that was higher than the street price would open the way once again for black markets and organized crime.

17   So, in the name of health, economics, and morality, there seems no alternative but to keep drugs illegal and to fight the criminals who traffic in them. Regardless of what legalization advocates say, this is now the overwhelming opinion of the public, the Reagan administration, the prospective candidates for president, and the Congress—not one of whose members has introduced legislation to decriminalize any drug. Congress is on the verge of forcing the administration to raise anti-drug spending next year from $3 billion to $5.5 billion.

18   There is, though, room to debate how best to wage this war. A consensus is developing that it has to be done both on the supply side (at overseas points of origin, through interdiction at U.S. borders and criminal prosecution of traffickers) and on the demand side (by discouraging use of drugs through education and treatment and/or by arrest and urine testing at workplaces). However, there is a disagreement about which side to emphasize and how to spend resources. Members of Congress, especially Democrats, want to blame foreigners and the Reagan administration for the fact that increasing amounts of cocaine, heroin, and marijuana are entering the country. They want to spend more money on foreign aid, use the U.S. military to seal the borders, and fund "nice" treatment and education programs, especially those that give ongoing support to professional social welfare agencies.

19   Conservatives, on the other hand, want to employ the military to help foreign countries stamp out drug laboratories, use widespread drug testing to identify—and, often, punish—drug users, and spend more on police and prisons. As Education Secretary William Bennett puts it, "How can we surrender when we've never actually fought the war?" Bennett wants to fight it across all fronts, and those who have seen drafts of a forthcoming report of the White House Conference for a Drug Free America say this will be the approach recommended by the administration, although with muted emphasis on use of the U.S. military, which is reluctant to get involved in what may be another thankless war.

20   However, DuPont and others, including Jeffrey Eisenach of the Heritage Foundation, make a strong case that primary emphasis ought to be put on the demand side—discouraging use in the United States rather than, almost literally, trying to become the world's policeman. Their argument, bolstered by a study conducted by Peter Reuter of the RAND Corporation, is that major profits in the drug trade are not made abroad (where the price of cocaine triples from farm to airstrip), but within the United States (where the markup from entry point to street corner is 12 times), and that foreign growing fields and processing laboratories are easily replaceable at low cost.

21   They say that prohibition policy should emphasize routine random urine testing in schools and places of employment, arrests for possession of drugs, and "coercive" treatment programs that compel continued enrollment as a condition of probation and employment. DuPont thinks that corporations have a right to demand that their employees be drug-free because users cause accidents and reduce productivity. He contends that urine testing is no more invasive than the use of metal detectors at airports.

22   "Liberals have a terrible time with this," says DuPont. "They want to solve every problem by giving people things. They want to love people out of their problems, while conservatives want to punish it out of them. What we want to do is take the profits out of drugs by drying up demand. You do that by raising the social cost of using them to the point where people say, 'I don't want to do this.' This isn't conservative. It's a way to save lives."

23   It is, and it's directly parallel to the way society is dealing with drunk driving and cigarette smoking—not merely through advertising campaigns and

surgeon general's warnings, but through increased penalties, social strictures—and prohibitions. Random testing for every employee in America may be going too far, but testing those holding sensitive jobs or workers involved in accidents surely isn't, nor is arresting users, lifting driver's licenses, and requiring treatment. These are not nosy, moralistic intrusions on people's individual rights, but attempts by society to protect itself from danger.

24   In the end, they are also humane and moral. There is a chance, with the public and policy-makers aroused to action, that ten years from now drug abuse might be reduced to its pre-1960s levels. Were drugs to be legalized now, we would be establishing a new vice—one that, over time, would end or ruin millions of lives. Worse yet, we would be establishing a pattern of doing the easy thing, surrendering, whenever confronted with a difficult challenge.

～

(2,469 words)

VOCABULARY

maiming (1)	carcinogenic (12)	susceptible (13)
extortion (14)	curtail (15)	interdiction (18)
bolstered (20)	coercive (21)	invasive (21)
strictures (23)		

THE FACTS

1. What parallels do advocates of drug legalization love to draw, according to the author?
2. What important differences between drugs and alcohol does the author cite?
3. According to the author, what is the addictive difference between marijuana and cocaine?
4. Which group of potential users, according to studies cited by the author, is most likely to get hooked on drugs?
5. What alternative proposals do some legalization advocates offer, and how does the author respond to them?

THE STRATEGIES

1. The author begins his argument by conceding that some things will get better if drugs are legalized. Because he is adamantly against the legalization of drugs, what is the benefit of this admission to his argument?

2. The author writes: "Of the 115 million Americans who consume alcohol, 85% rarely become intoxicated; with drugs, intoxication is the whole idea." What logical objection to this statement might an advocate of drug legalization make?

3. What is the thesis of the author's argument, and where is it stated?

4. In paragraphs 6 and 7, the author deduces probable drug addiction and usage from statistics about alcohol consumption before and after Prohibition. What is your opinion of the logic underlying this deduction?

5. In evaluating statistics and studies cited by the author from various agencies and institutes, what kind of questions should a cautious reader ask before accepting their validity?

THE ISSUES

1. Which of the author's arguments against the legalization of drugs do you find the most persuasive? Why?

2. The author says that tobacco smoking kills 320,000 people every year. Given this statistic, what is your opinion about the legalization of tobacco?

3. The author quotes an authority who claims that whereas liberals want to love people out of their problems, conservatives want to punish them. Based on your reading of these two articles, what other differences can you discern between the liberal and conservative mindset?

4. What is your opinion about mandatory drug testing in schools and places of employment?

5. Which drugs would you decriminalize, given the power and the opportunity? Why?

SUGGESTIONS FOR WRITING

1. Write an essay arguing for or against the banning of cigarette smoking in public places.

2. Defend or attack the proposal to decriminalize the use of marijuana.

—————— STUDENT CORNER ——————

1

Final Draft

Drug Use: The Continuing Epidemic

Linda Kunze, Glendale Community College

Brakes squeal as the late model Mercury Sable speeds down the street. Onlookers stare in amazement while the driver recklessly maneuvers in and out of traffic. Suddenly, the car jumps the curb and slams head on into a power pole. Moments later, police arrive to find the young female driver dead behind the steering wheel. In her hand she clutches the six-tenths of a gram of rock cocaine she had just purchased.

No, this scenario is not the opening scene from the latest big screen action adventure. Sadly, it is a true story taken from the Sunday, November 3, 1996, issue of the Daily News and is just another example of the death and destruction caused by the continued popularity and use of illicit drugs.

Drug use is far from new. It has been a major problem in America for decades. According to Linda Villarosa, author of *Body & Soul,* heroin and cocaine (two powerfully addictive drugs) were first introduced to consumers back at the turn of the century as ingredients in many over-the-counter medical remedies and soft drinks. In time, when the addictive properties of these narcotics were discovered, heroin, cocaine, and many other harmful drugs were outlawed, but this action came far too late. The overpowering problem of drug abuse and addiction had already begun to spread across America.

Kunze 2

Today, almost every adult American is aware of the dangers involved with the use of illegal substances. However, this knowledge has not stopped the rapid increase of drug abuse in this nation. In the September/October 1996 issue of *Psychology Today,* Owen Lipstein, Editor-in-Chief of the publication, states that currently, "More than 5 million [adults] smoke marijuana more than once a week; over 2 million are well acquainted with cocaine; an estimated 750,000 use heroin." Drug dependency and addiction are becoming far too common in this country and it is so tempting to close our eyes and turn our backs to the drug epidemic and just wish it away.

Unfortunately, denying the problems caused by the ever-growing use and abuse of narcotics, will not save anyone from the torments of drug abuse and addiction. Although there are no easy answers to this age-old problem, early education seems to be the only truly effective weapon the nation has against this equal opportunity destroyer known as drug abuse.

For education to be an effective deterrent to drug abuse, it must begin as early as grade school, because according to Schools Without Drugs, a recent pamphlet published by the United States Department of Education, "One out of every six 13-year-olds has used marijuana (at least once) and fifty-four percent of high school seniors have tried some type of illicit drug by the time they are ready to graduate." Children must be taught the dangers of drug abuse and strategies to avoid the use of these substances, prior to junior and senior high school where availability and peer pressure make drug use all too acceptable and easy to fall for.

Kunze 3

It is apparent that drug abuse is a problem that has grown in leaps and bounds over the years. It will not go away overnight, and there are no easy solutions to eliminate the stronghold drugs have in this country. However, we must continue to educate everyone, young and old, on the evils of illegal drugs and remain persistent in the fight against their use. We all deserve a drug free future.

How I Write

I always sit down and brainstorm—usually alone—before I write anything. In other words, I mull over ideas to see how they might work. I have never been gifted in the art of formal outlines, but I do jot down any idea that can be developed successfully. I like to work at home, with country music playing in the background.

How I Wrote This Essay

I located as many sources on drug abuse as time permitted. I then narrowed my sources down to the amount needed. I wrote one draft and put it away for a week. After the week was up, I reread my paper, changing what I didn't like and improving what I did like. The introduction is always the hardest for me to write. Everything else flows from there.

My Writing Tip

Write what you know and develop your own style. Always give yourself enough time to do the assignment well because a shoddy assignment leads only to embarrassment.

CHAPTER WRITING ASSIGNMENTS

1. Write an essay in which you provide illustrations from history, physics, biology, psychology, or literature to prove one of the following maxims:
   a. "Every man is the architect of his own fortune." (Seneca)
   b. "The injury of prodigality leads to this, that he who will not economize will have to agonize." (Confucius)
   c. "The foundation of every state is the education of its youth." (Diogenes)
   d. "The pull of gravity exerts far more influence than one might think." (Anonymous)
   e. "Satire is the guerrilla weapon of political warfare." (Horace Greeley)

2. Choose one of the following terms and write an essay giving examples of it.
   a. romance
   b. tyranny
   c. education
   d. humility
   e. prejudice
   f. law

WRITING ASSIGNMENTS FOR A SPECIFIC AUDIENCE

1. Addressing yourself to a group of eighth graders, write an essay about racism using examples from your own experience or that of acquaintances and friends.

2. Give examples to back up this statement: It was the best day of my life.

COLLABORATIVE WRITING PROJECT

Join a group of six other students. Brainstorm on the topic of race relations and racism. Ask yourself these questions: Have you ever been the victim of a racial snub or slur? Have race relations gotten better or worse? How do you feel about the present state of race relations? What can be done to improve relations between the races? After gathering opinions from the other students and making notes, write an essay on one of the following topics, backing up your stand with examples:

1. What are the personal effects of racism?

2. What can be done to improve race relations?

3. What can be done to change an individual's hostility toward certain races?

4. What is the impact of the past on today's race relations?

11

Definition

EDITORS' COUNSEL

What Definition Does

Definition means spelling out exactly what a word or phrase means. Articles, essays, and entire books have been written for the sole purpose of defining some abstract or disputed word, term, or phrase. Here is an example of a paragraph that defines *plot.*

> Let us define a plot. We have defined a story as a narrative of events arranged in their time-sequence. A plot is also a narrative of events, the emphasis falling on causality. "The king died and then the queen died," is a story. "The king died, and then the queen died of grief," is a plot. The time sequence is preserved, but the sense of causality overshadows it. Or again: "The queen died, no one knew why, until it was discovered that it was through grief at the death of the king." This is a plot with a mystery in it, a form capable of high development. It suspends the time sequence, it moves as far away from the story as its limitations will allow. Consider the death of the queen. If it is a story we say, "and then?" If it is a plot we ask, "why?" That is the fundamental difference between these two aspects of the novel. A plot cannot be told to a gaping audience of cavemen or to a tyrannical sultan or to their modern descendant the movie-public. They can only be kept awake by "and then-and then." They can only supply curiosity. But a plot demands intelligence and memory also.
>
> -E. M. Forster, Aspects of the Novel

In the preceding paragraph, the author not only defines *plot,* he distinguishes it from *story.* When he is done, we get a sense not only of what a plot is, but of what it is not.

When to Use Definition

What do words and phrases mean? Especially for abstract words and phrases, the answer is not always simple. It would be easy enough to explain to a Martian what the word *pencil* means because, as a last resort, we can produce one and wave it under the creature's antennas. But how do we explain the meaning of *love* to this alien? Or the meaning of *human rights?* Or even the meaning of *sovereignty?* None of these words overlays an object or thing to which we can point. Each is an idea or concept and, therefore, definable only by experience or words. The problem is that it is difficult, if not impossible, to find two people who have had such an identical experience with *love* or *human rights* or *sovereignty* that they will instantly agree on a common meaning. This is where words rush in to fill the gap.

Definitions are especially useful, then, if your essay hinges on one of these disputed abstractions. If you were writing an essay on *love,* for example, you could not take it for granted that your reader knows what you mean by that word. You would have to define it. You would have to write your definition in such a way as to make it instantly clear to your particular audience.

How to Use Definition

1. Begin your definition by saying what the term means. The traditional method of doing this is to first place the term in a general class and then show how it differs from others found there. Known as a *lexical definition,* this is the method of defining used by dictionaries. Here is an example:

A library is a repository for artistic and literary materials

Repository is identified as the general class to which *library* belongs, but a specialization in artistic and literary materials distinguishes it from other repositories.

Here are some more examples of lexical definitions:

A *motor scooter* is a two-wheeled vehicle with small wheels and a low-powered gasoline engine geared to the rear wheel.

An *oligarchy* is government by the few, especially a small group of people, such as one family.

Education is the process of systematic instruction in order to impart knowledge or skill.

Mercy is the kind and compassionate treatment of an offender.

This is a useful and preliminary way of saying what a term means. First show where the term belongs, then distinguish it from others in that same class. Consciously and unconsciously, we practice this method of defining every day.

2. Expand your definition, if necessary, with an etymological analysis of the term. The *etymology* of a word is an explanation of its roots, of what it originally meant, and is often useful in shedding light on how the current meaning of a word evolved. Here is an example of an etymological analysis that helps us to understand the meaning of the word *bible:*

> In the derivation of our word Bible lies its definition. It comes from the Greek word *biblion*[1], which in its plural *biblia* signifies "little books." The Bible is actually a collection of little books, of every sort and description, written over a long period of time, the very earliest dating, in part at least, as far back as 1200 B.C. or perhaps even earlier; the latest as late as A.D. 150. In its rich and manifold nature it might be called a *library* of Hebrew literature; in its slow production over a period of many centuries it might be termed a survey of that literature to be understood as we understand a *survey* of English literature, in which we become familiar with types of English prose and poetry from Anglo-Saxon times to our own.
>
> -Mary Ellen Chase, "What Is the Bible?"

3. Clarify your definition by stating what the word is not or does not mean. For instance, the meaning of *mythology* can be clarified by the statement that it is not merely "a story filled with lies." Likewise, *liberty* can be clarified by showing that it does not simply mean "doing anything one wants at any time." In the following paragraph, the term *empirical medicine* is partially defined by what it is not:

> By the practice of empirical medicine we mean that conclusions are reached as a result of experience and observation. Diagnoses are made and cures are found as a result of practical experience. Empirical medicine is not the practice of medicine based on scientific theories or knowledge but on what works. Because of its disregard for scientific knowledge, empirical medicine is often considered charlatanry by academicians.

In essays, the overriding aim of a defining paragraph is usually to clarify the meaning of a certain term. Occasionally, however, the technical or dictionary meaning of a word or phrase may not be what the writer is trying to convey. Indeed, some definitions may be philosophical or poetic, as in the following example:

> Home is where you hang your hat. Or home is where you spent your childhood, the good years when waking every morning was an excitement, when the round of the day could always produce something to fill your mind, tear your emotions, excite your wonder or awe or delight. Is home that, or is it the place where the people you love live, or the place where you have buried your dead, or the place where you want to be buried yourself? Or is it the place where you come in your last desperation to shoot yourself, choosing the garage or the barn

---

[1]Biblos was the name given to the inner bark of the papyrus; and the word biblion meant a papyrus roll, upon which the Bible was originally copied.

or the woodshed in order not to mess up the house, but coming back anyway to the last sanctuary where you can kill yourself in peace?

—Wallace Stegner, Big Rock Candy Mountain

4. Expand your definition with examples.   A well-chosen example can add volumes of clarity to your meaning. In the following paragraph, the author tells us what she thinks the word *manhood* means in America:

America has defined the roles to which each individual should subscribe. It has defined "manhood" in terms of its own interests and "femininity" likewise. An individual who has a good job, makes a lot of money and drives a Cadillac is a real man, and conversely, an individual who is lacking in these "qualities" is less of a man. The advertising media in this country continuously inform the American male of his need for indispensable signs of his virility—the brand of cigarettes that cowboys prefer, the whiskey that has a masculine tang or the label of the jock strap that athletes wear.

—Frances M. Beal, "Double Jeopardy: To Be Black and Female"

Whether or not you agree with this definition, you can at least grasp the author's meaning from her examples.

5. To define a complex term properly, you may need to practice a combination of techniques: You may have to cite examples, analyze etymology, and/or provide a lexical definition.   Here is a paragraph in which the writer uses all three devices to define *idiopathic diseases:*

examples

etymology

lexical

We have a roster of diseases which medicine calls "idiopathic," meaning that we do not know what causes them. The list is much shorter than it used to be; a century ago, common infections like typhus fever, tuberculosis, and meningitis were classed as idiopathic illnesses. Originally, when it first came into the language of medicine, the term had a different, highly theoretical meaning. It was assumed that most human diseases were intrinsic, due to inbuilt failures of one sort or another, things gone wrong with various internal humors. The word "idiopathic" was intended to mean, literally, a disease having its own origin, a primary disease without any external cause. The list of such disorders has become progressively shorter as medical science has advanced, especially within this century, and the meaning of the term has lost its doctrinal flavor; we use "idiopathic" now to indicate simply that the cause of one particular disease is unknown. Very likely, before we are finished with medical science, and with luck, we will have found that all varieties of disease are the result of one or another sort of meddling, and there will be no more idiopathic illness.

—Lewis Thomas, The Medusa and the Snail

Remember that your definition is incomplete if it leaves gaps in the meaning of a term or fails to clearly answer the question, "What does this mean?" Keep that question in mind when you write a definition and do your utmost to answer it until your meaning is unmistakably clear to your reader.

As you write your defining essays, beware of the most common student error—the circular definition. To say that "taxation is the act of imposing taxes" is repetitious. Better to say "Taxation is the principle of levying fees to support basic government services." Provide examples and details until you have answered the question "What is it?"

Warming Up to Write a Definition

1. Getting together with three or four of your classmates, sit down and discuss the best definition for each of the following terms. If needed, you may use a dictionary. Once you have agreed on the best definition, write it on a sheet of paper, using only one sentence. Refine the written definition until it could serve as a thesis statement for an essay.

   a. cleptomania

   b. astrology

   c. organ transplant

   d. terrorism

   e. deportation

2. In the following paragraph, the word *renaissance* needs to be defined for readers who are not familiar with it. Define the term by using at least three other words in the passage that explain what the word means. Write down your definition so that it could be used as the thesis of an essay about any community experiencing what Harlem is going through.

   Harlem, a community in northern Manhattan that hit bottom in the 1980s when poverty, neglected housing and drug-related crime took their toll, is enjoying a lively second *renaissance*. Some Harlemites dismiss the resurgence as little more than a real estate boom, because the neighborhood's magnificent 19th-century townhouses are being snapped up at a rapid rate. You'll also hear that the cultural scene doesn't compare with the Harlem's first flowering, in the 1920s, which was animated by extraordinary creativity in politics, the arts and especially the written word. But if it's true there are no stand-ins today for fiery W. E. B. DuBois, gentle Langston Hughes, or patrician Duke Ellington, the second renaissance is still taking shape. . .Highbrow, mainstream, pop, hippop, avant-garde—Harlem's cultural and artistic revival is evident on nearly every block.

   —From Peter Hellman, "Coming Up Harlem," *Smithsonian*, November 2002.

3. In the blank provided, check those definitions that are *not* correct; then provide the correct definition.

a. _____ *Charismatic* means disgusting.

b. _____ *Desolation* means a feeling of despair.

c. _____ A *skeptic* is one who is gullible.

d. _____ *Suburban* means out in the country.

e. _____ A *turret* is a tower or steeple.

f. _____ To *pay homage* means to ridicule.

g. _____ A *residue* is an evil citizen.

h. _____ *Genetic* means inherited.

i. _____ To *scrutinize* means to study or pore over.

j. _____ *Sovereignty* means debauchery.

———————— **EXAMPLES** ————————

WHO THE DEVIL IS THE DEVIL?

Robert Wernick

Writer Robert Wernick (b. 1918), a frequent contributor to Smithsonian *and other magazines, is based in Paris, France. He is the author of several books including* The Freebooters, *(1949),* The Hill of Fortune, *(1950), and* The Vikings *(1979).*

Known by a variety of names—Beelzebub, Abaddon, Apollyon, Dragon, Serpent, Evil One, God of this World, and Satan—the Devil is an ancient figure in Christian tradition, a former angel who rebelled against God and was cast out of heaven along with a troop of other fallen angels. This devilish crew, according to Christian tradition, now works to spread evil on earth and will continue to do so until the final showdown between the forces of good and evil. While the exact origin of the Devil is still blurry, this scholarly essay provides a revealing chronology of Satan's development over the years.

～

1   With the rapid approach of the third millenium, many people can't help wondering what role the Devil will be playing in it. But a cursory examination of the mainstream press of America reveals almost no mention of him, and even using the Internet services that promise to keep track of everything, it's much easier to find information on Monica Lewinsky than on the Devil.

2   What a humiliating comedown for one the mere mention of whose name was once enough to make the hair of kings stand up in terror; of whom Saint

Augustine said, "The human race is the Devil's fruit tree, his own property, from which he may pick his fruit."

3   To appreciate the full extent of that downfall, try to put yourself someplace in Western Europe in the year 999, as the second millennium was about to bow in.

4   In the tenth century and for at least half a millennium thereafter, the Devil was everywhere. He leered out of every church door, he capered through castle and church and cottage, and his plots and pranks and temptings of humans were spelled out in sermons, on the stage, in paintings, in pious books, and in stories told in taverns or in homes at bedtime.

5   No corner or cranny of daily life escaped him. He lurked outside every orifice of the human body, waiting for the chance to get at the human soul inside—one reason why to this day we say "God bless you" when we hear someone sneeze.

6   The Devil fathered children on sleeping women, he stirred up conspiracies and treasons, he led travelers astray. He caused boils, plagues, tempests, shipwrecks, heresies, barbarian invasions. Whatever he did, his name was on everyone's tongue, and he went by many names: Satan, Lucifer, Beelzebub, Belial, Mastema, the Prince of Darkness, the Lord of Lies. In the Bible be was the Accuser, the Evil One, the Prince of this World.

7   Today, a few scant hundred years later, he has dropped so far out of sight that some believe he is gone for good. It may be true that 48 percent of Americans tell the pollsters they believe in the existence of the Devil and another 20 percent find his existence probable. But though they use him often enough in common lighthearted expressions (give the devil his due, the devil is in the details) and in the privacy of their hearts may put the blame on him when they covet their neighbor's wife or cheat on their income tax, they do very little talking about him out loud. Reported physical appearances of the Devil are far rarer than sightings of UFOs. In practical terms, people have banished him from public life.

8   Yet most everyone who discusses moral standards in pulpits or on television talk shows or in the *New York Times* is agreed that morals are lower than ever before. The Devil should be out in the streets and on the airwaves, roaring like a lion about his triumphs. Where has he gone? It all depends on precisely what you mean by "the Devil."

9   Theologians have been arguing for centuries (and sometimes have gone to the stake for expressing the wrong opinion) to achieve a satisfactory definition. But today the average person with no theological axe to grind is apt to envisage the Devil as a sleek, dark-complexioned male figure, with black chin-whiskers, little horns and cloven hooves, perhaps with a foxy glint in his eye and a trace of a foreign accent, but on the whole handsome, worldly-wise, a persuasive talker, a friendly sort of customer. He may tell you anything, try to talk you into something too good to be true. Only later, when you've taken that risky bet or signed the shady contract, and he comes to collect his due, do you realize you have signed away your immortal soul. He is unquestionably the Lord of Lies.

10   This suave, sardonic Devil is actually a new kid on the block; he has been around for barely a few hundred years, a mere stutter in the long swell of human misery and woe. And the Devil in general, the Devil with a capital D, as opposed to the legions of lowercase devils, demons, imps, satyrs, fiends and so on, first entered human history less than 3,000 years ago.

11   But humans indistinguishable from us have been around for many thousands of years, and it seems fair to assume that from the very beginning they were all aware of unseen powerful presences affecting their lives and everything around them. Every ancient religion that we know of, as well as many modern religions with hundreds of millions of followers, perceives a bewildering array of such spirits: gods, demigods, angels, devils, demons, sprites, imps, goblins, ghosts, fairies, fauns, nymphs, jinns, poltergeists. Some of them are benevolent, some are malignant, though most of them alternate between the two extremes. The gods of ancient Greece are typical: Zeus was a wise ruler up on Mount Olympus, but he became a serial rapist when he came down to the lowlands; Persephone was goddess of life in spring and goddess of death in autumn. None of these ancient religions ever developed a single Devil concentrating all the essence of evil, any more than they ever concentrated the essence of good in a single God.

12   The Old Testament, which was composed between the tenth and the third centuries B.C., has little trace of the Devil with a capital *D*, and in its earlier books, none at all. God, speaking through the mouth of the prophet Isaiah, says, "I form the light and create darkness, I make peace and create evil, I the LORD do all these things." The serpent who tempted Adam and Eve in the Garden of Eden was later identified by Jewish rabbis and Christian church fathers with the Devil, the principle of Evil; but in the third chapter of Genesis as written, he is only a snake. It took another few hundred years before both snake and Devil were identified with Lucifer ("light-bearer," the Latin translation of the Hebrew and Greek words for the morning star, the planet Venus) who in Isaiah is thrown down from Heaven for having presumed to set his throne high above the stars of God.

13   Ancient Hebrew had a noun, *satan*, meaning "obstructor" or "accuser," and several satans appear in the Old Testament being sent by God on different errands, such as blocking the path of Balaam's ass or giving King Saul a fit of depression. When the Old Testament was translated into Greek beginning in the third century B.C., *satan* was rendered *diabolos*, "adversary," from which come the Latin *diabolus*, French *diable*, German *Teufel*, English "devil." The first time the word appears with a capital *S*, defining a particular person, is in the Book of Job, where Satan is a sort of celestial J. Edgar Hoover, sent by the Lord to check up on the loyalty of the folks down on earth.

14   The first Devil, the first concentration of all evil in a single personal form, appears in history some time before the Sixth century B.C., in Persia. His name is Ahriman, described by the prophet Zoroaster (Zarathustra) as the Principle of Darkness (evil) engaged in ceaseless conflict for control of the world with Ormazd or Mazda, the Principle of Light (good).

15   The Jews were under Persian domination for almost two centuries, and it is likely that Ahriman had some influence on the formation of the figure of their Satan. He appears for the first time acting independently in the third-century Book of Chronicles, where the text of the much older Book of Samuel is changed from "The LORD incited David," to read "Satan incited David." In the next few centuries of the so-called Intertestamentary Period between the compilation of the Old and New Testaments, when a major subject of theological speculation and literature was the apocalypse—the final struggle between good and evil at the imminent end of the world—this Satan grew in stature as the leader and embodiment of the forces of evil. The Jewish rabbis soon lost interest in him, and though he runs wild through folklore, he is a very minor figure in modern Judaism. He would be a major figure, however, as the Satan or Lucifer of the Christians or the Iblis or Shaytan of the Muslims. Whatever he does, and however powerful he may be at times, none of these religions have ever followed Zoroaster in allowing the Devil an independent existence apart from God. He is always separate but far from equal, though exactly to what extent separate and unequal has been the subject of perpetual debate on the questions that the postulation of a Devil naturally calls up: Why did a good God create an evil Devil in the first place? And if he had to, why did he give him so much power and let him reign so long? Or, as Friday asked Robinson Crusoe, "If God much strong, much might as the Devil, why God no kill the devil, no make him no more do wicked?" Such questions were being debated in Latin by 12th-century scholars in Paris in almost the same terms as by 12th-century scholars in Baghdad, and they are still being debated by scholars all over the world today.

16   The Christian Devil, who is the one most familiar in today's literature and art, appears often, but with only sketchy details, in the New Testament. It took three or four centuries of debate and speculation for the church to settle on a unified but not quite consistent picture of his history and functions. He was once an angel—some said the firstborn and chief of all the angels—who had led a rebellion in Heaven (some said out of pride; some said out of envy either of God himself or of the man, Adam, created in God's image; some said out of sexual lust for pretty women) and had been cast down to Hell (some said on the very first day or hour of the creation of the world, others after the creation of Adam, others after the Fall of Man, others during the time of Noah), had tempted humankind into sin, which allowed him to rule the world until the coming of Christ (Or until the Second Coming), and would on the Day of judgment be condemned to perpetual torment along with all the sinners of the race of Adam.

17   At the beginning there was curiously little interest in the particular features of this Devil, who does not appear at all in the first six or seven centuries of Christian art. Perhaps the early Christians, members of a small persecuted sect faced with the daily possibility of meeting the representatives of the Roman state in the form of gladiators, lions and howling mobs in arenas, did not need to dream up faces for the Devil. After Christianity became the state

religion of Rome in the early fourth century, the fight against the enemy changed in character. The heroes were not martyrs in an arena; they were monks who went out into the deserts to meet Satan face-to-face. Satan appeared to all of them to tempt them, and it was then that Satan first acquired a recognizable physical form, appearing variously as lion, bear, leopard, bull, serpent, hyena, scorpion and wolf.

18   Still, for hundreds of years no one thought of putting an image of the Devil on paper or a church wall. There is a sixth-century manuscript of the Gospels in Syriac that shows a couple of little black-winged creatures fleeing from the mouth of a man being exorcized. Not till the ninth century, in an illustrated manuscript known as the *Utrecht Psalter,* does a recognizable Devil appear, as a half-naked man holding a three-pronged pitchfork. The Devil would appear often like this in the next couple of centuries, human or at least humanoid in form, sometimes wearing the halo of his old angelic days in Heaven.

19   Then, some time around the pre-millennial tenth century, the Devil began, all over the Western world, to assume monstrous forms. He appeared on the illustrated pages of books now written for the first time in the vernacular languages, and on the painted walls and ceilings and the carved doors and columns and waterspouts of churches and cathedrals. Everywhere there were scenes from sacred history intended to teach the illiterate masses the way to salvation, and the Devil played a prominent, sometimes predominant, role in these scenes.

20   He appeared in a thousand grotesque and horrible guises. His features might be derived from those of old gods of Greece and Rome whose broken images still cluttered the soil of Europe, or the newer gods of the barbarian Germans and Scandinavians, or more ancient supernatural beings from Mesopotamia, Egypt, Persia, even China, who spread their wings on imported silks and tapestries. He borrowed horns and hairy legs with cloven hooves from the Greek god Pan, a hooked nose and grimacing lips from the Etruscan death god Charun, a pitchfork from the Roman sea god Neptune, an animal head from the Egyptian god Anubis. Sometimes he was a furry black monkey with great black bat's wings. Sometimes he was a snake, a wolf, a frog, a bear, a mouse, an owl, a raven, a tortoise, a worm. Often he appeared as a combination of human and animal forms, with a tail, spiky flame-like hair, an apish body, a goat's hairy thighs, an ass's feet, a boar's tusks, a wolfish mouth, an eagle's claws, a monkey's paws, a lizard's skin, a snake's tongue. When he led the revolt of the angels in Heaven, fighting Saint Michael, he was a scaly dragon. Enthroned in Hell, he was a potbellied imbecilic old man, with snakes growing out of his head and limbs, mindlessly chewing on the sterile souls of naked sinners as they dropped down to him on Judgment Day.

21   He was meant to be both frightening and disgusting, to demonstrate both the horror and the folly of sin. The fright was all the greater because the devices like bone-vices, spine-rollers and redhot prongs being used to torture sinners down in Hell were copied from those being used to torture heretics in public up on earth.

22   The static visions on the church walls were regularly brought to life in plays staged in front of churches or in public squares. Surrounded by elaborate scenery and firecrackers, the Devil was always a popular performer when, clothed in snakeskin and with a woman's face, he dangled an apple before our First Parents in Eden, or with fanged mask and hairy goat's body, he grimaced and grunted and growled as he prodded wailing sinners into a Mouth of Hell that could open and shut and spit flames.

23   One of the most popular stories throughout the Middle Ages, retold hundreds of times in many European languages, was that of Theophilus of Cilicia, a sixth-century ecclesiastic who signed a pact with the Devil, exchanging his soul for a powerful and profitable position in the church. He was then able to lead a life of unbridled pride and corruption till one day the Devil reappeared and demanded his payment. In terror, Theophilus repented and threw himself on the mercy of the Virgin Mary, who took pity on him, descended into Hell, grabbed the pact from Satan, then interceded for the sinner at the throne of God. He was pardoned, and the Devil was cheated of his due.

24   This tale played a major role in establishing the cult of the Virgin in Catholic Europe. It had the subsidiary effect of familiarizing everyone with the idea of diabolical pacts. The authorities of church and state took advantage of this when sometime in the 15th century they claimed to discover a vast conspiracy by a confederation of witches dedicated to the subversion of all order. There were, of course, plenty of supposed witches around, mostly old countrywomen who knew the traditional herbs and chants and charms that would attract a handsome lover or stop an unwanted pregnancy or blast the crops in an unfriendly neighbor's field. But for the space of two or three centuries, tens of thousands of accused witches, most of them women, most of them poor illiterates, were hanged or burned after being forced to confess to taking part in secret midnight meetings at which they ate babies, copulated with the Devil and signed blood compacts with him.

25   The Salem witch trials of 1692 are the most familiar to Americans, having left an indelible stain on the name of our Puritan forebears. Perhaps the most interesting thing about them is that, compared with what had been going on in Europe for the previous three centuries, they were on such a very small scale: 18 women, one man and two dogs put to death in obedience to the biblical command, "Thou shalt not suffer a witch to live." And there were no more witch trials in the Colonies after Salem.

26   For by the year 1700 few educated people really believed in witches anymore, and increasingly they were coming not to believe in the Devil himself. The reason was that Western Europe, followed in more or less short order by the rest of the world, was entering the modern era, the world of exploration, discovery, science, technology, individualism, capitalism, rationalism, materialism, democracy, progress. In such a world the old Devil was getting to seem both embarrassing and superfluous. When he appeared on the stage with his monkey suits and his conjuring tricks, he was only an unsightly clown—Ben Jonson summed it up in the title of one of his plays, *The Devil is an Ass*. And when you got down to the business of explaining what was going on around you, the Devil only got in the way. When Shakespeare's Othello

learns too late how he has been tricked into murdering his wife and losing his soul, his first, medieval instinct is to look down at Iago's feet; then he pulls himself together and says, "But that's a fable." Iago doesn't need supernatural cloven hooves; he has all the wickedness he needs stored up in his own human heart. Bit by bit, the Devil's possessions and prerogatives were stripped from him.

27   When Benjamin Franklin called down a great spark from Heaven with a mere key hanging on a kite, all the army of infernal spirits that had been swarming through the air vanished, and the atmosphere became nothing but a mass of nitrogen and oxygen and other atoms, whirling around according to laws that Satan had never heard of.

28   Where the 13th-century Cistercian abbot Richalm blamed the Devil for the "wondrous sound that would seem to proceed from some distemper" of his stomach or bowels, a modern monk sends for a gastroenterologist. Great storms are no longer conjured up by the Devil, but by El Nino currents, and no one blames the wreck of the Titanic on anything but errors of judgment and faults of design. People are still possessed by devils, and the Roman Catholic church among others provides means of exorcizing them. But their numbers are infinitesimal compared with the number of people who are daily put under the care of psychiatrists.

29   The old-fashioned horror-show Devil virtually disappeared from the fine arts with the coming of the Renaissance. In 1505 Raphael painted a traditional picture of Saint Michael beating the Devil out of Heaven. The Devil is a kind of outsize science-fiction insect with horns and wings and a madman's gasping face. Thirteen years later he did another painting on the identical theme, but the Devil this time, though a pair of bat wings grows out of his shoulders, is otherwise wholly human, a young man writhing in the despair of defeat, a much more arresting and moving figure than the bland self-satisfied saint who is poking him with a spear.

30   The real gravedigger of the old brutal, terrifying, physically threatening Devil was John Milton, whose *Paradise Lost* was to influence the world's conception of Satan in a way no other work of art has ever done, though not at all in the way the author intended. It was designed to be an epic poem like those of Homer or Virgil, but told to "justify God's ways to Man," and dealing with creation, sin and salvation. In outline, it is a very orthodox story of pride and sin eventually humbled and destroyed by the infinite wisdom and goodness of God. Milton's Satan follows the theologically correct process of transformation from the most radiant of angels to the loathsome crawling serpent of Book Ten. Few readers, however, get to Book Ten of Paradise Lost. They are more apt to let themselves be lost in fascination with the Satan of the first books, a heroic figure of the first order, young, proud, self-confident, self-reliant, inventive, ingenious, yielding to no obstacle, defiant, who will not accept defeat even if defeat is inevitable, who values his own freedom more than happiness, who would rather "reign in Hell than serve in Heaven." These might be considered features of the tireless visionary entrepreneurs

from Columbus to Bill Gates whose dreams and exploits have shaped so much of modern history, and provided the heroes for so many modern movies and novels.

31   But to the modern Devil, even more galling than his loss of physical power, his control of earthquakes and unholy wars, must be his loss of respect. The Prince of Darkness has become, in the view of Prof. Andrew Delbanco of Columbia University, in a book called *The Death of Satan*, a superannuated athlete who has gone on the lecture circuit.

32   He can always get a supporting role in a horror movie like *Rosemary's Baby* or a science-fiction thriller about a professor of comparative literature who carves up and cooks his more attractive students. But no one takes him really seriously. He is toned down, domesticated. Bowdlerized, he has become politically correct. As one of the tide characters in John Updike's *Witches of Eastwick* remarks, "Evil is not a word that we like to use. We prefer to say 'unfortunate' or 'lacking' or 'misguided' or 'disadvantaged.' " Even hellfire preachers who make a specialty of describing in detail the horrors of the afterlife no longer say, as the church fathers of a more robust age used to do, that one of the joys of being in Heaven will be to watch sinners writhing in the hands of the Devil.

33   To adjust to this pallid modern world, the Devil has had to change his ways. Always an expert shape-changer, he now comes on most often in the form of Mephistopheles. The name was made up in a 15th-century German updating of the old Theophilus legend, which has Mephistopheles signing a pact with Dr. Johann Faustus, a professor-turned-magician who is more than willing to trade his soul for 24 years of unbounded knowledge, power and sex. Christopher Marlowe's play of Doctor Faustus would launch both the Faust story and the character of Mephistopheles on a fabulously successful career. He was followed two centuries later by Goethe with his epic drama *Faust*. Between them they created the modern Devil, witty, ironic, disillusioned, a much more complex and interesting character than Doctor Faustus himself. Unlike Faust, however, Mephistopheles never *does* anything; he just talks.

34   He talks very well, of course. He talks very wittily and convincingly in Dostoyevsky's *Brothers Karamazov* and in George Bernard Shaw's *Man and Superman*. He is funny in a sinister kind of way when in C. S. Lewis' *Screwtape Letters* he becomes a conscientious bureaucrat filling reams of paper with instructions to an Englishman on how to get on his mother's nerves. He looks very handsome and winning when he is played by Al Pacino in the movies. But out in the world of commerce, politics, wars and gross national product, he is little more than a joke.

35   For some observers like Professor Delbanco and Prof. Jeffrey Burton Russell, of the University of California, Santa Barbara, whose five-volume biography of the Devil is the most authoritative, this is a tragic situation; it means that America, like the modern world generally, has lost its sense of evil, and without a sense of evil a civilization must go straight to Hell.

36   Perhaps, however, he is not dead after all; he may only be in hiding. A 17th-century Englishman, Richard Greenham, was apparently the first to coin the phrase, later borrowed or reinvented by Baudelaire, Dostoyevsky, G. K. Chesterton and Whittaker Chambers, "It is the policy of the Devil to persuade us that there is no Devil." The Devil, after all, if he is anything, is the personification of evil, and no one can deny that there is plenty of evil around even in today's comparative peace and prosperity.

37   The psychiatrist Viktor Frankl was a young doctor in Vienna in 1940 when he and his wife were picked up by Nazi thugs and sent off to concentration camps. She was soon murdered, but he managed to survive through all five years of the war. One night, as he climbed up to his wooden bunk, he found the man next to him moaning and roaring and thrashing, in prey to the worst nightmare Frankl had ever seen in his years of medical practice. His every humane instinct as a doctor told him to wake the man up before be hurt himself, but as he reached out to shake him, he suddenly remembered that the reality he would be waking the man up to was Auschwitz, with all its stenches and screams and heavy thudding blows, and that was a hundred times worse than anything the mere human imagination could make up in the confines of a narrow human skull. So he let the nightmare gallop on.

38   There were no devils running Auschwitz, only human beings doing an ill-paid job that they must have found unpleasant at times, but which was clearly preferable to being sent to die in the hell of the Russian front. That does not mean the Devil was not there.

39   Most everyone these days has taken the pledge that there will be no more Auschwitzes. But such pledges have been taken before. Common sense tells us that we will go on performing wicked deeds of one sort or another till an automated virtue machine is patented or (more likely) till the end of the world.

40   Madame Carmelita, a psychic on the Upper East Side of Manhattan, has assured me that the world will end on or about my 100th birthday, February 18, 2018. And a science-fiction scenario might have the world (meaning human life) come to an end when a giant comet hits the earth, clearing the ground for little polyps that will evolve into creatures much nicer and more spiritual than us mere mammals. A scientist has assured me that the world (meaning life on earth) will come to an end when our sun becomes a red giant in the year 4,000,001,999. If in the meanwhile a sleek gentleman dressed as a prosperous options-and-derivatives salesman offers you fantastic odds on a bet that he will not be around right up to the last second on any or all of those occasions, and you take him up on it, you will probably be making a bad bet.

~

(4,593 words)

VOCABULARY

cursory (1)
envisage (9)
apocalypse (15)
vernacular (19)
heretics (21)
subversion (24)
prerogatives (26)
exorcizing (28)
visionary (30)
bowdlerized (32)

orifice (5)
suave (10)
postulation (15)
grimacing (20)
ecclesiastic (23)
indelible (25)
distemper (28)
infinitesimal (28)
entrepreneurs (30)
pallid (33)

stake (9)
sardonic (10)
humanoid (18)
imbecilic (20)
interceded (23)
superfluous (26)
gastroenterologist (28)
ingenious (30)
superannuated (31)
scenario (40)

THE FACTS

1. According to Wernick's essay, is the Devil stronger or weaker today than he was centuries ago? Give reasons for your answer.

2. What evils were attributed to the Devil during the 10th century and for at least a half millenium thereafter? What would be the equivalent of these evils today? Why do you think people blamed the Devil for these evils?

3. In what light-hearted ways do people today still refer to the Devil? Can you give additional examples not listed in the essay?

4. According to Wernick's essay, at which point was the Devil identified with Lucifer, the chief archangel in heaven? Where in the Bible is his fall mentioned? Why was Lucifer thrown down from heaven?

5. At which point in history did the Devil take on a recognizable form—a half-naked creature holding a pitchfork? When did he begin to assume monstrous forms? What were the models for these forms?

THE STRATEGIES

1. What organization does the author use to give the reader a general review of the historical significance of the Devil? What advantage does this strategy have? What level of English is used throughout the essay?

2. What, according to the author, is the irony of the Devil being banished from our public life? Which paragraph mentions this irony? Where has the Devil reappeared? But is this the same Devil as before? Explain your answer.

3. What Biblical allusion does the author use to indicate his view that in the story of creation the Devil did not exist? What is your answer to this point?

4. How important is the author's reference to Persia in the 6th century B.C.? How does this reference possibly illuminate the character of Satan as the personification of all evil? How could this view have influenced the Judeo-Christian world?

5. To which medieval tale does the author allude as a major influence in strengthening the cult of the Virgin Mary in Catholic Europe? Does his idea make sense to you? Is it plausible?

THE ISSUES

1. What difference does it make to society whether or not its citizens believe in the Devil? To what do you attribute all of the evil in our world today?

2. What is your interpretation of the cryptic ending in paragraph 40? Who is the gentleman referred to?

3. Which forces, according to the author, have been most effective in creating a collapse in the belief that a personal Devil exists? Do you agree or do you have a totally different opinion of the Devil's role today? Explain your opinion.

4. Do you believe, as do many preachers and talk-show hosts, that the morals in our country are at an all-time low? If you do, what suggestions do you have for creating in people a heightened sense of morality?

5. What do you consider the worst evil existing in our country today? Consider such factors as extreme poverty, ignorance, lack of compassion, hedonism, or materialism. How can any of these evils be lessened or eradicated?

SUGGESTIONS FOR WRITING

1. Write an essay in which you suggest your own definition of evil. As you develop your essay, keep in mind that you must answer the question, "What is evil?"

2. Write a brief, 300-word essay defining one of the following terms, taken from Wernick's essay. Be sure to clarify the term so that the average reader will know what it means.

   a. bowdlerization

   b. apocalypse

   c. poltergeist

   d. Persephone

   e. Persia

THE COMPANY MAN

Ellen Goodman

Ellen Goodman (b. 1941) is a Pulitzer Prize-winning newspaper colum-
nist and editor. Born in Newton, Massachusetts, Goodman is considered
part of the "Eastern Establishment," having graduated from Radcliffe
and having worked for the Boston Globe *since 1967. Her column, "At*
Large," *is eagerly read by thousands of fans, who praise her for having*
intelligence combined with common sense. She has published several
volumes of her columns, including Close to Home *(1975) and* Value
Judgments *(1993). She also authored the influential book* Turning
Points *(1979), in which she examines the changes in men and women's*
lives as a result of the feminist movement.

Like many essays that define, this one delivers a definition almost in passing.
The writer tells the sad story of a "company man" who literally worked himself
to death and in the process ends up defining the term *company man.* We have
all known company men and women, all of whom share a compulsive devotion
to work. Some of us know, if not from experience then from hearsay, company
men and women who have neglected family and friends for the job only to become ill or even to die from work-related stress.

$\sim$

1   He worked himself to death, finally and precisely, at 3:00 A.M. Sunday morning. The obituary didn't say that, of course. It said that he died of a coronary
thrombosis—I think that was it—but everyone among his friends and acquaintances knew it instantly. He was a perfect Type A, a workaholic, a classic, they said to each other and shook their heads—and thought for five or ten
minutes about the way they lived.

2   This man who worked himself to death finally and precisely at 3:00 A.M.
Sunday morning—on his day off—was fifty-one years old and a vice-
president. He was, however, one of six vice-presidents, and one of three who
might conceivably—if the president died or retired soon enough—have
moved to the top spot. Phil knew that.

3   He worked six days a week, five of them until eight or nine at night, during a time when his own company had begun the four-day week for everyone but the executives. He worked like the Important People. He had no
outside "extracurricular interests," unless, of course, you think about a
monthly golf game that way. To Phil, it was work. He always ate egg salad
sandwiches at his desk. He was, of course, overweight, by 20 or 25 pounds.
He thought it was okay, though, because he didn't smoke.

4   On Saturdays, Phil wore a sports jacket to the office instead of a suit, because it was the weekend.

5   He had a lot of people working for him, maybe sixty, and most of them liked him most of the time. Three of them will be seriously considered for his job. The obituary didn't mention that.

6   But it did list his "survivors" quite accurately. He is survived by his wife, Helen, forty-eight years old, a good woman of no particular marketable skills, who worked in an office before marrying and mothering. She had, according to her daughter, given up trying to compete with his work years ago, when the children were small. A company friend said, "I know how much you will miss him." And she answered, "I already have."

7   "Missing him all these years," she must have given up part of herself which had cared too much for the man. She would be "well taken care of."

8   His "dearly beloved" eldest of the "dearly beloved" children is a hardworking executive in a manufacturing firm down South. In the day and a half before the funeral, he went around the neighborhood researching his father, asking the neighbors what he was like. They were embarrassed.

9   His second child is a girl, who is twenty-four and newly married. She lives near her mother and they are close, but whenever she was alone with her father, in a car driving somewhere, they had nothing to say to each other.

10   The youngest is twenty, a boy, a high-school graduate who has spent the last couple of years, like a lot of his friends, doing enough odd jobs to stay in grass and food. He was the one who tried to grab at his father, and tried to mean enough to him to keep the man at home. He was his father's favorite. Over the last two years, Phil stayed up nights worrying about the boy.

11   The boy once said, "My father and I only board here."

12   At the funeral, the sixty-year-old company president told the forty-eight-year-old widow that the fifty-one-year-old deceased had meant much to the company and would be missed and would be hard to replace. The widow didn't look him in the eye. She was afraid he would read her bitterness and, after all, she would need him to straighten out the finances—the stock options and all that.

13   Phil was overweight and nervous and worked too hard. If he wasn't at the office, he was worried about it. Phil was a Type A, a heart attack natural. You could have picked him out in a minute from a lineup.

14   So when he finally worked himself to death, at precisely 3:00 A.M. Sunday morning, no one was really surprised.

〜

(678 words)

VOCABULARY

obituary (1)   conceivably (2)

THE FACTS

1. What was the exact time of Phil's death? How often is the time stated, and why?

2. The medical cause of Phil's death is given as "coronary thrombosis," but what was the real cause?

3. What is meant by the phrase (paragraph 3) "Important People"? Do you recognize these people in your own sphere?

4. What did the widow mean when she answered "I already have" when a friend said, "I know how much you will miss him"? (See paragraph 6.)

5. In paragraph 7, we are told that the widow would be "well taken care of." What is the meaning of this phrase?

THE STRATEGIES

1. What is the relationship of the title to the content of the essay? What synonyms for the title are mentioned in the essay?

2. What kind of evidence does the author use to support her definition? Cite specific examples from the text. After reading the essay, do you feel you know what a "company man" is? Give reasons for your answer.

3. What level of reading difficulty does this essay present? To what kinds of audiences would it appeal?

4. How do the opening and closing of the essay function rhetorically?

5. What is the purpose in quoting Phil's son in paragraph 11?

THE ISSUES

1. What familiar warning to modern America does this essay give? Do you believe that the warning is warranted, or is the author being too alarmist?

2. How do you suggest that an ambitious father reconcile his duties at work with his responsibility to family? Suggest specific steps to follow.

3. What can a family do to prevent the father's becoming too involved in his work?

4. Why is it that the second child, a girl, has nothing to say to her father? Does this situation seem realistic?

5. Why is the story of the youngest child particularly tragic? How could the tragedy have been prevented?

WRITING ASSIGNMENTS

1. Write an essay about your father or another man you know well. Try to capture the essence of his character and your relationship with him.

2. Following Goodman's style, write an essay titled *The Company Woman.* Use personal experiences or your own imagination to develop the examples.

IN PRAISE OF THE HUMBLE COMMA

Pico Iyer

Pico Iyer is a freelance writer and contributing editorial writer for Time. *He has also written numerous books about exotic places and countries, among them* The Lady and the Monk: Four Seasons in Kyoto *(1992),* Falling off the Map: Some Lonely Places of the World *(1994),* Cuba and the Light *(1996), and the recent* Global Soul: Jet Lag, Shopping Malls, and the Search for Directions *(2000).*

This essay appeared as the featured essay on the back page of *Time* (June 13, 1988). Its purpose is to define punctuation in general and the comma specifically. Iyer suggests that punctuation marks are highly underrated because they give writing elegance as well as clarity, often keeping it from becoming a jumble of words strung along on a page.

～

1 The gods, they say, give breath, and they take it away. But the same could be said—could it not?—of the humble comma. Add it to the present clause, and, all of a sudden, the mind is, quite literally, given pause to think; take it out if you wish or forget it and the mind is deprived of a resting place. Yet still the comma gets no respect. It seems just a slip of a thing, a pedant's tick, a blip on the edge of our consciousness, a kind of printer's smudge almost. Small, we claim, is beautiful (especially in the age of the microchip). Yet what is so often used, and so rarely recalled, as the comma—unless it be breath itself?

2 Punctuation, one is taught, has a point: to keep up law and order. Punctuation marks are the road signs placed along the highway of our communication—to control speeds, provide directions and prevent head-on collisions. A period has the unblinking finality of a red light; the comma is a flashing yellow light that asks us only to slow down; and the semicolon is a stop sign that tells us to ease gradually to a halt, before gradually starting up again. By establishing the relations between words, punctuation establishes the relations between the people using words. That may be one reason why schoolteachers exalt it and lovers defy it ("We love each other and belong to each other let's don't ever hurt each other Nicole let's don't ever hurt each other," wrote

Gary Gilmore to his girlfriend). A comma, he must have known, "separates inseparables," in the clinching words of H. W. Fowler, King of English Usage.

3   Punctuation, then, is a civic prop, a pillar that holds society upright. (A run-on sentence, its phrases piling up without division, is as unsightly as a sink piled high with dirty dishes.) Small wonder, then, that punctuation was one of the first proprieties of the Victorian age, the age of the corset, that the modernists threw off: the sexual revolution might be said to have begun when Joyce's Molly Bloom spilled out all her private thoughts in 36 pages of unbridled, almost unperioded and officially censored prose; and another rebellion was surely marked when E. E. Cummings first felt free to commit "God" to the lower case.

4   Punctuation thus becomes the signature of cultures. The hot-blooded Spaniard seems to be revealed in the passion and urgency of his doubled exclamation points and question marks ("¡Caramba! ¿Quien sabe?"), while the impassive Chinese traditionally added to his so-called inscrutability by omitting directions from his ideograms. The anarchy and commotion of the '60s were given voice in the exploding exclamation marks, riotous capital letters and Day-Glo italics of Tom Wolfe's spray-paint prose; and in Communist societies, where the State is absolute, the dignity—and divinity—of capital letters is reserved for Ministries, Sub-Committees and Secretariats.

5   Yet punctuation is something more than a culture's birthmark; it scores the music in our minds, gets our thoughts moving to the rhythm of our hearts. Punctuation is the notation in the sheet music of our words, telling us when to rest, or when to raise our voices; it acknowledges that the meaning of our discourse, as of any symphonic composition, lies not in the units but in the pauses, the pacing and the phrasing. Punctuation is the way one bats one's eyes, lowers one's voice or blushes demurely. Punctuation adjusts the tone and color and volume till the feeling comes into perfect focus: not disgust exactly, but distaste; not lust, or like, but love.

6   Punctuation, in short, gives us the human voice, and all the meanings that lie between the words. "You aren't young, are you?" loses its innocence when it loses the question mark. Every child knows the menace of a dropped apostrophe (the parent's "Don't do that" shifting into the more slowly enunciated "Do not do that"), and every believer, the ignominy of having his faith reduced to "faith." Add an exclamation point to "To be or not to be . . ." and the gloomy Dane has all the resolve he needs; add a comma, and the noble sobriety of "God save the Queen" becomes a cry of desperation bordering on double sacrilege.

7   Sometimes, of course, our markings may be simply a matter of aesthetics. Popping in a comma can be like slipping on the necklace that gives an outfit quiet elegance, or like catching the sound of running water that complements, as it completes, the silence of a Japanese landscape. When V. S. Naipaul, in his latest novel, writes, "He was a middle-aged man, with glasses," the first comma can seem a little precious. Yet it gives the description a spin, as well as a subtlety, that it otherwise lacks, and it shows that the glasses are not part of the middle-agedness, but something else.

8   Thus all these tiny scratches give us breadth and heft and depth. A world that has only periods is a world without inflections. It is a world without shade. It has a music without sharps and flats. It is a martial music. It has a jackboot rhythm. Words cannot bend and curve. A comma, by comparison, catches the gentle drift of the mind in thought, turning in on itself and back on itself, reversing, redoubling and returning along the course of its own sweet river music; while the semicolon brings clauses and thoughts together with all the silent discretion of a hostess arranging guests around her dinner table.

9   Punctuation, then, is a matter of care. Care for words, yes, but also, and more important, for what the words imply. Only a lover notices the small things: the way the afternoon light catches the nape of a neck, or how a strand of hair slips out from behind an ear, or the way a finger curls around a cup. And no one scans a letter so closely as a lover, searching for its small print, straining to hear its nuances, its gasps, its sighs and hesitations, poring over the secret messages that lie in every cadence. The difference between "Jane (whom I adore)" and "Jane, whom I adore," and the difference between them both and "Jane—whom I adore—" marks all the distance between ecstasy and heartache. "No iron can pierce the heart with such force as a period put at just the right place," in Isaac Babel's lovely words; a comma can let us hear a voice break, or a heart. Punctuation, in fact, is a labor of love. Which brings us back, in a way, to gods.

~

(1,115 words)

VOCABULARY

pedant (1)	proprieties (3)	inscrutability (4)
ideograms (4)	enunciated (6)	ignominy (6)
aesthetics (7)	heft (8)	inflections (8)
martial (8)	nuances (9)	

THE FACTS

1. How does Iyer define *punctuation*? Which definition seems most helpful, and which least? Give reasons for your answers.
2. The author never gives a formal definition of the comma. What reason can you offer for this omission?
3. What does the author mean when he suggests that punctuation is the "signature of cultures"?
4. In the author's view, how is punctuation related to music?

5. According to the author, what would writing be like if it were deprived of the comma?

THE STRATEGIES

1. Why does the author entitle his essay *In Praise of the Humble Comma* when most of the essay deals with punctuation in general?

2. What is the author's style in this essay? How effective do you consider it?

3. What is the author's tone when he uses the word "humble" in connection with the comma?

4. What technique does the author use in closing his essay? How effective is it?

5. How does the author establish coherence between paragraphs 5 and 6?

THE ISSUES

1. If the author is correct that punctuation is "the signature of cultures," then how would you define our culture in terms of the way we use punctuation?

2. In your own writing, which punctuation mark gives you the most trouble? Which do you find the most helpful?

3. Review paragraph 3. What is your reaction to the author's view that our modern age has thrown off the Victorian restrictions of punctuation? If the author's view is true, has our new freedom improved writing? Why or why not?

4. How important is it for students to learn how to write with care? Support your answer with reasons.

5. What examples can you provide to support Isaac Babel's opinion that "[n]o iron can pierce the heart with such force as a period put at just the right place"? Use your imagination to create appropriate sentences.

SUGGESTIONS FOR WRITING

1. Write an essay in which you create your own definition of *punctuation.*

2. Write an essay in which you either support or attack the author's view that punctuation is a matter of care for what words imply.

3. Write an essay in which you assign responsibility for teaching punctuation to the proper educational institution.

KITSCH

Gilbert Highet

*Gilbert Highet (1906–1978) was born in Glasgow, Scotland, educated at
the University of Glasgow and at Oxford, and became an American citizen in 1951. A classicist, Highet was known for his scholarly and critical writing, including* The Classical Tradition *(1949) and* The
Anatomy of Satire *(1962).*

You probably have had some experience with "kitsch" even if you do not know
what the word means. You may have friends or relatives whose furniture, cu-
rios, or even favorite books are clearly kitschy. Gilbert Highet draws mainly on
literary examples to define *kitsch*; but, as you shall see, the concept applies
to nearly all matters of bad taste.

~

1   If you have ever passed an hour wandering through an antique shop (not
looking for anything exactly, but simply looking), you must have noticed
how your taste gradually grows numb, and then—if you stay—becomes perverted. You begin to see unsuspected charm in those hideous pictures of
plump girls fondling pigeons, you develop a psychopathic desire for spinning wheels and cobblers' benches, you are apt to pay out good money for a
bronze statuette of Otto von Bismarck, with a metal hand inside a metal frock
coat and metal pouches under his metallic eyes. As soon as you take the
things home, you realize that they are revolting. And yet they have a sort of
horrible authority; you don't like them; you know how awful they are; but it
is a tremendous effort to drop them in the garbage, where they belong.

2   To walk along a whole street of antique shops—that is an experience which
shakes the very soul. Here is a window full of bulbous Chinese deities; here
is another littered with Zulu assagais, Indian canoe paddles, and horse pis-
tols which won't fire; the next shopfront is stuffed with gaudy Italian majolica
vases, and the next, even worse, with Austrian pottery—tiny ladies and gentlemen sitting on lace cushions and wearing lace ruffles, with every frill,
every wrinkle and reticulation translated into porcelain: pink; stiff; but fortunately not unbreakable. The nineteenth century produced an appalling
amount of junky art like this, and sometimes I imagine that clandestine underground factories are continuing to pour it out like illicit drugs.

3   There is a name for such stuff in the trade, a word apparently of Russian
origin, *kitsch:*[1] it means vulgar showoff, and it is applied to anything that took
a lot of trouble to make and is quite hideous.

4   It is paradoxical stuff, kitsch: It is obviously bad: so bad that you can
scarcely understand how any human being would spend days and weeks

---

[1]The Russian verb *keetcheetsya* means to be haughty and puffed up.

making it, and how anybody else would buy it and take it home and keep it and dust it and leave it to her heirs. It is terribly ingenious, and terribly ugly, and utterly useless; and yet it has one of the qualities of good art—which is that, once seen, it is not easily forgotten. Of course it is found in all the arts: think of Milan Cathedral, or the statues in Westminster Abbey, or Liszt's settings of Schubert songs. There is a lot of it in the United States—for instance, the architecture of Miami, Florida, and Forest Lawn Cemetery in Los Angeles. Many of Hollywood's most ambitious historical films are superb kitsch. Most Tin Pan Alley love songs are perfect 100 per cent kitsch.

5   There is kitsch in the world of books also. I collect it. It is horrible, but I enjoy it.

6   The gem of my collection is the work of the Irish novelist Mrs. Amanda McKittrick Ros, whose masterpiece, *Delina Delaney,* was published about 1900. It is a stirringly romantic tale, telling how Delina, a fisherman's daughter from Erin Cottage, was beloved by Lord Gifford, the heir of Columbia Castle, and—after many trials and even imprisonment—married him. The story is dramatic, not to say impossible; but it is almost lost to view under the luxuriant style. Here, for example, is a sentence in which Mrs. Ros explains that her heroine used to earn extra cash by doing needlework:

> She tried hard to assist in keeping herself a stranger to her poor old father's slight income by the use of the finest production of steel, whose blunt edge eyed the reely covering with marked greed, and offered its sharp dart to faultless fabrics of flaxen fineness.

Revolting, but distinctive: what Mr. Polly called "rockockyo" in manner. For the baroque vein, here is Lord Gifford saying goodby to his sweetheart:

> My darling virgin! my queen! my Delina! I am just in time to hear the toll of a parting bell strike its heavy weight of appalling softness against the weakest fibers of a heart of love, arousing and tickling its dormant action, thrusting the dart of evident separation deeper into its tubes of tenderness, and fanning the flame, already unextinguishable, into volumes of blaze.

Mrs. Ros had a remarkable command of rhetoric, and could coin an unforgettable phrase. She described her hero's black eyes as "glittering jet revolvers." When he became ill, she said he fell "into a state of lofty fever"—doubtless because commoners have high fever, but lords have lofty fever. And her reflections on the moral degeneracy of society have rarely been equaled, in power and penetration:

> Days of humanity, whither hast thou fled? When bows of compulsion, smiles for the deceitful, handshakes for the dogmatic, and welcome for the tool of power live under your objectionable, unambitious beat, not daring to be checked by the tongue of candour because the selfish world refuses to dispense with her rotten policies. The legacy of your forefathers, which involved equity, charity, reason, and godliness, is beyond the reach of their frivolous, mushroom

offspring—deceit, injustice, malice and unkindness—and is not likely to be cod-
iciled with traits of harmony so long as these degrading vices of mock ambition
fester the human heart.

Perhaps one reason I enjoy this stuff is because it so closely resembles a
typical undergraduate translation of one of Cicero's finest perorations: sound
and fury, signifying nothing. I regret only that I have never seen Mrs. Ros's
poetry. One volume was called *Poems of Puncture* and another *Bayonets of Bastard Sheen*: alas, jewels now almost unprocurable. But at least I know the
opening of her lyric written on first visiting St. Paul's Cathedral:

> Holy Moses, take a look,
> Brain and brawn in every nook!

7   Such genius is indestructible. Soon, soon now, some earnest researcher will
be writing a Ph.D. thesis on Mrs. Amanda McKittrick Ros, and thus (as she
herself might put it) conferring upon her dewy brow the laurels of concrete
immortality.

8   Next to Mrs. Ros in my collection of kitsch is the work of the Scottish poet
William McGonagall. This genius was born in 1830, but did not find his vo-
cation until 1877. Poor and inadequate poets pullulate in every tongue, but
(as the *Times Literary Supplement* observes) McGonagall "is the only truly
memorable bad poet in our language." In his command of platitude and his
disregard of melody, he was the true heir of William Wordsworth as a descriptive poet.

9   In one way his talents, or at least his aspirations, exceeded those of
Wordsworth. He was at his best in describing events he had never witnessed,
such as train disasters, shipwrecks, and sanguinary battles, and in picturing
magnificent scenery he had never beheld except with the eye of the imagination. Here is his unforgettable Arctic landscape:

> Greenland's icy mountains are fascinating and grand,
> And wondrously created by the Almighty's command;
> And the works of the Almighty there's few can understand:
> Who knows but it might be a part of Fairyland?
>
> Because there are churches of ice, and houses glittering
>   like glass,
> And for scenic grandeur there's nothing can it surpass,
> Besides there's monuments and spires, also ruins,
> Which serve for a safe retreat from the wild bruins.
>
> The icy mountains they're higher than a brig's topmast,
> And the stranger in amazement stands aghast
> As he beholds the water flowing off the melted ice
> Adown the mountain sides, that he cries out, Oh! how nice!

10   McGonagall also had a strong dramatic sense. He loved to tell of agonizing adventures, more drastic perhaps but not less moving than that related in

Wordsworth's "Vaudracour and Julia." The happy ending of one of his "Gothic" ballads is surely unforgettable:

> So thus ends the story of Hanchen, a heroine brave,
> That tried hard her master's gold to save,
> And for her bravery she got married to the miller's eldest
>   son,
> And Hanchen on her marriage night cried Heaven's will be
>   done.

11   These scanty selections do not do justice to McGonagall's ingenuity as a rhymester. His sound effects show unusual talent. Most poets would be baffled by the problem of producing rhymes for the proper names General Graham and Osman Digna, but McGonagall gets them into a single stanza, with dazzling effect:

> Ye sons of Great Britain, I think no shame
> To write in praise of brave General Graham!
> Whose name will be handed down to posterity without any
>   stigma,
> Because, at the battle of El-Tab, he defeated Osman Digna.

12   One of McGonagall's most intense personal experiences was his visit to New York. Financially, it was not a success. In one of his vivid autobiographical sketches, he says, "I tried occasionally to get an engagement from theatrical proprietors and music-hall proprietors, but alas! 'twas all in vain, for they all told me they didn't encourage rivalry." However, he was deeply impressed by the architecture of Manhattan. In eloquent verses he expressed what many others have felt, although without adequate words to voice their emotion:

> Oh! Mighty City of New York, you are wonderful to
>   behold,
> Your buildings that magnificent, the truth be it told;
> They were the only thing that seemed to arrest my eye,
> Because many of them are thirteen stories high.
>
> And the tops of the houses are all flat,
> And in the warm weather the people gather to chat;
> Besides on the house-tops they dry their clothes,
> And also many people all night on the house-tops repose.

13   Yet McGonagall felt himself a stranger in the United States. And here again his close kinship with Wordsworth appears. The Poet Laureate, in a powerful sonnet written at Calais, once reproached the English Channel for delaying his return by one of those too frequent storms in which (reckless tyrant!) it will indulge itself:

> Why cast ye back upon the Gallic shore,
> Ye furious waves! a patriotic Son
> Of England?

In the same vein McGonagall sings with rapture of his return to his "ain countree":

> And with regard to New York, and the sights I did see,
> One street in Dundee is more worth to me,
> And, believe me, the morning I sailed from New York,
> For bonnie Dundee—my heart it felt as light as a cork.

15   Indeed, New York is a challenging subject for ambitious poets. Here, from the same shelf, is a delicious poem on the same theme, by Ezra Pound:

> My City, my beloved
> Thou art a maid with no breasts
> Thou art slender as a silver reed.
> Listen to me, attend me!
> And I will breathe into thee a soul,
> And thou shalt live for ever.

16   The essence of this kind of trash is incongruity. The kitsch writer is always sincere. He really means to say something important. He feels he has a lofty spiritual message to bring to an unawakened world, or else he has had a powerful experience which he must communicate to the public. But either his message turns out to be a majestic platitude, or else he chooses the wrong form in which to convey it—or, most delightful of all, there is a fundamental discrepancy between the writer and his subject, as when Ezra Pound, born in Idaho, addresses the largest city in the world as a maid with no breasts, and enjoins it to achieve inspiration and immortality by listening to him. This is like climbing Mount Everest in order to carve a head of Mickey Mouse in the east face.

17   Bad love poetry, bad religious poetry, bad mystical prose, bad novels both autobiographical and historical—one can form a superb collection of kitsch simply by reading with a lively and awakened eye. College songs bristle with it. The works of Father Divine[2] are full of it—all the more delightful because in him it is usually incomprehensible. One of the Indian mystics, Sri Ramakrishna, charmed connoisseurs by describing the Indian scriptures (in a phrase which almost sets itself to kitsch-music) as fried in the butter of knowledge and steeped in the honey of love.

Bad funeral poetry is a rich mine of the stuff. Here, for example, is the opening of a jolly little lament, "The Funeral" by Stephen Spender, apparently written during his pink period:

> Death is another milestone on their way,
> With laughter on their lips and with winds blowing round
>   Them
> They record simply
> How this one excelled all others in making driving belts.

Observe the change from humanism to communism. Spender simply took Browning's "Grammarian's Funeral," threw away the humor and the marching rhythm, and substituted wind and the Stakhanovist[3] speed-up. Such also

---

[2] A black evangelist of New York.—Ed.

[3] Alexei Stakhanov, a Russian miner who devised a worker incentive system.—Ed.

is a delicious couplet from Archibald MacLeish's elegy on the late Harry Crosby:

> He walks with Ernest in the streets in Saragossa
> They are drunk their mouths a.re hard they saw qué cosa.

18   From an earlier romantic period, here is a splendid specimen. Coleridge attempted to express the profound truth that men and animals are neighbors in a hard world; but he made the fundamental mistake of putting it into a monologue address to a donkey:

> Poor Ass! Thy master should have learnt to show
> Pity—best taught by fellowship of Woe!
> Innocent foal! thou poor despised forlorn!
> I hail thee brother. . . .

19

Once you get the taste for this kind of thing it is possible to find pleasure in hundreds of experiences which you might otherwise have thought either anesthetic or tedious: bad translations, abstract painting, grand opera. . .Dr. Johnson, with his strong sense of humor, had a fancy for kitsch, and used to repeat a poem in celebration of the marriage of the Duke of Leeds, composed by "an inferiour domestick. . .in such homely rhimes as he could make":

> When the Duke of Leeds shall married be
> To a fine young lady of high quality,
> How happy will that gentlewoman be
> In his Grace of Leed's good company.
>
> She shall have all that's fine and fair,
> And the best of silk and sattin shall wear;
> And ride in a coach to take the air,
> And have a house in St. James's Square.

20

Folk poetry is full of such jewels. Here is the epitaph on an old gentleman from Vermont who died in a sawmill accident:

> How shocking to the human mind
> The log did him to powder grind.
> God did command his soul away
> His summings we must all obey.

21

Kitsch is well known in drama, although (except for motion pictures) it does not usually last long. One palmary instance was a play extolling the virtues of the Boy Scout movement, called *Young England*. It ran for a matter of years during the 1930's, to audiences almost wholly composed of kitsch-fanciers, who eventually came to know the text quite as well as the unfortunate actors. I can still remember the opening of one magnificent episode. Scene: a woodland glade. Enter the hero, a Scoutmaster, riding a bicycle, and followed by the youthful members of his troop. They pile bicycles in silence.

Then the Scoutmaster raises his finger, and says (accompanied fortissimo by most of the members of the audience):

> Fresh water must be our first consideration.

22   In the decorative arts kitsch flourishes, and is particularly widespread in sculpture. One of my favorite pieces of bad art is a statue in Rockefeller Center, New York. It is supposed to represent Atlas, the Titan condemned to carry the sky on his shoulders. That is an ideal of somber, massive tragedy: greatness and suffering combined as in Hercules or Prometheus. But this version displays Atlas as a powerful moron, with a tiny little head, rather like the pan-fried young men who appear in the health magazines. Instead of supporting the heavens, he is lifting a spherical metal balloon: it is transparent, and quite empty; yet he is balancing insecurely on one foot like a furniture mover walking upstairs with a beach ball; and he is scowling like a mad baboon. If he ever gets the thing up, he will drop it; or else heave it onto a Fifth Avenue bus. It is a supremely ridiculous statue, and delights me every time I see it.

23   Perhaps you think this is a depraved taste. But really it is an extension of experience. At one end, Homer. At the other, Amanda McKittrick Ros. At one end, Hamlet. At the other, McGonagall, who is best praised in his own inimitable words:

> The poetry is moral and sublime
> And in my opinion nothing could be more fine.
> True genius there does shine so bright
> Like unto the stars of night.

~

(2,816 words)

VOCABULARY

psychopathic (1)	frock coat (1)	bulbous (2)
Zulu (2)	assagais (2)	majolica (2)
reticulation (2)	appalling (2)	illicit (2)
paradoxical (4)	ingenious (4)	luxuriant (6)
perorations (6)	unprocurable (6)	pullulate (8)
platitude (8)	sanguinary (9)	rapture (14)
incongruity (16)	enjoins (16)	mystical (17)
incomprehensible (17)	connoisseurs (17)	anesthetic (19)
palmary (21)	extolling (21)	fortissimo (21)
spherical (22)	depraved (23)	inimitable (23)

THE FACTS

1. Where in his essay does Highet give a succinct definition of *kitsch?* After reading the essay, how would you explain this term to a friend who has never heard it?

2. What examples of kitsch does Highet provide? Name the three that impressed you most. Give reasons for your choice.

3. What metaphor does Mrs. Ros use to describe her hero's black eyes? Provide a metaphor or simile that would not be kitsch.

4. What characteristics of William McGonagall's poetry make it kitsch? Give a brief critique of two or three excerpts reprinted by Highet.

5. What is the essence of kitsch, according to the author? In what paragraph is this essence revealed?

THE STRATEGIES

1. What is the predominant tone of the essay? Supply appropriate examples of this tone.

2. Point out some examples of striking figurative language in the essay. Are they serious or humorous?

3. What mode of development does Highet use more than any other? How does this method help his definition?

4. In the final paragraph, what is the irony of using McGonagall's own words to praise him?

THE ISSUES

1. Can you think of some well-known examples of kitsch in the United States besides those cited by Highet? What makes them kitsch?

2. Highet admits that certain kitsch items delight him. Explain how a person of taste might feel such delight.

3. How do you explain the overwhelming popularity of kitsch?

4. Popular lyrics are always a good source of kitsch. What lines from one of today's well-known songs can you quote as an example of kitsch? Do you still like the song even though it is kitsch? Give reasons for your answer.

5. Following are excerpts from two love poems (A and B). Which of them might be considered kitsch? Why?

A.

The time was long and long ago,
    And we were young, my dear;
The place stands fair in memory's glow,
    But it is far from here.

The springtimes fade, the summers come,
    Autumn is here once more;
The voice of ecstasy is dumb,
    The world goes forth to war.

But though the flowers and birds were dead,
    And all the hours we knew,
And though a hundred years had fled,
    I'd still come back to you.

B.

Ah, love, let us be true
To one another! for the world, which seems
To lie before us like a land of dreams,
So various, so beautiful, so new,
Hath really neither joy, nor love, nor light,
Nor certitude, nor peace, nor help for pain;
And we are here as on a darkling plain
Swept with confused alarms of struggle and flight,
Where ignorant armies clash by night.

SUGGESTIONS FOR WRITING

1. Using Gilbert Highet's definition of kitsch, choose one area of popular taste today and show how it fits the definition.

2. Write a paragraph in which you compare or contrast the meaning of *camp* with that of *kitsch.*

ARS POETICA

Archibald MacLeish

Archibald MacLeish (1892–1982), poet and playwright, was born in Glencoe, Illinois, and educated at Yale University. Trained as a lawyer, MacLeish served as librarian of Congress and as an adviser to President Franklin D. Roosevelt. A recurrent theme in his poetry was his deep apprehension about the rise of fascism. MacLeish won a Pulitzer Prize for a poetry collection, Conquistador *(1932), and another for his play* J. B. *(1958).*

In this famous poem, MacLeish proposes a succinct definition of poetry. The poem comes from a collection of poems spanning the years 1917 to 1982.

~

1 A poem should be palpable and mute
As a globed fruit,

Dumb
As old medallions to the thumb,

5 Silent as the sleeve-worn stone
Of casement ledges where the moss has grown—

A poem should be wordless
As the flight of birds.

A poem should be motionless in time
10 As the moon climbs,

Leaving, as the moon releases
Twig by twig the night-entangled trees,

Leaving, as the moon behind the winter leaves,
Memory by memory the mind—
15 A poem should be motionless in time
As the moon climbs.

A poem should be equal to:
Not true

For all the history of grief
20 An empty doorway and a maple leaf.

For love
The leaning grasses and two lights above the sea—

A poem should not mean
But be.

~

(144 words)

VOCABULARY

palpable (1)   medallions (4)   casement (6)

THE FACTS

1. The translation of the poem's Latin title is "The Art of Poetry." Why is the title in Latin? How does the title relate to the poem?

2. Where does MacLeish give an explicit definition of poetry? How does he convey to the reader what poetry is?

3. In lines 17 and 18, what does MacLeish mean by the words "equal to: /Not true"?

4. The final stanza contains MacLeish's summarized view of poetry. What is your interpretation of the stanza?

THE STRATEGIES

1. *Ars Poetica* is developed through a series of paradoxes. Analyze and interpret each.

2. MacLeish suggests that all the history of grief could be summarized by "an empty doorway and a maple leaf." Do you consider this an appropriate image? Can you suggest another equally appropriate image?

3. What image does MacLeish suggest for love? Do you find this image appropriate? Explain.

4. What synonyms for *mute* does the poet use? Cite them all.

5. What is the significance of repeating the fifth stanza in the eighth stanza?

THE ISSUES

1. What are some other definitions of *poetry*? What is your own definition? How does it compare to or contrast with MacLeish's definition?

2. How do you interpret MacLeish's statement that "A poem should be equal to / Not true"? Provide an example to clarify this statement.

3. What does the author mean when he writes in stanza 4 that "A poem should be wordless / As the flight of birds"? How does this statement relate to Highet's notion of kitsch? (See Highet's essay on pages 382–388.)

4. Find a short poem that, in your view, perfectly exemplifies MacLeish's view that a poem should "not mean / But be." Do you like this poem? Why or why not?

SUGGESTIONS FOR WRITING

1. Consult a collection of the works of Wordsworth, Coleridge, Keats, or Shelley, for a definition of poetry. Contrast that definition with the one in *Ars Poetica*. State which definition you like best and why.

2. Write a paragraph in which you give a definition of *love*, and support that definition with appropriate images. Then write another paragraph in which you do the same thing for *hate*.

───── ISSUE FOR CRITICAL ─────
THINKING AND DEBATE
GLOBAL WARMING

Global warming has become a hot topic lately, and there's no end in sight to the debate. The problem is that solid evidence is hard to come by and what there is of it is greeted with wildly differing interpretations. It is difficult for industrial nations to admit that the emissions of their factories and machines might be poisoning the entire world. Such admissions irk conservatives, who like to sectionalize the world in separate spheres of *us* and *them,* not think of it in terms of the "one boat" metaphor that liberals seem to love.

Yet, that we are all in the same boat is a fact of our collective lives. A nuclear blast in China, if immense enough, will affect the atmosphere of air-breathers in Iowa. Radiation leakage in India has the potential to destroy life a continent and an ocean away. We do not need pictures from satellites to tell us the obvious—that all human life is riding on the same ball of dirt adrift in the same ocean of space.

What is new about the global warming debate is that, for the first time in the history of humankind, individual nations have the capacity and the power to rock the global boat. Before, the idea of one nation or even a coalition of nations doing something to affect all the earth would be as preposterous as thinking that the weight of a single person could capsize the Titanic. But with nuclear power and the industrial might of the developed nations, our ship can not only be rocked, it is already rocking.

Two writers give us their opinion on this troubling subject. Mike Toner warns us that recent research demonstrates that ice sheets in the Arctic and Antarctic are melting at an alarming rate and posing the threat of flooding to many distant countries. The dissenting point of view is presented by Andrew Mercy, whose reply—*Global Warning and other Tales*—is dismissive. These two pieces, taken together, show how far apart we are on this issue. The famous paintings by Diego Rivera, on page 394, reminds us that industry is a powerful and relentless contributor to environmental decay, and the photo of smoke stacks on page 397 reinforces this unpleasant truth.

GLACIAL MELT IN GREENLAND CAUSES ALARM

Mike Toner

Mike Toner is an award-winning journalist who writes for the Atlanta Constitution. *In 1993, he won the Pulitzer prize for explanatory journalism.*

～

1 Greenland's glaciers, which had been expected to respond very slowly to global warming, are sliding toward the ocean faster than anticipated, NASA scientists reported Thursday. Coupled with recent evidence that Greenland's ice cover has been thinning rapidly in recent years, the findings add new urgency to the simmering political debate over Earth's changing climate.

Diego M. Rivera, Detroit Industry, North Wall *(detail) 1932–1933. Diego M. Rivera. Gift of Edsel B. Ford. Photograph © 1991 The Detroit Institute of Arts.*

2   Because Greenland contains 10 percent of the Earth's ice—enough to raise the sea level by nearly 20 feet if it all melted—scientists have been watching closely the island's response to increasing global temperatures.

3   Over the past 15 years, they have seen increased summer melting on the surface of the ice, but until now, it was expected that it would take centuries, perhaps thousands of years, for the warmer surface temperatures to speed the ice streams' movement toward the sea.

4   Now, in a report in the journal *Science,* scientists at NASA's Goddard Spaceflight Center in Greenbelt, Md., say water melting on the surface of Greenland's glaciers during the summer seeps swiftly through crevasses to bedrock, a half-mile or more below the ice surface. There, it acts as a lubricant, reducing the friction between the ice and the underlying rock—in effect greasing the skids for the glacier's journey to the sea.

5   "Previous models suggested that it might take hundreds, even thousands of years for changes in an ice sheet's surface to be felt at its base," said NASA glaciologist H. Jay Zwally. "This shows that summer melting can accelerate ice flow in a matter of weeks."

6   During the warmer-than-normal summers of 1998 and 1999, Zwally and his colleagues found that water seeping through one glacier more than doubled the speed of the ice. By the time Greenland's summer ended, the glacier had moved 18 feet.

7   "This effect has never been observed in ice sheets before," Zwally said. "It shows that large expanses of ice like this respond to climate warming faster than expected."

8   The latest report dovetails with earlier NASA satellite measurements showing that some of Greenland's outlet glaciers, which drain the mile-thick ice sheet into the sea, have thinned by as much as 30 feet since 1995.

9   Airborne laser measurements show that the ice sheet is losing 11 cubic miles of ice a year.

10   The changes in Greenland's ice sheet reflect only the change in climate there—not the causes of it—but NASA's latest findings come at a time when the politics of global warming also is heating up.

11   This week Japan became the 74th nation to ratify the 1997 Kyoto Protocol, an international accord that aims to reduce emissions of heat-trapping greenhouse gases, which come mostly from burning coal and oil. The 15-nation European Union ratified the treaty last week.

12   The Bush administration has cited uncertainty about the causes of climate change as a reason not to ratify the treaty. But last week it sent a report to the United Nations acknowledging human activity as a major cause of the problem. Still, Bush reiterated his opposition to the Kyoto treaty as a threat to America's economy.

13   Meanwhile, Australia, one of the world's largest coal-producing nations, announced this week that it would not sign the treaty unless the United States and developing nations took stronger action against global warming.

14   Greenland isn't the only harbinger of a warmer world. The United Nations Environment Program reported this week that the Himalayan glacier used during Sir Edmund Hillary's conquest of Mount Everest in 1953 has retreated three miles up the mountain.

15   There also are growing signs this year that Antarctica, Earth's largest repository of ice, is feeling the effects of global warming. Because temperatures are well below freezing throughout the year, Antarctica's interior ice cap is intact, but the continent's fringe of ice shelves has been disintegrating at what researchers say is a record rate.

16   Earlier this year, a 1,250-square mile section of the 600-foot thick Larsen B ice shelf collapsed in only 35 days, sending thousands of icebergs adrift in the Weddell Sea.

17   Glaciologists say the continued loss of Antarctica's ice shelves could hasten the flow of its now landlocked glaciers into the sea and rapidly increase global sea levels.

18   New research shows that the thick glaciers of Greenland are more susceptible to global warming than previously thought. Water from surface melting can flow down through the ice, speeding movement to the ocean.

VOCABULARY

crevasses (4)	bedrock (4)	lubricant (4)
glaciologist (5)	dovetails (8)	laser (9)
emissions (11)	greenhouse (11)	harbinger (14)
susceptible (18)		

THE FACTS

1. What other ice surfaces, besides the one in Greenland, are melting more rapidly than expected?

2. Why is it important to note that Greenland's ice cover is melting so rapidly?

3. What is the ultimate disaster that could occur as a result of global warming? Why is this disaster never mentioned by name in the essay?

4. How do previous models of changes in an ice sheet's surface differ from more recent models? How significant is the difference?

5. Who is H. Jay Zwally? How well is he qualified to comment on the matter of global warming?

THE STRATEGIES

1. Where does the author propose his thesis? What is the advantage of this placement?

2. Why does the author provide a detailed description of how the water can seep through crevasses to bedrock a half-mile or more below the ice surface?

3. Why does the author refer to the 1997 Kyoto Protocol? How is it related to the thesis of the essay?

4. Why is President George W. Bush alluded to in the essay? Does the author consider President Bush a friend or enemy to the cause of global warming?

5. What figurative images does the author use to make his language more vivid? Choose two or three and evaluate their contribution to the style of the essay.

THE ISSUES

1. What is the simmering debate over the earth's changing climate? Why does the debate often take place in the political arena? Do you think it belongs in politics? Give reasons for your answer.

2. Do you agree that what is happening in Greenland is important to the future of our earth? How high a priority should this problem receive? Give reasons for your answer.

3. Do you think the government of the United States is doing a good job of taking care of our environment? What are the positive moves it has made? What more could it do?

4. What role should the United States play in controlling the problem of global warming? Should it be an example? Should it lead? Should it stay out of the international debate concerning global warming?

5. What problem in our country should receive the most attention from our government? If it is not global warming, then what is it? How do you personally plan to help resolve this problem?

Smoke rising from industrial smoke stacks. Copyright © Chris Corrie/Index Stock Imagery.

SUGGESTIONS FOR WRITING

1. Focusing on a serious problem affecting our society, formulate a thesis about the problem and develop an essay to support your thesis. Try to convince your reader that this problem needs to be addressed and solved.

2. Write an essay in which you either back Toner's view of global warming or you consider his view one of doom saying.

GLOBAL WARMING AND OTHER TALES

Andrew Mercy

Andrew Mercy is a columnist for the University of California, Davis, newspaper, The Aggie.

~

1 One of the greatest threats to freedom and academic integrity is the politicization of scientific research and censorship. These two actions work hand-in-hand to rewrite the past, and even the present, to fit modern political agendas and silence the opposing viewpoint.

2   Unfortunately, this takes place on a university campus like ours more than elsewhere, threatening the academic freedom of everyone. There are numerous examples of this at the University of California-Davis and other campuses.

3   Perhaps the best example is the Chicken Little notion of global warming. Much like the doom-and-gloom theories on acid rain in the 1970s, global warming proponents are beginning to lose support for the idea that lacks any hard scientific evidence whatsoever.

4   More and more real scientific research has been conducted to debunk the threat of global warming as mere hysteria. The number of papers being published by geologists and meteorologists that find the variances in global temperatures and ozone layer to be natural and regulated by the Earth's atmosphere, not mankind, have increased.

5   In a March 2001 study out of the Massachusetts Institute of Technology, researchers found that certain types of clouds serve as a "heat vent" that releases any excess atmospheric heat into space. This contradicts the idea that the Earth is overheating due to industrial pollution.

6   Further, a study out of Harvard University found that the rise and fall of the Earth's temperatures align almost exactly with peaks and crests in the sun's magnetic field, again taking away credence to the pseudo-scientific view that global warming is an imminent threat.

7   If this is all true, why then do Greenies and environmental activists continue to promote their fading theories? At a university campus, the answer is simple: money.

8   An exorbitant amount of money each year is poured into scientific research from public and private sources. Many environmental researchers live off of global warming research, and as long as they can keep those checks coming, the academic establishment will oppose any effort to conduct balanced research.

9   Academic research is a vital part of university life, and academic freedom must be protected. Evidence that disproves profitable research should not be stifled in an effort to please left-wing faculty or to increase funding. These researchers know that scaring investors with a threat of something like global warming is a great way to get funding. If that threat is disproven, it becomes that much harder to attract funds.

10 While global warming is a prominent example of corruption in academia, it is not the only one. A few weeks ago *The Aggie* had a report as to how research out of UC Davis showed that moderate consumption of beer, not just wine, provides a cardiovascular health benefit.

11 Following that publication, there were letters to the editor complaining about alcoholism and that the initial article should not have been printed. The mere fact that some people abuse alcohol is no reason to stifle scientific evidence that responsible consumption can be a good thing.

12 Science and politics ought to be separate, but are seldom apart. It is the duty of every individual involved in academia to question whether their actions are based on curiosity or a political agenda.

∼

(538 words)

VOCABULARY

integrity (1)	politicization (1)	debunk (4)
hysteria (4)	ozone (4)	credence (6)
exorbitant (8)	prominent (10)	academia (10)
cardiovascular (10)		

THE FACTS

1. What, according to the author, is one of the greatest threats to academic integrity? Explain the threat as best you understand it.

2. What is the author's opinion of global warming? Do you agree with him?

3. According to the essay, what contradicts the view that the earth is overheating due to industrial pollution? Does the evidence presented seem convincing? Why or why not?

4. In the author's view, what is the simple reason so many Greenies and environmental activists continue to promote disproved theories? Is the author being fair in his accusation? Could other reasons exist? If so, what are they?

5. What force should motivate the actions of people at academic institutions? If this motivational force is not present, what negative effects could these people's actions have on society?

THE STRATEGIES

1. What metaphor does the author use to illustrate his accusation that the politicization of scientific research and censorship are threatening freedom and academic integrity? How effective is the metaphor?

2. What evidence does the author use to support his basic thesis? List the most important.

3. Paragraph 7 is the shortest paragraph in the essay. How does this brevity affect the paragraph's usefulness?

4. How does paragraph 9 provide insight into the author's own political views? Do you think these political views might affect his slant on global warming?

5. What is the purpose of the final paragraph?

THE ISSUES

1. How important do you consider the issue of global warming? What other issues, if any, do you consider more important? Explain your answer.

2. Which sources do you trust most when it comes to analyzing a social problem? In giving your answer, consider such sources as your teacher, your minister, priest or rabbi, a government representative, your parents, prestigious institutions of research, and the press.

3. What is your response to the report, mentioned in paragraph 10, that a moderate consumption of beer provides a cardiovascular health benefit?

4. The author refers to the belief in global warming as "pseudo-scientific." What is his motive in using this label? Is he being fair or prejudiced? Give reasons for your answer.

5. What criteria would you set up for yourself to avoid making decisions based on a political agenda? List the criteria.

SUGGESTIONS FOR WRITING

1. Write an essay offering your own view of global warming. Be sure to introduce expert opinions and other convincing evidence.

2. Using the Internet as a resource, summarize four essays that offer differing points of view on global warming.

—————— STUDENT CORNER ——————

1

Final Draft

Saving Life on Earth—It Doesn't Take an Education

Michèle Izzo, University of Maryland

Ecosystem, ecologically sound, biological diversity, global warming, chlorofluorocarbons, biosphere, ozone depletion. . .It seems as if we've added a lot of new terms to our vocabulary that are supposed to mean something to us in our everyday lives. In fact, admitting ignorance about their exact meaning would be very unfashionable. But what do all of these vogue words mean? Everywhere we look, information is dispersed on recycling, tropical rain forests, endangered species, greenhouse pollution, and toxic waste. We live in an age when the Vice-President of the United States has authored a national bestseller, *Earth in the Balance*, summarizing the state of the world environment today and giving thoughtful and concrete solutions to the environmental crisis. At the county public library recently, an informational brochure on composting lay beside one on how to deal with the pesky white-tailed neighborhood deer. Those aiming to maintain balance on the earth are at odds with those wishing to "simplify" our lives. Plastic is big business; reusing containers is not. To some it seems being environmentally conscious adds complexity and labor to our day. However, we don't have to keep abreast of the latest ecological crisis and political solution; we don't need to know the definition of all those ecological terms. We simply need to have common sense, a hate of waste, and a sense of caring. Our life is simplified when we respect life.

Izzo 2

The sudden rise in popularity of the environment in the last ten years is surprising. Surely the environment and the study of ecology existed before. It takes a disruption in the climate and the atmosphere, and a contamination of the seas to make people change old habits in order to fend off the crises which some have called the result of "The Earth fighting back." Are we suddenly enlightened into making the world a better place? No. While a few people hold themselves accountable to ensure a world fit for the future, most contribute to environmental abuse. The destruction we have caused should never have happened. Few fields of study can visibly be affected and changed by ordinary people like you and me. We can't change history; we can't suggest new answers to our mathematical problems; and we can't create new sentence structures, verb conjugations and spellings for the English language. The principles of physics remain the same, and the basic human anatomy does not transform. We can add new titles to the literary canon, but we can't change the content of the books we read. Ecology, however, is something that you and I and the guy next door can affect. We can change its course.

Some of us feel powerless in front of the magnitude of environmental disasters. We fail to make decisions with the environment in mind because we feel one person can't make a difference. Or we join the recycling efforts because we have to or because everyone else is joining, and we don't want to trail fashion. On the one hand, taking measures to preserve life on earth is trendy; on the other hand, people who recycle systematically or who crusade actively for the conservation of natural habitats and rare species are considered radical or fanatical, even miserly.

Izzo 3

Practical handbooks and videos have emerged on how to save the planet, suggesting, for example, 750 ways you can help clean up the earth, 50 simple things you can do to save the earth, 101 easy things you can do to save the animals, and 10 ways to save life's diversity. But wonderful as these are, you and I don't have the time to read them and calculate strategies to save the earth, nor do we have the funds to make charitable contributions to the World Wildlife Fund or the Nature Conservancy to enable them to do it for us.

Without knowing that styrofoam contains Benzene (a carcinogen) and gases which deplete the earth's vital ozone layer, common sense should keep us away from the unsightly, cumbersome white stuff. How could spraying chemicals from a can "freshen" the air? If something comes in a container labeled "hazardous," what makes it okay to toss it down the drain or to pour it onto the ground only to contaminate our drinking water? Why would we want to buy plastic bags when stores supply bags for each item purchased, no matter the size. Even so called biodegradable plastic will never completely disappear and often ends up in the ocean killing marine life. The ink on plastic bags contains the heavy metal toxic cadmium. Common sense dictates: "Bring canvas bags when you shop." While we leave the faucet running to brush our teeth, wash dishes, or shave, surely we don't assume the sink is a magical fountain sending the same water flowing back through? We don't need to know that a running faucet uses five gallons of water per minute to recognize the waste and instead fill a small basin and turn the faucet off. The thought of bleached coffee filters or flour should be enough to halt our appetite without knowing that the process of bleaching produces the deadly toxin dioxin which is dumped in America's waterways. We don't need to be told that many tropical forest plants have important medicinal and commercial uses in order to desire their conservation. We don't need a list of the 500 most endangered species to want to preserve their lives.

The real life of the heroes of our fiction—the wolves in *Dances with Wolves*, *White Fang*, the killer whales in *Free Willy*, *Orca*, the orangutan in the Clint Eastwood movies, the gorillas, the humpback whales—is not always romantic as these creatures are threatened by habitat loss, logging, international pet or animal parts trade, poaching, and carelessness by humans. It is unconscionable to subject animals to torture, maiming, and even death in order to find the right shade of golden blonde hair color, the right creamy texture of wineberry lipstick, the right scent of dandruff shampoo. Yet we are unconscionable when we purchase products from companies who practice animal testing.

When I was in high school, I always confused the word *ecology* with *agronomy*. I had a friend who was majoring in one or the other and to this day I don't know which one his degree is in. Yet in my family we always washed, saved, and reused containers. We always enjoyed the careful unwrapping of a gift and saved the paper for the following year. We never served our meals on paper or plastic. We always used, washed, and reused a cloth instead of tearing endless sheets of paper towels or wetwipes. We always bought large containers with little packaging rather than individually packaged products. We did this without thought or effort because we cared for life and despised waste. Human selfishness and greed have resulted in ever-increasing production,

Izzo 5

unlimited consumption, and depletion of nonrenewable resources. Leading a simple, wholesome lifestyle where people do not step on a treadmill of unbridled overconsumption needs to be advocated.

We don't need to be a throw-away society. Not only will recycling and avoiding items which contain toxins save us money individually, it will save our resources, our atmosphere, and most importantly, our lives. It does not take a workshop on recycling, a visit to the local aquarium, or an array of ecological knowledge; it takes individual common sense and caring. Eventually it has to come down to character. Albert Schweitzer, who believed in the sanctity of life, wrote, "A man is truly ethical only when he obeys the compulsion to help all life which he is able to assist, and shrinks from injuring anything that lives."

How I Write

Because I am gregarious, I like writing with people around me. Although I am easily distracted by the sounds of television, loud music, or incidental conversation (even smells hinder my concentration), talking with friends fuels rather than cools my inspiration to write. If I have a writing project to complete, one of my most successful strategies is to call up a friend and ask him or her to have dinner with me. In the restaurant, I will explain my task and suggest several ideas I have been incubating. Rather than using friends to give me ideas or state approval or disapproval, I use them as sounding boards. I suppose one could say that I am using their presence as an opportunity to run my ideas by me. Not only does this strategy serve as a brainstorming technique, but I actually do some of the writing right there on the spot—on a napkin if I neglected to bring paper.

Other times the setting is more spontaneous: I'm not planning to write nor am I seeking inspiration, but the situation—usually a room with several people in it talking—spurs me on, and I jot down words and sentences that I later merge into a written piece. The topic may or may not be related to the conversation at hand.

How I Wrote this Essay

I brainstormed in my usual manner, talking aloud in the presence of people—although this time it didn't help. (My favorite dinner friend has moved to California.) Then I turned on my laptop and between baby cries and baby feedings (I am a new mother), I typed in phrases and ideas as they popped into my head. I made a quick trip to my local library to get a list of titles that are out there to advise the general public on ecological matters. Then I sat and typed for a couple of hours. With a multitude of ideas bouncing around in my head, I had the hardest time with choosing a definite purpose. Should I define all of the ecosystems and list every possible area of crisis? Should I preach recycling and conservation? Should I list ways to save life on earth? In the end, I focused on what has always amazed me about all the environmental talk—people's indifference. If people only cared and used common sense, most of our environmental crisis would not exist. We should not have needed to be educated in the first place. I hope this approach comes across as the thesis of my essay. I tried to show that ecology is a very simple matter and that we don't even need to know what the word means. The easy part of completing this assignment was that the topic is one about which I had strong feelings; I cared about it. That is important when writing.

My Writing Tip

People often do not know how to end an essay or a report. I find it helpful to ask, "So what?" at the end of the essay. Now that you've proven what you set out to do as stated in your thesis, so what? What difference does it make to the big picture? Why is it so important? For instance, if you are writing about two characters in a novel, how do your ideas affect the work as a whole? You've proven that the two characters are in sharp contrast with each other—so what? The answer is likely to make a forceful conclusion. Asking "So what?" helps you end your essay with a bang rather than a whimper.

SUGGESTIONS FOR WRITING

1. Write a description of a typical landscape 100 years from today.
2. Write an essay describing the major effects on the environment if environmentalists lose out to economic growth.

   or

   Write an essay describing the major effects on the economically disadvantaged if environmentalists curtail economic growth.

CHAPTER WRITING ASSIGNMENTS

1. In an essay, define *history*.
2. Define *yourself* in an essay.
3. Write a definition of *superstition*.
4. Choose one of the following terms and write an essay in which you first define the term as a dictionary would. Then give an extended definition, using the development most suitable for answering the question, "What is it?"

Luxury Ignorance

Ambiance Catastrophic

Indignity Romance

Pest satisfaction

Deverseness Health

WRITING ASSIGNMENTS FOR A SPECIFIC AUDIENCE

1. Define the term *authority* for a seven-year-old child.
2. Write an essay to a relative defining *failure*.

COLLABORATIVE WRITING PROJECT

Join a group of six other students. Brainstorm on the topic of explorers such as Christopher Columbus who discovered the New World. Because there were people already living on the newly discovered land, write a definition of "discovered" as it applies to the findings of explorers. Define the term from Columbus's point of view and from the point of view of the people he "discovered."

12

Comparison/Contrast

EDITORS' COUNSEL

What Comparison/Contrast Does

To *compare* is to point out how two things are similar; to *contrast* is to stress how they are dissimilar. To say that both John Calvin and Martin Luther were persecuted by the Catholic Church, opposed to conservative theology, and personally against materialistic self-indulgence is to make a comparison. A contrast between the two men, however, might stress that Luther wanted the Church to return to the primitive simplicity of the apostles, whereas Calvin heartily supported the advancement of capitalism. In the following passage from a student essay, note how the Egyptian and Greek mythologies are contrasted:

> A brief consideration of Egyptian mythology contrasted with the mythology of the Greeks is enough to convince us of the revolution in thought that must have taken place from one age to the other. The Egyptian gods had no resemblance to anything in the real world, whereas the Greek gods were fashioned after real Greek people. In Egypt the gods typically worshiped consisted of a towering colossus, so immobile and so distorted that no human could imagine it alive; or a woman with a cat's head, suggesting inflexible, inhuman cruelty; or a monstrous mysterious sphinx, aloof from anything we might consider human. The Egyptian artists' interpretations of the divine were horrid bestial shapes that combined men's heads with birds' bodies or portrayed lions with eagle wings—creatures that could inhabit only terrifying nightmares. The monstrosities of an invisible world were what the Egyptians worshiped. The Greek interpretation of divinity stands in <u>opposition</u> to this dark picture. The Greeks were preoccupied with the visible world. <u>Unlike</u> the Egyptians, they found their desires satisfied in what they could actually see around them. The ancient statues of Apollo, for instance, resemble the strong young bodies of athletes contending in the Olympic games. Homer describes Hermes as if he were a splendid Greek citizen. Generally the Greek artists found their gods in the idealized beauty or intelligence of actual human counterparts. <u>In direct contrast</u> to the Egyptians, they had no wish to create some hideous fantasy that they then called god.

On the other hand, the following passage finds similarities between whales and human beings:

> Whales and human beings are like two nations of individuals who have certain characteristics <u>in common.</u> As mammals they both are warm-blooded, giving milk, and breathing air. As social creatures they <u>both</u> have basic urges for privacy <u>as well as</u> for fraternization. As species bent on reproduction they <u>both</u> show <u>similar</u> patterns of aggression during courtship, the male trying to gain the female's attention and the female responding. Finally, as mystical beings they <u>both</u> are caught in the net of life and time, fellow prisoners of the splendor, travail, and secrets of earth.

Comparisons that take the form of extended analogies are frequently used to clarify abstract or complex ideas. One of the most famous examples of this use comes from the biblical accounts of Jesus' remarks:

> The kingdom of heaven is like unto a grain of mustard seed, which a man took and sowed in his field: which indeed is less than all seeds; but when it is grown, it is greater than the herbs, and becometh a tree, so that the birds of the heaven come and lodge in the branches thereof.
>
> —Matthew 13:31–32.

By comparing the kingdom of heaven to a mustard seed, which would have been familiar to his agrarian listeners, Jesus explains the power and the influence that a life dedicated to God can exert.

When to Use Comparison/Contrast

The odds are that you will not get through college without having to write a comparison/contrast, either in an essay exam or in a research paper. An English exam may typically ask for a contrast between the tragic flaws of Oedipus and Othello. A sociology question may call for a comparison between the demands of the feminist and civil rights movements. You may be asked to catalogue the differences between substances of organic and inorganic chemistry, or you may be asked to write an essay contrasting the traits of apes in captivity with those of apes who live in the wild. Comparison/contrast questions, in fact, commonly occur in every imaginable discipline.

How to Use Comparison/Contrast

1. Use logical bases of contrast. Suppose you want to develop the key thought "My college experience is teaching me that good instructors are a different breed from bad ones." You must first decide on your bases for contrast. You must ask yourself in which areas of instruction you wish to contrast the activities of good teachers with bad teachers. The following three could be your choice: (1) time spent on lesson preparation; (2) willingness to tolerate dissent; (3) personal relationship with students. Having chosen your bases, write down the three areas under consideration on the left side of a sheet of paper and then create two columns (one for good instructors, the other for bad instructors) in which you will place comments, as follows:

	Good instructors	**Bad instructors**
1. Time spent on lesson preparation	Good instructors constantly revise lessons, including up-to-date reviews, newspaper clippings, research results, and other relevant material. They refer to more than one source work and give suggestions for further reading. Lectures and discussions are the result of clear objectives.	Bad instructors give the same lectures year in and year out, including the same dead jokes. They do nothing but spell out rudimentary facts, to be memorized verbatim for final tests. They often spend class time on dull workbook assignments. They show as many movies as possible, during which they nap.
2. Willingness to tolerate dissent	Good instructors welcome arguments as a way of bringing life into the classroom and of pointing out alternatives. Like Socrates, they believe the classroom dialectic is a valid teaching method.	Bad instructors see dissent or discussion as a threat to discipline and to their authority, so they avoid both. They feel safe only when they are parroting themselves or the textbook.
3. Personal relationships with students	Good instructors spend time beyond office hours listening to student questions or complaints. They willingly clarify difficult problems. They never embarrass or patronize students.	Bad instructors are usually too busy off campus to spend time in personal consultation with students. They deliver their lectures and disappear. They make students who ask for special help feel inferior.

2. Use either the alternating or block method of contrast.   Once you have made a preliminary sketch, you can develop it simply by adding a few transitional words and phrases, as has been done in the following passage (transitions are underlined):

My college experience is teaching me that good instructors are a different breed from bad ones. In terms of time spent on lesson preparation, good instructors constantly revise their lessons, including such items as up-to-date reviews, newspaper clippings, research results, or any other relevant material. They refer to more than one source work and give suggestions for further reading. Their lectures and discussions are the obvious result of clear objectives. In contrast, bad instructors give the same lectures year in and year out, including the same dead jokes. Only the rudimentary facts are spelled out in class, to be memorized verbatim and regurgitated on final tests. They often spend classroom time on dull workbook assignments or, as often as possible, a movie, during which they take a nap.

Another big difference between good and bad instructors is in their willingness to tolerate dissent. Good instructors welcome arguments as a way of bringing life into the classroom and of pointing up alternatives. Like Socrates, they believe that the classroom dialectic is a valid learning method. Bad instructors, however, take the opposite tack. They see dissent or discussion as a threat to their discipline and to their authority, so they avoid both. They feel safe only when they are parroting themselves or their textbooks.

Good and bad instructors differ markedly in their relationship to students. Good instructors spend time beyond office hours listening to student questions or complaints. They willingly clarify difficult problems, and they never embarrass or patronize students. Bad instructors, on the contrary, are usually too busy off campus to spend time in personal consultation with students. They deliver their lecture and disappear. The student who asks for special help is made to feel inferior.

The preceding example demonstrates the *alternating* method of comparison/contrast. The paragraph is written to alternate back and forth from one side of an issue to the other. Another system—called the *block* method—uses separate paragraphs for each side of the issue, as illustrated in the following passage that contrasts two views of Jewish history:

> On the one hand, the Diaspora Jews can say that this talk of a predestination drama is a lot of nonsense. What has happened is only an interesting constellation of accidental, impersonal events, which some people have distorted out of all proportions to reality. We were defeated in war, they could say, we lost our land, we were exiled, and now it is our turn to disappear, just as under similar circumstances the Sumerians, the Hittites, the Babylonians, the Assyrians, the Persians—yes, even the Jews in the Kingdom of Israel—disappeared.
>
> On the other hand, they can say that their ancestors could not have been pursuing a mere illusion for 2,000 years. They could say that if we are God's Chosen People as our forefathers affirmed, if we have been placed in an exile to accomplish a divine mission as our Prophets predicted, and since we did receive the Torah, then we must survive to fulfill our Covenant with God.
>
> —Max I. Dimont, The Indestructible Jews

The alternating and block methods of comparison/contrast are further clarified in the following two outlines contrasting the Toyota Camry and the Volkswagen Jetta on the basis of cost, performance, and looks:

	Alternating outline

First paragraph	I. Cost
	    A. Camry
	    B. Jetta

Second paragraph	II. Performance
	    A. Camry
	    B. Jetta

Third paragraph	III Looks
	    A. Camry
	    B. Jetta

	Block outline

First paragraph	I. Camry
	    A. Cost
	    B. Performance
	    C. Looks

Second paragraph	II. Jetta
	    A. Cost
	    B. Performance
	    C. Looks

3. Make sure that the items to be compared/contrasted belong to the same class.   Some common ground must exist between items in order for a comparison/contrast to be meaningful. For example, a comparison between a hummingbird and a cement mixer or between backgammon and Dutch Cleanser would be silly. On the other hand, some usefulness can be derived from a comparison between the Chinese and Japanese languages or between golf and tennis—pairings that belong to common groups: Oriental languages and sports, respectively. Moreover, the expression of the comparison/contrast must be grammatically accurate:

Wrong. Our telephone system is better than Russia.

Here, a telephone system is contrasted with all of Russia.

Right: Our telephone system is better than *that* of Russia.

or

Our telephone system is better than Russia's.

Wrong: Ed's income is less than his wife.

Here, Ed's income is contrasted with his wife.

Right: Ed's income is less than that of his wife.

or

Ed's income is less than his wife's.

4. Deal with both sides of the question. All comparisons and contrasts are concerned with two sides, and you must deal equally with both. Do not mention one side and assume that your reader will fill in the other side. If you are contrasting the summer weather in Death Valley with the summer weather at Donner Pass, you cannot say:

In Death Valley the heat is so intense that even lizards wilt.

and assume that your reader will fill in "but at Donner Pass the summers remain cool." You must draw the contrast fully, as in the following:

In Death Valley the heat is so intense that even lizards wilt, whereas at Donner Pass a cool breeze freshens even the hottest day.

5. Use expressions indicating comparison/contrast. Although comparison requires less back-and-forth movement than does contrast, you must nevertheless take both sides into account by stating exactly what traits they have in common. For instance, in pointing out that in some ways high schools are like prisons, you cannot restrict yourself to discussing the domineering principal, the snoopy truant officer, the pass required to leave campus, or the punitive grading system. You must mention both sides, indicating that the domineering principal in high school is *like* the stern warden in prison; that the snoopy truant officer who makes sure that students attend school has much *in common with the prison guards* who make sure that inmates stay in prison; that the pass required to leave campus *is similar* to the formal permission required to leave a locked ward; and that the punitive grading system of high schools is *like* the demerit system of prisons. These expressions serve as signposts in your text, telling your reader how your different points relate.

The following expressions indicate comparison:

also
as well as
bears resemblance to both . . .
and in common with
in like manner

like

likewise

neither . . . nor

similar

too

The following expressions indicate contrast:

although this may be true

at the same time

but

for all that

however

in contrast to

in opposition to

nevertheless

on the contrary

on the one hand . . . on the other hand

otherwise

still

unlike

whereas

yet

Contrast emphasizes the separate sides of an issue by pulling them apart as much as possible in order to clarify their differences. Comparison is less two-sided because it tries to draw together both sides of an issue in order to reveal what they have in common. In short, *contrasts diverge, comparisons converge.* Refer back to the contrast example on page 411, and note how Egyptian mythology and the Greek mythology are placed far apart so that their ideological differences stand out. Note also how the underlined expressions indicating contrast clarify the shift from one side to the other.

Warming Up to Write a Comparison/Contrast

Comparing and contrasting are normal ways people think, so you should not have too much difficulty completing these exercises.

1. In the left side of each column, write in three or four characteristics that describe the underlined heading; then write a contrasting characteristic for the heading at the right.

Example

Teacher Smith	*Teacher Brown*
Pleasant	Grouchy
Always prepared	Sometimes disorganized
Fascinating in his presentations	Usually boring

a.	*Historical romances*	*Myths*
b.	*Tornadoes*	*Cyclones*
c.	*Friend with bad ethics*	*Friend with good ethics*
d.	*Working in a restaurant*	*Working in a hospital*
e.	*Watching a movie on TV*	*Watching a movie at a cinema*

2. Write down three bases of contrast (not comparison) for each of the following subjects.

   a. Two close friends

   b. Two church services

   c. Two holidays

   d. Two sports teams (or persons)

   e. Two attitudes toward work

3. Write down at least three aspects in which each of the following pairs are similar.

   a. A farm and a garden

   b. A storm and a lover's quarrel

   c. An ant hill and city government

   d. Fishing and looking for a wife

   e. An eagle and a lion

——————— EXAMPLES ———————

THAT LEAN AND HUNGRY LOOK

Suzanne Jordan

Suzanne Jordan (b. 1946), formerly a university teacher of English, is now a feature writer for the Raleigh, North Carolina, News and Observer.

Flying in the face of today's admiration for slimly elegant people, Jordan gives the winning edge to the chubbies, favorably comparing them point by point with "that lean and hungry look" so mistrusted by Shakespeare.

~

1   Caesar was right. Thin people need watching. I've been watching them for most of my adult life, and I don't like what I see. When these narrow fellows spring at me, I quiver to my toes. Thin people come in all personalities, most of them menacing. You've got your "together" thin person, your mechanical thin person, your condescending thin person, your tsk-tsk thin person, your efficiency-expert thin person. All of them are dangerous.

2   In the first place, thin people aren't fun. They don't know how to goof off, at least in the best, fat sense of the word. They've always got to be adoing. Give them a coffee break, and they'll jog around the block. Supply them with a quiet evening at home, and they'll fix the screen door and lick S&H green stamps. They say things like "there aren't enough hours in the day." Fat people never say that. Fat people think the day is too damn long already.

3   Thin people make me tired. They've got speedy little metabolisms that cause them to bustle briskly. They're forever rubbing their bony hands together and eyeing new problems to "tackle." I like to surround myself with sluggish, inert, easygoing fat people, the kind who believe that if you clean it up today, it'll just get dirty again tomorrow.

4   Some people say the business about the jolly fat person is a myth, that all of us chubbies are neurotic, sick, sad people. I disagree. Fat people may not be chortling all day long, but they're a hell of a lot nicer than the wizened and shriveled. Thin people turn surly, mean and hard at a young age because they never learn the value of a hot-fudge sundae for easing tension. Thin people don't like gooey soft things because they themselves are neither gooey nor soft. They are crunchy and dull, like carrots. They go straight to the heart of the matter while fat people let things stay all blurry and hazy and vague, the way things actually are. Thin people want to face the truth. Fat people know there is no truth. One of my thin friends is always staring at complex, unsolvable problems and saying, "The key thing is . . ." Fat people never say that. They know there isn't any such thing as the key thing

5   about anything.

    Thin people believe in logic. Fat people see all sides. The sides fat people see are rounded blobs, usually gray, always nebulous and truly not worth worrying about. But the thin person persists. "If you consume more calories than you burn," says one of my thin friends, "you will gain weight. It's that simple." Fat

6   people always grin when they hear statements like that. They know better.

    Fat people realize that life is illogical and unfair. They know very well that God is not in his heaven and all is not right with the world. If God was up there, fat people could have two doughnuts and a big orange drink anytime

7   they wanted it.

    Thin people have a long list of logical things they are always spouting off to me. They hold up one finger at a time as they reel off these things, so I won't lose track. They speak slowly as if to a young child. The list is long and full of holes. It contains tidbits like "get a grip on yourself," "cigarettes kill," "cholesterol clogs," "fit as a fiddle," "ducks in a row," "organize" and "sound fiscal management." Phrases like that.

8   They think these 2,000-point plans lead to happiness. Fat people know happiness is elusive at best and even if they could get the kind thin people talk about, they wouldn't want it. Wisely, fat people see that such programs are too dull, too hard, too off the mark. They are never better than a whole cheesecake.

9   Fat people know all about the mystery of life. They are the ones acquainted with the night, with luck, with fate, with playing it by ear. One thin person I know once suggested that we arrange all the parts of a jigsaw puzzle into groups according to size, shape and color. He figured this would cut the time needed to complete the puzzle by at least 50 per cent. I said I wouldn't do it. One, I like to muddle through. Two, what good would it do to finish early? Three, the jigsaw puzzle isn't the important thing. The important thing is the fun of four people (one thin person included) sitting around a card table, working a jigsaw puzzle. My thin friend had no use for my list. Instead of joining us, he went outside and mulched the boxwoods. The three remaining fat people finished the puzzle and made chocolate, double-fudged brownies to celebrate.

10   The main problem with thin people is they oppress. Their good intentions, bony torsos, tight hips, neat corners, cerebral machinations and pat solutions loom like dark clouds over the loose, comfortable, spread-out, soft world of the fat. Long after fat people have removed their coats and shoes and put their feet up on the coffee table, thin people are still sitting on the edge of the sofa, looking neat as a pin, discussing rutabagas. Fat people are heavily into fits of laughter, slapping their thighs and whooping it up, while thin people are still politely waiting for the punch line.

11   Thin people are downers. They like math and morality and reasoned evaluation of the limitations of human beings. They have their skinny little acts together. They expound, prognose, probe and prick.

12   Fat people are convivial. They will like you even if you're irregular and have acne. They will come up with a good reason why you never wrote the great American novel. They will cry in your beer with you. They will put your name in the pot. They will let you off the hook. Fat people will gab, giggle, guffaw, gallumph, gyrate and gossip. They are generous, giving and gallant. They are gluttonous and goodly and great. What you want when you're down is soft and jiggly, not muscled and stable. Fat people know this. Fat people have plenty of room. Fat people will take you in.

∽

(1,035 words)

VOCABULARY

metabolism (3)   inert (3)   wizened (4)
surly (4)   nebulous (5)   elusive (8)
mulched (9)   boxwoods (9)   machinations (10)

rutabagas (10)   prognose (11)   convivial (12)
guffaw (12)   gallumph (12)   gyrate (12)
gluttonous (12)

THE FACTS

1. In a nutshell, what bothers the author most about thin people?

2. What is your view of the myth about the "jolly fat person" mentioned in paragraph 4? What evidence is there for your view?

3. In paragraph 9, what is the "list" objected to by the thin person? What is ironic about this objection?

4. The thesis of Jordan's essay is obvious, but what is her underlying purpose? Because the essay is humorous, you might say that she simply wants to entertain the reader; but what more serious purpose is revealed?

5. In paragraph 10, Jordan claims that thin people "oppress." What evidence does she cite to support this claim?

THE STRATEGIES

1. The title of the essay is a literary allusion that is echoed in the opening sentence. What is the origin of the allusion? What other allusion can you identify in the essay?

2. What rhetorical organization does the author use to develop her essay? What advantage does her organization present? What other type of organization could be used to contrast thin and fat people?

3. Paragraph 5 and other paragraphs open with short, declarative sentences. What is the effect?

4. Here and there throughout the essay, Jordan uses figurative language. Find three examples and label the kind of figure of speech used in each.

5. How does the author achieve humor in her essay? Cite appropriate examples of her techniques.

THE ISSUES

1. "Thin is in" is irrefutably one of the maxims of today. Why have we placed such emphasis on the slim look?

2. Reread John Leo's essay *Mirror, Mirror, on the Wall* on pages 336–338. What does Leo say about the slim-hipped look of today? Does your answer to question 1 fit in with his view? Why or why not?

3. Are you convinced by Jordan's logic about the superiority of fat people? How does it strike you? Be specific in your answer.

4. If you were to play devil's advocate, how would you describe the thin person as desirable and the fat person as undesirable? Give specific examples as does Jordan.

5. How much should a person's appearance affect his or her success on the job?

SUGGESTIONS FOR WRITING

1. Write an essay in which you compare the lifestyles, opportunities, and intellectual maturity of students at large universities with those of students attending small colleges.

2. Using Jordan's piece as a model, write a 500-word essay in which you contrast tall and short people.

DIOGENES AND ALEXANDER

Gilbert Highet

Gilbert Highet (1906–1978) was born in Glasgow, Scotland, educated at the University of Glasgow and at Oxford, and became an American citizen in 1951. A classicist, Highet was known for his scholarly and critical writing, including The Classical Tradition *(1949) and* The Anatomy of Satire *(1962).*

This essay describes a meeting between two sharply contrasting personalities in Greek history—the Greek Cynic philosopher Diogenes (c. 412–323 B.C.) and Alexander the Great (356–323 B.C.), King of Macedonia. As Highet shows, although the two men occupied strikingly different positions in Greek society, they shared at least one quality that made them unique among the people of their time.

~

1 Lying on the bare earth, shoeless, bearded, half-naked, he looked like a beggar or a lunatic. He was one, but not the other. He had opened his eyes with the sun at dawn, scratched, done his business like a dog at the roadside, washed at the public fountain, begged a piece of breakfast bread and a few olives, eaten them squatting on the ground, and washed them down with a few handfuls of water scooped from the spring. (Long ago he had owned a rough wooden cup, but he threw it away when he saw a boy drinking out of his hollowed hands.) Having no work to go to and no family to provide for, he was free. As the market place filled up with shoppers and merchants and gossipers and sharpers and slaves and foreigners, he had strolled through it for an hour or two. Everybody knew him, or knew of him. They would throw sharp questions at him and get sharper answers. Sometimes they threw jeers,

and got jibes; sometimes bits of food, and got scant thanks; sometimes a mischievous pebble, and got a shower of stones and abuse. They were not quite sure whether he was mad or not. He knew they were mad, each in a different way; they amused him. Now he was back at his home.

2   It was not a house, not even a squatter's hut. He thought everybody lived far too elaborately, expensively, anxiously. What good is a house? No one needs privacy; natural acts are not shameful; we all do the same things, and need not hide them. No one needs beds and chairs and such furniture: the animals live healthy lives and sleep on the ground. All we require, since nature did not dress us properly, is one garment to keep us warm, and some shelter from rain and wind. So he had one blanket—to dress him in the daytime and cover him at night—and he slept in a cask. His name was Diogenes. He was the founder of the creed called Cynicism (the word means "doggishness"); he spent much of his life in the rich, lazy, corrupt Greek city of Corinth, mocking and satirizing its people, and occasionally converting one of them.

3   His home was not a barrel made of wood: too expensive. It was a storage jar made of earthenware, something like a modern fuel tank—no doubt discarded because a break had made it useless. He was not the first to inhabit such a thing: the refugees driven into Athens by the Spartan invasion had been forced to sleep in casks. But he was the first who ever did so by choice, out of principle.

4   Diogenes was not a degenerate or a maniac. He was a philosopher who wrote plays and poems and essays expounding his doctrine; he talked to those who cared to listen; he had pupils who admired him. But he taught chiefly by example. All should live naturally, he said, for what is natural is normal and cannot possibly be evil or shameful. Live without conventions, which are artificial and false; escape complexities and superfluities and extravagances: only so can you live a free life. The rich man believes he possesses his big house with its many rooms and its elaborate furniture, his pictures and his expensive clothes, his horses and his servants and his bank accounts. He does not. He depends on them, he worries about them, he spends most of his life's energy looking after them; the thought of losing them makes him sick with anxiety. They possess him. He is their slave. In order to procure a quantity of false, perishable goods he has sold the only true, lasting good, his own independence.

5   There have been many men who grew tired of human society with its complications, and went away to live simply—on a small farm, in a quiet village, in a hermit's cave, or in the darkness of anonymity. Not so Diogenes. He was not a recluse, or a stylite, or a beatnik. He was a missionary. His life's aim was clear to him: it was "to restamp the currency." (He and his father had once been convicted for counterfeiting, long before he turned to philosophy, and this phrase was Diogenes' bold, unembarrassed joke on the subject.) To restamp the currency: to take the clean metal of human life, to erase the old false conventional markings, and to imprint it with its true values.

6   The other great philosophers of the fourth century before Christ taught mainly their own private pupils. In the shady groves and cool sanctuaries of the Academy, Plato discoursed to a chosen few on the unreality of this contingent existence. Aristotle, among the books and instruments and specimens and archives and research-workers of his Lyceum, pursued investigations and gave lectures that were rightly named esoteric "for those within the walls." But for Diogenes, laboratory and specimens and lecture halls and pupils were all to be found in a crowd of ordinary people. Therefore he chose to live in Athens or in the rich city of Corinth, where travelers from all over the Mediterranean world constantly came and went. And, by design, he publicly behaved in such ways as to show people what real life was. He would constantly take up their spiritual coin, ring it on a stone, and laugh at its false superscription.

7   He thought most people were only half-alive, most men only half-men. At bright noonday he walked through the market place carrying a lighted lamp and inspecting the face of everyone he met. They asked him why. Diogenes answered, "I am trying to find a man."

8   To a gentleman whose servant was putting on his shoes for him, Diogenes said, "You won't be really happy until he wipes your nose for you: that will come after you lose the use of your hands."

9   Once there was a war scare so serious that it stirred even the lazy, profit-happy Corinthians. They began to drill, clean their weapons, and rebuild their neglected fortifications. Diogenes took his old cask and began to roll it up and down, back and forward. "When you are all so busy," he said, "I felt I ought to do something!"

10   And so he lived—like a dog, some said, because he cared nothing for privacy and other human conventions, and because he showed his teeth and barked at those whom he disliked. Now he was lying in the sunlight, as contented as a dog on the warm ground, happier (he himself used to boast) than the Shah of Persia. Although he knew he was going to have an important visitor, he would not move.

11   The little square began to fill with people. Page boys elegantly dressed, spearmen speaking a rough foreign dialect, discreet secretaries, hard-browed officers, suave diplomats, they all gradually formed a circle centered on Diogenes. He looked them over, as a sober man looks at a crowd of tottering drunks, and shook his head. He knew who they were. They were the attendants of the conqueror of Greece, the servants of Alexander, the Macedonian king, who was visiting his newly subdued realm.

12   Only twenty, Alexander was far older and wiser than his years. Like all Macedonians he loved drinking, but he could usually handle it; and toward women he was nobly restrained and chivalrous. Like all Macedonians he loved fighting; he was a magnificent commander, but he was not merely a military automaton. He could think. At thirteen he had become a pupil of the greatest mind in Greece, Aristotle. No exact record of his schooling survives. It is clear, though, that Aristotle took the passionate, half-barbarous boy and

gave him the best of Greek culture. He taught Alexander poetry: the young prince slept with the *Iliad* under his pillow and longed to emulate Achilles, who brought the mighty power of Asia to ruin. He taught him philosophy, in particular the shapes and uses of political power: a few years later Alexander was to create a supranational empire that was not merely a power system but a vehicle for the exchange of Greek and Middle Eastern cultures.

13   Aristotle taught him the principles of scientific research: during his invasion of the Persian domains Alexander took with him a large corps of scientists, and shipped hundreds of zoological specimens back to Greece for study. Indeed, it was from Aristotle that Alexander learned to seek out everything strange which might be instructive. Jugglers and stunt artists and virtuosos of the absurd he dismissed with a shrug; but on reaching India he was to spend hours discussing the problems of life and death with naked Hindu mystics, and later to see one demonstrate Yoga self-command by burning himself impassively to death.

14   Now, Alexander was in Corinth to take command of the League of Greek States which, after conquering them, his father Philip had created as a disguise for the New Macedonian Order. He was welcomed and honored and flattered. He was the man of the hour, of the century: he was unanimously appointed commander-in-chief of a new expedition against old, rich, corrupt Asia. Nearly everyone crowded to Corinth in order to congratulate him, to seek employment with him, even simply to see him: soldiers and statesmen, artists and merchants, poets and philosophers. He received their compliments graciously. Only Diogenes, although he lived in Corinth, did not visit the new monarch. With that generosity which Aristotle had taught him was a quality of the truly magnanimous man, Alexander determined to call upon Diogenes. Surely Diogenes, the God-born, would acknowledge the conqueror's power by some gift of hoarded wisdom.

15   With his handsome face, his fiery glance, his strong supple body, his purple and gold cloak, and his air of destiny, he moved through the parting crowd, toward the Dog's kennel. When a king approaches, all rise in respect. Diogenes did not rise, he merely sat up on one elbow. When a monarch enters a precinct, all greet him with a bow or an acclamation. Diogenes said nothing.

16   There was a silence. Some years later Alexander speared his best friend to the wall, for objecting to the exaggerated honors paid to His Majesty; but now he was still young and civil. He spoke first, with a kindly greeting. Looking at the poor broken cask, the single ragged garment, and the rough figure lying on the ground, he said: "Is there anything I can do for you, Diogenes?"

17   "Yes," said the Dog, "Stand to one side. You're blocking the sunlight."

18   There was silence, not the ominous silence preceding a burst of fury, but a hush of amazement. Slowly, Alexander turned away. A titter broke out from the elegant Greeks, who were already beginning to make jokes about the Cur that looked at the King. The Macedonian officers, after deciding that Diogenes was not worth the trouble of kicking, were starting to guffaw and

nudge one another. Alexander was still silent. To those nearest him he said quietly, "If I were not Alexander, I should be Diogenes." They took it as a paradox, designed to close the awkward little scene with a polite curtain line. But Alexander meant it. He understood Cynicism as the others could not. Later he took one of Diogenes' pupils with him to India as a philosophical interpreter (it was he who spoke to the naked *addhus*). He was what Diogenes called himself, a cosmopolités, "citizen of the world." Like Diogenes, he admired the heroic figure of Hercules, the mighty conqueror who labors to help mankind while all others toil and sweat only for themselves. He knew that of all men then alive in the world only Alexander the conqueror and Diogenes the beggar were truly free.

~

(1,960 words)

VOCABULARY

expounding (4)	conventions (4)	superfluities (4)
stylite (5)	discoursed (6)	contingent (6)
archives (6)	superscription (6)	suave (11)
supranational (12)	virtuosos (13)	

Professor Highet explains the meanings of several words used in the essay. How does he interpret the following?

Cynicism (2)	esoteric (6)	Diogenes (14)
cosmopolités (18)		

THE FACTS

1. What characteristics do Diogenes and Alexander share?
2. In what ways are Diogenes and Alexander different?
3. What is Diogenes's rationale for living so humbly?
4. According to Diogenes, the richer a man is, the more enslaved he becomes. How does he explain this statement?
5. How did the teaching method of Diogenes differ from that of Plato or Aristotle?
6. Paragraph 12 states that Alexander was far older and wiser than his twenty years. How is this maturity indicated?
7. According to the essay, Alexander "understood Cynicism as the others could not." What is Cynicism? Why did Alexander understand it better than others?

THE STRATEGIES

1. In what paragraph does the focus shift from Diogenes to Alexander?

2. Does Highet draw his contrast by alternating back and forth between Diogenes and Alexander, or does he first draw a full portrait of Diogenes and then a full portrait of Alexander? What does Highet's method require of the reader?

3. How do you explain the paradox "If I were not Alexander, I should be Diogenes" (paragraph 18)?

4. The opening paragraph contains a sentence characterized by balance and parallelism. What are the opening words of this sentence?

5. What is the literary term for the phrase "to restamp the currency"? What is the meaning?

6. What topic sentence covers paragraphs 7, 8, and 9? How is it developed?

THE ISSUES

1. Which of the two men—Alexander or Diogenes—had a better chance for leading a contented life? Give reasons for your answer.

2. Reread the essay *My Wood* by E. M. Forster, pages 145–148, then make a connection between Alexander's and Diogenes's lives and the essay. Ask yourself which of the two world figures most closely resembles the owner of the wood. Why?

3. Respond to paragraph 2: Do you agree with the idea that man should live naturally and that we have become far too elaborate? Give reasons for your answer.

4. How important are philosophy, poetry, and the principles of scientific investigation—all subjects taught to Alexander by Aristotle—to a modern curriculum? What other subjects, if any, would you add to a balanced curriculum?

5. Which would you prefer to be—a person of power or a person of influence? Be specific in describing yourself, later in life, as having achieved either of these characteristics. What job would you be holding? What kind of family life would you lead?

SUGGESTIONS FOR WRITING

1. Write an essay in which you state why you admire Alexander more than Diogenes, or vice versa. Base your essay on the portraits of the two men as drawn by Highet.

2. Choosing one of the pairs listed here, write an essay developed by contrast. Begin with a thesis that summarizes the contrast. Keep in mind the basis of your contrast.

   a. Jealousy/envy

   b. Thoreau/Gandhi

   c. Wisdom/knowledge

   d. Statesman/politician

   e. Old age/youth

GRANT AND LEE: A STUDY IN CONTRASTS

Bruce Catton

Bruce Catton (1899–1978) is regarded as one of the most outstanding Civil War historians of the 20th century. His books include Mr. Lincoln's Army *(1951),* Glory Road *(1952),* A Stillness at Appomattox *(1953, Pulitzer Prize), and* This Hallowed Ground *(1956).*

The following essay contrasts two famous personalities in American Civil War history: Ulysses S. Grant (1822–1885), commander in chief of the Union army and, later, eighteenth president of the United States (1869–1877); and his principal foe in the Civil War, Robert E. Lee (1807–1870), general in chief of the Confederate armies, who surrendered his forces to Grant in April of 1865. The essay illustrates the development of a comparison/contrast between paragraphs, rather than within a paragraph.

~

1 When Ulysses S. Grant and Robert E. Lee met in the parlor of a modest house at Appomattox Court House, Virginia, on April 9, 1865, to work out the terms for the surrender of Lee's Army of Northern Virginia, a great chapter in American life came to a close, and a great new chapter began.

2 These men were bringing the Civil War to its virtual finish. To be sure, other armies had yet to surrender, and for a few days the fugitive Confederate government would struggle desperately and vainly, trying to find some way to go on living now that its chief support was gone. But in effect it was all over when Grant and Lee signed the papers. And the little room where they wrote out the terms was the scene of one of the poignant, dramatic contrasts in American history.

3 They were two strong men, these oddly different generals, and they represented the strengths of two conflicting currents that, through them, had come into final collision.

4 Back of Robert E. Lee was the notion that the old aristocratic concept might somehow survive and be dominant in American life.

5   Lee was tidewater Virginia, and in his background were family, culture, and tradition . . . the age of chivalry transplanted to a New World which was making its own legends and its own myths. He embodied a way of life that had come down through the age of knighthood and the English country squire. America was a land that was beginning all over again, dedicated to nothing much more complicated than the rather hazy belief that all men had equal rights and should have an equal chance in the world. In such a land Lee stood for the feeling that it was somehow of advantage to human society to have a pronounced inequality in the social structure. There should be a leisure class, backed by ownership of land; in turn, society itself should be keyed to the land as the chief source of wealth and influence. It would bring forth (according to this ideal) a class of men with a strong sense of obligation to the community; men who lived not to gain advantage for themselves, but to meet the solemn obligations which had been laid on them by the very fact that they were privileged. From them the country would get its leadership; to them it could look for the higher values—of thought, of conduct, of personal deportment—to give it strength and virtue.

6   Lee embodied the noblest elements of this aristocratic ideal. Through him, the landed nobility justified itself. For four years, the Southern states had fought a desperate war to uphold the ideals for which Lee stood. In the end, it almost seemed as if the Confederacy fought for Lee; as if he himself was the Confederacy . . . the best thing that the way of life for which the Confederacy stood could ever have to offer. He had passed into legend before Appomattox. Thousands of tired, underfed, poorly clothed Confederate soldiers, long since past the simple enthusiasm of the early days of the struggle, somehow considered Lee the symbol of everything for which they had been willing to die. But they could not quite put this feeling into words. If the Lost Cause, sanctified by so much heroism and so many deaths, had a living justification, its justification was General Lee.

7   Grant, the son of a tanner on the Western frontier, was everything Lee was not. He had come up the hard way and embodied nothing in particular except the eternal toughness and sinewy fiber of the men who grew up beyond the mountains. He was one of a body of men who owed reverence and obeisance to no one, who were self-reliant to a fault, who cared hardly anything for the past but who had a sharp eye for the future.

8   These frontier men were the precise opposites of the tidewater aristocrats. Back of them, in the great surge that had taken people over the Alleghenies and into the opening Western country, there was a deep, implicit dissatisfaction with a past that had settled into grooves. They stood for democracy, not from any reasoned conclusion about the proper ordering of human society, but simply because they had grown up in the middle of democracy and knew how it worked. Their society might have privileges, but they would be privileges each man had won for himself. Forms and patterns meant nothing. No man was born to anything, except perhaps to a chance to show how far he could rise. Life was competition.

9   Yet along with this feeling had come a deep sense of belonging to a national community. The Westerner who developed a farm, opened a shop, or set up in business as a trader, could hope to prosper only as his own community prospered—and his community ran from the Atlantic to the Pacific and from Canada down to Mexico. If the land was settled, with towns and highways and accessible markets, he could better himself. He saw his fate in terms of the nation's own destiny. As its horizons expanded, so did his. He had, in other words, an acute dollars-and-cents stake in the continued growth and development of his country.

10   And that, perhaps, is where the contrast between Grant and Lee becomes most striking. The Virginia aristocrat, inevitably, saw himself in relation to his own region. He lived in a static society which could endure almost anything except change. Instinctively, his first loyalty would go to the locality in which that society existed. He would fight to the limit of endurance to defend it, because in defending it he was defending everything that gave his own life its deepest meaning.

11   The Westerner, on the other hand, would fight with an equal tenacity for the broader concept of society. He fought so because everything he lived by was tied to growth, expansion, and a constantly widening horizon. What he lived by would survive or fall with the nation itself. He could not possibly stand by unmoved in the face of an attempt to destroy the Union. He would combat it with everything he had, because he could only see it as an effort to cut the ground out from under his feet.

12   So Grant and Lee were in complete contrast, representing two diametrically opposed elements in American life. Grant was the modern man emerging; beyond him, ready to come on the stage, was the great age of steel and machinery, of crowded cities and a restless, burgeoning vitality. Lee might have ridden down from the old age of chivalry, lance in hand, silken banner fluttering over his head. Each man was the perfect champion of his cause, drawing both his strengths and his weaknesses from the people he led.

13   Yet it was not all contrast, after all. Different as they were—in background, in personality, in underlying aspiration—these two great soldiers had much in common. Under everything else, they were marvelous fighters. Furthermore, their fighting qualities were really very much alike.

14   Each man had, to begin with, the great virtue of utter tenacity and fidelity. Grant fought his way down the Mississippi Valley in spite of acute personal discouragement and profound military handicaps. Lee hung on in the trenches at Petersburg after hope itself had died. In each man there was an indomitable quality . . . the born fighter's refusal to give up as long as he can still remain on his feet and lift his two fists.

15   Daring and resourcefulness they had, too; the ability to think faster and move faster than the enemy. These were the qualities which gave Lee the dazzling campaigns of Second Manassas and Chancellorsville and won Vicksburg for Grant.

16   Lastly, and perhaps greatest of all, there was the ability, at the end, to turn quickly from war to peace once the fighting was over. Out of the way these

two men behaved at Appomattox came the possibility of a peace of reconciliation. It was a possibility not wholly realized, in the years to come, but which did, in the end, help the two sections to become one nation again . . . after a war whose bitterness might have seemed to make such a reunion wholly impossible. No part of either man's life became him more than the part he played in their brief meeting in the McLean house at Appomattox. Their behavior there put all succeeding generations of Americans in their debt. Two great Americans, Grant and Lee—very different, yet under everything very much alike. Their encounter at Appomattox was one of the great moments of American history.

~

(1,438 words)

VOCABULARY

poignant (2)	deportment (5)	embodied (6)
sanctified (6)	obeisance (7)	tenacity (11)
diametrically (12)	burgeoning (12)	

THE FACTS

1. What was Lee's background? What ideal did he represent?
2. What was Grant's background? What did he represent?
3. What was Grant's view of the past? What was his attitude toward society and democracy?
4. What was the most striking contrast between Grant and Lee?
5. Catton writes that the behavior of Grant and Lee at Appomattox "put all succeeding generations of Americans in their debt" (paragraph 16). Why?

THE STRATEGIES

1. Although the article is entitled *Grant and Lee: A Study in Contrasts*, Catton begins by examining what Lee represented. Why? What logic is there to his order?
2. What function does paragraph 4 serve? Why is this one sentence set off in a separate paragraph?
3. What common contrast phrase does paragraph 11 use?
4. In paragraph 8, the author writes: "These frontier men were the precise opposites of the tidewater aristocrats." What do these types have to do with a contrast between Grant and Lee?
5. What function does paragraph 8 serve?

THE ISSUES

1. Does an aristocracy still survive in our multicultural United States? If you believe it has survived, describe what and where it is. If you believe it has vanished, then describe what has taken its place.

2. Which kind of citizen do you admire most—the aristocrat or the frontiersman? Which do you believe is needed most for the betterment of our society today? Give reasons for your answers.

3. The aristocrat believes in form and tradition. How important are these ideas, in your view? Which traditions would you be willing to part with? Which would you want to keep?

4. What two women from history present an interesting contrast in two cultures? Describe both women and their contrasting cultures.

5. Which U.S. president, besides Ulysses S. Grant, is known for his support of economic growth and expansion? Do you favor continued growth and expansion, or are there other values you cherish more?

SUGGESTIONS FOR WRITING

1. Examine and analyze the organization of the contrast in this essay. In what various respects are Grant and Lee contrasted? How does Catton order and structure his contrast?

2. Discuss the idea that a society can benefit from the presence of a privileged class. Or, conversely, take the position that a society can benefit from the presence of an underprivileged class.

BRICKLAYER'S BOY

Alfred Lubrano

Alfred Lubrano is a writer on the staff of the Philadelphia Inquirer. *He has written articles for magazines such as* GQ *and regularly contributes commentaries on* National Public Radio.

What happens when a son, through the labors and sacrifices of his blue-collar father, becomes an educated, white-collar professional? How will his newly acquired white-collar values affect his relationship with his father? This situation, which is really quite common in opportunity-laden America, occurred to the author of this essay. In telling his appealing story, the author also develops a touching contrast between blue-collar father and white-collar son.

~

1 My father and I were college buddies back in the mid 1970s. While I was in class at Columbia, struggling with the esoterica du jour, he was on a brick-layer's scaffold not far up the street, working on a campus building.

2   Sometimes we'd hook up on the subway going home, he with his tools, I with my books. We didn't chat much about what went on during the day. My father wasn't interested in Dante, I wasn't up on arches. We'd share a New York Post and talk about the Mets.

3   My dad has built lots of places in New York City he can't get into: colleges, condos, office towers. He makes his living on the outside. Once the walls are up, a place takes on a different feel for him, as if he's not welcome anymore. It doesn't bother him, though. For my father, earning the dough that paid for my entrée into a fancy, bricked-in institution was satisfaction enough, a vicarious access.

4   We didn't know it then, but those days were the start of a branching off, a redefining of what it means to be a workingman in our family. Related by blood, we're separated by class, my father and I. Being the white-collar son of a blue-collar man means being the hinge on the door between two ways of life.

5   It's not so smooth jumping from Italian old-world style to U.S. yuppie in a single generation. Despite the myth of mobility in America, the true rule, experts say, is rags to rags, riches to riches. According to Bucknell University economist and author Charles Sackrey, maybe 10 percent climb from the working to the professional class. My father has had a tough time accepting my decision to become a mere newspaper reporter, a field that pays just a little more than construction does. He wonders why I haven't cashed in on that multi-brick education and taken on some lawyer-lucrative job. After bricklaying for thirty years, my father promised himself I'd never pile bricks and blocks into walls for a living. He figured an education—genielike and benevolent—would somehow rocket me into the consecrated trajectory of the upwardly mobile, and load some serious loot into my pockets. What he didn't count on was his eldest son breaking blue-collar rule No. 1: Make as much money as you can, to pay for as good a life as you can get.

6   He'd tell me about it when I was nineteen, my collar already fading to white. I was the college boy who handed him the wrong wrench on help-around-the-house Saturdays. "You better make a lot of money," my blue-collar handy dad wryly warned me as we huddled in front of a disassembled dishwasher I had neither the inclination nor the aptitude to fix. "You're gonna need to hire someone to hammer a nail into a wall for you."

7   In 1980, after college and graduate school, I was offered my first job, on a now-dead daily paper in Columbus, Ohio. I broke the news in the kitchen, where all the family business is discussed. My mother wept as if it were Vietnam. My father had a few questions: "Ohio? Where the hell is Ohio?"

8   I said it's somewhere west of New York City, that it was like Pennsylvania, only more so. I told him I wanted to write, and these were the only people who'd take me.

9   "Why can't you get a good job that pays something, like in advertising in the city, and write on the side?"

10   "Advertising is lying," I said, smug and sanctimonious, ever the unctuous undergraduate. "I wanna tell the truth."

11   "The truth?" the old man exploded, his face reddening as it does when he's up twenty stories in high wind. "What's truth?" I said it's real life, and writing about it would make me happy. "You're happy with your family," my father said, spilling blue-collar rule No. 2. "That's what makes you happy. After that, it all comes down to dollars and cents. What gives you comfort besides your family? Money, only money."

12   During the two weeks before I moved, he reminded me that newspaper journalism is a dying field, and I could do better. Then he pressed advertising again, though neither of us knew anything about it, except that you could work in Manhattan, the borough with the water-beading high gloss, the island polished clean by money. I couldn't explain myself, so I packed, unpopular and confused. No longer was I the good son who studied hard and fumbled endearingly with tools. I was hacking people off.

13   One night, though, my father brought home some heavy tape and that clear, plastic bubble stuff you pack your mother's second-string dishes in. "You probably couldn't do this right," my father said to me before he sealed the boxes and helped me take them to UPS. "This is what he wants," my father told my mother the day I left for Columbus in my grandfather's eleven-year-old gray Cadillac. "What are you gonna do?" After I said my good-byes, my father took me aside and pressed five $100 bills into my hands. "It's okay," he said over my weak protests. "Don't tell your mother."

14   When I broke the news about what the paper was paying me, my father suggested I get a part-time job to augment the income. "Maybe you could drive a cab." Once, after I was chewed out by the city editor for something trivial, I made the mistake of telling my father during a visit home. "They pay you nothin', and they push you around too much in that business," he told me, the rage building. "Next time, you gotta grab the guy by the throat and tell him he's a big jerk."

15   "Dad, I can't talk to the boss like that."

16   "Tell him. You get results that way. Never take any shit." A few years before, a guy didn't like the retaining wall my father and his partner had built. They tore it down and did it again, but the guy still bitched. My father's partner shoved the guy into the freshly laid bricks. "Pay me off," my father said, and he and his partner took the money and walked. Blue-collar guys have no patience for office politics and corporate bile-swallowing. Just pay me off and I'm gone. Eventually, I moved on to a job in Cleveland, on a paper my father has heard of. I think he looks on it as a sign of progress, because he hasn't mentioned advertising for a while.

17   When he was my age, my father was already dug in with a trade, a wife, two sons and a house in a neighborhood in Brooklyn not far from where he was born. His workaday, family-centered life has been very much in step with his immigrant father's. I sublet what the real-estate people call a junior one-bedroom in a dormlike condo in a Cleveland suburb. Unmarried and unconnected in an insouciant, perpetual-student kind of way, I rent movies during the week and feed single women in restaurants on Saturday nights. My dad asks me about my dates, but he goes crazy over the word "woman." "A

girl," he corrects. "You went out with a girl. Don't say 'woman.' It sounds like you're takin' out your grandmother."

18   I've often believed blue-collaring is the more genuine of lives, in greater proximity to primordial manhood. My father is provider and protector, concerned only with the basics: food and home, love and progeny. He's also a generation closer to the heritage, a warmer spot nearer the fire that forged and defined us. Does heat dissipate and light fade further from the source? I live for my career, and frequently feel lost and codeless, devoid of the blue-collar rules my father grew up with. With no baby-boomer groomer to show me the way, I've been choreographing my own tentative shuffle across the wax-shined dance floor on the edge of the Great Middle Class, a different rhythm in a whole new ballroom.

19   I'm sure it's tough on my father, too, because I don't know much about bricklaying, either, except that it's hell on the body, a daily sacrifice. I idealized my dad as a kind of dawn-rising priest of labor, engaged in holy ritual. Up at five every day, my father has made a religion of responsibility. My younger brother, a Wall Street white-collar guy with the sense to make a decent salary, says he always felt safe when he heard Dad stir before him, as if Pop were taming the day for us. My father, fifty-five years old, but expected to put out as if he were three decades stronger, slips on machine-washable vestments of khaki cotton without waking my mother. He goes into the kitchen and turns on the radio to catch the temperature. Bricklayers have an occupational need to know the weather. And because I am my father's son, I can recite the five-day forecast at any given moment.

20   My father isn't crazy about this life. He wanted to be a singer and actor when he was young, but that was frivolous doodling to his Italian family, who expected money to be coming in, stoking the stove that kept hearth fires ablaze. Dreams simply were not energy-efficient. My dad learned a trade, as he was supposed to, and settled into a life of pre-scripted routine. He says he can't find the black-and-white publicity glossies he once had made.

21   Although I see my dad infrequently, my brother, who lives at home, is with the old man every day. Chris has a lot more blue-collar in him than I do, despite his management-level career; for a short time, he wanted to be a construction worker, but my parents persuaded him to go to Columbia. Once in a while he'll bag a lunch and, in a nice wool suit, meet my father at a construction site and share sandwiches of egg salad and semolina bread.

22   It was Chris who helped my dad most when my father tried to change his life several months ago. My dad wanted a civil-service bricklayer foreman's job that wouldn't be so physically demanding. There was a written test that included essay questions about construction work. My father hadn't done anything like it in forty years. Why the hell they needed bricklayers to write essays I have no idea, but my father sweated it out. Every morning before sunrise, Chris would be ironing a shirt, bleary-eyed, and my father would sit at the kitchen table and read aloud his practice essays on how to wash down a wall, or how to build a tricky corner. Chris would suggest words and approaches.

23   It was so hard for my dad. He had to take a Stanley Kaplan–like prep course in a junior high school three nights a week after work for six weeks. At class time, the outside men would come in, twenty-five construction workers squeezing themselves into little desks. Tough blue-collar guys armed with No. 2 pencils leaning over and scratching out their practice essays, cement in their hair, tar on their pants, their work boots too big and clumsy to fit under the desks.

24   "Is this what finals felt like?" my father would ask me on the phone when I pitched in to help long-distance. "Were you always this nervous?" I told him yes. I told him writing's always difficult. He thanked Chris and me for the coaching, for putting him through school this time. My father thinks he did okay, but he's still awaiting the test results. In the meantime, he takes life the blue-collar way, one brick at a time.

25   When we see each other these days, my father still asks how the money is. Sometimes he reads my stories; usually he likes them, although he recently criticized one piece as being a bit sentimental: "Too schmaltzy," he said. Some psychologists say that the blue-white-collar gap between fathers and sons leads to alienation, but I tend to agree with Dr. Al Baraff, a clinical psychologist and director of the Men-Center in Washington, D.C. "The core of the relationship is based on emotional and hereditary traits," Baraff says. "Class [distinctions] just get added on. If it's a healthful relationship from when you're a kid, there's a respect back and forth that'll continue."

26   Nice of the doctor to explain, but I suppose I already knew that. Whatever is between my father and me, whatever keeps us talking and keeps us close, has nothing to do with work and economic class.

27   During one of my visits to Brooklyn not long ago, he and I were in the car, on our way to buy toiletries, one of my father's weekly routines. "You know, you're not as successful as you could be," he began, blue-collar blunt as usual. "You paid your dues in school. You deserve better restaurants, better clothes." Here we go, I thought, the same old stuff. I'm sure every family has five or six similar big issues that are replayed like well-worn videotapes. I wanted to fast-forward this thing when we stopped at a red light.

28   Just then my father turned to me, solemn and intense. His knees were aching and his back muscles were throbbing in clockable intervals that registered in his eyes. It was the end of a week of lifting fifty-pound blocks. "I envy you," he said quietly. "For a man to do something he likes and get paid for it—that's fantastic." He smiled at me before the light changed, and we drove on. To thank him for the understanding, I sprang for the deodorant and shampoo. For once, my father let me pay.

∽

(2,332 words)

VOCABULARY

esoterica (1)	vicarious (3)	lawyer-lucrative (5)
consecrated (5)	sanctimonious (10)	unctuous (10)

isouciant (17)   proximity (18)   primordial (18)
progeny (18)   dissipate (18)   choreographing (18)

THE FACTS

1. Despite the American dream, what does the author say the rule really is about mobility in American society?
2. The author says he broke blue-collar rule number 1. What is that rule?
3. Where was the author's first newspaper job?
4. What ambition did the author's father have but never fulfilled?
5. What was the outcome of the civil service test the author's father took?

THE STRATEGIES

1. In paragraph 1, the author says he was in class, struggling with "esoterica du jour." What is the meaning of this phrase? Where does it come from?
2. Although this is not formally structured as a contrasting essay, it still draws many contrasts between father and son. What are some of these contrasts, and how are they presented?
3. Throughout, the author peppers his language with slang phrases, such as, "I wasn't up on arches," or "I was hacking people off." Why do you think he does this?
4. Which paragraph sums up the thesis of this essay? What is its thesis?
5. Which of the two contrast patterns, interparagraph or intraparagraph, does the author chiefly use? Which pattern do you think better suits his purpose? Why?

THE ISSUES

1. How do you think a college education is likely to affect your relationship with your own family?
2. The author talks about the implicit rules of blue-collar life. What rule or rules can you think of that apply to white-collar life?
3. If blue-collar people work primarily for money, what do you think white-collar people primarily work for?
4. Which of the two lifestyles do you personally prefer, blue-collar or white-collar? Why?
5. The author reports being scolded by his father for saying "women" instead of "girls." What does this say about the relative sexism between the two classes?

SUGGESTIONS FOR WRITING

1. Write an essay about any class or generational conflict you have had with your own family.

2. Write a contrast between you and one of your parents.

————————— ISSUE FOR CRITICAL —————————
THINKING AND DEBATE

THE EXISTENCE OF GOD

"God is dead. Nietzsche," wrote some unknown wit on a bathroom wall, to which another unknown writer replied, "Nietzsche is dead. God." As an example of the everyday debate that has long raged about the existence of God, this exchange is a classic. Yet, what Friedrich Nietzsche, the German philosopher, actually wrote was considerably more complex: "God is dead, but considering the state species Man is in, there will perhaps be caves, for ages yet, in which his shadow will be shown." The shorthand version of what Nietzsche actually said is perhaps catchier, but the fuller version is a more accurate summation about the condition of God among modern thinkers. Even today, and not only in caves, the shadow of God is everywhere around us. God may or may not be dead, but the argument about his alleged death is very much alive.

Of all the questions we ask about our world, none is more profound than "Does God exist?" Every generation asks this question anew and answers it in its own way. Every generation has its own attitudes and its own relationship with the concept of a divinity. But one truth is constant: Wherever human beings have made history, they have talked about or written about God. Rare indeed is the mythology that does not contain some story of creation, of the origin of evil, and of an ultimate power ruling the universe and directing its destiny.

The variations of belief or nonbelief in God are also staggering. Some highly educated people base their faith on a simple acceptance of the four Biblical Gospels. Others base complex beliefs on astronomical numbers, Cabalistic mysteries, or prophetic interpretations. Some people who think themselves moral are staunch atheists, whereas others who profess to be religious behave in ways that strike many of us as immoral. Some people follow the teachings of Jesus, some of Buddha, some of Mohammed, and some of latter-day prophets like Scientology's L. Ron Hubbard. Still others search for God in nature, in mystery, or in coincidence and tea leaves.

Regardless of who we are, all of us occasionally experience a twinge of wonder about where we came from, about who made our world, and where it and we are headed. It also mystifies us to contemplate that so far, in peering out with gigantic telescopes into the endless expanse of space, we still have not found any evidence of other civilizations. The speculations and beliefs go on as they have throughout the ages, with many of us—believers or nonbelievers—hovering between acceptance of an all-powerful, all-knowing, and ever-present force—God—and the aloneness of believing in a Godless universe in which we make our own destiny. Whether or not there is a God is a question that lies at the core of our being.

This chapter offers two viewpoints on whether or not God exists. First, there is a reasoned sermon from a minister of religion in which he gives ten reasons for believing in immortality and therefore in God. This is followed by a systematic listing by a secular humanist of quotations by the famous who denied that God existed. The painting below is a reproduction of Michelangelo's powerful depiction of God creating Adam, and in the Student Corner, a student writer weighs in with his own opinion about the existence of God.

Michelangelo, *The Creation of Adam,* detail from The Sistine Chapel restoration.

TEN REASONS FOR BELIEVING IN IMMORTALITY

John Haynes Holmes

John Haynes Holmes (1897–1964) was an American minister and social activist, known for fearlessly defending many controversial causes, including pacifism and civil liberties for all. He was a prolific writer who wrote twenty books, including Religion for Today *(1917),* My Ghandi *(1953),* The Collected Hymns of John Haynes Holmes *(1960), and an autobiography,* I Speak for Myself *(1959).*

~

1   Nobody can speak on the immortality of the soul at this late date without being acutely conscious of the fact that there is nothing new that can be said. Since the time of Plato, at least, five hundred years before the birth of Jesus, the discussion of immortality has been conducted by the greatest minds upon the highest levels of human thought. Theology, philosophy, psychology and science have all been called upon to make their contributions to the theme. Poetry has offered its voice and religion its faith, with the result that every corner of knowledge has been explored, every depth of truth uncovered and revealed! There is always the possibility, of course, that the veil which hangs over every grave to divide this life from the mystery that lies beyond, may some day be lifted to our gaze. There are those who claim—not without some reason, it seems to me—that they have penetrated this veil, and thus have looked upon the reality of survival after death. But short of some such remarkable discovery as this, there is nothing new to be anticipated in this field. Everything has been said that can be said. The case for immortality is in!

2   Now it is this case which I want to present to you this morning. Since I cannot hope to say anything that is new, I want to see what I can do in the way of saying something that is old. I cannot say much, to be sure, for no discourse however merciless in length, can compass the range and beauty of the argument for immortality. But since ten is a goodly number, I take ten of the reasons which have brought conviction to the minds of men and offer these as the case for immortality today. I trust that it may be interesting, and also persuasive, especially to the members of our younger generation, to be reminded of what has been thought upon this question for many years.

3   By way of introduction, may I make mention of some two or three reasons for believing in immortality which do not concern me. I speak of these not because they are important, but because some of you may wonder, if I am silent, why they do not appear in my list of ten.

4   Thus I do not see any reason for believing in immortality because Jesus is reputed to have risen from the dead. In the first place, I do not believe that he rose from the dead. There is no evidence to substantiate this miracle. In the second place, even if he did break the barriers of the tomb, I fail to see what the resurrection of the body has to do with the immortality of the soul. The

two things are irrelevant, the one to the other. What we have here is one of the myths of Christianity which, even if it were true, would have nothing seriously to do with our question.

5   Again, I find no argument for immortality in the succession of the seasons, the revival of nature of the spring, the blossoming of the flowers after the winter's cold. Poets are fond of this idea, as Shelley, for example, when he wrote his famous line,

> If winter comes, can spring be far behind?

I think we may see in it a pretty parable, a rather beautiful poetic concept. But as an argument for immortality, it is what Ruskin called an instance of the "pathetic fallacy." The flowers that blossom in the spring are not the flowers that died the preceding autumn. The tide of life that flows on through nature, season after season, is the tide that flows on through humanity, generation after generation, and it touches as little in the one case as in the other the survival of the individual. Like most parables, this does not hold when applied rigorously to the issue that is involved.

6   Again, I must confess that I am not convinced by the argument that men must be immortal because the heart demands it. It is natural that we should cling to those we love. It is inevitable that we should believe that providence, if it be beneficent, must give answer to our plea that we have not permanently separated from our friends and kindred. Whittier was yielding to the deepest impulses of the soul when he suggested in his "Snow Bound" that "Life is ever Lord of Death," because "Love can never lose its own." This is the cry of the human heart, and I personally believe that it is not destined to go unanswered. But a longing is one thing, and a reason is another. I see no evidence, in the scheme of things, that what we want we are therefore going to have. On the contrary, Felix Adler has taught us that frustration is the basic principle of life, that experience is "permeated with the sense of incompleteness," and that this "sense of incompleteness" is a perpetual doom that is laid upon us as "a necessary instrument of spiritual development." Whether this be true or not I do not know, but in either case I still believe that love gives no guarantee of its own survival.

7   But there are arguments for immortality which seem to suggest that it is true. Surveying all the field, I find myself agreeing with William James that, while we are under no compulsion to believe in immortality, as we are under a compulsion, for example, to believe that "things equal to the same thing are equal to each other," yet we are free to believe, if we so desire, without being guilty of superstition. "You may believe henceforward," said Professor James, "whether you care to profit by the permission or not." There are perfectly good and sufficient reasons, in other words, why an intelligent man may intelligently believe in immortality. Ten of these reasons I propose to submit to you this morning, beginning with those which open up the question, so to speak, and ending with those which close it as a conviction of the soul.   •

8   (1) First of all, may I offer the suggestion, not important in itself and yet of real significance to the thinking mind, that we may believe in immortality because there is no reason for not believing in it. In discussions of this question we are constantly reminded that immortality has never been proved. To which there is the immediate and inevitable reply that immortality has never been disproved! As there is no positive testimony to prove it true, so is there no negative testimony to prove it untrue. What we have here is an absence of testimony, and such "absence of testimony;" says John Fiske, "does not even raise a negative presumption, except in cases where testimony is accessible." In this case, testimony is not accessible. Therefore the question is open "for those general considerations of philosophic analogy and moral probability which are the grounds upon which we can call for help in this arduous inquiry." As the question is open, so must our minds be open. My first reason, therefore, for believing in immortality or for being ready to believe in immortality, is the primarily interesting fact that there is no reason for not believing in immortality. My mind is absolutely at one with that of John Stuart Mill when he said upon his question, "To anyone who feels it conducive either to his satisfaction or to his usefulness to hope for a future state, . . . there is no hindrance to his indulging that hope."

9   (2) My second reason for believing in immortality is to be found in the universality of the idea. In saying this, I am not seeking to substantiate my position by taking a majority vote upon the question. I am not arguing that a proposition is necessarily true because most persons have believed it. All too many beliefs have clung pertinaciously to the human mind, only in the end to be revealed as superstitions, and it may very well be that this concept of immortality is one of them.

10   What I have in mind here is the very different consideration that immortality is not merely a belief to be accepted but an idea to be explained. "Here is this wonderful thought," says Emerson, "Wherever man ripens, this audacious belief presently appears. . . . As soon as thought is exercised, this belief is inevitable. . . . Whence came it? Who put it in the mind?" In itself it is remarkable, this idea that the death of the body is not the extinction of personality. Who has ever looked upon a dead body without marveling that man has ever thought of survival beyond the grave? Emerson could not explain the fact, as it has appeared in all ages and among all peoples, except upon the supposition that the thought of immortality is "not sentimental" but "elemental"—elemental in the sense that it is "grounded in the necessities and forces we possess."

11   That this idea is something more than idle speculation is shown by the whole philosophy of evolution, which has given to us that fundamental interpretation of life as "the continuous adjustment of inner relations to outer relations." An organism lives by successfully adjusting itself to the conditions of its environment, by developing itself inwardly in such a way as to meet the conditions of reality. When we find in plant or animal some inner faculty or attitude which is universally present, and which persists from generation to generation, we may be perfectly sure that it represents some correspondence

with reality which has made survival possible. Life, in other words, is so definitely a matter of the successful coordination of inner relations with outer relations, that it is altogether impossible to conceive that in any specific relation the subjective term is real and the objective term is non-existent. What exists within is the sign and symbol, and guarantee, of what exists without.

12   Now man has never existed without the thought of immortality. From the earliest period of his life upon the earth, he has been profoundly concerned with this idea. He has never been able to live without it; even when he has tried to deny it, he has not been able to get rid of it. The immortal life is part of his being, as a line on the surface of a coin is a part of the pattern of its design. And as the line upon the coin could not have been set there except as the impression of the die which stamped its mark upon the metal, so the idea of immortality could not have appeared within the consciousness of man, except as the impression of the reality which made it what it is. Our faculties, our attributes, our ideas, as we have seen, are the reflection of the environment to which we adapt ourselves as the condition of survival. What we feel within is the reaction upon what exists without. As the eye proves the existence of light, and the ear the existence of sound, so the immortal hope may not unfairly be said to prove the existence of the immortal life. It is this that we mean when we say that the universality of the idea is an argument for the acceptance of the idea. In his great essay on "Immortality," Emerson tells us of two men who early in life spent much of their time together in earnest search for some proof of immortality. An accident separated them, and they did not meet again for a quarter of a century. They said nothing, "but shook hands long and cordially. At last his friend said, 'Any light, Albert?' 'None', replied Albert. 'Any light, Lewis?' 'None,' he replied." And Emerson comments "that the impulse which drew these two minds to this inquiry through so many years was a better affirmative evidence for immortality than their failure to find a confirmation was a negative."

13   (3) This universal diffusion of the idea of immortality takes on an added significance when I come to my third reason for believing in immortality. I refer to the fact so memorably stated by Cicero. "There is in the minds of men," he says, "I know not how, a certain presage, as it were, of a future existence; and this takes deepest root in the greatest geniuses and the most exalted souls." The leaders of the race, in other words, have always believed in immortality. They are not separated in this case, as in so many cases, from the masses of ignorant and superstitious men by doctrines of dissent. On the contrary, in this case the ideas of the highest are at one with the hopes of the humblest among mankind.

14   In referring thus to the great names that are attached to the idea of immortality, I would not have you believe that I am making any blind appeal to the concept of authority. I have never seen any reason for arbitrarily separating our minds from the companionship of other minds. There is such a thing, even for the independent thinker, as a consensus of best opinion which cannot be defied without the weightiest of reasons. And in this matter of immortality there is a consensus of best opinion which constitutes, to my mind,

one of the most remarkable phenomena in the whole history of human thinking. I have no time this morning to list the names of those who have believed in the immortality of the soul. If I did so, I should have to include the names of scientists from Aristotle to Darwin and Eddington, of philosophers from Plato to Kant and Bergson, of poets from Sophocles to Goethe and Robert Browning, of ethical teachers and public leaders from Socrates to Tolstoi and Mahatma Gandhi. There are dissenters from the doctrine, like Epictetus yesterday and Bernard Shaw today, but the consensus of opinion the other way is remarkable. Even the famous heretics stand in awe before this conception of eternity. Thus, Voltaire declared that "reason agrees with revelation . . . that the soul is immortal." Thomas Paine affirmed that he did not "trouble (himself) about the manner of future existence," so sure he was that "the Power which gave existence is able to continue it in any form." Even Robert G. Ingersoll confessed, as he stood by his brother's grave, that love could "hear the rustle of an angel's wing:" In the light of such testimony as this, are we not justified in believing that there is reason for believing in immortality? If not, then we know, with James Martineau, "who are those who are mistaken. Not the mean and grovelling souls who never reached to so great a thought. . . . No, the deceived are the great and holy, whom all men revere; the men who have lived for something better than their happiness and spent themselves on the altar of human good. Whom are we to reverence, and what can we believe, if the inspirations of the highest nature are but cunningly-devised fables?"

15   (4) This conviction of immortality as rooted in the minds of men, and the greatest men, brings us immediately to the consideration of human nature itself as evidence for its own survival. Thus, my fourth reason this morning for believing in immortality is found in what I would call man's over-endowment as a creature of this earth, his surplus equipment for the adventure of his present life. If we want to know what is needed for successful existence upon this planet, we have only to look at any animal. His equipment of physical attributes and powers seems perfectly adapted to the necessities of his natural environment. The outfit of man, on the contrary, seems to constitute something like "a vast over-provision" for his necessities. If this life is all, in other words, what need has man for all these mental faculties, moral aspirations, spiritual ideals, which make him to be distinctly a man as contrasted with the animal? If existence upon the earth is his only destiny, why should man not prefer the swiftness of the deer, the strength of the lion, the vision of the eagle, to any endowment of mind and heart, as more adequate provision for the purely physical task of physical survival in a physical world? What we have here is a fundamental discrepancy between the endowment of man and the life he has to live; and this constitutes, if this life be all, an unparalleled violation of the creative economy of the universe. In every other form of life, an organism is equipped to meet the exactions of its immediate environment. Man is equipped for this environment, and also for something more. Why is this not proof that he is destined for something more? As we estimate the length of the voyage of a ship by the character of its equipment, never confusing a little coasting vessel with a transatlantic

liner or an arctic exploration steamer, why should we not estimate the length of man's voyage upon the seas of life in exactly the same way? What man bears within himself is evidence that he is destined for some farther port than any upon these shores. What he is in mind and heart and spirit, in the range of his interests and the lift of his soul, can only be explained on the supposition that he is preparing for another and a vaster life. I believe that man is immortal because already the signs of immortality are upon him.

16   (5) This consideration is basic, and sums up our whole case for immortality as rooted in human nature. But it opens out into other considerations which may well be taken as other reasons for believing in immortality. Thus, I would specify as my fifth reason for believing in immortality the lack of co-ordination, or proportion, between a man's body and a man's mind. If these two are to be regarded as aspects of a single organism, adapted only to the conditions of this present life, why do they so early begin to pull apart, and the weakness of the one to retard and at last to defeat the other? For a while, to be sure, there seems to be a real coordination between soul and body, between the personality, on the one hand, and the physical frame which it inhabits, on the other. Thus the child is in nothing so delightful as in the fact that it is a perfect animal. Then, as maturity approaches, two exactly opposite processes begin to take place within the life of the human being. On the one hand, the body begins to lose its resiliency and harden, to stop its growth and become static, then to decay and at last to dissolve. There is a definite cycle, in other words, in the physical life of the individual. There is a beginning, then a pause, and then an end. It is from first to last a process of completion. But there is no completion in the life of the soul. "Who dares speak the word 'completed,' " says Professor Munsterberg, the great psychologist. "Do not our purposes grow? Does not every newly-created value give us the desire for further achievement? Is our life ever so completely done that no desire has still a meaning?" The personality of man is an enduring thing. As the body weakens through the years, so the soul only grows the stronger and more wonderful. As the body approaches irrevocably to its end, so the soul only mounts to what seems to be a new beginning. We come to death, in other words, only to discover within ourselves exhaustless possibilities. The aged have testified again and again to this amazing truth that as the body turns to ashes, the spirit mounts as to a flame. Victor Hugo, protesting against the waning of his powers, said, "For half a century I have been writing my thoughts in prose and verse . . . but I feel that I have not said a thousandth part of what is in me." Said James Martineau, on his 80th birthday, "How small a part of my plans have I been able to carry out! Nothing is so plain as that life at its fullest on earth is but a fragment." Robert Browning catches this thought in his poem, "Cleon," where he makes his hero say,

> . . . Every day my sense of joy
> Grows more acute, my soul . . . enlarged, more keen,
> While every day my hairs fall more and more,
> My hand shakes, and the heavy years increase
> The horror quickening still from year to year,

When I shall know most, and yet least enjoy.
What to do, in such emergency, except what Cleon did,
. . . imagine to (our) need
Some future state . . .

17   (6) But there is a lack of coordination not only between our personalities
and our physical bodies, but also between our personalities and the physical
world. This is my sixth reason for believing in immortality—that our souls
have potentialities and promises which should not, as indeed they cannot, be
subject to the chance vicissitudes of earthly fortune. What are we going to
say, for example, when we see some life of eminent utility, of great achievement, of character and beauty and noble dedication to mankind, not merely
borne down by the body, but cut off sharply before its time by an automobile
accident, a disease germ, a bit of poisoned food? What shall we think when
we see a Shelley drowned in his thirtieth year by the heedless sea, a Phillips
Brooks stricken in the prime of his manhood by a diphtheric sore-throat, a
Captain Scott frozen in mid-career by an accident of weather? Is it possible
that these lives of ours are dependent upon a fall of snow, a grain of dust, a
passing breeze upon the sea? Is it conceivable that our personalities, with all
their potencies of spirit, can be destroyed, as our bodies can be broken, by the
material forces of the world? Are we to believe that eternal powers can be annihilated by transient accidents? I cannot think so! Rather must I think, as
Professor George Herbert Palmer thought, as he looked upon the dead body
of his wife, one of the greatest and most beautiful women of her time, stricken
ere her years were ripe. "Though no regrets are proper for the manner of her
death," said this noble husband, "yet who can contemplate the fact of it and
not call the world irrational if, out of deference to a few particles of disor-
dered matter, it excludes so fair a spirit?"

18   (7) But this question of the irrationality of a world which would allow
death to exercise mastery over a radiant spirit, has application not merely to
the individual but also to the race. This brings me to my seventh reason for
believing in immortality—a reason drawn from the logic of evolution. There
is nothing more familiar, of course, than the fact that this world is the result
of a natural process of development which has been going on for unnum-
bered millions of years. If this process is rational, as man's processes are rational, it must have been working all these eons of time to the achievement of
some permanent and worthy end. What is this end? It is not the physical
world itself, for the day must come when this earth will be swallowed up by
the sun, and all the universe be merged again into the original fire-mist from
which it sprang. It is not the works of man, for these perish even as man lives,
and must vanish utterly in the last cataclysm of ruin. It is not man himself, for
man, like the earth on which he lives, must finally disappear. Is there nothing
that will remain as the evidence and vindication of this cosmic process? Or
must we believe that, from the beginning, it has been like a child's tower of
blocks built up only to be thrown down?

19   It was the challenge of this contingency, of evolution coming in the end to
naught that moved no less a man than Charles Darwin, agnostic though he

was, to proclaim the conviction that "it is an intolerable thought that man and all other sentient beings are doomed to complete annihilation after such long-continued slow process." Unless the universe is crazy, something must remain. The process must justify itself by producing something that endures. And what can this thing be but the spiritual essence of man's nature—the soul which is immortal? "The more thoroughly we comprehend the process of evolution," says John Fiske in an unforgettable statement, "the more we are likely to feel that to deny the everlasting persistence of the spiritual element in man is to rob the whole process of its meaning. Its goes far toward putting us to permanent intellectual confusion." Which led him to his famous verdict upon all the evidence: "I believe in the immortality of the soul as a supreme act of faith in the reasonableness of God's work."

20   (8) This leads us deep into the realm of science—to a fundamental principle that provides my eighth reason for believing in immortality. I refer to the principle of persistence or conservation. The gist of this doctrine is that nothing in the universe is ever lost. All energy is conserved. No matter what changes take place in any particular form of energy, that energy persists, if not in the old form then in a new, and the sum total of energy in the universe remains the same. "Whatever is," says Sir Oliver Lodge, speaking of forms of energy in the physical universe, "whatever is, both was and shall be." And he quotes the famous statement of Professor Tait, that "persistence, or conservation, is the test or criterion of real existence."

21   Now if this principle applies to the "real existence" of the material world, why not to the "real existence" of the spiritual world as well? If it is impossible to think of physical energy as appearing and disappearing, coming into and going out of existence, why is it not equally impossible to think of intellectual or moral or spiritual energy as acting in this same haphazard fashion? We would laugh at a man who contended that the heat in molten metal, which disappears under the cooling action of air or water, had thereby been destroyed. Why should we not similarly laugh at a man who argues that the personality of a human being, which disappears under the chilling influence of death, has thereby been annihilated? What the personality may be, I do not know. Whether it is a form of energy itself, as some scientists assert, or "belongs to a separate order of existence," as Sir Oliver Lodge, for example, argues, I cannot say. But of this thing I am sure—that the soul of man is just as much a force in the world as magnetism or steam, or electricity, and that if the cosmic law of conservation forbids the destruction of the latter, it must as well forbid the destruction of the former. Anything else is inconceivable. The universe cannot be so thrifty of its physical, and so wasteful of its spiritual, resources. It is madness to conceive that the heat of an engine must be preserved, while the love of a heart may be thrown away. What prevails in the great realm of matter can be only an anticipation of what must equally prevail in the greater realm of spirit. For the universe is one. Its laws are everywhere the same. What science has discovered about the conservation of energy is only the physical equivalent of what religion has discovered about the immortality of the soul.

22   (9) We are coming now to ultimate things—to those first and last questions of origins and meanings. This brings me to my ninth reason for believing in immortality—the fact, namely, that all the values of life exist in man, and in man alone. For the world as we know it and love it is not the world as we receive it, but the world as we make it by the creative genius of the inward spirit. Consider this earthly scene with man eliminated! The sun would be here, and the stars. Mountains would still lift themselves to the skies, and oceans spread afar to vast horizons. Birds would sing, and leaves rustle, and sunsets glow. But what would it all mean without man to see and hear, to interpret? What do the stars mean to the eagle, or the sea to the porpoise, or the mountain to the goat? It is man's ear which has heard the cuckoo as a "wandering voice," his eye which has seen "the floor of heaven thick inlaid with patines of bright gold," his mind which has found "sermons in stone, books in the running brooks, and good in everything." All that is precious in the world—all its beauty, its wonder, its meaning—exists in man, and by man, and for man. The world is what man has done with it in the far reaches of his soul. And we are asked to believe that the being who sees and glorifies shall perish, while the world which he has seen and glorified endures! Such a conclusion is irrational. The being who created the world must himself be greater than the world. The soul which conceives Truth, Goodness and Beauty, must itself be as eternal as the Truth, Goodness, and Beauty which it conceives. Nothing has any value without man. Man, therefore, is the supreme value. Which is the essence of the Platonic philosophy of eternal life for man!

23   "Tell me, then," says Socrates in the *Phaedo,* "what is that the inherence of which renders the body alive?"

24   "The soul," Cebes replied.

25   "Then whatever the soul possesses, to that she comes bearing life?"

26   "Yes, certainly."

27   "And is there any opposite to life?"

28   "There is—Death."

29   "And will the soul ever receive the opposite of what she brings?"

30   "Impossible," replied Cebes.

31   "Then," said Socrates, "the soul is immortal!"

32   (10) These, now, are my main reasons for believing in immortality. I have but one more, the tenth to add. It is the pragmatic argument that faith in an eternal life beyond the grave justifies itself in terms of the life that we are now living upon this side of the grave. For immortality does not concern the future alone; it concerns, also, the present. We are immortal today, if we are ever going to be immortal tomorrow. And this means that we have the chance to put to the test, even now and here, the belief to which we hold. It is the essence of the pragmatic philosophy that what is true will conduce to life, as food conduces to health, and that what is false will destroy life, as poison the body. Whatever is true enlarges and lifts and strengthens the life of man; whatever is false represses and weakens and disintegrates his life. Now what does immortality do when we put its affirmation to this test? What are the consequences which follow if we live as though we were eternal spirits? Can there be any doubt as to the answer?

33   We see a universe where spiritual values, not material forces, prevail; where personality, whether in ourselves or in others, is precious, and therefore to be conserved; where principles, not possessions, are the supreme concern of life; where man is equal to his task, and labors not in vain for the high causes of humanity; where sacrifice is not foolish but wise, and love "the greatest thing in the world." The man who lives an immortal life takes on immortal qualities. His character assumes the proportions of his faith, and his work the range of his high destiny. "Immortality makes great living;" says Dr. Fosdick. Therefore I believe in immortality.

34   Ten reasons! Are these all? No, they are not all! They are simply ten of the many reasons for the most persistent faith which has ever beset the heart of man. In choosing these ten, I have sought to gather reasons which were reasons, and not mere superstitions—arguments which appeal to intellect rather than emotion, and which are based upon experience rather than credulity. That these reasons prove the idea of immortality to be true, I cannot claim. But there is many an idea which we accept for good reasons, even though it be not proved, as there is many a verdict in court which is returned for good reasons, even though it be not proved, and immortality is one of them. What impresses me, as I follow the course of this great argument through the ages, is what impressed the mind of James Martineau when he said, "We do not believe immortality because we have proved it, but we forever try to prove it because we believe it." Hence the judgment of the poet, Tennyson—

> O, yet we trust that somehow good
> Will be the final goal of ill,
> pangs of nature, sins of will,
> Defects of doubt, and taints of blood.
>
> That nothing walks with aimless feet;
> That not one life shall be destroyed,
> cast as rubbish to the void,
> When God hath made the pile complete. . . .
>
> I stretch lame hands of faith, and grope
> And gather dust and chaff, and call
> To what I feel is Lord of all,
> And faintly trust the larger hope.

~

(5,622 words)

VOCABULARY

immortality (title)	penetrated (1)	discourse (2)
parables (5)	providence (6)	beneficent (6)
permeated (6)	testimony (8)	presumption (8)
pertinaciously (9)	speculation (11)	organism (11)
correspondence (11)	diffusion (13)	presage (13)
consensus (14)	endowment (15)	discrepancy (15)
constitutes (15)	unparalleled (15)	violation (15)

economy (15)   transient (17)   cataclysm (18)
vindication (18)   contingency (19)   naught (19)
sentient (19)   persistence (20)   conservation (20)
annihilated (21)   pragmatic (32)   disintegrates (32)
credulity (34)

THE FACTS

1. Does the author offer proof of immortality or does he base his argument on other claims? In what way does he compare the belief in immortality to experience in a courtroom? Explain how he achieved his belief in immortality.

2. Does the author come up with some telling, new ideas in support of immortality? If so, what are they; if not, why not?

3. What three existing reasons favoring immortality does the author dismiss? Why do these reasons not concern him?

4. What is the first reason the author presents for believing in immortality? How strong do you consider the logic behind this reason? Offer your own reaction.

5. What idea from the evolutionary theory does the author borrow in order to strengthen his second reason for believing in immortality— namely that whenever human beings think deeply, the idea of immortality surfaces?

THE STRATEGIES

1. How does the author assure that the reader can follow his ten reasons for believing in immortality without getting lost in the catalogue? What advantage does this system have? What other system could he have used?

2. Who are "those who claim," referred to in paragraph 1? What do you make of this reference? Does it help the author's argument? Why or why not? Explain yourself.

3. Compared with the other essays in this book, what level of English does this essay use? How easy or difficult was it for you to follow the argument? Analyze the style and voice. Consider such matters as vocabulary, allusions, figurative language, and sentence structure.

4. Which paragraph begins the author's reasons for believing in immortality? How does he indicate that this is where he intends to start? What other purpose does the paragraph serve?

5. In paragraph 17, the author alludes to Shelley, Phillips Brooks, and Captain Scott—all men with lives of great promise cut off by early deaths. Who are these men and what was their contribution to history? What other talented young people can you cite who died while they were young?

THE ISSUES

1. What is your response to the author's view that because immortality cannot be disproved, anyone who feels that a belief in immortality would bring satisfaction and hope should hold such a belief with impunity? How logical is this argument?

2. How comfortable are you with the author's third reason for believing in immortality—that because the leaders and greatest geniuses of the human race have always believed in immortality, therefore such a belief is rational? How does the author support this reason?

3. Do you agree that if human beings are not immortal, then why are they so over-endowed with mental and spiritual faculties not necessary to a successful existence? Why, in your view, do we not have the swiftness of the deer, the strength of the lion, or the vision of the eagle? Would you prefer more brawn and less brain? Explain your answer.

4. Do you agree with the author's view that as human beings age and lose their physical abilities they develop deeper desires for spiritual gifts? What distinction do you see between the life of the body and the life of the soul? Explain your answer.

5. Do you agree with the author's view that because nothing is ever destroyed in the physical world, this same law can apply to the spiritual world as well? An answer to this question requires that you closely evaluate the similarities of the physical and spiritual worlds. In other words, are these two realms really alike or are there significant differences between them?

SUGGESTIONS FOR WRITING

1. Using Alfred Lord Tennyson's lines at the end of the essay as a springboard, write an essay on the subject of hope beyond this life.

2. Write an essay in which you use the seasonal cycles—spring, summer, autumn, and winter—as symbols of either hope or fate.

BREAKING THE LAST TABOO

James A. Haught

James A Haught (b. 1932) is an editor and writer who has won many awards, including the National Headliner Award (1971). He is the author of several books, among them Holy Horrors: An Illustrated History of Religious Murder and Madness *(1990) and* Two Thousand Years of Disbelief: Famous People with the Courage to Doubt *(1996).*

~

1　Few Americans know that Thomas Jefferson wrote, in a letter to John Adams:

2   "The day will come when the mystical generation of Jesus, by the supreme being as his father in the womb of a virgin, will be classed with the fable of the generation of Minerva in the brain of Jupiter."

3   Or that Albert Einstein wrote in the *New York Times* in 1930:

4   "I cannot imagine a God who rewards and punishes the objects of his creation, whose purposes are modeled after our own—a God, in short, who is but a reflection of human frailty. Neither can I believe that the individual survives the death of his body, although feeble souls harbor such thoughts through fear or ridiculous egotism."

5   Or that Mark Twain wrote in his journal:

6   "I cannot see how a man of any large degree of humorous perception can ever be religious—unless he purposely shut the eyes of his mind and keep them shut by force."

7   Or that Emily Brontë wrote in 1846:
      "Vain are the thousand creeds that move men's hearts, unutterably vain, worthless as withered weeds."

8   Or that Sigmund Freud wrote, in a letter to a friend:

9   "Neither in my private life nor in my writings, have I ever made a secret of being an out-and-out unbeliever."

10   Or that Thomas Paine wrote in *The Age of Reason*:

11   "All national institutions of churches, whether Jewish, Christian or Turkish, appear to me no other than human inventions, set up to terrify and enslave mankind, and monopolize power and profit."

12   Or that Thomas Edison told the *New York Times* in 1910:

13   "I cannot believe in the immortality of the soul. . . . No, all this talk of an existence for us, as individuals, beyond the grave is wrong. It is born of our tenacity of life—our desire to go on living—our dread of coming to an end."

14   Or that Voltaire wrote, in a letter to Frederick the Great:

15   "Christianity is the most ridiculous, the most absurd, and bloody religion that has ever infected the world."

16   Or that Beethoven shunned religion and scorned the clergy.

17   Or that Abraham Lincoln never joined a church, and once wrote a skeptical treatise, which friends burned in a stove, to save him from wrecking his political career.

18   Or that the motto of Margaret Sanger's birth-control newsletter was: "No gods, no masters."

19   Or that Clarence Darrow said, in a 1930 speech in Toronto:

20   "I don't believe in God because I don't believe in Mother Goose."

21   Or that President William Howard Taft said, in a letter declining the presidency of Yale University:

22   "I do not believe in the divinity of Christ, and there are many other of the postulates of the orthodox creed to which I cannot subscribe."

23   Or that Luther Burbank told a newspaper interviewer in 1926:

24   "As a scientist, I cannot help feeling that all religions are on a tottering foundation. . . . I am an infidel today. I do not believe what has been served to me to believe. I am a doubter, a questioner, a skeptic. When it can be proved

to me that there is immortality, that there is resurrection beyond the gates of death, then I will believe. Until then, no."

25 Or that Bertrand Russell wrote in 1930:

26 "My own view of religion is that of Lucretius. I regard it as a disease born of fear and as a source of untold misery to the human race."

27 Or that George Bernard Shaw wrote, in the preface to one of his plays:

28 "At present there is not a single credible established religion in the world."

29 Or that Leo Tolstoy wrote, in response to his excommunication by the Holy Synod of the Russian Orthodox church:

30 "To regard Christ as God, and to pray to him, are to my mind the greatest possible sacrilege."

31 Or that Charles Darwin said:

32 "The mystery of the beginning of all things is insoluble by us, and I for one must be content to remain an agnostic."

33 Or that Kurt Vonnegut said:

34 "Say what you will about the sweet miracle of unquestioning faith, I consider a capacity for it terrifying and absolutely vile."

35 Or that Gloria Steinem said:

36 "By the year 2000, we will, I hope, raise our children to believe in human potential, not God."

37 Many, perhaps most, of the world's outstanding thinkers, scientists, writers, reformers—people who changed Western life—have been religious skeptics. But this fact is little known in America. Why?

38 Because our nation has one last taboo, one unmentionable topic: religious doubt.

39 In the daily tumult, it's permissible to challenge any idea, save one. Supernatural religion—invisible gods and devils, heavens and hells—is off limits. It's acceptable to write that Elvis is alive on a UFO, but not that God is a figment of the imagination. A few "freethought" journals do so, but mainstream media mostly stay mum.

40 There's an unspoken consensus that the subject is too touchy, that it is "impolite" to question anyone's religion. In a nation of 100 million church members, with an upsurge of fundamentalism, too many feelings would be hurt.

41 Why are some believers angered by disbelief? Bertrand Russell offered this explanation:

42 "There is something feeble and a little contemptible about a man who cannot face the perils of life without the help of comfortable myths. Almost inevitably, some part of him is aware that they are myths, and that he believes them only because they are comforting. But he dares not face this thought! Moreover, since he is aware, however dimly, that his opinions are not rational, he becomes furious when they are disputed."

43 Maybe that's the reason why, for many centuries, you could be killed for doubting dogmas. Believers killing non-believers was a pattern long before the Ayatollah Khomeini ordered a holy hit on Salman Rushdie.

44 In the fifth century B.C.E., the Greek teacher Protagoras wrote:

45   "As to the gods, I have no way of knowing either that they exist or do not exist, or what they are like."

46   Protagoras was charged with impiety, as were other Greek thinkers. Unlike Socrates and Anaxagoras, who were sentenced to death, Protagoras merely was banished from Athens, and his books were burned. As he sailed into exile, he drowned.

47   In the year 415, the woman scientist Hypatia, head of the legendary Alexandria library, was beaten to death by Christian monks who considered her a pagan. The leader of the monks, Cyril, was canonized a saint.

48   In the eleventh century, Omar Khayyam wrote his exquisite Persian verses on the futility of trying to discern any purpose of life. He scoffed at believers yearning for heaven—"Fools, your reward is neither here nor there"—and belittled divine prophecies:

49
>   The revelations of the devout and learn'd
>   Who rose before us and as prophets burn'd
>   Are all but stories, which, awoke from sleep
>   They told their comrades, and to sleep return'd.

50   How did Omar escape execution in the Muslim world, which is known for beheading "blasphemers"? Actually, Omar is a mystery, and the verses attributed to him didn't begin surfacing until two centuries after his death.

51   In the 1500s, Michel de Montaigne, who created the essay as a literary form, wrote comments such as:

52   "Man is certainly stark mad: he cannot make a worm, yet he will make gods by the dozen."

53   Although Montaigne lived at a time when "heretics" were burned, he eluded prosecution. Other thinkers weren't so lucky. In 1553, the physician Michael Servetus, who discovered the pulmonary circulation of blood, was burned alive in John Calvin's Geneva for doubting the Trinity. (In my Unitarian church, the youth group holds a yearly "Michael Servetus Wiener Roast" in his memory.)

54   In 1600, the philosopher Giordano Bruno was burned for teaching that the earth circles the sun, and that the universe is infinite. He was among thousands of Inquisition victims.

55   Later in the 1600s, the Englishman Thomas Hobbes, generally deemed the first major thinker in what is now called the Age of Reason, wrote:

56   "Opinion of ghosts, ignorance of second causes, devotion to what men fear, and taking of things casual for prognostics, consisteth the natural seeds of religion."

57   A bishop accused Hobbes of atheism. Parliament ordered an investigation. Hobbes hastily burned his manuscripts, and escaped with only a ban against future writings.

58   Baruch Spinoza, a Jew in Amsterdam, doubted theological dogmas and wrote lines such as:

59   "Popular religion may be summed up as a respect for ecclesiastics."

60　He was excommunicated by the Dutch synagogue, and lived as a semi-outcast.

61　Gradually, the iron fist of religion lost its grip in the West, and disbelief became a bit safer. But there were relapses. For example, a French teen-ager was beheaded and burned in 1766 for marring a crucifix, singing irreverent songs, and wearing his hat while a church procession passed. Voltaire tried to save him, but the clergy demanded death, and the French parliament decreed it.

62　And Denis Diderot, creator of the first encyclopedia, was jailed for skepticism, and his writings burned. And English publishers who printed Thomas Paine's *The Age of Reason* were jailed for blasphemy.

63　Despite the risks, thinkers kept on questioning, and the right to doubt gradually was established—in the West, but not in the Muslim world, where "blasphemers" still face death today.

64　Although the right was won, it remains partly muzzled in America. What schoolchild is taught that Thomas Jefferson wrote many sneers at "priest-craft"—that he was denounced as a "howling atheist"—and that his famous vow of "eternal hostility against every form of tyranny over the mind of man," which is engraved in his memorial in Washington, was written of the clergy?

65　What student hears scientific explanations of religion, such as this one: Sigmund Freud said the widespread belief in a father-god arises from psychology. Each tiny child is awed by his or her father as a seemingly all-powerful protector and punisher. As maturity comes, the real father grows less awesome. But the infantile image remains hidden in the subconscious, and becomes attached to an omnipotent, magical father in an invisible heaven. Unknowingly, Freud said, believers worship the loner forgotten toddler impression of the biological father, "clothed in the grandeur in which he once appeared to the small child."

66　Although open agnosticism is a no-no in America—and although fundamentalism is booming—supernatural religion is fading among educated people. America's mainline Protestant churches, formerly the domain of the elite, have lost millions of members since the 1960s. Intelligent people don't take miracles seriously, and realize there's no evidence of a spirit realm.

67　The old church "thou shalt nots" against sex, liquor, gambling, birth control, dancing, Sunday shopping, etc., have subsided in our lifetime. Fundamentalism may be rising, but so is secularism. Educated Americans are becoming like Europeans, who have mostly abandoned religion. In England, for example, only a tiny fringe attends church today.

68　Soon it may be acceptable to challenge the supernatural, as so many great figures have done. The tacit code of silence—the last taboo—may be near an end. I certainly hope so.

～

(1,898 words)

Sources of Quotations (in sequence as they appear in the article)

Thomas Jefferson—letter to John Adams, April 11, 1823

Albert Einstein—*New York Times* commentary, November 9, 1930

Mark Twain—*Mark Twain's Notebooks and Journals,* edited by Frederick Anderson, 1979, notebook 27, August 1887–July 1888

Emily Bronte—*No Coward Soul,* January 1846

Sigmund Freud—letter to Charles Singer

Thomas Paine—*The Age of Reason,* 1794

Thomas Edison—interview in the *New York Times,* October 2, 1910, front of magazine section, by Edward Marshall

Voltaire—letter to Frederick the Great, quoted in the *Encyclopedia of Unbelief,* Prometheus Books, 1985, p. 715

Margaret Sanger—masthead of her newsletter, *The Woman Rebel,* quoted in the 1994 *Women of Freethought Calendar* by Carole Gray, Columbus, Ohio

Clarence Darrow—speech at Toronto, 1930, cited in *The Great Quotations* by George Seldes, Lyle Stuart publisher, 1960, p. 190

William Howard Taft—*The Life and Times of William Howard Taft,* by Harry F. Pringle, Farrar & Rinehart, Inc., New York, 1939, p. 373

Luther Burbank—*San Francisco Bulletin,* January 22, 1926, p. 1, by Edgar Waite, headline: "I'm an Infidel, Declares Burbank, Casting Doubt *on Soul* Immortality Theory"

Bertrand Russell—opening lines of essay "Has Religion Made Useful Contributions to Civilization," 1930

George Bernard Shaw—*Major Barbara,* preface, final paragraph

Leo Tolstoy—letter April 4, 1901, to the Holy Synod of the Russian Orthodox church, in response to his excommunication, cited in *Tolstoy,* by Henri Troyat, Doubleday, 1967, p. 591; and In *The Life of Lyof N. Tolstoy,* by Nathan Haskell Dole, Scribner's, 1923, pp. 371–372

Charles Darwin—*Life and Letters,* cited in Peter's *Quotations,* by Laurance J. Peter, Wm. Morrow & Co., 1977, p. 45

Kurt Vonnegut—*Peter's Quotations,* p. 191

Gloria Steinem—*Peter's Quotations,* p. 103

Russell again—*Human Society in Ethics and Politics,* 1954

Protagoras—*On the Gods*

Omar Khayyam—*The Rubaiyat of Omar Kiayyam,* translated by Edward Fitzgerald, fifth translation, *1889,* verse 65, reprinted by Dover Thrift Editions, 1990, p. 41

Michel de Montaigne—*Apology to Raimond Sebond.* 1580, Essays book 2, chapter 12

Thomas Hobbes—quoted by *Rufus* K. Noyes in *Yews of Religion,* L. K. Washburn publisher, Boston, 1906, p. 30

Baruch Spinoza—quoted by Eugene Brussell in *The Dictionary of Quotable Definitions,* Prentice Hall, 1970, p. 490

Thomas Jefferson—vow against tyranny, letter to Dr. Benjamin Rush, September 23, 1800

Sigmund Freud—father-God explanation from "The Future of an Illusion," in *The Freud Reader,* edited by Peter Gay, W. W. Norton, 1989, pp. 694–696; quote is from *New Introductory Lectures on Psychoanalysis,* cited by Seldes in *The Great Quotations,* p. 261

VOCABULARY

mystical (2)	fable (2)	perception (6)
creeds (7)	unutterably (7)	monopolize (11)
tenacity (13)	treatise (17)	postulates (22)
orthodox (22)	infidel (24)	excommunication (29)
sacrilege (30)	insoluble (32)	taboo (38)
tumult (39)	mum (39)	consensus (40)
contemptible (42)	disputed (42)	impiety (44)
futility (48)	discern (48)	eluded (53)
pulmonary (53)	dogmas (58)	ecclesiastics (59)
tacit (68)		

THE FACTS

1. What is a *taboo?* Look up the word if you don't understand it. What is the particular taboo about which the author writes?

2. Who is Clarence Darrow, referred to in paragraph 19? Do you consider him a viable reference for the author's position on the supernatural? What is the meaning of Darrow's reference to Mother Goose?

3. Charles Darwin called himself an *agnostic.* What are the differences among an *agnostic,* a *skeptic,* and an *atheist?* Look up each word in a dictionary so that you understand its meaning. Which of these attitudes is most likely to develop into a *believer?*

4. According to Bertrand Russell, believers are dangerous because they get deeply angered by disbelief. Why are they so angered? Do you agree with this opinion? Explain your answer.

5. What explanation does Sigmund Freud, the father of psychiatry, give for the widespread belief in a father-God? What is your response to Freud's explanation?

THE STRATEGIES

1. What is the main rhetorical mode used by the author to support his thesis that a belief in God is going out of style? Do you think this same mode could be used to support a thesis stating the opposite view?

2. Which quotation impressed you the most—either positively or negatively? Explain your answer.

3. Who is the first person quoted by the author at the start of his essay? Why do you think he placed this particular reference at the outset of his essay? What is your personal reaction to the allusion?

4. Why is the allusion to Hypatia (paragraph 47) rather unusual in this essay? What irony does it point out?

5. What is the purpose of repeating the word "or" so often in the first part of the essay? What effect does this repetition have? Where does the author express his own view of "the last taboo"? How effective is this placement?

THE ISSUES

1. How important is it to live in a country that allows its citizens to question sacred beliefs? How is this right guaranteed in the United States? What dangers, if any, might be associated with freedom of expression?

2. If you are a believer, how do you feel about unbelievers? If you are an unbeliever, how do you feel about believers?

3. In your view, what happens when scientific discoveries are suppressed as soon as they disagree with truths that are held sacred? Give examples that support your answer.

4. What would it take for a person like Luther Burbank to believe in immortality? What proof would he need? Is this kind of proof available?

5. For most believers, what is the crux of their belief? Is this an intelligent approach? Why or why not? How do you think unbelievers should be treated in our country?

SUGGESTIONS FOR WRITING

1. After comparing the essay by John Haynes Holmes with that of James A. Haught, write an essay in which you support one view or the other. Write a clear thesis in the opening paragraph of your essay; then support that thesis with appropriate reasoning and evidence.

2. Write an essay in which you state your own approach to the existence of God and immortality. Whatever your position, state it clearly as a thesis and then support it with appropriate evidence.

CHILDREN'S LETTERS TO GOD

Dear God, Thank you for the baby brother but what I asked for was a puppy. You can look it up.

Joyce

Dear God, It rained for our whole vacation and is my father mad! He said some things about you that people are not supposed to say, but I hope you will not hurt him anyway. Your friend (I am not going to tell you who I am).

Unsigned

Dear God, How did you know you were God?

Charlene

Dear God, What does it mean you are a jealous God? I thought you had everything.

Jane

Dear God, We read Thomas Edison made light. But in Sunday School they said you did it. I bet he stoled your Idea.

Sincerely, Donna

Dear God, I am doing the best I can. It's hard sometimes.

Frank

Dear God, I didn't think orange went with purple until I saw the sunset you made on Tuesday. That was Cool. Thank you.

Eugene

Dear God, I do not think anybody could be a better God. Well, I just want you to know that. And I am not just saying that because you are God.

Charles

—————— STUDENT CORNER ——————

I

Final Draft

The Existence of God

Ara Babaian, Loyola Law School

Whether viewed as a single deity or a collection of deities, God used to perform a larger role in society than he (or she) does today. In fact, human beings of bygone eras would plead to God for everything in their lives, giving him the power to rule over them in every situation. When something good happened, these people explained the good as God's favor. Conversely, when something bad happened, they understood it to be God's wrath, punishing humans for being sinful, or sometimes God's fickleness, done for no apparent reason. For instance, the cavemen begged God for a successful hunt. The Greeks pleaded to their gods and goddesses for a bountiful harvest of grapes. In the middle ages, Europeans and Middle Easterners alike prayed to God to prevail in war. However, as people began to better understand the science of things, they reduced the role that God played in their lives. They no longer needed to pray to God for rain, because they understood how water evaporates and turns into clouds which, in turn, make rain. They understood that it was not the devil who possessed certain individuals, but chemical and psychological disturbances that produce schizophrenia, manic depression, and other personality disorders. As such, science made God smaller.

Babaian 2

Now, people still invoke God's name in times of despair, as when natural disaster strikes or when someone dies, and also in times of celebration, as when a child is born or when two people marry. Of course, many sectors of society remain devout followers of one religion or another. These people uphold traditions, old and new, and call to God more regularly than most other people for spiritual support and guidance. Still, many people are not as fervent in their religious practice as were humans in the past.

Nevertheless, it would be false to say that Americans lack spirituality in today's world. During the 1990s, "religions" have gained a certain popularity. People study religions like Buddhism, the Cabbala, and New Age philosophies. They pick and choose tenets from these and other doctrines to form their own, idiosyncratic faith. Even die-hard Christians, at the very least, use terms in their daily vocabulary that stem from other religions, terms like *karma, nirvana,* and *yin* and *yang.*

Thus, although many Americans are no longer religious in the traditional sense, we are nevertheless spiritual in a more organic and all-inclusive sense. True, parts of American society stand firm in their belief of one God or another, and there is definitely a good share of new religions that may or may not deserve merit. It is doubtful that these phenomena will change in the future. However, in this highly technological world where the role of God has essentially atrophied to a smaller stature, Americans are looking to a variety of beliefs not only for spiritual nourishment, but also to contemplate the final, unanswerable question—death.

How I Write

I admit it: I enjoy writing. Writing is a difficult process; you have to sit alone and pull words from your mind, put them in an intelligible sequence, and hopefully do it in an interesting way. When I write an essay, I go around for days or, if I have time, weeks just thinking about the topic. Most people call this procrastination, but it's really not because I am constantly thinking about the things I want to say. When I finally sit in front of my computer, I write whatever comes to my mind, however it comes. I then go back and rewrite portions, copy and paste parts of my essay to other parts, and just generally make it better.

How I Wrote This Essay

Writing this essay was like going to the dentist. I didn't pick the topic, and I don't like writing about "The Existence of God." The topic just sounds too daunting—but then again so is going to the dentist. Nevertheless, I went around for a month thinking about what I wanted to say, with the deadline of when I had to turn in the essay in mind. Finally, I sat in front of my computer, wrote, rewrote, and finalized the essay.

My Writing Tip

Write about a topic that you like and want to learn more about. Write after you have thought about your topic for at least a couple of days. When you write, do not be afraid of making typographical, punctuation, or grammatical errors. Just write. Later, you will have plenty of time to edit your paper. Always make several drafts; nobody's first product is a final product. If you have the time, put what you've written away for a couple of days (or at least hours) and read it again with a "fresh eye," making any necessary edits. Make your edits on a hard copy of the essay, not on the computer screen. Read your essay aloud; awkward sentences sound awkward. I strongly urge you to use your spell check, but after you do, read your essay again for spelling errors; your computer can't tell the difference between "here" and "hear" or "their" and "there." Finally, if you like what you wrote, try to publish it in a school or community magazine. It's worth the effort.

CHAPTER WRITING ASSIGNMENTS

1. Write an essay in which you contrast one of the following pairs of concepts:
   a. Hearing–listening
   b. Liberty–license
   c. Servant–slave
   d. Democracy–demagoguery
   e. Art–craft
   f. Having an opinion–being opinionated
   g. Talent–ability
2. Write an essay comparing any two jobs you've ever had.

WRITING ASSIGNMENTS FOR A SPECIFIC AUDIENCE

1. Write a letter to a younger brother or sister—or an imaginary one—contrasting college with high school. Be sure to choose appropriate bases for the contrast, such as academic rigor, social life, relationships with teachers, and independence.

2. Write an essay to one of your parents contrasting your former boss with your present one.

COLLABORATIVE WRITING PROJECT

Assemble students who are literature lovers into two groups. Each group will select a modern author for a study. By consensus, choose one short work from the author for reading and study. In an oral session, compare and contrast the single representative work of both authors using mutually agreed upon bases of comparison/contrast. From your notes, team-write a comparison contrast of the chosen authors.

13

Division/Classification

EDITORS' COUNSEL

What Division/Classisification Does

To write a division/classification means to break down a subject into its constituent types. If you write a paragraph on the kinds of books in your library, the types of cars in your miniature-car collection, or the varieties of humor in Mark Twain's works, you are classifying. A prime purpose of a division/classification is to discover the nature of a subject by a study of its parts and their relationship to the larger whole. For example, the following paragraph tries to explain and understand people by grouping them together into two primary categories:

> A simple experiment will distinguish two types of human nature. Gather a throng of people and pour them into a ferry-boat. By the time the boat has swung into the river you will find that a certain proportion have taken the trouble to climb upstairs in order to be out on deck and see what is to be seen as they cross over. The rest have settled indoors to think what they will do upon reaching the other side, or perhaps lose themselves in apathy or tobacco smoke. But leaving out those apathetic, or addicted to a single enjoyment, we may divide all the alert passengers on the boat into two classes: those who are interested in crossing the river, and those who are merely interested in getting across. And we may divide all the people on the earth, or all the moods of people, in the same way. Some of them are chiefly occupied with attaining ends, and some with receiving experiences. The distinction of the two will be more marked when we name the first kind practical, and the second poetic, for common knowledge recognizes that a person poetic or in a poetic mood is impractical, and a practical person is intolerant of poetry.
>
> —Max Eastman, "Poetic People"

Division and classification are common to the way we think. We divide and classify the plant and animal kingdoms into phyla, genera, families, and species; we divide the military into the Army, Navy, Air Force, Marines, and Coast Guard. We divide and classify people into kinds and types. When we ask, "What kind of person is he?" we are asking for information developed by division and classification. An assignment asking for an essay developed by division, therefore, is an exercise in this common mode of thinking.

When to Use Division/Classification

Division/classification is especially useful in analyzing big, complex subjects. All of us draw on categories—some accurate, some prejudicial—in our attempts to understand the world around us. We wonder what type of person a certain man or woman is, and when we think we know, we react accordingly. This is not necessarily bad, so long as we do not hold false categories about people that function as prejudices. We speculate on the experiences that happen to us and try to sort them into understandable types. We say that yesterday was that kind of day and that last year was that sort of year. We have theories about kinds of love, types of friends, varieties of personalities. Science, philosophy, and even the practical arts are largely based on classifications. Biology sorts animals and plants into genera and species; medicine organizes diseases into types; chemistry classifies substances; and literature classifies writing. The concept of types rescues us from the tyranny of uniqueness and spares us from having to individually study every event, object, person, or thing. Without categories that tell us that this is like that, experience would have no predictive value and we would be overwhelmed by the uniqueness of every butterfly, thunderstorm, or love affair.

How to Use Division/Classification

1. *All good writing is based on clear thinking, but division/classification most decidedly so.* To classify is to think and analyze, to see relationships between individual items where none are obvious. You are, in a sense, superimposing your mind's filing cabinet onto the world. To classify accurately, then, you must base your typing and sorting on a single principle. This means that your sorting must be done on the basis of one criterion or your scheme will be a muddle. A simple example would be if you were to classify sports by whether or not they involve physical contact and lumped tennis in with football. Obviously, tennis is a noncontact sport, and your sorting would be inaccurate. Likewise, if you were writing a paper on the works written by Samuel Johnson and came up with the following list:

   a. Johnson's poetry

   b. Johnson's prose

   c. Johnson's dictionary

   d. Boswell's *Life of Johnson*

   your division/classification would also be false. Boswell's *Life of Johnson* is not by Johnson but about him and, therefore, does not belong in your list.

In a more formal context, we see this error repeated in the following paragraph, whose division/classification is not based on a single principle:

Mass production in American industry is made up of four distinct elements: division of labor, standardization through precision tooling, assembly line, and consumer public. First is the division of labor, which means that a complicated production process is broken down into specialized individual tasks that are performed by people or machines who concentrate on these tasks only. Second is the standardization of parts as a result of precision tooling. This means that each part can be produced by machines both for interchangeability and for assembly by semiskilled workers. Third is the assembly line, which is a method of moving the work from one person to another in a continual chain of progress until the item is completed. This is a way of moving the work to the person, instead of the person to the work. The last element is the consumer public. Without it mass production would be a futile endeavor, for it is the public that buys up all the mass-produced items as fast as they roll off the assembly line.

Clearly, the division/classification is not based on a single principle. Division of labor, standardization through precision tooling, and the use of an assembly line may be part of the mass-production process, but the consumer public plainly is not. Only after production has been completed and an item is ready to be marketed does the consumer enter into the picture. As it stands, the paragraph has misrepresented the elements involved in mass production.

2. *Make your division/classification complete.* A complete division/classification is one that includes all the parts of the subject being divided. If you were to classify sports by whether or not they involve the use of a ball and left out soccer, your division/classification would be incomplete. If you omitted the short story from an essay classifying types of literature, you would likewise be guilty of this error. Similarly, if you were to divide the family of Equidae into its main categories, you would have to include the horse, the ass, and the zebra. Leave out any of these, and your division/classification would be incomplete.

3. *Avoid the overlapping of categories.* Here is an example of an overlapping division in the division/classification of literature according to genres:

   a. Poetry
   b. Short story
   c. Humor
   d. Drama
   e. Novel

   Humor is not a genre but a characteristic of poetry, a short story, a drama, or a novel. Therefore, it does not belong in this list.

Warming Up to Write a Classification

1. Here's a good exercise to get your brain to think in terms of classification—that is, inventing categories into which to divide a subject and then placing items into each category. As quickly as possible, divide each of the following subjects into as many categories as seems sensible. Keep a list of the categories. If, after rereading your list, a category doesn't fit, delete it.

   a. Books

   b. Clothing

   c. Friends

   d. Weather

   e. TV programs

   f. Pets

   g. Music

2. In the following classifications, check the category that does not fit and write down the reasons why it should be excluded.

   a. Dreams

   _____1.   sexual

   _____2.   paralyzing

   _____3.   imagining

   _____4.   replaying the day

   b. Cars

   _____1.   SUVs

   _____2.   trucks

   _____3.   sedans

   _____4.   electric cars

   c. Family games

   _____1.   card games

   _____2.   ping pong

   _____3.   domino games

   _____4.   board games

   d. Houses in which to live

   _____1.   sheds

   _____2.   cottages

   _____3.   mansions

   _____4.   tract homes

e. Jobs

_____1.   technical

_____2.   waitress

_____3.   professional

_____4.   hard labor

Looking back at Exercise 1, choose one of the subjects you classified into categories; then pick one of the categories and place at least three items in it. For instance, if you classified meals into *hors d'oeuvres, main dishes, side dishes,* and *desserts,* you might choose "main dishes" as your category and then list the following items as belonging to it: meat, poultry, fish, and vegetarian substitute. Make sure that your items are appropriately related to the category.

―――――――― **EXAMPLES** ――――――――

STYLES OF LOVING

John Alan Lee

John Alan Lee (b. 1933) is a retired Canadian sociologist who has done research in healing, educational television, and minorities.

The following essay is the result of answers to a questionnaire distributed and collected by the author. After studying the answers, Lee was able to classify love into several types. The essay originally appeared in the October, 1974 issue of *Psychology Today* and was adapted by the author from his book, *Colours of Love,* published in Canada. The types of love described are as recognizable today as they were in the 1970s.

∼

1   We will accept variety in almost anything, from roses and religions to politics and poetry. But when it comes to love, each of us believes we know the real thing, and we are reluctant to accept other notions. We disparage other people's experiences by calling them infatuations, mere sexual flings, unrealistic affairs.

2   For thousands of years writers and philosophers have debated the nature of love. Many recognized that there are different kinds of love, but few accepted them all as legitimate. Instead, each writer argues that his own concept of love is the best. C. S. Lewis[1] thought that true love must be unselfish

―――――――――――――――

[1]C. S. Lewis, British novelist and critic (1898–1963)

and altruistic, as did sociologist Pitirim Sorokin. Stendhal,[2] by contrast, took the view that love is passionate and ecstatic. Others think that "real" love must be wedded to the Protestant ethic, forging a relationship that is mutually beneficial and productive. Definitions of love range from sexual lust to an excess of friendship.

3   The ancient Greeks and Romans were more tolerant. They had a variety of words for different and, to them, equally valid types of love. But today the concept has rigidified; most of us believe that there is only one true kind of love. We measure each relationship against this ideal in terms of degree or quantity. Does Tom love me more than Tim does? Do you love me as much as I love you? Do I love you enough? Such comparisons also assume that love comes in fixed amounts—the more I give to you, the less I have for anyone else; if you don't give me everything, you don't love me enough.

4   "There is hardly any activity, any enterprise, which is started with such tremendous hopes and expectations, and yet which fails so regularly, as love," wrote Erich Fromm. I think that part of the reason for this failure rate is that too often people are speaking different languages when they speak of love. The problem is not how much love they feel, but which kind. The way to have a mutually satisfying love affair is not to find a partner who loves "in the right amount," but one who shares the same approach to loving, the same definition of love.

5   *The Structure of Love*   My research explored the literature of love and the experiences of ordinary lovers in order to distinguish these approaches. Color served me as a useful analogy in the process. There are three primary colors— red, yellow and blue—from which all other hues are composed. And empirically I found three primary types of love, none of which could be reduced to the others, and a variety of secondary types that proved to be combinations of the basic three. In love, as in color, "primary" does not mean superior; it simply refers to basic structure. Orange is no more or less a color than red, and no less worthy. In love, as in color, one can draw as many distinctions as one wishes; I have stopped, somewhat arbitrarily, with nine types.

6   *EROS*   Stendhal called love a "sudden sensation of recognition and hope." He was describing the most typical symptom of eros: an immediate, powerful attraction to the physical appearance of the beloved. "The first time I saw him was several weeks before we met," a typical erotic lover said in an interview, "but I can still remember exactly the way he looked, which was just the way I dreamed my ideal lover would look." Erotic lovers typically feel a chemical or gut reaction on meeting each other; heightened heartbeat is not just a figment of fiction, it seems, but the erotic lover's physiological response to meeting the dream.

7   Most of my erotic respondents went to bed with their lovers soon after meeting. This was the first test of whether the affair would continue, since erotic love demands that the partner live up to the lover's concept of bodily perfection. They may try to overlook what they consider a flaw, only to find

---

[2]Stendhal, pen name of Marie Henri Beyle, French novelist and biographer (1783–1842)

that it undermines the intensity of their attraction. There is no use trying to persuade such a lover that personal or intellectual qualities are more lasting or more important. To do so is to argue for another approach to love.

8   My erotic respondents all spoke with delight of the lover's skin, fragrance, hair, musculature, body proportions, and so on. Of course, the specific body type that each lover considered ideal varied, but all erotics had such an ideal, which they could identify easily from a series of photographs. Erotic lovers actively and imaginatively cultivate many sexual techniques to preserve delight in the partner's body. Nothing is more deadly for a serious erotic lover than to fall in love with a prudish partner.

9   Modern usage tends to define *erotic* as *sexual;* we equate erotic art with pornography. But eros is not mere sexual attraction; it is a demanding search for the lover's ideal of beauty, a concept that is as old as Pygmalion.[3] Eros involves mental as well as sexual attraction, which is faithful to the Platonic concept. Most dictionaries define Platonic love as "devoid of sensual feeling," which is certainly not what Plato had in mind. On the contrary, it was sensual feeling for the beautiful body of another person that evoked eros as the Greeks understood it.

10   *The Dream of the Ideal*   The fascination with beauty that marks eros is the basis for personal and psychological intimacy between the lovers. The erotic lover wants to know everything about the beloved, to become part of him or her. If an erotic relationship surpasses the initial hurdles of expectation and physical ideals, this desire for intimacy can sustain the relationship for years. (And this knowledge must be first-hand. The playful lover may ask a friend what so-and-so is like in bed. No erotic lover would dream of relying on such vicarious evidence.)

11   An essential component of successful erotic love is self-assurance. It takes confidence to reveal oneself intensely to another. A lover who doubts himself, who falls into self-recriminations if his love is not reciprocated, cannot sustain eros.

12   The typical erotic lovers in my sample avoided wallowing in extremes of emotion, especially the self-pity and hysteria that characterize mania. They recalled happy and secure childhoods, and reported satisfaction with work, family, and close friends. They were ready for love when it came along, but were not anxiously searching. They consider love to be important, but they do not become obsessive about it; when separated from the beloved, they do not lose their balance, become sick with desire, or turn moody. They prefer exclusive relationships but do not demand them, and they are rarely possessive or afraid of rivals. Erotic lovers seek a deep, pervasive rapport with their partners and share development and control of the relationship.

13   But because the erotic lover depends on an ideal concept of beauty, he is often disappointed. The failure of eros has littered our fiction with bitter and cynical stories of love, and caused conventional wisdom to be deeply suspicious of ideal beauty as a basis for relationships. Indeed, I found that the

---

[3]Paygmalion, King of Cyprus, who fell in love with a statue

purer the erotic qualities of a respondent's love experience, the less his chances of a mutual, lasting relationship.

14   An erotic lover may eventually settle for less, but he or she never forgets the compromise, and rarely loses hope of realizing the dream. However, I found several cases of "love at first sight" in which initial rapture survived years of married life. The success of a few keeps the dream alive for many more.

15   *LUDUS*   About the year One A.D. the Roman poet Ovid came up with the term *amor ludens*, playful love, love as a game. Ovid advised lovers to enjoy love as a pleasant pastime, but not to get too involved. The ludic lover refuses, then, to become dependent on any beloved, or to allow the partner to become overly attached to him or her, or too intimate.

16   Other types of lovers dismiss ludus as not a kind of love at all; erotic types disdain its lack of commitment, moralists condemn its promiscuity and hedonism. But to make a game of love does not diminish its value. No skilled player of bridge or tennis would excuse inept playing because "it's only a game," and ludus too has its rules, strategies, and points for skill. Ludus turns love into a series of challenges and puzzles to be solved.

17   *Ludis Strategies*   For example, ludus is most easily and most typically played with several partners at once, a guarantee against someone on either side getting too involved. "Love several persons," a 17th-century manual advises, for three lovers are safer than two, and two much safer than one. A ludic lover will often invent another lover, even a spouse, to keep the partner from becoming too attached.

18   But most of my ludic respondents had other tactics. They were careful not to date a partner too often; they never hinted at including the partner in any long-range plans; they arranged encounters in a casual, even haphazard, way: "I'll give you a call"; "See you around sometime." Such indefiniteness is designed to keep the partner from building up expectations or from becoming preoccupied with the affair.

19   Of course, as in many games, one must be on guard against cheats. Cheats in ludic love are cynical players who don't care how deeply involved the partner becomes, who may even exploit such intensity. Such players scandalize ludic lovers who believe in fair play. Insincerity and lies may be part of the game, so long as both partners understand this.

20   The ludic lover notices differences between bodies, but thinks it is stupid to specialize. As the ludic man said in Finian's Rainbow, when he is not near the girl he loves, he loves the girl he's near. But ludus is not simply a series of sexual encounters. A lover could get sex without the rituals of conversation, candles and wine. In ludus, the pleasure comes from playing the game, not merely winning the prize.

21   Actually, sexual gratification is only a minor part of the time and effort involved in ludic love. Of any group, ludic respondents showed the least interest in the mutual improvement of sex techniques. Their attitude was that it is easier to find a new sex partner than to work out sexual problems and explore new sexual pleasures with the current one; this view contrasts sharply

with that of erotic and storgic lovers. Ludic people want sex for fun, not emotional rapport.

22   ***Don Juans Aren't Always Doomed***   Ludus had enjoyed recurring popularity through history. Montesquieu[4] could write of 18th-century France: "A husband who wishes to be the only one to possess his wife would be regarded as a public killjoy." The first Don Juan emerged in Tirso de Molina's The Trickster of Seville in 1630, the diametric opposite of the erotic Tristan,[5] the courtly ideal. Tirso's hero conquered only four women, but a century later Mozart's Don Giovanni won a thousand and three in Espana alone.

23   Of course the various fates of the legendary ludic lovers reflect society's ambivalence toward them. They usually go to hell, get old and impotent, or meet their match and surrender. Rarely is ludus tolerated, much less rewarded.

24   But I was struck by the fact that most of my ludic respondents neither suffered nor regretted their ways. Like successful erotics, they play from a base of self-confidence. They believe in their own assets so much that they convince themselves that they do not "need" other people, like most mortals. These ludic lovers prefer to remain in perfect control of their feelings; they do not think that love is as important as work or other activities; they are thus never possessive or jealous (except as a teasing ploy in the game). They typically recall their childhoods as "average," and their current lives as "OK, but occasionally frustrating."

25   My ludic respondents seemed quite content with their detachment from intense feelings of love, but most failed the acid test of ludus: the ability to break off with a partner with whom they were through. Their intentions were ludic, but they had Victorian hangovers. They tended to prolong the relationship for the sake of the partner, until the inevitable break was painful. Ovid would not have approved. "Extinguish the fire of love gradually," he admonished, "not all at once . . . it is wicked to hate a girl you used to love."

26   The legendary ludic lovers, like Don Juan and Alfie, were generally men, and only in recent years—with the pill and penicillin—have women won entry into the game. Ludus is also frequently identified with male homosexual love; the term "gay" may have originated from the assumption that homosexuals adopt a noncommittal, playful approach to sex and love, which is not necessarily so.

27   There is a variant of this type of love that I call manic ludus, in which the lover alternates between a detached, devil-may-care attitude toward the partner, and a worried, lovesick desire for more attention. People in this conflicting state would like to be purely ludic, but they lack the vanity or self-sufficiency to remain aloof from intimacy. They both need and resent love, and they cannot control their emotions long enough to maintain a cool relationship.

---

[4]Baron de la Brede e de Montesquieu, French political philosopher, jurist, and writer (1689–1755)

[5]Tristan was a prince at King Arthur's Court who fell in love with the Irish princess Iseult and died with her.

28   *STORGE* (pronounced stor-gay) is, as Proudhon described it, "love without fever, tumult or folly, a peaceful and enchanting affection" such as one might have for a close sibling. It is the kind of love that sneaks up unnoticed; storgic lovers remember no special point when they fell in love. Since storgic lovers consider sex one of the most intimate forms of self-disclosure, sex occurs late in the relationship.

29   Storge is rarely the stuff of dramatic plays or romantic novels, except perhaps as a backdrop or point of comparison. In *Of Human Bondage,* the hero, Philip, follows a manic love affair with Mildred with a storgic marriage to Sally, whom he has known all along.

30   Storge superficially resembles ludus in its lack of great passion, but the origins of the two types are quite different. The ludic lover avoids intensity of feeling consciously aware of its risks. The storgic lover is unaware of intense feeling. It simply doesn't occur to him that a lover should be dewy-eyed and sentimental about a beloved. Such behavior is as out of place in storgic love as it would be for most of us in relating to a close friend. Storgic love "just comes naturally" with the passage of time and the enjoyment of shared activities. You grow accustomed to her face.

31   In most modern cities people do not live near each other long enough to develop the unself-conscious affection that is typical of storgic love. I found some such cases among people who grew up in rural areas. However, among my urban respondents, who usually had few lasting contacts with their childhood friends, there were some storgic types who based their love on friendship and companionship. This characteristic distinguishes storge from other types of love, in which the partners may not treat each other at all like friends.

32   When a storgic lover gets involved with another type of lover, serious misunderstandings are likely to occur. The goals of storge, for instance, are marriage, home and children, avoiding all the silly conflicts and entanglements of passion. But to the erotic or ludic lover, storge is a bore. Storge implies a life that is reasonable and predictable; why make it more complicated by engaging in emotionally exhausting types of love? Erotic lovers would never understand that question.

33   *The Strengths of Storge Storge*   is a slow-burning love, rarely hectic or urgent, though of course storgic lovers may disagree and fight. But they build up a reservoir of stability that will see them through difficulties that would kill a ludic relationship and greatly strain an erotic one. The physical absence of the beloved, for instance, is much less distressing to them than to other lovers; they can survive long separations (Ulysses and Penelope are a classic example of that ability).

34   Even if a break-up occurs, storgic lovers are likely to remain good friends. A typical storgic lover would find it inconceivable that two people who had once loved each other could become enemies, simply because they had ceased to be lovers.

35   In a ludic or erotic relationship, something is happening all the time. In eros, there is always some secret to share, a misunderstanding to mend, a separation to survive with letters and poems. In ludus, inactivity quickly leads

to boredom, and a search for new amusement. In storge, there are fewer campaigns to fight and fewer wounds to heal. There is a lack of ecstasy, but also a lack of despair.

36   Eros, ludus and storge are the three primary types of love, but few love affairs and few colors, are pure examples of one type. Most reds have a little yellow or blue in them, and most cases of eros have a little storge or ludus.

37   The color analogy led me to distinguish mixtures from blends (compounds). You can mix two colors and be aware of both components. But it may happen that two primary colors are so evenly blended that an entirely new color emerges, unclassifiable as a hue of either, with unique properties. This is the case with mania, a fourth color of love.

38   *MANIA*   The Greeks called it *theia mania*, the madness from the gods. Both Sappho and Plato, along with legions of sufferers, recorded its symptoms: agitation, sleeplessness, fever, loss of appetite, heartache. The manic lover is consumed by thoughts of the beloved. The slightest lack of enthusiasm from the partner brings anxiety and pain; each tiny sign of warmth brings instant relief, but no lasting satisfaction. The manic lover's need for attention and affection from the beloved is insatiable. Cases of mania abound in literature, for its components—furious jealousy, helpless obsession, and tragic endings—are the stuff of human conflict. Goethe made his own unhappy bout with mania the subject of his novel, The Sorrows of Young Werther, and Somerset Maugham did the same in Of Human Bondage. The manic lover alternates between peaks of ecstasy when he feels loved in return, and depths of despair when the beloved is absent. He knows his possessiveness and jealousy are self-defeating, but he can't help himself.

39   *From God's Curse to Popular Passion*   Rational lovers throughout the ages, from Lucretius[6] to Denis de Rougemont,[7] have warned us to avoid mania like the plague. Fashions in love, of course, change. To the ancient Greeks, a person who fell head-overheels, "madly" in love, had obviously been cursed by the gods. Many parents in the Middle Ages strongly disapproved of love matches, preferring their children to arrange "sensible marriages." But mania has gained popularity in the West since the 13th century; today many young people would consider it wrong to marry unless they loved "romantically."

40   So popular is mania in literature and love that I originally assumed it would be a primary type. But green, a color that occurs in nature more than any other, is not a primary, but a blend of yellow and blue. Similarly, the data from my interviews refused to reduce mania to one clear type. Instead, mania respondents derive their unique style of love from the primaries of eros and ludus.

41   These yearning, obsessed, often unhappy manic lovers are typical of frustrated eros. With eros, they share the same intensity of feeling, the same urgency to find the ideal beloved. But erotic lovers are not crushed by

---

[6]Titus Lucretius Carus, Roman poet and philosopher (96?–55 B.C.)

[7]Denis de Rougement (1906-1985). Swiss thinker and writer who wrote over 30 books including the influential *Love in the Western World* (1939)

disappointment as manic lovers are; they keep their self-respect. Manic lovers, by contrast, are self-effacing, ambivalent, lacking in confidence. They don't have a clear idea of what they are looking for, as erotic lovers do, and they feel helpless, out of control of their emotions. "I know it was crazy, but I couldn't help myself," was a favorite explanation.

42   Oddly, manic lovers persist in falling in love with people they say they don't even like. "I hate and I love," wailed the Roman poet Catullus. "And if you ask me how, I do not know. I only feel it, and I'm torn in two." Aldous Huxley's hero in *Point Counter-Point* "wanted her against all reason, against all his ideals and principles, madly, against his wishes . . . for he didn't like Lucy, he really hated her."

43   For these reasons, some psychologists consider mania to be neurotic, unhealthy. Freud was most critical of obsessive love, and Theodor Reik, in *Of Love and Lust*, explains the obsessiveness of mania as a search for the qualities in a partner that the lover feels lacking in himself. The typical manic lover in my samples seemed to feel, as the song suggests, that he was nobody until somebody loved him.

44   Paradoxically, manic lovers also behave in ways similar to ludus. They try to hold back to manipulate the lover, to play it cool. But unlike successful ludic types, manic lovers never quite succeed at detachment. Their sense of timing is off. They try to be noncommittal, only to panic and surrender in ignominious defeat.

45   *The Telephone Trauma*   Consider this typical caper. The manic realizes that he has been taking the initiative too often in calling his beloved, so he asks her to call the next time. This is a consciously ludic ploy, since no erotic or storgic lover would keep count or care. But it is part of the game in ludus to keep things in balance.

46   The hour of the expected call arrives, and the phone sits silent. The true ludic lover would not be terribly bothered; he or she would quickly make a few calls and get busy with other lovers. The manic lover falls into a frenzy of anxiety. Either he breaks down and calls the lover, or he is in such a state of emotional upset that he is incapable of ludic detachment when the lover does call: "Where were you? I was so worried!"

47   Manic lovers, in short, attempt to play by the rules of ludus with the passion of eros, and fail at both. They need to be loved so much that they do not let the relationship take its own course. They push things, and thereby tend to lose; mania rarely ends happily. Few lovers go to such extremes as violence or suicide, but most remain troubled by the experience for months, even years. Like malaria, it may return to seize the manic lover with bouts of nostalgia and unrest.

48   It is theoretically possible for mania to develop into lasting love, but the manic lover must find an unusual partner—who can ride out the storms of emotion, return the intensity of feeling, and ultimately convince the manic lover that he or she is lovable. A ludic partner will never tolerate the emotional extremes, and a storgic lover will be unable to reciprocate the feelings. A strong-willed erotic partner might manage it.

49   *Ludic Eros*   Mania can be reduced by resolving the underlying conditions that create and sustain the lover's lack of self-esteem and his desperate need to be in love. Then the lover may move toward a more confident eros or, perhaps, a more playful ludus. This is the part of the color chart labeled ludic eros, the sector between the two primaries.

50   What enables one lover to mix ludus and eros in a pleasant compromise, while another finds them compounded into mania? Having previous experience in love and many good relationships is one factor. The manic lovers in my sample were discontented with life, but ludic-erotic lovers were basically content and knew what kind of partners they wanted. Ludic-erotic people resemble ludus in their pluralism, their desire for many relationships, but they resemble eros in their preference for clearly-defined types. They do not easily accept substitutes, as ludic types do.

51   Ludic-erotic love walks an exacting tightrope between intensity and detachment. Most people think this approach is too greedy, and therefore immoral. To the ludic-erotic lover, it is just good sense.

52   *The Art of Passionate Caution*   The tightrope isn't always easy. The lover may spend an evening in the most intense intimacy with his partner, but will always back off in a ludic direction at critical moments. Just when you, the beloved, are about to react to his passion with a murmur of confirmation, he leaps from the couch to make a cup of coffee. Or just when he is about to blurt out that he loves you; he bites his lips and says something less committal: "You really turn me on."

53   The successful combination of ludus and eros is rare, but it exists. The journals of Casanova are a classic example of the bittersweet taste of this type of love. Today many attempts at "open marriages" are in fact advocating a ludic-erotic approach to love: the spouses remain primarily involved with each other, yet may have intense involvements with others so long as these remain temporary.

54   *PRAGMA*   is love with a shopping list, a love that seeks compatibility on practical criteria. In traditional societies, marriages were arranged on similarities of race, social class, income, and so on. In modern society the pragmatic approach to love argues that lovers should choose each other on the basis of compatible personalities, like interests and education, similar backgrounds and religious views, and the like. Computer-match services take a pragmatic view.

55   The pragmatic lover uses social activities and programs as a means to an end, and will drop them if there is no payoff in partners. By contrast, a storgic lover goes out for the activities he enjoys, and thereby meets someone who shares those interests. The storgic lover never consciously chooses a partner.

56   Pragma is not a primary type of love but a compound of storge and ludus. The pragmatic lover chooses a partner as if she had grown up with him (storge) and will use conscious manipulation to find one (ludus). Pragma is rather like manufactured storge, a faster means of achieving the time-honored version. If a relationship does not work out, the pragmatic lover will move rationally on, ludic-fashion, to search for another.

57   The pragmatic approach is not as cold as it seems. Once a sensible choice is made, more intense feelings may develop; but one must begin with a solid match that is practically based. Oriental matchmakers noted that in romantic love "the kettle is boiling when the young couple first starts out"—and cools with time, bringing disappointment. An arranged marriage, they say, is like a kettle that starts cold and slowly warms up. Pragmatic love grows over the years.

58   As pragma is the compound, so storge and ludus may combine as a mixture. The distinguishing features of a storgic-ludic affair are convenience and discretion. A typical example is that of a married boss and his secretary, in which the relationship is carefully managed so as to disrupt neither the boss's marriage nor the office routine. Of course, such affairs don't always stay in neat storgic-ludic boxes. In the film, *A Touch of Class,* the affair becomes too intense, threatening to interfere with the man's comfortably companionate marriage.

59   *AGAPE* (pronounced ah-ga-pay) is the classical Christian view of love: altruistic, universalistic love that is always kind and patient, never jealous, never demanding reciprocity. When St. Paul wrote to the Corinthians that love is a duty to care about others, whether the love is deserved or not, and that love must be deeply compassionate and utterly altruistic, he used the Greek word, *agape.* But all the greater religions share this concept of love, a generous, unselfish, giving of oneself.

60   I found no saints in my sample. I have yet to interview an unqualified example of agape, although a few respondents had had brief agapic episodes in relationships that were otherwise tinged with selfishness. For instance, one of my subjects, seeing that his lover was torn between choosing him or another man, resolved to save her the pain of deciding; he bowed out gracefully. His action fell short of pure agape, however, because he continued to be interested in how well his beloved was doing, and was purely and selfishly delighted when she dropped the other man and returned to him.

61   Yet my initial sample of 112 people did contain eight case histories that came quite close to the sexual restraint, dutiful self-sacrifice, universality and altruism that characterize agape. These respondents mixed storge and eros; they had an almost religious attitude toward loving, but they fell short of the hypothetical ideal in loving the partner more than anyone else. They felt intense emotion, as erotic lovers do, along with the enduring patience and abiding affection of storge.

62   Storgic-erotic respondents felt an initial attraction to their partners, distinguishable from erotic attraction by the absence of physical symptoms of excitement. And unlike eros, these people felt little or no jealousy; they seemed to find enough pleasure in the act of loving another person so that the matter of reciprocity was almost irrelevant.

63   *Testing One's Type of Love*   Why construct a typology of love in the first place? Love is a delicate butterfly, runs a certain sentiment, that can be ruined with clumsy dissection. Who cares how many species it comes in; let it fly.

64   As far as I am concerned, any analysis that helps reduce misunderstandings is worthwhile, and there is no human endeavor more ripe for misunderstandings than love. Consider. A person who has just fallen in love is often
tempted to test his sensations to prove it's "really" love. Usually such tests
are based on a unidimensional concept of love, and therefore they are usually
180° wrong.

65   For example, the decision to test love by postponing sex would be disastrous for an erotic love affair, the equivalent of depriving a baby of food for a
week to see if it is strong enough to live. A budding erotic love thrives on sexual intimacy. But delaying sex would be absolutely natural and right for a
storgic lover, and it might be a positive incentive to a manic lover.

66   The advantage of my typology, preliminary as it is, is that it teases apart
some very different definitions of love, and suggests which types of love
are most compatible. Generally, the farther apart two types are on the color
chart, the less likely that the lovers share a common language of love. One
of my ludic respondents berated his storgic lover for trying to trap him into
a commitment, while she accused him of playing games just to get her
body. Different types, different languages. Eros insists on rapid intimacy,
storge resents being rushed. Same feelings of "love," but opposite ways to
express it.

67   Obviously, two lovers who represent unlike primaries will have trouble
getting along unless they both bend toward a mixture or compromise. But it
all depends on what each individual wants out of a relationship. Two storgic
lovers have the best chance for a lasting relationship, and two ludic lovers
have the worst chance-but they will have fun while it lasts.

68   One swallow does not a summer make, and neither does one manic
binge confirm you as an obsessive lover. One playful affair in a storgic marriage does not define you as ludus. While some people have enjoyed a variety of love experiences equally, most of us definitely prefer one type. We
live with other kinds, as we live with many colors, but we still have our
favorites.

~

(5,264 words)

VOCABULARY

altruistic (2)	rigidified (3)	empirically (5)
arbitrarily (5)	Platonic (9)	devoid (9)
vicarious (10)	self-recriminations (11)	reciprocated (11)
rapture (14)	disdain (16)	hedonism (16)
diametric (22)	ambivalence (23)	impotent (23)
ploy (24)	insatiable (38)	ignominious (44)
nostalgia (47)	compatibility (54)	pragmatic (54)
hypothetical (61)	typology (63)	unidimensional (64)

THE FACTS

1. According to the author, people tend to seek partners who love by quantity—that is, in the right amount—a hunt that leads to failure. Instead, what should they be looking for and why?

2. What main types of love are identified in the essay? Can you cite a personal experience you had with any of the types? Give an example of one of the main characteristics of this relationship.

3. Which type of love do you think has the best chance of survival? Give reasons for your answer. Provide examples with which you are familiar.

4. What are the characteristics associated with the first type of love described? Do you recognize any of these characteristics in love relationships you have observed? How did you react to these characteristics?

5. Who is "Don Juan"? What kind of love does he represent? Do you admire this kind of lover? Would you like to have him as a lover? Give reasons for your answer.

THE STRATEGIES

1. What is the basis for Lee's classification? How does he use the color wheel to structure his essay?

2. How does the author let his readers know when he is moving to the next type of love? How helpful is this strategy? Explain.

3. What keeps the essay from being silly, tasteless, or in any other way inappropriate? Point to specific passages from the essay to make your point.

4. What is the author's purpose in presenting his typology of love? Do you think his purpose may come close to being fulfilled by those who read the essay? Do you find the typology useful? Give reasons for your answer.

5. What point does the author make at the end of his essay? Do you consider this point important in keeping a balanced view of love? Explain your answer.

THE ISSUES

1. Do you think that Lee's typology should be taken seriously by anyone who is about to fall in love? Should this typology be publicized to lessen the risk of bad marriages? Will knowing what kind of lover you are keep you from falling into the trap of a wrong alliance?

2. Do you agree with the author that the erotic lover is often disappointed in love because he has an idealized concept of what his lover should be? Why are novels, plays, and films filled with the bitterness and cynicism of lovers?

3. How, in modern divorces, does the *storge* love often reveal itself? What is your own view of *storge* love? Would you choose it for yourself? Why or why not?

4. In paragraph 53, the author alludes to "open marriages" as an example of the combination of *eros* and *ludus* love. Do you think open marriages have any value in our society? Can they work? What would be your reaction to a wife or husband who would suggest an open marriage to you?

5. Why do you think the author was unable to find an unqualified example of *agape* love? What is your definition of this kind of love? Where might you come closest to finding it?

SUGGESTIONS FOR WRITING

1. Creating your own typology of hate, write an essay in which you suggest the major types of hatred existing in our society. Be sure to use the same basis of classification for each type. For instance, you might base your classification on causes for the hatred, on manifestations of the hatred, or on some other basis of your own choice.

2. Write an essay in which you define the kind of love that leads to marriage. Be sure to provide enough examples or experiences to make the definition clear. Begin your essay with a dictionary-type definition of *love*.

THINKING AS A HOBBY

William Golding

English novelist William Golding (1911–1993) was educated at Oxford. Golding once described his hobbies as "thinking, classical Greek, sailing, and archaeology." His works include The Pyramid *(1964),* The Scorpion God *(1971), and* Paper Work *(1984), but he is best known for his novel* Lord of the Flies *(1954). In 1983, Golding won the Nobel Prize for Literature.*

Division and classification are often creative thinking exercises in which the essayist looks for patterns and relationships that are not immediately obvious. In this essay, for example, William Golding concludes that there are three grades of thinking, which he explains with examples and anecdotes. Are there really only three grades of thinking? That is beside the point. The essayist is not a scientific researcher, but an expresser and shaper of opinion. As a professional writer, Golding takes liberties with his classification and does here what any essayist should do: He makes us think.

~

1   While I was still a boy, I came to the conclusion that there were three grades of thinking; and since I was later to claim thinking as my hobby, I came to an even stranger conclusion—namely, that I myself could not think at all.

2   I must have been an unsatisfactory child for grownups to deal with. I remember how incomprehensible they appeared to me at first, but not, of course, how I appeared to them. It was the headmaster of my grammar school who first brought the subject of thinking before me—though neither in the way, nor with the result he intended. He had some statuettes in his study. They stood on a high cupboard behind his desk. One was a lady wearing nothing but a bath towel. She seemed frozen in an eternal panic lest the bath towel slip down any farther, and since she had no arms, she was in an unfortunate position to pull the towel up again. Next to her, crouched the statuette of a leopard, ready to spring down at the top drawer of a filing cabinet labeled A–AH. My innocence interpreted this as the victim's last, despairing cry. Beyond the leopard was a naked, muscular gentleman, who sat, looking down, with his chin on his fist and his elbow on his knee. He seemed utterly miserable.

3   Some time later, I learned about these statuettes. The headmaster had placed them where they would face delinquent children, because they symbolized to him the whole of life. The naked lady was the Venus of Milo. She was Love. She was not worried about the towel. She was just busy being beautiful. The leopard was Nature, and he was being natural. The naked, muscular gentleman was not miserable. He was Rodin's Thinker, an image of pure thought. It is easy to buy small plaster models of what you think life is like.

4   I had better explain that I was a frequent visitor to the headmaster's study, because of the latest thing I had done or left undone. As we now say, I was not integrated. I was, if anything, disintegrated; and I was puzzled. Grownups never made sense. Whenever I found myself in a penal position before the headmaster's desk, with the statuettes glimmering whitely above him, I would sink my head, clasp my hands behind my back and writhe one shoe over the other.

5   The headmaster would look opaquely at me through flashing spectacles. "What are we going to do with you?"

6   Well, what *were* they going to do with me? I would writhe my shoe some more and stare down at the worn rug.

7   "Look up, boy! Can't you look up?"

8   Then I would look up at the cupboard, where the naked lady was frozen in her panic and the muscular gentleman contemplated the hindquarters of

the leopard in endless gloom. I had nothing to say to the headmaster. His spectacles caught the light so that you could see nothing human behind them. There was no possibility of communication.

9   "Don't you ever think at all?"

10   No, I didn't think, wasn't thinking, couldn't think—I was simply waiting in anguish for the interview to stop.

11   "Then you'd better learn—hadn't you?"

12   On one occasion the headmaster leaped to his feet, reached up and plonked Rodin's masterpiece on the desk before me.

13   "That's what a man looks like when he's really thinking."

14   I surveyed the gentleman without interest or comprehension.

15   "Go back to your class."

16   Clearly there was something missing in me. Nature had endowed the rest of the human race with a sixth sense and left me out. This must be so, I mused, on my way back to the class, since whether I had broken a window, or failed to remember Boyle's Law, or been late for school, my teachers produced me one, adult answer: "Why can't you think?"

17   As I saw the case, I had broken the window because I had tried to hit Jack Arney with a cricket ball and missed him; I could not remember Boyle's Law because I had never bothered to learn it; and I was late for school because I preferred looking over the bridge into the river. In fact, I was wicked. Were my teachers, perhaps, so good that they could not understand the depths of my depravity? Were they clear, untormented people who could direct their every action by this mysterious business of thinking? The whole thing was incomprehensible. In my earlier years, I found even the statuette of the Thinker confusing. I did not believe any of my teachers were naked, ever. Like someone born deaf, but bitterly determined to find out about sound, I watched my teachers to find out about thought.

18   There was Mr. Houghton. He was always telling me to think. With a modest satisfaction, he would tell me that he had thought a bit himself. Then why did he spend so much time drinking? Or was there more sense in drinking than there appeared to be? But if not, and if drinking were in fact ruinous to health—and Mr. Houghton was ruined, there was no doubt about that—why was he always talking about the clean life and the virtues of fresh air? He would spread his arms wide with the action of a man who habitually spent his time striding along mountain ridges.

19   "Open air does me good, boys—I know it!"

20   Sometimes, exalted by his own oratory, he would leap from his desk and hustle us outside into a hideous wind.

21   "Now, boys! Deep breaths! Feel it right down inside you—huge draughts of God's good air!"

22   He would stand before us, rejoicing in his perfect health, an open-air man. He would put his hands on his waist and take a tremendous breath. You could hear the wind, trapped in the cavern of his chest and struggling with all the unnatural impediments. His body would reel with shock and his

ruined face go white at the unaccustomed visitation. He would stagger back to his desk and collapse there, useless for the rest of the morning.

23   Mr. Houghton was given to high-minded monologues about the good life, sexless and full of duty. Yet in the middle of one of these monologues, if a girl passed the window, tapping along on her neat little feet, he would interrupt his discourse, his neck would turn of itself and he would watch her out of sight. In this instance, he seemed to me ruled not by thought but by an invisible and irresistible spring in his nape.

24   His neck was an object of great interest to me. Normally it bulged a bit over his collar. But Mr. Houghton had fought in the First World War alongside both Americans and French, and had come—by who knows what illogic?— to a settled detestation of both countries. If either country happened to be prominent in current affairs, no argument could make Mr. Houghton think well of it. He would bang the desk, his neck would bulge still further and go red. "You can say what you like," he would cry, "but I've thought about this—and I know what I think!"

25   Mr. Houghton thought with his neck.

26   There was Miss Parsons. She assured us that her dearest wish was our welfare, but I knew even then, with the mysterious clairvoyance of childhood, that what she wanted most was the husband she never got. There was Mr. Hands—and so on.

27   I have dealt at length with my teachers because this was my introduction to the nature of what is commonly called thought. Through them I discovered that thought is often full of unconscious prejudice, ignorance and hypocrisy. It will lecture on disinterested purity while its neck is being remorselessly twisted toward a skirt. Technically, it is about as proficient as most businessmen's golf, as honest as most politicians' intentions, or—to come near my own preoccupation—as coherent as most books that get written. It is what I came to call grade-three thinking, though more properly, it is feeling, rather than thought.

28   True, often there is a kind of innocence in prejudices, but in those days I viewed grade-three thinking with an intolerant contempt and an incautious mockery. I delighted to confront a pious lady who hated the Germans with the proposition that we should love our enemies. She taught me a great truth in dealing with grade-three thinkers; because of her, I no longer dismiss lightly a mental process which for nine-tenths of the population is the nearest they will ever get to thought. They have immense solidarity. We had better respect them, for we are outnumbered and surrounded. A crowd of grade-three thinkers, all shouting the same thing, all warming their hands at the fire of their own prejudices, will not thank you for pointing out the contradictions in their beliefs. Man is a gregarious animal, and enjoys agreement as cows will graze all the same way on the side of a hill.

29   Grade-two thinking is the detection of contradictions. I reached grade two when I trapped the poor, pious lady. Grade-two thinkers do not stampede easily, though often they fall into the other fault and lag behind. Grade-two thinking is a withdrawal, with eyes and ears open. It became my hobby and

brought satisfaction and loneliness in either hand. For grade-two thinking destroys without having the power to create. It set me watching the crowds cheering His Majesty the King and asking myself what all the fuss was about, without giving me anything positive to put in the place of that heady patriotism. But there were compensations. To hear people justify their habit of hunting foxes and tearing them to pieces by claiming that the foxes like it. To hear our Prime Minister talk about the great benefit we conferred on India by jailing people like Pandit Nehru and Gandhi. To hear American politicians talk about peace in one sentence and refuse to join the League of Nations in the next. Yes, there were moments of delight.

30   But I was growing toward adolescence and had to admit that Mr. Houghton was not the only one with an irresistible spring in his neck. I, too, felt the compulsive hand of nature and began to find that pointing out contradiction could be costly as well as fun. There was Ruth, for example, a serious and attractive girl. I was an atheist at the time. Grade-two thinking is a menace to religion and knocks down sects like skittles. I put myself in a position to be converted by her with an hypocrisy worthy of grade three. She was a Methodist—or at least, her parents were, and Ruth had to follow suit. But, alas, instead of relying on the Holy Spirit to convert me, Ruth was foolish enough to open her pretty mouth in argument. She claimed that the Bible (King James Version) was literally inspired. I countered by saying that the Catholics believed in the literal inspiration of Saint Jerome's Vulgate, and the two books were different. Argument flagged.

31   At last she remarked that there were an awful lot of Methodists, and they couldn't be wrong, could they—not all those millions? That was too easy, said I restively (for the nearer you were to Ruth, the nicer she was to be near to) since there were more Roman Catholics than Methodists anyway; and they couldn't be wrong, could they—not all those hundreds of millions? An awful flicker of doubt appeared in her eyes. I slid my arm round her waist and murmured breathlessly that if we were counting heads, the Buddhists were the boys for my money. But Ruth had really wanted to do me good, because I was so nice. She fled. The combination of my arm and those countless Buddhists was too much for her.

32   That night her father visited my father and left, red-cheeked and indignant. I was given the third degree to find out what had happened. It was lucky we were both of us only fourteen. I lost Ruth and gained an undeserved reputation as a potential libertine.

33   So grade-two thinking could be dangerous. It was in this knowledge, at the age of fifteen, that I remember making a comment from the heights of grade two, on the limitations of grade three. One evening I found myself alone in the school hall, preparing it for a party. The door of the headmaster's study was open. I went in. The headmaster had ceased to thump Rodin's Thinker down on the desk as an example to the young. Perhaps he had not found any more candidates, but the statuettes were still there, glimmering and gathering dust on top of the cupboard. I stood on a chair and rearranged them. I stood Venus in her bath towel on the filing cabinet, so that now the top

drawer caught its breath in a gasp of sexy excitement. "A-ah!" The portentous Thinker I placed on the edge of the cupboard so that he looked down at the bath towel and waited for it to slip.

34   Grade-two thinking, though it filled life with fun and excitement, did not make for content. To find out the deficiencies of our elders bolsters the young ego but does not make for personal security. I found that grade two was not only the power to point out contradictions. It took the swimmer some distance from the shore and left him there, out of his depth. I decided that Pontius Pilate was a typical grade-two thinker. "What is truth?" he said, a very common grade-two thought, but one that is used always as the end of an argument instead of the beginning. There is a still higher grade of thought which says, "What is truth?" and sets out to find it.

35   But these grade-one thinkers were few and far between. They did not visit my grammar school in the flesh though they were there in books. I aspired to them, partly because I was ambitious and partly because I now saw my hobby as an unsatisfactory thing if it went no further. If you set out to climb a mountain, however high you climb, you have failed if you cannot reach the top.

36   I did meet an undeniably grade-one thinker in my first year at Oxford. I was looking over a small bridge in Magdalen Deer Park, and a tiny mustached and hatted figure came and stood by my side. He was a German who had just fled from the Nazis to Oxford as a temporary refuge. His name was Einstein.

37   But Professor Einstein knew no English at that time and I knew only two words of German. I beamed at him, trying wordlessly to convey by my bearing all the affection and respect that the English felt for him. It is possible—and I have to make the admission—that I felt here were two grade-one thinkers standing side by side; yet I doubt if my face conveyed more than a formless awe. I would have given my Greek and Latin and French and a good slice of my English for enough German to communicate. But we were divided; he was as inscrutable as my headmaster. For perhaps five minutes we stood together on the bridge, undeniable grade-one thinker and breathless aspirant. With true greatness, Professor Einstein realized that any contact was better than none. He pointed to a trout wavering in midstream.

38   He spoke: "Fisch."

39   My brain reeled. Here I was, mingling with the great, and yet helpless as the veriest grade-three thinker. Desperately I sought for some sign by which I might convey that I, too, revered pure reason. I nodded vehemently. In a brilliant flash I used up half of my German vocabulary. *"Fisch. Ja. Ja."*

40   For perhaps another five minutes we stood side by side. Then Professor Einstein, his whole figure still conveying good will and amiability, drifted away out of sight.

41   I, too, would be a grade-one thinker. I was irreverent at the best of times. Political and religious systems, social customs, loyalties and traditions, they

all came tumbling down like so many rotten apples off a tree. This was a fine hobby and a sensible substitute for cricket, since you could play it all the year round. I came up in the end with what must always remain the justification for grade-one thinking, its sign, seal and charter. I devised a coherent system for living. It was a moral system, which was wholly logical. Of course, as I readily admitted, conversion of the world to my way of thinking might be difficult, since my system did away with a number of trifles, such as big business, centralized government, armies, marriage . . .

42   It was Ruth all over again. I had some very good friends who stood by me, and still do. But my acquaintances vanished, taking the girls with them. Young women seemed oddly contented with the world as it was. They valued the meaningless ceremony with a ring. Young men, while willing to concede the chaining sordidness of marriage, were hesitant about abandoning the organizations which they hoped would give them a career. A young man on the first rung of the Royal Navy, while perfectly agreeable to doing away with big business and marriage, got as red-necked as Mr. Houghton when I proposed a world without any battleships in it.

43   Had the game gone too far? Was it a game any longer? In those prewar days, I stood to lose a great deal, for the sake of a hobby.

44   Now you are expecting me to describe how I saw the folly of my ways and came back to the warm nest, where prejudices are so often called loyalties, where pointless actions are hallowed into custom by repetition, where we are content to say we think when all we do is feel.

45   But you would be wrong. I dropped my hobby and turned professional.

46   If I were to go back to the headmaster's study and find the dusty statuettes still there, I would arrange them differently. I would dust Venus and put her aside, for I have come to love her and know her for the fair thing she is. But I would put the Thinker, sunk in his desperate thought, where there were shadows before him—and at his back, I would put the leopard, crouched and ready to spring.

∼

(3,084 words)

VOCABULARY

statuettes (2)	integrated (4)	penal (4)
opaquely (5)	ruinous (18)	draughts (21)
impediments (22)	monologues (23)	detestation (24)
clairvoyance (26)	disinterested (27)	proficient (27)
proposition (28)	solidarity (28)	skittles (30)
flagged (30)	restively (31)	libertine (32)
inscrutable (37)	veriest (39)	revered (39)
amiability (40)		

THE FACTS

1. Into what three types does Golding divide all thinking? Describe each type in your own words. Is there a value judgment implied in the division?

2. Why does Golding take up so much time describing some of his grade-school teachers? How are they related to the purpose of the essay?

3. Why is it so difficult to find grade-one thinkers? Describe someone whom you consider a grade-one thinker.

4. How do you interpret Golding's last two paragraphs? Has the author reverted to grade-three or grade-two thinking, or is he still a grade-one thinker? Comment.

5. What does the encounter between Golding and Albert Einstein indicate?

THE STRATEGIES

1. In paragraph 2, the author describes three statuettes on a cupboard behind the headmaster's desk. In what paragraph is each of the statuettes explained? Why is the explanation necessary?

2. Much of the article reflects a young boy's point of view. How is this point of view achieved? Point to some specific passages.

3. Paragraphs 24, 25, and 27 refer to the word *neck* repeatedly. What has the neck come to symbolize in this context?

4. What is the analogy used in paragraph 28 to describe grade-three thinkers? Is the analogy effective? Explain.

5. What is Golding's purpose in alluding to the jailing of Nehru and Gandhi, and to the Americans' refusal to join the League of Nations?

THE ISSUES

1. To be a grade-one thinker, must one do away with big business, centralized government, armies, marriages, and so on? How could one be a grade-one thinker without wanting to destroy these?

2. Golding seems to indicate that his teachers were conformists, hypocrites, or men of prejudice. What kinds of thinkers do you remember your grade-school teachers to have been? Give examples of their thinking.

3. What groups in our society reveal typical grade-three thinking? Give reasons for your choices.

4. What, if anything, is important about grade-two thinking? Does one need to be a grade-two thinker before going on to grade-one?

5. How does nature assist or resist grade-one thinking?

SUGGESTIONS FOR WRITING

1. Write an essay in which you answer the question "Does a college education help to eliminate prejudice and hypocrisy?" Support your answer with examples from your own experience.

2. Write an essay in which you divide your acquaintances into types according to the kinds of behavior they project. Be sure that your categories are mutually exclusive and that they take in as many of your acquaintances as possible.

KINDS OF DISCIPLINE

John Holt

John Holt (1923–1985), education theorist, was born in New York. He has taught at Harvard University and the University of California, Berkeley. His works include How Children Fail *(1964),* How Children Learn *(1967),* Freedom and Beyond *(1972), from which this selection was taken,* Escape from Childhood *(1974),* Instead of Education *(1976), and* Teach Your Own *(1981).*

Because *discipline* is an ambiguous and often misunderstood word, the author attempts to give it a clearer meaning by focusing on three specific kinds of discipline.

~

1   A child, in growing up, may meet and learn from three different kinds of disciplines. The first and most important is what we might call the Discipline of Nature or of Reality. When he is trying to do something real, if he does the wrong thing or doesn't do the right one, he doesn't get the result he wants. If he doesn't pile one block right on top of another, or tries to build on a slanting surface, his tower falls down. If he hits the wrong key, he hears the wrong note. If he doesn't hit the nail squarely on the head, it bends, and he has to pull it out and start with another. If he doesn't measure properly what he is trying to build, it won't open, close, fit, stand up, fly, float, whistle, or do whatever he wants it to do. If he closes his eyes when he swings, he doesn't hit the ball. A child meets this kind of discipline every time he tries to do something, which is why it is so important in school to give children more chances to do things, instead of just reading or listening to someone talk (or pretending to). This discipline is a great teacher. The learner never has to wait long for his answer; it usually comes quickly, often instantly. Also it is clear, and very often points toward the needed correction; from what happened he can not only see that what he did was wrong, but also why, and what he needs to do instead. Finally, and most important, the giver of the answer, call it Nature, is impersonal, impartial, and indifferent. She does not give opinions, or make

judgments; she cannot be wheedled, bullied, or fooled; she does not get angry or disappointed; she does not praise or blame; she does not remember past failures or hold grudges; with her one always gets a fresh start, this time is the one that counts.

2   The next discipline we might call the Discipline of Culture, of Society, of What People Really Do. Man is a social, a cultural animal. Children sense around them this culture, this network of agreements, customs, habits, and rules binding the adults together. They want to understand it and be a part of it. They watch very carefully what people around them are doing and want to do the same. They want to do right, unless they become convinced they can't do right. Thus children rarely misbehave seriously in church, but sit as quietly as they can. The example of all those grownups is contagious. Some mysterious ritual is going on, and children, who like rituals, want to be part of it. In the same way, the little children that I see at concerts or operas, though they may fidget a little, or perhaps take a nap now and then, rarely make any disturbance. With all those grownups sitting there, neither moving nor talking, it is the most natural thing in the world to imitate them. Children who live among adults who are habitually courteous to each other, and to them, will soon learn to be courteous. Children who live surrounded by people who speak a certain way will speak that way, however much we may try to tell them that speaking that way is bad or wrong.

3   The third discipline is the one most people mean when they speak of discipline—the Discipline of Superior Force, of sergeant to private, of "you do what I tell you or I'll make you wish you had." There is bound to be some of this in a child's life. Living as we do surrounded by things that can hurt children, or that children can hurt, we cannot avoid it. We can't afford to let a small child find out from experience the danger of playing in a busy street, or of fooling with the pots on the top of a stove, or of eating up the pills in the medicine cabinet. So, along with other precautions, we say to him, "Don't play in the street, or touch things on the stove, or go into the medicine cabinet, or I'll punish you." Between him and the danger too great for him to imagine we put a lesser danger, but one he can imagine and maybe therefore wants to avoid. He can have no idea of what it would be like to be hit by a car, but he can imagine being shouted at, or spanked, or sent to his room. He avoids these substitutes for the greater danger until he can understand it and avoid it for its own sake. But we ought to use this discipline only when it is necessary to protect the life, health, safety, or well-being of people or other living creatures, or to prevent destruction of things that people care about. We ought not to assume too long, as we usually do, that a child cannot understand the real nature of the danger from which we want to protect him. The sooner he avoids the danger, not to escape our punishment, but as a matter of good sense, the better. He can learn that faster than we think. In Mexico, for example, where people drive their cars with a good deal of spirit, I saw many children no older than five or four walking unattended on the streets. They understood about cars, they knew what to do. A child whose life is full of the threat and fear of punishment is locked into babyhood. There is no way

for him to grow up, to learn to take responsibility for his life and acts. Most important of all, we should not assume that having to yield to the threat of our superior force is good for the child's character. It is never good for anyone's character. To bow to superior force makes us feel impotent and cowardly for not having had the strength or courage to resist. Worse, it makes us resentful and vengeful. We can hardly wait to make someone pay for our humiliation, yield to us as we were once made to yield. No, if we cannot always avoid using the Discipline of Superior Force, we should at least use it as seldom as we can.

4   There are places where all three disciplines overlap. Any very demanding human activity combines in it the disciplines of Superior Force, of Culture, and of Nature. The novice will be told, "Do it this way, never mind asking why, just do it that way, that is the way we always do it." But it probably is just the way they always do it, and usually for the very good reason that it is a way that has been found to work. Think, for example, of ballet training. The student in a class is told to do this exercise, or that; to stand so; to do this or that with his head, arms, shoulders, abdomen, hips, legs, feet. He is constantly corrected. There is no argument. But behind these seemingly autocratic demands by the teacher lie many decades of custom and tradition, and behind that, the necessities of dancing itself. You cannot make the moves of classical ballet unless over many years you have acquired, and renewed every day, the needed strength and suppleness in scores of muscles and joints. Nor can you do the difficult motions, making them look easy, unless you have learned hundreds of easier ones first. Dance teachers may not always agree on all the details of teaching these strengths and skills. But no novice could learn them all by himself. You could not go for a night or two to watch the ballet and then, without any other knowledge at all, teach yourself how to do it. In the same way, you would be unlikely to learn any complicated and difficult human activity without drawing heavily on the experience of those who know it better. But the point is that the authority of these experts or teachers stems from, grows out of their greater competence and experience, the fact that what they do works, not the fact that they happen to be the teacher and as such have the power to kick a student out of the class. And the further point is that children are always and everywhere attracted to that competence, and ready and eager to submit themselves to a discipline that grows out of it. We hear constantly that children will never do anything unless compelled to by bribes or threats. But in their private lives, or in extracurricular activities in school, in sports, music, drama, art, running a newspaper, and so on, they often submit themselves willingly and wholeheartedly to very intense disciplines, simply because they want to learn to do a given thing well. Our Little-Napoleon football coaches, of whom we have too many and hear far too much, blind us to the fact that millions of children work hard every year getting better at sports and games without coaches barking and yelling at them.

～

(1,512 words)

VOCABULARY

wheedled (1)   ritual (2)   impotent (3)
autocratic (4)

THE FACTS

1. What principle or basis of division does Holt use?
2. How does Holt clarify for the reader what he means by "Discipline of Nature or of Reality"? Is this method of clarification effective? Why?
3. What are the advantages of learning from nature or reality?
4. According to the author, when should the discipline of superior force be used? Do you agree?
5. At the end of his essay, Holt identifies the most successful motivation for discipline. What is it?

THE STRATEGIES

1. In the last sentence of paragraph 1, the author uses the feminine pronouns *she* and *her* in referring to nature. What is his purpose?
2. What transitional guideposts does the author use to gain coherence and organization?
3. What is the effect of labeling certain football coaches "Little Napoleons"?

THE ISSUES

1. What additional examples can you supply of the ways in which children submit to the discipline of culture or society?
2. What tips can you provide for someone who has no discipline in studying college courses? What method has worked best for you?
3. Holt warns adults that the use of superior force in order to punish children is never good for the children's characters (see paragraph 3) and should therefore be used as little as possible. What, in your opinion, is the result of never using this superior force in the training of children? Give examples to support your point.
4. Our society is witnessing the self-destruction of many young people through chemical abuse of one kind or another. How is this abuse tied to Holt's idea of discipline?
5. How important is discipline in your life? Do you choose friends who are strongly disciplined, or do you prefer those who are more "laid back"? Give reasons for your answers.

SUGGESTIONS FOR WRITING

1. Write an essay in which you divide discipline according to the kinds of effects it produces; for example, discipline that results in strong study habits.

2. Develop the following topic sentence into a three-paragraph essay: "To be successful, a person must have three kinds of discipline: of the intellect, of the emotions, and of the body." Use Holt's essay as a model for your organization.

THE IDOLS

Francis Bacon

Francis Bacon (1561–1626) was born in London and educated at Trinity College, Cambridge, and Gray's Inn. Bacon is generally credited with applying the inductive method of logic to scientific investigation. His essays, which are notable for their aphoristic style, are his best-known works.

This excerpt comes from *Novum Organum* (1620), possibly Bacon's most famous work. Bacon was struggling against the traditions of medieval scholasticism, which assumed a given and unchangeable set of premises from which, by deductive logic, one could infer truths about the world. Our way of thinking today, especially in science, is just the opposite, thanks in part to Bacon. We begin not with givens but with questions. We proceed by gathering data and using induction to draw conclusions. (See the discussion of logic in chapter 15.) This method of thinking does not completely safeguard us from Bacon's Idols, but it does help keep them at bay.

~

1   The *Idols* and false notions which have already preoccupied the human understanding, and are deeply rooted in it, not only so beset men's minds, that they become difficult to access, but even when access is obtained, will again meet and trouble us in the instauration of the sciences, unless mankind, when forewarned, guard themselves with all possible care against them.

2   Four species of *Idols* beset the human mind: to which (for distinction's sake) we have assigned names: calling the first *Idols of the Tribe;* the second *Idols of the Den;* the third *Idols of the Market;* the fourth *Idols of the Theater.*

3   The formation of notions and axioms on the foundations of true induction, is the only fitting remedy, by which we can ward off and expel these *Idols.* It is however of great service to point them out. For the doctrine of *Idols* bears the same relation to the interpretation of nature, as that of the confutation of sophisms does to common logic.

4   The *Idols of the Tribe* are inherent in human nature, and the very tribe or race of man. For man's sense is falsely asserted to be the standard of things. On

the contrary, all the perceptions, both of the senses and the mind, bear reference to man, and not to the universe, and the human mind resembles those uneven mirrors, which impart their own properties to different objects, from which rays are emitted, and distort and disfigure them.

5   The *Idols of the Den* are those of each individual. For every body (in addition to the errors common to the race of man) has his own individual den or cavern, which intercepts and corrupts the light of nature; either from his own peculiar and singular disposition, or from his education and intercourse with others, or from his reading, and the authority acquired by those whom he reverences and admires, or from a different impression produced on the mind, as it happens to be preoccupied and predisposed, or equable and tranquil, and the like: so that the spirit of man (according to its several dispositions) is variable, confused, and as it were actuated by chance; and Heraclitus[8] said well that men search for knowledge in lesser worlds and not in the greater or common world.

6   There are also *Idols* formed by the reciprocal intercourse and society of man with man, which we call *Idols of the Market*, from the commerce and association of men with each other. For men converse by means of language; but words are formed at the will of the generality; and there arises from a bad and unapt formation of words a wonderful obstruction to the mind. Nor can the definitions and explanations, with which learned men are wont to guard and protect themselves in some instances, afford a complete remedy: words still manifestly force the understanding, throw everything into confusion, and lead mankind into vain and innumerable controversies and fallacies.

7   Lastly there are *Idols* which have crept into men's minds from the various dogmas of peculiar systems of philosophy, and also from the perverted rules of demonstration, and these we denominate *Idols of the Theater*. For we regard all the systems of philosophy hitherto received or imagined, as so many plays brought out and performed, creating fictitious and theatrical worlds. Nor do we speak only of the present systems, or of the philosophy and sects of the ancients, since numerous other plays of a similar nature can be still composed and made to agree with each other, the causes of the most opposite errors being generally the same. Nor, again, do we allude merely to the general systems, but also to many elements and axioms of sciences, which have become inveterate by tradition, implicit credence and neglect. We must, however, discuss each species of *Idols* more fully and distinctly in order to guard the human understanding against them.

~

(645 words)

---

[8]Greek philosopher of the Sixth Century B.C.—Ed.

VOCABULARY

beset (1)	instauration (1)	axioms (3)
induction (3)	confutation (3)	sophism (3)
inherent (4)	predisposed (5)	equable (5)
reciprocal (6)	wont (6)	dogmas (7)
denominate (7)	sects (7)	inveterate (7)
implicit (7)	credence (7)	

THE FACTS

1. Exactly what is being divided in this essay? Why does Bacon use the term *idols?*

2. Using your own words, describe each idol in the order listed by Bacon. Supply an example for each from your own experience.

3. According to Bacon, what is the remedy for all these idols? How will this remedy work?

THE STRATEGIES

1. What connection is there between Bacon's thought and his style?

2. Point out specific words or phrases to show that Bacon's style is archaic.

3. What method of thinking does Bacon use to conclude that idols preoccupy the human understanding? Trace his use of the method in the essay.

4. What is the analogy used to illustrate the last idol? Explain how this analogy helps clarify the idol.

THE ISSUES

1. Compare Bacon's division with some more contemporary ideas on the same subject. Is his essay still valid, or is it out of date? Give reasons for your answer.

2. What specific examples can you cite to illuminate Bacon's "idols of the tribe"?

3. How dangerous to present society are "idols of the market"? Give reasons for your opinion.

4. What examples can you cite from your own upbringing to indicate that you have bowed to "idols of the den"?

5. In your view, what ideas marketed publicly today are dangerous but highly seductive—especially for the naïve?

SUGGESTIONS FOR WRITING

1. Write an essay in which you divide your bad habits into three or four categories. Make sure that these categories are mutually exclusive and that they include the entire range of your bad habits.

2. Write a brief report on Francis Bacon's major contributions to society. In the report, organize these contributions into separate divisions.

ENGLISH 101

Bart Edelman

Bart Edelman (b. 1951) is a contemporary American poet who spent his childhood in Teaneck, New Jersey, the subject of many of his poems. Today he lives in southern California, where he gives poetry readings at colleges all over the United States. He has been the recipient of numerous grants and fellowships to study literature in India, Egypt, Nigeria, and Poland. He is presently a professor of English at Glendale College in California. His poetry collections include Crossing the Hackensack *(1993),* Under Damaris' Dress *(1996), and* The Alphabet of Love *(1999), and* The Gentle Man *(2001).*

This poem conjures up familiar memories in anyone who has taken freshman composition and remembers the opening session when students are introduced to the requirements and goals of the course. The poet uses concrete language to convey vivid portraits of three kinds of students in class on opening day.

⁓

ENGLISH 101

1   They appear-
    Always-
    That first day,
    Astray;
5   Some wait to fall,
    Others to rise:

    Here rests the tired boy,
    The hour long,
    He drops his brain

10 Upon the desk
    And thinks he'd be better off dead,
    Five worlds away
    From Frost and Twain . . .
    (He'll have no part of 101).

15 A fair-haired girl in knots
Twists her braids so tight
They make her ache;
She takes good notes,
Does what she's told,
20 If asked a quote
She knows it cold . . .
(But could a smile unclench those lips?)

Then the hand,
One resolute voice
25 Speaks through the bell
And the great stampede-
Engaged in speculation
We turn wheat to notion,
Sifting through each tiny grain . . .
30 (The composition now complete).

∼

(118 words)

VOCABULARY

astray (4)   resolute (24)   stampede (26)

THE FACTS

1. Where does the action of the poem take place? How do you know?

2. Who are "They" in the first stanza? Why are they described as "astray"?

3. What is meant by "He drops his brain/Upon the desk" in the second stanza? Explain the figure of speech.

4. What kind of student is described in stanza 3? Describe her in your own words.

5. What is the meaning of the phrase "One resolute voice/Speaks through the bell"?

THE STRATEGIES

1. In what sense is this poem a classification? What is being classified? How many items belong to the classification? List them.

2. After listing the first two students as a boy and a girl, why does the poet then refer to a "hand" and "voice" as the third student?

3. Why do you suppose the author chose the title "English 101" rather than, say, "Math 220" or "Economics 300"?

4. What comparison does the poet draw in stanza 4? What other simile might be used? Use your poetic imagination to find one.

THE ISSUES

1. What is the theme (thesis) of this poem? State it in one sentence.
2. According to the poem, wherein lies a teacher's greatest classroom challenge?
3. If you were a teacher, which student would bother you more—the student of stanza 2 or the student of stanza 3? Give reasons for your answer.
4. What is your opinion on the basic importance of freshman composition? Should it be a requirement? Why or why not?
5. In stanza 2, the poet refers to Frost and Twain. How are these two literary figures related to the theme of the poem?

SUGGESTIONS FOR WRITING

1. Write an essay in which you classify the various kinds of teachers who have taught you. For your bases of classification, consider such aspects as ability to communicate, personality, values, and attitude toward the subject matter.
2. Using Edelman's poem as a springboard, choose three or four friends who are representative types to classify your most intimate friends. Try to make each type come to life by using vivid details in describing him or her.

———— ISSUE FOR CRITICAL ———— THINKING AND DEBATE

RACISM

Even to the casual observer, racism in America remains a festering problem. Its toxic influence ranges from blatant discrimination in the housing market, where minorities are deliberately steered to specific neighborhoods, to subtle hiring practices wherein deserving employees are denied promotions because of skin color. Blacks live shorter lives than whites, earn less money, and make up over half of U.S. murder victims (ninety-four percent of whom are killed by other blacks). Compared to whites, blacks are also imprisoned more often and are more likely to be executed.

To remedy the inequality between whites and blacks, the U.S. Congress passed Civil Rights Act of 1964 and set in place laws promoting affirmative action. Although the effect of these measures was to narrow the educational

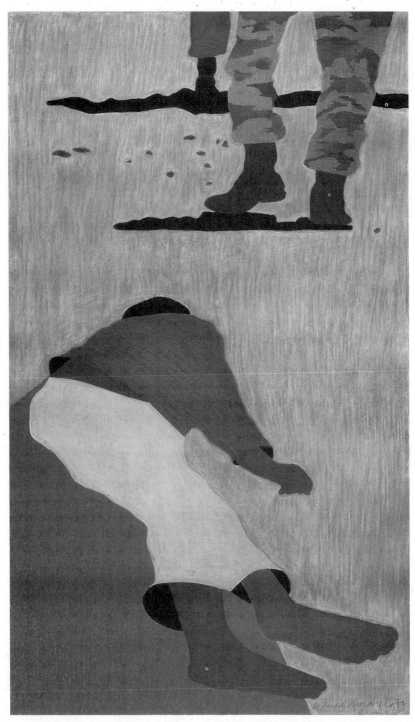

Rupert Garcia, Mexico, Chile, Soweto . . . , *1977. Pastel on paper 51 × 35 inches. Courtesy of the artist and Rena Bransten Gallery, San Francisco, California and Galerie Claude Samuel, Paris, France.*

Two Fists Tattooed with Love and Hate. Copyright © V.C.L./Taxi/GETTY.

gap between blacks and whites, nearly one-third of all black families and nearly one-half of all black children still live in poverty. Indeed, black married couples still earn about three-quarters the income of their white counterparts and are more than twice as likely to be poor (Shulman, Steven, "The causes of black poverty: Evidence and interpretation," *Journal of Economic Issues*, December 1990).

How this inequality is viewed depends as much on the viewer's race as on any facts. The stark differences in racial perception between whites and blacks burst into the public consciousness with the October 1995, not-guilty verdict in the O. J. Simpson trial. Whites generally thought Simpson guilty and believed that a murderer had been set free; blacks typically thought him innocent and celebrated. Moreover, there was an odder response exemplified by some black intellectuals who thought Simpson guilty, yet still gloated over his acquittal. One black professor who had been a federal prosecutor in the Bush administration even praised the defense tactic of encouraging jurors to forget the facts and, instead, render a verdict based on race (*Commentary*, December 1995). The prosecutor went on to argue in the *Yale Law Review* that "jury nullification," or playing the "race card" in high-stakes trials, is "morally as well as legally right," because "African-Americans live in a police state."

The inequality between the races is so plain and stark that statistics do no more than confirm what the eye already sees. Predictably, the explanations for the causes of the inequality are divided along liberal/conservative fault lines. Liberals blame white racism and its poisonous legacy, arguing that the remedy for racial inequality is more government intervention. Conservatives argue that the time has come for racially neutral laws, with no affirmative action boost for minorities. Neither side denies the historical effects of racism. But whereas conservatives assert that the past is past and opportunities are now equal, liberals insist that the damage done to black consciousness by past injustices cannot be so casually dismissed.

These two themes are implicit in the pieces we have chosen for this debate. The first is a wrenching chapter from a book, *Warriors Don't Cry*, by an African

American woman who helped desegregate Central High School in Little Rock, Arkansas, in 1954. Because this woman dared to want an education equal to what white Americans regard as their birthright, she was hounded with obscene phone calls, pelted with rocks, threatened by mobs, and tormented by her fellow students. The second reading is by a remarkable set of black sisters—Sarah and A. Elizabeth Delany—who wrote their memoirs when both were over 100 years old. The art work of the chapter also reflects the problem of racism. In the painting on page 499, a black victim lies, lifeless, on the ground as two soldiers walk away, seemingly indifferent to the plight of the slain man. Tha photo on page 500 emphasizes the choice we all make between love and hate.

The turmoil caused by racism is as unsettling as it is unsettled. The liberal/conservative argument over race boils down to these questions: How much is the past really past? What can we do to ensure that the ugly legacy of racism won't continue to poison the efforts of those men and women who try to make race relations better?

WARRIORS DON'T CRY

Melba Patillo Beals

Melba Patillo Beals (b. 1941) earned a B.A. degree from San Francisco State and a graduate degree from Columbia. She has worked as a reporter for NBC. Today she works as a communications consultant and has written books on public relations and marketing. In 1957, she was one of nine students chosen to integrate Central High School in Little Rock, Arkansas, in the wake of the 1954 Supreme Court decision Brown v. Board of Education of Topeka, Kansas, *which declared segregated schools illegal. This reading is the opening chapter from her memoir of that traumatic experience,* Warriors Don't Cry *(1994).*

1

~

In 1957, while most teenage girls were listening to Buddy Holly's "Peggy Sue," watching Elvis gyrate, and collecting crinoline slips, I was escaping the 2 hanging rope of a lynch mob, dodging lighted sticks of dynamite, and washing away burning acid sprayed into my eyes.

During my junior year in high school, I lived at the center of a violent civil rights conflict. In 1954, the Supreme Court had decreed an end to segregated schools. Arkansas Governor Orval Faubus and states' rights segregationists defied that ruling. President Eisenhower was compelled to confront Faubus—to use U.S. soldiers to force him to obey the law of the land. It was a historic confrontation that generated worldwide attention. At the center of 3 the controversy were nine black children who wanted only to have the opportunity for a better education.

On our first day at Central High, Governor Faubus dispatched gun-toting Arkansas National Guard soldiers to prevent us from entering. Mother and I got separated from the others. The two of us narrowly escaped a rope-carrying lynch mob of men and women shouting that they'd kill us rather than see me go to school with their children.

4   Three weeks later, having won a federal court order, we black children maneuvered our way past an angry mob to enter the side door of Central High. But by eleven that morning, hundreds of people outside were running wild, crashing through police barriers to get us out of school. Some of the police sent to control the mob threw down their badges and joined the rampage. But a few other brave members of the Little Rock police force saved our lives by spiriting us past the mob to safety.

5   To uphold the law and protect lives, President Eisenhower sent soldiers of the 101st Airborne Division, the elite "Screaming Eagles"—Korean War heroes.

6   On my third trip to Central High, I rode with the 101st in an army station wagon guarded by jeeps with turret guns mounted on their hoods and helicopters roaring overhead. With the protection of our 101st bodyguards, we black students walked through the front door of the school and completed a full day of classes.

7   But I quickly learned from those who opposed integration that the soldiers' presence meant a declaration of war. Segregationists mounted a brutal campaign against us, both inside and out of school.

8   My eight friends and I paid for the integration of Central High with our innocence. During those years when we desperately needed approval from our peers, we were victims of the most harsh rejection imaginable. The physical and psychological punishment we endured profoundly affected all our lives. It transformed us into warriors who dared not cry even when we suffered intolerable pain.

9   I became an instant adult, forced to take stock of what I believed and what I was willing to sacrifice to back up my beliefs. The experience endowed me with an indestructible faith in God.

10   I am proud to report that the Little Rock experience also gave us courage, strength, and hope. We nine grew up to become productive citizens, with special insights about how important it is to respect the value of every human life.

11   I am often asked, in view of the state of race relations today, if our effort was in vain. Would I integrate Central if I had it to do over again? My answer is yes, unequivocally yes. I take pride in the fact that, although the fight for equality must continue, our 1957 effort catapulted the civil rights movement forward a giant step and shifted the fight to a more dignified battlefield. For the first time in history, a President took a very bold step to defend civil rights—our civil rights.

12   Back then, I naively believed that if we could end segregation in the schools, all barriers of inequality would fall. If you had asked me in 1957 what I expected, I would have told you that by this time our struggle for human rights would have been won. Not so. But I am consoled by the words my grandmother spoke: "Even when the battle is long and the path is steep, a true warrior does not give up. If each one of us does not step forward to

claim our rights, we are doomed to an eternal wait in hopes those who would usurp them will become benevolent. The Bible says, WATCH, FIGHT, and PRAY."

13   Although I am perplexed by the state of race relations in this country today, I am at the same time very hopeful because I have ample evidence that what Grandmother promised me is true. With time and love, God solves all our problems. When we returned to Central High School for our first reunion in 1987, many Little Rock residents, white and black, greeted the nine of us as heroines and heroes. Hometown white folk in the mall smiled and said hello and offered directions even when they did not recognize us from our newspaper photos.

14   During all the fancy ceremonies, some of Arkansas's highest officials and businessmen came from far and wide to welcome us. And perhaps the most astounding evidence that things have indeed changed for the better was the attitude of Governor Bill Clinton.

15   "Call me Bill," he said, extending his hand, looking me in the eye. "You'all come on up to the house and sit a while." He flashed that charming grin of his. A few minutes of conversation assured me that his warm invitation was genuine. He is, after all, a man my brother refers to as "good people," based on their working relationship over the years.

16   So my eight friends and I found ourselves hanging out at the governor's mansion, the one Faubus built. Governor Clinton sauntered about serving soft drinks and peanuts. He and his wife, Hillary, were the kind of host and hostess who could make me feel at home even in the place where Faubus had hatched his devilish strategies to get the nine of us out of Central High School by any means possible.

17   "You'all ought to think about coming on back home now. Things are different," Governor Clinton said. He had been eleven years old when Faubus waged his segregationist battle against us. He displayed genuine respect for our contribution to the civil rights struggle. That visit was to become an evening I shall always treasure. As Chelsea played the piano and Bill and Hillary talked to me as though we'd known each other always, I found myself thinking, "Oh, Mr. Faubus, if only you and your friends could see us now."

18   My grandmother India always said God had pointed a finger at our family, asking for just a bit more discipline, more praying, and more hard work because He had blessed us with good health and good brains. My mother was one of the first few blacks to integrate the University of Arkansas, graduating in 1954. Three years later, when Grandma discovered I would be one of the first blacks to attend Central High School, she said the nightmare that had surrounded my birth was proof positive that destiny had assigned me a special task.

19   First off, I was born on Pearl Harbor Day, December 7, 1941. Mother says while she was giving birth to me, there was a big uproar, with the announcement that the Japanese had bombed Pearl Harbor. She remembers how astonished she was, and yet her focus was necessarily on the task at hand. There was trouble with my delivery because Mom was tiny and I was nine pounds.

The doctor used forceps to deliver me and injured my scalp. A few days later, I fell ill with a massive infection. Mother took me to the white hospital, which reluctantly treated the families of black men who worked on the railroad. A doctor operated to save my life by inserting a drainage system beneath my scalp.

20   Twenty-four hours later I wasn't getting better. Whenever Mother sought help, neither nurses nor doctors would take her seriously enough to examine me. Instead, they said, "Just give it time."

21   Two days after my operation, my temperature soared to 106 and I started convulsing. Mother sent for the minister to give me the last rites, and relatives were gathering to say farewell.

22   That evening, while Grandmother sat in my hospital room, rocking me back and forth as she hummed her favorite hymn, "On the Battlefield for My Lord," Mother paced the floor weeping aloud in her despair. A black janitor who was sweeping the hallway asked why she was crying. She explained that I was dying because the infection in my head had grown worse.

23   The man extended his sympathy. As he turned to walk away, dragging his broom behind him, he mumbled that he guessed the Epsom salts hadn't worked after all. Mother ran after him asking what he meant. He explained that a couple of days before, he had been cleaning the operating room as they finished up with my surgery. He had heard the doctor tell the white nurse to irrigate my head with Epsom salts and warm water every two or three hours or I wouldn't make it.

24   Mother shouted the words "Epsom salts and water" as she raced down the hall, desperately searching for a nurse. The woman was indignant, saying, yes, come to think of it, the doctor had said something about Epsom salts. "But we don't coddle niggers," she growled.

25   Mother didn't talk back to the nurse. She knew Daddy's job was at stake. Instead, she sent for Epsom salts and began the treatment right away. Within two days, I was remarkably better. The minister went home, and the sisters from the church abandoned their death watch, declaring they had witnessed a miracle.

26   So fifteen years later, when I was selected to integrate Central High, Grandmother said, "Now you see, that's the reason God spared your life. You're supposed to carry this banner for our people."

~

(1,669 words)

VOCABULARY

decreed (2)	endowed (9)	unequivocally (11)
usurp (12)	benevolent (12)	sauntered (16)
convulsing (21)		

THE FACTS

1. What president ordered in the troops to ensure the integration of the high school that the author attended?
2. What does the author admit she naively believed would happen if the segregation of schools could be ended?
3. Who was governor of Arkansas when the author returned to her former high school for her reunion?
4. What happened to the author when she was born?
5. Whose muttered remark resulted in the author's getting the treatment that saved her life?

THE STRATEGIES

1. The author wrote her memoir some forty years after the actual event. What kinds of problems do you think she encountered in writing this piece so many years after it happened?
2. How would you characterize the person who is telling the story? How old do you think she is? What characteristics of her language help project her onto the page?
3. What technique does the writer use to grab our interest in the opening paragraph?
4. The author tells the story of how she almost died when she was a baby, but does so with little or no editorial comment. Why is this an effective technique?
5. In addition to the author's religious convictions, what does the story about her illness as a newborn dramatically illustrate?

THE ISSUES

1. What effect do you think living through such a traumatic experience is likely to have on someone? How does it seem to have affected the author?
2. The author says that she is perplexed by the state of race relations today. How do you feel about the relationship between the races in the United States today?
3. What do you regard as the most pressing issue in race relations today? What solution do you have for that issue?
4. The author says that the experience of desegregating Central High made her an "instant adult." What do you think she meant by that? What is an *instant adult?*
5. What, in your opinion, is necessary to end racism in the United States?

SUGGESTIONS FOR WRITING

1. Write an essay about a personal encounter you have had with prejudice.

2. Write an essay about any side of racism.

INCIDENTS WITH WHITE PEOPLE

Sarah L. and A. Elizabeth Delany

Sarah (Sadie) L. Delany (1890–1999) and Dr. A. Elizabeth (Bessie) Delany (1891–1995) were African American centenarian sisters who found fame and fortune in 1993 with the publication of their co-authored memoirs Having Our Say: The Delany Sisters First 100 Years, *written in collaboration with Amy Hill Hearth. The book was on the* New York Times *bestseller list for two years and has been translated into seven languages. The Delany sisters left one million dollars to St. Augustine College, on whose campus they were born, lived, and were educated.*

In this excerpt from *Having Our Say*, Bessie tells of leaving home in 1911 at age twenty to teach school in Boardman, North Carolina, where she boarded with a couple, Mr. and Mrs. Atkinson. We learn of her reaction to the news that the *Titanic* had sunk (1912) and how she narrowly escaped being lynched in Georgia. As you read the essay, ask yourself how you would react to the encounter with the drunken white man she relates.

～

1   Mr. Atkinson was the ugliest man I ever saw, and not at all well educated, but he was an absolute gentleman. He never bothered me once. His first name was Spudge, which was short for Spudgeon, or so he told me. He said he was named after a Baptist preacher who was legendary in those parts, and he was just appalled that this little Episcopalian girl had never heard of him.

2   There was no Episcopal Church in Boardman, so I attended Baptist or Methodist services. They were poor and had no hymnals. The Methodists had the words to their hymns scratched out in the margins of old pieces of paper, like the Sears catalog.

3   The food we ate in Boardman was about the worst diet I have ever been on. I have always been a slim thing, but Honey, I got fat while I was there! When I came home at Christmas I weighed 153 pounds, and people came from everywhere to see this fat Bessie. But I lost that weight eventually, and never gained it back. Sadie says it was from eating all that fatback and collards and sweet potatoes in Boardman.

4   Those people didn't know the first thing about vitamins or minerals. They were so poor and ignorant. It was the same thing Sadie was running into as Jeanes Supervisor in Wake County. Mama was worried about me, and she

would send me these little care packages. She would go to a store in Raleigh called the California Fruit Company, and buy some grapefruits and ship them to me.

5   Well, Mr. Spudge Atkinson had never seen a grapefruit before. He said, "Miss Delany, what is that ugly-looking piece of fruit?" Now, I gave him a piece and he just puckered up and spit it out and said it was the worst, most sour, miserable thing he'd ever put in his mouth! And I said, "Mr. Atkinson, if you're just going to waste my grapefruit, then please give it back to me." And he gave me the rest back, gladly. He sure did think that Miss Delany from Raleigh was peculiar, sitting on his porch sucking down grapefruit.

6   Mr. Atkinson tended to be a rather dramatic man. One time he came into my classroom and said, "Oh, Miss Delany! Miss Delany!" And I said, "What's the matter, Mr. Atkinson?" And he fell to the ground and said, "It's terrible, it's just terrible!" And I said, "What's terrible?" And he said, "That ship they said could not sink, well, it's done sunk! And all those rich white people have gone down with it, in that icy water!"

7   I didn't say it out loud, but I remember thinking, Too bad the *Titanic* didn't take more rich white people down with it, to its watery grave! Especially some of the rebby boys around here! Now, isn't that awful of me? Isn't it vicious? You see why this child is worried about getting into Heaven? Sadie is just shocked by me sometimes. Sadie just says, "Live, and let live."

8   But in a way, I was a sweet child, too. You know, when I was in Boardman and got my first paycheck—$40 a month—I paid nine dollars for my room and board and sent the rest home to Papa immediately. No one had asked me to do that. It just seemed like the right thing to do.

9   Well, I got a letter back from Mama. She thanked me for the money but she told me not to send any more. She told me to save it for myself, or I'd never get to college.

10   I saved most of my money, but I will admit that I spent some on a silk dress, yes, sir! Papa wouldn't let me have a silk dress—I guess because it was so expensive but also kind of sexy. So, when I was in Boardman I ordered several yards of silk. I think it was blue, with a thin white stripe. And I made myself a dress. Skirts were going up, and you could see the ankle when you walked. And when the men would see a glimpse of ankle they would say, "Oooooh-weeee!" Papa didn't like that at all. When Sadie and I would wear those dresses, he would just scowl at us!! Today women show everything. They're crazy. Trust me, you can get in enough trouble just with a little ankle showing.

11   Now, after two years in Boardman, it was time for me to move on to a new teaching assignment. The people didn't want to see me go, but I was ready for a new challenge. So in 1913 I went to Brunswick, Georgia, to teach at Saint Athanasius, an Episcopal school for colored children. I wanted to see the world!

12   Brunswick was a sophisticated place compared to Boardman. The faculty lived together in a dormitory, and that is how I met my lifelong friend, Elizabeth Gooch. "Gooch," as I always called her, was the oldest one of us, and I was the youngest, and so the principal assigned the two of us to room

together. I guess he thought Gooch would be a good influence on me, but I think I was a good influence on Gooch!

13   I didn't like Gooch that much at first. She didn't treat me the way I would have liked to be treated. For instance, she took the bed away from the window, so that I'd get the draft at night. But after a while, Gooch and I became good friends. Sometimes, we'd go to the beach and see the turtles come in from the sea to nest.

14   Now, Georgia was a mean place—meaner than North Carolina. You know that song about Georgia, that sentimental song? Well, they can have it! They can have the whole state as far as I'm concerned.

15   In Georgia, they never missed a chance to keep you down. If you were colored and you tried on a hat or a pair of shoes, Honey, you owned 'em. What a rebby state! To be fair, I can understand why they didn't want Negroes to try on hats without buying them: because in those days, Negroes would grease their hair. And the store couldn't sell the hat if it got grease on it. So, to be fair, I think that was OK.

16   But it was on my way to my job in Brunswick in 1913 that I came close to being lynched. You see, I had to change trains in Waycross, Georgia. I was sitting in the little colored waiting room at the station, and I took my hair down and was combing it. I was fixing myself up. I was going to my new job, and I wanted to look nice.

17   Well, there I was with my long hair down when this white man opened the door, to the colored waiting room. There was no one in there except me and two colored teachers from New York who were traveling with me to Brunswick. The white man stuck his head in and started, well, leering at me. He was drunk, and he smelled bad, and he started mumbling things. And I said, "Oh, why don't you shut up and go wait with your own kind in the white waiting room?"

18   What happened next was kind of like an explosion. He slammed the door and I could hear him shouting at the top of his lungs outside, "The nigger bitch insulted me! The nigger bitch insulted me!"

19   The two colored teachers traveling with me slipped out the back without a word and made a beeline for the woods. They hid in the woods! I guess I can't blame them. A colored porter came in to see what this was all about, and he whispered to me, "Good for you!" But then he ran out on me, too. He left me there by myself.

20   Well, I could see a crowd begin to gather on the platform, and I knew I was in big trouble. Papa always said, "If you see a crowd, you go the other way. Don't even hang around long enough to find out what it's about!" Now, this crowd was outside, gathering for me.

21   By now, there were dozens of white people in the crowd, and the white man kept yelling, "Nigger bitch insulted me!" I was just waiting for somebody to get a rope. Thousands of Negroes had been lynched for far less than what I had just done. But I just continued to sit on the bench, combing my

hair, while that white man was a-carrying on! I realized that my best chance was to act like nothing was happening. You see, if you acted real scared, sometimes that spurred them on.

22 Two things saved me: That glorious, blessed train rounded the bend, breaking up the crowd and giving me my way to get on out of there. And it helped that the white man was drunk as a skunk, and that turned off some of the white people.

23 But I wasn't afraid to die! I know you ain't got to die but once, and it seemed as good a reason to die as any. I was ready. Lord, help me, I was ready.

24 You know what Sadie says? Sadie says I was a fool to provoke that white man. As if I provoked him! Honey, he provoked me! Sadie says she would have ignored him. I say, how do you ignore some drunk, smelly white man treating you like trash? She says, child, it's better to put up with it, and live to tell about it. She says at the very least I should have run off into the woods with those other two teachers. She says I am lucky to be alive. But I would rather die than back down, Honey.

~

(1,667 words)

VOCABULARY

legendary (1)	appalled (1)	vicious (7)
sophisticated (12)	lynched (16)	spurred (21)

THE FACTS

1. Which of the three religions in Boardman—Methodist, Baptist, Episcopalian—had the poorest membership? How was the poverty revealed? Who do you think made up the membership of the churches mentioned by the narrator?

2. What kind of diet made Bessie gain weight? What do we find out about Bessie's family and its knowledge of healthy foods? What kinds of foods should be blamed today for making so many youngsters obese?

3. What was your reaction to Bessie's admission that she wished more rich white people had sunk with the *Titanic?*

4. What is the difference between Bessie's personality and that of the rest of her family? Which attitude do you admire most? Explain your answer.

5. According to Bessie, what saved her from being lynched? Do you think she really was in danger of being lynched? Give reasons for your answer.

THE STRATEGIES

1. How does the author keep this story a dramatic monologue in which the speaker is telling her story to an unseen, trusted interviewer? Give examples of the author's technique.

2. The title of the story is "Incidents with White People." How do the incidents portray the white people? Is the portrait flattering or not? Support your answer with examples from the narration.

3. What is the reference to "that sentimental song about Georgia" that Bessie discredits? What is the title of the song? Why does Bessie dislike Georgia?

4. How does Bessie refer to black people in this narration? Is this how blacks refer to themselves today in most American locations or do they use other terminologies? Cite examples.

5. How well does the narrator handle the scene with the white drunk? What strategies does she use to keep the reader interested in the scene?

THE ISSUES

1. How is Mr. Atkinson portrayed in the narrative? How does the narrator seem to feel about him? Does the portrayal seem realistic or fantastic? Give reasons for your answer.

2. What reputation did silk dresses have among the conscientious parents of black girls at the time of this story? What might the equivalent be today?

3. What is your view of the black teachers who slipped out the back without a word and made a beeline for the woods? What is your view of the black porter who said, "Good for you!" and then ran away? What kinds of people today are fearless and stand to be counted? Give examples.

4. What is your reaction to the advice from Bessie's father—"If you see a crowd, you go the other way. Don't even hang around long enough to find out what it's about!"? Is this sound advice, even today?

5. Bessie felt that she would rather die than back down in front of this crowd of whites when she had been insulted. She also felt that she could not just ignore the white drunk. Do you think she was right? Would you be willing to lay your life on the line if you were in a similar situation? What issue would you be willing to die for?

SUGGESTIONS FOR WRITING

1. Write an essay in which you offer your opinion as to why blacks were treated the way they were at the time Bessie and Sadie lived in the South.

2. In an ideal world, how would ethnic, economic, religious, and gender differences be treated? Answer this question in an essay.

STUDENT CORNER

1

Final Draft

Racism: How Far Have We Come?

Nancey Phillips, California State University at Long Beach

"I have a dream my four little children will one day live in a nation where they will not be judged by the color of their skin but by the content of their character"

—Martin Luther King, Jr.

Dr. Martin Luther King, Jr. had great hopes for racial harmony in this country. The 1960s saw many advancements towards that end; the destruction of segregation and the passage of the Civil Rights Amendment were giant steps toward equality. But today, as the Twenty-First Century approaches, one sensational crime has split the country along racial lines and revealed the continuing problem of deep-seated racism in the U.S. The arrest and trial of O. J. Simpson for double murder has sparked heated debate in every level of American society, proving that there still remains a great divide between black and white.

On June 12, 1994, Nicole Brown Simpson and Ronald Goldman were stabbed to death outside of Brown's California condominium. In the days that followed the murders, famous football hero O. J. Simpson was arrested for the crime. The case soon became a national obsession as millions tuned in to watch the notorious slow-speed Bronco chase. The fact that Simpson, a convicted spousal abuser, was thought to have killed his ex-wife could have set off hostility between genders. The fact that Simpson was an extremely wealthy celebrity, capable of assembling a virtual "dream team" of defense attorneys, could have sparked controversy among opposed socioeconomic classes. But the O. J. Simpson trial did not pit men against women or rich against poor; instead the country was divided by race with black America crying "innocent" and white America crying "guilty."

After the lengthy and highly publicized trial, a predominately black jury found Simpson not guilty, triggering the worst wave of racial tension since the beating of Rodney King. The evidence against Simpson was considerable: his blood was found at the murder scene, the victim's blood was found in his car, he had a history of violence against Ms. Brown, and he had no alibi. Despite this mountain of evidence, Simpson went home a free man. Prosecutor Marcia Clark sharply criticized jurors and implied that race was the paramount factor in their decision. USA Today quoted her as saying, "Liberals don't want to admit it, but a majority black jury won't convict in a case like this. They won't bring justice."

Simpson's supporters seem to fall into two distinct categories. There are those who believe that he is guilty of the crime, but deserves to go free to make up for the injustices that African Americans have suffered through the years. Many black men have been wrongly prosecuted and imprisoned due to the color of their skin. In addition, many white men have gone free simply because their victims were black. The Medgar Evers murder case is one example where a white jury would not convict a white defendant for killing the civil rights leader. The black community longs for atonement from the justice system, and O.J. is it. Although this theory of making up for the past is flawed, the sentiment behind it is understandable to blacks and whites alike.

Phillips 3

The second group of Simpson advocates truly believe in his innocence. It is here that black and white divide. The difference in opinion goes far beyond basic prejudice, although it is a contributing factor. The main issue here seems to be differing experiences with the criminal justice system. A large majority of African Americans distrust the police force, whereas most white Americans have nothing but confidence in these officers. When the defense team suggested that much of the evidence in the case was planted by racist cops, the prosecutors balked at such a preposterous notion. The jurors had quite the opposite reaction. Psychologist Craig Haney, an expert on the role of race in the courtroom, states, "My guess is they went into the jury room and someone voiced concern about racism and a police conspiracy, and then there was widespread agreement that they couldn't trust the evidence." Quoted by USA Today, he continues, "That's a seemingly far-fetched idea to white folks who don't distrust the system, but in the African American community, it's not a hard sell at all."

Therefore, the seemingly overwhelming mountain of evidence is nullified in the mind of anyone who is suspicious of policework; the fact that most of those distrusting the police are black indicates a problem far more serious than the guilt or innocence of a football star. Black Americans are not receiving equal treatment at the hands of police or there would not be such wide-spread doubt regarding the validity of evidence. Positions on the Simpson case are not chosen randomly; different opinions are based on different experiences. Blacks and whites are simply not experiencing the same America.

Phillips 4

And so, more than thirty years after Dr. King's landmark speech, Americans find themselves still in the midst of racial crisis. One must surmise that if racist behavior is present on the police force, it is surely present in other factions of society. O. J. Simpson has illuminated the on-going problem of racism in this country, not because of his guilt or innocence, but because of America's polarized reaction to the case.

How I Write

I need absolute quiet when I write, so I usually lock myself away in my bedroom to work. My list of necessary tools is quite succinct: my powerbook and a strong cup of tea. Inspiration tends to strike late at night . . . and very often the night before the assignment is due. (I suppose that would be desperation rather than inspiration.) Nevertheless, you can now understand my need for the tea; the powerbook, of course, is self-explanatory. My writing tends to be highly structured, and so I simply cannot begin a paper without having a clear outline in my head. I rarely write down a formal outline, but I will jot down on paper my main points and the order in which I will use them. Once I know where I'm going with a paper, I sometimes write the body paragraphs first, and go back to construct the introduction later. I find it difficult to give my reader a preview of coming attractions when I'm not even sure what's ahead; once the body is done, the introduction practically writes itself. I compose very slowly, agonizing over each sentence as I go, instead of simply getting the basic idea down and rewriting later. As a result, my first draft is generally pretty close to the final product. I know plenty of people who can breeze through their first draft and then spend time perfecting their work; but I simply cannot write that way. My time on a project is spent mentally categorizing and organizing my points, and then physically sitting at the computer, choosing the best words to express my ideas. Once I start writing, I don't like to stop until I'm finished with the project or until I run out of tea . . . and actually it appears that my cup is now empty.

How I Wrote This Essay

The most difficult part of writing this essay was narrowing down the topic. Volumes and volumes have been written on the topic of racism, and so I had to find the one small area that I could manage in an essay of this length. I must admit that I was absolutely addicted to the Simpson trial, and with the issue of race being so prominent in the case, it seemed natural to write about it. I did my research on the Internet. I searched under "Racism in the Simpson Case" and came up with over one thousand matches; there was no shortage of information to sift through. I found using the Internet quick and easy compared to digging through microfiche at the library. After compiling my information, I jotted down a few main points and went to work on writing the essay. I spent about four hours writing the first draft and another hour revising it.

My Writing Tip

My best writing tip is to have someone else read your paper before you print the final draft. I mean ANYONE! It doesn't have to be a tutor or an English major; even your Mom or Dad will suffice. I find that after writing a paper, I am too used to looking at the words to be objective, and I often miss simple spelling or punctuation errors. An outsider will give you a fresh perspective and often find errors that you missed.

CHAPTER WRITING ASSIGNMENTS

1. In an essay, divide and classify one of the following subjects:
   a. Your friends
   b. Your relatives
   c. Things or activities that give you pleasure
   d. Classes you like to take
   e. Classes you don't like to take
2. Write an essay dividing and classifying the various techniques you have used over the years to make yourself a better writer.

WRITING ASSIGNMENTS FOR A SPECIFIC AUDIENCE

1. Pretending that you're writing to a prospective employer, divide and classify your life into various stages leading up to the present.
2. Write a letter to anyone you admire, dividing and classifying into stages the changes you have undergone in your career ambitions since you were young.

COLLABORATIVE WRITING PROJECT

Get together with a panel of eight other students in your class. The purpose of the panel is to gather crime statistics for the neighborhood around your school. Go through the public records available either on-line or through your police department and classify the crimes by any basis agreed on by a panel—whether by frequency, severity, or any other yardstick. Assemble and report on the results of your investigation in a team-written essay that you present to the class.

14

Causal Analysis

EDITORS' COUNSEL

What Causal Analysis Does

Causal analysis focuses specifically on explanations that show a connection between a situation and its cause or effect. It either answers the question "Why did this happen?" or "What will this do?" An answer to the first question will result in an explanation of cause; an answer to the second, a prediction of effect. An essay based on the controlling idea that "The lack of tough antipollution laws is the cause of multiple illnesses, including cancer, in the United States" is analyzing cause. If the essay was based on the controlling idea that "A law to stiffen penalties against toxic polluters will clear our drinking water from cancer-causing chemicals," it would be forecasting effect. As the diagram illustrates, cause points to past occurrences, whereas effect predicts future consequences.

$$cause \quad \leftarrow \quad situation \quad \rightarrow \quad effect$$

Here, for example, is a causal analysis written to answer the question "Why are so many couples unable to discuss their marital problems?"

> Barriers between husbands and wives are often caused by timidity. Many couples are embarrassed to discuss intimate problems, such as sexual maladjustment, personal hygiene, or religious beliefs. They prefer to let their discontent fester rather than confront it openly. A wife says, "I wouldn't hurt my husband by telling him that his dirty hands offend me." A husband says, "I dislike the way my wife compares me to her father in everything I do, from mowing the lawn to smoking my pipe, but I could never tell her so." Guilt feelings can reinforce this sort of timidity. If a wife or husband knows that a frank talk about sex, for instance, will uncover some past indiscretion, he or she will avoid the confrontation either out of personal guilt or fear of knowing about the other partner's past. The longer this silence is kept, the stronger and more destructive it becomes. Many a broken marriage can trace the break back to barriers in communication.

On the other hand, a slight shift in the approach to this topic leads naturally to a discussion of effect. An essay based on the question, "What happens when two people no longer discuss their marital problems?" would now focus on the effect, rather than the cause, of no communication in a marriage:

> Barriers between husband and wife result in a tension-filled home. When marriage partners constantly overlook a problem or pretend it does not exist, they eventually become frustrated and angry. They develop feelings of isolation and rejection, as their unfulfilled yearnings become a gnawing hunger. Lacking communication, the marriage is left without an emotional safety valve to let off pent-up frustration. The ensuing strain increases as the angry partners take out hidden, unexpressed resentments on their children, using them as scapegoats for their own great void. In the beginning the tension may show itself only in minor misunderstandings or brief pout sessions, but as the barriers remain, these little hurts turn into large wounds. The husband may become belligerent toward the wife, belittling her in front of friends or ignoring her until she retreats in cold indignation. The wife may feel so rejected and worthless that she seeks another man to comfort her or to treat her with sensitivity. The tension grows. Soon the home has become a place of bitter hostility, where love and warmth are impossible.

When to Use Causal Analysis

Use causal analysis when you are trying to explain why something happened or to predict the likely results if an event does or does not occur. Throughout your college study you will probably be given many assignments that require writing in the causal-analysis mode of development. A history paper might ask you to analyze the causes of the Louisiana Purchase in 1803; an astronomy exam, to explain the cause of the aurora borealis. In economics, you might be asked to predict what will happen to the American economy if oil prices surge. A psychology exam might require you to examine three results on the work of Carl Jung caused by his break with Sigmund Freud. Causal analysis is also commonly employed in argumentative papers written in all fields and disciplines.

How to Use Causal Analysis

Know the Differences among Necessary, Sufficient, and Contributory Cause   Three kinds of cause can create a given effect:

1. *A necessary cause is one that must be present for the effect to occur, but it alone cannot make the effect occur.* For instance, irrigation is necessary for a crop of good grapes, but irrigation alone will not cause a good crop. Enough sunshine, correct pruning, proper pesticides, and good soil are also required.

2. *A sufficient cause is one that can produce a given effect by itself.* For instance, an empty gasoline tank alone can keep a car from running, even though other problems such as a bad spark plug, a leaking hose, or ignition trouble may also be present.

3. *A contributory cause is one that might produce an effect but cannot produce the effect by itself.* For instance, vitamin E may help a long-distance runner win a race but cannot by itself determine the performance of a runner who got a bad start, trained haphazardly, or is not properly conditioned. The runner may also win the race without the help of vitamin E.

Understanding the differences among these three causes will help you in your investigations of cause and effect and keep you from making dogmatic statements such as these.

A vegetarian diet will prevent cancer.

Acupuncture is the answer to anesthesiology problems in America.

Violence on television is the cause of today's growing criminal violence.

Rather, you will soften your statements by inserting such phrases as "may be," "is a contributing factor," "is one of the reasons," or "is a major cause." A careful study of cause and effect teaches that few causes are sufficient; most are merely necessary or contributory.

Make Your Purpose Clear   The excerpt from Jim Corbett's book, reprinted later in this chapter, opens with this clear statement: "As many of the stories in this book are about man-eating tigers, it is perhaps desirable to explain why these animals develop man-eating tendencies." It proceeds to explain exactly that. This sort of definiteness early in the piece adds a guiding focus to any explanation of cause.

Be Modest in Your Choice of Subject   It is difficult enough to analyze the causes of simple effects without compounding your problem through the choice of a monstrously large subject. The student who tries to write an essay on the causes of war is already in deep trouble; such a complex phenomenon bristles with thousands of causes. Selecting a more manageable subject for causal analysis will make your task much easier.

Concentrate on Immediate Rather than Remote Cause   It is easy in analysis of cause to become entangled in the infinite. In a series of causations, the most likely cause is always the nearest. For example, take the case of a student—John Doe—who gets a poor grade on a test. Why? Probably because he failed to study. On the other hand, perhaps John failed to study because he thought he was doomed to fail anyway, and didn't see the point in exerting himself. Why? Probably because the instructor scared him with a lecture on how high her standards were and how hard it was to pass her class. Why did she do that? Probably because of pressure from the Regents, who accused her and her department of grading too easily. Why? The Regents, in turn, may have gotten tough because of an article critical of the department's standards that appeared in a newspaper and was written by a cub reporter who played loose with the facts. This story, in turn, was approved by an editor who had a toothache caused by a badly filled tooth. Yet, in spite of this chain of events, it is a stretch to claim that John Doe failed the test because of sloppy dentistry. Common sense must guide your thinking in this sort of analysis; but because infinity lies behind even the reason why someone purchases a popsicle, it is safer, as a rule of thumb, to stay with immediate cause and ignore the remote.

Don't Be Dogmatic about Cause   Institutions of learning rigorously demand that students analyze cause with caution and prudence. The reasoning is simple enough: Colleges and universities are quite determined to impress on their students the complexity of the world. It is advisable, therefore, that you be modest in your claims of causation. You can easily temper a dogmatic statement by interjecting qualifiers into your claims. Instead of writing:

> Violence in America is *caused* by violent television programs.

you could more prudently write:

> Violence in America is *influenced* by television programs.

If a student had written the following paragraph, it would no doubt have drawn the instructor's criticism:

> This brings me to the major cause of unhappiness, which is that most people in America act not on impulse but on some principle, and that principles upon which people act are usually based upon a false psychology and a false ethic. There is a general theory as to what makes for happiness and this theory is false. Life is conceived as a competitive struggle in which felicity consists in getting ahead of your neighbor. The joys which are not competitive are forgotten.

Yet, this paragraph is from a Bertrand Russell article, *The Unhappy American Way,* which readers have read with much sagacious head-nodding. Bertrand Russell was a Nobel laureate, a mathematician, and a noted philosopher when he wrote this. No doubt it is unfair, but his obvious accomplishments gain for him a temporary suspension of the rules against dogmatizing. Students, however, are not readily granted such license. We advise that, for the time being, anyway, you generalize about cause prudently.

Use Common Sense in Asserting Cause   Most writers do not rigidly follow the principles of causal analysis except when they argue a technical question that must be explained according to the rules of logic. The following passage is an example of the free use of the principles of causal analysis:

> The association of love with adultery in much of medieval love poetry has two causes. The first lies in the organization of feudal society. Marriages, being matters of economic or social interest, had nothing whatever to do with erotic love. When a marriage alliance no longer suited the interests of the lord, he got rid of his lady with as much dispatch as he got rid of a horse. Consequently, a lady who might be nothing more than a commodious piece of property to her husband, could be passionately desired by her vassal. The second cause lies in the attitude of the medieval Christian church, where the desire for erotic, romantic love was considered wicked and a result of Adam's sin in the Garden of Eden. The general impression left on the medieval mind by the church's official teachers was that all erotic pleasure was wicked. And this impression, in addition to the nature of feudal marriage, produced in the courtly poets the perverse desire to emphasize the very passion they were told to resist.

The student who wrote this paragraph does not demonstrate cause according to precise rules, but rather shows the commonsense result of her research into why medieval poetry emphasized adulterous love.

Warming Up to Write a Causal Analysis

Remember that causes look backward to the source of an event whereas effects look forward to consequences. Here are some warm-up exercises that will help you focus on cause and effect.

1. List at least three causes for each of the following situations:
   a. Teenage smoking
   b. Recent increase in obesity
   c. Deadlock between executives and strong labor unions
   d. Children's feelings of guilt during a divorce
   e. Grownups not knowing how to use a computer
2. List at least three effects that result from the following situations:
   a. Loss of a parent while one is still young
   b. Having one's car stolen
   c. The fear of further terrorist attacks in the United States and other countries
   d. Listening to classical music
   e. Discovering a rat infestation in one's cellar
3. Write a thesis for each of the answers you gave to Exercise 1. Then pick the thesis that you think would lead to the best essay.

4. Write a thesis for each of the answers you gave to Exercise 2. Then pick the thesis that you think would lead to the best essay.

───── EXAMPLES ─────

A PEACEFUL WOMAN EXPLAINS WHY SHE CARRIES A GUN

Linda M. Hasselstrom

Linda M. Hasselstrom (b. 1943) is a writer and teacher who grew up in rural South Dakota. Her works include Roadkill *(1984), a collection of her poetry, and* Land Circle *(1991), a collection of her essays.*

Living alone on an isolated ranch may seem romantic to some who love nature or solitude, but it can involve some hair-raising encounters, as we find out from the close calls related in the essay that follows. Embedded within the story line is the issue of who, if anyone, should have legal access to a gun.

～

1   I am a peace-loving woman. But several events in the past 10 years have convinced me I'm safer when I carry a pistol. This was a personal decision, but because handgun possession is a controversial subject, perhaps my reasoning will interest others.

2   I live in western South Dakota on a ranch 25 miles from the nearest town: for several years I spent winters alone here. As a free-lance writer, I travel alone a lot—more than 100,000 miles by car in the last four years. With women freer than ever before to travel alone, the odds of our encountering trouble seem to have risen. Distances are great, roads are deserted, and the terrain is often too exposed to offer hiding places.

3   A woman who travels alone is advised, usually by men, to protect herself by avoiding bars and other "dangerous situations," by approaching her car like an Indian scout, by locking doors and windows. But these precautions aren't always enough. I spent years following them and still found myself in dangerous situations. I began to resent the idea that just because I am female, I have to be extra careful.

4   A few years ago, with another woman, I camped for several weeks in the West. We discussed self-defense, but neither of us had taken a course in it. She was against firearms, and local police told us Mace was illegal. So we armed ourselves with spray cans of deodorant tucked into our sleeping bags. We never used our improvised Mace because we were lucky enough to camp beside people who came to our aid when men harassed us. But on one occasion we visited a national park where our assigned space was less than 15 feet from other campers. When we returned from a walk, we found our closest neighbors were two young men. As we gathered our cooking gear, they

drank beer and loudly discussed what they would do to us after dark. Nearby campers, even families, ignored them: rangers strolled past, unconcerned. When we asked the rangers pointblank if they would protect us, one of them patted my shoulder and said, "Don't worry girls. They're just kidding." At dusk we drove out of the park and hid our camp in the woods a few miles away. The illegal spot was lovely, but our enjoyment of that park was ruined. I returned from the trip determined to reconsider the options available for protecting myself.

5   At that time, I lived alone on the ranch and taught night classes in town. Along a city street I often traveled, a woman had a flat tire, called for help on her CB radio, and got a rapist who left her beaten. She was afraid to call for help again and stayed in her car until morning. For that reason, as well as because CBs work best along line-of-sight, which wouldn't help much in the rolling hills where I live, I ruled out a CB.

6   As I drove home one night, a car followed me. It passed me on a narrow bridge while a passenger flashed a blinding spotlight in my face. I braked sharply. The car stopped, angled across the bridge, and four men jumped out. I realized the locked doors were useless if they broke the windows of my pickup. I started forward, hoping to knock their car aside so I could pass. Just then another car appeared, and the men hastily got back in their car. They continued to follow me, passing and repassing. I dared not go home because no one else was there. I passed no lighted houses. Finally they pulled over to the roadside, and I decided to use their tactic: fear. Speeding, the pickup horn blaring, I swerved as close to them as I dared as I roared past. It worked: they turned off the highway. But I was frightened and angry. Even in my vehicle I was too vulnerable.

7   Other incidents occurred over the years. One day I glanced out at a field below my house and saw a man with a shotgun walking toward a pond full of ducks. I drove down and explained that the land was posted. I politely asked him to leave. He stared at me, and the muzzle of the shotgun began to rise. In a moment of utter clarity I realized that I was alone on the ranch, and that he could shoot me and simply drive away. The moment passed: the man left.

8   One night, I returned home from teaching a class to find deep tire ruts in the wet ground of my yard, garbage in the driveway, and a large gas tank empty. A light shone in the house: I couldn't remember leaving it on. I was too embarrassed to drive to a neighboring ranch and wake someone up. An hour of cautious exploration convinced me the house was safe, but once inside, with the doors locked, I was still afraid. I kept thinking of how vulnerable I felt, prowling around my own house in the dark.

9   My first positive step was to take a kung fu class, which teaches evasive or protective action when someone enters your space without permission. I learned to move confidently, scanning for possible attackers. I learned how to assess danger and techniques for avoiding it without combat.

10   I also learned that one must practice several hours every day to be good at kung fu. By that time I had married George: when I practiced with him, I learned how close you must be to your attacker to use martial arts, and

decided a 120-pound woman dare not let a six-foot, 220-pound attacker get that close unless she is very, very good at self-defense. I have since read articles by several women who were extremely well trained in the martial arts, but were raped and beaten anyway.

11   I thought back over the times in my life when I had been attacked or threatened and tried to be realistic about my own behavior, searching for anything that had allowed me to become a victim. Overall, I was convinced that I had not been at fault. I don't believe myself to be either paranoid or a risk-taker, but I wanted more protection.

12   With some reluctance I decided to try carrying a pistol. George had always carried one, despite his size and his training in martial arts. I practiced shooting until I was sure I could hit an attacker who moved close enough to endanger me. Then I bought a license from the county sheriff, making it legal for me to carry the gun concealed.

13   But I was not yet ready to defend myself. George taught me that the most important preparation was mental: convincing myself I could actually shoot a person. Few of us wish to hurt or kill another human being. But there is no point in having a gun; in fact, gun possession might increase your danger unless you know you can use it. I got in the habit of rehearsing, as I drove or walked, the precise conditions that would be required before I would shoot someone.

14   People who have not grown up with the idea that they are capable of protecting themselves—in other words, most women—might have to work hard to convince themselves of their ability, and of the necessity. Handgun ownership need not turn us into gunslingers, but it can be part of believing in, and relying on, ourselves for protection.

15   To be useful, a pistol has to be available. In my car, it's within instant reach. When I enter a deserted rest stop at night, it's in my purse, with my hand on the grip. When I walk from a dark parking lot into a motel, it's in my hand, under a coat. At home, it's on the headboard. In short, I take it with me almost everywhere I go alone.

16   Just carrying a pistol is not protection; avoidance is still the best approach to trouble. Subconsciously watching for signs of danger, I believe I've become more alert. Handgun use, not unlike driving, becomes instinctive. Each time I've drawn my gun—I have never fired it at another human being—I've simply found it in my hand.

17   I was driving the half-mile to the highway mailbox one day when I saw a vehicle parked about midway down the road. Several men were standing in the ditch, relieving themselves. I have no objection to emergency urination, but I noticed they'd dumped several dozen beer cans in the road. Besides being ugly, cans can slash a cow's feet or stomach.

18   The men noticed me before they finished and made quite a performance out of zipping their trousers while walking toward me. All four of them gathered around my small foreign car, and one of them demanded what the hell I wanted.

19   "This is private land. I'd appreciate it if you'd pick up the beer cans."

20   "What beer cans?" said the belligerent one, putting both hands on the car door and leaning in my window. His face was inches from mine, and the beer fumes were strong. The others laughed. One tried the passenger door, locked; another put his foot on the hood and rocked the car. They circled, lightly thumping the roof, discussing my good fortune in meeting them and the benefits they were likely to bestow upon me. I felt very small and very trapped and they knew it.

21   "The ones you just threw out," I said politely.

22   "I don't see no beer cans. Why don't you get out here and show them to me, honey?" said the belligerent one, reaching for the handle inside my door.

23   "Right over there," I said, still being polite. "—there, and over there." I pointed with the pistol, which I'd slipped under my thigh. Within one minute the cans and the men were back in the car and headed down the road.

24   I believe this incident illustrates several important principles. The men were trespassing and knew it: their judgment may have been impaired by alcohol. Their response to the polite request of a woman alone was to use their size, numbers, and sex to inspire fear. The pistol was a response in the same language. Politeness didn't work: I couldn't match them in size or number. Out of the car, I'd have been more vulnerable. The pistol just changed the balance of power. It worked again recently when I was driving in a desolate part of Wyoming. A man played cat-and-mouse with me for 30 miles, ultimately trying to run me off the road. When his car passed mine with only two inches to spare, I showed him my pistol, and he disappeared.

25   When I got my pistol, I told my husband, revising the old Colt slogan, "God made men *and women*, but Sam Colt made them equal." Recently I have seen a gunmaker's ad with a similar sentiment. Perhaps this is an idea whose time has come, though the pacifist inside me will be saddened if the only way women can achieve equality is by carrying weapons.

We must treat a firearm's power with caution. "Power tends to corrupt, and absolute power corrupts absolutely," as a man (Lord Acton) once said. A pistol is not the only way to avoid being raped or murdered in today's world, but, intelligently wielded, it can shift the balance of power and provide a measure of safety.

∼

(1,902 words)

VOCABULARY

improvised (4)	angled (6)	evasive (9)
assess (9)	martial (10)	paranoid (11)
reluctance (12)	urination (17)	trespassing (24)

THE FACTS

1. How many times did the author actually use her pistol? In each case, what was the pistol's role? How do you feel about her use of a pistol?

2. Why is a woman who travels alone believed to be more vulnerable than a man who does the same? What other precautions besides avoiding bars, approaching her car carefully, and locking doors and windows can a woman traveling alone observe?

3. Why did the author have to go to town at night when she lived on a ranch out in the country? Could she have avoided the regular trips to town?

4. According to the author, why is the martial art of kung fu not an ideal deterrent to anyone with a criminal intent?

5. Why did the author buy a license from the county sheriff after she had practiced shooting and had purchased a gun? Do you think all gun owners should follow her example? Why or why not?

THE STRATEGIES

1. Where is the thesis of the essay most clearly stated? Evaluate the merits of this particular position.

2. What rhetorical strategy does the author use to convince her readers that she did the appropriate thing by purchasing a pistol that she could easily hide from view? Were you convinced by her argument? Why or why not?

3. At what point in the essay does the author seem to be in the most danger? Explain your answer.

4. Which paragraphs of the essay constitute a fascinating drama with an exciting climax and a happy ending? What technique makes this passage so absorbing?

5. What is the purpose of the famous quotation by Lord Acton? In what context is this quotation usually used? Why does it fit the context of this essay as well?

THE ISSUES

1. How do you interpret the old Colt slogan, "God made men and women, but Sam Colt made them equal"? What do you think of the notion that carrying a gun is one way for women to achieve equality with men? Why does the author express sorrow at the thought that carrying weapons might be the only way women can achieve equality with men?

2. Do you believe the author was paranoid or an excessive risk taker? Did she in any way contribute to her own insecurity while living at

the ranch? What, if anything, could she have done to better protect herself?

3. What are some useful ways in which women in general can learn to protect themselves when they are forced to be in an environment where they could be victims of criminals?

4. What is the most frightening encounter you have ever had? If you were a victim, how did you handle the situation?

5. What is your opinion of gun control? Support your opinion with logic and strong evidence.

SUGGESTIONS FOR WRITING

1. Write an essay in which you propose an effective solution for the crime of rape.

2. Using Hasselstrom's essay as a counterpoint, write an essay entitled *The Dangers of Carrying a Gun.*

COMING INTO LANGUAGE

Jimmy Santiago Baca

Jimmy Santiago Baca (b. 1952) is one among several admired "Barrio" writers, so-called because they emerged from the poverty and squalor of barrio life to portray their background with power and vividness. An ex-convict, Baca taught himself to read and write while in prison, eventually winning the American Book Award of 1988. Part Chicano and part Indian, he was abandoned by his parents when he was two and lived with his grandparents. By the time he was five, his mother had been murdered by her second husband, his father had died of alcoholism, and Baca had lived in an orphanage, from which he escaped to survive on the streets. In time, he landed in prison on a drug charge (which he claimed was false) and was sent to maximum security and later placed in isolation because of his combative nature. Through an outside mentor, his writings gradually received international attention, and he was released from prison. Despite his tragic life, his writing—mostly poetry—dwells on rebirth rather than bitterness. Among his works are Immigrants in Our Own Land *(1979),* Swords of Darkness *(1981),* What's Happening? *(1982),* Martin and Meditations on the South Valley *(1987),* Black Mesa Poems *(1989), and* Working in the Dark: Reflections of a Poet of the Barrio *(1990), from which the following essay is taken.*

What follows is a horrifying yet heartwarming autobiographical account of the author's personal journey toward poetic birth. We are allowed an intimate glance into a man's scarred and demon-filled soul and we witness how he faces the horrors of prison life, including solitary confinement and the mental ward. We see and feel his torment and hellish despair, but we also watch his slow development as a writer as he is purged of crime and violence through an appreciation of the beauty of language.

~

1   On weekend graveyard shifts at St. Joseph's Hospital I worked the emergency room, mopping up pools of blood and carting plastic bags stuffed with arms, legs, and hands to the outdoor incinerator. I enjoyed the quiet, away from the screams of shotgunned, knifed, and mangled kids writhing on gurneys outside the operating rooms. Ambulance sirens shrieked and squad car lights reddened the cool nights, flashing against the hospital walls: gray–red, gray–red. On slow nights I would lock the door of the administration office, search the reference library for a book on female anatomy and, with my feet propped on the desk, leaf through the illustrations, smoking my cigarette. I was seventeen.

2   One night my eye was caught by a familiar-looking word on the spine of a book. The title was *450 Years of Chicano History in Pictures.* On the cover were black-and-white photos: Padre Hidalgo exhorting Mexican peasants to revolt against the Spanish dictators; Anglo vigilantes hanging two Mexicans from a tree; a young Mexican woman with rifle and ammunition belts crisscrossing her breast; César Chávez and field workers marching for fair wages; Chicano railroad workers laying creosote ties; Chicanas laboring at machines in textile factories; Chicanas picketing and hoisting boycott signs.

3   From the time I was seven, teachers had been punishing me for not knowing my lessons by making me stick my nose in a circle chalked on the blackboard. Ashamed of not understanding and fearful of asking questions, I dropped out of school in the ninth grade. At seventeen I still didn't know how to read, but those pictures confirmed my identity. I stole the book that night, stashing it for safety under the slop-sink until I got off work. Back at my boardinghouse, I showed the book to friends. All of us were amazed; this book told us we were alive. We, too, had defended ourselves with our fists against hostile Anglos, gasping for breath in fights with the policemen who outnumbered us. The book reflected back to us our struggle in a way that made us proud.

4   Most of my life I felt like a target in the cross hairs of a hunter's rifle. When strangers and outsiders questioned me I felt the hang-rope tighten around my neck and the trapdoor creak beneath my feet. There was nothing so humiliating as being unable to express myself, and my inarticulateness increased my sense of jeopardy, of being endangered. I felt intimidated and vulnerable, ridiculed and scorned. Behind a mask of humility, I seethed with mute rebellion.

5   Before I was eighteen, I was arrested on suspicion of murder after refusing to explain a deep cut on my forearm. With shocking speed I found myself handcuffed to a chain gang of inmates and bused to a holding facility to await trial. There I met men, prisoners, who read aloud to each other the works of

Neruda, Paz, Sabines, Nemerov, and Hemingway. Never had I felt such free-dom as in that dormitory. Listening to the words of these writers, I felt that invisible threat from without lessen—my sense of teetering on a rotting plank over swamp water where famished alligators clapped their horny snouts for my blood. While I listened to the words of the poets, the alligators slumbered powerless in their lairs. Their language was the magic that could liberate me from myself, transform me into another person, transport me to other places far away.

6   And when they closed the books, these Chicanos, and went into their own Chicano language, they made barrio life come alive for me in the fullness of its vitality. I began to learn my own language, the bilingual words and phrases explaining to me my place in the universe. Every day I felt like the paper boy taking delivery of the latest news of the day.

7   Months later I was released, as I had suspected I would be. I had been guilty of nothing but shattering the windshield of my girlfriend's car in a fit of rage.

8   Two years passed. I was twenty now, and behind bars again. The federal marshals had failed to provide convincing evidence to extradite me to Ari-zona on a drug charge, but still I was being held. They had ninety days to prove I was guilty. The only evidence against me was that my girlfriend had been at the scene of the crime with my driver's license in her purse. They had to come up with something else. But there was nothing else. Eventually they negotiated a deal with the actual drug dealer, who took the stand against me. When the judge hit me with a million-dollar bail, I emptied my pockets on his booking desk: twenty-six cents.

9   One night in my third month in the county jail, I was mopping the floor in front of the booking desk. Some detectives had kneed an old drunk and hand-cuffed him to the booking bars. His shrill screams raked my nerves like a hacksaw on bone, the desperate protest of his dignity against their inhuman-ity. But the detectives just laughed as he tried to rise and kicked him to his knees. When they went to the bathroom to pee and the desk attendant walked to the file cabinet to pull the arrest record, I shot my arm through the bars, grabbed one of the attendant's university textbooks, and tucked it in my overalls. It was the only way I had of protesting.

10   It was late when I returned to my cell. Under my blanket I switched on a pen flashlight and opened the thick book at random, scanning the pages. I could hear the jailer making his rounds on the other tiers. The jangle of his keys and the sharp click of his boot heels intensified my solitude. Slowly I enunciated the words. . .p-o-n-d, ri-pple. It scared me that I had been reduced to this to find comfort. I always had thought reading a waste of time, that nothing could be gained by it. Only by action, by moving out into the world and confronting and challenging the obstacles, could one learn anything worth knowing.

11   Even as I tried to convince myself that I was merely curious, I became so absorbed in how the sounds created music in me and happiness, I forgot where I was. Memories began to quiver in me, glowing with a strange but

familiar intimacy in which I found refuge. For a while, a deep sadness overcame me, as if I had chanced on a long-lost friend and mourned the years of separation. But soon the heartache of having missed so much of life, that had numbed me since I was a child, gave way, as if a grave illness lifted itself from me and I was cured, innocently believing in the beauty of life again. I stumblingly repeated the author's name as I fell asleep, saying it over and over in the dark: Words-worth, Words-worth.

12   Before long my sister came to visit me, and I joked about taking her to a place called Kubla Khan and getting her a blind date with this *vato* named Coleridge who lived on the seacoast and was *malias* on morphine. When I asked her to make a trip into enemy territory to buy me a grammar book, she said she couldn't. Bookstores intimidated her, because she, too, could neither read nor write.

13   Days later, with a stub pencil I whittled sharp with my teeth, I propped a Red Chief notebook on my knees and wrote my first words. From that moment, a hunger for poetry possessed me.

14   Until then, I had felt as if I had been born into a raging ocean where I swam relentlessly, flailing my arms in hope of rescue, of reaching a shoreline I never sighted. Never solid ground beneath me, never a resting place. I had lived with only the desperate hope to stay afloat; that and nothing more.

15   But when at last I wrote my first words on the page, I felt an island rising beneath my feet like the back of a whale. As more and more words emerged, I could finally rest: I had a place to stand for the first time in my life. The island grew, with each page, into a continent inhabited by people I knew and mapped with the life I lived.

16   I wrote about it all—about people I had loved or hated, about the brutalities and ecstasies of my life. And, for the first time, the child in me who had witnessed and endured unspeakable terrors cried out not just in impotent despair, but with the power of language. Suddenly, through language, through writing, my grief and my joy could be shared with anyone who would listen. And I could do this all alone; I could do it anywhere. I was no longer a captive of demons eating away at me, no longer a victim of other people's mockery and loathing, that had made me clench my fist white with rage and grit my teeth to silence. Words now pleaded back with the bleak lucidity of hurt. They were wrong, those others, and now I could say it.

17   Through language I was free. I could respond, escape, indulge; embrace or reject earth or the cosmos. I was launched on an endless journey without boundaries or rules, in which I could salvage the floating fragments of my past, or be born anew in the spontaneous ignition of understanding some heretofore concealed aspect of myself. Each word steamed with the hot lava juices of my primordial making, and I crawled out of stanzas dripping with birth-blood, reborn and freed from the chaos of my life. The child in the dark room of my heart, that had never been able to find or reach the light switch, flicked it on now; and I found in the room a stranger, myself, who had waited so many years to speak again. My words struck in me lightning crackles of elation and thunderhead storms of grief.

18   When I had been in the county jail longer than anyone else, I was made a trustee. One morning, after a fist fight, I went to the unlocked and unoccupied office used for lawyer-client meetings, to think. The bare white room with its fluorescent tube lighting seemed to expose and illuminate my dark and worthless life. And yet, for the first time, I had something to lose—my chance to read, to write; a way to live with dignity and meaning, that had opened for me when I stole that scuffed, second-hand book about the Romantic poets. In prison, the abscess had been lanced.

19   "I will never do any work in this prison system as long as I am not allowed to get my G.E.D." That's what I told the reclassification panel. The captain flicked off the tape recorder. He looked at me hard and said, "You'll never walk outta here alive. Oh, you'll work, put a copper penny on that, you'll work."

20   After that interview I was confined to deadlock maximum security in a subterranean dungeon, with ground-level chicken-wired windows painted gray. Twenty-three hours a day I was in that cell. I kept sane by borrowing books from the other cons on the tier. Then, just before Christmas, I received a letter from Harry, a charity house Samaritan who doled out hot soup to the homeless in Phoenix. He had picked my name from a list of cons who had no one to write to them. I wrote back asking for a grammar book, and a week later received one of Mary Baker Eddy's treatises on salvation and redemption, with Spanish and English on opposing pages. Pacing my cell all day and most of each night, I grappled with grammar until I was able to write a long true-romance confession for a con to send to his pen pal. He paid me with a pack of smokes. Soon I had a thriving barter business, exchanging my poems and letters for novels, commissary pencils, and writing tablets.

21   One day I tore two flaps from the cardboard box that held all my belongings and punctured holes along the edge of each flap and along the border of a ream of state-issue paper. After I had aligned them to form a spine, I threaded the holes with a shoestring, and sketched on the cover a hummingbird fluttering above a rose. This was my first journal.

22   Whole afternoons I wrote, unconscious of passing time or whether it was day or night. Sunbursts exploded from the lead tip of my pencil, words that grafted me into awareness of who I was; peeled back to a burning core of bleak terror, an embryo floating in the image of water, I cracked out of the shell wide-eyed and insane. Trees grew out of the palms of my hands, the threatening otherness of life dissolved, and I became one with the air and sky, the dirt and the iron and concrete. There was no longer any distinction between the other and I. Language made bridges of fire between me and everything I saw. I entered into the blade of grass, the basketball, the con's eye and child's soul.

23   At night I flew. I conversed with floating heads in my cell, and visited strange houses where lonely women brewed tea and rocked in wicker rocking chairs listening to sad Joni Mitchell songs.

24   Before long I was frayed like a rope carrying too much weight, that suddenly snaps. I quit talking. Bars, walls, steel bunk and floor bristled with

millions of poem-making sparks. My face was no longer familiar to me. The only reality was the swirling cornucopia of images in my mind, the voices in the air. Mid-air a cactus blossom would appear, a snake-flame in blinding dance around it, stunning me like a guard's fist striking my neck from behind.

25   The prison administrators tried several tactics to get me to work. For six months, after the next monthly prison board review, they sent cons to my cell to hassle me. When the guard would open my cell door to let one of them in, I'd leap out and fight him—and get sent to thirty-day isolation. I did a lot of isolation time. But I honed my image-making talents in that sensory-deprived solitude. Finally they moved me to death row, and after that to "nut-run," the tier that housed the mentally disturbed.

26   As the months passed, I became more and more sluggish. My eyelids were heavy, I could no longer write or read. I slept all the time.

27   One day a guard took me out to the exercise field. For the first time in years I felt grass and earth under my feet. It was spring. The sun warmed my face as I sat on the bleachers watching the cons box and run, hit the handball, lift weights. Some of them stopped to ask how I was, but I found it impossible to utter a syllable. My tongue would not move, saliva drooled from the corners of my mouth. I had been so heavily medicated I could not summon the slightest gesture. Yet inside me a small voice cried out, I am fine! I am hurt now but I will come back! I am fine!

28   Back in my cell, for weeks I refused to eat. Styrofoam cups of urine and hot water were hurled at me. Other things happened. There were beatings, shock therapy, intimidation.

29   Later, I regained some clarity of mind. But there was a place in my heart where I had died. My life had compressed itself into an unbearable dread of being. The strain had been too much. I had stepped over that line where a human being has lost more than he can bear, where the pain is too intense, and he knows he is changed forever. I was now capable of killing, coldly and without feeling. I was empty, as I have never, before or since, known emptiness. I had no connection to this life.

30   But then, the encroaching darkness that began to envelop me forced me to re-form and give birth to myself again in the chaos. I withdrew even deeper into the world of language, cleaving the diamonds of verbs and nouns, plunging into the brilliant light of poetry's regenerative mystery. Words gave off rings of white energy, radar signals from powers beyond me that infused me with truth. I believed what I wrote, because I wrote what was true. My words did not come from books or textual formulas, but from a deep faith in the voice of my heart.

31   I had been steeped in self-loathing and rejected by everyone and everything—society, family, cons, God and demons. But now I had become as the burning ember floating in darkness that descends on a dry leaf and sets flame to forests. The word was the ember and the forest was my life.

32   I was born a poet one noon, gazing at weeds and creosoted grass at the base of a telephone pole outside my grilled cell window. The words I wrote then sailed me out of myself, and I was transported and metamorphosed into the images they made. From the dirty brown blades of grass came bolts of electrical light that jolted loose my old self; through the top of my head that self was released and reshaped in the clump of scrawny grass. Through language I became the grass, speaking its language and feeling its green feelings and black root sensations. Earth was my mother and I bathed in sunshine. Minuscule speckles of sunlight passed through my green skin and metabolized in my blood.

33   Writing bridged my divided life of prisoner and free man. I wrote of the emotional butchery of prisons, and of my acute gratitude for poetry. Where my blind doubt and spontaneous trust in life met, I discovered empathy and compassion. The power to express myself was a welcome storm rasping at tendril roots, flooding my soul's cracked dirt. Writing was water that cleansed the wound and fed the parched root of my heart.

34   I wrote to sublimate my rage, from a place where all hope is gone, from a madness of having been damaged too much, from a silence of killing rage. I wrote to avenge the betrayals of a lifetime, to purge the bitterness of injustice. I wrote with a deep groan of doom in my blood, bewildered and dumbstruck; from an indestructible love of life, to affirm breath and laughter and the abiding innocence of things. I wrote the way I wept, and danced, and made love.

∼

(3,131 words)

VOCABULARY

incinerator (1)	inarticulateness (4)	lairs (5)
extradite (8)	enunciated (10)	primordial (17)
subterranean (20)	Samaritan (20)	treatises (20)
regenerative (30)	creosoted (32)	metamorphosed (32)

THE FACTS

1. Why did the author drop out of school in ninth grade?

2. What reason does the author offer for his having been sent to prison on a murder charge?

3. Who are Wordsworth and Coleridge? How do they relate to the author?

4. What was the "island" on which the author finally could rest while he was in jail? (See paragraph 15.)

5. When a prison guard finally took the author out to the exercise field, why couldn't he talk or even make the slightest gesture?

THE STRATEGIES

1. Who is the voice in this essay? What kind of person is revealed? How do you feel about him? Why does he seem to be writing the essay?

2. The author's experience is rendered in separate steps that could be called "the process of regeneration." What are the steps?

3. Where in this essay does the author reveal his poetic talent? Find specific examples of poetic utterances.

4. How does the author indicate the passage of time?

5. What do you think the author meant when he made the following statement: "Most of my life I felt like a target in the cross hairs of a hunter's rifle"? Explain this statement in your own words.

THE ISSUES

1. Which aspect of the author's artistic journey do you consider the climax of his experience as related in this essay? In other words, at which point does he recognize the possibilities inherent in language? Give reasons for your choice.

2. How can you explain the author's grasp of English grammar despite the fact that he was a school dropout?

3. How would you characterize the essence of Baca's life before he became a writer? How was it possible for him to become a writer?

4. What is your opinion of the punishment meted out by the author's teachers from the time he was seven years old? What typical results does this kind of pedagogy win?

5. Do you consider it a good idea to encourage prison inmates to develop their talents while in prison? Why or why not? If you believe the idea to have merit, what process would you suggest for assessing and promoting the prisoners' talents? If you believe the idea has no merit, indicate why.

SUGGESTIONS FOR WRITING

1. Language reached Baca in a way nothing else had. Write an essay that answers these questions: "Can every criminal be 'reached' on some level?" "Is there a good person inside even the most violent and apparently unrepentant criminal?"

2. Write an essay either attacking or defending our prison system in the way it helps inmates to improve themselves intellectually.

WHY TIGERS BECOME MAN-EATERS

Jim Corbett

James Edward Corbett (1875–1955) was born in Nainital, India, and worked with a railroad company for twenty years. He served first as a captain then as a major during World War I. From 1907 to 1938, he was a tiger hunter in the remote regions of India, where he was often summoned to destroy man-eaters preying on villagers. His memoirs, Man-Eaters of Kumaon, was first published in 1944 in India.

The big-game hunter has dwindled into something of a movie spoof. But not so many years ago, such a figure was a godsend to helpless remote villagers being preyed upon by rogue animals. Although he has hunted many such predators, the author tells us in an opening note to his famed book, *Man-Eaters of Kumaon*, that when an animal becomes a man-eater, the transformation is rare, unnatural, and never without cause. In this, his opening chapter, the author explains why tigers change suddenly into man-eaters, giving us a sympathetic view of the tiger, which has today been hunted by humans to the brink of extinction.

~

1   As many of the stories in this book are about man-eating tigers, it is perhaps desirable to explain why these animals develop man-eating tendencies.

2   A man-eating tiger is a tiger that has been compelled, through stress of circumstances beyond its control, to adopt a diet alien to it. The stress of circumstances is, in nine cases out of ten, wounds, and in the tenth case old age. The wound that has caused a particular tiger to take to man-eating might be the result of a carelessly fired shot and failure to follow up and recover the wounded animal, or be the result of the tiger having lost his temper when killing a porcupine. Human beings are not the natural prey of tigers, and it is only when tigers have been incapacitated through wounds or old age that, in order to live, they are compelled to take to a diet of human flesh.

3   A tiger when killing its natural prey, which it does either by stalking or lying in wait for it, depends for the success of its attack on its speed and, to a lesser extent, on the condition of its teeth and claws. When, therefore, a tiger is suffering from one or more painful wounds, or when its teeth are missing or defective and its claws worn down, and it is unable to catch the animals it has been accustomed to eating, it is driven by necessity to killing human beings. The change-over from animal to human flesh is, I believe, in most cases accidental. As an illustration of what I mean by "accidental" I quote the case of the Muktesar man-eating tigress. This tigress, a comparatively young animal, in an encounter with a porcupine lost an eye and got some fifty quills,

varying in length from one to nine inches, embedded in the arm and under the pad of her right foreleg. Several of these quills after striking a bone had doubled back in the form of a U, the point and the broken-off end being quite close together. Suppurating sores formed where she endeavored to extract the quills with her teeth, and while she was lying up in a thick patch of grass, starving and licking her wounds, a woman selected this particular patch of grass to cut as fodder for her cattle. At first the tigress took no notice, but when the woman had cut the grass right up to where she was lying the tigress struck once, the blow crushing in the woman's skull. Death was instantaneous, for, when found the following day, she was grasping her sickle with one hand and holding a tuft of grass, which she was about to cut when struck, with the other. Leaving the woman lying where she had fallen, the tigress limped off for a distance of over a mile and took refuge in a little hollow under a fallen tree. Two days later a man came to chip firewood off this fallen tree, and the tigress who was lying on the far side killed him. The man fell across the tree and, as he had removed his coat and shirt and the tigress had clawed his back when killing him, it is possible that the smell of the blood trickling down his body as he hung across the bole of the tree first gave her the idea that he was something that she could satisfy her hunger with. However that may be, before leaving him she ate a small portion from his back. A day later she killed her third victim deliberately, and without having received any provocation. Thereafter she became an established man-eater and had killed twenty-four people before she was finally accounted for.

4   A tiger on a fresh kill, or a wounded tiger, or a tigress with small cubs will occasionally kill human beings who disturb them; but these tigers cannot, by any stretch of imagination, be called man-eaters, though they are often so called. Personally I would give a tiger the benefit of the doubt once, and once again, before classing it as a man-eater, and whenever possible I would subject the alleged victim to a post-mortem before letting the kill go down on the records as the kill of a tiger or a leopard, as the case might be. This subject of post-mortems of human beings alleged to have been killed by either tigers or leopards or, in the plains, by wolves or hyenas, is of great importance, for, though I refrain from giving instances, I know of cases where deaths have wrongly been ascribed to carnivora.

5   It is a popular fallacy that all man-eaters are old and mangy, the mange being attributed to the excess of salt in human flesh. I am not competent to give any opinion on the relative quantity of salt in human or animal flesh; but I can, and I do, assert that a diet of human flesh, so far from having an injurious effect on the coat of man-eaters, has quite the opposite effect, for all the man-eaters I have seen have had remarkably fine coats.

6   Another popular belief in connection with man-eaters is that the cubs of these animals automatically become man-eaters. This is quite a reasonable supposition; but it is not borne out by actual facts, and the reason why the cubs of a man-eater do not themselves become man-eaters is that human beings are not the natural prey of tigers, or of leopards.

7   A cub will eat whatever its mother provides, and I have even known of tiger cubs' assisting their mothers to kill human beings; but I do not know of a single instance of a cub, after it had left the protection of its parent, or after that parent had been killed, taking to killing human beings.

8   In the case of human beings killed by carnivora, the doubt is often expressed as to whether the animal responsible for the kill is a tiger or leopard. As a general rule—to which I have seen no exceptions—tigers are responsible for all kills that take place in daylight, and leopards are responsible for all kills that take place in the dark. Both animals are semi-nocturnal forest-dwellers, have much the same habits, employ similar methods of killing, and both are capable of carrying their human victims for long distances. It would be natural, therefore, to expect them to hunt at the same hours; and that they do not do so is due to the difference in courage of the two animals. When a tiger becomes a man-eater it loses all fear of human beings and, as human beings move about more freely in the day than they do at night, it is able to secure its victims during daylight hours and there is no necessity for it to visit their habitations at night. A leopard on the other hand, even after it has killed scores of human beings, never loses its fear of man; and, as it is unwilling to face up to human beings in daylight, it secures its victims when they are moving about at night, or by breaking into their houses at night. Owing to those characteristics of the two animals, namely, that one loses its fear of human beings and kills in the daylight, while the other retains its fear and kills in the dark, man-eating tigers are easier to shoot than man-eating leopards.

9   The frequency with which a man-eating tiger kills depends on (a) the supply of natural food in the area in which it is operating; (b) the nature of the disability which has caused it to become a man-eater; and (c) whether it is a male or a female with cubs.

10   Those of us who lack the opportunity of forming our own opinion on any particular subject are apt to accept the opinions of others, and in no case is this more apparent than in the case of tigers—here I do not refer to man-eaters in particular, but to tigers in general. The author who first used the words "as cruel as a tiger" and "as bloodthirsty as a tiger," when attempting to emphasize the evil character of the villain of his piece, not only showed a lamentable ignorance of the animal he defamed, but coined phrases which have come into universal circulation, and which are mainly responsible for the wrong opinion of tigers held by all except that very small proportion of the public who have the opportunity of forming their own opinions.

11   When I see the expression "as cruel as a tiger" and "as bloodthirsty as a tiger" in print, I think of a small boy armed with an old muzzle-loading gun—the right barrel of which was split for six inches of its length, and the stock and barrels of which were kept from falling apart by lashings of brass wire—wandering through the jungles of the terai and bhabar in the days when there were ten tigers to every one that now survives; sleeping anywhere he happened to be when night came on, with a small fire to give him company and warmth, wakened at intervals by the calling of tigers, sometimes in the

distance, at other times near at hand; throwing another stick on the fire and turning over and continuing his interrupted sleep without one thought of unease; knowing from his own short experience and from what others, who like himself had spent their days in the jungles, had told him, that a tiger, unless molested, would do him no harm; or during daylight hours avoiding any tiger he saw, and when that was not possible, standing perfectly still until it had passed and gone, before continuing on his way. And I think of him on one occasion stalking half-a-dozen jungle fowl that were feeding in the open, and, on creeping up to a plum bush and standing up to peer over, the bush heaving and a tiger walking out on the far side and, on clearing the bush, turning round and looking at the boy with an expression on its face which said as clearly as any words, "Hello, kid, what the hell are you doing here?" and, receiving no answer, turning round and walking away very slowly without once looking back. And then again I think of the tens of thousands of men, women, and children who, while working in the forests or cutting grass or collecting dry sticks, pass day after day close to where tigers are lying up and who, when they return safely to their homes, do not even know that they have been under the observation of this so-called "cruel" and "bloodthirsty" animal.

12   Half a century has rolled by since the day the tiger walked out of the plum bush, the latter thirty-two years of which have been spent in the more or less regular pursuit of man-eaters, and though sights have been seen which would have caused a stone to weep, I have not seen a case where a tiger has been deliberately cruel or where it has been bloodthirsty to the extent that it has killed, without provocation, more than it has needed to satisfy its hunger or the hunger of its cubs.

13   A tiger's function in the scheme of things is to help maintain the balance in nature and if, on rare occasions when driven by dire necessity, he kills a human being, or when his natural food has been ruthlessly exterminated by man he kills two percent of the cattle he is alleged to have killed, it is not fair that for these acts a whole species should be branded as being cruel and bloodthirsty.

14   Sportsmen are admittedly conservative, the reason being that it has taken them years to form their opinions, and as each individual has a different point of view, it is only natural that opinions should differ on minor, or even in some cases on major, points, and for this reason I do not flatter myself that all the opinions I have expressed will meet with universal agreement.

15   There is, however, one point on which I am convinced that all sportsmen— no matter whether their point of view has been a platform on a tree, the back of an elephant, or their own feet—will agree with me, and that is, that a tiger is a largehearted gentleman with boundless courage and that when he is exterminated—as exterminated he will be unless public opinion rallies to his support—India will be the poorer by having lost the finest of her fauna.

16   Leopards, unlike tigers, are to a certain extent scavengers and become man-eaters by acquiring a taste for human flesh when unrestricted slaughter of game has deprived them of their natural food.

17   The dwellers in our hills are predominantly Hindu, and as such cremate their dead. The cremation invariably takes place on the bank of a stream or river in order that the ashes may be washed down into the Ganges and eventually into the sea. As most of the villages are situated high up on the hills, while the streams or rivers are in many cases miles away down in the valleys, it will be realized that a funeral entails a considerable tax on the manpower of a small community when, in addition to the carrying party, labor has to be provided to collect and carry the fuel needed for the cremation. In normal times these rites are carried out very effectively; but when disease in epidemic form sweeps through the hills and the inhabitants die faster than they can be disposed of, a very simple rite, which consists of placing a live coal in the mouth of the deceased, is performed in the village and the body is then carried to the edge of the hill and cast into the valley below.

18   A leopard, in an area in which his natural food is scarce, finding these bodies very soon acquires a taste for human flesh, and when the disease dies down and normal conditions are established, he very naturally, on finding his food supply cut off, takes to killing human beings.

19   Of the two man-eating leopards of Kumaon, which between them killed five hundred and twenty-five human beings, one followed on the heels of a very severe outbreak of cholera, while the other followed the mysterious disease which swept through India in 1918 and was called "war fever."

~

(2,443 words)

VOCABULARY

incapacitated (2)   suppurating (3)   ascribed (4)
carnivora (4)   fallacy (5)   semi-nocturnal (8)
habitations (8)   defamed (10)   fauna (15)
entails (17)

THE FACTS

1. In nine cases out of ten, what is the cause of a tiger's suddenly becoming a man-eater? What is the cause in the tenth case?

2. What animal was responsible for wounding the Muktesar tigress, making her incapable of hunting her natural prey?

3. What popular fallacy does the author cite about the condition of man-eaters?

4. In the author's opinion, what are the chances that a tiger cub whose mother has become a man-eater will also prey on humans?

5. What phrases often applied to the tiger does the author find untrue and objectionable? Why?

THE STRATEGIES

1. Aside from explaining why tigers become man-eaters, what do the early paragraphs do? Why is this task necessary to the author's purpose?

2. What kinds of support does the author offer for most of his assertions about tigers?

3. In paragraph 11, the author relates his boyhood experiences with tigers, using the third-person singular rather than the first person. Why do you think he makes this odd choice of pronouns? What effect does this usage have on the story?

4. The author is a big-game hunter, not a writer, and his style reflects an expected roughness. What example of this roughness can you cite from paragraph 12?

5. Throughout the explanation of why tigers become man-eaters, the author subtly contrasts the tiger with the leopard. Why? What effect does that contrast have on his explanation?

THE ISSUES

1. What can you infer about the author's childhood from his writing?

2. What would you imagine would be the author's initial reaction if he were asked to hunt down a tiger that had allegedly become a man-eater?

3. Considering that, by the author's own admissions, tigers and leopards have killed hundreds of humans, why should these animals be saved from extinction?

4. The author says in paragraph 14 that sportsmen are conservative. What is your opinion of sportsmen?

5. Of the two animals, tigers and leopards, which has the greater claim on the public imagination? How do you account for this difference?

SUGGESTIONS FOR WRITING

1. Find a poem or short work about the tiger and write an essay on the way the work depicts the animal.

2. Write an essay for or against hunting as a sport.

WHY I WENT TO THE WOODS

Henry David Thoreau

Henry David Thoreau (1817–1862), essayist, lecturer, and moralist, was born in Concord, Massachusetts and educated at Harvard University. He is regarded as one of the seminal influences on American thought and literature. His most famous work is Walden *(1854), which grew out of the journal recording his solitary existence in a cabin beside Walden Pond, near Concord. His essay* Civil Disobedience *(1849) has been enormously influential since it was first published and has affected the actions and thoughts of such men as Mahatma Gandhi and Martin Luther King, Jr.*

In this excerpt from *Walden*, Thoreau explains why he went to the woods to live by himself. Unlike many of the writers in this section, Thoreau writes in a voice rich with metaphors, allusions, and images.

~

1   I went to the woods because I wished to live deliberately, to front only the essential facts of life, and see if I could not learn what it had to teach, and not, when I came to die, discover that I had not lived. I did not wish to live what was not life, living is so dear; nor did I wish to practice resignation, unless it was quite necessary. I wanted to live deep and suck out all the marrow of life, to live so sturdily and Spartanlike as to put to rout all that was not life, to cut a broad swath and shave close, to drive life into a corner, and reduce it to its lowest terms, and, if it proved to be mean, why then to get the whole and genuine meanness of it, and publish its meanness to the world; or if it were sublime, to know it by experience, and be able to give a true account of it in my next excursion. For most men, it appears to me, are in a strange uncertainty about it, whether it is of the devil or of God, and have somewhat hastily concluded that it is the chief end of man here to "glorify God and enjoy him forever."

2   Still we live meanly, like ants; though the fable tells us that we were long ago changed into men; like pygmies we fight with cranes; it is error upon error, and clout upon clout, and our best virtue has for its occasion a superfluous and evitable wretchedness. Our life is frittered away by detail. An honest man has hardly need to count more than his ten fingers, or in extreme cases he may add his ten toes, and lump the rest. Simplicity, simplicity, simplicity! I say, let your affairs be as two or three, and not a hundred or a thousand; instead of a million count half a dozen, and keep your accounts on your thumbnail. In the midst of this chopping sea of civilized life, such are the clouds and storms and quick sands and thousand-and-one items to be allowed for, that a man has to live, if he would not founder and go to the bottom and not make his port at all, by dead reckoning, and he must be a great calculator indeed

who succeeds. Simplify, simplify. Instead of three meals a day, if it be necessary eat but one; instead of a hundred dishes, five; and reduce other things in proportion. Our life is like a German Confederacy, made up of petty states, with its boundary forever fluctuating, so that even a German cannot tell you how it is bounded at any moment. The nation itself, with all its so-called internal improvements, which, by the way are all external and superficial, is just such an unwieldy and overgrown establishment, cluttered with furniture and tripped up by its own traps, ruined by luxury and heedless expense, by want of calculation and a worthy aim, as the million households in the lands; and the only cure for it, as for them, is in a rigid economy, a stern and more than Spartan simplicity of life and elevation of purpose. It lives too fast. Men think that it is essential that the Nation have commerce, and export ice, and talk through a telegraph, and ride thirty miles an hour, without a doubt, whether they do or not; but whether we should live like baboons or like men, is a little uncertain. If we do not get our sleepers, and forge rails, and devote days and nights to the work, but go to tinkering upon our lives to improve them, who will build railroads? And if railroads are not built, how shall we get to heaven in season? But if we stay at home and mind our business, who will want railroads? We do not ride on the railroad; it rides upon us. Did you ever think what those sleepers[1] are that underlie the railroad? Each one is a man, an Irishman, or a Yankee man. The rails are laid on them, and they are covered with sand, and the cars run smoothly over them. They are sound sleepers, I assure you. And every few years a new lot is laid down and run over; so that, if some have the pleasure of riding on a rail, others have the misfortune to be ridden upon. And when they run over a man that is walking in his sleep, a supernumerary sleeper in the wrong position, and wake him up, they suddenly stop the cars, and make a hue and cry about it, as if this were an exception. I am glad to know that it takes a gang of men for every five miles to keep the sleepers down and level in their beds as it is, for this is a sign that they may sometimes get up again.

3   Why should we live with such hurry and waste of life? We are determined to be starved before we are hungry. Men say that a stitch in time saves nine, and so they take a thousand stitches to-day to save nine to-morrow. As for work, we haven't any of any consequence. We have the Saint Vitus' dance, and cannot possibly keep our heads still. If I should only give a few pulls at the parish bell-rope, as for a fire, that is, without setting the bell, there is hardly a man on his farm in the outskirts of Concord, notwithstanding that press of engagements which was his excuse so many times this morning, nor a boy, nor a woman, I might almost say, but would forsake all and follow that sound, not mainly to save property from the flames, but, if we will confess the truth, much more to see it burn, since burn it must, and we, be it known, did not set it on fire,—or to see it put out, and have a hand in it, if that is done as handsomely; yes, even if it were the parish church itself. Hardly a man takes a half-

---

[1]Cross ties; Thoreau is playing on the word.—Ed.

hour's nap after dinner, but when he wakes he holds up his head and asks, "What's the news?" as if the rest of mankind had stood his sentinels. Some give directions to be waked every half-hour, doubtless for no other purpose; and then, to pay for it, they tell what they have dreamed. After a night's sleep the news is as indispensable as the breakfast. "Pray tell me anything new that has happened to a man anywhere on this globe,"—and he reads it over his coffee and rolls, that a man has had his eyes gouged out this morning on the Wachito River; never dreaming the while that he lives in the dark unfathomed mammoth cave of this world, and has but the rudiment of an eye himself.

4   For my part, I could easily do without the post-office. I think that there are very few important communications made through it. To speak critically, I never received more than one or two letters in my life—I wrote this some years ago—that were worth the postage. The penny-post is, commonly, an institution through which you seriously offer a man that penny for his thoughts which is so often safely offered in jest. And I am sure that I never read any memorable news in a newspaper. If we read of one man robbed, or murdered, or killed by accident, or one house burned, or one vessel wrecked, or one steamboat blown up, or one cow run over on the Western Railroad, or one mad dog killed, or one lot of grasshoppers in the winter,—we never need read of another. One is enough. If you are acquainted with the principle, what do you care for a myriad instances and applications? To a philosopher all news, as it is called, is gossip, and they who edit and read it are old women over their tea. Yet not a few are greedy after this gossip. There was such a rush, as I hear, the other day at one of the offices to learn the foreign news by the last arrival, that several large squares of plate glass belonging to the establishment were broken by the pressure,—news which I seriously think a ready wit might write a twelvemonth, or twelve years, beforehand with sufficient accuracy. As for Spain, for instance, if you know how to throw in Don Carlos and the Infanta, and Don Pedro and Seville and Granada, from time to time in the right proportions,—they may have changed the names a little since I saw the papers,—and serve up a bullfight when other entertainments fail, it will be true to the letter, and give us as good an idea of the exact state or ruin of things in Spain as the most succinct and lucid reports under this head in the newspapers: and as for England, almost the last significant scrap of news from that quarter was the revolution of 1649; and if you have learned the history of her crops for an average year, you never need attend to that thing again, unless your speculations are of a merely pecuniary character. If one may judge who rarely looks into the newspapers, nothing new does ever happen in foreign parts, a French revolution not excepted.

5   What news! how much more important to know what that is which was never old! "Kieou-he-yu (great dignitary of the state of Wei) sent a man to Khoung-tseu to know his news. Khoung-tseu caused the messenger to be seated near him, and questioned him in these terms: What is your master doing? The messenger answered with respect: My master desires to diminish the number of his faults, but he cannot come to the end of them. The messenger being gone, the philosopher remarked: What a worthy messenger!

What a worthy messenger!" The preacher, instead of vexing the ears of drowsy farmers on their day of rest at the end of the week,—for Sunday is the fit conclusion of an ill-spent week, and not the fresh and brave beginning of a new one,—with this one other draggle-tail of a sermon, should shout with thundering voice, "Pause! Avast! Why so seeming fast, but deadly slow?"

6   Shams and delusions are esteemed for soundless truths, while reality is fabulous. If men would steadily observe realities only, and not allow themselves to be deluded, life, to compare it with such things as we know, would be like a fairy tale and the Arabian Nights' Entertainments. If we respected only what is inevitable and has a right to be, music and poetry would resound along the streets. When we are unhurried and wise, we perceive that only great and worthy things have any permanent and absolute existence, that petty fears and petty pleasures are but the shadow of the reality. This is always exhilarating and sublime. By closing the eyes and slumbering, and consenting to be deceived by shows, men establish and confirm their daily life of routine and habit everywhere, which still is built on purely illusory foundations. Children, who play life, discern its true law and relations more clearly than men, who fail to live it worthily, but who think that they are wiser by experience, that is, by failure. I have read in a Hindoo book, that "there was a king's son, who, being expelled in infancy from his native city, was brought up by a forester, and, growing up to maturity in that state, imagined himself to belong to the barbarous race with which he lived. One of his father's ministers having discovered him, revealed to him what he was, and the misconception of his character was removed, and he knew himself to be a prince. So soul," continues the Hindoo philosopher, "from the circumstances in which it is placed, mistakes its own character, until the truth is revealed to it by some holy teacher, and then it knows itself to be Brahme." I perceive that we inhabitants of New England live this mean life that we do because our vision does not penetrate the surface of things. We think that that is which appears to be. If a man should walk through this town and see only the reality, where, think you, would the "Mill-dam" go to? If he should give us an account of the realities he beheld there, we should not recognize the place in his description. Look at the meetinghouse, or a court-house, or a jail, or a shop, or a dwelling-house, and say what that thing really is before a true gaze, and they would all go to pieces in your account of them. Men esteem truth remote, in the outskirts of the system, behind the farthest star, before Adam and after the last man. In eternity there is indeed something true and sublime. But all these times and places and occasions are now and here. God himself culminates in the present moment, and will never be more divine in the lapse of all the ages. And we are enabled to apprehend at all what is sublime and noble only by the perpetual instilling and drenching of the reality that surrounds us. The universe constantly and obediently answers to our conceptions; whether we travel fast or slow, the track is laid for us. Let us spend our lives in conceiving then. The poet or the artist never yet had so fair and noble a design but some of his posterity at least could accomplish it.

7   Let us spend one day as deliberately as Nature, and not be thrown off the track by every nutshell and mosquito's wing that falls on the rails. Let us rise early and fast, or breakfast, gently and without perturbation; let company come and let company go, let the bells ring and the children cry,—determined to make a day of it. Why should we knock under and go with the stream? Let us not be upset and overwhelmed in that terrible rapid and whirlpool called a dinner, situated in the meridian shallows. Weather this danger and you are safe, for the rest of the way is down hill. With unrelaxed nerves, with morning vigor, sail by it, looking another way, tied to the mast like Ulysses.[2] If the engine whistles, let it whistle till it is hoarse for its pains. If the bell rings, why should we run? We will consider what kind of music they are like. Let us settle ourselves, and work and wedge our feet downward through the mud and slush of opinion, and prejudice, and tradition, and delusion, and appearance, that alluvion which covers the globe, through Paris and London, through New York and Boston and Concord, through Church and State, through poetry and philosophy and religion, till we come to a hard bottom and rocks in place, which we can call reality, and say, This is, and no mistake; and then begin, having a point d'appui,[3] below freshet and frost and fire, a place where you might found a wall or a state, or set a lamp-post safely, or perhaps a gauge, not a Nilometer, but a Realometer, that future ages might know how deep a freshet of shams and appearances had gathered from time to time. If you stand right fronting and face to face to a fact, you will see the sun glimmer on both its surfaces, as if it were a cimeter, and feel its sweet edge dividing you through the heart and marrow, and so you will happily conclude your mortal career. Be it life or death, we crave only reality. If we are really dying, let us hear the rattle in our throats and feel cold in the extremities; if we are alive, let us go about our business.

8   Time is but the stream I go a-fishing in. I drink at it; but while I drink I see the sandy bottom and detect how shallow it is. Its thin current slides away, but eternity remains. I would drink deeper; fish in the sky, whose bottom is pebbly with stars. I cannot count one. I know not the first letter of the alphabet. I have always been regretting that I was not as wise as the day I was born. The intellect is a cleaver; it discerns and rifts its way into the secret of things. I do not wish to be any more busy with my hands than is necessary. My head is hands and feet. I feel all my best faculties concentrated on it. My instinct tells me that my head is an organ for burrowing, as some creatures use their snout and fore paws, and with it I would mine and burrow my way through these hills. I think that the richest vein is somewhere hereabouts; so by the divining-rod and thin rising vapors, I judge; and here I will begin to mine.

∽

(2,857 words)

---

[2]tied . . . Ulysses: In Homer's *Odyssey*, Ulysses had himself tied to the mast of his boat so that he could listen, but not respond, to the irresistible songs of the sirens, who were believed to lure ships to their doom.—Ed.

[3]point d'appui: point of stability.—Ed.

VOCABULARY

superfluous (2)	evitable (2)	supernumerary (2)
rudiment (3)	myriad (4)	succinct (4)
pecuniary (4)	culminates (6)	posterity (6)
perturbation (7)	meridian (7)	alluvion (7)
freshet (7)		

THE FACTS

1. Why did Thoreau go to the woods? What, in his opinion, was wrong with the nation?
2. Thoreau writes: "We do not ride on the railroad; it rides upon us." What does he mean?
3. What is Thoreau's definition of "news"? What is his definition of "gossip"? According to Thoreau, how does news differ from gossip?
4. What does Thoreau mean when he says that the "universe constantly and obediently answers to our conceptions" (paragraph 6)? How, then, is truth possible?
5. Where, according to Thoreau, is truth to be found? What prevents us from finding it?

THE STRATEGIES

1. Reread the final sentence of paragraph 1. What tone does Thoreau use?
2. Thoreau uses two anecdotes in this excerpt (paragraphs 5 and 6). What do these have in common? What do they indicate about the writer's philosophy?
3. "We have the Saint Vitus' dance, and cannot possibly keep our heads still" (paragraph 3). What figure of speech is this? Can you find other examples of this same figure of speech in the text? What effect do they have on Thoreau's writing?
4. "Our life is like a German Confederacy, made up of petty states, with its boundary forever fluctuating, so that even a German cannot tell you how it is bounded at any moment" (paragraph 2). What figure of speech is this? How does it differ from the example in the preceding question?
5. An allusion is a figure of speech in which some famous historical or literary figure or event is casually mentioned. Can you find an allusion in Thoreau's text? (Hint: Examine paragraph 7.) What effect does the allusion have on the writer's style?

THE ISSUES

1. Reread the essay *Diogenes and Alexander,* on pages 422–426. What views about society do Diogenes and Thoreau share? Do you agree with these views? Why or why not?

2. Thoreau witnessed the creation of the railroad and felt that it was an intrusion on life. In paragraph 2, he states, "We do not ride on the railroad; it rides upon us." What new industrial creation of your time might evoke a similar statement from some social commentator like Thoreau?

3. Do you agree with Thoreau that few important communications reach you through the post office? Why or why not?

4. In paragraph 6, Thoreau follows in Plato's footsteps when he tells us that only great and worthy things have absolute existence, but that petty things are a mere shadow of reality. Imagine yourself to be like Thoreau, living alone out in the woods. What would be essential to your life? What would seem petty? Give examples.

5. What memorable experience, if any, have you had of being alone in nature? How did this experience affect you? What did you learn from it?

SUGGESTIONS FOR WRITING

1. Write an essay describing the clutter of petty affairs in an average person's life. Suggest some ways of simplifying life.

2. Pretend that you are Thoreau and that you have just been brought back to life and introduced to 20th-century America. Write a diary putting down your first impressions.

TERM PAPER SUGGESTION

Thoreau was once sent to jail for refusing to pay his taxes. Research this episode and write about it.

THE STORM

Kate Chopin

Kate O'Flaherty Chopin (1851–1904) was an American author of Creole-Irish descent, born in St. Louis. In 1870, she married a Louisiana businessman and lived with him in Natchitoches parish and New Orleans, where she acquired an intimate knowledge of Creole and Cajun life, on which she based most of her best stories. After her husband's death in 1883, she returned with their six children to St. Louis and began to write seriously. Her novel The Awakening *(1899) caused a furor among readers because of its treatment of feminine sexuality that seemed to ignore the mores of the time. For the next sixty years, Chopin was virtually ignored. Today, her work is praised for its regional flavor and for its remarkable independence of mind and feeling. Among her works are two collections of short stories,* Bayou Folk *(1894), and* A Night in Acadie *(1897).*

This story, *The Storm*, makes light of an adulterous episode that takes place during a storm. Notice the parallels between the passion of the lovers and the ferocity of the storm as well as the serenity in both human and nature that follows afterwards. As you read this story, ask yourself if it seems to represent a particular feminist ideology toward sexuality.

~

I

1   The leaves were so still that even Bibi thought it was going to rain. Bobinôt, who was accustomed to converse on terms of perfect equality with his little son, called the child's attention to certain sombre clouds that were rolling with sinister intention from the west, accompanied by a sullen, threatening roar. They were at Friedheimer's store and decided to remain there till the storm had passed. They sat within the door on two empty kegs. Bibi was four years old and looked very wise.

2   "Mama'll be 'fraid, yes," he suggested with blinking eyes.

3   "She'll shut the house. Maybe she got Sylvie helpin' her this evenin'," Bobinôt responded reassuringly.

4   "No; she ent got Sylvie. Sylvie was helpin' her yistiday," piped Bibi.

5   Bobinôt arose and going across to the counter purchased a can of shrimps, of which Calixta was very fond. Then he returned to his perch on the keg and sat stolidly holding the can of shrimps while the storm burst. It shook the wooden store and seemed to be ripping great furrows in the distant field. Bibi laid his little hand on his father's knee and was not afraid.

II

6   Calixta, at home, felt no uneasiness for their safety. She sat at a side window sewing furiously on a sewing machine. She was greatly occupied and did not notice the approaching storm. But she felt very warm and often stopped to mop her face on which the perspiration gathered in beads. She unfastened her white sacque[1] at the throat. It began to grow dark, and suddenly realizing the situation she got up hurriedly and went about closing windows and doors.

---

[1]Work dress, house dress.—Ed.

7   Out on the small front gallery she had hung Bobinôt's Sunday clothes to air and she hastened out to gather them before the rain fell. As she stepped outside, Alcée Laballière rode in at the gate. She had not seen him very often since her marriage, and never alone. She stood there with Bobinôt's coat in her hands, and the big rain drops began to fall. Alcée rode his horse under the shelter of a side projection where the chickens had huddled and there were plows and a harrow piled up in the corner.

8   "May I come and wait on your gallery till the storm is over, Calixta?" he asked.

9   Come 'long in, M'sieur Alcée."

10   His voice and her own startled her as if from a trance, and she seized Bobinôt's vest. Alcée, mounting to the porch, grabbed the trousers and snatched Bibi's braided jacket that was about to be carried away by a sudden gust of wind. He expressed an intention to remain outside, but it was soon apparent that he might as well have been out in the open: the water beat in upon the boards in driving sheets, and he went inside, closing the door after him. It was even necessary to put something beneath the door to keep the water out.

11   "My! what a rain! It's good two years sence it rain' like that," exclaimed Calixta as she rolled up a piece of bagging and Alcée helped her to thrust it beneath the crack.

12   She was a little fuller of figure than five years before when she married; but she had lost nothing of her vivacity. Her blue eyes still retained their melting quality; and her yellow hair, dishevelled by the wind and rain, kinked more stubbornly than ever about her ears and temples.

13   The rain beat upon the low, shingled roof with a force and clatter that threatened to break an entrance and deluge them there. They were in the dining room—the sitting room—the general utility room. Adjoining was her bed room, with Bibi's couch along side her own. The door stood open, and the room with its white, monumental bed, its closed shutters, looked dim and mysterious.

14   Alcée flung himself into a rocker and Calixta nervously began to gather up from the floor the lengths of a cotton sheet which she had been sewing.

15   "If this keeps up, Dieu sait[2] if the levees goin' to stan' it!" she exclaimed.

16   "What have you got to do with the levees?"

17   "I got enough to do! An' there's Bobinôt with Bibi out in that storm—if he only didn' left Friedheimer's!"

18   "Let us hope, Calixta, that Bobinôt's got sense enough to come in out of a cyclone."

19   She went and stood at the window with a greatly disturbed look on her face. She wiped the frame that was clouded with moisture. It was stiflingly hot. Alcée got up and joined her at the window, looking over her shoulder. The rain was coming down in sheets obscuring the view of far-off cabins and enveloping the distant wood in a gray mist. The playing of the lightning was

---

[2]French for *God Knows*.—Ed.

incessant. A bolt struck a tall chinaberry tree at the edge of the field. It filled all visible space with a blinding glare and the crash seemed to invade the very boards they stood upon.

20   Calixta put her hands to her eyes, and with a cry, staggered backward. Alcée's arm encircled her, and for an instant he drew her close and spasmodically to him.

21   "Bonté!"[3] she cried, releasing herself from his encircling arm and retreating from the window, "the house'll go next! If I only knew w'ere Bibi was!" She would not compose herself; she would not be seated. Alcée clasped her shoulders and looked into her face. The contact of her warm, palpitating body when he had unthinkingly drawn her into his arms, had aroused all the old-time infatuation and desire for her flesh.

22   "Calixta," he said, "don't be frightened. Nothing can happen. The house is too low to be struck, with so many tall trees standing about. There! aren't you going to be quiet? say, aren't you?" He pushed her hair back from her face that was warm and steaming. Her lips were as red and moist as pomegranate seed. Her white neck and a glimpse of her full, firm bosom disturbed him powerfully. As she glanced up at him the fear in her liquid blue eyes had given place to a drowsy gleam that unconsciously betrayed a sensuous desire. He looked down into her eyes and there was nothing for him to do but to gather her lips in a kiss. It reminded him of Assumption.

23   "Do you remember—in Assumption, Calixta?" he asked in a low voice broken by passion. Oh! she remembered; for in Assumption he had kissed her and kissed and kissed her; until his senses would well nigh fail, and to save her he would resort to a desperate flight. If she was not an immaculate dove in those days, she was still inviolate; a passionate creature whose very defenselessness had made her defense, against which his honor forbade him to prevail. Now—well, now—her lips seemed in a manner free to be tasted, as well as her round, white throat and her whiter breasts.

24   They did not heed the crashing torrents, and the roar of the elements made her laugh as she lay in his arms. She was a revelation in that dim, mysterious chamber; as white as the couch she lay upon. Her firm, elastic flesh that was knowing for the first time its birthright, was like a creamy lily that the sun invites to contribute its breath and perfume to the undying life of the world.

25   The generous abundance of her passion, without guile or trickery, was like a white flame which penetrated and found response in depths of his own sensuous nature that had never yet been reached.

26   When he touched her breasts they gave themselves up in quivering ecstasy, inviting his lips. Her mouth was a fountain of delight. And when he possessed her, they seemed to swoon together at the very borderland of life's mystery.

27   He stayed cushioned upon her, breathless, dazed, enervated, with his heart beating like a hammer upon her. With one hand she clasped his head,

---

[3]French for *Goodness!*—Ed.

her lips lightly touching his forehead. The other hand stroked with a sooth-ing rhythm his muscular shoulders.

28   The growl of the thunder was distant and passing away. The rain beat softly upon the shingles, inviting them to drowsiness and sleep. But they dared not yield.

29   The rain was over; and the sun was turning the glistening green world into a palace of gems. Calixta, on the gallery, watched Alcée ride away. He turned and smiled at her with a beaming face; and she lifted her pretty chin in the air and laughed aloud.

III

30   Bobinôt and Bibi, trudging home, stopped without at the cistern to make themselves presentable.

31   "My! Bibi, w'at will yo' mama say! You ought to be ashame'. You oughtn' put on those good pants. Look at 'em! An' that mud on yo' collar! How you got that mud on yo' collar, Bibi? I never saw such a boy!" Bibi was the picture of pathetic resignation. Bobinôt was the embodiment of serious solicitude as he strove to remove from his own person and his son's the signs of their tramp over heavy roads and through wet fields. He scraped the mud off Bibi's bare legs and feet with a stick and carefully removed all traces from his heavy brogans. Then, prepared for the worst—the meeting with an over-scrupulous housewife, they entered cautiously at the back door.

32   Calixta was preparing supper. She had set the table and was dripping cof-fee at the hearth. She sprang up as they came in.

33   "Oh, Bobinôt! You back! My! but I was uneasy. W'ere you been during the rain? An' Bibi? he ain't wet? he ain't hurt?" She had clasped Bibi and was kiss-ing him effusively. Bobinôt's explanations and apologies which he had been composing all along the way, died on his lips as Calixta felt him to see if he were dry, and seemed to express nothing but satisfaction at their safe return.

34   "I brought you some shrimps, Calixta," offered Bobinôt, hauling the can from his ample side pocket and laying it on the table.

35   "Shrimps! Oh, Bobinôt! you too good fo' anything!" and she gave him a smacking kiss on the cheek that resounded. "J'vous réponds,[4] we'll have a feas' to night! umph-umph!"

36   Bobinôt and Bibi began to relax and enjoy themselves, and when the three seated themselves at table they laughed much and so loud that anyone might have heard them as far away as Laballière's.

IV

37   Alcée Laballière wrote to his wife, Clarisse, that night. It was a loving letter, full of tender solicitude. He told her not to hurry back, but if she and the babies

---

[4]French for *I answer you*.—Ed.

liked it at Biloxi, to stay a month longer. He was getting on nicely; and though he missed them, he was willing to bear the separation a while longer—realizing that their health and pleasure were the first things to be considered.

V

38   As for Clarisse, she was charmed upon receiving her husband's letter. She and the babies were doing well. The society was agreeable; many of her old friends and acquaintances were at the bay. And the first free breath since her marriage seemed to restore the pleasant liberty of her maiden days. Devoted as she was to her husband, their intimate conjugal life was something which she was more than willing to forego for a while.

39   So the storm passed and every one was happy.

～

(1,895 words)

VOCABULARY

sombre (1)	projection (7)	harrow (7)
gallery (8)	deluge (13)	monumental (13)
levees (15)	incessant (19)	spasmodically (20)
palpitating (21)	sensuous (22)	immaculate (23)
inviolate (23)	revelation (24)	enervated (27)
cistern (30)	resignation (31)	embodiment (31)
solicitude (31)	brogans (31)	effusively (33)
conjugal (38)		

THE FACTS

1. What relationship exists between Calixta and Alcée? What do you infer from their past?
2. How does the storm contribute to the love tryst that takes place?
3. What caused the lovers to act so impetuously? Do you consider the cause valid and acceptable?
4. How do the lovers react to their mates after the love affair? Does the reaction seem plausible? Give reasons for your answer.
5. In paragraph 13, what is the significance of describing Calixta's bedroom as "dim and mysterious"? Explain the reference.

THE STRATEGIES

1. What setting forms the backdrop for this story? What does the setting contribute?
2. What is the purpose of the Roman numerals dividing the story?

3. What kind of language does the author resort to in describing the passion of the two lovers? Point to specific examples.

4. What do you think of the title of this story? Is the story really about a storm? Explain your answer.

5. Where does the climax of the story take place? Explain your answer.

THE ISSUES

1. In your opinion, did the lovers handle the situation as morally as possible, given that they yielded to the temptation of the situation? If you disagree with their reactions, what should they have done?

2. The narrator tells us that Calixta's flesh "was knowing for the first time its birthright" (paragraph 24). What is meant by this statement? What similar comment is made about Alcée?

3. As indicated in the biographical headnote about Kate Chopin, the author's work was criticized for its "feminine sexuality." What do you think readers of her day thought about a story like *The Storm*? How does your view of the story compare with the view of Chopin's contemporaries?

4. What kind of conjugal life do the couples described seem to share? What, if anything, is good about it?

5. What is the theme (main point) of the story? Express it in one sentence.

SUGGESTIONS FOR WRITING

1. Write an analysis of what happens when people lose control of their passions. Use examples to prove your point.

2. Write an essay offering your views about the causes of the widespread marital infidelity so common in our society today.

DESIGN

Robert Frost

Robert Frost (1874–1963) was a lecturer, poet, and teacher. When he was nineteen and working in a mill in Lawrence, Massachusetts, the Independent accepted and published My Butterfly, an Elegy—*the poem that began Frost's career as one of America's great poets. Rugged New England farm life was the inspiration for many of his poems.*

Like much of Frost's poetry, *Design* appears on the surface to be simple and plain, but a closer study reveals subtleties and depth. The speaker observes nature with a philosophic mind.

⌒

1 I found a dimpled spider, fat and white,
   On a white heal-all, holding up a moth
   Like a white piece of rigid satin cloth—
   Assorted characters of death and blight
5 Mixed ready to begin the morning right,
   Like the ingredients of a witches' broth—
   A snow-drop spider, a flower like a froth,
   And dead wings carried like a paper kite.

   What had that flower to do with being white,
10 The wayside blue and innocent heal-all?
   What brought the kindred spider to that height,
   Then steered the white moth thither in the night?
   What but design of darkness to appall?—
   If design govern in a thing so small.

⌒

(110 words)

VOCABULARY

characters   blight   kindred
appall

THE FACTS

1. The heal-all is a wildflower—usually blue or violet, but occasionally white—commonly found blooming along footpaths and roads. The name derives from the belief that this flower possessed healing qualities. As described in the first stanza, what do the spider, the heal-all, and the moth have in common?

2. Three questions are asked in the second stanza. How can these be condensed into one question? What answer is implied in the poem?

3. The "argument from design" was a well-known 18th-century argument for the existence of God. It proposed a broad view of history and the cosmos, which revealed that some divine intelligence fashioned and then sustained existence. What twist does Frost give this argument?

4. Is the poem probing a sufficient, a necessary, or a contributory cause?

THE STRATEGIES

1. What five examples of figurative language are used in the first stanza? Tell what effect each has.

2. In the second stanza, why does the poet use the adjective *kindred* in connection with the spider?

3. In the second stanza, what synonyms does the poet use to repeat the concept of design?

THE ISSUES

1. The question of whether or not our destinies are controlled by some higher intelligence concerns many thinking people. Why do you suppose human beings wrestle so often with this question?

2. How would you argue against Frost's theme? Use an example from nature to take the opposite viewpoint.

3. Judging from your experience, which of your intimate acquaintances are better able to cope with life—those with a strong belief in a God who controls human destiny, or those with the belief that existence is simply experience and that no God controls any aspect of the universe?

SUGGESTIONS FOR WRITING

1. Using an example from nature, write a brief essay showing how an incontrovertible harmony seems to regulate the activities of the world as a whole.

2. Write a brief essay in which you explain what in the poem causes you to like or dislike it.

——— ISSUE FOR CRITICAL ——— THINKING AND DEBATE

THE STATUS OF WOMEN

Women are better off today than ever before. We can make that statement boldly on the evidence of statistics and from our own experience. In 1900, women could not vote, could not own property, and derived their legal status from whether or not they had husbands. Women, who did not win the right to vote until 1920, now vote in larger numbers than men. In a recent poll conducted by *USA Today*, eighty-one percent of the sampled women predicted the election of a woman president within the next twenty-five years.

Woman conducting a business meeting. Copyright © Randy Taylor/Index Stock Imagery.

Today, women work in as varied a range of occupations as men. Some are senators, CEOs, TV anchors, stock brokers, and university presidents. Some have made financial fortunes while their husbands took care of the children. Only a few years ago, when a woman's place was thought to be in the home and her job to care for her husband and family, such achievements would have been unthinkable.

In spite of these victories, the war for equality between men and women in the workplace and in society at large continues. One lingering bone of contention is the disparity between the salaries of men and the salaries of women for the same work. The 2000 census showed that for 1999, the median income of men was $35,922, in contrast to $26,292 for women. This inequality has persisted since record-keeping began.

Anyone with even a scant knowledge of history would have to admit that the significant gains made in the status of woman were mainly won by the feminist movement. It is therefore a paradox that feminism has lost its appeal to many women of the upcoming generation. Daughters who today enjoy the benefits won by yesterday's militants regard feminism as their mother's movement, not theirs. In an ironic way, that attitude is a triumph for feminism, whose central aim has always been the empowerment of the individual to do, say, and think as he/she feels.

The change in the status of women, however, comes at a price. Women now face a world that no longer regards them as delicate and needing protection. If the *Titanic* disaster had happened in our era, the cry heard on deck would not be the chivalrous one that rang out in 1912 aboard the doomed ship, "Women and children first!" It would more likely be, "Every person for himself/herself!" For some conservative women, this has been too high a price to pay. For many other women, it's a bargain. The photo on page 556 is a declaration of what women have gained in the race for equality with men—the right to hold high executive jobs. Conversely, the cartoon on page 558 argues that the price of equality for some women is an overburdened life.

Our essayists take predictably different tacks on the subject. Kate Gubata declares firmly that women should continue to work toward achieving total equality with men in every nook of life—from politics to economics. Rebecca E. Rubins believes that women have already achieved equality with men, making the feminist movement obsolete. The student essay, written by Paula Rewa, of East Tennessee State University, argues that the word *woman* now mainly functions as an adjective—as in *woman* lawyer—but should be reclaimed as a noun. *Woman*—used as a noun—remains a woman, no matter how she dresses or what she does.

THE NEW FEMINISM

Kate Gubata

Kate Gubata writes a column for the Brown University student newspaper.

~

1   Jane is pro-choice. Jane loves chocolate. She backs candidates who strive to change the wages inequity that exists in this country. She likes boys who wear Abercrombie & Fitch. She wishes she looked a little more like Jennifer Lopez. She believes in human rights and equality for men and women.

2   Is she a feminist? Possibly. Is she a young woman in America? Without a doubt.

3   At a time when the term *feminism* often suggests the impression of the radical, almost militantly liberal rival of the male-dominated status quo, many young women are hesitant, if not outright opposed, to associate themselves with this exclusive group.

4   After all, that is feminism, right? Feminism defines my mother's generation. It represents at one extreme the assemblage of hairy-legged, men-hating conspirators to overthrow professional men's sports; on the softer side, feminists gather together to hold hands and listen to Helen Reddy. Why on earth would a young woman today deny herself the title of feminist?

5   One of the greatest barriers opposing the feminist movement today is the lack of interest of young women due to their misconceptions of the feminists' aims. Feminism is a progressive movement that seeks to bring about the change that will embed equality for men and women in all aspects of life, from the larger spheres of political, social and economic structure, to the ways in which men and women perceive each other throughout the course of common interaction. Feminism is not an abstract, ideological construct. It represents not

an exclusive body of individual motivations but a movement that reaches everyone who believes in human rights.

6   How can we bridge the gap between feminist rhetoric and everyday life? How can feminists illuminate the aspects of the movement that affect the ways in which we on this campus live our lives?

7   Feminism is a movement of action. The goal of feminism today is to stimulate men and women to transform the aims of equality into reality. This is not an ideological mission. The causes of feminism are about action; as Brown students we can all become active participants. Choice, pay inequity, the recent passage of mifeprestone—"the abortion drug"—by the FDA, and the legal battles over homosexual marriage are some of the issues pertinent to feminists today. The various on-campus events intend to educate the Brown community as a whole and to promote a sense of unity among students who have an interest in these types of issues. The movements both on campus and

Super Mom drawing. Copyright © Artville/GETTY.

in the local community to promote change are the mechanisms by which young people can use their ideas and energies to fuel united action.

8   Feminism does not have a feminist-checklist. Feminists embody the characteristics of free thought, openness to ideas, and the desire to pool resources with all people willing to work for equality. Feminism represents an inclusive, not exclusive assembly. The key to encompassing a wide range of interest is the resolution of the conflict many people sense between the abstract concepts of feminism and their personal emotions and ideas. A young woman who does not identify with her impression of the radical image of a feminist must not deny herself the opportunity to share her opinions and ideas with a group that is in fact more than willing to listen and learn. There is no dress code or behavior code for a feminist; the term feminist characterizes anyone who aspires to achieve equality and who believes in the power of the united fight for human rights.

9   What's the solution for Jane and others seeking the balance between the persona of the radical feminist ideology and feminism's role in the modern lifestyle? Get involved. Keep an eye out for campus and community events that pertain to important feminist issues and goals. If a group interests you, dive in and make yourself heard; but leave your preconceptions at the door. Be prepared to find a diverse group of people who may share nothing but the will to achieve equality. Move over Helen Reddy; a new group of activists is ready to roar.

~

(676 words)

VOCABULARY

Feminism (title)	militantly (3)	assemblage (4)
ideological (5)	illuminate (6)	persona (9)
preconceptions (9)		

THE FACTS

1. At the time of writing this essay, where is the author? What does her location bring to the essay?

2. According to the author, what is the goal of feminism today? What other goal(s), if any, do you consider important for women to pursue?

3. In paragraph 5 and again in paragraph 7, the author insists that feminism must not be an "ideological" movement. Why does the author shun ideology? What is more important to her than ideology? Do you agree with her? Explain yourself.

4. According to the author, what issues should be of major concern to feminists today? Respond to each issue by evaluating its importance within the total social fabric of your environment.

5. What does the author mean when she writes that "Feminism does not have a feminist-checklist"? Do you think the movement *should* have a checklist? Explain your answer.

THE STRATEGIES

1. In what paragraph does the author define feminism by stating what it is not? Is this a good technique to use when defining a term?

2. In what paragraph does the author associate feminism with a past generation? What effect does the association have? Offer your personal response.

3. What is the purpose of the question posed at the start of paragraph 9? Is the question ever answered? If yes, what is the answer; if no, why is no answer given?

4. Who is the "Jane" referred to at the beginning and at the end of the essay? Explain her function in the essay.

5. What is the author's tone in the final sentence of the essay? Explain why you think the author uses this tone to end her essay.

THE ISSUES

1. What does the term *feminist* conjure up in your mind? Do you react favorably or unfavorably to this term? Explain your answer.

2. In your view, what have women gained so far and what have they lost as a result of the feminist movement? Whom does the movement favor most? Whom does it favor least?

3. Do you agree with the author that one of the greatest barriers opposing the feminist movement today is the lack of interest on the part of young women? If the author is right, what do you think are the reasons for today's apathy on the part of young women? If you think the author is wrong, give reasons why you think so.

4. If a woman prefers to stay home and be a housewife once she is married, does she still have an obligation to get involved in feminist issues? Or, should she focus more on matters of family values? Give reasons for your stand.

5. If you are a man, do you want your wife to have her own career, or would you prefer to have her be a full-time homemaker? Explain your choice. If you are a woman, would you prefer to have a career or to remain at home as a full-time homemaker? Explain your choice. Consider also the possibility of combining a career with homemaking.

SUGGESTIONS FOR WRITING

1. Write an essay in which you define the term *feminism* as you understand it. Clarify your definition by using illustration, comparison/contrast, causal analysis, or any other rhetorical mode that helps you answer the question, "What is feminism?"

2. Re-read the question at the beginning of paragraph 9 to make sure you understand what is meant by feminist ideology and by the feminist's role in today's lifestyle. Then write an essay answering the question. Be sure to formulate a thesis that you support with appropriate evidence. For instance, you might write "The true feminist will support human rights while remaining nonmasculine in her manner." Or, if you really detest feminism, your thesis might read: "The feminist movement has done nothing but destroy family values, which are the foundation of a strong nation."

THE FARCE OF FEMINISM

Rebecca E. Rubins

Rebecca E. Rubins writes a column for the Harvard Crimson.

∼

1 Strolling through the Freshman Week Activities Fair, I was accosted by an energetic young woman from a women's issues group who asked me fiercely, "Do you support women?"—As I took my time answering, my interrogator laughingly remarked, "It'd be really sad if you didn't."

2 Although at the time I shrugged my shoulders and signed my name to the mailing list, the feeling of having been grouped into a general category against my will simply because of my sex haunted me. For the question being asked was not "Do I support women?"—which I certainly do—but "Do I support feminism?"—which I emphatically do not. Feminism is an outdated, misdirected ideology that perpetuates the very ills it condemns and harms women much more than it helps them.

3 Perhaps there was once a time when feminism was warranted, when its name was not synonymous with self-pitying whining but with active efforts toward positive change. In the early 20th century, when women still had not gained the right to vote, the suffragettes showed remarkable dedication in bringing the system's inherent inequality to the forefront of public awareness.

4 In recent years, however, feminism in America has found itself hopelessly bereaved of a cause for which to fight. Women in this country are now on an entirely equal footing with men and are sometimes even given preferential

treatment. Instead of focusing on areas of the world where women are truly being oppressed, where they cannot show their ankles on the street without fear of being shot and killed, feminists of today spend their time creating support groups for one another and debating the relative disadvantages faced by girls in science and math classrooms. Feminism keeps women from naturally asserting their equality to men in an environment which is now conducive to such equality.

5   Feminism also creates a double standard for men and women, thus promoting the societal ills it supposedly opposes. Feminists laud women-only discussion groups, dance teams and drama clubs, but when men try to create or maintain similar men-only groups, they are accused of discrimination. The feminist movement operates on the principle that past wrongs done to women can be remedied by preferential treatment now—that two wrongs will make a right. This reverse discrimination is not only unethical but also belies their alleged opposition to judgment or exclusion based on gender alone.

6   Finally, and most importantly, feminism accomplishes the exact opposite of what it intends. Instead of raising women's social status, it burdens them with a weighty sense of victimization that neither empowers them nor motivates men to view them as equals. Girls are not born feeling inferior to boys. Rather, it is their exposure to feminism that causes them to develop a slave-like mentality.

7   This is particularly evident in school, where the "feminist aspect: of every subject is now played up, thereby bringing social activism into the classroom where it only detracts from the learning process. English teachers ask students to apply feminist criticism to books with no semblance of a feminist outlook. History textbooks try to compensate for the fact that women were in the kitchen for most of recorded time by highlighting the life of one particular female or another regardless of how little she matters to history. Other programs, such as Take Your Daughter to Work Day, also impress upon young girls the notion that they are inherently inferior citizens who need rewritten history books and politically correct semi-holidays to raise them up to the level of their male peers who, incidentally, seem to do just fine without such support. In this way, the movement marginalizes women by reminding them constantly of their former subservient status and instilling in them at a very young age a dependency on the support of other women and on feminism to "survive" in a horribly male-dominated world.

8   If feminists were to take a step back and view the current situation of women in the country objectively, they might realize that women no longer need interest groups, support networks, activism and doctored curriculae—that they, in fact, are better off without feminists' supposed help. But that objective view would leave feminists without a viable *raison d'etre*, and so they continue to ignore, for example, the possibility that the average female college student walking through an activities fair might support women but not support feminism, that she might instead consider feminism a threat to her own sense of self and empowerment.

9   Maybe feminists should start asking themselves the question, "Do we support women?" And maybe it's time someone said, "It's sad, but you don't."

⌒

(772 words)

VOCABULARY

Farce (title)	accosted (1)	interrogator (1)
ideology (2)	inherent (3)	preferential (4)
conducive (4)	discrimination (5)	belies (5)
alleged (5)	victimization (6)	marginalizes (7)
subservient (8)	curriculae (curriculum) (8)	empowerment (8)

THE FACTS

1. Why does the author entitle her essay *The Farce of Feminism*? Look up the word *farce* to make sure you understand its full meaning. In what way is the feminist movement a farce in the eyes of the author?

2. The author states that feminism promotes the very ills it condemns and thus harms women (see paragraph 2). To what ills is the author referring? Can you name other ills promoted by feminism?

3. According to the author, why do women no longer need feminism? Do you agree with her reasoning? Why or why not?

4. What is the difference between *feminine* and *feminism*? How important is it for the reader to be aware of the distinction?

5. What activities of feminism does the author particularly discredit? How do you feel about these activities? How important are they today? Evaluate them critically.

THE STRATEGIES

1. What grabber does the author use to capture the reader's attention? How effective is it in keeping you interested in what follows?

2. Where does the author place her thesis? Why is it not in the opening or final paragraph? Is the placement effective? Explain your opinion.

3. How does the author make a transition from the past to the present as it concerns feminism? What is the purpose of such a transition? Where does it take place?

4. Paragraph 5 refers to a "double standard" created by feminism. What example does the author use to illustrate the double standard? In what other areas in politics or society do double standards occur? Provide some examples.

5. Why does the author return to the activities fair at the end of the essay? Is she being redundant or is there a good reason for the repeated reference? Explain your answer.

THE ISSUES

1. Do you agree that feminism has reached the point at which it perpetuates the very ills it condemns? If you agree, what are some of the ills that feminism perpetuates? Provide examples. If you believe that feminism must continue to fight for its rights, what are these rights?

2. Do you think that women who have not had the advantage of a higher education and women with advanced degrees hold different attitudes toward feminism?

3. What is *reverse discrimination* as the author uses the term? What are some of the examples of reverse discrimination not mentioned in the essay? How can it be prevented?

4. Do you agree with the author that women today are better off without the help of feminism? What contribution might feminism still make to the cause of women?

5. What would your answer be the question, "Do you support feminism?" What would your answer be to the question, "Do you support women?"

SUGGESTIONS FOR WRITING

1. Using the Internet as your research source, find out what contributions the suffragettes (see paragraph 3) made to the cause of feminism and write an essay using the information you uncovered.

2. Write an essay in which you contrast the position of Kate Gabata with that of Rebecca Rubins concerning feminism. Be sure to find some clear bases for the contrast. Review the Editor's Counsel for chapter 12.

STUDENT CORNER

I

Final Draft

"Woman" Is a Noun

Paula Rewa, East Tennessee State University

From a local playground, a brave voice yells, "Are you a boy or a girl?" A cluster of children grin as they wait for my answer. They think they've caught me. "I'm a girl," I answer with a forced but friendly smile. I picture myself as they must see me...my stubble hair, my chunky black glasses and overloaded backpack. In my standard jeans and plain t-shirt, I'm not the collegiate Barbie they expect. I'm a curious blur as I walk past their games—an oddity.

In a restaurant, an older man at the bar asks me, "What are you, a man or a woman? I wonder, if he thought I was a man, would he have asked? "I am a woman," I answer as he looks me over. I feel his eyes on me as I leave.

In the mirror, I ask myself, "Who am I?" I know the answer. I am a woman.

No matter what advances women have made in present day society, we are still restricted by cultural expectations. If we choose to pursue a career, we become women in the workplace. If we have a family and a job, we become working mothers. We are women bankers, women lawyers, and women plumbers.

Today, it seems 'woman' is used as an adjective. Defined positively, 'woman' means feminine in appearance, even while wearing a suit. A woman person exists in a male world while retaining female qualities. Ideally, she is someone's wife. She is never taken for a 'man'. Defined negatively, 'woman' also means potentially bossy, overzealous, or emotionally driven (…the phrase "woman lawyer" makes more sense now, doesn't it?).

The adjective 'woman' confers many, if not all, of these qualities. So where does this leave the woman person who does not fit? She is stripped of her womanhood. Her sexual orientation often is questioned. It may be said that she is trying to be a man. Society pressures her to become the adjectival 'woman'.

The image of the working woman is simply a modern version of the homemaker dress of the fifties. The codes of womanly appearance dictate what is appropriate. It is acceptable for a woman to have short hair if she wears cosmetics. If she chooses not to wear cosmetics, she should have a naturally pretty face and wear feminine clothing. We may now have access to the world of business, but we are still put in our place as much as ever. Our suit jackets proclaim us as equals, while our skirts hint that we are really just women underneath.

Codes of appearance apply not only in corporate America, but also in society in general. The look has changed, but we are still expected to conform. Today, women can wear anything that men wear. In fact, many popular stores carry only clothing that can be worn by both men and women. Yet the expectations persist: when a woman wears it, she must still look "woman."

Our culture must reclaim 'woman' as a noun, and recognize that women remain women, regardless of what they wear or what they do. If they are accountants, call them accountants. To say "woman accountant" is unnecessary, and the implications of such a title are not appreciated. If a woman has short hair and prefers

Rewa 3

suits to skirts, do not assume that she wants to be a man. Instead, consider how secure she must be to feel comfortable without conforming to society's expectations.

Women must learn to cherish themselves without being slaves to femininity. Many women enjoy wearing dresses, and they should be applauded for their own expression of self. But dresses should not be mandatory, and neither should long hair, painted nails, or push-up bras. The true woman is the person inside, not the image she projects.

I have been asked many times if I am a man or a woman. Children ask out of curiousity, men ask with mockery. I answer without hesitation, because I know that 'woman' is a noun. I may have very short hair. I may wear cosmetics only occasionally. But I am proud to be a woman, just as I am proud to be myself.

How I Write

When I sit down to write, the most important factor in my productivity is comfort. I do all my writing on a computer, but I don't sit directly in front of the screen, feet flat on the floor, and all that jazz. My high school typing teacher would probably be appalled to see me lounging on my couch with my keyboard on my knees, an extension cord reaching across the living room to my PC.

I never have any music playing when I need to concentrate. I used to play my favorite artists as inspiration, but I tended to get carried away. As a result, the flavor of my writing was often influenced by the mood of the music.

I like to do all my writing on a computer, because it is much easier to revise over and over. I tend to revise as I write, and then over again several times as my essay develops. I find that this helps me maintain clarity and stay connected to what I'm writing. I find it frustrating to do first, second, and third drafts, because I feel I should wait for the next official "draft" to change something I don't like. In order to write effectively, it is essential that I give myself permission to change things any time I want. I do save different versions of my paper as it evolves, for reference and in case I decide I like something better the way it was. I also print out my paper several times, in order to make notes for necessary changes.

How I Wrote This Essay

When I get a new assignment or idea, I try to get something on paper immediately. Even if I don't end up using any of it, the writing gets my mind moving in a direction. It also solidifies the images and phrases that fly through my head when I'm excited about a new project.

For this essay, I was given the subject of "Women's Status: Gains or Losses?" I started by breaking down the subject. My first thought was "why not gains and losses?" Other questions followed, such as "What is our status?" "How are women perceived?" "What does 'woman' really mean?" I recorded these questions and others at the top of my paper, and kept them there for reference throughout the writing process.

The first time I sat down to work on this essay, I had so many thoughts swimming around in my head that the result was five different introductory paragraphs, all strung together with no connections. Instead of worrying about this, I set the essay aside for a few days, and thought about what it was that I truly wanted to say. When I came back to my computer, my thoughts were much clearer, and I was able to mold what I had into a clear idea.

My Writing Tip

Above all, don't get frustrated when you start writing. I have my bouts with writer's block, but I try to keep writing: Write anything that pops into your head. Don't worry about if it's in the right place. I tend to have three or four good sentences pushing along ahead of my cursor, just waiting for a good place for me to stick them in.

The trick is to keep going. Eventually, you'll hit on an idea, a sentence, or even a combination of words that say just what you want it to say, and the rest will flow from there.

Good luck!

CHAPTER WRITING ASSIGNMENTS

1. Write a causal analysis for one of the following conditions:
    a. The poor writing habits of today's students
    b. The lack of popular financial support for museums, concerts, and other art forms
    c. The decline of the stock market
    d. The need for prison reform
    e. The worldwide popularity of rock music
    f. The rise in child pornography
    g. The failure of the rapid transit system in most large cities
    h. The need to conserve our beaches
    i. Our tendency to buy throwaway items

2. Write a causal analysis explaining the reason behind the breakup of a relationship.

WRITING ASSIGNMENTS FOR A SPECIFIC AUDIENCE

1. Write a letter to a teacher you once had (but don't send it!) analyzing why you did badly or well in his/her class.
2. Write an essay explaining why you chose a certain major in college.

COLLABORATIVE WRITING PROJECT

Join a group of four other students. After reviewing all the material in this chapter on women's status today, brainstorm about why the steam has gone out of the feminist movement. Assign research on the topic to the group's members and work as one to team-write an essay entitled: *Why the Feminist Movement has Lost its Punch.*

15

Argumentation and Persuasion

EDITORS' COUNSEL

What Argumentation and Persuasion Do

Argumentation and persuasion are the fraternal twins of rhetoric. The difference between them is this: An argument appeals strictly by reason and logic; persuasion appeals by both logic and emotion. If you're pleading for more funding for diabetes research and you base your appeal primarily on numbers, you're making an argument. If you supplement the number crunching with testimony from diabetes sufferers who have been horribly affected by the disease, you're being persuasive. The forum in which the argument takes place will determine which tactic you should adopt. A formal paper for a philosophy class should be worded as an argument. An essay or article written for your student newspaper, depending on the topic, should be both logical as well as persuasive.

Argumentation, unlike the other modes of writing, is a term of rhetorical intent, not of form. It refers to any essay or speech whose aim is to sway or persuade a reader or listener. Because writers resort to many techniques and devices to achieve this aim, the argumentation essay tends to be a mixture of rhetorical forms; that is, you are likely to find the writer defining, describing, narrating, or even dividing during the course of the argument. The tone of the essay can vary from the savage sarcasm of Jonathan Swift's *A Modest Proposal* to the chilling, matter-of-fact tone of Andrew Vachss's *Sex Predators Can't Be Saved*. The subject matter can include any topic from the nearly infinite spectrum of issues about which people argue.

When to Use Argumentation and Persuasion

Some people think that all writing is persuasive. Their reasoning is that even if you're describing a scene, what you're really doing is trying to persuade your reader to see through your eyes. If you are comparing two friends, you are hoping to convince your reader that your observations about them are true. Trace elements of the techniques of persuasion are no doubt present in other kinds of writing, but we formally apply the techniques of argumentation and persuasion when we're trying to bring someone around to our opinion or point of view. This may be in a debate or in an essay on a topic that requires you to advocate one side over another.

How to Use Argumentation and Persuasion

What elements are most likely to sway us in an argumentative essay—to make us change our minds and believe a writer's arguments? Research suggests some clues. First, there is our perception of the writer's credentials to hold an opinion on the subject. If we think the writer is competent and qualified on the subject—a medical doctor writing on a medical topic, for example—we are more likely to believe the advocated opinion. If you hold a particular qualification to write on the subject, then mentioning it will probably help. You do not have to blare out your credentials, but you can do it subtly. For example, in his essay on the sexual predators, Vachss tells us that he has interviewed many sex predators over the years—a revelation that leaves us more likely to accept his views of them. If you are not an expert yourself, quoting an expert can certainly lend weight to your view.

Another element that inclines us to believe an argumentative essay is the quality of its reasoning. If the writer's logic is sound, if the facts and supporting details strike us as reasonable and strong, then we are likely to be swayed by the conclusions. Presenting your facts in all their glory, while making the links between the propositions of your argument instantly clear, will make it difficult for anyone to easily dismiss your conclusions.

Finally, arguments are persuasive if they appeal to our self-interests. We are more likely to believe an argument if we think there is something in it for us. This insight explains why arguers huff and puff to portray themselves and their views as if they agreed exactly with our self-interests, even if the correspondence is far-fetched. The underlying appeal of Jonathan Swift's ironic proposal, for instance, is to the self-interests of Irish citizens who Swift thinks would be better off in a unified Ireland free from British exploitation.

If your argument is not reasoned logically, it is unlikely to be effective. And if it is not backed with solid evidence, its claims will most likely arouse disbelief. When the issue at stake is a practical one, these two elements—logical reasoning and solid evidence—are basic requirements for any effective argument.

There are, in addition, some common strategies that writers use to make their arguments persuasive. Being persuasive involves more than being strictly logical; it takes in the whole range of writing skills—conciseness, clarity, and the ability to infuse a prose style with a distinctive personality. To write a persuasive argument, then, you should try to practice the following techniques:

1. Begin your argument at the point of contention. This means that your initial paragraph should immediately focus on the issue being argued. Consider this opening from an argument:

"We have room for but one language here, and that is the English language, for we intend to see that the crucible turns our people out as Americans and not as dwellers in a polyglot boarding house." Theodore Roosevelt

In the store windows of Los Angeles, gathering place of the world's aspiring peoples, the signs today ought to read, "English spoken here." Supermarket price tags are often written in Korean, restaurant menus in Chinese, employment-office signs in Spanish. In the new city of dreams, where gold can be earned if not found on the sidewalk, there are laborers and businessmen who have lived five, ten, 20 years in America without learning to speak English. English is not the common denominator for many of these new Americans. Disturbingly, some of them insist it need not be.

"Against a Confusion of Tongues," William A. Henry III.

As you can see, the writing begins with a quotation from Theodore Roosevelt and a pointed paragraph that makes it immediately clear what he is arguing against: immigrants who refuse to learn English. He wastes no time in pointless preamble or beating around the bush.

Here are two openings from student essays arguing against offshore drilling. One begins with an ominous drift; the other gets immediately to the point.

Unfocused: I oppose offshore drilling for oil. But before I give my reasons for making this statement, I would like to review the various present sources of crude oil in our country. . . .

Focused: I oppose offshore drilling for oil because such a project could, in the name of energy, destroy thousands of miles of our oceans and add to the already staggering amount of pollution on the earth . . .

Your opening sentence or sentences should underscore your stand as well as your preliminary reasoning.

2. Draw your evidence from multiple sources.   This is a self-evident observation. If your argument is based on a single book or the testimony of one expert, it will be invariably weaker than if it draws support from many sources. Ideally, the direction and force of your research should lead you to different kinds and sources of evidence. However, we often get papers that are based on the writer's devotion to a single book or the point of view of one expert. This can be a crippling limitation, especially if your one book or one expert hold views that turn out to be wrong. The antidote for overreliance on a single source of evidence is to find a topic you're truly interested in.

3. Pace your argument with some obvious movement.   Don't allow your argument to become clogged with a dreary recital of evidence or bogged down with pointless hairsplitting. We suggest that you imagine the typical reader's reactions to any argumentative essay or speech:

Reader or Listener	Your Response
Ho hum!	(Wake up the reader with provocative introduction.)
Why bring that up?	(State your argument in clear, forceful language.)
For instance?	(Supply evidence and facts.)
So what?	(Restate the thesis, say what you expect the reader to do.)

Responding to these four imagined reader/listener attitudes will give your argument a discernible movement.

4. Begin your argument with an assumption that is either grounded in evidence or defensible. You should not attempt to argue the unarguable or prove the unprovable. While the realm of the arguable is constantly expanding before an onslaught of mysticism and fantasy, many instructors would nevertheless find the following theses entirely unacceptable in an argumentative essay:

Hell exists as a place of punishment for sinners to atone for wrongdoing committed on earth.

The Great Depression of the 1930s was caused by a destructive astrological conjunction between the planets Venus and Mars.

Cats and all manner of feline creatures are despicable, nauseating beasts.

Arthur Conan Doyle, creator of Sherlock Holmes, was the greatest detective-story writer of all times.

All four propositions are based on personal belief and, therefore, unprovable in a strictly logical sense.

5. Anticipate the opposition. For instance, if you are arguing that a controversial cancer drug should be legalized, you must not only marshal evidence to show the effectiveness of the drug, you must also answer the arguments of those opposed to its legalization. You might, for instance, introduce these arguments this way:

Opponents to the legalization of this drug claim that its use will prevent the cancer patient from using other remedies proven effective against cancer. This claim, however, misses the point.

Then get down to the point that has been missed.

A frequent tactic used in arguments is not only to sum up the opposition's viewpoint but also to point out any inconsistencies in it. Here is an example of this from an argument in favor of using animals in medical research:

Extremists within the animal-rights movement take the position that animals have rights equal to or greater than those of humans. It follows from this that even if humans might benefit from animal research, the cost to animals is too high. It is ironic that despite this moral position, the same organizations condone—and indeed sponsor—activities that appear to violate the basic rights of animals to live and reproduce. Each year 10,000,000 dogs are destroyed by public pounds, animal shelters and humane societies. Many of these programs are supported and even operated by animal-protectionist groups. Surely there is a strong contradiction when those who profess to believe in animal rights deny animals their right to life. A similar situation exists with regard to programs of pet sterilization, programs that deny animals the right to breed and to bear offspring and are sponsored in many cases by antivivisectionists and animal-rights groups. Evidently, animal-rights advocates sometimes recognize and subscribe to the position that animals do not have the same rights as humans. However, their public posture leaves little room for examining these subtleties or applying similar standards to animal research.

Frederick A. King, "Animals in Research: The Case for Experimentation"

Moral logic requires us to practice what we preach; if it can be shown that the opposition is more likely to preach than to practice, that is grounds for calling into question the sincerity of its views.

6. Supplement your reasoning and evidence with an emotional appeal. This tactic must, however, be used with discretion and caution—as we said, depending on the topic and the forum. Emotional appeal is no substitute for reasoned argument or solid evidence. However, used in supplementary doses, emotional appeal can be highly persuasive in dramatizing an outcome or condition in a way that evidence and facts alone cannot. Here is an example: A speaker is trying to persuade an audience to donate blood for the benefit of hemophiliacs. A hemophiliac himself, he spends the first half of his speech explaining factually what hemophilia is—reciting statistics about its incidence and discussing its symptoms. Then, to dramatize the awfulness of the disease, he resorts to an emotional appeal, using his own experience with the pain of hemophilia:

> Because medical science had not advanced far enough, and fresh blood not given often enough, my memories of childhood and adolescence are memories of pain and heartbreak. I remember missing school for weeks and months at a stretch-of being very proud because I attended school once for four whole weeks without missing a single day. I remember the three long years when I couldn't even walk because repeated hemorrhages had twisted my ankles and knees to pretzel-like forms. I remember being pulled to school in a wagon while other boys rode their bikes, and being pushed to my table. I remember sitting in the dark empty classroom by myself during recess while the others went out in the sun to run and play. And I remember the first terrible day at the big high school when I came on crutches and built-up shoes carrying my books in a sack around my neck.
>
> But what I remember most of all is the pain. Medical authorities agree that a hemophilic joint hemorrhage is one of the most excruciating pains known too mankind.

To concentrate a large amount of blood into a small compact area causes a pressure that words can never hope to describe. And how well I remember the endless pounding, squeezing pain. When you seemingly drown in your own perspiration, when your teeth ache from incessant clenching, when your tongue floats in your mouth and bombs explode back of your eyeballs; when darkness and light fuse into one hue of gray; when day becomes night and night becomes daytime stands still—and all that matters is that ugly pain. The scars of pain are not easily erased.

Ralph Zimmerman, "Mingled Blood"

The appeal is moving and effective and contributes to the persuasiveness of the speaker's plea.

Warming Up to Write an Argument

1. Write down at least three objections to each of the following propositions:
    a. Women should be drafted into the military.
    b. The United Nations should have its own army.
    c. The euro should now be used in every country of the world.
    d. Every official meeting of Congress should begin with prayer.
    e. "I am not responsible for saving the world."
2. For each of the following areas, list three topics you think you could develop into a persuasive argument:
    a. Something in your personal life you would like to change
    b. A social or political problem that needs solving
    c. An area of education you would like to see improved
3. Sketch out some ideas you would use to support the following quotations:
    a. "Opinions founded on prejudice are always sustained with the greatest violence."
        —Francis Jeffrey
    b. "The most tragic paradox of our time is to be found in the failure of nation-states to recognize the imperatives of internationalism."
        —Chief Justice Earl Warren
    c. "There is no greater lie than a truth misunderstood."
        —William James
    d. "To be a success in business, be daring, be first, be different."
        —Marchant
    e. "The drive toward complex technical achievement offers a clue to why the U.S. is good at space gadgetry and bad at slum problems."
        —John Kenneth Galbraith

—————— EXAMPLES ——————

IN DEFENSE OF GENDER

Cyra McFadden

Cyra McFadden (b. 1937) is a freelance writer and teacher who lives in California. She is a contributor of articles to many popular magazines such as Nation, McCall's, *and* Smithsonian. *Among her other works is the novel* The Serial *1977.*

English is sexist in its use of pronouns. The third-person singular pronoun, when a specific person is not identified, is always "he." One result of this is a prejudice against women. In the 1960s, with the rise of the feminist movement, came a determined attempt to correct this inequity, leading to strange coinages such as "mailpersons" and "salespersons." Predictably, this sparked a backlash, particularly among highly literary people such as the author. Even today, a solution to satisfy everyone has not yet been found, and writers continue to muddle their way through on a case-by-case basis, sometimes saying "he/she" or putting the sentence in the plural to avoid altogether having to use a sexist pronoun.

~

1   So pervasive is the neutering of the English language on the progressive West Coast, we no longer have people here, only persons: male persons and female persons, chairpersons and doorpersons, waitpersons, mailpersons—who may be either male or female mailpersons—and refuse-collection persons. In the classified ads, working mothers seek childcare persons, though one wonders how many men (archaic for "male person") take care of child persons as a full-time occupation. One such ad, fusing nonsexist language and the most popular word in the California growth movement, solicits a "nurtureperson."

2   Dear gents and ladies, as I might have addressed you in less troubled times, this female person knows firsthand the reasons for scourging sexist bias from the language. God knows what damage was done me, at fifteen, when I worked in my first job—as what is now known as a newspaper copyperson—and came running to the voices of men barking, "Boy!"

3   No aspirant to the job of refuse-collection person myself, I nonetheless take off my hat (a little feathered number, with a veil) to those of my own sex who may want both the job and a genderless title with it. I argue only that there must be a better way, and I wish person or persons unknown would come up with one.

4   Defend it on any grounds you choose; the neutering of spoken and written English, with its attendant self-consciousness, remains ludicrous. In print, those "person" suffixes and "he/she's" jump out from the page, as distracting as a cloud of gnats, demanding that the reader note the writer's virtue. "Look what a nonsexist writer person I am, voiding the use of masculine forms for the generic."

5   Spoken, they leave conversation fit only for the Coneheads on "Saturday Night Live." "They have a daily special," a woman at the next table told her male companion in Perry's, a San Francisco restaurant. "Ask your waitperson." In a Steig cartoon, the words would have marched from her mouth in the form of a computer printout.

6   In Berkeley, Calif., the church to which a friend belongs is busy stripping its liturgy of sexist references. "They've gone berserk," she writes, citing a reading from the pulpit of a verse from 1 Corinthians. Neutered, the once glorious passage becomes "Though I speak with the tongues of persons and of angels. . . ." So much for sounding brass and tinkling cymbals.

7   The parson person of the same church is now referring to God as "He/She" and changing all references accordingly—no easy undertaking if he intends to be consistent. In the following, the first pronoun would remain because at this primitive stage of human evolution, male persons do not give birth to babies: "And she brought forth her firstborn son/daughter, and wrapped him/her in swaddling clothes, and laid him/her in a manger; because there was no room for them in the inn. . . ."

8   As the after-dinner speaker at a recent professional conference, I heard a text replete with "he/she's" and "his/hers" read aloud for the first time. The hapless program female chairperson stuck with the job chose to render these orally as "he-slash-she" and "his-slash-her," turning the following day's schedule for conference participants into what sounded like a replay of the Manson killings.

9   Redress may be due those of us who, though female, have answered to masculine referents all these years, but slashing is not the answer; violence never is. Perhaps we could right matters by using feminine forms as the generic for a few centuries, or simply agree on a per-woman lump-sum payment.

10   Still, we would be left with the problem of referring, without bias, to transpersons. These are not bus drivers or Amtrak conductors but persons in transit from one gender to the other—or so I interpret a fund-drive appeal asking me to defend their civil rights, along with those of female and male homosexuals.

11   Without wishing to step on anyone's civil rights, I hope transpersons are not the next politically significant pressure group. If they are, count on it, they will soon want their own pronouns.

12   In the tradition of the West, meanwhile, feminists out here wrestle the language to the ground, plant a foot on its neck and remove its masculine appendages. Take the local art critic Beverly Terwoman.

13   She is married to a man surnamed Terman. She writes under "Terwoman," presumably in the spirit of *vive la différence*. As a letter to the editor of the paper for which she writes noted, however, "Terwoman" is not ideologically pure. It still contains "man," a syllable reeking of all that is piggy and hairy-chested.

14   Why not Beverly Terperson? Or better, since "Terperson" contains "son," Terdaughter"? Or a final refinement, Beverly Ter?

15   Beverly Terwoman did not dignify this sexist assault with a reply. The writer of the letter was a male person, after all, probably the kind who leaves his smelly sweat socks scattered around the bedroom floor.

16   No one wins these battles anyway. In another letter to the same local weekly, J. Seibert, female, lets fire at the printing of an interview with Phyllis Schlafly. Not only was the piece "an offense to everything that Marin County stands for," but "it is even more amusing that your interview was conducted by a male.

17   "This indicates your obvious assumption that men understand women's issues better than women since men are obviously more intelligent (as no doubt Phyllis would agree)."

18   A sigh suffuses the editor's note that follows: "The author of the article, Sydney Weisman, is a female."

19   So the war of the pronouns and suffixes rages, taking no prisoners except writers. Neuter your prose with all those clanking "he/she's," and no one will read you except Alan Alda. Use masculine forms as the generic, and you have joined the ranks of the oppressor. None of this does much to encourage friendly relations between persons, transpersons or—if there are any left—people.

20   I also have little patience with the hyphenated names more and more California female persons adopt when they marry, in the interests of retaining their own personhood. These accomplish their intention of declaring the husband separate but equal. They are hell on those of us who have trouble remembering one name, much less two. They defeat answering machines, which can't handle, "Please call Gwendolyn Grunt-Messerschmidt." And in this culture, they retain overtones of false gentility.

21   Two surnames, to me, still bring to mind the female writers of bad romances and Julia Ward Howe.

22   It's a mug's game, friends, this neutering of a language already fat, bland and lethargic, and it's time we decide not to play it. This female person is currently writing a book about rodeo. I'll be dragged behind a saddle bronc before I will neuter the text with "cowpersons."

〜

(1,121 words)

VOCABULARY

pervasive (1)	archaic (1)	scourging (2)
aspirant (3)	generic (4)	replete (8)
hapless (8)	redress (9)	suffuses (18)
gentility (20)	lethargic (22)	

THE FACTS

1. What is the author's main complaint against the movement to neuter English of its sexist pronouns?

2. To what popular television character does the author think neutered English is suited?

3. In Berkeley, California, what has the movement to neuter English led to? What have been the results, according to the author?

4. According to the author, what is due to women for having had to endure centuries of pronouns with masculine referents?

5. What solution does the author propose? Do you agree with her solution?

THE STRATEGIES

1. Very early in her essay, as if we couldn't tell from her name, the author tells us that she is female. What rhetorical advantage you think she gets from doing this?

2. Where in the first three paragraphs does the author assert what is the closest thing to a thesis? What is this sentence?

3. What technique of tone does the author use repeatedly to get her opinions across?

4. In paragraph 2, the author tells us about her experience with sexist language in her first job. Why do you think she shares this experience with us? What does it add to her argument?

5. Although this essay definitely makes an argument against gender neutering of the language, the author draws heavily on one of the modes of development. Which one is it, and how does it suit her purpose?

THE ISSUES

1. What are your views on the neutering of English? Do you agree with the author or do you think she's being hypercritical and extraordinarily fussy?

2. What do you think the English language will lose if all of its pronouns become nonsexist?

3. Reread paragraph 8. What metaphor here would strike some as being in bad taste?

4. What does the author propose in paragraph 9? Do you think she's serious? What is your opinion of this proposal?

5. Assuming that the movement to neuter English began with the feminist movement of the 1960s, what changed circumstances of women would seem to make that issue irrelevant? Or, do you believe that the change is still necessary? Why?

SUGGESTIONS FOR WRITING

1. Find a piece of writing from an old magazine or newspaper that uses "he" as a generic pronoun and commits other sexist-language sins. Rewrite it to make the passage completely nonsexist. Compare the two and say which one is better.

2. In an essay, argue for or against McFadden's opinion that neutering the language has led to some ludicrous constructions.

A MODEST PROPOSAL

For Preventing the Children of Poor People from Being a Burden to Their Parents or the Country and for Making Them Beneficial to the Public

Jonathan Swift

Considered one of the greatest satirists in the English language, Jonathan Swift (1667–1745) was born in Dublin and educated at Trinity College. His satirical masterpiece, Gulliver's Travels, *was published in 1726, by which time Swift was already regarded by the Irish as a national hero for his* Drapier's Letters *(1724). Originally published as a pamphlet,* A Modest Proposal *first appeared in 1729.*

In this famous satire, Swift, assuming the role of a concerned and logical citizen, turns society's indifference to the value of human life into an outraged attack against poverty in Ireland.

~

1 It is a melancholy object to those who walk through this great town, or travel in the country, when they see the streets, the roads, and cabin doors crowded with beggars of the female sex followed by three, four, or six children, all in rags and importuning every passenger for an alms. These mothers, instead of being able to work for their honest livelihood, are forced to employ all their time in strolling, to beg sustenance for their helpless infants, who, as they grow up, either turn thieves for want of work or leave their dear native country to fight for the Pretender in Spain or sell themselves to the Barbadoes.[1]

2   I think it is agreed by all parties that this prodigious number of children, in the arms or on the backs or at the heels of their mothers and frequently of their fathers, is in the present deplorable state of the kingdom a very great additional grievance, and therefore whoever could find out a fair, cheap, and easy method of making these children sound and useful members of the commonwealth would deserve so well of the public as to have his statue set up for a preserver of the nation.

3   But my intention is very far from being confined to provide only for the children of professed beggars; it is of a much greater extent, and shall take in

---

[1]Swift refers to the exiled Stuart claimant of the English throne, and to the custom of poor emigrants to commit themselves to work for a number of years to pay off their transportation to a colony.—Ed.

the whole number of infants at a certain age who are born of parents in effect as little able to support them as those who demand our charity in the streets.

4   As to my own part, having turned my thoughts for many years upon this important subject and maturely weighed the several schemes of other projectors, I have always found them grossly mistaken in their computation. It is true, a child just dropped from its dam may be supported by her milk for a solar year, with little other nourishment, at the most not above the value of two shillings, which the mother may certainly get, or the value in scraps, by her lawful occupation of begging; and it is exactly at one year old that I propose to provide for them in such a manner as, instead of being a charge upon their parents or the parish or wanting food and raiment for the rest of their lives, they shall on the contrary contribute to the feeding, and partly to the clothing, of many thousands.

5   There is likewise another great advantage in my scheme, that it will prevent those voluntary abortions and that horrid practice of women murdering their bastard children, alas! too frequent among us, sacrificing the poor innocent babes, I doubt more to avoid the expense than the shame, which would move tears and pity in the most savage and inhuman breast.

6   The number of souls in this kingdom being usually reckoned one million and a half, of these I calculate there may be about two hundred thousand couple whose wives are breeders, from which number I subtract thirty thousand couple who are able to maintain their own children (although I apprehend there cannot be so many, under the present distresses of the kingdom); but this being granted, there will remain a hundred and seventy thousand breeders. I again subtract fifty thousand for those women who miscarry or whose children die by accident or disease within the year. There only remain a hundred and twenty thousand children of poor parents annually born. The question therefore is how this number shall be reared and provided for, which, as I have already said, under the present situation of affairs is utterly impossible by all the methods hitherto proposed. For we can neither employ them in handicraft or agriculture; we neither build houses (I mean in the country) nor cultivate land; they can very seldom pick up a livelihood by stealing, till they arrive at six years old, except where they are of towardly parts, although I confess they learn the rudiments much earlier, during which time they can, however, be properly looked upon only as probationers; as I have been informed by a principal gentleman in the County of Cavan who protested to me that he never knew above one or two instances under the age of six, even in a part of the kingdom so renowned for the quickest proficiency in that art.

7   I am assured by our merchants that a boy or a girl before twelve years old is no saleable commodity, and even when they come to this age they will not yield above three pounds or three pounds and a half a crown at most on the exchange, which cannot turn to account either to the parents or the kingdom, the charge of nutriment and rags having been at least four times that value.

8   I shall now, therefore, humbly propose my own thoughts, which I hope will not be liable to the least objection.

9   I have been assured by a very knowing American of my acquaintance in London that a young, healthy child well nursed is, at a year old, a most deli-

cious, nourishing, and wholesome food, whether stewed, roasted, baked, or boiled; and I make no doubt that it will equally serve in a fricassee or a ragout.

10   I do therefore humbly offer it to public consideration that of the hundred and twenty thousand children already computed, twenty thousand may be reserved for breed, whereof only one fourth part to be males, which is more than we allow to sheep, black cattle, or swine; and my reason is that these children are seldom the fruits of marriage, a circumstance not much regarded by our savages; therefore one male will be sufficient to serve four females. That the remaining hundred thousand may, at a year old, be offered in sale to the persons of quality and fortune through the kingdom, always advising the mother to let them suck plentifully in the last month, so as to render them plump and fat for a good table. A child will make two dishes at an entertainment for friends; and when the family dines alone, the fore-or hind-quarter will make a reasonable dish, and seasoned with a little pepper or salt, will be very good boiled on the fourth day, especially in winter. I have reckoned, upon a medium, that a child just born will weigh twelve pounds, and in a solar year, if tolerably nursed, will increase to twenty-eight pounds.

11   I grant this food will be somewhat dear, and therefore very proper for the landlords, who, as they have already devoured most of the parents, seem to have the best title to the children.

12   Infant's flesh will be in season throughout the year, but more plentifully in March and a little before and after; for we are told by a grave author, an eminent French physician, that fish being a prolific diet, there are more children born in Roman Catholic countries about nine months after Lent than at any other season; therefore, reckoning a year after Lent, the markets will be more glutted than usual, because the number of Popish infants is at least three to one in this kingdom; and therefore it will have one other collateral advantage, by lessening the number of Papists among us. I have already computed the charge of nursing a beggar's child (in which list I reckon all cottagers, laborers, and four fifths of the farmers) to be about two shillings per annum, rags included; and I believe no gentleman would repine to give ten shillings for the carcass of a good fat child, which, as I have said, will make four dishes for excellent nutritive meat, when he has only some particular friend or his own family to dine with him. Thus the squire will learn to be a good landlord and grow popular among his tenants; the mother will have eight shillings net profit and be fit for work till she produces another child.

13   Those who are more thrifty (as I must confess the times require) may flay the carcass, the skin of which, artificially dressed, will make admirable gloves for ladies and summer boots for fine gentlemen.

14   As to our city of Dublin, shambles[2] may be appointed for this purpose in the most convenient parts of it; and butchers, we may be assured, will not be wanting, although I rather recommend buying the children alive than dressing them hot from the knife as we do roasting pigs.

---

[2]Slaughterhouses—Ed.

15   A very worthy person, a true lover of his country, and whose virtues I highly esteem, was lately pleased in discoursing on this matter to offer a refinement upon my scheme. He said that many gentlemen of his kingdom having of late destroyed their deer, he conceived that the want of venison might be well supplied by the bodies of young lads and maidens, not exceeding fourteen years of age nor under twelve, so great a number of both sexes in every country being now ready to starve for want of work and service; and these to be disposed of by their parents if alive, or otherwise by their nearest relations. But with due deference to so excellent a friend and so deserving a patriot, I cannot be altogether in his sentiments; for as to the males, my American acquaintance assured me, from frequent experience, that their flesh was generally tough and lean, like that of our schoolboys, by continual exercise, and their taste disagreeable; and to fatten them would not answer the charge. Then as to the females, it would, I think, with humble submission, be a loss to the public, because they would soon become breeders themselves, and besides, it is not improbable that some scrupulous people might be apt to censure such a practice (although indeed very unjustly) as a little bordering upon cruelty, which, I confess, has always been with me the strongest objection against any project, however so well intended.

16   But in order to justify my friend, he confessed that this expedient was put into his head by the famous Psalmanazar, a native of the island Formosa, who came from thence to London above twenty years ago and in conversation told my friend that in his country, when any young person happened to be put to death, the executioner sold the carcass to persons of quality as a prime dainty and that in his time the body of a plump girl of fifteen, who was crucified for an attempt to poison the emperor, was sold to his imperial Majesty's prime minister of state and other great mandarins of the court in joints from the gibbet at four hundred crowns. Neither, indeed, can I deny that if the same use were made of several plump young girls in this town who, without one single groat to their fortunes, cannot stir abroad without a chair, and appear at playhouse and assemblies in foreign fineries which they never will pay for, the kingdom would not be the worse.

17   Some persons of a desponding spirit are in great concern about that vast number of poor people who are aged, diseased, or maimed, and I have been desired to employ my thoughts what course may be taken to ease the nation of so grievous an encumbrance. But I am not in the least pain upon the matter, because it is very well known that they are every day dying and rotting by cold, and famine, and filth, and vermin, as fast as can be reasonably expected. And as to the young laborers, they are now in almost as hopeful a condition; they cannot get work and consequently pine away for want of nourishment to a degree that if at any time they are accidentally hired to common labor, they have not strength to perform it; and thus the country and themselves are happily delivered from the evils to come.

18   I have too long digressed and therefore shall return to my subject. I think the advantages by the proposal which I have made are obvious and many, as well as of the highest importance.

19   For first, as I have already observed, it would greatly lessen the number of Papists, with whom we are yearly overrun, being the principal breeders of the nation as well as our most dangerous enemies, and who stay at home on purpose to deliver the kingdom to the Pretender, hoping to take their advantage by the absence of so many good Protestants, who have chosen rather to leave their country than stay at home and pay tithes, against their conscience, to an Episcopal curate.

20   Secondly, the poorer tenants will have something valuable of their own which by law may be made liable to distress and help to pay their landlord's rent, their corn and cattle being already seized and money a thing unknown.

21   Thirdly, whereas the maintenance of a hundred thousand children from two years old and upward cannot be computed at less than ten shillings apiece per annum, the nation's stock will thereby be increased fifty thousand pounds per annum, beside the profit of a new dish introduced to the tables of all gentlemen of fortune in the kingdom who have any refinement in taste. And the money will circulate among ourselves, the goods being entirely of our own growth and manufacture.

22   Fourthly, the constant breeders, beside the gain of eight shillings sterling per annum by the sale of their children, will be rid of the charge of maintaining them after the first year.

23   Fifthly, this food would likewise bring great custom to taverns, where the vintners will certainly be so prudent as to procure the best receipts for dressing it to perfection and consequently have their houses frequented by all the fine gentlemen who justly value themselves upon their knowledge in good eating; and a skillful cook who understands how to oblige his guests will contrive to make it as expensive as they please.

24   Sixthly, this would be a great inducement to marriage, which all wise nations have either encouraged by rewards or enforced by laws and penalties. It would increase the care and tenderness of mothers toward their children when they were sure of a settlement for life to the poor babes, provided in some sort by the public, to their annual profit or expense. We could see an honest emulation among the married women, which of them could bring the fattest child to the market. Men would become as fond of their wives during the time of their pregnancy as they are now of their mares in foal, their cows in calf, or sows when they are ready to farrow, nor offer to beat or kick them (as is too frequent a practice) for fear of a miscarriage.

25   Many other advantages might be enumerated. For instance, the addition of some thousand carcasses in our exportation of barreled beef; the propagation of swine's flesh and improvement in the art of making good bacon, so much wanted among us by the great destruction of pigs, too frequent at our table, which are no way comparable in taste or magnificence to a well-grown fat yearling child, which, roasted whole, will make a considerable figure at a lord mayor's feast or any other public entertainment. But this and many others I omit, being studious of brevity.

26   Supposing that one thousand families in this city would be constant customers for infant's flesh, beside others who might have it at merry-meetings,

particularly at weddings and christenings, I compute that Dublin would take off annually about twenty thousand carcasses and the rest of the kingdom (where probably they will be sold somewhat cheaper) the remaining eighty thousand.

27   I can think of no one objection that will possibly be raised against this proposal unless it should be urged that the number of people will be thereby much lessened in the kingdom. This I freely own, and it was indeed one principal design in offering it to the world. I desire the reader will observe that I calculate my remedy for this one individual kingdom of Ireland and for no other that ever was, is, or I think ever can be, upon earth. Therefore let no man talk to me of other expedients; of taxing our absentees at five shillings a pound; of using neither clothes nor household furniture except what is of our own growth and manufacture; of utterly rejecting the materials and instruments that promote foreign luxury; of curing the expensiveness of pride, vanity, idleness, and gaming in our women; of introducing a vein of parsimony, prudence, and temperance; of learning to love our country, in the want of which we differ even from Laplanders and the inhabitants of Tupinamba; of quitting our animosities and factions, nor acting any longer like the Jews, who were murdering one another at the very moment their city was taken; of being a little cautious not to sell our country and conscience for nothing; of teaching landlords to have at least one degree of mercy toward their tenants; lastly, of putting a spirit of honesty, industry, and skill into our shop-keepers, who, if a resolution could now be taken to buy only our native goods, would immediately unite to cheat and exact upon us in the price, the measure, and the goodness, nor could ever yet be brought to make one fair proposal of just dealing, though often and earnestly invited to it.

28   Therefore, I repeat, let no man talk to me of these and the like expedients till he has at least some glimpse of hope that there will be ever some hearty and sincere attempt to put them in practice.

29   But as to myself, having been wearied out for many years with offering vain, idle, visionary thoughts and at length utterly despairing of success, I fortunately fell upon this proposal, which, as it is wholly new, so it has something solid and real, of no expense and little trouble, full in our own power, and whereby we can incur no danger in disobliging England. For this kind of commodity will not bear exportation, the flesh being of too tender a consistence to admit a long continuance in salt, although perhaps I could name a country which would be glad to eat up our whole nation without it.

30   After all, I am not so violently bent upon my own opinion as to reject any offer proposed by wise men which shall be found equally innocent, cheap, easy, and effectual. But before some thing of that kind shall be advanced in contradiction to my scheme and offering a better, I desire the author or authors will be pleased maturely to consider two points: first, as things now stand, how they will be able to find food and raiment for a hundred thousand useless mouths and backs; and secondly, there being a round million of creatures in human figure throughout this kingdom whose whole subsistence, put into a common stock, would leave them in debt two millions of pounds sterling, adding those who are beggars by profession to the bulk of farmers, cot-

tagers, and laborers, with the wives and children who are beggars in effect, I desire those politicians who dislike my overture, and may perhaps be so bold as to attempt an answer, that they will first ask the parents of these mortals whether they would not at this day think it a great happiness to have been sold for food at a year old in the manner I prescribe, and thereby have avoided such a perpetual scene of misfortunes as they have since gone through by the oppression of landlords, the impossibility of paying rent without money or trade, the want of common sustenance, with neither house nor clothes to cover them from the inclemencies of the weather, and the most inevitable prospect of entailing the like of greater miseries upon their breed forever.

31   I profess in the sincerity of my heart that I have not the least personal interest in endeavoring to promote this necessary work, having no other motive than the public good of my country, by advancing our trade, providing for infants, relieving the poor, and giving some pleasure to the rich. I have no children by which I can propose to get a single penny, the youngest being nine years old and my wife past childbearing.

~

(3,393 words)

VOCABULARY

importuning (1)	sustenance (1)	prodigious (2)
proficiency (6)	collateral (12)	censure (15)
gibbet (16)	encumbrance (17)	digressed (18)
propagation (25)	parsimony (27)	overture (30)
inclemencies (30)		

THE FACTS

1. On what premise is *A Modest Proposal* based? What is the chief assumption of its argument?

2. Reread paragraph 11. Why do the landlords have "the best title to the children"?

3. Swift's satire redefines children in economic terms. What does this say about his view of the society in which he lived?

4. What does the satire imply about religious feelings in Ireland during Swift's time?

5. Given the state of affairs as the author describes them, is his argument logical? Explain.

THE STRATEGIES

1. What is the effect of the word "modest" in the title?

2. Swift describes people with words like *breeder, dam, carcass,* and *yearling child.* What are the effects of these words?

3. Satire usually provides hints of the true state of things as it proposes its own alternatives. How does Swift hint at the true state of things? Give examples.

4. How would you characterize the tone of this piece?

5. Reread the final paragraph. What is its purpose?

THE ISSUES

1. Do you consider satire an effective way to call attention to social ills? Why or why not?

2. Which paragraphs reveal Swift's real suggestions for improving the economic condition of the Irish? How do these paragraphs fit into the general scheme of Swift's essay?

3. How persuasive do you consider this essay? Would a straightforward essay be more effective? Why or why not?

4. Is Swift's essay simply a literary masterpiece to be studied within its context, or does it have a message for us today?

5. What condition existing in our country today would make an excellent subject for the kind of satire used by Swift? What satirical proposal can you suggest?

SUGGESTIONS FOR WRITING

1. Infer from *A Modest Proposal* the state of life in Ireland during Swift's time. Make specific references to the article to justify your inferences.

2. Using your answer to question 5, write a satirical proposal for curing some aspect of today's society.

I WANT A WIFE

Judy Syfers Brady

Judy Syfers Brady (b. 1937) is a freelance writer who espouses the feminist cause. Born in San Francisco, she studied at the University of Iowa, where she earned a B.F.A. in painting (1962). In 1973, her feminist convictions led her to Cuba to study class relationships as a means of understanding how social change can occur. She is best known for the essay reprinted here, which has become a classic and has been hailed as the feminist manifesto of the modern woman's emancipation from male domination.

Syfers's-Brady's argument is based on the premise that all wives are completely devoted to their husbands and ardently diligent about promoting their husbands' causes and tending to their needs while remaining glamorous and sexual. Once you accept that premise, Syfers's argument makes perfect sense and seems incontrovertible. But more critical reading reveals some flaws in the argument. Pay particular attention to tone.

～

1   I belong to that classification of people known as wives. I am a Wife. And, not altogether incidentally, I am a mother.

2   Not too long ago a male friend of mine appeared on the scene fresh from a recent divorce. He had one child, who is, of course, with his ex-wife. He is obviously looking for another wife. As I thought about him while I was ironing one evening, it suddenly occurred to me that I, too, would like to have a wife. Why do I want a wife?

3   I would like to go back to school so that I can become economically independent, support myself, and, if need be, support those dependent on me. I want a wife who will work and send me to school. And while I am going to school I want a wife to take care of my children. I want a wife to keep track of the children's doctor and dentist appointments. And to keep track of mine, too. I want a wife to make sure that my children eat properly and are kept clean. I want a wife who will wash the children's clothes and keep them mended. I want a wife who is a good nurturant attendant to my children, who arranges for their schooling, makes sure they have an adequate social life with their peers, takes them to the park, the zoo, etc. I want a wife who takes care of the children when they are sick, a wife who arranges to be around when the children need special care, because, of course, I cannot miss classes at school. My wife must arrange to lose time at work and not lose the job. It may mean a small cut in my wife's income from time to time, but I guess I can tolerate that. Needless to say, my wife will arrange and pay for the care of the children while my wife is working.

4   I want a wife who will take care of my physical needs. I want a wife who will keep the house clean. A wife who will pick up after me. I want a wife who will keep my clothes clean, ironed, mended, replaced when need be, and who will see to it that my personal things are kept in their proper place so that I can find what I need the minute I need it. I want a wife who cooks the meals, a wife who is a *good* cook. I want a wife who will plan the menus, do the necessary shopping, prepare the meals, serve them pleasantly, and then do the cleaning up while I do my studying. I want a wife who will care for me when I am sick and sympathize with my pain and loss of time from school. I want a wife to go along when our family takes a vacation so that someone can continue to care for me and my children when I need a rest and change of scene.

5   I want a wife who will not bother me with rambling complaints about a wife's duties. But I want a wife who will listen to me when I feel the need to explain a rather difficult point I have come across in my course of studies. And I want a wife who will type my papers for me when I have written them.

6   I want a wife who will take care of the details of my social life. When my wife and I are invited out by my friends, I want a wife who will take care of the babysitting arrangements. When I meet people at school that I like and

want to entertain, I want a wife who will have the house clean, prepare a special meal, serve it to me and my friends, and not interrupt when I talk about the things that interest me and my friends. I want a wife who will have arranged that the children are fed and ready for bed before my guests arrive so that the children do not bother us. I want a wife who takes care of the needs of my guests so that they feel comfortable, who makes sure that they have an ashtray, that they are passed the hors d'oeuvres, that they are offered a second helping of the food, that their wine glasses are replenished when necessary, that their coffee is served to them as they like it.

7   And I want a wife who knows that sometimes I need a night out by myself.

8   I want a wife who is sensitive to my sexual needs, a wife who makes love passionately and eagerly when I feel like it, a wife who makes sure that I am satisfied. And, of course, I want a wife who will not demand sexual attention when I am not in the mood for it. I want a wife who assumes the complete responsibility for birth control, because I do not want more children. I want a wife who will remain sexually faithful to me so that I do not have to clutter up my intellectual life with jealousies. And I want a wife who understands that *my* sexual needs may entail more than strict adherence to monogamy. I must, after all, be able to relate to *people* as fully as possible.

9   If, by chance, I find another person more suitable as a wife than the wife I already have, I want the liberty to replace my present wife with another one. Naturally, I will expect a fresh, new life; my wife will take the children and be solely responsible for them so that I am left free.

10   When I am through with school and have a job, I want my wife to quit working and remain at home so that my wife can more fully and completely take care of a wife's duties.

11   *My God, who wouldn't want a wife?*

～

(990 words)

VOCABULARY

nurturant (3)   replenished (6)   entail (8)
adherence (8)

THE FACTS

1. According to Syfers-Brady, what dual role does a wife play in the family?
2. What physical needs of the husband does the wife take care of?
3. What does Syfers-Brady say about the sexual expectations and behavior of husbands?
4. According to the author, for what details of a husband's social life are wives responsible?

5. According to the essay, what should happen if a more suitable wife comes along?

THE STRATEGIES

1. What part does hyperbole or exaggeration play in this essay? What flaws do you detect in Syfers-Brady's argument?
2. How would you characterize the tone of this essay?
3. What pronoun does the author use to refer to a "wife"? Why?
4. How and where does the author use italics in this essay? To what effect?
5. What kinds of evidence does the author use to support her argument?

THE ISSUES

1. Do you think Syfers-Brady has fairly characterized the expectations men have of their wives or has she grossly exaggerated?
2. Syfers-Brady's article was first published in 1970. Do you think her criticisms still apply today or has the relationship between men and women changed so much that they are now dated?
3. Would you want a spouse, male or female, as obliging and eager to please as the one Syfers-Brady parodies in her essay? Why or why not?
4. What qualities and characteristics would you expect to find in the perfect spouse?

SUGGESTIONS FOR WRITING

1. Write a similar essay, from a man's point of view, about wanting a husband.
2. Write a serious essay describing your ideal mate.
3. Write an essay telling why you would not want a wife like the one Syfers-Brady has described.

SEX PREDATORS CAN'T BE SAVED

Andrew Vachss

Andrew Vachss (b. 1942) is a New York-based lawyer whose professional focus has been representing children. From 1965 to 1966, he served as a field interviewer and investigator for the Task Force on the Eradication of Syphilis for the U.S. Public Health Service in Ohio. He also worked for numerous community organizations concerned with youth problems. Since 1976, he has been in private law practice and has been a lecturer at numerous law schools in New York. His writing includes a book, Life-Style Violent Juvenile: The Secure Treatment Approach *(1979), and two novels—*Flood *(1985) and* Strega *(1996). He has written numerous magazine articles.*

All of us have seen and read media accounts of violent sexual crimes, which force us to wonder what a fitting punishment for violent offenders should be. In Vachss's essay, a criminal lawyer provides what he considers the only possible solution to violent sex offenses.

$\sim$

1   Westley Allan Dodd was scheduled to be hanged at 12:01 A.M. this morning at the Washington State Penitentiary in Walla Walla. Sentenced to execution for the torture-murder of three boys, Mr. Dodd has refused all efforts to appeal his case. He may not have exhausted his legal remedies, but he has certainly exhausted society's efforts at "rehabilitation."

2   A chronic, calcified sexual sadist, Mr. Dodd stated in a recent court brief, "If I do escape, I promise you I will kill and rape again, and I will enjoy every minute of it."

3   Mr. Dodd's threat demands a response because we know he is not unique. There can be no dispute that monsters live among us. The only question is what to do with them once they become known to us.

4   The death penalty is not a response. Racially and economically biased and endlessly protracted, it returns little for its enormous economic and social costs. Though it is effective—the killer will not strike again—the death penalty is limited to murderers; it will not protect us from rapists and child molesters who are virtually assured of release and who are almost certain to commit their crimes again.

5   If we do not intend to execute sex criminals, does our hope lie in killing their destructive impulses? Mr. Dodd and his ilk are sociopaths. They are characterized by a fundamental lack of empathy. All children are born pure egoists. They perceive their needs to the exclusion of all others. Only through socialization do they learn that some forms of gratification must be deferred and others denied. When a child's development is incomplete or perverted— and child abuse is the most dominant cause in that equation—he or she tends not to develop empathy. There's a missing card, one that cannot be put back in the deck once the personality is fully formed.

6   While early childhood experiences may impel, they do not compel. In the end, evil is a matter of choice. Sociopaths can learn to project a veneer of civilization—for predators, it is part of their camouflage—but they will always lack the ability to feel any pain but their own, pursuing only self-gratification. Not all sociopaths choose sexual violence. For some, the outlet can be political or economic skullduggery. But those for whom blood or pain is the stimulus act no less efficiently and at a terrible and unacceptable cost.

7   Some predatory sociopaths can be deterred. None can be rehabilitated, since they cannot return to a state that never existed. The concept of coercive therapy is a contradiction; successful psychiatric treatment requires participants, not mere recipients. What makes sexual predators so intractable and dangerous is that, as Mr. Dodd candidly acknowledged, they like what they do and intend to keep doing it.

8   The obsession of sexual predators is typified in the case of Donald Chapman, a New Jersey rapist who was released in November after serving 12 years, the maximum for his crime. He underwent continual therapy in prison, and was utterly unaffected by it. He vows to continue to attack women—a threat that reflects his total absorption with sexual torture. As a result of his threat, he sits in his house in Wyckoff, N.J., surrounded by a 24-hour police guard.

9   A 1992 study of 767 rapists and child molesters in Minnesota found those who completed psychiatric treatment were arrested more often for new sex crimes than those who had not been treated at all. A Canadian survey that tracked released child molesters for 20 years revealed a 43 percent recidivism rate regardless of the therapy. The difference between those simply incarcerated and those subjected to a full range of treatment appears statistically negligible. And the more violent and sadistic the offense, the more likely it is to be repeated.

10   Another factor that thwarts rehabilitation is the need for offenders to seek higher and higher levels of stimulation. There is no observable waning of their desires over time: sexual predators do not outgrow their behavior. Thus, while most sadistic sex offenders are not first arrested for homicide, they may well try to murder someone in the future.

11   What about a traditional self-help program? Should we concentrate on raising their self-esteem? Imprisoned predators receive as much fan mail as rock stars. They are courted by the news media, studied by devoted sociologists, their every word treasured as though profound. Their paintings are collected, their poetry published. Trading cards celebrate their bloody passage among us.

12   I recently received a letter from a young woman who gushed that, after a long exchange of letters, she was "granted visiting privileges" with Mr. Dodd and subsequently appeared on "Sally Jessy Raphael" "due to my relationship" with "Wes," who she believes is "sincere." So do I. We simply disagree about the object of his sincerity.

13   Sexual predators are already narcissistic; they laugh behind their masks at our attempts to understand and rehabilitate them. We have earned their contempt by our belief that they can change—by our confusion of "crazy" with "dangerous," and "sick" with "sickening."

14   If we don't intend to execute sexual predators, and we have no treatment, what is our final line of defense? Washington State has a so-called sexual predator law permitting indefinite confinement of sex offenders deemed to be dangerous if released. The law's critics argue that psychiatry has been a woefully inadequate forecaster. Others cite the constitutional problems of imprisonment based on prospective conduct.

15   Recently there has been much discussion of voluntary castration. Such a "remedy" ignores reality. Sexual violence is not sex gone too far, it is violence with sex as its instrument. Rage, sadism and a desire to control or debase others are the driving forces. Castration can be reversed chemically with black-market hormones, and sex murders have been committed by physically castrated rapists. People have been raped by blunt objects. And how do you castrate female offenders?

16   Our response to sexual predators must balance the extent and intensity of the possible behavior with the probability of its occurrence. An ex-prisoner likely to expose himself on a crowded subway may be a risk we are willing to assume. A prisoner with even a moderate probability of sexual torture and murder is not. Such violence is like a rock dropped into a calm pool—the concentric circles spread even after the rock has sunk. More and more victims will be affected.

17   When it comes to sexual violence, the sum of our social and psychiatric knowledge adds up to this: Behavior is the truth.

18   Chronic sexual predators have crossed an osmotic membrane. They can't step back to the other side—our side. And they don't want to. If we don't kill or release them, we have but one choice: Call them monsters and isolate them.

19   When it comes to the sexual sadist, psychiatric diagnoses won't protect us. Appeasement endangers us. Rehabilitation is a joke.

20   I've spoken to many predators over the years. They always exhibit amazement that we do not hunt them. And that when we capture them, we eventually let them go. Our attitude is a deliberate interference with Darwinism—an endangerment of our species.

21   A proper experiment produces answers. Experiments with sexual sadists have produced only victims. Washington State's sexual predator law will surely be challenged in the courts and it may take years before constitutional and criminological criteria are established to incarcerate a criminal beyond his or her sentence.

22   Perhaps no-parole life sentences for certain sex crimes would be a more straightforward answer. In any event, such laws offer our only hope against an epidemic of sexual violence that threatens to pollute our society beyond the possibility of its own rehabilitation.

∽

(1,284 words)

VOCABULARY

rehabilitation (1)	calcified (2)	protracted (4)
ilk (5)	sociopaths (5)	empathy (5)
impel/compel (6)	predators (6)	camouflage (6)
skullduggery (6)	intractable (7)	recidivism (9)
narcissistic (13)	castration (15)	osmotic (18)
appeasement (19)		

THE FACTS

1. What particular crime does the essay analyze? How does this crime differ from other crimes?
2. What are the main causes that lead human beings to become sex offenders? When are these causes developed?
3. According to the author, do sex offenders have a choice in the way they act?
4. According to Allan Dodd's testimony, why will he continue to kill and rape?
5. According to the author, what has research found out about the efficacy of psychiatric treatment for violent sex criminals?

THE STRATEGIES

1. Where does the author place the proposition (main point) of his argument? How does this placement affect his argument?
2. What kinds of argumentative strategies does the author use to support his proposition? Cite specific strategies.
3. What is the point of view from which the essay is written? How effective is this point of view? Give reasons for your answer.
4. How soon in the essay is the audience introduced to the idea that sex offenders cannot be rehabilitated?
5. Where does the author use figurative language? Is this helpful, or does it detract from the seriousness of the topic? For instance, how apt is the analogy of the missing card in paragraph 5?

THE ISSUES

1. Do you agree completely with the author's view that there is no hope for the rehabilitation of sex offenders, or do you believe the author has neglected some aspect of healing? Explain your answer.
2. How important is self-esteem in the socialization of human beings? Provide examples from your own experience to show what happens when individuals lack self-esteem and also examples to show the effect of having self-esteem.
3. What do you think of the idea of castrating violent sex offenders? Does such a policy seem logical, humane, and appropriate for our times? Explain your answers.
4. Why do you think the woman who befriended Allan Dodd while he was in prison could possibly have been attracted to such a man?
5. What is your own solution to the problem of sex predators? How do you propose that we protect society from their heinous crimes?

SUGGESTIONS FOR WRITING

1. Write an essay in which you argue for your own solution to the social menace posed by sex predators. Use facts, statistics, experience, and expert testimony to bolster your proposition. Also, be sure to take into account any opposition to your argument.

2. Write a letter to a person—real or imaginary—who is in prison because of a violent sex crime. Even though the letter will not be mailed, it should reveal your honest thoughts.

DOOLEY IS A TRAITOR

James Michie

James Michie (b. 1927), British poet and translator, is director of The Bodley Head Ltd. publishers, London, and a former lecturer at London University. His works include Possible Laughter *(1959),* The Odes of Horace *(trans. 1964), and* The Epigrams of Martial *(trans. 1973).*

In this humorous poem, a murderer makes a spirited defense against being compelled to fight a war not of his own making.

~

"So then you won't fight?"
"Yes, your Honour," I said, "that's right."
"Now is it that you simply aren't willing,
Or have you a fundamental moral objection to killing?"
5 Says the judge, blowing his nose
And making his words stand to attention in long rows.
I stand to attention too, but with half a grin
(In my time I've done a good many in).
"No objection at all, sir," I said
10 "There's a deal of the world I'd rather see dead—
Such as Johnny Stubbs or Fred Settle or my last landlord, Mr. Syme.
Give me a gun and your blessing, your Honour, and I'll be killing
    them all the time.
But my conscience says a clear no
15 To killing a crowd of gentlemen I don't know.
Why, I'd as soon think of killing a worshipful judge,
High-court, like yourself (against whom, God knows, I've got no
    grudge—
20 So far), as murder a heap of foreign folk.
If you've got no grudge, you've got no joke
To laugh at after."
Now the words never come flowing

Proper for me till I get the old pipe going.
And just as I was poking
Down baccy, the judge looks up sharp with "No smoking,
25   Mr. Dooley. We're not fighting this war for fun.
And we want a clearer reason why you refuse to carry a gun.
This war is not a personal feud, it's a fight
Against wrong ideas on behalf of the Right.
Mr. Dooley, won't you help to destroy evil ideas?"
30   "Ah, your Honour, here's
The tragedy," I said. "I'm not a man of the mind.
I couldn't find it in my heart to be unkind
To an idea. I wouldn't know one if I saw one. I haven't one of my
      own.
35   So I'd best be leaving other people's alone."
"Indeed," he sneers at me, "this defence is
Curious for someone with convictions in two senses.
A criminal invokes conscience to his aid
To support an individual withdrawal from a communal crusade
40   Sanctioned by God, led by the Church, against a godless, churchless
      nation!"
I asked his Honour for a translation.
"You talk of conscience," he said. "What do you know of the
Christian creed?"
45   "Nothing, sir, except what I can read,
That's the most you can hope for from us jail-birds.
I just open the Book here and there and look at the words.
And I find when the Lord himself misliked an evil notion
He turned it into a pig and drove it squealing over a cliff into the
50   ocean,
And the loony ran away
And lived to think another day.
There was a clean job done and no blood shed!
Everybody happy and forty wicked thoughts drowned dead.
55   A neat and Christian murder. None of your mad slaughter
Throwing away the brains with the blood and the baby with the
      bathwater.
Now I look at the war as a sportsman. It's a matter of choosing
The decentest way of losing.
60   Heads or tails, losers or winners,
We all lose, we're all damned sinners.
And I'd rather be with the poor cold people at the wall that's shot
Than the bloody guilty devils in the firing-line, in Hell and keeping
      hot."
65   "But what right, Dooley, what right," he cried,
"Have you to say the Lord is on your side?"
"That's a dirty crooked question," back I roared.
"I said not the Lord was on my side, but I was on the side of the Lord."

70   Then he was up at me and shouting,
      But by and by he calms: "Now we're not doubting
      Your sincerity, Dooley, only your arguments,
      Which don't make sense."
      ('Hullo,' I thought, 'that's the wrong way round.
75   I may be skylarking a bit, but my brainpan's sound.')
      Then biting his nail and sugaring his words sweet:
      "Keep your head, Mr. Dooley. Religion is clearly not up your street.
      But let me ask you as a plain patriotic fellow
80   Whether you'd stand there so smug and yellow
      If the foe were attacking your own dear sister."
      "I'd knock their brains out, mister,
      On the floor," I said. "There," he says kindly, "I knew you were no
          pacifist.
85   It's your straight duty as a man to enlist.
      The enemy is at the door." You could have downed
      Me with a feather. "Where?" I gasp, looking round.
      "Not this door," he says angered. "Don't play the clown.
      But they're two thousand miles away planning to do us down,
90   Why, the news is full of the deeds of those murderers and rapers.
      "Your Eminence," I said, "my father told me never to believe the papers
      But to go by my eyes,
      And at two thousand miles the poor things can't tell truth from lies."
      His fearful spectacles glittered like the moon: "For the last time what
95   right
      Has a man like you to refuse to fight?"
      "More right," I said, "than you.
      You've never murdered a man, so you don't know what it is I won't
100   do.
      I've done it in good hot blood, so haven't I the right to make bold
      To declare that I shan't do it in cold?"
      Then the judge rises in a great rage
      And writes DOOLEY IS A TRAITOR in black upon a page
105 And tells me I must die.
      "What, me?" says I.
      "If you still won't fight."
      "Well, yes, your Honour," I said, "that's right."

                              ∼

                                                    (896 words)

THE FACTS

1. Dooley is an admitted murderer, yet he refuses to fight. Why? What
    is his primary objection to war?

2. How many arguments does the judge use in trying to persuade
    Dooley? What are they, and in what order are they used?

3. Are the judge's arguments logical? Do they appeal to reason and
    evidence or to emotion?

THE STRATEGIES

1. The poem is written in rhyming couplets. What does the rhyme contribute to the poem's tone?
2. How is Dooley characterized? What techniques are used?
3. How is the judge characterized? What techniques are used?

THE ISSUES

1. Evaluate critically the saying "All's fair in love and war." Has this attitude prevailed throughout history? Is it morally valid?
2. What is the poet's point in reflecting a pacifist view through a criminal rather than, say, a minister or a respected private citizen?
3. Do you perceive a difference between killing a rapist who attacked your sister and killing an unknown enemy during war? Explain your answer.

SUGGESTIONS FOR WRITING

1. Analyze the logic in the exchanges between Dooley and the judge. Pinpoint the difference between their respective ways of thinking.
2. Assume that you are in Dooley's position and must argue against your participation in a war. Formulate an argument in your defense.

———— ISSUE FOR CRITICAL ———— THINKING AND DEBATE

HOMELESSNESS

Homelessness would seem to be a nondebatable issue. Everyone is against it, at least in principle. The debate begins not on whether or not homelessness is terrible—everyone agrees that it is—but on its causes. The division of opinion is predictably political: Conservatives, as a whole, blame homelessness on lapses and addictions in the individual; liberals tend to blame economic causes.

Adding to the muddle is the blurry definition of homelessness. Is a person who lives in a government-funded shelter, say a hotel that houses the poor through a system of voucher payments from the state, homeless? Or is the homeless person one with no permanent residence, who sleeps on the street, in a car, or in a bus station? Most government statistics count both groups among the homeless. Yet, government-funded housing, as some critics point out, may be drawing people who had been doubling up with family members into the ranks of the counted homeless. The result is the more the government funds shelters for the homeless, the greater the homeless population seems to grow (Ellickson, Robert, The homelessness muddle, *Public Interest*, April 1990).

Dorothea Lange, Migrant Mother, *Nipomo Valley, 1936. Copyright The Dorothea Lange Collection, Oakland Museum of California, City of Oakland. Gift of Paul S. Taylor.*

How many people are homeless in America? No one knows for sure. Homelessness advocates say there are three million. Other studies have put the figure at around 400 thousand. The Department of Housing and Urban Development estimated in 1994 that there were about "600,000 people on the streets on any given night and that 7 million Americans experienced homelessness at some point in the latter half of the 1980s" (Who's homeless and why, *Christian Century*, September 7, 1994). One recent report claims that nearly one percent of American families, even in a robust economy, will go through episodes of homelessness within a year. (The Urban Institute: available on-line at http://www.urban.org/news/pressrel/pr000201.html). These figures—whether high or low—are difficult to trust because they are always based on different methods of counting. Added to the roster of the un-countable are the so-called "invisible homeless," who have no residence of their own but live in makeshift arrangements with relatives.

The two essays in this section typify the debate about homelessness. The first essay, *Homeless: Expose the Myths,* by a conservative writer, argues that the individual, not the system or the economy, is to blame for homeless-ness. Having spent a night in New York's Grand Central Station, the au-thor reports that he saw no dispossessed yuppies, only dysfunctional people. The other point of view is represented by a columnist who exam-ines the complexities behind the homeless problem and shows us an ex-ample, Greg, who ended up being homeless because of a change in Boston's rent control laws. Here, the author lays the blame at the doorstep of a badly run government bureaucracy and an out-of-kilter economy. The art work in this chapter offers a concrete view of the problem. On page 600, a homeless migrant worker, holding a child, sends a look of anguished de-spair from her tired eyes. The photo on page 602 makes the viewer wonder what the thoughts of this homeless woman will be when she wakes up form her nap.

Which view is right? It is impossible to say. Certainly, one can imagine a scenario where an individual, even a family, can fall on hard times that result in homelessness. Yet, anyone who lives in a city also knows from plain ob-servation that many dysfunctional, tormented souls haunt the streets. Why homelessness exists in such an affluent country as ours may be impossible to explain, but one thing is certain: It should not exist.

HOMELESS: EXPOSE THE MYTHS

Joseph Perkins

Joseph Perkins (b. 1960) is a regular columnist for The San Diego Union-Tribune.

According to the author, the homeless people out on our streets do not suffer from poverty as much as they suffer from mental illness or substance abuse.

∼

1 Back in the days when the homeless problem was in vogue, I decided to in-vestigate for myself whether economic policies were to blame for the grow-ing legions of street people who seemed to have invaded America's cities.

Homeless woman napping by shopping cart. Copyright © David Doody/Index Stock Imagery.

2   So I spent a night at New York's Grand Central Station, which was a favorite gathering place for many of the city's homeless.

3   I quickly discovered that contrary to the news reportage at that time, the
homeless were not "people like you and me" who simply had fallen upon
hard times. I saw no yuppies in threadbare suits sifting through the trash
bins. I saw no middle-class families huddled on benches.

4   What I did see were dozens upon dozens of pitiable men and women who
were suffering from some dysfunction or another. Some were afflicted with
mental problems. Others were drug or alcohol abusers. Clearly their homelessness owed not to economic dislocation, but simply to self-destruction.

5   It is now eight years later, yet homeless advocates continue to promulgate
the myth that homelessness is primarily an economic problem rather than a
mental health and substance-abuse problem.

6   Among the more prominent purveyors of this misinformation is the National Law Center on Homelessness and Poverty. It notes that 40 percent of
poor people spend two-thirds of their income on housing. "This means that
for growing millions of Americans, a missed paycheck, a health crisis or a
high utility bill brings the threat of homelessness," the lawyers assert.

7   The law center advocates were less than happy with President Clinton's
recent executive order calling for a homeless plan to be developed within
nine months. They saw no reason why he shouldn't have given his impri-
matur to a plan that they already have drawn up.

8   So what is the lawyers' solution? Have the federal government turn over
former military bases and other vacant property to the homeless. Create a

jobs program for them. Give them income assistance. Offer them day care and health care.

9   It's the typical liberal response to a problem—spend more money, create programs. They miss the boat. In 1963, there were as many poor people as there are today. Yet, in 1963, the only homeless people were the occasional bums and hobos.

10   Two things happened between 1963 and 1993 to give us today's homeless population: All but the most dangerous patients were disgorged from state mental hospitals, and illegal drug use exploded.

11   This is born out by a 1992 survey conducted by the U.S. Conference of Mayors. The mayors found that 28 percent of the homeless population in the cities were mentally ill and 41 percent substance abusers.

12   This means that at least seven of 10 street people have either a mental or chemical problem. Even if the economy were booming, jobs were plentiful and affordable housing abundant, these unfortunates probably would still be out on the streets.

13   By linking homelessness to poverty, advocates obscure the real root of the problem. If we really wanted to help the homeless, we would pay far more attention to their mental health and substance abuse problems.

~

(518 words)

VOCABULARY

vogue (1)	legions (1)	dysfunction (4)
promulgate (5)	purveyors (6)	imprimatur (7)
disgorged (10)		

THE FACTS

1. How did the author find out whether government policies were really to blame for the growing street people population—as often claimed by liberals?

2. What was the author's first discovery? How long did this discovery take?

3. What about the National Law Center on Homelessness and Poverty annoys the author?

4. According to the author, what happened between 1963 and the present to change the statistics concerning the homeless population?

5. What is the author's answer to our desire to help the homeless?

THE STRATEGIES

1. In your view, how does the brevity of the essay affect its ability to convince? Why or why not?

2. Why does the author word his proposition as a conditional clause ("If we really wanted to help the homeless . . .")? What might an alternate wording be?

3. How does the author maintain coherence between paragraphs 10 and 11?

4. What does the word *myths* refer to in the title of the essay?

5. How would you describe the author's style of writing?

THE ISSUES

1. The author says that in 1963, the only homeless people were occasional bums and hobos. How are bums and hobos different from today's homeless?

2. How much influence do economic policies have on people's standard of living?

3. What is the author's most compelling support for his proposition?

4. In your opinion, which is more effective—the liberals' response of spending more money on programs for the homeless or the conservatives' response of tending to their mental illnesses? Give reasons for your stance.

5. What is your opinion of the suggestion that military bases be turned into housing for the poor? What other solution would you propose?

SUGGESTIONS FOR WRITING

1. Write an essay in which you propose a solution to the problem of begging that is so prevalent in our cities today. Support your argument with facts, experience, expert testimony, and logic.

2. Write an essay in which you describe a plan of action should you suddenly find yourself homeless and foodless. Base your plan on reality, not fantasy.

THE HOMELESS LACK A POLITICAL VOICE, BUT NOT AMERICAN IDEALS

Matt Lynch

Matt Lynch writes a column for University Wire.

Exactly who are the homeless and how did they get that way? The answer you get depends on whom you ask. Conservatives maintain that the homeless mainly consist of people with addiction problems or those who are mentally ill. Liberals reply that anyone can become homeless during difficult economic times, that elements of bad luck and bad timing are often responsible for homelessness. These two points of view have a radical effect not only on our attitudes toward the homeless, but on government policy. If we believe that people become homeless because of bad economics, we are inclined to help. If we think that addiction is to blame, we are more inclined to punish. This writer demonstrates that the stereotypes about the homeless are often off the mark and hollow.

~

1   Greg is a conservative's dream.

2   He wakes up every morning before 6:00 A.M., showers, eats breakfast, and dons a suit and tie. He goes to his office job every day, puts in more than forty hours per week, saves his money and doesn't drink. He gets back in time for dinner, watches the news and is in bed by 10:00 P.M.

3   Greg is not his real name. Homeless shelter volunteers are not permitted to give out the names of those staying in the facility, for fear of discrimination. It's a fear that is well-founded.

4   The prevailing attitudes toward the homeless in America are not particularly sympathetic. Most people view them as a minor annoyance; their only exposure to the homeless comes when someone on the street bothers them for change. Many would characterize them as a bunch of degenerates and alcoholics, fully deserving of their unfortunate fate.

5   If they would only get themselves together and get a job like everyone else, most say, they wouldn't find themselves in this predicament.

6   But it's a bit more complicated than that.

7   Homelessness in the wealthiest nation on earth is caused by a variety of factors and they are not always the result of repeated bad judgment by those who are homeless. For Greg, it came from the skyrocketing rents and housing prices in Boston, which did away with rent-control laws in 1997.

8   For others, it comes from an untimely lay-off and a lack of close relatives to take them in. Some, like a former Boston College basketball player and account coordinator whose story appeared in a recent Boston Globe column, just made one mistake—in his case, incurring the wrath of the I.R.S.

9   Walking into a homeless shelter in Cambridge, Massachusetts, the shelter where Greg sleeps, is not setting foot into the armpit of society. It's more akin to walking into a hospital waiting room: residents play cards, watch the news or read magazines. At dinnertime, they are as orderly and polite as anyone else.

10   The shelter is dry; anyone who is intoxicated is turned away at the door. Fights and rude language are no more common than in the rest of society. Residents are early to bed and early to rise, and strive to look as presentable as everyone else.

11   For most at this shelter, homelessness is not a career. They have fallen on hard times, and are trying to pull themselves up by their bootstraps. Anyone who buys into the American work ethic, particularly politicians, should be proud.

12   Yet efforts to help the homeless remain woefully under-funded, and the only legislation that deals with homelessness—the oft-amended McKinney-Vento Bill of 1987—addresses the effects rather than the causes of the problem. The National Coalition for the Homeless called for $4.3 billion for their efforts in the 2002 budget, an amount it says will still leave many of its programs without adequate funding. Bush requested just over half that amount for efforts to help the homeless.

13   In today's political climate, this is not surprising. Requests for homeless programs are seen as bleeding-heart-liberal garbage, further evidence of the liberals' tax-and-spend nature. They do not understand that efforts to help the homeless are compatible with the historical, mythical allure of America: the opportunity to start over, to begin anew. It brought colonists here as the continent was being settled, and it brought them to the frontier as the country grew.

14   But the frontier is gone; those with economic troubles can no longer escape to the West. Greg will probably escape homelessness through his shelter's progressive work-contract program, but he is one of the lucky ones.

15   Today's economy is struggling, and most homeless shelters do not have enough beds to go around. Not all of them have the resources for the kind of work-contract program Greg takes part in. Few can offer the necessary treatment for diseases that sometimes contribute to homelessness, namely mental illness and alcoholism.

16   Unfortunately, the problem will probably not be addressed until stereotypes disappear, until those begging on the street are no longer taken to represent the group as a whole, until people understand that those who are homeless often appear no different than anyone else. Most strive for the same goals and possess the same virtue, but do not have the same luck.

17   Politicians must change their attitudes, as well. They do deal with the effects of homelessness; no one enjoys hearing stories of the homeless freezing to death in winter months, and usually there are places for them to stay for some period of time. But the politicians need to get over their instinctive reactions against funding programs to address the roots of homelessness and helping people out of it.

18   The cause is not a helpless one; it has simply never been given the resources it needs and deserves. Republicans and Democrats alike must recognize that though the homeless lack a strong political voice in this country, most do not lack its ideals.

∽

(824 words)

VOCABULARY

prevailing (4)	degenerates (4)	woefully (12)
mythical (13)	allure (13)	stereotypes (16)

THE FACTS

1. What is it that makes Greg a conservative's dream? Do you agree that he is a conservative's dream? Why or why not?

2. What is the prevailing attitude toward homelessness, according to the author? What is your own attitude?

3. What is the reason for Greg's homeless condition? What other reasons, besides irresponsibility and drug abuse, can you cite for the homelessness of certain people?

4. What institution does Greg's shelter resemble? What factors contribute to the resemblance?

5. According to the author, programs to help the homeless reflect the American Dream. What is the American Dream, and how can government programs help the homeless achieve it?

THE STRATEGIES

1. What is the author's thesis, and where is it stated?

2. How does the author try to capture your attention at the start of his essay? How successful is he? What other effective introduction can you suggest?

3. What figures of speech does the author use to enliven his language? Name at least two and explain the meaning of each.

4. In paragraph 13, what effect does the expression "historical, mythical allure" create? Explain why you think the author used this phrase.

5. Why does the author insist that real help for the homeless cannot come until we get rid of stereotyping? What does stereotyping do to retard the general cause of helping the homeless?

THE ISSUES

1. What plan for helping people like Greg would you propose if you were mayor of your city or governor of your state? How would you propose to fund your plan?

2. What is the best method of demolishing established stereotypes— whether of the homeless, of certain ethnic groups, or of class levels?

3. In paragraph 12, the author mentions that current legislation deals with the effects, rather than the roots, of homelessness. What effects does he have in mind? What is the difference between cause and effect in this case?

4. How is the pursuit of the American Dream different today from, say, two centuries ago? What can we do to help the homeless pursue the American Dream?

5. Do you agree with the notion that anyone in a homeless shelter has the right to live there anonymously in order to avoid discrimination? Explain your answer.

SUGGESTIONS FOR WRITING

1. Write a proposal in which you suggest practical ways of helping the homeless re-establish themselves.

2. Write an essay in which you describe how a friend, relative, or acquaintance lost all possessions and the living conditions that person was forced to accept. If help was offered, mention that as well.

———— STUDENT CORNER ————

I

Final Draft

People Out on a Limb

Antoinette Poodt, Furman University

A disease plagues our people. This disease can be seen in every great city and far beyond that. As one walks the streets, it is all over the place. What is it? The Homeless! The main cause of the homeless is poverty. In 1993, according to the U.S. Bureau of the Census, more than one million Americans fell into poverty. Despite the increasing economic growth and the decrease in unemployment, economic gaps are increasing. In 1993, the top fifth of all households held approximately 48% of the national income, whereas the share of national income going to the bottom fifth of the households (3.6%) was the lowest ever recorded. So it is evident for all to see that, although there has been increasing economic growth, little of it has gone to the poor. We are becoming a polarized nation, with a great divide developing between the "haves" and the "have nots."

Who is responsible for this, and who should bear the burden is an issue that is unclear to many. Although the responsibility is unclear, evidently the gap in economic status between households can be blamed on some of the following factors: insufficient minimum wage, insufficient affordable housing, and inadequate government benefits. In today's economy, due to the astronomically high cost of a college education, many people that come from homeless families cannot afford to attend college.

Poodt 2

Moreover, children growing up in such an environment are not stimulated enough to attain the higher standards needed for scholarships or grant money. As a result, the jobs chiefly available to them are minimum wage jobs. From January 1981 through March 1990, the minimum wage was frozen at $3.35 an hour, while the cost of living increased by 48%. Then in 1990 the government decided to raise the minimum wage to $4.25 an hour, which hardly made up for the ground lost during the inflation of the '80s. Even now the cost of living has risen since 1991, and it has taken six years for the minimum wage to be raised to $5.25 an hour.

Government benefits, another side of the issue, have taken more cuts in the past three years than in the past 25 years. Rent increases have also risen immensely in the past few years, making the issue hit closer to home than many ever imagined. As a college student myself, who is earning below the poverty line, cannot afford housing on her own, and receives little or no government benefits, I can empathize with the homeless in some way. When it comes right down to it, the only difference between me and a homeless person is that I have a family who cares.

It is easy for me to sit in judgment when I see a "bum" on the side of the street, or for me to think to myself that he should get a job, because I am not in his position. When I think that I, or someone close to me, could easily be in that position, then I am not so quick to judge. The burden of the cross is unclear to me, but I do believe that if one is blessed enough to have a roof over one's head, one should want to help people who are less fortunate. I have always thought that America was the land of equal opportunity where anyone could do anything. This was why

Poodt 3

the issue of the homeless was so difficult for me to understand. Now I know that the issue is more complicated than I ever realized. As I see it, the plight of the homeless is they lack hope and the chance of achieving their dreams. Should society have sympathy for them and would people feel differently if they walked in the shoes of the homeless? I think so!

How I Write

Writing has always been a challenge for me, and it is usually very difficult for me to get started. Once I get the introduction down, however, the rest of the paper usually flows. Before I begin writing, I gather information about my topic, which I get from the Internet or the library. Then I go to my computer and begin typing. I cannot write in pen or pencil, and then type a paper. Instead I type as I write. This is easier for me because it is simple to make corrections as I go along. When writing a paper or essay, I usually begin with a story, quote, or statement that will grab the reader's attention. Then, taking into account the audience and depending on the type of writing I am to do, I follow with an outline covering specific points. If the paper is a story about me, or something I am very familiar with, I do not follow an outline.

After I write the first draft, I begin with a spell check followed by a computer grammar check. Then I print out the paper and do at least three to five revisions. Once I think the paper is good, I give it to someone else to read. I feel that I do much better on a paper when I spend a few days revising it instead of writing, revising, and turning it in all in one day. When I leave a paper for a while, and then go back to look at it, I see new things that I can do to improve it. Once I have made all the revisions, I read it over one more time and then turn it in.

How I Wrote This Essay

I began this paper by doing research to get some facts on the homeless. It took me a while to figure out what spin I was going to take. I actually started this essay three or four times before I found the spin I wanted to use. Once I got started on the one I wanted, the essay flowed for me. After a very rough first draft, I revised the paper six times. Then I had my mom read over it to make any last-minute changes. While doing my corrections, my improvements were more instinctive than for any specific reason. When I thought I could not change the paper any more, I printed out the last copy.

My Writing Tip

One word of wisdom I can give to fellow writers is to learn to type on a computer as they write. Being a college student, I do not know where I would find the time if I had to write, say in pen or pencil, and then type. Corrections are so much quicker and easier to make when you can see them on the computer screen. It saves so much time, leading to less stress and hence better writing.

Another tip I would give is not to follow a cookie-cutter style of writing. Find your style, become comfortable with it, and use it whenever you write. Do not let one teacher discourage your writing ability because he or she doesn't like your style. We all have our own style. Write in your own style and your paper will turn out better than if you try to write like everyone else. In other words, trust your own personality.

CHAPTER WRITING ASSIGNMENTS

1. Write an essay discussing the idea that religion is a conditioned reflex.
2. Analyze the logic in *Dooley Is a Traitor*.
3. Construct an argument for or against competitiveness in business.
4. Should a belief in creation be taught along with Darwin's theory of evolution? Write an essay arguing for or against this question.
5. Write an essay suggesting ways of achieving sexual equality.

TERM PAPER SUGGESTIONS

Investigate the major arguments related to any one of the following subjects:

a. The influence of the church in our country today
b. Animal experimentation
c. Better care for the poor
d. Increased emphasis on physical fitness
e. Careful monitoring of the ecosystems on our planet
f. Equal rights for women (or another minority) in our country
g. Maintaining ethnic identities in a pluralistic environment
h. Smoke-free overseas flights
i. The need for a national health program that allows for long-term health care

WRITING ASSIGNMENTS FOR A SPECIFIC AUDIENCE

1. Write an essay arguing for a campus completely free from smoking. Your audience consists of the readers of your college paper. State your proposition clearly and support it with convincing evidence about the hazards of secondhand smoke.
2. Write an essay in which you argue that movies often portray minorities inaccurately or offensively. Be specific with your facts and examples.

COLLABORATIVE WRITING PROJECT

This assignment requires a minimum of three students, each researching one aspect of homelessness in our cities: (1) homelessness due to job loss, (2) homelessness due to illness or some other catastrophe, or (3) homelessness due to laziness or irresponsibility or drug and alcohol abuse. The bulk of the research should represent specific statistics and examples. The three students should make copies of their research for distribution to each other. After the members of your group have read each other's work, you should come up with a group paper offering solutions to the problem, arguing that as citizens of a civilized and compassionate democracy, we have a sacred duty to end homelessness.

16

Combining the Modes

EDITORS' COUNSEL

What Combining the Modes Does

The rhetorical modes are an idealization. In the rough-and-tumble writing of the everyday world, they exist only in hit-or-miss practice. It is possible to find a paragraph or even an entire essay that is written strictly in one mode; it is far more typical to find essays that blend the modes rather than observe them faithfully. Writing, a creative art, is nothing if not unpredictable.

Here are two examples that illustrate what we mean. The first is a paragraph that we would say was developed by *illustration*. It opens with the traditional topic sentence (underlined), which it then supports with a series of examples.

> <u>Considerations of what makes for good English or bad English are to an uncomfortably large extent matters of prejudice and conditioning.</u> Until the eighteenth century it was correct to say "you was" if you were referring to one person. It sounds odd today, but the logic is impeccable. *Was is* a singular verb and *were* a plural one. Why should *you* take a plural verb when the sense is clearly singular? The answer—surprise, surprise—is that Robert Lowth[1] didn't like it. "I'm hurrying, are I not?" is hopelessly ungrammatical, but "I'm hurrying, aren't I?"—merely a contraction of the same words—is perfect English. *Many is* almost always a plural (as in "Many people were there"), but not when it is followed by *a*, as in "Many a man was there." There's no inherent reason why these things should be so. They are not defensible in terms of grammar. They are because they are.
>
> —Bill Bryson, *The Mother Tongue: English and How it Got That Way*

Here, however, is an example of a mixed-mode paragraph that is even more typical of everyday writing:

causal
analysis

> English grammar is so complex and confusing for the one very simple reason that its rules and terminology are based on Latin—a language with which it has precious little in common. In Latin,

---

[1] An amateur grammarian whose influental book, *A short Introduction to English Grammar* (1762), enshrined many of the stupid rules of English usage still observed today.

illustration   to take one example, it is not possible to split an infinitive. So in English, the early authorities decided, it should not be possible to split an infinitive either. But there is no reason why we shouldn't, *comparison*   any more than we should forsake instant coffee and air travel because they weren't available to the Romans. Making English grammar conform to Latin rules is like asking people to play baseball using the rules of football. It is a patent absurdity. But once *argument*   this insane notion became established grammarians found themselves having to draw up ever more complicated and circular arguments to accommodate the inconsistencies. As Burchfield notes in *The English Language,* one authority, F. Th. Visser, found it necessary to devote 200 pages to discussing just one aspect of the present participle. That is as crazy as it is amazing.

—Bill Bryson, *The Mother Tongue: English and How it Got That Way*

The writer begins with a causal analysis, gives an illustration, makes a comparison, and then develops an argument.

This is exactly how writers actually write. They treat the rhetorical modes the way a baker might treat a cookie cutter. The object is to produce cookies, not exalt the cutter. It is the same with the rhetorical modes—they exist to make writing easier for beginners. When you're no longer a beginner, you will discard them.

When to Combine the Modes

Combining modes is a tactic many writers follow, especially for long and complex subjects. You should use a combination of modes only when you feel comfortable with it and when your subject is a particularly demanding one that requires a complex form. If you're ranging far afield on an unfamiliar topic, you may not wish to follow any strict pattern and might prefer to improvise as you go along. This is the ideal time to combine the rhetorical modes.

How to Use Combined Modes

The key in writing a mixed-mode essay is to stick to the point and use ample transitions. Essays that are written in a combination of modes have a tendency to either drift from the point or to be herky-jerky rather than smooth. Writers overcome these tendencies by using the techniques of paragraph writing covered in chapter 6 (now would be a good time to review this material). If you use transitions to guide the reader from one point to the next and if you faithfully stick to your announced topic, your mixed-mode essays will read as smoothly as anything you've ever written in any single pattern.

Here is an example of a mixed-mode paragraph that sticks to the point. The writer is discussing the implements that the Arawak Indians, who lived in Jamaica at the time of Columbus, used in their daily lives. He begins with a description, moves to a process, and ends with a definition. He is able to do all of these things without losing the reader because his focus is so tight and his transitions skillful.

> Apart from earthen pots and other utensils, the main items of furniture were hammocks and wooden stools. The hammock was an Indian invention (even the original name, which was *hamac*), one which was not known in Europe before the discovery of the West Indies. These hammocks were made either of cotton string "open-work," or of a length of woven cotton cloth, sometimes dyed in bright colours. Jamaica was well known at that period for the cultivation of cotton, and much of the women's time was spent spinning and weaving it. In fact Jamaica supplied hammocks and cotton cloth to Cuba and Haiti for some time after those islands had been occupied by Spain, and the Spaniards themselves had sail-cloth made in Jamaica. Because of this one of the many suggested origins of the name *Jamaica* attempts to link it with the Indian word for hammock and to prove that it means "land of cotton." The name Jamaica is of great interest. Some of the early Spanish historians, substituting X for J as they often did, write the name *Xaymaca*, but it also appears in its present form in a work published as early as 1511. Columbus called the island *St. Jago* (Santiago), but as with the other islands of the Greater Antilles, the Indian name has survived the Spanish. It is commonly thought that Xaymaca in the Arawak language meant "land of springs," but since the discoverers do not give the meaning of the name (as they do in the case of various place-names in Haiti) it is possible that the meaning had already been forgotten by the Indians themselves.
>
> —Clinton V. Black, *The Story of Jamaica*

Notice, for example, the repetition of the word *hammocks*, the variant forms of *Jamaica*, and the writer's use of the transitional sentence "The name Jamaica is of great interest." These little transitional touches are designed to nudge the reader along the writer's line of thought.

To sum up, if you do not now do it, eventually you will find yourself commonly writing essays that conform more to the mixed mode pattern than to any other. The rhetorical modes are useful tools for the beginning writer, but less so for the veteran. As you make your way through school, you, too, will become a practiced writer who has outgrown them.

—————— EXAMPLES ——————

SHREW—THE LITTLEST MAMMAL

Alan DeVoe

Alan DeVoe (1909–1955) wrote many naturalist essays that were much admired by his readers. He also contributed widely to numerous magazines, among them the American Mercury, Audubon, *and* Readers' Digest. *Additionally, he was the author of numerous books, including* Phudd Hill *(1937),* Down to Earth *(1940), and* This Fascinating Animal World *(1951).*

DeVoe's description of the tiniest mammal, the shrew, tells us how this fren-
zied little beast got its reputation for ferocity. The shrew, having features similar to those of a mouse, is so rabid about pursuing its one mission in life—to
eat—that it will attack animals twice its size. DeVoe uses paragraphs of different modes to portray the life cycle of this tiny creature whose nature is
driven by a giant appetite.

～

1   The zoological Class to which we human beings belong is the Mammalia.
There has been some dispute as to whether we possess immortal souls and
the capacity for a unique kind of intellection, but we do possess unquestionably the " . . . four-chambered heart, double circulatory system, thoracic cavity separated from abdominal cavity by muscular diaphragm, and habit of
bearing the young alive and nursing them at the breast" which classically establish our membership in that group of warm-blooded animals which are
guessed to have come into being on the planet some hundred-odd million
years ago.

2   It is today a large and various group, this mammalian kindred. With some
of our fellow-mammals it is not hard to feel relationship: with apes, for instance, or with the small sad-eyed monkeys that we keep for our beguilement
as flea-bitten captives in our pet shops. But with others of the group our tie is
less apparent; and the reason, often enough, is disparity of size and shape. It
is such disparity, no doubt, that prevents our having much fellow-feeling for
the hundred-ton sulphur-bottomed whales that plunge through the deep waters of both Pacific and Atlantic, though whales' blood is warmed as ours is,
and the females of their kind have milky teats; and likewise it is doubtless in
part because we have two legs and attain to some seventy inches of height
that we do not take as much account as otherwise we might of the little animal that is at the opposite end of the mammal size-scale: the little four-footed
mammal that is rather smaller than a milkweed pod and not as heavy as a cecropia cocoon.

3   This tiniest of mammals is the minute beast called a shrew. A man need go
to no great trouble to look at it, as he must to see a whale; he can find it now
in the nearest country woodlot. Despite its tininess a shrew is still after a fashion a relative of ours; and on that account, even if on no other, should merit a
little knowing.

4   In the narrow twisting earth-burrow dug by a mouse or a mole the least of
the mammals is usually born. Its fellows in the litter may number four or five,
and they lie together in the warm subterranean darkness of their tiny nest-
chamber in a little group whose whole bulk is scarcely that of a walnut. The
infant shrew, relative of whales and elephants and us, is no more than a
squirming pink speck of warm-fleshed animal aliveness. Totally defenseless
and unequipped for life, it can only nuzzle the tiny dugs of its mother, wrig-
gle tightly against its brothers to feel the warmth of the litter, and for many
hours of the twenty-four lie asleep in the curled head-to-toes position of a minuscule foetus.

5   The baby shrew remains a long time in the birth-chamber. The size of even an adult shrew is very nearly the smallest possible for mammalian existence, and the young one cannot venture out into the world of adult activity until it has almost completely matured. Until then, therefore, it stays in the warm darkness of the burrow, knowing the universe only as a heat of other little bodies, a pungence of roots and grasses, a periodic sound of tiny chittering squeakings when its mother enters the burrow after foraging-trips, bringing food. She brings in mostly insects—small lady-beetles whose brittle spotted wing-covers must be removed before they can be eaten, soft-bodied caterpillars, ants, and worms. The young shrew, after its weaning has come about, acquires the way of taking this new food between its slim delicate forepaws, fingered like little hands, and in the under-earth darkness nibbles away the wing-covers and chitinous body-shells as adroitly as a squirrel removes the husk from a nut.

6   When at last the time comes for the young shrew to leave its birthplace, it has grown very nearly as large as its mother and has developed all the adult shrew-endowments. It looks, now, not unlike a mouse, save that its muzzle is more sharply pointed, but a mouse reduced in size to extreme miniature. The whole length of its soft-furred little body is only a fraction more than two inches, compared to the four-inch length of even the smallest of the white-footed woods-mice; its tail is less than half as long as a mouse's. The uniquely little body is covered with dense soft hair, sepia above and a paler buffy color underneath—a covering of fur so fine and close that the shrew's ears are nearly invisible in it, and the infinitesimal eyes are scarcely to be discerned. The shrew's hands and feet are white, smaller and more delicate than any other beast's; white also is the underside of the minute furry tail. The whole body, by its softness of coat and coloring and its tininess of bulk, seems far from kinship with the tough strong bodies of the greater mammals. But it is blood-brother to these, all the same; warm blood courses in it; the shrew is as much mammal as a wolf. It sets forth, with its unparalleledly tiny physical equipments, to live as adventurous a life as any of its greater warm-blooded relatives.

7   The life-adventure of Man, "the medium-sized mammal," is shaped by such diverse motives and impulses that it is difficult to say what may be the most powerful of the driving urges that direct it. In the life-adventure of the littlest mammal, the shrew, the driving urge is very plain and single: it is hunger. Like hummingbirds, smallest of the aves, this smallest of the mammals lives at a tremendous pitch of nervous intensity. The shrew's little body quite literally quivers with the vibrance of life-force that is in it; from tiny pointed snout to tailtip the shrew is ever in a taut furor of aliveness. Its body-surface, like a hummingbird's, is maximally extensive in relation to its minimal weight; its metabolism must proceed with immense rapidity; to sustain the quivering nervous aliveness of its mite of warm flesh it must contrive a food-intake that is almost constant. It is possible on that account to tell the shrew's life-story almost wholly in terms of its feeding. The shrew's life has other ingredients, of course—the seeking of its small mate, the various rituals of copulating and

sleeping and dung-dropping and the rest, that are common to all mammal-lives—but it is the process of feeding that is central and primary, and that is the distinguishing preoccupation of the littlest mammal all its days.

8   The shrew haunts mostly moist thick-growing places, the banks of streams and the undergrowth of damp woods, and it hunts particularly actively at night. Scuttling on its pattery little feet among the fallen leaves, scrabbling in the leaf-mould in a frenzy of tiny investigation, it looks ceaselessly for food. Not a rodent, like a mouse, but an insectivore, it seizes chiefly on such creatures as crickets, grasshoppers, moths, and ants, devouring each victim with nervous eagerness and at once rushing on with quivering haste, tiny muzzle incessantly a-twitch, to look for further provender.

9   Not infrequently the insects discoverable in the shrew's quick scampering little sallies through the darkness are inadequate to nourish it, so quick is its digestion and so intense the nervous energy it must sustain. When this is the case, the shrew widens its diet-range, to include seeds or berries or earthworms or any other sustenance that it can stuff with its little shivering forepaws into its tiny muzzle. It widens its diet to include meat; it becomes a furious and desperate carnivore. It patters through the grass-runways of the meadow-mice, sniffing and quivering; it darts to the nest of a deer-mouse. And presently, finding deer-mouse or meadowmouse, it plunges into a wild attack on this "prey" that is twice its size. The shrew fights with a kind of mad recklessness; it becomes a leaping, twisting, chittering, squeaking speck of hungering fury. Quite generally, when the battle is over, the shrew has won. Its thirty-two pinpoint teeth are sharp and strong, and the wild fury of its attack takes the victim by surprise. For a little while, after victory, the shrew's relentless body-needs are appeased. For a little while, but only a little; and then the furry speck must go pattering and scuttling forth into the night again, sniffing for food and quivering with need.

10   That is the pattern of shrew-life: a hunting and a hungering that never stops, an endless preoccupied catering to the demands of the kind of metabolism which unique mammalian smallness necessitates. The littlest mammal is a mammal in all ways; it breathes and sleeps and mates and possibly exults, as others do; but chiefly, as the price of unique tininess, it engages in restless never-ending search for something to eat.

11   The way of a shrew's dying is sometimes curious. Sometimes, of course, it dies in battle, when the larger prey which it has tackled proves too strong. Sometimes it dies of starvation; it can starve in a matter of hours. But often it is set upon by one of the big predators—some fox or lynx or man. When that happens, it is usually not the clutch of fingers or the snap of the carnivorous jaws that kills the shrew. The shrew is usually dead before that. At the first instant of a lynx's pounce—at the first touch of a human hand against the shrew's tiny quivering body—the shrew is apt to shiver in a quick violent spasm, and then lie still in death. The littlest of the mammals dies, as often as not, of simple nervous shock.

~

(1,616 words)

VOCABULARY

beguilement (2)	disparity (2)	minuscule (4)
chitinous (5)	adroitly (5)	infinitesimal (6)
discerned (6)	diverse (7)	impulsions (7)
extensive (7)	contrive (7)	provender (8)
exults (10)		

THE FACTS

1. About which zoological fact is the author sure? About which element is he less sure? Why is he so much more sure about one than the other?

2. Where is the shrew usually born? What does this tell us about shrew parents?

3. In terms of its impulses, how does the shrew differ from its other mammal relatives? What causes this difference?

4. If the shrew can't find enough insects to feed its hunger, what will it do?

5. If insects and vegetation are not available, what will the shrew do to get the food it so badly needs to stay alive? What attitude does the shrew convey? How do you view this attitude?

THE STRATEGIES

1. This essay reveals the use of more than one rhetorical mode. What other modes are used? Try to name these modes paragraph by paragraph.

2. What dominant impression of the shrew did you receive from this essay?

3. What is the purpose of the quotation in the opening paragraph? What, if anything, does it add to the essay?

4. Of what help is paragraph 10 as you learn about the shrew?

5. Why does the author sprinkle specialized terms throughout the essay (e.g., *cecropia, cocoon, chitinous body shells*)? How do these terms affect the author's style?

THE ISSUES

1. The author declares a kinship among whales, monkeys, shrews, and humans. Of the nonhuman mammals, which do you feel closest to? Why? Of all animals, which one would you prefer to have as a pet? Why?

2. Do you agree with the author that because the shrew is related to us, we should know something about this mammal? Give reasons for

your answer. What other reasons are there to encourage us to learn more about animals?

3. If a woman is called a "shrew," what is meant by the label? What connection can you see between this metaphor and the tiniest mammal?

4. Do you think that laboratory experiments on the mammalian shrew would be justified if the purpose were to benefit humans?

5. What is the largest mammal? Where have you seen this mammal other than in pictures? How do you react toward it?

SUGGESTIONS FOR WRITING

1. Describe the most interesting animal you have ever observed. If needed, use more than one rhetorical mode for this assignment.

2. Choose one of the following creatures and write an essay describing in what ways it is superior to human beings: lion, tiger, cat, dog, eagle, snake, or ant.

CRICKET

Robert MacNeil

Robert MacNeil (1930) is a Canadian-born writer and television news commentator. He is the co-anchor and executive editor of the popular MacNeil/Lehrer News Hour. *He is also the co-author of* The Story of English *(1986), a companion volume to the PBS television series of the same name.*

Even readers who have never had the slightest interest in the game of cricket will be entertained by this sprightly explanation of an old English tradition.

~

1 I played soccer, hockey, and Canadian football badly. I was twenty-fourth man on a twenty-four-man football team. Once, out of pity, in the dying light of a raw November day, I was sent in for one play in one game. My hands were cold and I dropped the pass thrown to me. Here beginneth and here endeth the football career. But I had a football sweater with a number, and afterwards, with muscles tingling from a hot shower, I could affect the elastic swagger of the real stars, entering the dining hall glowing and hungry. Those were the days when to be cheered for glories on the football field seemed the pinnacle of human bliss.

2 I was better at long-distance running and scraped on to the school ski team. But I found my spiritual home, my lifetime apogee of athletic prowess, and a hint of the adulation real school sports stars enjoy—playing cricket.

3   That quintessentially English game was, even in the 1940s, as foreign to Canada as to the United States. There were a few adult cricket clubs peopled by expatriate Brits, retired officers, diplomats, and West Indians. And it was played by a handful of boys' private schools like Ashbury—still living in some colonial autumn; staffed by British masters exiled by the war and trying to perpetuate the ideals of British public schooling.

4   Cricket was the most conspicuous anachronism, perverse in cutting a small number of Canadian boys off from their national summer sport, which was baseball. As I later found out, it is a game widely ridiculed by North Americans. You have only to name the fielders (*wicket-keeper, slips, cover, square-leg, mid-off, mid-on, silly-mid-off,* and *silly-mid-on*) to start them laughing. And try explaining the rules!

5   "Well, you see, there are two home plates called wickets and you have two batters called *batsmen in* up at once . . ."

6   "Two batters go up at once?"

7   "No, the batsmen are *in* not *up.* And there are two pitchers, called *bowlers,* who *bowl* six balls from either end . . ."

8   "Two pitchers at the same time?"

9   "No, they take turns. When one of the *batsmen* hits the ball, he can run or not as he chooses . . ."

10   "He hits the ball and he doesn't have to run?"
      "And there are no foul balls, he can hit it in any direction he likes . . ."
      "No foul balls. How do they get him out?"
      "If he's run out or caught on a fly like baseball, or if he lets the ball hit his *wicket.*"
      "What's the *wicket?*"

11   "That's three sticks stuck in the ground side by side, with two small turned pieces of wood called *bails* laid across the top. If the ball knocks them off, the *batsman* is out. He is also out if he puts his leg or another part of his body in front of the *wicket.* It's called *lbw, leg before wicket.*"

12   "How do you score runs?"

13   "When the *batsman* receiving the *bowling* hits a ball away from a fielder, he runs *down the pitch* to the other end—"

14   "What's the *pitch?*"
      "It's the playing area between the *stumps.*"
      "What in hell are the *stumps?*"

15   "It's another name for the sticks that make up the *wicket.* If the batsman steps out of his *crease,* the *wicket-keeper* can get him out by using the ball to knock the *bails* off. It's called being *stumped.*"

16   "So if the guy who hits the ball runs, what happens to the other batter?"

17   "He runs to the opposite end. If they have time, they run twice or three times. Each time is a run. But if he hits the ball over the boundary on the ground, it's an automatic four runs. If he hits it over in the air, it's six runs."

18   "How many times do they get up to bat?"
      "Just once in each *innings.*"
      "You mean each inning,"

"No, an *innings* is one."

"How many *innings*?"

19   "Usually only one to a match. Sometimes two, especially if the match lasts more than one day."

20   "More than one day? How long does it take?"

"Usually all day."

"All day, for Christ's sake!"

"Sure, it usually takes the morning to get one side out and the afternoon for the other."

"All morning! How long can one batter stay up?"

21   "As long as he can avoid getting out. Often a good batsman can make a hundred runs or more, a *century*. Sometimes the best batsman can stay in till the end of the game and is never out."

22   "What do you mean, never out?"

23   "One man is always *not out*. They say he *carried his bat*."

"That's an awful long time!"

"Oh, they break for lunch."

"In the middle of the game they have lunch?"

"Sure, and they break again for tea in the middle of the afternoon."

"They drink tea in the middle of the game?"

24   "Yes, with little sandwiches and cakes, and in June bowls of strawberries and cream. Now let me explain the scoring . . . If the bowler bowls six balls— it's called an *over*—with no runs, it's called a *maiden over*. They say he *bowled a maiden over*—"

25   "Come on! I'm getting out of here!"

"What's wrong? Americans played cricket long before they played baseball."

26   "We played that pansy game? I don't believe it. No wonder they kicked the British out. *Bowled a maiden over*? Jesus!"

27   All these terms used to be perfectly familiar to Americans, who played cricket long after the hated British had left. Baseball did not really take over until the middle of the nineteenth century, and the first hardball used was a cricket ball, made smaller. Cricket is the oldest bat-and-ball team game still in existence, popular since the time of Henry VIII.

28   Except for the accelerated version played on television, cricket is the most leisurely of games—chess on grass, someone called it. People watch as much to see the subtle duel between batsman and bowler, each with a repertoire of fine points to display, as to know who wins.

29   Curiously, the game which appears so effete to Americans is disparaged by some English intellectuals; they consider cricket the preserve of hearty dolts and village bumpkins. In fact, it is one English sport with no class associations. The game took root all over the British Empire, yet the poet of Empire, Rudyard Kipling, sneered at cricketers as "the flannelled fools at the wicket."

30   For all that, it is great fun to play. It is often rough: you catch balls harder than a baseball, sometimes hit only a few feet away, in your bare hands—no gloves for fielders. I broke two fingers that way. But it is also a game of nu-

ances. The flat willow and ash bat can be used for a cunning variety of drives, snicks, cuts, glances, pulls, and blocks. To watch a skilled batsman defend his wicket for hours at a time, testing himself against a variety of bowling—fast, slow, spin—is both exciting and soothing.,

31   I loved the atmosphere, usually a beautifully-mown ground surrounded by trees at a distance. I wasn't much good as a batsman, tending under the tension to revert to a baseball swing. But I could bowl and in my last year won the school trophy for the best bowler. Like baseball, that meant getting the biggest number of outs for the smallest number of runs scored against you.

32   My hour came in the annual match between the school team called the First XI, and the staff, a tradition started when all the staff were Englishmen who played cricket. Now, in 1949, only a few leftover and nearly retired Englishmen still did. The faculty filled out the team with Canadians who came goodnaturedly but weren't all as talented. The staff had as captain the deputy headmaster, a rock-hard Brit named A. D. Brain. He had a square, chunky body. . . When he entered a classroom, his black gown billowing and his pipe puffing, he looked so solid you felt he could have walked through the wall without effort.

33   Brain taught French, Latin, and Greek, and was the master for the sixth form. He was also the school administrator and chief executioner. Boys called to his office quaked outside because he decided whether an offence merited a caning and, if it did, he administered it. In some schools, like Rothesay, senior boys and any master could beat a boy. Ashbury was more progressive— only Brain had the painful duty, but he was thought to relish it.

34   Brain always looked at me, I thought, with contempt, because I was Canadian and, therefore, inferior. He was the kind of Englishman whose condescension makes Canadians hate the British, yet fawn on them. Even when I became a sixth-former, prefect, captain of the cadet corps, and other dizzying honours in the tiny scale of school life—the icy, pale blue eyes in the square, Henry VIII face strongly implied that he thought me a shallow, trivial, lazy fellow. Doubtless my own guilt was an ingredient, but he bore down on me very heavily. When I gave up Latin for German, he behaved as though I had abandoned all pretence of seriousness. He was a bully, psychologically and physically. In class one day he asked me a question, standing to answer, I began, "Well, sir—"

35   Brain snapped out, "Don't patronise me, boy!"

I had no idea what he meant, and when he waved me to go on, I said again: "Well, sir—"

"Don't patronise me, I say!" his voice rising in exasperation.

"Well, sir—"

36   This time he bellowed. "Are you being impertinent MacNeil, or deliberately obtuse? I told you not to patronise me."

37   It dawned on me that my starting with *well* offended him, and when I finally answered without, he, huffed and squared his shoulders impatiently and went on. But he never explained.

38   His classes were dreaded; no one whispered for the hour. Today's schoolboys would call him a *pain in the ass.* We called him, less colourfully, a *prick.*

39   This was the man who presented himself on the playing field, first in the batting order for the masters' side on the day of the cricket match. It was a very fine day in May. I felt extraordinarily loose and detached about my bowling. When I delivered a ball, I was confident it would go exactly where I intended, as though some invisible hand were guiding my arm.

40   The entrance of the batsman is one of cricket's highly theatrical moments. It is usually a long walk in his leg pads, with his bat tucked under his arm, adjusting the cotton gloves that have rubber guards to protect the backs of the fingers. Some batsmen scamper in half-apologetically; some walk confidently but modestly; some swagger, some prance. The opposing team size them up psychologically by their gait. Brain came in like General Patton taking command of an army. You could imagine a band playing "Land of Hope and Glory." His vanity about cricket was legendary. He had confided to us (he confided every year) that "if my fingers had been a quarter of an inch longer, I would have been one of the best medium-pace bowlers in England." And, we embroidered, if another part of his anatomy had been a quarter of an inch longer, it would have been doubled.

41   His boast was in my mind as he took his place at the wicket. I too was a medium-pace bowler. Brain made another ostentatious show *of taking his guard,* asking the umpire to signal when his bat was in the position he wanted relative to the bowler's approach. The batsman then makes a mark in the dust, and that is where he takes his stand to receive the bowling. Brain elaborated the exercise, as cocky batsmen will, slapping his pads, adjusting his gloves, looking around in a leisurely and disdainful way to see how the fielders were placed and, with a final "harrumph!" indicated he was ready.

42   Our captain was a thin, funny French Nicaraguan named Henrique Dreyfus. As I walked back to begin my runup to bowl the first ball, Dreyfus whispered, "A dollar if you bowl him out first ball!" I laughed and turned. Brain was a very competent batsman and we all expected him to be in there for hours, knocking up a respectable thirty or forty runs before lunch. Brain expected it too.

43   He dispatched my first few balls smartly, earning three runs. I gave the next ball no particular thought. The invisible hand guided it to a perfect length, exactly between his two outside stumps, with a slight spin that made it break inwards. He put his front leg out in the proper fashion, made the conventional blocking stroke, and bit the ball smartly—straight into my hands. The umpire shouted "Out" and he was out—*caught and bowled,* in the cricket expression: both by me. He was totally astonished. So was I. He straightened up, muttered "Extraordinarily good ball," and walked off the field—the very long walk back—humiliated. My teammates confined their jubilation behind the traditional polite clapping, and Dreyfus said, "Oh, tough luck, sir." But the air was electric with joy. The bastard who terrorized us all was vanquished. "Thy right hand, O Lord, hath dashed in pieces the enemy."

44   I had a blissful moment and then, in the long wait for another batsman, felt some regret for the man whose moment of glory had been snuffed out. Suddenly I knew him: not the monster I believed, but a competent man, not more, hiding his inadequacies by making himself haughty and feared. Life has never dealt me as pure a moment since. I took six more wickets in that match. Is there a life after high school? I must have doubted it that day.

45   I have played cricket only twice in the nearly forty years since then, but have cherished the game and its absurd language: its *googlies* (balls with deceptive spin), *sticky wickets* (damp pitches that take spin bowling), and *stone-walling* (batsmen who play extra-defensively). *Sticky wicket* has become a general metaphor for an awkward situation and *stone-walling* for being uncooperative. Many cricket expressions developed a wider currency: *hit him for six, off his own bat, stumped, up stumps,* and the Englishman's ultimate protest over bad sportsmanship or unfairness: *It isn't cricket,* or *That's hardly cricket, old boy*!

46   In her book *Edward VIII*, Frances Donaldson uses one: "King George, who is normally represented as being completely bowled out at this time by his sense of his own inadequacy. . ."

47   If you define yourself by the language you acquire as you enter different spheres, cricket was another piece of my self-definition.

~

(2,454 words)

VOCABULARY

apogee (2)	quintessentially (3)	perpetuate (3)
conspicuous (4)	anachronism (4)	perverse (4)
dolts (29)	bellowed (36)	obtuse (36)
scamper (40)	legendary (40)	ostentatious (41)
dispatched (43)	jubilation (43)	

THE FACTS

1. Write a brief description of *cricket*. Where did this game originate?

2. According to the author, why did North Americans ridicule cricket? After reading the essay, what is your reaction to this sport? Do you find it ridiculous or not? Explain your answer.

3. Who are the speakers in the dialogue of paragraphs 5 to 26? What purpose does the dialogue serve?

4. What surprising fact does the American find out about cricket? What is his reaction?

5. How would you describe the author's victory over Brain, described in paragraphs 32 to 44? What was your reaction to this victory?

THE STRATEGIES

1. How many rhetorical modes can you identify in this essay? Try to label the paragraphs with the appropriate modes Hint: Paragraphs 1 and 2 are narration.

2. In paragraph 1, the author uses the verbs "endeth" and "beginneth"—verb forms used frequently in the King James Version of the *Bible* or in Shakespeare's works. In paragraph 43, he quotes a passage from one of the Old Testament prophets. Why do you think the author used this style?

3. How does the author feel about the surroundings in which cricket is usually played? Where do Americans find similar surroundings?

4. What kind of language does the author use to describe Brain? How appropriate is this language, and how does it add or detract from Brain's portrait?

5. In what way has cricket had a lasting effect on the English language? What other sports have had a similar effect?

THE ISSUES

1. Why are some games quintessentially American, English, French, or Russian or some other nationality? Is it important for every nation to have its own quintessential sport? What does such a sport contribute to the national character?

2. How should students handle a person in authority like Brain? How would you have handled him?

3. How are nonathletic students looked upon in your school? Can students still be popular and take on positions of leadership if they do not participate in any sport? What is your view of the role of sports in college?

4. Do you believe that people are defined by the language they acquire through sports or other spheres (see the final paragraph of the essay)? If so, what sport or sphere in your life has helped define you? Explain your answer.

5. Have you ever felt the satisfaction of vanquishing an enemy? If yes, what were the circumstances and how did you feel afterwards? If no, is there a person you wished you could vanquish? What were the circumstances?

SUGGESTIONS FOR WRITING

1. Using MacNeil's essay as a model, write a description of your favorite sport. Use any combination of rhetorical modes to make the essay lively and genuine.

2. Write an essay in which you describe an incident in which a bully received his or her deserved punishment.

ONCE MORE TO THE LAKE

E. B. White

Elwyn Brooks White (1899–1985) was one of the wittiest and most admired observers of contemporary American society. As a member of The New Yorker *magazine staff, he wrote a number of essays for the section called "Talk of the Town"; some of these essays have been collected in* The Wild Flag *(1946) and* Writings from The New Yorker *(1991). With James Thurber, White wrote* Is Sex Necessary? *(1929). His other well-known works include* One Man's Meat *(1942),* Here Is New York *(1949), and two beloved children books,* Stuart Little *(1945) and* Charlotte's Web *(1952).*

This essay ends with a bang, not a whimper. The writer tackles what might seem at first glance a humdrum subject—an annual vacation trip to a lake—and describes in evocative and lovely prose the carefree summer days he spent hiking and fishing with his son. Then, at the very end, the trap is sprung and the true meaning of the essay is revealed.

~

August 1941

1   One summer, along about 1904, my father rented a camp on a lake in Maine and took us all there for the month of August. We all got ringworm from some kittens and had to rub Pond's Extract on our arms and legs night and morning, and my father rolled over in a canoe with all his clothes on; but outside of that the vacation was a success and from then on none of us ever thought there was any place in the world like that lake in Maine. We returned summer after summer—always on August 1 for one month. I have since become a salt-water man, but sometimes in summer there are days when the restlessness of the tides and the fearful cold of the sea water and the incessant wind that blows across the afternoon and into the evening make me wish for the placidity of a lake in the woods. A few weeks ago this feeling got so strong I bought myself a couple of bass hooks and a spinner and returned to the lake where we used to go, for a week's fishing and to revisit old haunts.

2   I took along my son, who had never had any fresh water up his nose and who had seen lily pads only from train windows. On the journey over to the lake I began to wonder what it would be like. I wondered how time would have marred this unique, this holy spot—the coves and streams, the hills that the sun set behind, the camps and the paths behind the camps. I was sure that the tarred road would have found it out, and I wondered in what other ways it would be desolated. It is strange how much you can remember about places

like that once you allow your mind to return into the grooves that lead back. You remember one thing, and that suddenly reminds you of another thing. I guess I remembered clearest of all the early mornings, when the lake was cool and motionless, remembered how the bedroom smelled of the lumber it was made of and of the wet woods whose scent entered through the screen. The partitions in the camp were thin and did not extend clear to the top of the rooms, and as I was always the first up I would dress softly so as not to wake the others, and sneak out into the sweet outdoors and start out in the canoe, keeping close along the shore in the long shadows of the pines. I remembered being very careful never to rub my paddle against the gunwale for fear of disturbing the stillness of the cathedral.

3   The lake had never been what you would call a wild lake. There were cottages sprinkled around the shores, and it was in farming country although the shores of the lake were quite heavily wooded. Some of the cottages were owned by nearby farmers, and you would live at the shore and eat your meals at the farmhouse. That's what our family did. But although it wasn't wild, it was a fairly large and undisturbed lake and there were places in it that, to a child at least, seemed infinitely remote and primeval.

4   I was right about the tar: it led to within half a mile of the shore. But when I got back there, with my boy, and we settled into a camp near a farmhouse and into the kind of summertime I had known, I could tell that it was going to be pretty much the same as it had been before—I knew it, lying in bed the first morning smelling the bedroom and hearing the boy sneak quietly out and go off along the shore in a boat. I began to sustain the illusion that he was I, and therefore, by simple transposition, that I was my father. This sensation persisted, kept cropping up all the time we were there. It was not an entirely new feeling, but in this setting it grew much stronger. I seemed to be living a dual existence. I would be in the middle of some simple act, I would be picking up a bait box or laying down a table fork, or I would be saying something and suddenly it would be not I but my father who was saying the words or making the gesture. It gave me a creepy sensation.

5   We went fishing the first morning. I felt the same damp moss covering the worms in the bait can, and saw the dragonfly alight on the tip of my rod as it hovered a few inches from the surface of the water. It was the arrival of this fly that convinced me beyond any doubt that everything was as it always had been, that the years were a mirage and that there had been no years. The small waves were the same, chucking the rowboat under the chin as we fished at anchor, and the boat was the same boat, the same color green and the ribs broken in the same places, and under the floorboards the same fresh water leavings and débris—the dead helgramite, the wisps of moss, the rusty discarded fishhook, the dried blood from yesterday's catch. We stared silently at the tips of our rods, at the dragonflies that came and went. I lowered the tip of mine into the water, tentatively, pensively dislodging the fly, which darted two feet away, poised, darted two feet back, and came to rest again a little farther up the rod. There had been no years between the ducking of this dragonfly and the other one—the one that was part of memory. I looked at the boy, who was

silently watching his fly, and it was my hands that held his rod, my eyes watching. I felt dizzy and didn't know which rod I was at the end of.

6   We caught two bass, hauling them in briskly as though they were mackerel, pulling them over the side of the boat in a businesslike manner without any landing net, and stunning them with a blow on the back of the head. When we got back for a swim before lunch, the lake was exactly where we had left it, the same number of inches from the dock, and there was only the merest suggestion of a breeze. This seemed an utterly enchanted sea, this lake you could leave to its own devices for a few hours and come back to, and find that it had not stirred, this constant and trustworthy body of water. In the shallows, the dark, water-soaked sticks and twigs, smooth and old, were undulating in clusters on the bottom against the clean ribbed sand, and the track of the mussel was plain. A school of minnows swam by, each minnow with its small individual shadow, doubling the attendance, so clear and sharp in the sunlight. Some of the other campers were in swimming, along the shore, one of them with a cake of soap, and the water felt thin and clear and unsubstantial. Over the years there had been this person with the cake of soap, this cultist, and here he was. There had been no years.

7   Up to the farmhouse to dinner through the teeming dusty field, the road under our sneakers was only a two-track road. The middle track was missing, the one with the marks of the hooves and the splotches of dried, flaky manure. There had always been three tracks to choose from in choosing which track to walk in; now the choice was narrowed down to two. For a moment I missed terribly the middle alternative. But the way led past the tennis court, and something about the way it lay there in the sun reassured me; the tape had loosened along the backline, the alleys were green with plantains and other weeds, and the net (installed in June and removed in September) sagged in the dry noon, and the whole place steamed with midday heat and hunger and emptiness. There was a choice of pie for dessert, and one was blueberry and one was apple, and the waitresses were the same country girls, there having been no passage of time, only the illusion of it as in a dropped curtain—the waitresses were still fifteen; their hair had been washed, that was the only difference—they had been to the movies and seen the pretty girls with the clean hair.

8   Summertime, oh, summertime, pattern of life indelible with fade-proof lake, the wood unshatterable, the pasture with the sweetfern and the juniper forever and ever, summer without end; this was the background, and the life along the shore was the design, the cottages with their innocent and tranquil design, their tiny docks with the flagpole and the American flag floating against the white clouds in the blue sky, the little paths over the roots of the trees leading from camp to camp and the paths leading back to the outhouses and the can of lime for sprinkling, and at the souvenir counters at the store the miniature birch-bark canoes and the postcards that showed things looking a little better than they looked. This was the American family at play, escaping the city heat, wondering whether the newcomers in the camp at the head of the cove were "common" or "nice," wondering whether it was true

that the people who drove up for Sunday dinner at the farmhouse were turned away because there wasn't enough chicken.

9   It seemed to me, as I kept remembering all this, that those times and those summers had been infinitely precious and worth saving. There had been jollity and peace and goodness. The arriving (at the beginning of August) had been so big a business in itself, at the railway station the farm wagon drawn up, the first smell of the pine-laden air, the first glimpse of the smiling farmer, and the great importance of the trunks and your father's enormous authority in such matters and the feel of the wagon under you for the long ten-mile haul, and at the top of the last long hill catching the first view of the lake after eleven months of not seeing this cherished body of water. The shouts and cries of the other campers when they saw you, and the trunks to be unpacked, to give up their rich burden. (Arriving was less exciting nowadays, when you sneaked up in your car and parked it under a tree near the camp and took out the bags and in five minutes it was all over, no fuss, no loud wonderful fuss about trunks.)

10   Peace and goodness and jollity. The only thing that was wrong now, really, was the sound of the place, an unfamiliar nervous sound of the outboard motors. This was the note that jarred, the one thing that would sometimes break the illusion and set the years moving. In those other summertimes all motors were inboard; and when they were at a little distance, the noise they made was a sedative, an ingredient of summer sleep. They were one-cylinder and two-cylinder engines, and some were make-and-break and some were jump-spark, but they all made a sleepy sound across the lake. The one-lungers throbbed and fluttered, and the twin-cylinder ones purred and purred, and that was a quiet sound, too. But now the campers all had outboards. In the daytime, in the hot mornings, these motors made a petulant, irritable sound; at night in the still evening when the afterglow lit the water, they whined about one's ears like mosquitoes. My boy loved our rented outboard, and his great desire was to achieve single-handed mastery over it, and authority, and he soon learned the trick of choking it a little (but not too much), and the adjustment of the needle valve. Watching him I would remember the things you could do with the old one-cylinder engine with the heavy flywheel, how you could have it eating out of your hand if you got really close to it spiritually. Motorboats in those days didn't have clutches, and you would make a landing by shutting off the motor at the proper time and coasting in with a dead rudder. But there was a way of reversing them, if you learned the trick, by cutting the switch and putting it on again exactly on the final dying revolution of the flywheel, so that it would kick back against compression and begin reversing. Approaching a dock in a strong following breeze, it was difficult to slow up sufficiently by the ordinary coasting method, and if a boy felt he had complete mastery over his motor, he was tempted to keep it running beyond its time and then reverse it a few feet from the dock. It took a cool nerve, because if you threw the switch a twentieth of a second too soon you would catch the flywheel when it still had speed enough to go up past center, and the boat would leap ahead, charging bull-fashion at the dock.

11   We had a good week at the camp. The bass were biting well and the sun shone endlessly, day after day. We would be tired at night and lie down in the accumulated heat of the little bedrooms after the long hot day and the breeze would stir almost imperceptibly outside and the smell of the swamp drift in through the rusty screens. Sleep would come easily and in the morning the red squirrel would be on the roof, tapping out his gay routine. I kept remembering everything, lying in bed in the mornings—the small steamboat that had a long rounded stern like the lip of a Ubangi, and how quietly she ran on the moonlight sails, when the older boys played their mandolins and the girls sang and we ate doughnuts dipped in sugar, and how sweet the music was on the water in the shining night, and what it had felt like to think about girls then. After breakfast we would go up to the store and the things were in the same place—the minnows in a bottle, the plugs and spinners disarranged and pawed over by the youngsters from the boys' camp, the Fig Newtons and the Beeman's gum. Outside, the road was tarred and cars stood in front of the store. Inside, all was just as it had always been, except there was more Coca-Cola and not so much Moxie and root beer and birch beer and sarsaparilla. We would walk out with the bottle of pop apiece and sometimes the pop would backfire up our noses and hurt. We explored the streams, quietly, where the turtles slid off the sunny logs and dug their way into the soft bottom; and we lay on the town wharf and fed worms to the tame bass. Everywhere we went I had trouble making out which was I, the one walking at my side, the one walking in my pants.

12   One afternoon while we were at that lake a thunderstorm came up. It was like the revival of an old melodrama that I had seen long ago with childish awe. The second-act climax of the drama of the electrical disturbance over a lake in America had not changed in any important respect. This was the big scene, still the big scene. The whole thing was so familiar, the first feeling of oppression and heat and a general air around camp of not wanting to go very far away. In midafternoon (it was all the same) a curious darkening of the sky, and a lull in everything that had made life tick; and then the way the boats suddenly swung the other way at their moorings with the coming of a breeze out of the new quarter, and the premonitory rumble. Then the kettle drum, then the snare, then the bass drum and cymbals, then crackling light against the dark, and the gods grinning and licking their chops in the hills. Afterward the calm, the rain steadily rustling in the calm lake, the return of light and hope and spirits, and the campers running out in joy and relief to go swimming in the rain, their bright cries perpetuating the deathless joke about how they were getting simply drenched, and the children screaming with delight at the new sensation of bathing in the rain, and the joke about getting drenched linking the generations in a strong indestructible chain. And the comedian who waded in carrying an umbrella.

13   When the others went swimming my son said he was going in, too. He pulled his dripping trunks from the line where they had hung all through the shower and wrung them out. Languidly, and with no thought of going in, I

watched him, his hard little body, skinny and bare, saw him wince slightly as he pulled up around his vitals the small, soggy, icy garment. As he buckled the swollen belt, suddenly my groin felt the chill of death.

~

(2,884 words)

VOCABULARY

incessant (1)   desolated (2)   primeval (3)
transposition (4)   tentatively (5)   pensively (5)
undulating (6)   unsubstantial (6)   cultist (6)
indelible (8)   sedative (10)   imperceptibly (11)
premonitory (12)

THE FACTS

1. How old was White when he first went to the lake with his father? How old was he when he took his own son there?

2. What illusion did White begin to sustain on hearing his own son sneaking out to go down to the boat on the lake?

3. What changes did the author notice in the road leading from the lake to the farmhouse? What did this change say about the passing of time?

4. What difference did the author note between the way guests arrived at the lake in his own boyhood days and their arrival now?

5. What experience precipitated White's realization that time had passed, that he was no longer young, that he was mortal?

THE STRATEGIES

1. Aside from description, what other mode of development is implicitly part of the structure of this essay? What is the purpose of holding back the true meaning of the essay until the final paragraph?

2. In paragraph 2, White writes that he "was sure that the tarred road would have found it [the lake] out." What is odd about the phrasing of this sentence? What do you think White was trying to achieve in phrasing it that way?

3. Examine the author's boyhood recollections of the lake (paragraph 2). To which of our senses do his details and images appeal?

4. Examine the description of the fishing boat in paragraph 5. How does White manage to convey such a vivid picture of the boat?

5. In what part of his body did White feel the chill of death? In the context of the essay, why is this such an appropriate place?

THE ISSUES

1. In paragraph 2, why does White refer to the lake as a "holy spot"? What is the connotation of this term, given that the place was not a religious shrine? What, in your life, would be a similar spot? Give reasons for your choice.

2. The author states that he missed the "middle track" of the road leading up to the farmhouse for dinner. Try to imagine yourself in a similar situation forty years hence. What vehicles of transportation, not yet commonly used, might invade your road then?

3. What is the social implication of the words *common* and *nice* in paragraph 8? Have times changed, or are these distinctions still made?

4. Not everyone would have reacted in the way the author describes his own reaction in the final sentence of the essay. What might be another realistic reaction?

5. What are some clear signs in your life to indicate that you are not immortal? What are your feelings about these signs?

SUGGESTIONS FOR WRITING

1. Write a mixed-mode essay about anything you really like to do. Be specific in your details.

2. Write an essay in any mode about your favorite author.

——— ISSUE FOR CRITICAL ——— THINKING AND DEBATE

SEPARATION OF CHURCH AND STATE

The First Amendment to the Constitution declares that "Congress shall make no law respecting an establishment of religion, or prohibiting the free exercise thereof. . . .," a clause whose wording is the nub of the disagreement between the pro and con sides in the debate about the separation of church and state. One side believes that the clause was intended to ban the establishment of a national religion, nothing else. The other holds that the clause means that the state must stay out of religion.

Over the years, the courts have more or less interpreted this passage as requiring a strict separation between the images and icons of religion and the conduct of business by the state. Typical of the court's attitude is a decision handed down by the Alabama Supreme Court on November 18, 2002, which ruled that a 10-ton monument engraved with the Ten Commandments and installed in an Alabama state judicial building had to come down because it promoted the Christian religion. To many religious people, this decision once

Elderly woman with ProLife sign.
Copyright © Stephanie Maze/CORBIS.

again confirmed their fears that the country is drifting toward atheism. To others, it is one in a line of many court decisions that confirm the bedrock principle requiring separation of church and state. Believers, however, should take heart in this odd fact: In spite of all the uproar, Congress continues to maintain a House Chaplin at a cost of $277,000 per year, and sessions of Congress open and close with a prayer.

The debate sputters on to this day, with no end in sight. It has yielded close examination of the wording of the First Amendment clause, with entire essays devoted to analyzing the meaning of the word "respecting." Of all the areas of disagreement over the Constitution or anything else, this one stands to be the most polarizing and inflammatory, with neither side giving an inch.

The writers in this debate approach the muddle almost obliquely. James Watkins points out that law and religious morality cannot be separated no matter how hard we struggle to keep them apart. Richard W. Whitrock focuses his argument on the recent California court ruling that decided that the Pledge of Allegiance was unconstitutional. The student essay by Adam Winkler offers yet another opinion on the matter. Two photos focus on specific social problems that often blur the line between church and state. On page 636, we see a woman carrying a poster pleading the cause against abortion, and on page 637, we see a political demonstration in favor of gay rights.

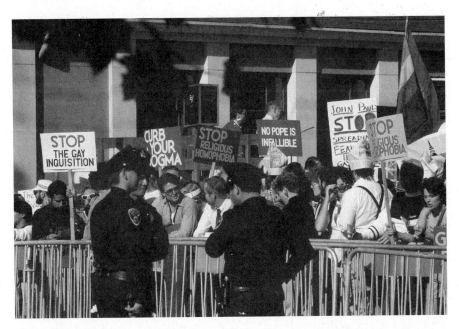

Gay rights demonstration for John Paul II. Copyright © Allen Russell/Index Stock Imagery.

SEPARATING SIDES IN THE CHURCH-STATE CONFLICT

James Watkins

James Watkins writes a newspaper column for University Wire.

~

1   The "separation of church and state" debate is as strong as it's ever been in Texas. Right now, the battle is raging as to whether the Ten Commandments should be displayed on the grounds of the Capitol. Just last January, there was a rally there to advocate the removal of the monument. The Atheist Community of Austin and the Austin chapter of Americans United for the Separation of Church and State were represented at the event.

2   Unfortunately, there is a lot of confusion when people debate this issue. Both sides are fighting for what they believe in, and these beliefs are based upon different interpretations of the First Amendment and what religion really means.

3   The side of this debate that advocates a "separation of church and state" believes that the establishment clause of the First Amendment mandates this. Therefore, the government cannot favor one religion over another when laws are passed and when symbols are displayed in the public sector. They also reference Thomas Jefferson as coining the phrase "wall of separation between church and state" in a letter he wrote to the Danbury Baptist Association.

4   Another important distinction this side makes is that one can separate morality and religion. Therefore, when reason is used to determine what a law should be—such as the illegality of murder—this is not a religious belief, and therefore "separation of church and state" is not violated.

5   There are some serious fallacies to this reasoning. For instance, when Jefferson mentions the "wall of separation" in his letter, he is not advocating that the government be neutral in all religious matters. He uses this metaphor to illustrate that the government should allow us to worship in whatever manner we see fit without intrusion. This is what the Danbury Baptists were concerned about when they wrote him in 1808. However, he is not saying that there should not be religious symbols and principles in the public sector of this country.

6   Another inconsistency is that it is impossible to separate religion and morality. The belief that murder is wrong—as well as every other belief—is a religious belief. In fact, a religion is simply a system of beliefs. Therefore, Atheism, Christianity, Judaism and Islam are all religions.

7   Consequently, it is impossible for the government to be religiously "neutral" in all matters. Whenever a symbol is displayed in the public sector, a religious belief is conveyed. The Ten Commandments displayed on the Capitol grounds convey religious beliefs. However, religious beliefs are also displayed when the picture of a witch is displayed at a public school on Halloween. Whenever a law is created, society adopts a standard that is rooted in religion. When the Supreme Court legalized abortion in 1973, a religious belief was abandoned while another replaced it.

8   This debate is a battle of ideas and we—as a nation—must determine which religious principles are to be taught in the public schools and conveyed in our laws and court rulings.

9   Unfortunately, the nuts and bolts of these principles can be difficult to determine in a nation as diverse as the United States. It was a lot easier when the country was primarily of one religious faith. But now, with surging diversity, it can be very difficult to come to any kind of a consensus about tough issues like abortion or whether or not gays should be allowed to marry.

10   So this is the challenge we, as Americans, face. Let's continue to debate these tough issues and grow as a nation. Hopefully, we will grow in a positive way as we adopt principles that work for the betterment of the nation and its people.

～

(614 words)

VOCABULARY

advocate (1)   mandates (2)   fallacies (4)
metaphor (4)   conveyed (6)   diverse (8)
surging (8)   consensus (8)

THE FACTS

1. Where was this essay published? Is this area fairly representative of the debate concerning separation of church and state? What specific issue caused the essay to be written?

2. Who coined the phrase "wall of separation between church and state"? Why is this statement subject to contrary interpretations? How does the author interpret the phrase?

3. What is another popular interpretation of this phrase not mentioned by the author? What is your own interpretation?

4. The author believes that because every moral decision is a religious one, it is impossible for the government to be religiously neutral. What examples does he use to support his view? How might one disagree with the author?

5. What is the author's basis for stating that when the picture of a witch is displayed at a public school, a religious belief is exhibited?

THE STRATEGIES

1. What is the author's thesis and where is it stated? What proof, if any, does the author offer in support of his thesis?

2. From which belief is the entire argument developed? What does the author think we must do, given his belief?

3. In what paragraph does the author begin to demonstrate his opposition to people who want to make a total separation between church and state? How does he introduce his opposition?

4. What are the "nuts and bolts" of these principles? Explain this figure of speech.

5. What voice does the author use in the final paragraph of the essay? Why do you think he used this voice?

THE ISSUES

1. Do you believe that the separation of church and state is an important issue or should we turn our attention to other matters, such as the threat of war or the high cost of medicine? What is your personal view on the separation of church and state?

2. How should our society deal with the enormous diversity of religions in our country? Would we be better off if we had just one religion to which every American belonged?

3. What moral principles, if any, do you think should be taught in our public schools?

4. Do you believe that department stores should be allowed to display crèches or other Christian symbols as part of their Christmas window decors, or should such displays be forbidden on the grounds that they would offend non-Christians?

5. Of the following acts, which should be dealt with by the church, which by the government, and which by both the church and the government?

   a. Child abuse

   b. Abortion

   c. Luxury taxation

   d. Child adoption by gays

   e. Molestation of a minor by a priest

   f. Running a red light

   g. Refusing to attend church

SUGGESTIONS FOR WRITING

1. Make a journal entry in which you analyze what freedom of religion means to you.

2. Write an essay in which you indicate how the church and the government can work together to help correct social injustice, such as oppression of the poor or prejudice against certain segments of society.

PLEDGE RULING JUST PLAIN WRONG

Richard W. Whitrock

Richard W. Whitrock writes a column for University Wire.

~

1 In perhaps the most historic decision in recent memory, California courts have ruled that the Pledge of Allegiance is unconstitutional. Despite the proclaimed facade of protecting the separation of church and state, the decision was wrong.

2 Supporters of the ruling have many arguments why the Pledge of Allegiance should not be said in schools, mostly about the phrase "one nation under God." To them, the Pledge of Allegiance is a state endorsement of religion, which violates the constitution and separation of church and state.

3 Second, they argue that making the pledge optional forces the student into an unconstitutionally coercive situation: following the crowd and espousing beliefs they do not hold, or protesting publicly.

4   Finally, they argue that since America does not mention God in the constitution, and the insertion of "under God" into the pledge was religiously motivated, the pledge forces religion on children.

5   To be succinct, these are some of the worst arguments in the history of mankind.

6   First, the issue of unconstitutionality. It is true that God is not mentioned in the Constitution, and that the Constitution is very clear about the separation of church and state.

7   What supporters of the ruling fail to realize, however, is that the Constitution also mentions that "Congress shall make no law respecting an establishment of religion, or prohibiting the free exercise thereof." In other words, ladies and gentlemen, not allowing the expression of a belief in God is every bit as unconstitutional as forcing or endorsing one.

8   Furthermore, the idea of a separation between church and state (derived from the phrase "no law respecting an establishment of religion") means only that the state cannot sanction a church.

9   The reasoning for that restriction is to allow the free practice of religion, not to force its absence in all things public. The answer, then, is to allow for the voluntary practice of religion—not to ban religion.

10   Additionally, the argument is false because it is not a state endorsement of religion and therefore does not violate the terms of separation. To be clear, allowing the pledge to continue on a voluntary basis is not a violation for two reasons.

11   First, "voluntary" by definition excludes endorsement. Allowing someone to espouse a belief has never been akin to endorsement. Second, the term "under God" does not specify a religion. The term does not mean a Christian God any more than an Islamic, Hindu, or Navajo god for that matter.

12   To make the argument that the state is endorsing a religion, the religion it is supposedly endorsing must at the minimum be identified.

13   Second, the argument that an optional pledge forces the student into a coercive situation is just as invalid.

14   Since when is standing up for one's beliefs a bad thing? Forcing students to have an opinion or belief and follow through with it builds character, a quality that is in short supply in today's world.

15   Avoiding the issue by not allowing anyone to say the pledge is not the American way, it's the cowards way.

16   Protesting can be as simple as not saying the "offensive" words.

17   Finally, it deprives students of the ability to express their belief in public (anyone remember free expression and free press in the First Amendment?). That force is worse than coercion.

18   The third argument supporters have is that the inclusion of the term "under God" was religiously motivated.

19   Since no religion is identified, this is hardly the case. Whether those that included it clearly meant a Christian God or not is irrelevant—the words themselves are unspecific and very open to interpretation.

20   The phrase "under God" doesn't need to be seen as a mention of the existence of God but as an acknowledgement of Man's equality.

21   The Declaration of Independence mentions God for just that purpose. Because two people utter the phrase "under God" does not mean that the two use the phrase in the same sense.

22   The pledge ruling has not resolved the issue.

23   In the coming months, America should be ready not only for a strong and passionate response to that irresponsible and indefensible ruling. To survive the onslaught, supporters of the California ruling will need better arguments, ones that make sense.

~

(697 words)

VOCABULARY

facade (1)	endorsement (2)	optional (3)
coercive (3)	succinct (5)	sanction (8)
voluntary (9)	espouse (11)	offensive (16)
irrelevant (19)	indefensible (23)	

THE FACTS

1. In paragraph 1, what is the "historic decision" to which the author refers? Why is it historic?

2. What reason did the California courts give for ruling that the Pledge of Allegiance is unconstitutional? Regardless of whether or not you agree, is the ruling logical? Give reasons for your answer.

3. Do you agree that even if students are given the choice to utter the Pledge or to remain silent, the situation is still coercive? Defend your answer.

4. What important part of our Constitution, according to the author, do supporters of the ruling ignore? Why is this part important?

5. Why does the author think that students should make the decision to either say the Pledge or remain silent? Do you agree with this view? Support your answer.

THE STRATEGIES

1. What purpose does the title of the essay serve? Is it an appropriate title?

2. What voice does the author use in paragraph 4? How effective is this voice?

3. How does the author organize his essay to help the reader follow his reasoning? Point to specific passages in the essay.

4. In paragraph 16, what are the "offensive words" alluded to? How do you know for sure?

5. What style does the author use to convey his argument? What advantage does his style have? What disadvantage?

THE ISSUES

1. The "under God" clause was added to our Constitution in the 1950s during the Cold War when the United States wanted to let the atheistic Soviet Union know that we were a nation of people who believed in God. In retrospect, do you think it was wise for our government to add this clause? Supply reasons and examples for your answer.

2. Why do you think religious beliefs often cause vicious fights between people? Why are people so sensitive about their religions?

3. Do you agree with the author that the phrase "under God" does not need to be seen as an acknowledgement of God's existence, but rather as an acknowledgement that all humans are equal? Explain your answer.

4. The author believes that America should respond with passion to the California ruling. What do you think he hopes passion will accomplish?

5. As you recite the Pledge of Allegiance, what feelings does it evoke in you? Are these good or bad feelings? Explain.

SUGGESTIONS FOR WRITING

1. After thinking about your answer to question 5, write an essay explaining just what the Pledge of Allegiance means to you.

2. Write an essay in which you analyze whether or not our government did the right thing by adding the phrase "under God" to the Pledge of Allegiance.

—————— STUDENT CORNER ——————

1

Final Draft

The Modern Reformation

Adam Winkler, Georgia State University

In 1620 a group of English puritans fled religious persecution in England and arrived in New England on the *Mayflower*. Their presence in America was the direct result of the inextricable link between the English monarchy and the religious establishment. This troublesome link is well documented in England's history, notably in the 12th century when Thomas Becket was murdered in a cathedral, and in the 16th century's Protestant reformation. Since England was America's umbilical link to their "mother land," the founding fathers borrowed the bulk of their political ideas from the Magna Carta and coupled them with new strains of radical thought emerging from France. Consequently, when Thomas Jefferson framed the Constitution, he sought "a wall of separation" between the church and the state, the aim being to make it virtually impossible for America to ever have an official national religion. In theory, the separation of church and state is the keystone of the American Constitution that has upheld its original purpose. In practice, the United States remains insensitive toward non-Christian religions and has not completely separated religion from government.

The separation of church and state is set forth in the First Amendment of the Bill of Rights as follows:

Winkler 2

Congress shall make no law respecting an establishment of religion, or prohibiting the free exercise thereof; or abridging the freedom of speech, or of the press, or the right of the people peaceably to
assemble, and to petition the Government for a redress of grievances.

The same amendment that guarantees the freedom of speech,
the press, and assembly also protects citizens' rights to worship
whatsoever they please and protects them from being forced to
support someone else's religion. Its seems very plain and simple—
there will be no collaboration between the church and the
government—but certain government sponsored institutions, such
as the schools and the courts, give preference to Christian
religious ideas, beliefs, and values that blur the separation of
church and state.

For example, public school systems have the word *Christmas* on
the school calendar, even though Christmas is a Christian festival.
By having Christmas and not Hanukkah on the public school
calendar, the government is subtly expressing a religious
preference. The politically neutral term for the season should just
be *holidays*. It is true that Christmas was declared a federal holiday
in 1870 by Ulysses S. Grant. But it is also true that there are no
non-Christian holidays on the American public school calendar.
For example, the Newton County school board in Covington,
Georgia, removed the word *Christmas* from the school calendar
only when some agitated parents, joined with the American Civil
Liberties Union, threatened to sue. Now Christmas is under wraps
in Newton County.

Sometimes the quarrel over the separation of church and state
can result in bitter fights over symbols. For example, most public

schools across the country usually present a Christmas pageant or play in December. Under pressure, the school board at South Orange Middle School in New Jersey replaced the school's seasonal play, "A Christmas Carol" by Charles Dickens, with "The Great Railroad Race." In a way, this was a trivial dispute because Dickens's play uses Christmas merely as a seasonal backdrop to illustrate Ebenezer Scrooge's emerging sympathy and compassion in the season that is supposed to bring out the good will in men towards men. But the school board was, strictly speaking, correct in this decision. Christmas plays should be performed at churches, not in public schools. If the American government wants to stop indoctrinating non-Christian children with Christian holidays, beliefs, and ideas, it needs to truly separate religion from state sponsored institutions and allow individual households to teach and celebrate other religious festivals.

Another example of how tangled the issue of separation of church and state can become occurred in Alabama. There the state's chief justice (a conservative Christian named Roy Moore who campaigned as the "Ten Commandments Judge") moved a 5,280-pound stone monument depicting the original stone tablets of the Ten Commandment into the rotunda of the state judicial building in the middle of the night on the 31st of July, 2001. The American Civil Liberties Union, in collaboration with the Southern Poverty Law Center, filed suit on behalf of three Alabama lawyers who felt that the monument was offensive and in violation of the separation of church and state. Roy Moore testified that he was only recognizing the source of our system of justice.

Winkler 4

In this argument he was absolutely wrong. Although the Ten
Commandments complement our justice system, four out of
those ten do not belong in any American courthouse because
they are exclusively Christian: 1) "Thou shalt have no other Gods
before me," 2) "Thou shalt not make unto thee any graven image,"
3) "Thou shalt not take the name of the Lord thy God in vain,"
4) "Remember the Sabbath and keep it Holy." If the chief judicial
officer of Alabama thought the monument wasn't violating the
separation of the church and state, then he wouldn't have moved
the monument in the middle of the night and he wouldn't have had
a film crew from a Christian ministry tape the event.

Moore's confusion is understandable. After all, every piece of
American currency, from the 50 cent piece to the 100 dollar bill,
has *In God We Trust* inscribed or written on it. Federal offices are
closed on Good Friday—an exclusively Christian festival. Our
courts still administer oaths on the Bible. Although one can refuse,
if you testify in court, you place your right hand on the Bible
(because Jesus was seated at the right hand of the father) and a
court official asks you, "Do you swear or affirm to tell the truth,
the whole truth, and nothing but the truth, so help you God?" Our
Pledge of Allegiance describes America as "one nation under
God."

But religion is completely separate from our government, and
there is in fact a "wall of separation" between the government and
any religious establishment. Right? If there isn't, there should be.

How I Write

Before I write an essay, I brainstorm heavily. I sit down and fill about four or five pages of my brainstorming notebook with pictures, ideas, and even flow charts. Usually, I listen to music when I write in my idea notebook so that I never stop writing. Even if I have to write down the lyric of the song that I'm listening to, I never stop scribbling down either pictures or ideas. Once I have 4 or 5 pages of ideas, I just organize the thoughts and make an outline. I don't write from the outline, but I use it to organize the essay. When I begin typing the first draft and every draft that follows, I do it in a quiet place with no music, but I consult my outline and my special notebook frequently.

How I Wrote This Essay

I wrote the introduction of this essay in my brainstorming journal. After that it really began to write itself. Half way through the essay I changed the argument completely because I had more examples that defended the lack of separation of church and state than examples that defended the separation of church and state. I was anticipating and countering the other side of the argument and collected examples that overwhelmed my original argument. So I edited and rewrote and I was pleased with the results.

My Writing Tip

Get a notebook and scribble in it. Don't think; just write and don't stop writing. Put the pen to the paper and use multiple colored pens if you want. Draw pictures. Don't worry about spelling or grammar—just get the thoughts down, and if you don't have any thoughts that directly support your thesis, start writing a descriptive passage about anything that relates to your topic.

CHAPTER WRITING ASSIGNMENTS

1. Write an essay about your favorite Internet site.
2. Write an imaginative essay that predicts and describes useful gadgets yet to be invented.
3. Who is your favorite actor for playing the "heavy" or a villain in movies? Write an essay on that theme.
4. Write an essay about the job you would least like to have.
5. Write an essay about your favorite board game.

WRITING ASSIGNMENTS FOR A SPECIFIC AUDIENCE

1. Write to the Internal Revenue Service outlining your expenses for a semester of school.
2. Explain baseball to a foreigner who has never heard of the game.

COLLABORATIVE WRITING PROJECT

Get together with five or six students who hold different views about the separation of church and state. Discuss your positions and make a note of the differences of opinion. Then write a report to the class suggesting a compromise that could be worked out to the satisfaction of both sides.

PART III

Rewriting Your Writing

_____

The Editing Booth

> Revising is part of writing.
> Few writers are so expert that they can
> produce what they are after on the first try.
>
> —William Strunk, Jr., and E. B. White

Rewriting is a necessary part of the composing process. That a writer's best comes gushing out spontaneously at the first and only sitting is true only in some rare instances. Most of the time, it must be coaxed out of the pen, drop by drop, by labored rereading and rewriting. Rewriting means reviewing what you have written and making changes to your text. It may be broadly classified into revising and editing.

Revising literally means "seeing again." You take a second look at your paragraphs, sentences, and words and change them until they express your intended meaning. You make major changes to the essay's structure, sentences, and paragraphs. You are trying to stick to a thesis, present evidence in a logical order, and project a tone appropriate to your audience. Accomplishing any of these three tasks may require you to move or insert paragraphs, cut out sentences, add transitions, rewrite your essay's beginning or ending, or even do more research.

Editing, on the other hand, means focusing your rewriting efforts mainly on individual words and sentences. It entails making small changes to the text, often with an eye to improving syntax and overall smoothness. It means choosing a better synonym, correcting a misspelling, inventing a sharper image, improving punctuation, conforming to a specific format, and pruning unnecessary words or phrases.

Both revising and editing are important parts of any rewriting effort. And although it is true that revising usually comes before editing, even this sequence does not necessarily always apply. You may find yourself making small changes to individual words and sentences when you go over your text the first time. On a second reading, you may find an obvious defect missed earlier, causing you to make major changes in the material. As with writing, rewriting is hard to segment into absolute steps.

REVISING

Essential to all rewriting is careful and purposeful rereading. You reread your work with an eye on its intended audience and overall purpose. As you reread what you have written, you ask yourself whether your audience is likely to understand it. You ask yourself whether this paragraph, sentence, word is appropriate, whether this passage makes your views emphatic and plain. You read with pen in hand or fingers on the keyboard, slashing away here and there, scribbling in the margins, striking out and rewriting some sentences. And as you progress through multiple rereadings, your text will gradually begin to get better.

But the key is rereading, and its importance to a writer cannot be overstated. If you wish to write well, you must be willing to reread your work constantly. You must reread it not only when it is done, but also while you are doing it. If you should even become temporarily stuck—and virtually every writer occasionally does—don't stare vacantly into space or at the ceiling. Reread your work from the beginning. If no new ideas occur to you and you're still stuck, reread your work again. Sooner or later you will see where your text made a lurch in the wrong direction and be able to correct it.

Writing and rewriting are part of the recursive pattern of composing. Some revising to your rough plan or purpose will take place in your head even before you have scribbled a first draft. But most will occur immediately after or during the act of composition. You will set down a sentence or two on the page, glance at it, and see a way to make it better. Or you will write a paragraph, begin another and become stuck, then go back to the first and insert some details or transitional material. Regardless of your personal method of ments the changes she proposed to make. Since this section emphasizes revising, as opposed to editing, we have corrected the errors that would have been caught in the editing process and have left only those that could be improved through revising. In the next part of this chapter, we shall stress editing.

THE EXPLOITATION OF ENDANGERED WILDLIFE

The fascination with endangered wildlife within the affluent nations of the world increases the market for illegal poaching and exporting of wildlife goods. Wildlife is big business. Exotic-bird collectors will pay as much as $10,000 for a hyacinth macaw. At Saks Fifth Avenue in New York a pair of cowboy boots, trimmed in lizard skin, will sell for $250. A Christian Dior coat, made from only the belly fur of 17 lynx cats, will cost a staggering $100,000. These are rather mild examples of what is being done with animals stolen from wildlife retreats across the world.

Move to end of paragraph.

For stronger opening, begin here.

Of course, it's not that anyone cares if people spend their thousands on nonessentials. Instead, the act of murdering innocent and lovely animals for vanity's sake is an irreversible and despicable crime. For example, the baby seals, so prized for their exquisitely soft furs, are repeatedly beaten over the head with heavy clubs until they lie spread out on the ground, unconscious. To the poachers who routinely do the butchering, death is not relevant to this ugly scenario, nor are humane methods of killing. All they care about is the blood money extracted from the skins of these helpless little creatures. Another example is the thousands of wild birds imported live from Brazil and Australia. Since these countries have laws banning such exports, each cage of birds is smuggled aboard the smugglers' boat and has a weight attached to it. In case of being spotted by some police official, the cages can easily be thrown overboard, and no implicating evidence will remain. Still another species of endangered wildlife being exploited is the elephant. Investigators have found as many as twenty of these enormous pachyderms, gunned down with automatic weapons or shot with poison darts, lying close together as if they were victims of some cruel genocide. Their tusks have been carved from their heads and carried away, leaving the bloody carcasses to rot and waste away on the plains.

Delete: adds nothing. Is too informal.

More commentary needed here. Add a transition.

of . . .

How often? For what purpose?

Where? Add detail.

The irreversible effect of this illegal murdering could mean the extinction of many exotic wildlife species. In the 17th century, 13,200 species of mammals and birds were known, but today more than 130 species have gone. An estimated 240 more are considered seriously endangered. Almost all of the cases can be traced to human activity. It's not because we needed these animals for food, nor because their unique traits could help us find cures for diseases, nor because killing them taught us anything relevant, except that perhaps when they are gone forever, taking with them their natural mystery, beauty, and grace, then we may learn how ignorant we have been.

Be more direct.

Add a transition.

Rewrite to make stronger appeal to reader's sense of fair play. Make more coherent.

Following is the revised version of the first draft:

THE EXPLOITATION OF ENDANGERED WILDLIFE

Wildlife is big business. Exotic-bird collectors will pay as much as $10,000 for a hyacinth macaw. At Saks Fifth Avenue in New York a pair of cowboy boots, trimmed in lizard skin, will sell for $250. A Christian Dior coat, made from only the belly fur of 17 lynx cats, will cost a staggering $100,000. These are rather mild examples of what is being done with animals stolen from wildlife retreats across the world. The fascination with endangered wildlife within the affluent nations of the world increases the market for illegal poaching and exporting of wildlife goods.

The act of murdering innocent and lovely animals for vanity's sake is an irreversible and despicable crime. It is a way of saying that animals have no feelings and that human beings have the right to plunder and kill the lower orders if doing so will enhance the human life-style. For example, the baby seals, so prized for their exquisitely soft furs, are repeatedly beaten over the head with heavy clubs until they lie spread out on the ground, unconscious. To the poachers who routinely do the butchering, death is not relevant to this ugly scenario, nor are humane methods of killing. All they care about is the blood money extracted from the skins of these helpless little creatures. Another example of this savage and unnecessary rape is the thousands of wild birds imported yearly live from Brazil and Australia—to end up either in cages gracing the living rooms of tycoons who like to collect birds, or as ornaments on sweaters and hats of rich and fashion-conscious women. But since most countries have laws banning such exports, each cage of birds is smuggled aboard the smugglers' boat and has a weight attached to it. In case of being spotted by some police official, the cages can easily be thrown overboard, and no implicating evidence will remain. Still another species of endangered wildlife being exploited is the elephant. Investigators in West Africa have found as many as twenty of these enormous pachyderms, gunned down with automatic weapons or shot with poison darts, lying close together as if they were victims of some cruel genocide. Their tusks have been carved from their heads and carried away, leaving the bloody carcasses to rot and waste away on the plains.

The irreversible effect of this illegal murdering will certainly eventually lead to the extinction of many exotic wildlife species. Already time has witnessed the demise of many exotic animals. In the 17th century, 13,200 species of mammals and birds were known, but today more than 130 species are extinct. An estimated 240 more are considered seriously endangered. In almost all cases, the extinction can be traced to greedy plunder by human beings. And the tragic part is that we did not commit the plunder because we needed these animals for food, nor because their unique traits could help us find cures for diseases, nor because killing them taught us anything useful. But perhaps when they are gone forever—taking with them their natural mystery, beauty, and grace—then we may see how ignorant and foolish we were. Then we will realize, much too late, that we sold our birthright for a mess of pottage.

EDITING

After revising—in most cases—comes editing. You now concentrate on the smaller elements of your writing—on individual words and sentences—with the goal of improving them. Again, careful editing begins with close rereading. You remember whom you are writing for and why, and you use your intended audience and purpose to judge the suitability of both your syntax and diction.

What follows is a checklist of some fundamental rules of editing. Have your own work in front of you as you go over this list. If your writing suffers from mechanical problems, such as fragments, comma splices, and dangling modifiers, you should consult a good handbook.

Rule 1: Make Your Title Descriptive

The title of a paper should describe its content. Avoid puffy, exotic titles like this one on a paper dealing with the use of fantasy in Keats' poetry:

> *Poor:* Keats: The High Priest of Poetry
>
> *Rewrite:* The Use of Fantasy in Keats's Poetry

Rule 2: Begin with a Simple Sentence

It is stylistically good sense to open your paper with a short and simple sentence. A long and involved opening will repel, rather than attract, a reader:

> *Poor:* The problem that has come up again and again before various workers in the social sciences, and especially before sociologists and anthropologists, and one that has been debated at length in the journals of both disciplines as well as in the classrooms of various universities and colleges across the country, and one to which various answers, none satisfactory, have been proposed, is this: Are social scientists politically neutral, or are they *ipso facto* committed by their research?

To open with such a cumbersome sentence is like compelling a friend to view a clear landscape through a dirty windowpane. It is better to begin with an easily grasped sentence:

> *Rewrite:* The question is this: Are social scientists politically neutral, or are they committed by their research?

Rule 3: Prune Deadwood

Deadwood refers to any word, phrase, or sentence that adds bulk without meaning. It accumulates wherever the writing is roundabout and indistinct. Some styles of writing are so vested in wordiness that it is impossible to assign blame to any single word or phrase:

> *Poor:* There are many factors contributing to the deficiencies of my writing, the most outstanding being my unwillingness to work.
>
> *Rewrite:* I write badly mainly because I am lazy.
>
> *Poor:* Anthropologists carrying their studies of primate behavior deep into the tropical forests of Malaysia contribute, through the pursuit of their specialized interest, to the one field that in fact gives us our broadest perspective of human beings.
>
> *Rewrite:* Anthropologists add to our knowledge of human beings by studying primate behavior in the forests of Malaysia.

The solution to wordiness is to be plain and direct—to state your ideas without fluff or pretension.

Aside from wordiness there are other, more specific kinds of deadwood:

a. Cut *there are* and *there is* whenever possible, thereby tightening a sentence.

> *Poor:* There are many reasons why businesses fail.
>
> *Rewrite:* Businesses fail for many reasons.
>
> *Poor:* There is a cause for every effect.
>
> *Rewrite:* Every effect has a cause.

b. Cut *I think, I believe,* and *in my opinion.* Such phrases make the writer sound insecure.

> *Poor:* I think that Freud's approach to psychology is too dominated by sex.
>
> *Rewrite:* Freud's approach to psychology is too dominated by sex.
>
> *Poor:* I believe that women should be paid as much as men for the same work.
>
> *Rewrite:* Women should be paid as much as men for the same work.
>
> *Poor:* In my opinion, marriage is a dying institution.
>
> *Rewrite:* Marriage is a dying institution.

c. Cut all euphemistic expressions.

> *Poor:* He went to Vietnam and paid the supreme sacrifice.
>
> *Rewrite:* He was killed in Vietnam.

Poor: Last year for the first time I exercised the right of citizens on election day.

Rewrite: Last year I voted for the first time.

d. Cut *-wise, -ly,* and *-type* word endings. Such words, easily concocted from adverbs and adjectives, have become popular in college writing, but they add bulk, not meaning.

Poor: Moneywise, she just didn't know how to be careful.

Rewrite: She didn't know how to be careful with her money.

Poor: Firstly, let me point out some economic problems.

Rewrite: First, let me point out some economic problems.

Poor: A jealous-type man annoys me.

Rewrite: A jealous man annoys me.

a. Eliminate all redundant phrases or expressions. Here are some typical examples, followed by possible substitutes:

Redundancy	Rewrite
bright in color	bright
large in size	large
old in age	old
shiny appearance	shiny
in this day and age	today
true and accurate	accurate *Or* true
important essentials	essentials
end result	result
terrible tragedy	tragedy
free gift	gift
unexpected surprise	surprise
each and every	each *Or* every
beginning preparation	preparation
basic and fundamental	basic *Or* fundamental

In the preceding cases, all you have to do is cross out the words that *do not add* any meaning.

Another kind of redundancy is the use of ready-made phrases that could be replaced by a single word:

Ready-made Phrase	Rewrite
owing to the fact that	because
plus the fact that	and
regardless of the fact that	although
in the event that	if
in a situation in which	when
concerning the matter of	about
it is necessary that	must
has the capacity for	can
it could happen that	may, can, could, might
prior to	before
at the present time	now *Or* today
at this point in time	now *Or* today
as of this date	today
in this day and age	nowadays
in an accurate manner	accurately
in a satisfactory manner	satisfactorily
subsequent to	after
along the lines of	like

Unfortunately, we cannot give you a comprehensive guide to all unnecessary phrases. Only by a thorough rereading of your text can you spot these redundancies.

However, some chronic redundancies are caused by such words as *process, field, area, systems,* and *subject* being unnecessarily attached by the preposition *of* to certain nouns. Usually, these words and the preposition can be eliminated with no damage whatsoever to your meaning and a considerable lightening of your style. Here are some examples:

The *process of law* is not free of faults.

The *field of education* needs creative minds.

Some incompetency exists in the *area of medicine.*

People employed in *systems of management* make good salaries.

They know little about the *subject of mathematics.*

In each case, if you delete the "of" phrase, the redundancy disappears:

The law is not free of faults.

Education needs creative minds.

Some incompetency exists in medicine.

People employed in management make good salaries.

They know little about mathematics.

Context, activity, concept, factor, problem are similar offenders.

f. Cut all preamble phrases such as *the reason why . . . is that.*

Poor: The reason why wars are fought is that nations are not equally rich.

Rewrite: Wars are fought because nations are not equally rich.

Poor: The thing I wanted to say is that history has shown the human being to be a social predator.

Rewrite: History has shown the human being to be a social predator.

Poor: The point I was trying to make is that reality is sometimes confused with fantasy in Keats's poetry.

Rewrite: Reality is sometimes confused with fantasy in Keats's poetry.

In all such cases the rewrite principle is the same: lift out the heart of the idea and state it plainly.

g. Cut most rhetorical questions.

That illusion, though deceptive, is more consoling and less hostile to human needs than reality appears to be a central theme in Keats's poetry. Why would anyone feel this way? Why did Keats himself feel this way? Possibly because he had tuberculosis and knew he was going to waste away and die.

Rewrite: That illusion, though deceptive, is more consoling and less hostile to human needs than reality appears to be a central theme in Keats's poetry. Keats possibly felt this way because he had tuberculosis and knew he was going to waste away and die.

Rule 4: Do Not Overexplain

Poor: Some critics sneered at Keats for being an apothecary-surgeon, which is what he was trained for.

Rewrite: Some critics sneered at Keats for being an apothecary-surgeon.

If Keats was an apothecary-surgeon, then that is obviously what he was trained to be.

Poor: As president of the company, which is an executive-type position, he never scheduled work for himself during April.

Rewrite: As president of the company, he never scheduled work for himself during April.

The term *president* already lets the reader know that the position is an executive one.

> *Poor:* The car is blue in color and costs $15,000 in price.
> *Rewrite:* The car is blue and costs $15,000.

That blue is a color and that $15,000 is the price is self-evident.

Rule 5: Be Specific

Lack of specific detail will infect your prose with a pallid vagueness.

> *Poor:* The effect of the scenery was lovely and added a charming touch to the play.
> *Rewrite:* The scenery, which consisted of an autumn country landscape painted on four flats extended to cover the entire background of the stage, added a charming touch to the play.

Being specific is simply calling things by their proper names. In speech, it might pass as cute to call things *thingamajigs* or *thingamabobs* or *widgets,* but in prose, any sort of vagueness caused by the writer's not calling things by their proper names will leave a bad impression. Consider the following examples:

> *Poor:* James Boswell, the famous writer, died from living badly.
> *Rewrite:* James Boswell, the famous *biographer,* died of *uremia following a gonorrheal infection.*

The writer of the second sentence, who has simply named Boswell's terminal infection, appears more competent than the writer of the first.

> *Poor:* Browning wrote poetry in which a speaker talked either to himself or to someone else.
> *Rewrite:* Browning wrote *dramatic monologues.*

In the first sentence, for want of a name, the writer is forced into a roundabout description of the kind of poetry Browning wrote. A little research on Browning would have yielded the term *dramatic monologue.*

Rule 6: Avoid Trite Expressions

Some words, phrases, or expressions through overuse have become unbearably hackneyed and should be avoided. Following are some of the most glaring offenders.

in conclusion, I wish to say

last, but by no means least

slowly but surely

to the bitter end

it goes without saying

by leaps and bounds

few and far between

in the final analysis

Rule 7: Use the Active Voice

The active voice is more vigorous and understandable than the passive because it allows the subject of a sentence to stand in its familiar position in
front of the verb, for example, "I took a walk." The subject *I* occupies the position immediately in front of the verb *took*. The same sentence in the passive
voice denies this familiar immediacy between subject and verb, "A walk was
taken by me." The subject and verb stand at opposite ends of the sentence,
with *by* intervening between them. In some passive constructions, the subject
is even dropped:

> Information about the suspect could not be obtained.

By whom? you might ask. The answer is not evident in this sentence. Because
of this tendency to implicate no one as the doer of an action, the passive voice
enjoys widespread use among bureaucratic writers. Notice how converting
the above sentence to the active voice not only makes the sentence more vigorous, but also makes some agency or person its subject and, therefore, responsible:

> The police could not obtain any information about the suspect.

The strongest argument to be given for using the active instead of the passive
voice, however, is the simplest one: the active voice is easier to read and understand. Here are some more examples of the passive voice, followed by appropriate revisions:

> *Passive:* Her makeup was applied in thick, daubing strokes by her.
> *Active:* She applied her makeup in thick, daubing strokes.
> *Passive:* To see their hero in person was the fans' most cherished dream.
> *Active:* The fans' most cherished dream was to see their hero in person.
> *Passive:* It was determined by the committee that the new tax law would
>   benefit middle-income people.

Active: The committee determined that the new tax law would benefit middle-income people.

Passive: My last trip to Jamaica will always be remembered.

Active: I shall always remember my last trip to Jamaica.

The use of the passive voice is stylistically justified only when an action or the object of an action is more important than the subject:

There, before our eyes, two human beings were burned alive by gasoline flames.

In this case the object, *human beings,* is more important than the subject, *gasoline flames,* and the passive voice is therefore effective. Here are two more examples of the passive voice appropriately used:

Cancer-producing particles are released into the atmosphere by spray guns applying asbestos during building construction.

In this context, cancer-producing particles are more important than spray guns.

Widespread death and injury were caused when 20,000 tons of TNT were dropped on Hiroshima in an atomic bomb.

Obviously the human dead and injured are more important than the atomic bomb.

Rule 8: Make Your Statements Positive

Statements that hedge, hesitate, or falter in the way they are worded tend to infuse your style with indecision. Whenever possible, word your statements positively:

Poor: He was not at all a rich man.

Rewrite: He was a poor man.

Poor: "The Cherry Orchard" is not a strong play; it does not usually sweep the audience along.

Rewrite: "The Cherry Orchard" is a weak play that usually bores its audience.

Poor: A not uncommon occurrence is for rain to fall this time of the year.

Rewrite: It commonly rains this time of the year.

Rule 9: Keep to One Tense

Once you have decided to summarize an action or event in one tense, you must thereafter stick to that tense. Don't start in the past and shift to the present, nor start in the present and shift to the past. Notice the corrections in the following passage.

> Here is what I saw: For two acts the ballerina pirouetted, leapt, and floated
>   fell
> like a silver swallow; then suddenly, she ~~falls~~ to the ground like a heavy boul-
>   was
> der. Her leg ~~is~~ fractured. For years before I observed this spectacular drama,
>   had   was watching
> I often heard of this artist's brilliant career. Now I ~~am watching~~ her final per-
> ^
>
> formance.

Rule 10: Place Key Words at the Beginning or End of a Sentence

Poor: Workers today have forgotten the meaning of the word *quality,* so most craftsmen tell us.

Rewrite: Workers today, so most craftsmen tell us, have forgotten the meaning of the word *quality.*

Poor: Generally speaking, *wars* turn civilized nations into barbaric tribes.

Rewrite: Wars, generally speaking, turn civilized nations into barbaric tribes.

Rule 11: Prune Multiple *Ofs*

A double *of* construction is tolerable; a triple *of* construction is not.

> *Poor:* The opinions *of* the members *of* this panel *of* students are their own.
>
> *Rewrite:* The opinions expressed by this panel of students are their own.

A good way to break up an *of* construction is to add another verb. In the preceding example the verb *expressed* is inserted in the sentence.

Rule 12: Break up Noun Clusters

A noun cluster is any string of noun + adjective combinations occurring at length without a verb. The cluster is usually preceded by either *the* or *a.* Noun clusters contribute a tone of unarguable objectivity to prose and have consequently found favor in the writing styles of textbooks, the government, and the social sciences. Note the italicized noun clusters in the following:

> We therefore recommend *the use of local authorities for the collection of information on this issue.*

> *The increased specialization and complexity of multicellular organisms* resulted from *evolution according to the principles of random variation and natural selection.*

> The *general lessening of the work role in our society* does not mean that we have abandoned *the work basis for many of our values.*

> One cannot doubt *the existence of polarized groups in America.*

The test for a noun cluster is whether or not it can be replaced by a single pronoun. Each of the above can be.

To rewrite noun clusters, convert one of the nouns to an equivalent verb form:

> We therefore recommend using local authorities *to collect* information on this issue.

> Multicellular organisms *specialized and evolved* in complexity by the principles of random variation and natural selection.

> Because people today *work* less than they used to is no reason to believe that we have abandoned work as a basis for many of our values.

> One cannot doubt that polarized groups *exist* in America.

Noun clusters clot the flow of a sentence. Avoid them by being generous in your use of verbs.

Rule 13: Use Exclamation Points Sparingly

The exclamation point should be used rarely and only when urgency or strong emotion is being expressed, as in the following:

> This is what we fought our wars for!
> Hooray! They found the prize!

Otherwise, it adds a forced breeziness to your prose.

> We must have urban renewal; and we must have it now!
> One cannot construct a science with unreliable instruments!

Rule 14: Vary Your Sentences

Do not begin two sentences in a row with the same word or phrase unless you are deliberately aiming for an effect.

> *Poor:* The true Keats scholar is as familiar with the poet's life as with his poetry and can instantly relate any stage of the two. The true

Keats scholar has a tendency to use Keats's poetry to explicate his life, and to use his life to explicate his poetry.

Rewrite: Scholars of Keats know the poet's life as well as they know his poetry and can instantly relate any stage of the two. They use Keats's poetry to explain his life, and his life to explain his poetry.

Vary the length of your sentences.

Poor: The man was angry and wanted his money back. But the officer would not give it back and told him to leave. That made the man angrier, and he threatened to call the police.

Rewrite: The man was angry; he wanted his money back. But the officer would not give it back to him, and told him to leave, which made the man angrier. He threatened to call the police.

The rewrite is more effective because the sentences have a greater variety in length and style.

Rule 15: Keep Your Point of View Consistent

If you begin a sentence by referring to yourself first as "I" and then as "one," you have made the error known as shift in point of view. Such shifts can occur because of the several ways in which you can refer to yourself, your audience, and people in general. You can refer to yourself as *the writer, I,* or *we.* You can refer to your audience as *you, we,* or *all of us.* You can refer to people in general as *people, one,* and *they.* The rule is that once you have chosen your point of view, it must remain consistent:

Poor: Do not buy Oriental rugs at an auction, because if we do, we may get cheated.

Better: Do not buy Oriental rugs at an auction, because if you do, you may get cheated.

Poor: I try to take good care of my car, for when one does not, they usually pay a big price.

Better: I try to take good care of my car, for when I do not, I usually pay a big price.

Poor: Everyone stood aghast when I told them about the accident.

Better: They all stood aghast when I told them about the accident.

Rule 16: Use Standard Words

College students can be unrelenting in their invention of newfangled vocabulary and often fall prey to the excesses of neologisms—new or coined words. Voguish words fade as quickly as they appear. By the time this book sees print, such words as *nerd, cool, rad, vibes, stoned, grody, jive,* and *fox* will begin to sound dated and old-fashioned. You should use neologisms sparingly—if at all—in your writing. Instead, draw your primary stock of words from the vocabulary established over the centuries.

Remember, too, standard words must be written in standard spelling. Double-check any doubtful spelling in a dictionary.

Rule 17: End with Impact

The ending of your essay should either clinch your argument, summarize your main point, reassert your thesis, urge some kind of action, or suggest a solution. Avoid committing the following common errors in your ending:

a. Endings that are trite:

In conclusion I wish to say . . .

And now to summarize . . .

Such endings are too obvious. If your essay has been properly developed, no special announcement of the conclusion is necessary.

b. Endings that introduce a new idea:

Wealth, position, and friends, then, made him what he is today, although his father's death may also have influenced him.

If an idea has not been covered earlier, do not be tempted to introduce it as a novelty item in the final paragraph.

c. Endings that are superfluous:

And so these are my thoughts on the subject.

As you can see; my essay proves that carbohydrates are bad for our health.

From these thoughts you will clearly see that Diaghilev was a dominant figure in modern ballet.

These endings do not reflect thoughtfulness on the part of the writer; they are useless in an essay.

Editing an Actual Essay   Following is the first draft of a student paper, with revisions marked in boldface. In the left margin is the corresponding number of the rule in this section that has been broken.

I

The Loss of Horror in Horror Movies

Rule 1   ~~Goose Pimples, Where Are You?~~

Rule 6   ~~For various and sundry reasons~~ Audiences are no longer

scared as they once were by the old-fashioned horror

movies. Over the years people have been exposed to so

                                    vampires, werewolves, zombies, and mummies
Rule 5   many ~~monsters~~ that such creatures have lost their

Rule 3g   effectiveness as objects of terror. ~~Why do you think this~~

~~happened?~~

Lack of novelty has produced indifference. Originally, a

movie monster, such as the one created by Frankenstein,

terrified audiences simply because the concept of a man

                              was
Rules 9/3e creating human life ~~is~~ new. ~~Plus the fact that~~ Frankenstein's

monster had a sinister plausibility that people of the 1930s

had not experienced. But then the public was inundated by

a deluge of other film monsters as studios tried to

capitalize on the success of the original. Gradually audiences

grew bored as these creations became trite and shopworn.

Fearing loss of business, ambitious movie producers tried to

Rule 3d   invent fresh ~~type,~~ grisly shapes that would lure moviegoers

back into the theaters. But their attempts had no effect on

a public surfeited with horror, so Frankenstein's monster,

2

Wolfman, and Dracula eventually became comic creatures

in Abbott and Costello films.

to produce

Rule 3e   Most modern horror films fail ~~in the production of~~

genuine, goose-pimply terror in their audiences. Of course,

it may be argued that films like "The Exorcist" and "Jaws"

hysterical screams.

Rule 5   scared many people—even to the point of ~~great fear.~~ But

these films relied heavily on shock rather than on fear.

differs from fear.

Rule 8   Shock ~~and fear are not the same.~~ Genuine fear involves the

It

unknown or the unseen. ~~Genuine fear~~ seduces the

and appeals

Rule 14   imagination into fantastic realms, ~~Genuine fear appeals~~ to

our innate store of nightmares. But shock is merely

synonymous with repulsion. People are shocked when they

see something they don't want to see. For example, the

scene of a man being devoured by a shark will shock. The

flaw here is that the shock value of such a scene serves

repulse or offend

Rule 16   more to ~~give the creeps or the heebie-jeebies~~ than to

frighten.

Today shock devices are used far too frequently in

motion pictures; yet, the sad truth is that these graphic

displays of blood and gore lack imagination. In older horror

movies, the audience was not privy to the horrible details

3

Rule 7   of murder. Scenes ~~which~~ merely suggested evil ~~were used~~
audience's imagination supplied the details.
instead, and the ~~details were supplied by the audience's~~

Rule 4   ~~imagination.~~ This approach is more effective ~~in its results~~

than shock because it spurs the viewers to conjure up

their own images of the unseen. The old movie formulas

did not have to use shock devices, such as bloody murders,

to achieve a pinnacle of horror. Unfortunately, today's

audiences have become "shockproof" in the sense that it
bigger and more bizarre doses of horror

Rule 5   takes ~~more and more~~ to scare them. ~~In conclusion, horror~~
One wonders what the ultimate horror movie will be.

Rule 17a   ~~movies have truly lost their effect.~~

Here is the polished version of the paper, ready to be submitted to the instructor.

I

The Loss of Horror in Horror Movies

Audiences are no longer scared as they once were by the old-fashioned horror movies. Over the years people have been exposed to so many vampires, werewolves, zombies, and mummies that such creatures have lost their effectiveness as objects of terror.

Lack of novelty has produced indifference. Originally, a movie monster, such as the one created by Frankenstein, terrified audiences simply because the concept of a man creating a human life was new. Frankenstein's monster had a sinister plausibility that people of the 1930s had not experienced. But then the public was inundated by a deluge of other film monsters as studios tried to capitalize on the success of the original. Gradually audiences grew bored as these creations became trite and shopworn. Fearing loss of business, ambitious movie producers tried to invent fresh, grisly shapes that would lure moviegoers back into the theaters. But their attempts had no effect on a public surfeited with horror, so Frankenstein's monster, Wolfman, and Dracula eventually became comic creatures in Abbott and Costello films.

2

Most modern horror films fail to produce genuine, goose-pimply terror in their audiences. Of course, it may be argued that films like "The Exorcist" and "Jaws" scared many people—even to the point of hysterical screams. But these films relied heavily on shock rather than on fear. Shock differs from fear. Genuine fear involves the unknown or the unseen. It seduces the imagination into fantastic realms and appeals to our innate store of nightmares. But shock is merely synonymous with repulsion. People are shocked when they see something they don't want to see. For example, the scene of a man being devoured by a shark will shock. The flaw here is that the shock value of such a scene serves more to repulse or offend than to frighten.

Today shock devices are used far too frequently in motion pictures; yet, the sad truth is that these graphic displays of blood and gore lack imagination. In older horror movies, the audience was not privy to the horrible details of murder. Scenes merely suggested evil, and the audience's imagination supplied the details. This approach is more effective than shock because it spurs the viewers to conjure up their own images of the unseen. The old movie formulas did not have to use shock devices, such as bloody

3

murders, to achieve a pinnacle of horror. Unfortunately, today's

audiences have become "shockproof" in the sense that it takes

bigger and more bizarre doses of horror to scare them. One

wonders what the ultimate horror movie will be.

EXERCISES

1. What follows is the opening paragraph of a student essay. Revise it to improve its effectiveness. Remember that your lead sentence should captivate your audience.

   Wars are always destructive and rarely worth the devastation they cause. Today, Europe is still recuperating from World War II. Endless statistics attempt to project what would happen if a nuclear war were to break out today; yet, nobody really knows the actual effects. The most accurate picture to date was provided by the bombing of Hiroshima in 1945. This terrible historical event provided actual evidence of what a super weapon has the capability of accomplishing. For the first time the world saw the greatest disaster ever created by man. The effects were unforgettably horrifying and disastrous. No one had bargained for the ensuing nightmare.

2. From the following pairs, choose the more descriptive title.
   a. (1) The Dreadful Nightmare of 1945
      (2) The Crippling Effects of the Atom Bomb on Hiroshima
   b. (1) Whence Did We Come and Why Are We Here?
      (2) What Is Philosophy?
   c. (1) China and Europe: Two Different Cultures
      (2) Dynamic Growth versus Static Social Principles
   d. (1) The People of the Black Moccasin
      (2) The Plains Culture of the Blackfoot Indians
   e. (1) Francisco Pizarro, Conqueror of Peru
      (2) Mighty Conquistador of the New World

3. Rid the following sentences of all deadwood:
   a. There are many ways in which light can be diffracted.
   b. No one has the right, in my opinion, to dictate to another human being whom to worship.
   c. Educationwise Will Rogers never did go to college.
   d. It has been said many times that power corrupts.
   e. There were thousands of teachers who attended the conference.
   f. The attitude-adjustment hour will begin at 5:00 P.M. and will be "no host."

4. Eliminate all redundant or imprecise phrases from the following sentences. Rewrite passages if necessary.
   a. Owing to the fact that it rained, Napoleon was defeated at Waterloo.
   b. We asked for a full and complete list of the passengers.

    c. One-man-one-vote should be a basic and fundamental reality of any political system.

    d. The room is square in shape, pale blue in color, and cheerful in appearance.

    e. The custodian was fired on the grounds that he slept on the job.

    f. A huge celebration marked the occasion of Martin Luther King's birthday.

    g. Those engaged in the profession of writing should be the guardians of grammar.

5. Rewrite the following sentences in the active voice:

    a. From early times on stucco was used by the Romans as a finish for important buildings.

    b. Immortality was not believed in by the Sadducees of Jerusalem.

    c. The *Brahmanas,* originally written in Sanskrit, were produced by Indian priests.

    d. Chewing mouths are used by termites to eat wood.

    e. A good time was had by all of us.

    f. Sometimes no symptoms are exhibited by victims of trichinosis.

6. Rewrite the following sentences to break up the noun clusters:

    a. The way to avoid a future fuel crisis is the construction of a mass transportation system and the investing in quality insulation.

    b. The inspecting of the chemical-disposal plant was never accomplished.

    c. One can hope for the existence of an afterlife.

    d. The making of great strides by medical technology gives hope to people with incurable heart diseases.

    e. The development of a good ear is necessary to the writing of effective prose.

7. Rewrite the following sentences to correct an inconsistent point of view or shift in tense:

    a. They left early for the big city of San Francisco. Once there, they take the cable car to the top of Nob Hill. At five in the evening, they eat at a restaurant on the wharf.

    b. One must have respect for the flag of our country. If you don't, how can we expect others to respect it?

    c. Swarms of bees attacked him, so he quickly hides his face inside his heavy wool jacket.

    d. If one has ever lived by the sea, you always tend to miss the roar of the waves and the sound of seagulls.

APPENDIX

Optional Assignments

—————— **ASSIGNMENT I** ——————

The Research Paper

WHY ENGLISH INSTRUCTORS ASSIGN RESEARCH PAPERS

Students rarely greet the research paper with joy, but it still remains one of the most important college assignments. Writing one entails thinking critically about a subject, tracking down and evaluating facts for relevance and truth, organizing materials in support of a thesis, and cultivating a readable style. Success in college depends largely on the acquisition of these skills, which are also essential for accomplishment in business, the major professions, and even in private life. Salespeople often research a market and analyze it for trends; lawyers track down facts and organize them in preparing briefs and contracts; journalists depend on investigative research to gather material for stories. Engineers, nurses, secretaries, actors, architects, insurance agents—virtually all the professions—rely on the research techniques exemplified in this chapter.

HOW TO CHOOSE YOUR TOPIC

Typically, English instructors grant students the freedom to choose their own research topics, thus promoting exploration and self-discovery. If such a choice is indeed available to you, we recommend some preliminary browsing through the library until you come across a subject that arouses your curiosity—be it primitive Indians, the reign of the last empress of China, some influential sports figure, the complexities of the New York Stock Exchange, children's psychological problems, or the fiction or poetry of a modern writer. Here are some tips on finding a suitable topic:

1. Work with a familiar subject. For instance, you may have been fascinated by historical attempts of the superrich to manipulate the U.S. economy such as the Gould-Fisk scheme to corner gold in 1869, with the consequent Black Friday market panic. Now you must find out more about Jay Gould, who became symbolic of autocratic

business practices and was hated by most American businesspeople. Research will supply the necessary information.

2. If familiarity fails, try an entirely new area. Perhaps you have always wanted to learn about Lenin's philosophy of government, genetic engineering, evolution in the Paleozoic era, the Roman empress Galla Placidia, the causes of earthquakes, pre-Columbian art, or the historical causes for the political unrest in Ireland. A research paper finally gives you the opportunity.

3. Books and magazines can suggest possible topics. The library is a gold mine of hidden information. Browse through book stacks and magazine racks. Some topic of interest is bound to leap out at you.

Avoid topics for which a single source can provide all the needed information; those that require no development but end as soon as started; those so popular that virtually everything about them has already been written and said; those so controversial that you have only fresh fuel to add to the already raging fire; or those decidedly unsuited to your audience, for example, a paper advocating radical revision of the U.S. Constitution written for an instructor who is a conservative Republican.

HOW TO NARROW YOUR SUBJECT

Good research papers deal with topics of modest and workable proportions. To attempt a paper on the galaxies of the universe or on World War II is to attempt the impossible. A simple but practical way to narrow your subject is to subdivide it into progressively smaller units until you reach a topic specific enough for a paper. The following diagram on the sport of fencing illustrates what we mean:

Any of the entries found on the lowest subdivision are properly narrowed subjects. For instance, you could write a useful paper on the sixteenth-century German schools that taught fencing to European gentlemen, on the use of the saber in fencing, or on the rules of modern team fencing. But a paper just on fencing would be overambitious and tricky to write.

Another point to bear in mind is that unlike the typical class-written paper, in which you must first formulate a thesis and then write the text, in the research paper you, gather evidence, study it, and only then deduce a thesis. The assembled facts, statistics, graphs, schematics, arguments, expert testimony, and so on will suggest a conclusion that will be your thesis. What you learn in this process of writing the research paper is not only how to write, but also how to infer a reasonable conclusion from a body of evidence.

THE PROCESS OF WRITING THE PAPER

You have narrowed your subject. You do not yet have a thesis or a definite topic, but you have a likely subject area to explore. You can do it in these simple steps:

Find and Evaluate Sources

To do this, you must spend time in a library, which is your systematized retrieval network. Materials for your subject will be listed in the card catalog, in appropriate indexes, in reference works, on shelves, in files, and—in many libraries—on a computer screen. Evaluate each source by scanning titles, tables of contents, chapter headings, or article summaries. Check the date of publication to make sure the information in the source is still valid. Ask the reference librarian for help. As you work, list each possible source on its own bibliography card, providing the information necessary for easy retrieval. Here is an example:

813.409   College Library
Sch.

Schneider, Robert W. *Five Novelists of the*
  Progressive Era.
  New York: Columbia University Press, 1965
Chapter 5 evaluates the novels of Winston Churchill, stating why
they were loved by contemporaries but scorned by succeeding generations.

Take Notes

Using your pile of bibliography cards, retrieve the books, magazines, pamphlets, and other identified sources and place them in front of you. Skim each source to get the drift of its content. Decide if it contains material relevant enough to warrant a more detailed reading. Once you have skimmed your sources, you can start taking four basic kinds of notes:

1. summary—record the gist of a passage;
2. paraphrase—restate in your own words what the source says;
3. direct quotation—copy the exact words of a source; and
4. personal comments—express your own views on the subject or source.

Write your notes on cards, which can be easily shuffled or discarded when you get down to the business of writing the paper. For easier reorganization of your notes, restrict each card to a single idea. To guard against unintentional plagiarism, copy down only exact quotations from your sources while digesting and expressing all other ideas in your own words. At some point in this stage (it varies from paper to paper), a thesis will occur to you. When it does, write it down on a card for permanent reference. This will be the starting point for your paper.

Write the First Draft

With a jumble of notes strewn on your desk, you may feel bewildered about what to include or exclude as you tackle your first draft. This may be the time for an outline, which can be adjusted later to fit your paper, or your paper can subsequently be adjusted to fit your outline.

In any case, by now you should have become something of an expert on your subject. Using your outline, start composing your first draft. If you are using computerized word processing, you can easily correct or rewrite; if you are using a typewriter, you will more likely progress by writing, striking out, and rewriting. As you write, you will be backing up your own opinions and views with source material uncovered by your research and recorded in your notes.

Use Proper Documentation

Except for statements that are common knowledge ("Abraham Lincoln was shot by Wilkes Booth"), all information taken from your sources—whether quoted, paraphrased, or summarized—must be accompanied by a source citation given in parentheses and conforming to the proper format. We provide two sample papers in this chapter—one in the Modern Language Association

(MLA) format, the other in the American Psychological Association (APA) format. Use the MLA author-work format if your instructor tells you to or if your paper is on a subject in the liberal arts, such as literature, philosophy, history, religion, or fine arts. For a paper in a more scientific field, such as psychology, sociology, or anthropology, the APA author-date format should be used. In any event, check with your instructor about the documentation format that is expected and appropriate. One caution: Do *not* mix styles.

The two annotated student papers represented in this appendix serve as general models and illustrate most of the documenting problems you are likely to encounter. For more complex citations, we recommend that you consult a style sheet or a research paper handbook. Both MLA and APA have gone to a system of parenthetical documentation, which gives brief but specific information about the sources within the text itself. The MLA style cites the author's surname or the title of a work, followed by a page number; the APA style cites the author's surname, followed by a date and a page number. In both styles, the author's name, work, and date can be omitted from the parentheses if they have already been supplied within the text. The rule of thumb is this: If the citation cannot be smoothly worked into the text, it should be supplied within parentheses. This kind of parenthetical documentation is obviously simpler than footnotes or endnotes because the citation can be given as the paper is being written and is not tediously repeated in the text, the note, and the bibliography. Moreover, the writer does not have to contend with typing in superscript notes (always a chore) and keeping track of a note sequence.

Flexibility in citations is a characteristic of both the MLA and APA styles. For example, you might choose to cite the author's name in the text while putting the page (MLA) or year and page (APA) in parentheses:

MLA example:
> In her autobiography, Agatha Christie admits that often she felt the physical presence of Hercule Poirot (263).

APA example:
> According to 800-Cocaine by Mark S. Gold (1985, p. 21), cocaine has exploded into a business with brand names.

Or you might choose to include the title of the citation in the parentheses:

MLA example:
> The author began to realize how much she liked Poirot and how much a part of her life he had become (Christie, Autobiography 421).

APA example:
> During the airing of ABC's *Good Morning, America* (Ross & Bronkowski, 1986), case histories were analyzed in an extremely serious tone.

In any case, the overriding aim should be to cite the necessary information without interrupting the flow of the text. What cannot be worked elegantly into the text is cited within parentheses.

PREPARE "WORKS CITED" OR "REFERENCES"

The sources cited in your text must be alphabetically listed in full at the end of your paper. In the MLA style of documentation, the list is titled "Works Cited"; in the APA style, it is titled "References." Both styles require the same general information, but differ slightly in details of capitalization and order. MLA entries, for example, begin with a surname, followed by a full (first and last) name; on the other hand, APA requires a surname, followed only by initials. In MLA entries, the author's name is followed by the title of the work, whereas in APA entries, the author's name is followed by the date. Both APA and MLA entries use hanging indentations (second and subsequent lines are indented five spaces). Other differences are also minor: MLA requires titles of books or periodicals to be underlined, articles or chapters to be placed within quotation marks, and all words of a title to be capitalized. On the other hand, APA italicizes the titles of books and magazines but uses no quotation marks around the titles of chapters or articles within these longer works. APA capitalizes only the first word of a book or article title, the first word of a subtitle (if there is one), and any proper nouns; all other words are lowercase. See the sample student papers for specific examples of how to handle various bibliographical matters.

WRITE THE FINAL COPY

Revising and editing your paper is the final step. Do not be easy on yourself. Pretend that the paper is someone else's and badly in need of work. Check for logical progression, completeness of development, and mechanical correctness. The task of rewriting and revising can be simplified if you know how to use a word processor, which will spare you the tedious chore of retyping every page that needs changing. Still, the only way to produce an excellent paper is to pore over it paragraph by paragraph for weaknesses or faults. After careful review and editing, type the final copy using one of the formats exemplified by the two student papers. If you are following the APA format, you will also need to write an abstract summarizing your findings (see student sample, pages 717–747). Remember that the appearance of a paper can add to or detract from its quality. Here are some important tips on manuscript appearance:

1. Use 8½ by 11 white paper. Double space throughout the paper.

2. Except for page numbers, use one-inch margins at the top, bottom, and sides of the paper. (For page numbers, see item 6.)

3. Avoid fancy fonts such as script.

4. Place a balanced and uncluttered outline before the text of the paper. Double-space throughout the outline. (See item 6 for paginating the outline.)

5. Do not use a title page unless your instructor specifies otherwise. Instead, type your name, instructor's name, course number, and date on the first page of the outline, repeating this information in the upper left-hand corner on the first page of the text. The title should be centered and double spaced below the date. (See sample papers.)

6. Number pages consecutively throughout the paper in the upper right-hand corner. Do not follow page numbers with hyphens, parentheses, periods, or other characters. Number the outline with lower-case Roman numerals (i, ii, iii, and so on). Number the first page of the paper itself, beginning with an Arabic 1 and continuing throughout the paper, including "Works Cited" or "Reference List."

7. Double-check the appropriate format (MLA or APA) for citing and documentation.

8. Note that APA papers feature an abstract and a running header. See sample paper for a model.

ANNOTATED STUDENT RESEARCH PAPER
Modern Language Association (MLA) Style

——————— **1** ———————

*The first page seen by your reader is the outline of your paper. Paginate the outline with small Roman numerals. Write your name in the top left-hand margin, followed by your instructor's name, the course title and number, and the date the paper is due.

——————— **2** ———————

Center the title of your paper. A good title should tell the reader what the paper is about. Double space throughout the outline.

——————— **3** ———————

The thesis consists of a single declarative sentence preceded by the word *Thesis.* The rest of the outline follows the rules for correct sentence outlining. Some instructors allow topic outlines, which consist of phrases rather than full sentences. Do not make the outline too long. A rule of thumb is to have one page of outline for every five pages of writing. The outline leaves out the details of the paper, mentioning only major points.

———————

*The Arabic numerals in the margins of the research paper correspond to the comments that follow.

i

1   Stephanie Hollingsworth

Dr. Ronald Dekker

English 101

September 30, 2003

2   Choosing Single Motherhood: A Sign of Modern Times?

3   Thesis: Increases in educational and career opportunities for women,

advances in medical technology, and diminishing social stigma

all contribute to the rising number of women who are choos-

ing to become single mothers.

  I. Women are waiting longer to start families.

    A. A shift in women's consciousness has occurred since the

1960s.

      1. Marriage is no longer a necessary component to

childbearing.

      2. The use of birth control gave women more choices over

when or even if to get pregnant.

    B. There are more opportunities for women today.

      1. More women are taking advantage of higher education.

      2. The number of career opportunities for women has

increased.

    C. Women are more willing to wait for the right partner.

      1. Personal fulfillment plays a higher role in the consciousness

of today's woman.

ii

    2. Many of today's women are children of divorce and would like to avoid that situation in their own marriages.

  D. Waiting longer creates concern for some women who fear the biological clock's ticking.

II. Advances in fertility technology are providing women with more options as to when and how to have a child.

  A. Women can have children later in life.

  B. Single women have the option of conceiving a child through donor insemination.

III. The social stigma of a single woman having a child has diminished.

  A. More adults today are children of divorce and therefore more tolerant of single parenting.

  B. The formation of support groups for single mothers has given single parenting a boost.

IV. Although many critics argue that single mothering by choice represents a breakdown of traditional family values, some studies indicate otherwise.

  A. Critics fear that the traditional nuclear family is quickly becoming the exception.

  B. Some studies argue that a father is not necessary for the healthy upbringing of a child.

    1. These studies show that children do not necessarily fare better when a father is present.

    2. Many fathers spend less than two and a half hours a day with their children.

4

College papers require no title page. Simply write your name in the top left-hand margin of the first page, your teacher's name, followed by the course title and number, and the date the paper is due—all of this information double spaced, each entry on a separate line. Then double space again, center the title (capitalizing only the first, last, and principal words and without underlining). Continue double spacing throughout the paper. Number all pages in the upper right-hand corner, one-half inch from the top and adjacent to the right margin. Place your name followed by a space before each page number (so that misplaced pages can be easily found). A one-inch margin is required on all sides. Do not staple the paper or place it in a folder; just use a large paper clip to hold the pages together.

5

The first paragraph grabs the reader by drawing attention to the difference between the traditional view of having babies and some modern women's views. The last sentence of the paragraph is the thesis. It is placed in the classical position at the end of the opening paragraph, where it controls the remainder of the paper. The parenthetical citation refers the reader to the bibliographical "Works Cited" list at the end of the paper. The abbreviation "qtd. in" means that the author is quoted in someone else's work. Integrating documentary sources into the flow of the paper takes considerable skill. Notice that the final period follows the final parenthesis of the citation except in case of a long quotation set off from the main text. Study the parenthetical documentation of this paper to see the various possibilities for handling source citations.

1

4

Stephanie Hollingsworth

Dr. Ronald Dekker

English 101

September 30, 1999

Choosing Single Motherhood: A Sign of Modern Times?

5

First comes love, then comes marriage, then comes baby in the baby carriage . . . not necessarily so. Today, an increasing number of children are being reared in single parent households, usually headed by the mother. These are women who, for whatever reason, have remained single and decided to have a child but don't believe that a husband is necessary for them to achieve motherhood. This trend is boosted by increased career opportunities for women that lessen the need for a husband's financial support. Consequently, the notion that a woman must be married in order to have a child is becoming less and less true. In an article written for *Time,* Dr. Nachtigall, a fertility specialist, captured the new trend in these words: "The biological drive to reproduce may be stronger than the cultural yearning to get married" (qtd. in Stonesifer 130–31). With increases in educational and career opportunities for women, advances in medical technology making single motherhood a safe and relatively affordable choice, and diminishing social stigma, America's rising number of single mothers by choice comes as little surprise.

6

The second paragraph introduces the student writer's first major subidea, that women are waiting longer to start families. Along with this change has come a substantial rise in the number of children born to unmarried women. The writer observes research convention by introducing the source of a long or important quotation, especially when referring to the source for the first time. A prose quotation longer than four lines should be indented one inch (left-hand margin only) and should not be enclosed in quotation marks. Also, do not single space quotations. The parenthetical citation follows the final period of the quotation.

7

A parenthetical citation is not necessary following the indented quotation for two reasons: the corporate author of this source is mentioned in the introduction to the indented quotation; and the source is a Website, which has no pagination (see pp. 693 and 697 for other examples of indented quotations.) The superscript "1" at the end of the paragraph refers the reader to the "Notes" on p. 10 of the paper. On p. 6, superscript "2" appears. It, too, refers the reader to the "Notes" on p. 10.

8

Because the author and title of the work have been introduced, only the page number needs to be placed in parentheses. Notice how in this sentence and the following paragraphs the quoted material is so well integrated into the grammatical structure of the text that it does not interrupt the natural flow of the ideas.

6　　According to the National Center for Health Statistics, there has been a substantial rise in the number of children born to unmarried mothers:

> Out-of-wedlock childbearing has been increasing in the United States for over half a century. The rate of non-marital births in 1993 was more than six times the rate in 1940, and the proportion of births that occur outside marriage has risen from four to thirty-one percent. By most measures, the increase has accelerated sharply over the past fifteen years.[1]

7　　Some of this new attitude can be attributed to the dramatic shift in the consciousness of women since the 1960s. The women's movement created feelings of empowerment and self-sufficiency, and the advent of the birth control pill gave a woman control over when to become a mother, if at all. These twin events also emboldened women to challenge the established paradigms on marriage and childbearing. Marriage became more optional as having a child on one's own became possible. In her book, *Going Solo: Single Mothers by Choice,* Jean Renvoize claims that it is "impossible to look at the subject of single parenting by choice without considering what effect the women's movement has had and is continuing to have on women all over the world" (3).

8　　The movement also opened a myriad of job opportunities for women, which many took advantage of, resulting in the postponement or relinquishment of marriage and children. In fact, it has been found that there is a direct correlation between the amount of education a

——————— **9** ———————

The parenthetical citation indicates that this information is found on pages 116 and 117 in the source authored by Ludtke and fully documented in the works cited.

Hollingsworth 3

woman has and her likelihood of having children. A survey conducted

by Molly McKaughan in her book, *The Biological Clock,* reported that,

". . . only a third of the women who did not attend college are child-

less, whereas over half of the college grads are in this position and over

two thirds of the MBAs and women with PhDs or MDs hear the clock

ticking" (3).

More women are pursuing higher education and professional occu-

pations before beginning families, resulting in a higher median age for

first-time brides and mothers, with some women forgoing marriage

altogether and opting for single motherhood. The National Center for

Health Statistics reports that among all unmarried women aged 35–39,

the increase in birthrates from 1984–1994 was 82% (Ludtke 116–17).

Many women come from families of divorce and are waiting longer

to get married, if only to avoid becoming involved in a messy divorce

themselves. Women whose mothers married right after high school are

pursuing academic and career ambitions rather than setting those aside

and beginning a family immediately. The increase in opportunities has

restructured women's priorities; and because fulfillment of personal

goals has become more important to women than in previous years,

many are willing to wait for their ideal partner. Today's woman doesn't

need to rush into a marriage for reasons of financial security alone. She

is often more economically independent than her mother and doesn't

feel the pressure to succumb to society's antiquated convention of

marrying a good provider. Instead, today's woman feels she deserves

9

Hollingsworth 4

more and is willing to wait for it. The National Center for Health Sta-

tistics indicates the following:

> Among . . . women in the early childbearing ages, the decline in
>
> the married population largely reflects delays in the timing of
>
> first marriage. The percent of women aged twenty-five to
>
> twenty-nine who had never been married tripled from eleven to
>
> thirty-three percent, between 1950 and 1992. (Online. *The*
>
> *Demography*)

Consequently, because of these choices, more women are finding

themselves approaching middle age unmarried and childless—a situa-

tion that can create feelings of disappointment in women who want to

have a family. Melissa Ludtke, author of *On Our Own: Unmarried Mother-*

hood in America, offers the following assessment:

> Today, because cultural and economic forces encourage women
>
> to delay marriage and childbearing, many more women, married
>
> and single, arrive at their middle to late thirties feeling that
>
> they've missed out on a big part of what their lives were meant
>
> to include. (104)

Unfortunately a woman's childbearing years are finite and a "biological

clock panic" may hit when a single woman who wants children nears

forty. In an article titled "Saga of a Midlife Single Mom," one woman is

quoted as making the following observation:

> I was starting to approach my 40th birthday. Up until then I was
>
> never around kids very much and, frankly, preferred the idea of a
>
> house full of dogs and cats. The 40th approach must have made

my biological clock start ticking more loudly. I didn't want to be one of those women who at age 50 said "Oops, I forgot to have a baby." I began to feel like I was missing something that was a really important experience—something that would really mean something.

Concerned about their ability to conceive as they grow older, a number of these women begin to think about the possibility of having a child on their own. As Molly McKaughan states the case, "If a woman hears the clock ticking and is filled with anxiety about how much time she has left, she is more likely to consider going ahead on her own" [citation should be (89)]. A study conducted by The Institute for Social Science Research in Los Angeles found that "half the women surveyed said they would consider having and rearing a child by themselves if they were childless by the time they reached their forties" (Ludtke 22).

The decision to opt for single motherhood is rarely taken lightly, and it is often not the woman's first choice. According to author Molly McKaughan,

> Eighty percent of women who say they are considering single motherhood plan on waiting three to five years before going ahead. Most are hoping that the elusive right man for them will show up and they will be able to have babies under normal circumstances. [citation should be (104)].

Many of these women have not disregarded marriage; however, they do not feel they must hinge their childbearing future on whether or not the right man comes along, and most are unwilling to settle for an

————————— **10** —————————

The second major subidea is introduced—namely that advances in fertility technology are providing women with more options as to when and how to have children (see II of outline). This assertion is then supported through documented evidence.

Hollingsworth 6

inadequate partner and potential father of their children merely to fulfill this desire. Cynthia, "one of the first in the wave of single professional women to choose deliberately to birth and raise a child without
a partner," sums up her decision in these words: "I'm a single mother
by choice, which doesn't mean that I'm choosing not to be in relationship with a man. It means that I was not in a relationship with a man
and I chose to have a child. That's different" (Alexander 26).[2]

10   Technology today is moving at an incredible pace, and some of the
most amazing scientific discoveries have dealt with reproduction.
Advances in fertility technology are providing women with numerous
options, including when and how to conceive a child. Older women
who have delayed pregnancy are not faced with the medical risks taken
by earlier generations. In the past, single women who had chosen to
conceive were forced to engage in risky sexual behavior, but sperm
banks now offer a safe alternative along with a myriad of potential
donors. Women can screen for everything from cultural background
to IQ. California Cryobank, a Los Angeles sperm bank, estimates that
25% of the women seeking donor insemination are single. According
to *When Baby Makes Two: Single Mothers by Chance or by Choice*,
authored by Jene Stonesifer, "increasingly, single women who don't have
a steady are turning to artificial insemination as a way to experience motherhood. Its appeal lies in that it is relatively safe, simple and
affordable" (128–29). For costs ranging from $50.00 to $150.00 a day,
donor insemination allows a woman to choose a deliberate pregnancy

——————— 11 ———————

Subidea number 3 is introduced (see III of outline). Here the writer shows that the social stigma of being a single mother has diminished.

——————— 12 ———————

The source of the quotation is given as having been found on the Internet, its author's last name being Thornton. The full reference, of course, is found in "Works Cited."

Hollingsworth 7

in a safe, accessible fashion ("Donor Insemination Resources"). Moreover, there has been a dramatic alteration of society's perception of single mothers. In an article titled, "Attitudes, Values and Norms Related to
Non-marital Fertility," Arland Thornton gives this description:

> Recent data reveal fundamental shifts in values, attitudes, and
> norms concerning a wide range of family issues, including mar-
> riage, sexuality, and childbearing . . . In addition, attitudes and
> norms prohibiting . . . premarital sexual relationships, and child-
> bearing outside of marriage have dramatically receded. Thus,
> many behaviors that were previously restricted by prevailing
> social norms and personal attitudes have become accepted by
> substantial fractions of Americans.

11   Whereas previously a woman who found herself unmarried and pregnant would either try to hide the fact from society or rush to get married, today's single mother experiences less societal opposition to her
lifestyle. Because the single parent phenomenon has become so widespread, its stigma has lessened dramatically and many Americans "agree
that there is no reason why single women shouldn't have children and
12   rear them if they want to" (Thorton).

No longer is the single mother regarded as a social deviant, and
many single mothers are finding support from family, friends, and
organized groups. This is true also for women who are consciously
choosing this lifestyle. Single Mothers By Choice, a nation-wide group
devoted to providing information and support to single mothers, was

——————— **13** ———————

The fourth and final subidea is introduced (see outline IV). Here the writer deftly indicates that she realizes that some opposition exists to the modern idea of single mothers. But she quickly minimizes the opposing point of view by offering documentation supporting her thesis that single motherhood is here to stay and is a sign of the times.

Hollingsworth 8

described by one member as a group of "single women who chose to become single mothers; single mothers who are mature and responsible and who feel empowered rather than victimized" (*Mattes* xxi).

13   There are, however, opponents to the single mother phenomenon. Critics argue that single motherhood signals a breakdown of traditional family values; yet these same critics fail to recognize that the traditional nuclear family is quickly becoming a thing of the past and that "in an era in which close to one half of all marriages end in divorce, belief in marriage as a secure, supportive relationship has greatly diminished" (Ludtke 117). By the mid-1990s, three of every ten families with young children had only one parent (usually the mother) living with them (25). Critics also argue that the absence of a father in the house causes harm to children growing up. However, they neglect to mention that the father, even if he still lives at home, often spends little time actually caring for the child. A study by Karl Zinsmeister, a DeWitt Wallace Fellow at the American Enterprise Institute, found that three-fourths of modern dads do not take regular responsibility for the daily care of their children; and studies of children from kindergarten to tenth grade found that daily father-child interaction averages only between thirty minutes to two and a half hours (*Stonesifer* ii). And author Trish Wilson, in a critique of "Deconstructing the Essential Father," an article written by Louise B. Silverstein and Carl F. Auerbach, found that "Mothers, not fathers, continue to take on the bulk of the day-to-day childrearing and housekeeping, whether or not they work outside the home" (qtd. in Wilson).

——————— 14 ———————

Like all good research papers, this one reflects mostly the ideas of outside sources, not the writer's own. Nevertheless, the student provides enough commentary of her own to make a convincing case for her thesis. As is proper in a formal research paper, the writer expresses her opinions without using the personal pronouns *I, me,* and *my.*

Hollingsworth 9

14 On the whole, women's lives have changed dramatically in the last few decades, with one of the most significant lifestyle changes being the increasing numbers of women who are choosing the single motherhood lifestyle. Pursuing her own goals and unwilling to settle for an unsatisfactory partner, today's single-mother-by-choice is truly a sign of the times.

—————— 15 ——————

Both notes are listed on a separate page, under the "Notes" (not underlined and without quotation marks), centered and one inch from the top of the page. The Notes page appears at the end of the paper but before Works Cited page. The notes are double spaced throughout.

15

Notes

[1] An informal poll of my female friends indicated that the majority of them would not consider giving birth to a baby without a father to help in his or her upbringing.

[2] It must be noted that some sociologists see a backlash occurring and predict that the difficulties of being the sole breadwinner and parent are leading women to return to the traditional approach of waiting until they have a husband before planning to give birth.

———————— **16** ————————

The heading "Works Cited" (not underlined and without quotation marks) is centered on the page one inch from the top. The entire page is double spaced. Notice that the second and subsequent lines of each entry are indented one-half inch. The entries appear in alphabetical order according to the first letter of the entry. Left and right margins are one inch.

———————— **17** ————————

Typical entry for a book.

———————— **18** ————————

Typical entry for a source found on the Internet.

Hollingsworth 11

16   Works Cited

17   Alexander, Shoshana. <u>In Praise of Single Parents: Mothers and Fathers</u>

            <u>Embracing Challenges</u>. New York: Houghton Mifflin, 1994.

18   "Donor Insemination Resources." 2 Aug. 2003. 6 Sept. 2003

            <http://www.parentsplace.com/family/singleparent/gen/

            0,3375,10660,00.html>.

        Fabe, Marilyn, and Norma Wikler. <u>Up against the Clock: Career</u>

            <u>Women Speak on the Choice to Have Children</u>. New York:

            Random, 1979.

        Ludtke, Melissa. <u>On Our Own: Unmarried Motherhood in America</u>.

            New York: Random, 1997.

        Mattes, Jane. <u>Single Mothers by Choice: A Guidebook for Single</u>

            <u>Women Who Are Considering or Have Chosen Single Mother-</u>

            <u>hood</u>. New York: Random, 1994.

        McKaughan, Molly. <u>The Biological Clock</u>. New York: Doubleday, 1987.

        National Center for Health Statistics. <u>The Demography of Out-of-</u>

            <u>Wedlock Childbearing</u>. 11 Sept. 2003. 18 Sept. 2003

            <http://www.cdc.gov/nchswww/data/Wedlock.pdf>.

        Renvoize, Jean. <u>Going Solo: Single Mothers by Choice</u>. New York:

            Routledge, 1985.

        "Saga of a Midlife Single Mom." 15 September 1999. 20 Sept. 2003

            <http://www.midlifemommies.com/singlemompart1.html>.

        Stonesifer, Jene. <u>When Baby Makes Two: Single Mothers by Chance or by</u>

            <u>Choice</u>. Los Angeles: Lowell, 1994.

—————— **19** ——————

Typical entry for a periodical with an annual volume as well as issue number.

Hollingsworth 12

Thorton, Arland. "Attitudes, Values and Norms Related to Non-marital
   Fertility." Institute for Social Research, Department of Sociology
   and Population Studies Center at the University of Michigan. 20
   Sept. 2003. 25 Sept. 2003.<http://www.cdc.gov/nchswww/data/
   Wedlock.pdf>.
Wilson, Trish. "Deconstructing Fatherhood Propaganda." <u>Feminista</u> 3.4
   (1999): 34–38.

ANNOTATED RESEARCH PAPER
American Psychological Association (APA) Style

DEVELOPMENT OF A SCALE

I

Development of a Scale to

Detect Sexual Harassers:

The Potential Harasser Scale (PHS)

Leanne M. Masden

and

Rebecca B. Winkler

DePaul University

——————— I ———————

The Abstract should not exceed 120 words. Any numbers present in the Abstract should appear as Arabic numerals (except a number that begins a sentence).

Abstract

The current study was an attempt to design a scale to detect one's propensity to sexually harass women. The Likelihood to Sexually Harass (LSH) scale designed by Pryor (1987) was used as a starting point in probing the characteristics held by men who sexually harass women. Using existing research, an initial scale was designed and tested on a pilot sample of men known to the authors. After the scale was completed by the participants, statistics were calculated and explored to determine which items needed to be retained and which needed to be dropped. Following these analyses, the Potential Harasser Scale (PHS) was determined to be statistically sound and ready for future use.

2

This is a typical citation, appearing at the sentence's conclusion and followed by a period. This work has three authors.

3

Because the information mentioned in this sentence is derived from three different sources, the paper's authors have chosen to place each citation adjacent to the corresponding element. Note that the first citation identifies a source with two authors, the second citation has three authors, and the third citation has one author.

DEVELOPMENT OF A SCALE

3

Development of a scale to detect sexual harassers:

The Potential Harasser Scale (PHS)

Our interest in the current topic was first sparked as a result of sexual

harassment being the focus of one team member's master's thesis. Current

estimates state that approximately one out of every two women will be

2   sexually harassed at least once during her working or educational life

(Fitzgerald, Swan, & Magley, 1997). But why do so many women experience

sexual harassment? Researchers have found evidence to support a power-

threat motive for offenders, where women who possess certain

characteristics that would put them in direct competition with men for

resources are more likely to be harassed, apparently in an attempt to

dissuade them from entering the male-dominated sphere of privilege and

3   power. Some such female characteristics are having egalitarian sex-role

attitudes (Dall'Ara & Maass, 1999), being single, having more education and

longer tenure within the organization (DeCoster, Estes, & Mueller, 1999),

and being young (Gruber, 1998). However, there is not pure consensus in

the field regarding the effect of age on the risk of being sexually harassed

(O'Connell & Korabik, 2000). Because men are more likely than women to

be perpetrators of sexual harassment (Fitzgerald, Magley, Drasgow, & Waldo,

1999), this particular population will be the focus of the present study.

During the initial research process, we discovered the Likelihood to

Sexually Harass (LSH) scale, originally developed by Pryor (1987). This scale

was designed to measure one's propensity to sexually harass based on the

possession of certain characteristics that perpetrators of sexual

—————— **4** ——————

Because the authors are mentioned in the sentence, a citation is not necessary at the sentence's conclusion.

—————— **5** ——————

The paper's first internal heading appears centered, using upper case and lower case.

—————— **6** ——————

The paper's second internal heading appears flush with the left margin, using upper case and lower case.

DEVELOPMENT OF A SCALE

4

harassment tend to have. This scale gave us the direction we needed to conduct further research in order to identify the relevant constructs this topic contained. Luckily, the LSH scale has generated a fair amount of research as a result of others attempting to find exactly what constructs this scale measures. For example, Driscoll, Kelly, and Henderson (1998) found that men who scored high on the LSH also held more traditional views toward women, more negative views toward women, and had a more masculine personality. Other researchers also found that aggression, acceptance of interpersonal violence, fraternity affiliation, and sex-role stereotyping were related to scoring high on the LSH (Lackie & de Man, 1997). In addition, Pryor (1987) showed that men scoring high on the LSH found it more difficult to view things from another's perspective and had higher authoritarian beliefs. As a result of this research, we now knew what we needed to include when we started to develop our own Potential Harasser Scale (PHS).

Method

Item and Scale Development

After reading the relevant research on our topic, we decided that our scale should include eight dimensions plus a few demographic questions. We also decided that each dimension should have four items. Our eight dimensions were as follows: Aggression, sex role stereotyping (i.e., holding traditional views toward women), egalitarianism/negative views towards women, masculinity, acceptance of interpersonal violence, lack of empathy, authoritarianism, and hostile environment behaviors.

The first seven dimensions were derived from the current literature on the topic of sexual harassment and related concepts. However, the last dimension was developed to fill a gap in the existing LSH scale. The LSH scale is designed to detect sexual harassers who exhibit *quid pro quo* behaviors, meaning those who attempt to exchange sexual favors for work-related promotions or other advantages (Pryor, 1987). However, this focus fails to address other forms of sexual harassment, such as hostile environment behaviors. This type of sexual harassment is considered to be less severe but even more pervasive (Fitzgerald, Gelfand, & Drasgow, 1995). Therefore, we thought it would be important to attempt to capture this dimension in our PHS instrument.

We also included a few demographic questions to see if age, race, or marital status were related to one's potential to sexually harass. In addition, a short section about fraternity membership and extent of one's involvement were included as a result of this affiliation being significantly related in previous research (Lackie & de Man, 1997). Therefore, our total scale had 37 items, 32 in the actual scale and 5 demographic questions. Furthermore, we renamed our instrument the *Personal Beliefs Questionnaire* so that those who completed our instrument would not be alerted to what it was attempting to measure.

Characteristics of the Pilot Sample

We recruited male classmates, co-workers, fathers, and significant others to complete our scale. As a result of our efforts, we had 14 respondents. All of them were Caucasian with the exception of one Hispanic. In addition, three individuals in our sample were married, five were single, and six currently

DEVELOPMENT OF A SCALE

6

lived with a partner. Our respondents ranged in age from 23 to 60, with a mean age of 30.28. Concerning fraternity affiliation, 35.7% of our sample were members of a fraternity, and 40% reported being "very involved."

Results

Results of Preliminary Item Analyses

First, we cleaned the data by looking at the frequencies and descriptive statistics. All values were within the expected range, so we considered our data to be clean. By taking a closer look at our means and standard deviations, we immediately noticed some items had extremely low standard deviations. For example, item 11 asks about one's acceptance of domestic violence. Whether the answers reflected socially desirable responses due to lack of anonymity with only fourteen respondents or true beliefs, everyone in our sample strongly disagreed with the appropriateness of hitting one's spouse.

We scanned the correlation matrix including all of our items, and with the exception of item 11, which had no correlations due to its lack of variance, every other item exhibited at least one theoretically meaningful correlation with another item. For example, two items relating to aggression were significantly correlated (i.e., "I am an aggressive driver" and "I enjoy playing sports with a lot of physical contact"). The only items that were not significantly correlated with anything else on the scale were those that tapped into fraternity affiliation and involvement.

We also ran an intraclass correlation analysis to determine our scale's internal consistency. As a result, our Cronbach's alpha was r = .8069, which shows that our scale had high internal consistency.

——————— **7** ———————

The authors refer the reader to the Appendix, which appears at the paper's conclusion and following the References.

DEVELOPMENT OF A SCALE

7

Final Scale Revision

Based on our initial item analyses, we determined that a few changes could be made that would improve our scale's psychometric properties. Therefore, we removed the items on fraternity affiliation and involvement. Although previous research has shown these constructs to be related to one's likelihood to sexually harass (Lackie & de Man, 1997), our analyses showed that these items were the only ones that were not significantly correlated to any other item in our scale. Since these items were in the demographics section, they were not included in the intraclass correlation analysis. Therefore, this analysis was not re-run, because no improvement would have been noted here.

    Although traditional scale construction theory would normally guide us to remove a few other items due to their low standard deviations, we decided that the low variance on these items was most likely due to the restrictions placed on us to our small sample. If we were to administer our scale to more people in a more anonymous setting, perhaps we would not see the same restricted variance due to the greater chance of people answering truthfully. In our small and familiar sample, we found many answers that may have been driven by a socially desirable and appropriate manner of responding. See the Appendix for the final version of the PHS.

Discussion

This project taught us many valuable lessons. To begin with, we were pleased with the fact that we were able to construct a theoretically

DEVELOPMENT OF A SCALE

8

meaningful instrument that also displayed desirable psychometric properties, such as our high Cronbach's alpha. In addition, it was an interesting experience to design items that fit into our proposed dimensions. We also had a fun time piloting it on our sample and gathering the reactions from our participants, in addition to analyzing their answers to draw the relevant conclusions on our new tool. However, there are also many things we would have done differently had this been a "real world" project.

First, merely masking our scale's true intent by designing a new label did not do much to mask the content and what we were trying to measure. Our participants (especially our classmates) could tell by the transparency of many of our items what we were aiming for. In addition, although we believe our sample to be well-educated and fairly liberal overall in their views toward women, they all still knew that we would be analyzing their responses and would probably be able to tell who was who if we really wanted to. Therefore, there may have been some socially desirable responding that caused many of our items to have low variances.

Some improvements in methodology could prevent this type of responding from occurring. For example, administering this scale in a more anonymous format with many other respondents (e.g., in an auditorium setting) would probably allow more truthful answers to emerge. Furthermore, if the scale items could be embedded within a larger instrument, the aim of the Potential Harasser Scale would also be less obvious. Overall, however, we were pleased with both the process and the results.

During the course of this project, we each also attempted to contact a publisher who had designed a relevant scale. One person contacted the

DEVELOPMENT OF A SCALE

9

company Risk and Needs Assessment, Inc., to obtain their Sexual Adjustment Inventory. The other person contacted Sigma Assessment Systems to obtain their Sex-Role Egalitarianism Scale.

Both of us were successful in our endeavors and did not have to endure any trouble at all. One team member simply called the publisher and received a sample packet in a matter of days that included one test book, two answer sheets, one training manual, one example report, and a computer disk that provided the scoring key program. The other person e-mailed the publisher and received a sample brochure in the mail a few days later. Therefore, the ease in contacting the publishers was about equal between the two team members, but the amount of scale information given varied greatly.

In summary, working on this project allowed us to put into action much of the theory that we have spent the past 10 weeks learning. It was interesting to us to experience the process of developing a scale as well as learning to deal with some of the pitfalls that inevitably occur with not having a large group of people we don't know to pilot our instrument on. However, all in all, we think we will be better survey and test developers in the future as a result of constructing the Potential Harasser Scale.

—————— **8** ——————

The list of references appears on a separate page (or pages), with the label References centered at the top of the page. All references cited in the text must appear in the Reference list; and each entry in the Reference list must be cited in the text of the paper.

—————— **9** ——————

References with the same first author and different second, third, or fourth authors are alphabetized by the surname of the second author (or, if the second author is the same, the surname of the third).

DEVELOPMENT OF A SCALE

10

8

References

Dall'Ara, E., & Maass, A. (1999). Studying sexual harassment in the laboratory: Are egalitarian women at higher risk? Sex Roles, 41(9/10), 681–704. Retrieved December 9, 2002, from Proquest Education Complete database.

DeCoster, S., Estes, S. B., & Mueller, C. W. (1999). Routine activities and sexual harassment in the workplace. Work and Occupations, 26(1), 21–49.

Driscoll, D. M., Kelly, J. R., & Henderson, W. L. (1998). Can perceivers identify likelihood to sexually harass? Sex Roles, 38(7/8), 557–588.

Fitzgerald, L. F., Gelfand, M. J., & Drasgow, F. (1995). Measuring sexual harassment: Theoretical and psychometric advances. Basic and Applied Social Psychology, 17, 425–427.

Fitzgerald, L. F., Magley, V. J., Drasgow, F., & Waldo, C. R. (1999). Measuring sexual harassment in the military: The sexual experiences questionnaire (SEQ-DoD). Military Psychology, 11(3), 243–263. Retrieved December 9, 2002, from Academic Search Elite database.

Fitzgerald, L. F., Swan, S., & Magley, V. J. (1997). But was it really sexual harassment? Legal, behavioral, and psychological definitions of the workplace victimization of women. In W. O'Donohue (Ed.), Sexual harassment: Theory, research, and treatment (pp. 5–28). Boston: Allyn & Bacon.

Gruber, J. E. (1998). The impact of male work environments and organizational policies on women's experiences of sexual harassment. Gender and Society, 12(3), 301–320.

9

DEVELOPMENT OF A SCALE

11

Lackie, L., & de Man, A. F. (1997). Correlates of sexual aggression among male university students. <u>Sex Roles</u>, *37*(5/6), 451–457.

O'Connell, C. E., & Korabik, K. (2000). Sexual harassment: The relationship of personal vulnerability, work context, perpetrator status, and type of harassment to outcomes. <u>Journal of Vocational Behavior</u>, *56*, 299–329.

Pryor, J. B. (1987). Sexual harassment proclivities in men. *Sex Roles, 17*(5/6), 269–290.

---------------- **10** ----------------

If the paper has only one appendix, label it Appendix. If your paper has more than one appendix, label each one with a capital letter (e.g., Appendix A, Appendix B). Provide a title for each appendix.

DEVELOPMENT OF A SCALE

12

10

Appendix: Personal Beliefs Questionnaire

Please rate how strongly you agree or disagree with the following statements using the scale provided below. Please answer all questions honestly; note that all of your answers will remain anonymous.

1=**Strongly Disagree**

2=**Disagree**

3=**Neither Agree nor Disagree**

4=**Agree**

5=**Strongly Agree**

1. Being around strong women makes me   1   2   3   4   5
   uncomfortable.

2. I am an aggressive driver (e.g. I cut   1   2   3   4   5
   people off, honk the horn often).

3. I believe some women are to blame   1   2   3   4   5
   for being raped (e.g., by wearing sexy
   clothes, flirting, etc.).

4. I believe that every citizen should have   1   2   3   4   5
   the right to carry a gun.

5. I believe that it is important for a woman   1   2   3   4   5
   to take care of her body so that she
   looks good for her man.

6. I believe that it is important to volunteer   1   2   3   4   5
   time or donate money to help others
   in need.

DEVELOPMENT OF A SCALE

13

I=Strongly Disagree

2=Disagree

3=Neither Agree nor Disagree

4=Agree

5=Strongly Agree

7. I believe that men should be the primary   I   2   3   4   5
   breadwinners for their families.

8. I believe that most homeless people are   I   2   3   4   5
   still homeless because they are lazy.

9. I believe that people should respect their   I   2   3   4   5
   place within an organizational hierarchy.

10. I believe that some women are still paid   I   2   3   4   5
    less than men for doing the same work.

11. I believe that sometimes it is OK for a   I   2   3   4   5
    husband to hit his wife.

12. I believe that too many women are   I   2   3   4   5
    focusing too much on their careers,
    to the detriment of their families.

13. I believe that too many women are trying   I   2   3   4   5
    to enter occupations that are better suited
    for men.

14. I believe that women should be primarily   I   2   3   4   5
    responsible for taking care of children.

15. I believe that women should not play sports I   2   3   4   5
    with a lot of physical contact (e.g., football).

DEVELOPMENT OF A SCALE

14

1=Strongly Disagree

2=Disagree

3=Neither Agree nor Disagree

4=Agree

5=Strongly Agree

16. I display pictures of naked/near naked women at work/school.	1	2	3	4	5
17. I do not question the decisions made by the President.	1	2	3	4	5
18. I enjoy cooking for others.	1	2	3	4	5
19. I enjoy magazines that display pictures of scantily clad women.	1	2	3	4	5
20. I enjoy participating in cultural events (e.g., attending dramatic plays, museums, poetry readings).	1	2	3	4	5
21. I enjoy playing sports with a lot of physical contact.	1	2	3	4	5
22. I enjoy playing video games that allow you to fight and kill others.	1	2	3	4	5
23. I enjoy watching action movies with scenes involving car crashes, fights, and guns.	1	2	3	4	5
24. I flirt with women at my place of work/school.	1	2	3	4	5
25. I often get into fights.	1	2	3	4	5
26. I tell lewd jokes at work/school.	1	2	3	4	5

DEVELOPMENT OF A SCALE

15

1=Strongly Disagree

2=Disagree

3=Neither Agree nor Disagree

4=Agree

5=Strongly Agree

27. I tend to raise my voice when I am upset.   1   2   3   4   5

28. I think it is important to obey   1   2   3   4   5

authority figures.

29. I try to put myself in others' shoes to   1   2   3   4   5

help me understand their situation.

30. In spousal disagreements, I believe that   1   2   3   4   5

the man should have the final say.

31. Watching the nightly news   1   2   3   4   5

can be depressing.

32. When it comes to asking a girl for a date,   1   2   3   4   5

I don't take no for an answer.

DEVELOPMENT OF A SCALE

16

Demographics

33. How old are you?_____

34. What is your race? Check one.

☐ Caucasian   ☐ African American   ☐ Hispanic

☐ Asian   ☐ Native American   Other_____

35. Please indicate your marital status. Check one.

☐ Married   ☐ Single   ☐ Divorced

☐ Widowed   ☐ Living with partner

36. Did you belong to a fraternity? Circle one.   Yes   No

If so, how involved were you? Circle one.

Not at all involved   Somewhat involved   Very involved

SUGGESTIONS FOR WRITING

1. Following the style advocated by your instructor, write a five- to eight-page research paper on one of the following psychological problems:

    a. Anorexia nervosa in teenage girls

    b. Effects of loneliness and alienation on the elderly

    c. The effects of divorce on children under the age of ten

    d. Alcoholism among high school students

    Be sure to document any significant statement not your own.

2. Write a paper on the relationship between art and social class. Focus your research on the following queries:

    a. Does art reflect a class bias?

    b. Do different classes hold to different standards for judging art?

    c. Are these standards related to the ways different classes perceive the world?

    d. Is there a sociology of art?

3. Choosing any poem or short story in this book, write a literary analysis focusing on theme, character, action, or form.

APPENDIX WRITING ASSIGNMENTS

Write a research paper, following the format suggested by your instructor. Above all, choose a topic in which you have a genuine interest. The following titles and restricted theses are presented to stimulate your own investigation.

Title	Thesis
"A Look at Thomas Wolfe"	The inconsistencies in Thomas Wolfe's writing can be directly attributed to constant family conflicts, to his doubts concerning his country's economic stability, and to his fear of not being accepted by his reading public.
"American Architectural Development"	The development of American architecture was greatly attenuated until the eighteenth century because of the lack of adequate transportation and manufacturing facilities, and because city life had not formed prior to that century.
"Wordsworth and Coleridge: Their Diverse Philosophies"	Although Wordsworth and Coleridge were both Romantic poets, they believed in two completely different philosophies of nature.
"Why Jazz Was What We Wanted"	This paper deals with the various trends that led to the rise, development, and recognition of jazz as an important part of American musical culture during the nineteenth and twentieth centuries.

Title	Thesis
"The Influence of Imagism on Twentieth-Century Poetry"	Imagism, a self-restricted movement, has greatly influenced twentieth-century poetry.
"Automation and Employment"	The current fear of humans being displaced by machines, or what alarmists term the "automation hysteria," is based on insubstantial reports.
"Needed: A New Definition of Insanity"	Our courts need a better definition of insanity because neither the M'Naghten Rule nor the psychological definition is adequate.
"The Proud Sioux"	In this paper, I shall prove that the Sioux Indians, although confined to a shabby reservation, still fought on stubbornly against their captors—the white man and his hard-to-accept peace terms.
"Women's Fashions after the World Wars"	The First and the Second World Wars had significant effects on women's fashions in America.
"Charlie Chaplin"	This paper deals with the various factors that made Charlie Chaplin the master of silent movies.
"The Funnies"	Today's funnies reflect a change in America's attitude toward violence, ethnic minorities, and ecology.
"The Decline of the Mayans"	The four most popular theories that have been advanced to explain the abrupt end of the Mayan civilization are: the effects of natural disaster, physical weaknesses, detrimental social changes, and foreign influence.
"Relief Paintings in Egyptian Mastabas"	The relief paintings found in the mastabas depict the everyday life of the Egyptian people.
"Athena"	The goddess Athena bestowed her favors not on those who worshipped her, but on those who fought for their own beliefs.
"Goldfish"	Originally from China, goldfish have been bred into one of the most beautiful and marketable species of fish.

ASSIGNMENT 2

The Literary Paper

HOW TO WRITE A PAPER ABOUT LITERATURE

Literature is a difficult subject to write about. First, it is a subject about which there is no shortage of opinions; a famous play such as *Hamlet* has been so thoroughly studied and interpreted that it would take a tome or two to collect everything that has been written about it. Beginning writers must therefore always live in dread that what they have to say about a work may be blasphemously contrary to established opinion.

Second, the beginning writer is often unaware of the tradition or era into which a piece of literature falls. Yet to write intelligently about a piece of literature, a student must be able to distinguish the qualities of its literary tradition from the properties singular to the particular work. It is nearly impossible, for instance, to write comprehensibly about the work of a Romantic poet unless one knows something about the disposition of Romanticism.

However, the beginning student is rarely called upon to perform any such feat of interpretation. Instead, what an instructor generally wishes to evoke from a student writer is simply an intelligent exploration of a work's meaning, along with a straightforward discussion of one or two of its techniques. The student might therefore be asked to analyze the meaning of a sonnet and to comment briefly on its prosody, to discuss the theme of a short story and to examine the actions and attitudes of a principal character, or to explain the social customs upon which a certain play is based.

Even so, there are numerous pitfalls awaiting the beginning commentator on literature. The first of these is a tendency to emote over a literary favorite. Students who fall victim to this trait mistake sentimentality for judgment, and write enthusiastically about how much they like a particular work. But this is not what the instructor is generally looking for in a student's essay. What is desired is not an outpouring of affection, but the careful expression of critical judgment.

A second mistake beginning students of literature often make is assuming that one opinion about a literary piece is as valid and as good as another. It is only in literature classes that one finds such extreme democracy. Geologists do not assume that one opinion about a rock is the same as another, nor do chemists or astronomers blithely accept every theory about chemicals and planets. This fallacious view of criticism has its origin in the mistaken belief that one's primary reaction toward literature is emotional. But the emotional response evoked by the literary work is not what a writing assignment is designed to draw out of a student. Instead, what the instructor is looking for is reasoned opinion based on a close reading of the text. Disagreements in interpretation can then be referred to the text, and evidence can be gathered to support one view over another. It is very much like two lawyers getting together to interpret the fine print on a contract. It is not at all like two people trying to reconcile their differing reactions to anchovy pizza. Interpretations that cannot be supported by the text may be judged farfetched or simply wrong; those that can be supported may be judged *more* right.

But perhaps the most common mistake of the student-critic is a tendency to serve up inconsistent, unproven, and fanciful interpretations of the literary work. Often, these take the guise of rather exotic meanings that the student has inferred and for which scanty (if any) evidence exists. In its most extreme form, this tendency leads to rampant symbol hunting, where the writer finds complex and knotty meanings bristling behind the most innocent statements. The only known cure is the insistence that all interpretations be grounded in material taken from the text itself. If you have devised an ingenious explanation or reading of a work, be certain that you can point to specific passages from it that support your interpretations, and always make sure that other passages do not contradict your thesis.

THE IN-CLASS ESSAY ON LITERATURE

Often students are asked to analyze and interpret literature in class-written essays. The literary work may consist of a poem, a passage from a novel being read by the class, a short story, or a play. Depending on how the assignment is worded, the student may be required to find and express the theme, analyze an action, interpret a symbol, or comment on form.

FINDING AND EXPRESSING A THEME

The theme of a literary work is its central or dominant idea, its comment on life. Finding and expressing this idea involves a form of literary algebra that requires students to think logically from cause to effect. Of course, writers say more than any summary theme can possibly express; finding a theme should not involve smothering a writer's work under a crude and simplistic summary. Instead, in the summary you should compress into a few brief sentences what you interpret as the emphasis of the work.

Consider the poem "Design" (p. 553). A moth has been found dead in a spider's web spun on a heal-all flower. The poet wonders what could have brought the moth to this particular flower, where a web was spun and a spider was waiting. Why didn't the moth go to another, safer flower? This apparently trivial discovery leads the poem to speculate that destiny operates in random and mysterious ways, which is more or less the central emphasis or theme of the poem.

This theme can, of course, be stated in several ways. So, for that matter, can the theme of any poem or other literary work. What you must do, after you have deciphered the theme of the work, is to make a statement and prove it. Proof can be supplied by quoting lines and passages from the work. The instructor can then reconstruct the process of thinking behind your conclusion. If you have misinterpreted the work, the proof allows the instructor to see how your misreading occurred.

ANALYZING CHARACTER AND ACTION

Fictional characters behave according to the same hopes, fears, hates, and loves that motivate real people, but the characters of fiction are found in exotic dilemmas real people hardly ever encounter. Consequently, fiction provides us with an opportunity to ponder how common people might react in uncommon situations; we can then draw moral lessons, psychological principles, and philosophical insights from their behavior. Without fiction, we would remain hemmed in by the narrow horizons of reality and experience.

By asking you to write an essay explaining why a certain character performed a certain action, your instructor is fostering valuable skills of social analysis. If you can understand the rage and jealousy of Othello or the isolated pride of Hester Prynne, you are better equipped to understand these emotions in yourself or in your acquaintances.

When you state that a certain character behaves a certain way, the burden of proof is on you. It is not enough to say that Hamlet was indecisive or weak, or that Lear was overweening and arrogant, or that the unidentified male character in "Hills Like White Elephants" is petty and selfish. In every instance, you must quote passages that prove your interpretation.

INTERPRETING SYMBOLS

In its most literal sense, a symbol is a thing that stands for something beyond itself. The dove is a symbol of peace; the flag is the symbol of a country. In literature, a symbol is created when an author invests an object, an idea, or an action with a significance far beyond itself. A person may also be treated in such a way as to symbolize a class or a group of people.

Most of the time, symbolism is implicit in literature. The reader is left to unravel the meaning of the symbol. Indeed, the effect of a symbol would otherwise be ruined by preachiness. But occasionally an author will come out and say what a certain symbol means. For instance, in "Ars Poetica" (p. 390), the poet tells us explicitly that "An empty doorway and a maple leaf" are symbols that stand for "all the history of grief."

In the interpretation of symbols, it is less a matter of who is right or wrong than of who has proven a point and who has not. Symbols rarely have cut-and-dried, unarguable meanings. Considerable variation in the interpretation of symbols is not only possible, but extremely likely. Whatever your interpretation, however, it must be supported by material quoted from the text.

COMMENTING ON FORM

For the most part, this type of assignment applies to poetry, where the student has numerous opportunities to express a knowledge of the terms and concepts of prosody. (Fiction and drama contain fewer nameable techniques.) In writing about a poem, you may be asked to describe its verse form or its meter, or to label and identify various tropes and figures of speech.

Wherever possible, use the formal names of any techniques present in a work. If you know that the poem you are analyzing is an Italian sonnet, it does no harm to say so. If you know that a certain action in a play occurs in its *denouement*, you should not be bashful about using that term. If a story begins *in media res* and then proceeds in *flashbacks*, you should say so. Your use of such labels will show an instructor that you have not only mastered the meaning of the work, but have also grasped its form.

In summary, when writing about literature, you should do more than simply ascribe a certain interpretation to the literary work. Your prime purpose should be to prove that your reading of the work is reasonable and logical. Passages from the work should be liberally quoted to support your paper's interpretation of it. Above all, never assume that any reading of a work, no matter how unsupported or farfetched, will do.

Bear one thing in mind before you begin to write your paper: Famous literary works, especially works regarded as classics, have been thoroughly studied to the point where prevailing opinion on them has assumed the character of orthodoxy. What may seem to you a brilliant insight may, in fact, be nothing more than what critics have been saying about the writer and his or her works for years. Saying that Hemingway's male characters suffer from *machismo* is a little like the anthropology student opining that humans are bipedal. Both remarks are undoubtedly true, but they are neither original nor insightful. You should, therefore, check out the prevailing critical opinions on a writer before attempting to dogmatize on your own.

THE LITERARY PAPER

The following literary paper is one student's response to the following assignment: "Write a 500-word critical analysis of Eudora Welty's 'A Worn Path,' (see pp. 754–763) focusing on character, action, mood, setting, and literary techniques such as diction, figurative language, and symbolism. Choose those strategies that best illumine the theme of the narrative."

——————— **I** ———————

*The introductory paragraph captures the reader's attention by creating a "jewel" metaphor. It also presents the reviewer's unqualified literary judgment—that "A Worn Path" is an excellent, moving story.

——————— **2** ———————

Paragraph two provides a summary of the story's literal level, allowing even the uninitiated reader to comprehend the reviewer's coming comments and interpretations.

---

*The Arabic numerals in the margins of the research paper correspond to the comments that follow.

I

Douglas B. Inman
English 102
Professor McCuen
March 15, 1988

A Worn, but Lightly Traveled Path

1   In this day when mediocrity is praised as inspiration and
chaos as art, it is refreshing to find among the literary dung
heaps a jewel, shining and glittering and making one forget, for
the moment, the overwhelming stench and filth that threatens
to suffocate, and squeeze the very life from one's literary soul.
Eudora Welty's "A Worn Path" is such a rare jewel. Here is a
story that exudes craftsmanship from every pore. It is filled with
finely turned phrases, distinctly vivid imagery, and carefully
constructed moods; but, more importantly, it tells its story well,
communicating on many different levels. Ms. Welty demonstrates
a firm command of the art of storytelling, and the way she
weaves this particular tapestry of words will convince the reader
that here is a lady who could turn a sow's ear into silk.

2   "A Worn Path" is the portrait of Phoenix Jackson, an old
Negro woman, seen making a trip to town to retrieve badly
needed medicine for her ailing grandchild. Burdened by age
and faced with obstacles, she nevertheless presses on, stoically
pursuing her goal. On the most obvious level, this is the
story of an eccentric but delightful woman whose spirit

——————— **3** ———————

Paragraph three begins the most important part of this critical review. The student has chosen to focus on the symbolic level of the story. For him, the importance of the narrative lies in its relationship to the history of black freedom in America.

——————— **4** ———————

Here, as in several other passages, the reviewer carefully quotes from the story in order to bolster his argument—that the plight of Phoenix Jackson is also the history of blacks in America. Notice that each quotation is smoothly integrated into the main text of the essay. Note also that when Phoenix Jackson, the character, is speaking, the student writer uses single quotation marks within double quotation marks. But when the student is quoting the narrator, he uses double quotation marks only. In this way the reader can distinguish what the narrator says from what the character says in monologue or dialogue.

——————— **5** ———————

The reviewer is straightforward in his explication of the thorn bush as a significant individual symbol within the total allegorical framework.

Inman 2

belies her advanced years. She makes the long and arduous trip to town despite the great distance, the many obstacles she encounters, and an encroaching senility that gently touches the soul of the reader. She climbs hills, crosses a creek by way of a suspended log, crawls under a barbed wire fence, marches through fields, confronts a stray dog, and comes to grips with exhaustion, hallucinations, and a failing memory. And throughout these ordeals, the author reveals a character filled with pride and dignity.

But there is another story here, one played out on a much deeper level. It is the story of black people in America, and their struggle for freedom and equality. The path Phoenix follows is the road of life for her people, and the obstacles she encounters on the way become the challenges of being black.

For instance, she comes to a hill. "'Seems like there is chains about my feet, time I get this far,'" she says, and we know that it is the hill out of slavery that she must climb. And she does it, although "'something,'" white people perhaps, "'pleads I should stay.'" And when she gets to the top, she turns and gives a "full, severe look behind her where she had come." Doubtless this action represents the black race scrutinizing in retrospect some especially difficult scene in the drama of their freedom. Phoenix encounters opposition to her newfound freedom in the form of a thorny bush, and here her dress is a symbol of that freedom, as she struggles to free herself from the thorns without tearing her garment. But

─────────── **6, 7** ───────────

Two more symbols—the marble cake and the scarecrow—are interpreted.

─────────── **8** ───────────

The reviewer alludes to Egyptian mythology in order to draw attention to the special significance of the heroine's name.

─────────── **9** ───────────

The reviewer points out other bird symbols and interprets them. Even the little grandson is seen as a bird symbol. Again, quotations from the story are used as primary sources to support the reviewer's claims.

Inman 3

6   she maintains her dignity, showing no spite for the thorns, saying
"'you doing your appointed work. Never want to let folks
past—.'" And finally, trembling from the experience, "she stood
free."

7   But freedom for blacks is an illusive thing, as the reader
understands when a small boy seems to bring Phoenix a slice of
marble-cake, "but when she went to take it there was just her
own hand in the air." Like the cake, freedom for the blacks has
historically often been a seductive picture that seemed real; yet,
when the blacks tried to claim it, it dissolved back into fantasy.

8   Phoenix passes through the childhood of her race when she
traverses fields of "withered cotton" and "dead corn." She
encounters "something tall, black, and skinny," and it is both a
scarecrow and the image of slavery past. "'Who be you the
ghost of?'" she asks, but there is only silence and the scarecrow
dancing in the wind. And here Phoenix is the Negro of the past
giving way to the future, as she intones, "'Dance, old scarecrow,
while I dancing with you.'"

9   In this story, birds are used repeatedly to symbolize freedom.
The character's very name, Phoenix, is an illustration of this
strategy, for the phoenix was a bird in Egyptian mythology
which, every five hundred years, would consume itself in fire
and then rise renewed from the ashes, as blacks rose from
slavery after the Civil War. Other bird symbols occur. For
instance, Phoenix comes to a place where quail are walking
about, and she tells then, as she would young Negroes, "'Walk

────────────── **10** ──────────────

The reviewer begins to summarize by focusing on the mood of the story, calling it "optimistic." In other words, the summary appraisal is that this is a story of hope and triumph, not of bitterness and despair.

Inman 4

pretty. This is the easy place. This is the easy going,'" referring to the new time of freedom after the Civil War. And when she encounters a white hunter, she sees in his sack a bobwhite, "with its beak hooked bitterly to show it was dead," indicating that even though slavery has been abolished, whites still managed to oppress blacks, and the struggle for black freedom is not yet complete.

Phoenix's grandson represents the new generation of blacks who never knew slavery, but still feel its impact, and he too is portrayed as a bird of freedom. "'He suffer and it don't seem to put him back at all. He got a sweet look. He going to last. He wear a little patch quilt and peep out, holding his mouth open like a little bird,'" she tells a nurse in town.

10   Overall, the story is an optimistic outlook on the black experience. Though much of the action focuses on earlier hardship, it ends with hope for the future, as can be seen when Phoenix finally reaches town. There, it is Christmas time, while during her journey it is simply a cold December day. In town, dozens of black children whirl around her in the street, bells are ringing, and colorful lights abound. "'Here I be,'" she says, indicating the end of the journey, the attaining of freedom and new life. And already the past is being forgotten; all the slavery, the fight for freedom, the long and painful road to happiness is but a dim memory. "'It was my memory had left me,'" she says near the end, "'There I sat and forgot why I made my long trip.'"

"'Forgot?'" asks the nurse. "'After you came so far?'"

——————— **I I** ———————

The final paragraph makes the point that it is Phoenix Jackson, the heroine and major character of the story, who gives the story its meaning and beauty. The concluding sentence brings the analysis full circle by using the same jewel/gem metaphor used in the introduction.

Inman 5

11   This is the story of a courageous and dignified old woman on a long journey, but it is also the story of a courageous and dignified race, and their long struggle for freedom and equality. With wonderful artistry, Eudora Welty takes the reader along, to travel this worn path of struggle that has been trudged by so many peoples over the ages. She shows the dignity in the struggle and the hope of a new generation. And she does so with the craftsmanship of a fine watchmaker. One cannot help but be changed in some way by this beautiful story. "A Worn Path" is truly a gem.

Glossary

abstract Words or phrases denoting ideas, qualities, and conditions that exist but cannot be seen. *Love,* for example, is an abstract term; so are *happiness, beauty,* and *patriotism.* The opposite of abstract terms are concrete ones—words that refer to things that are tangible, visible, or otherwise physically evident. *Hunger* is abstract, but *hamburger* is concrete. The best writing blends the abstract with the concrete, with concrete terms used in greater proportion to clarify abstract ones. Writing too steeped in abstract words or terms tends to be vague and unfocused.

ad hominem **argument** A fallacious argument that attacks the integrity or character of an opponent rather than the merits of an issue. (*Ad hominem* is Latin for "to the man.") It is also informally known as "mud-slinging."

ad populum **argument** A fallacious argument that appeals to the passions and prejudices of a group rather than to its reason. (*Ad populum* is Latin for "to the people.") An appeal, for instance, to support an issue because it's "the American Way" is an *ad populum* argument.

allusion A casual reference to some famous literary work, historical figure, or event. For example, to say that a friend "has the patience of Job" means that he is as enduring as the biblical figure of that name. Allusions must be used with care lest the audience miss their meaning.

ambiguity A word or an expression having two or more possible meanings is said to be ambiguous. Ambiguity is a characteristic of some of the best poetry, but it is not a desired trait of expository writing, which should clearly state what the writer means.

analogy A comparison that attempts to explain one idea or thing by likening it to another. Analogy is useful if handled properly, but it can be a source of confusion if the compared items are basically unlike.

argumentation A writer's attempt to convince the reader of a point. It is based on appeals to reason, evidence proving the argument, and sometimes emotion to persuade. Some arguments attempt merely to prove a point, but others go beyond proving to inciting the reader to action. At the heart of all argumentation lies a debatable issue.

audience The group for whom a work is intended. For a writer, the audience is the reader whom the writer desires to persuade, inform, or entertain. Common sense tells us that a writer should always write to the level and needs of the particular audience for whom the writing is meant. For example, if you are writing for an unlettered audience, it is pointless to cram your writing with many literary allusions whose meanings will likely be misunderstood.

balance In a sentence, a characteristic of symmetry between phrases, clauses, and other grammatical parts. For example, the sentence "I love Jamaica for its weather, its lovely scenery, and its people" is balanced. This sentence —"I love Jamaica for its weather, its lovely scenery, and because its people are friendly"—is not. See also **parallelism.**

causal analysis A mode of developing an essay in which the writer's chief aim is to analyze cause or predict effect. For example, in "Why Tigers Become Man-Eaters," Jim Corbett's chief aim is to explain why some tigers start to prey on people.

cliché A stale image or expression, and the bane of good expository writing. "White as a ghost" is a cliché; so is "busy as a bee." Some clever writers can produce an effect by occasionally inserting a cliché in their prose, but most simply invent a fresh image rather than cull one from the public stock.

coherence The principle of clarity and logical adherence to a topic that binds together all parts of a composition. A coherent essay is one whose parts—sentences, paragraphs, pages—are logically fused into a whole. Its opposite is an incoherent essay—one that is jumbled, illogical, and unclear.

colloquialism A word or expression acceptable in informal usage but inappropriate in formal discourse. A given word may have a standard as well as a colloquial meaning. *Bug,* for example, is standard when used to refer to an insect; when used to designate a virus, for example "She's at home recovering from a *bug,*" the word is a colloquialism.

comparison/contrast A rhetorical mode used to develop essays that systematically match two items for similarities and differences. See the comparison/contrast essay examples in Chapter 12.

conclusion The final paragraph or paragraphs that sum up an essay and bring it to a close. Effective conclusions vary widely, but common tacks used by writers to end their essays include summing up what has been said, suggesting what ought to be done, specifying consequences that are likely to occur, restating the beginning, and taking the reader by surprise with an unexpected ending. Most important of all, however, is to end the essay artfully and quietly in a way that emphasizes your main point without staging a grand show for the reader's benefit.

concrete Said of words or terms denoting objects or conditions that are palpable, visible, or otherwise evident to the senses. *Concrete* is the opposite of *abstract.* The difference between the two is a matter of degree. *Illness,* for example, is abstract; *ulcer* is concrete; "sick in the stomach" falls somewhere between the two. The best writing usually expresses abstract propositions in concrete terms.

connotation The implication or emotional overtones of a word rather than its literal meaning. *Lion,* used in a literal sense, denotes a beast (see **denotation**). But to say that Winston Churchill had "the heart of a lion" is to use the connotative or implied meaning of *lion.*

deduction Something inferred or concluded. Deductive reasoning moves from the general to the specific.

denotation The specific and literal meaning of a word, as found in the dictionary. The opposite of *connotation.*

description A rhetorical mode used to develop an essay whose primary aim is to depict a scene, person, thing, or idea. Descriptive writing evokes the look, feel, sound, and sense of events, people, or things. See Chapter 8 for instructions on writing a descriptive essay.

diction The choice of words a writer uses in an essay or other writing. Implicit in the idea of diction is a vast vocabulary of synonyms—words that have more or less equivalent meanings. If only one word existed for every idea or condition, diction would not exist. But because we have a choice of words with various shades of meaning, a writer can and does choose among words to express ideas. The diction of skilled writers is determined by the audience and occasion of their writing.

division and classification A rhetorical mode for developing an essay whose chief aim is to identify the parts of a whole. A division and classification essay is often an exercise in logical thinking. See, for example, "Thinking as a Hobby," by William Golding in Chapter 13.

documentation In a research paper, the support provided for an assertion, theory, or idea, consisting of references to the works of other writers. Different styles of documentation exist. Most disciplines now use the parenthetical style of documentation—see the sample research paper, "Choosing Single Motherhood: A Sign of the Times," in the Appendix—where citations are made within the text of the paper rather than in footnotes or endnotes.

dominant impression The central theme around which a descriptive passage is organized. For example, a description of an airport lobby would most likely use the dominant impression of rush and bustle, which it would support with specific detail, even though the lobby may contain pockets of peace and tranquility. Likewise, a description of Cyrano de Bergerac—the famous dramatic lover whose nose was horrendously long—would focus on his nose rather than on an inconspicuous part of his face.

emotion, appeal to An appeal to feelings rather than to strict reason; a legitimate ploy in an argument as long as it is not excessively and exclusively used.

emphasis A rhetorical principle that requires stress to be given to important elements in an essay. Emphasis may be given to an idea in various parts of a composition. In a sentence, words may be emphasized by placing them at the beginning or end or by judiciously italicizing them. In a paragraph, ideas may be emphasized by repetition or by the accumulation of specific detail.

essay From the French word *essai*, or "attempt," the essay is a short prose discussion of a single topic. Essays are sometimes classified as formal or informal. A formal essay is aphoristic, structured, and serious. An informal essay is personal, revelatory, humorous, and somewhat loosely structured.

evidence The logical bases or supports for an assertion or idea. Logical arguments consist of at least three elements: propositions, reasoning, and evidence. The first

of these consists of the ideas that the writer advocates or defends. The logical links by which the argument is advanced make up the second. The statistics, facts, anecdotes, and testimonial support provided by the writer in defense of the idea constitute the evidence. In a research paper, evidence consisting of paraphrases or quotations from the works of other writers must be documented in a footnote, endnote, or parenthetical reference. See also **argumentation** and/or **documentation.**

example An instance that is representative of an idea or claim or that otherwise illustrates it. The example mode of development is used in essays that make a claim and then prove it by citing similar and supporting cases. See, for example, the essays in Chapter 11.

exposition Writing whose chief aim is to explain. Most college composition assignments are expository.

figurative Said of a word or expression used in a nonliteral way. For example, the expression "to go the last mile" may have nothing at all to do with geographical distance, but may mean to complete a task or job.

focus In an essay, the concentration or emphasis on a certain subject or topic.

generalization A statement that asserts some broad truth based on a knowledge of specific cases. For instance, the statement "big cars are gas guzzlers" is a generalization about individual cars. Generalizations are the products of inductive reasoning, where a basic truth may be inferred about a class after experience with a representative number of its members. However, one should beware of rash or faulty generalizations—those made on insufficient experience or evidence. It was once thought, for example, that scurvy sufferers were malingerers, which led the British navy to the policy of flogging the victims of scurvy aboard its ships. Later, medical research showed that the lethargy of scurvy victims was an effect rather than the cause of the disease. The real cause was found to be a lack of vitamin C in their diet.

image   A phrase or expression that evokes a picture or describes a scene. An image may be either literal, in which case it depicts what something looks like, or figurative, in which case an expression is used that likens the thing described to something else (e.g., "My love is like a red, red rose").

induction   A form of reasoning that proceeds from specific instances to a general inference or conclusion. Inductive reasoning is the cornerstone of the scientific method, which begins by examining representative cases and then infers some law or theory to explain them as a whole. See Chapter 9.

interparagraph   Between paragraphs. A comparison/contrast, for example, may be drawn between several paragraphs rather than within a single paragraph. For an example of an interparagraph comparison/contrast, see Chapter 6.

intraparagraph   Within a single paragraph. For an example of an intraparagraph comparison/contrast, see Chapter 6.

inversion   The reversal of the normal order of words in a sentence to achieve some desired effect, usually emphasis. Inversion is a technique long used in poetry, although most modern poets shun it as too artificial. For examples of inversion, see Shakespeare's "That Time of Year" (Sonnet 73) in Chapter 5.

irony   The use of language in such a way that apparent meaning contrasts sharply with real meaning. One famous example (in Shakespeare's *Julius Caesar*) is Antony's description of Brutus as "an honorable man": Because Brutus was one of Caesar's assassins, Antony meant just the opposite. Irony is a softer form of sarcasm and shares with it the same contrast between apparent and real meaning.

jargon   The specialized or technical language of a trade, profession, class, or other group of people. Jargon is sometimes useful, but when used thoughtlessly it can become meaningless

expression bordering on gibberish, as in the following sentence from a psychology text: "Her male sibling's excessive psychogenic outbursts were instrumental in causing her to decompensate emotionally." A clearer statement would be the following: "Her brother's temper eventually caused her to have a nervous breakdown."

literal   *Literal* and *figurative* are two opposing characteristics of language. The literal meaning is a statement about something rendered in common, factual terms: "Good writers must be aggressive and daring." The figurative meaning is clouded in an image: "Good writers must stick out their necks." See **figurative.**

logical fallacies   Errors in reasoning used by speakers or writers, sometimes in order to dupe their audiences. Most logical fallacies are based on insufficient evidence ("All redheads are passionate lovers"); or irrelevant information ("Don't let him do the surgery; he cheats on his wife"); or on faulty reasoning ("If you don't quit smoking, you'll die of lung cancer").

metaphor   A figurative image that implies a similarity between things otherwise dissimilar, such as the poet Robert Frost's statement "I have been acquainted with the night," meaning that he has suffered despair.

mood of a story   The pervading impression made on the feelings of the reader. For instance, Edgar Allan Poe often created a mood of horror in his short stories. A mood can be gloomy, sad, joyful, bitter, frightening, and so forth.

mood of verbs   A verb form expressing the manner or condition of the action. The moods of verbs are *indicative* (statements or questions), *imperative* (requests or commands), and *subjunctive* (expressions of doubt, wishes, probabilities, and conditions contrary to fact).

narration   An account of events that happened. A narrative organizes material on the basis of chronological order or pattern, stressing the sequence of events and pacing these events according to the emphasis desired. Narration is often distinguished from three other modes of writing: argumentation, description, and exposition. See "How to Write a Narration," Chapter 7.

objective and subjective writing Two attitudes toward writing. In *objective* writing, the author tries to present the material fairly and without bias; in *subjective* writing, the author stresses personal responses and interpretations. For instance, news reporting should be objective, whereas poetry can be subjective.

pacing The speed at which a piece of writing moves along. Pacing depends on the balance between summarizing action and representing the action in detail. See "How to Write a Narration," Chapter 6.

parallelism The principle of coherent writing requiring that coordinate elements be given the same grammatical form, as in Daniel Webster's dictum, "I was born an American; I will live an American; I will die an American."

paraphrase A restatement of a text or passage in another form or in other words, often to clarify the meaning. Paraphrase is commonly used in research papers to assimilate the research into a single style of writing and thereby avoid a choppy effect. See also **plagiarism.**

personification Attributing human qualities to objects, abstractions, or animals: "'Tis beauty calls and glory leads the way."

plagiarism Copying words from a source and then passing them off as one's own. Plagiarism is considered dishonest scholarship. Every writer is obligated to acknowledge ideas or concepts that represent someone else's thinking.

point of view The perspective from which a piece of writing is developed. In nonfiction, the point of view is usually the author's. In fiction, the point of view can be first- or third-person point of view. In the first-person point of view, the author becomes part of the narration and refers to him/herself as "I." In the third-person point of view, the narrator simply observes the action of the story. Third-person narrative is either *omniscient* (the narrator knows everything about all of the characters) or *limited* (the narrator knows only those things that might be apparent to a sensitive observer).

premise An assertion or statement that is the basis for an argument. See **syllogism.**

process A type of development in writing that stresses how a sequence of steps produces a certain effect. For instance, explaining to the reader all of the steps involved in balancing a checkbook would be a *process* essay. See Chapter 7 for examples of process writing.

purpose The commitment on the part of authors to explain what they plan to write about. Purpose is an essential part of unity and coherence. Most teachers require students to write a statement of purpose, also called a *thesis*: "I intend to argue that our Federal Post Office needs a complete overhaul."

red herring A side issue introduced into an argument to distract from the main argument. It is a common device of politicians: "Abortion may be a woman's individual right, but have you considered the danger of the many germ-infested abortion clinics?" Here the side issue of dirty clinics clouds the ethical issue of having an abortion.

repetition A final review of all of the main points in a piece of writing; also known as *recapitulation*. In skillful writing, repetition is a means of emphasizing important words and ideas, of binding together the sentences in a passage, and of creating an effective conclusion. Its purpose is to accumulate a climactic impact or to cast new light on the material being presented.

rhetoric The art of using persuasive language. This is accomplished through the author's diction and sentence structure.

rhetorical question A question posed with no expectation of receiving an answer. This device is often used in public speaking to launch or further discussion. For example, a speaker might say, "What is the meaning of life anyway?" as a way of nudging a talk toward a discussion of ethics.

satire   Often an attack on a person. Also the use of wit and humor to ridicule society's weaknesses so as to correct them. In literature, two types of satire have been recognized: *Horatian satire,* which is gentle and smiling, and *Juvenalian satire,* which is sharp and biting.

simile   A figure of speech that, like the metaphor, implies a similarity between things otherwise dissimilar. The simile, however, always uses *like, as,* or *so* to introduce the comparison: "My word is like a steel plate, never to be broken."

slanting   The characteristic of selecting facts, words, or emphasis to achieve a preconceived intent:

favorable intent: "Although the Senator looks bored, when it comes time to vote, she is on the right side of the issue."

unfavorable intent: "The Senator may vote on the right side of issues, but she always looks bored."

specific   A way of referring to the level of abstraction in words; the opposite of *general.* A *general* word refers to a group or class, whereas a *specific* word refers to a member of a group or class. Thus, the word *nature* is general, the word *tree* more specific, and the word *oak* even more specific. The thesis of an essay is general, but the details supporting that thesis are specific. See also **abstract** and **concrete.**

Standard English   The English of educated speakers and writers. Any attempt to define Standard English is controversial because no two speakers of English speak exactly alike. What is usually meant by "Standard English" is what one's grammar book dictates.

statement of purpose   What an author is trying to tell an audience; the main idea of an essay. Traditionally, what distinguishes a statement of purpose from a *thesis* is wording, not content. A statement of purpose includes words such as "My purpose is . . . " and "In this paper I

intend to . . . " A statement of purpose is often the lead sentence of an essay. See Chapter 4.

straw man   An opposing point of view, set up so that it can easily be refuted. This is a common strategy used in debate.

style   The expression of an author's individuality through the use of words, sentence patterns, and selection of details. Our advice to fledgling writers is to develop a style that combines sincerity with clarity. See F. L. Lucas's "What Is Style?" in Chapter 10.

subordination   Expressing in a dependent clause, phrase, or single word any idea that is not significant enough to be expressed in a main clause or an independent sentence:

lacking subordination: John wrote his research paper on Thomas Jefferson; he was interested in this great statesman.

with subordination: Because John was interested in Thomas Jefferson, he wrote his research paper on this great statesman.

syllogism   In formal logic, the pattern by which a deductive argument is expressed:

All men are mortal. (major premise)

John Smith is a man. (minor premise)

Therefore John Smith is mortal. (conclusion)

symbol   An object or action that in its particular context represents something else. For instance, in Ernest Hemingway's novel *A Farewell to Arms,* the rain represents impending disaster because when it rains something terrible happens.

synonym   A word or phrase that has the same meaning as another. For instance, the words *imprisonment* and *incarceration* are synonyms. The phrases "fall short" and "miss the mark" are synonymous.

syntax   The order of words in a sentence and their relationships to each other. Good syntax requires correct grammar as well as effective sentence patterns, including unity, coherence, and emphasis.

theme   See **thesis.**

thesis   The basic idea of an essay, usually stated in a single sentence. In expository and argumentative writing, the thesis (or *theme*) is the unifying force that every word, sentence, and paragraph of the essay must support.

tone   The reflection of the writer's attitude toward subject and audience. The tone can be personal or impersonal, formal or informal, objective or subjective, or expressed in irony, sarcasm, anger, humor, satire, hyperbole, or understatement.

topic sentence   The *topic sentence* is to a paragraph what the *thesis* or *theme* is to the entire essay—that is, it expresses the paragraph's central idea.

transition   Words, phrases, sentences, or even paragraphs that indicate connections between the writer's ideas. These transitions provide landmarks to guide readers from one idea to the next. The following are some standard transitional devices:

time: soon, immediately, afterward, later, meanwhile, in the meantime

place: nearby, on the opposite side, further back, beyond

result: as a result, therefore, thus, as a consequence

comparison: similarly, likewise, also

contrast: on the other hand, in contrast, nevertheless, but, yet, otherwise

addition: furthermore, moreover, in addition, and, first, second, third, finally

example: for example, for instance, to illustrate, as a matter of fact, on the whole, in other words

understatement   Deliberately representing something as less than it is in order to stress its magnitude. Also called *litotes.* A good writer will restrain the impulse to hammer home a point and will use understatement instead. An example is the following line from Oscar Wilde's play *The Importance of Being Earnest:*

"To lose one parent, Mr. Worthing, may be regarded as a misfortune; to lose both looks like carelessness."

unity   The characteristic in writing of having all parts contribute to an overall effect. An essay or paragraph is described as having *unity* when all of its sentences develop one central idea. The worst enemy of unity is irrelevant material. A good rule is to delete all sentences that do not advance or prove the thesis or topic sentence of an essay.

voice   The presence or the sound of self chosen by an author. Most good writing sounds like someone delivering a message. The aim in good student writing is to sound natural. Of course, the voice will be affected by the audience and occasion for writing. See Chapter 3, "What Is a Writer's Voice?"

Literary Credits

Maya Angelou, "My Name Is Margaret" copyright © 1969 and renewed 1997 by Maya Angelou from *I Know Why the Caged Bird Sings* by Maya Angelou. Used by permission of Random House, Inc.

Geoff Axford, "Children Don't Need to be Spanked to Learn a Lesson" by Geoff Axford from *The London Free Press,* December 26, 2001. Reprinted by permission.

Jimmy Santiago Baca, "Coming Into Language" from *Working in the Dark: Reflections of a Poet of the Barrio.* Copyright © 1992 by Jimmy Santiago Baca.

Sheridan Baker, "The Thesis" from *The Complete Stylist and Handbook,* 3rd Edition. Copyright © 1984 by Harper & Row, Publishers, Inc.

Melba Pattillo Beals, Reprinted with the permission of Atria Books, a Division of Simon & Schuster Adult Publishing Group, from *Warriors Don't Cry: A Searing Memoir of the Battle to Integrate Little Rock's Central High* by Melba Pattillo Beals. Copyright © 1994 by Melba Beals.

Judy (Syfers) Brady, "Why I Want a Wife" from *Ms.* (1971). Copyright © 1971 by Judy Brady. Reprinted with the permission of the author.

Mort Castle, "Tone: The Writers Voice on the Readers Mind" by Mort Castle. Copyright © 1997-2000 by Writer's Write, Inc. Reprinted by permission.

Bruce Catton, "Grant and Lee: A Study in Contrasts" from *The American Story,* edited by Earl Schenk Miers. Copyright © 1956 by the United States Capitol Historical Society.

Jim Corbett, From *The Man-Easters of Kumaon* by Jim Corbett. Reproduced by permission of Oxford University Press India, New Delhi.

Malcolm Cowley, "The View From 80" from *The View from 80* by Malcolm Cowley, copyright © 1976, 1978, 1980 by Malcolm Cowley. Used by permission of Viking Penguin, a division of Penguin Putnam Inc.

Sarah and A. Elizabeth Delany with Amy Hill Hearth, From *Having Our Say* by Sarah and A. Elizabeth Delany with Amy Hill Hearth. Reprinted by permission of Kodansha America, Inc.

Alan DeVoe, "Shrew—The Littlest Mammal."

Bart Edelman, "English 101." Copyright © 1995 by Bart Edelman.

E.M. Forster, "My Wood" from *Abinger Harvest* by E.M. Forster. Copyright 1936 and renewed 1964 by Edward M. Forster. Reprinted by permission of Harcourt, Inc. and The Provost and Scholars of King's College, Cambridge and the Society of Authors as the Literary Representatives of the Estate of E.M. Forster.

Robert Frost, "Design" and "The Flood" from *The Poetry of Robert Frost* edited by Edward Connery Lathem. Copyright 1928, 1936, © 1969 by Henry Holt and Company, © 1956 by Robert Frost, © 1964 by Lesley Frost Ballantine. Reprinted by permission of Henry Holt and Company, LLC.

William Golding, "Thinking as a Hobby" from *Holiday* (July 18, 1961). Copyright © 1961 by The Curtis Publishing Company.

Ellen Goodman, "The Company Man" reprinted with the permission of Simon & Schuster Adult Publishing Group from *Close to Home* by Ellen Goodman. Copyright © 1979 by The Washington Post Company.

Dick Gregory, "Shame" from *Nigger: An Autobiography* by Dick Gregory, copyright © 1964 by Dick Gregory Enterprises, Inc. Used by permission of Dutton, a division of Penguin Putnam Inc.

Arthur Grimble, From *A Pattern of Islands* by Arthur Grimble. Reprinted by permission of John Murray (Publishers) Ltd.

Kate Gubata, "The New Feminism" by Kate Gubata. Reprinted by permission of U-Wire.

Betsy Hart, "The Need for Spanking" by Betsy Hart. Reprinted by permission of U-Wire.

Linda Hasselstrom, "Why One Peaceful Woman Carries a Gun" by Linda Hasselstrom from *Land Circle: Writings Collected form the Land.* Copyright © 1991 by Linda Hasselstrom. Reprinted by permission of Fulcrum Publishing.

James A. Haught, "Breaking the Last Taboo" by James A. Haught from *Free Inquiry,* Winter 1996/1997. Reprinted by permission of Counsel for Secular Humanism.

George Orwell, "Shooting an Elephant" from *Shooting an Elephant* by George Orwell. Copyright 1950 by Harcourt, Inc. and renewed 1979 by Sonia Brownell Orwell, reprinted by permission of Harcourt, Inc. and by permission of Bill Hamilton as the Literary Executor of the Estate of the Late Sonia Brownell Orwell and Secker & Warburg Ltd.

Barry Parr, "The Buck Stops Here" from *American West* by Barry Parr. Reprinted by permission of the author.

Kenneth Patchen, "How To Be an Army" by Kenneth Patchen, from *The Collected Poems of Kenneth Patchen*, copyright 1943 by New Directions Publishing Corp. Reprinted by permission of New Directions Publishing Corp.

Joseph Perkins, "Homeless: Expose the Myths" by Joseph Perkins from *The San Diego Union Tribune*, June 9, 1993. Reprinted by permission.

Adrienne Rich, "Living in Sin" copyright © 2002, 1955 by Adrienne Rich, from *The Fact of a Doorframe: Selected Poems 1950-2001* by Adrienne Rich. Used by permission of W. W. Norton & Company, Inc.

Paul Roberts, "How to Say Nothing in Five Hundred Words" from *Understanding English* by Paul Roberts. Copyright © 1958 by Paul Roberts. Reprinted by permission of Pearson Education, Inc.

Roxanne Roberts, "The Grieving Never Ends" by Roxanne Roberts from *The Los Angeles Times*, June 12, 1996. Copyright © 1996, The Washington Post. Reprinted with permission.

Roger Rosenblatt, "Rules for Aging" by Roger Rosenblatt from *Modern Maturity*, May-June 1999. Reprinted with the permission of the author

Rebecca E. Rubins, "The Farce of Feminism" by Rebecca E. Rubins. Reprinted by permission of U-Wire.

Salman Rushdie, "American and Anti-Americans" by Salman Rushdie from *The New York Times*, February 4, 2002. Copyright © 2002 The New York Times Co. Reprinted by permission.

William Shirer, "Hitler's Workday" from *Berlin Diary* by William Shirer. (Boston: Little, Brown, 1940). Reprinted by permission of Estate of William Shirer.

May Swenson, "Pigeon Woman" from *New and Selected Things Taking Place* (Boston: Little, Brown and Company). Originally published in *The New Yorker*, 1962. Copyright © 1962 by May Swenson.

Lewis Thomas, "On Disease" copyright © 1979 by Lewis Thomas from *The Medusa and the Snail* by Lewis Thomas. Used by permission of Viking Penguin, a division of Penguin Putnam Inc.

Edward T. Thompson, "How to Write Clearly" from *Power of the Printed Word* series.

James Thurber, "The Catbird Seat" from *The Thurber Carnival* (New York: Harper, 1945). Copyright © 1945 by James Thurber, renewed 1973 by Helen Thurber and Rosemary A. Thurber.

Am. Tibbetts and Charlene Tibbetts, "Writing Successful Paragraphs" by Am. Tibbetts and Charlene Tibbetts from *Strategies of Rhetoric*. Copyright © 1969, 1974 by Scott Foresman & Co. Reprinted by permission of Pearson Education, Inc.

Mike Toner, "Glacial Melt in Greenland Causes Alarm Report Comes as the Politics of Global Warming Heats Up" by Mike Toner from *Atlanta Journal and Constitution*, June 7, 2002. Copyright © 2002. Reprinted by permission of the publisher via Copyright Clearance Center.

Andrew Vachss, "Sex Predators Can't Be Saved" from *The New York Times*, January 5, 1993. Copyright © 1993 by The New York Times Co.

Gore Vidal, "Drugs" by Gore Vidal, copyright © 1968, 1970, 1971, 1972 by Gore Vidal, from *Homage to Daniel Shays: Collected Essays* by Gore Vidal. Used by permission of Random House, Inc.

James Watkins, "Separating Sides in the Church-State Conflict" by James Watkins. Reprinted by permission of U-Wire.

Eudora Welty, "A Worn Path" from *A Curtain of Green and Other Stories*, copyright 1941 and renewed 1969 by Eudora Welty, reprinted by permission of Harcourt, Inc.

Robert Wernick, "Who the Devil is the Devil?" by Robert Wernick from *Smithsonian*, October 1999, pp. 113-118. Reprinted by permission.

E.B. White, "One More to the Lake" from *One Man's Meat* by E.B. White. Text copyright 1941 by E.B. White. Copyright renewed. Reprinted by permission of Tilbury House, Publishers, Gardiner, Maine.

Richard W. Whitrock, "Pledge Ruling Just Plain Wrong" by Richard W. Whitrock. Reprinted by permission of U-Wire.

Oscar Wilde, "Letter to the Rev. J. Page Hopps" from *The Letters of Oscar Wilde* (New York: Harcourt Brace & World, 1962). Copyright © 1962 by Vyvyan Holland.

Anthony C. Winkler and Jo Ray McCuen, "The Editing Booth" from *Rhetoric Made Plain* by Anthony C. Winkler and Jo Ray McCuen.

Peter Worthington, "The Rules of Fighting Terror" by Peter Worthington from *The Ottawa Sun*, September 22, 2002. Reprinted by permission.

Index